LBJ
The Mastermind
of the JFK
Assassination

Phillip F. Nelson

Skyhorse Publishing

This book is dedicated to my wonderful wife, Karen,
without whose love, understanding, and patience I would
not have been able to complete it.

Skyhorse Publishing books may be purchased in bulk at special discounts for sales promotion, corporate gifts, fund-raising, or educational purposes. Special editions can also be created to specifications. For details, contact the Special Sales Department, Skyhorse Publishing, 307 West 36th Street, 11th Floor, New York, NY 10018 or info@skyhorsepublishing.com.

Skyhorse® and Skyhorse Publishing® are registered trademarks of Skyhorse Publishing, Inc.®, a Delaware corporation.

www.skyhorsepublishing.com

10 9 8

Library of Congress Control Number: 2011032137
Paperback ISBN: 978-1-62087-610-7

Printed in the United States of America

CONTENTS

ACKNOWLEDGMENTS

I want to extend a heartfelt thanks to the people who have been immensely helpful to me in the process of completing this book.

Four years before I started to work on this book, I was fortunate to see one of the broadcasts by The History Channel of the video "The Guilty Men," which is also referred to as Episode Nine of *The Men Who Killed Kennedy*. The 2003 broadcasts provoked a knee-jerk reaction amongst those who were still highly invested in the maintenance of the official governmental lies about Lyndon Johnson's faux "legacy"; these included Jack Valenti, who Lyndon Johnson had placed in Hollywood knowing that he would be in a position to censor future films which did not conform to the "official story" of how he had come into office, as well as Lady Bird Johnson, former President Jerry Ford and Johnson's high level aide Bill Moyers. Their threats caused The History Channel—in an action not unlike the practice of "book burning"—to cancel any further rebroadcasts of this episode, and with it, episodes seven ("The Smoking Guns") and eight ("The Love Affair") though all three are still available, along with the original six episodes, on internet websites such as Youtube.

It was the broadcast of "The Guilty Men"—which I regard as the single best video ever recorded about the JFK assassination—that reawakened my interest in "the crime of the century", leading me to further research on the subject. This video became the "proximate cause"—the original catalyst —which caused my subsequent immersion into the analysis of previously discovered evidence and conclusions presented by the authors of a number of books, as outlined below. I should have previously acknowledged this in earlier editions of the book but neglected to do so; clearly, the video had more influence on the creation of this book than any single book or other resource. So, Kudos to Ed Tatro, Rick Russo, Barr McClellan, Walt Brown, Greg Burnham, Nigel Turner and all others associated with the production of this video! These researchers and authors prompted me to read all of the books listed in the Bibliography and to eventually come into contact with a number of the authors and researchers who created these books and videos.

For the first edition, they included Noel Twyman, Doug Horne, and Larry Hancock, the authors of some of the best, most comprehensive works on the assassination of John F. Kennedy. Noel's book covered the complexities of this subject more comprehensively than any other author, and

Doug's book added even more depth to that body of information. Larry's book, originally published in 2006, contains a wealth of information he had gathered from his review of thousands of documents, White House diaries, telephone logs, and tape recordings. Moreover, Larry assisted me by doing a "peer review" of an early draft of the manuscript and continued to offer suggestions as further work on the first—and then the second—edition of the book was prepared.

The author of the most important book ever published on the Warren Commission, Gerald McKnight, PhD, was also very supportive to me before and after the first edition of the book was published. Douglas Caddy, the former attorney for Billie Sol Estes who assisted Estes in his attempt to "come clean" with the Justice Department in 1984, has also been very helpful to me in gaining a better understanding about that incident and the reasons the effort was unsuccessful. Author James H. Fetzer, PhD, has been particularly accomodating in assisting with a number of improvements for this edition—including the revision to the "shot sequence" narrative that is arguably the best summary ever written on that point—as well as supporting the book through his book reviews, essays, and his postings on various Internet forums.

Thanks to one of many acts of kindness by researcher Robert P. Morrow, of Austin, Texas, I made contact with other longtime researchers, including Connie Kritzberg, who was a news reporter/editor for the Dallas *Times Herald* in 1963; her firsthand memories have troubled her ever since that tragic weekend. Connie's account of having a news report she wrote on November 22, 1963, surreptitiously co-opted by the FBI has been added to this edition because of its gravity; it was one of the first indications that unseen forces were already at work to manage the outcome of the case and was one more incident among the many which must not be lost in the shuffle as so many of the details become more and more blurred with time.

The many other books listed in the bibliography have all contributed in some way to the development of this book. They represent the "most likely" aspects which have been combined and distilled into a story which probably could have been proven in court decades ago, if the facts now known had then been available.

Finally, I am very indebted to Tony Lyons, of Skyhorse Publishing, for the opportunity of having the book professionally redone, and David Schwartz, for his valuable work in transforming the original manuscript into a much easier read while simultaneously strenghening the case regarding Johnson's involvement in JFK's assassination. I am also grateful to Yvette Grant in the Skyhorse production department, whose help with numerous corrections and her meticulous eye was much appreciated. The result is a greatly improved book, one that will be much more likely to eventually cause the general public to begin to accept the awful truth of what happened in Dallas nearly fifty years ago.

INTRODUCTION

When you have excluded the impossible, whatever remains,. however improbable, must be the truth.

—SHERLOCK HOLMES
(A. C. DOYLE'S *THE ADVENTURE OF THE BERYL CORONET*)

In 1963, I was a recent high school graduate who had begun working at Chicago's O'Hare Airport to save money for college; like everyone else alive at that time, I was stunned at the assassination of JFK and confused about the character of the new president, Lyndon Johnson. The only thing widely known about him were stories that magazines such as *Look, Collier's, Life*, and *Time* had recently printed; the stories were generally discomforting because they seemed to produce more questions than answers about the new president.

While working in the main terminal one day in the summer of 1964, Henry Wade, the Dallas district attorney, and his wife approached the counter to check in for a flight to Traverse City, Michigan; Wade's name had often appeared in news accounts coming from Dallas. They both looked bored and tired after their flight from Dallas but immediately responded when I asked, "Are you *the* Henry Wade of Dallas?" Mrs. Wade was the first to respond with a smile and an excited "Yes!" Henry also managed a little smile, and nodded; there was at least a streak of shyness about him, which came as a surprise for some reason. Apparently, no one else had recognized them, and neither would I have if I hadn't seen their tickets. This was before the Warren Report was published, and I resisted the urge to ask Mr. Wade any questions regarding his most important, if fleeting, case; I merely stated my hope that their work (by *their*, meaning everyone involved in the investigation and adjudication) would soon resolve the confusion and distress that continued to afflict the country. He said thanks, and left with Mrs. Wade to board the airplane.

What I know now, but didn't then, is that Henry Wade was merely one man of many who were being managed by that same new president to go along with a number of odd requests from Washington, all of which were shrouded in a mysterious blanket of national security concerns related to Kennedy's assassination. The cold war was reaching the boiling point; in fact, it had remained on high heat since the Cuban Missile Crisis, and people argued over whether Kennedy had handled it well or not. Those who felt he had not thought he had missed an opportunity to invade Cuba and send Castro packing and rid the Western Hemisphere of the Soviet Union and the menace of Communism. When the verdict of the Warren Commission was announced—that the assassination was the work of a single "lone nut"— the continued declaration of the "national security" canard, especially with respect to locking away all the remaining evidence (that which wasn't already destroyed) for seventy-five years, began to ring hollow: If the crime was such a simple case of a lone nut, a misguided Communist, why exactly was so much of the case being treated so secretly?

What were once considered "facts"—photographs and films, autopsy records, FBI reports, eyewitness testimony—have since been proven to have been fabricated, lost, or distorted. The enormity of the cover-up, beginning with the Warren Commission, reveals the breadth and depth of the pre- and postassassination conspiracies that are emerging now only because of the work done by previous researchers and authors. A number of meticulously documented books have proven that the analysis presented by the President's Commission on the Assassination of John F. Kennedy— the Warren Commission—was a lie. Some will have difficulty in accepting this premise because there is a natural tendency to want to believe the government, especially a commission of supposedly learned and august men who have served it throughout their lives. For people still experiencing doubt, a careful reading of Gerald McKnight's *Breach of Trust: How the Warren Commission Failed the Nation and Why* will disabuse them of any remaining questions about the validity of this point. The majority of Americans (and people around the world) already generally believe that much of the so-called investigation of events conducted by the FBI and the Warren Commission's imprimatur was flawed; the consensus on this point has only grown since 1964. They were, and are, absolutely correct, despite the decades of deception foisted upon them by apologists for the completely discredited "official" version of events.

For over forty years it has become more and more apparent that much of the evidence originally put forward by the FBI and Warren Commission was invented or modified to fit the assertion that Lee Harvey Oswald was the lone gunman, just as other original evidence has disappeared (including JFK's brain). Furthermore, the false evidence was developed quickly, in some cases overnight, to prove that Oswald, a man his fellow marines would say "lacked coordination" and call "a very poor rifle marksman,"[1] shot three bullets, two of which very precisely hit their moving target, in the space of a little

---

1. Hurt (photo section after p. 138).

over six seconds—a shooting feat, incidentally, that has never been replicated, even by expert sharpshooters. The proofs of these claims have appeared in numerous books, newspapers, and websites; they contain the kernels of truth that can be harvested and swept into the narrative as conclusive evidence. Each item we cite along the way can be represented as a "dot" on a very large historical matrix; the narrative will connect those dots and lead us to conclusions in a process guided by the Sherlock Holmes epigraph referenced above. Every investigation that preceded mine into the most famous cold case ever, the unsolved murder of the thirty-fifth president of the United States, contributed in some way to the distillation of information and interpretation of facts that are now being presented; I am indebted to all authors of such work, regardless of whether they have been cited here.

It is not the intent of this book to provide a complete list of all the errors, anomalies, inconsistencies, and impossibilities of the Warren Report since that has already been done by other cited authors, but to build upon preexisting research and provide a succinct but comprehensive overview of the entire plot and its cover-up. A cohesive and compelling account that combines the respective findings of earlier works—in a way that includes the best evidence from each of them while replacing the incongruities of discarded accounts—into a "most plausible" single story has not previously been written. Moreover, other books on the subject become so absorbed in the minutia of the crime that they fail to examine the resulting vacuum of "who was the mastermind." That most of the people who were involved, directly or indirectly, in the events in Dallas are now deceased means it is highly unlikely that the whole truth behind the crime of the century will ever be known; the possibility of such knowledge has been eroded by almost five decades of deceit. Nevertheless, enough circumstantial evidence has surfaced to make a persuasive case. A figurative whole cloth can be woven from these threads of evidence, both empirical and anecdotal; documented facts and reasonable hearsay will be considered. Pending a complete and unredacted release of 100 percent of all secret government files, this is as close to the complete picture as it is now possible to achieve.

John F. Kennedy's assassination changed the culture and historical direction of the United States. The event plunged Americans into collective shock, leaving all grasping for answers about who would commit such an audacious and unspeakable crime; at this juncture, how citizens viewed the motives and actions of their government took a decidedly more jaded and cynical turn. Suspicions remained of a larger unknown force behind the accused suspect, accompanied by an enormous, albeit suppressed, anxiety, as fear and group paranoia descended upon the American people. An ephemeral void, as though left by the departed spirit of John F. Kennedy, lurked throughout the nation in the days and weeks following his death, the result of lingering questions about an unthinkable possibility. The void eventually morphed into a ghostly, shadowy presence that grew larger and larger as more details of the assassination emerged. The shadows withdrew as the days became weeks and then months while the enigmatic persona of Lyndon B. Johnson became more familiar. LBJ, with his colloquial Texan toughness and coarseness—together with his insecurities and oversized ego, his contradictions—became one of the most distrusted presidents ever known in America.

JFK's murder has never been solved because the public gave LBJ the benefit of the doubt, while he was alive and for four decades beyond, effectively removing him from scrutiny. That the official government's accusatory finger pointed in other directions, and that LBJ was the primary pointer, precluded an examination of the most likely candidate, the one true suspect with an actual motive (unlike the hapless Mr. Oswald). Most people realized that the new president had infinitely more motive to kill Kennedy than did Oswald, a man who had said he actually liked JFK.[2] But they suppressed this conclusion, because it was dangerous, the implications unfathomable. Johnson got his pass because the alternative was simply an unspeakable thought: The notion that a president could be killed in a conspiracy by others in his administration, especially his own vice president, was impossible for people to confront. That someone so highly placed could possibly be so evil was simply an outrageous idea. Such thinking was so awful, it induced a corollary paranoia. While this mood prevailed throughout the country, Lyndon Johnson presented himself on higher and higher levels as a creditable and earnest politician and was given the deference accorded to senior officials in those days. Reporters were hesitant to write negative personal stories about presidents then (imagine that!) or to critically examine presidential decisions and policies, much less stand up to the president, with a few specific exceptions like Clark Mollenhoff of the *Des Moines Register*. Most were swayed by the temptation of gaining favorable access to the president and keeping it through self-censorship.

Because most people consider the well-marketed, good side of LBJ (that of a magnanimous, consensus-seeking, backslapping, generous liberal politician) a mitigating factor to his bad side, the natural inclination, aided by a dearth of information about his negatives until now, is to give him the benefit of the doubt. To do so, however, means the malevolent characteristics that shaped his rise in politics, that catapulted him into the Oval Office, and with which he governed as president, are put aside and ignored, much as they

---

2. Baker, *Me & Lee*, p. 457.

have been for almost fifty years. The lies that have already replaced the truth about Johnson will never be cleansed from the American consciousness if they are allowed to continue to usurp the real story about John F. Kennedy's demise.

The first three books of an eventual four-part series of biographies (the last volume is still being written) by Robert Caro, *The Years of Lyndon Johnson*, examine Johnson's life from boyhood through high school and college; his short stint as a teacher; his time as congressional assistant and head of the National Youth Administration; his election to Congress in 1937; his failed attempt to run for the Senate in 1941; his tainted election to the Senate in 1948; and his years in the Senate thereafter, leading to his election as vice president in 1960. The unparalleled detail with which Caro has documented Johnson's experiences and the picture it reveals of Lyndon B. Johnson make this series the essential resource for understanding the motives, the morality (or amorality), the obsessive ambition, drive, and narcissistic personality of the thirty-sixth president. Instead of the popular, even charismatic campus figure described in other biographies—written by authors who never interviewed the people who knew him best, who accepted without question the stories of his youth that LBJ manufactured—his true persona becomes clear: He was a crude, condescending, duplicitous, ruthless, and deceitful man not above the use of criminal means to attain his objective. Caro, arguably a man who has studied Lyndon Johnson more than any other person, concluded, among other things, that Johnson could be trusted *only* to do what would benefit *himself;* his singular lifetime goal was to be the president of the United States and one who would be considered for all time among the greatest.[3] It could even be argued, using conclusions from Caro's books, that becoming president was much more than a goal—it was a compulsion he didn't try to control: It was his obsession.

The best possible theory of a "lone nut" scenario was represented by the Warren Report; a comparable, comprehensive scenario for a consensus theory of conspiracy has never previously been written. There are aspects of the story you are about to read that nearly defy belief. But as the story proceeds page by page and chapter by chapter, a common thread will emerge that seamlessly connects one to the other. That thread weaves together people, events, and defining points in Lyndon Johnson's sixty-four-year lifeline; it follows his continual move up the political ladder that started when, as a young boy following his sometime-delegate father around the

---

3. Caro, Path pp. 275, 535.

Austin Capitol Building, he first tasted the perquisites of political influence and power over others–a taste he became addicted to and relished for as long as he lived. The threads Lyndon Johnson wove as he put his plan together, starting three years before the assassination, are now faded and frayed, but many still remain as evidence of his omnipresence. Many more of them are visible from the day of the assassination through the critical period to the end of the following year, the publication of the Warren Report, and the 1964 election. In fact, when he left the White House, his ultimate base of power, he quickly languished into a pitiful shadow of his former self, dying almost exactly four years later—what would have been the end of his second term, if he hadn't created the disaster of Vietnam during his first.

As the new president Lyndon B. Johnson became more familiar to the American people, they also found out more and more about his background. Earlier stories about the TFX scandal had circulated for a couple of years and had not yet gone away. The Billie Sol Estes and Bobby Baker scandals had similarly surfaced later, only after Johnson was the vice president and able to insulate himself from his long-term involvement with his former friends-in-fraud. LBJ told his Senate friends that one should not be judged by the actions of others; he maintained that he "hardly knew" these men, Billie Sol and Bobby, even though they were both close friends and longtime associates, and with each of whom he had been criminally engaged, as will be examined in chapter 4. Before the scandals broke, however, Johnson had proudly announced to the whole world that if he had had a son, Bobby Baker would have been him and that "Bobby is my strong right arm. He is the last person I see at night and the first person I see in the morning." Upon becoming president, the investigations into LBJ's criminal past were immediately curtailed, and then quietly closed.

The events and actions attributed to Lyndon Johnson were well hidden by him all along his lifetime journey. Through his many enablers—his attorneys, Ed Clark, Don Thomas, John Cofer, and even the famed but flawed Abe Fortas and his extensive staff of aides willing to do anything he asked—Johnson was able to keep himself distanced from the worst of the crimes. But the tendons that connected him to those crimes, from the financial frauds and stolen elections to the murders of anyone who stood in his way, lay just beneath the surface, such that they were even exposed on a number of occasions but caught in time and safely covered back up. In those instances, criminal activities originating in the 1950s, during which he was majority leader of the U.S. Senate before continuing into his term as vice president, started unraveling on the front pages of major newspapers: the TFX scandal, the Billie Sol Estes scandal, the Bobby Baker scandals. All of these played out in the national media of the day, sometimes even making the cover of *Life* and *Time* and the other news magazines. The aggregation of these lesser crimes gave Johnson the confidence and resolve that inexorably led to the plot to assassinate John F. Kennedy and put himself into the office of the president of the United States.

Lyndon B. Johnson was given the benefit of the doubt hundreds of times—by his mother first, then his peers in college, his constituents, his wealthy benefactors, his wife, his colleagues in the House and the Senate, and finally by his political appointees* and the judicial system itself, which he found was malleable enough in certain key areas to be controlled through bribery and extortion. His most effective tool was his unique, well-practiced talent for ingratiating himself with others; this as well as the rest of his methods will be closely examined throughout the book. Johnson's criminal activities, including his brazenly illegal fund-raising controversies and the fraud connected to his elections, culminating in the famous "Box 13" bogus ballots that at the last minute materialized to give him his Senate seat in 1948, will be reviewed. His political future came close to crashing a number of times; one of the closest, which involved the stunningly high-risk legal gambit created by Abe Fortas to get Supreme Court Justice Hugo Black to fix the legal impasse of the 1948 election by awarding it to Johnson on a jurisdictional technicality, will also be examined in detail. Finally, his astonishing accumulation of wealth during the period of his congressional service will be explored, all in the context of how he was able to get people to look the other way as they repeatedly gave him the benefit of the doubt.

Then there were the several early murders to which LBJ has been linked by his former partners in crime and his longtime mistress, with whom he fathered a child. He did not need a pass or forgiveness for these sins because they were swept under the rug; the people who were involved had to wait until Johnson died to step forward, after having kept quiet for years as a result of his intimidation. Even after his death, the silence of news media afraid to expose such dark secrets about someone they had protected for so long kept the secrets locked away. All of his many successes in his criminal conduct led Johnson to believe he was beyond the reach of the law, because he knew he could pull enough strings to avoid getting caught, as he always

---

*According to Evelyn Lincoln (Kennedy and Johnson, p. 140), these measured into the hundreds, just on the senatorial staff when he was majority leader; he had placed many others in high positions throughout the federal government's departments and agencies, including his favorites, the Federal Communications Commission and the Department of Agriculture. Even as vice president, he had coerced Kennedy into giving him unprecedented additional power over patronage appointments throughout the federal government, including all appointments for Texas, a particularly sore point (one of many) which Senator Ralph Yarborough was continually upset about, since that was normally a plum which he would have enjoyed.

had. When he became president, he knew he would be in a position to fully control the investigation that would inevitably follow the assassination of his predecessor.

In 1960, Johnson realized that his lifelong dream of becoming president of the United States was finally within his grasp if he planned it well. But he also realized that it would be impossible to achieve through the conventional process according to which he would stand for election to the office. He knew that it would require a few more years of intense planning and the help of some key individuals acting outside their official roles. He also knew that the biggest benefit of the doubt he would ever need had to come from the American people, who were still respectful of their leaders and willing to suspend any natural suspicions they may have had, to give the new president ample opportunity to continue the government as seamlessly as possible. By exploiting their fears, he would gain their confidence in due course, allowing him to be elected in his own right after "proving himself" through the passage of important legislation that he himself had impeded throughout Kennedy's term; such a triumph would allow him to be portrayed in the months before his own election as a great leader, having just arrived in town on his white horse, ready to fix all the world's problems.

It is not difficult to understand how Johnson became deluded enough to have vigorously pursued his dream at the expense of the country generally and John F. Kennedy in particular. Time and time again, he cheated at the election box, collected hundreds of thousands (millions in the aggregate) of dollars under the table through kickbacks and bribery, and eventually, according to certain of his associates, ordered the murder of a number of people who got in his way—all to advance his career. The evolution of the LBJ character was a long, slow process entailing the maturation of distinctive personality traits into a singularly unique individual: Lyndon B. Johnson was a nominally educated cowboy gifted with the genius required to formulate complex schemes involving multiple participants; a master psychologist's skill at seeing inside the soul of others to determine their every weakness; and finally, a charisma that could attract and hold vulnerable men and women, that could impel them to do his bidding almost without regard to the moral implications of their actions—notwithstanding the fact that many of these men and women were seemingly well-grounded people of high moral character; others were not. Johnson's unique talent, practiced since his youth and perfected by the time he was in Congress, was his ability to take all of his associates as close to the edge of their own ethical margins where each could venture before falling into their own abyss.

Of all the possible candidates mentioned variously in hundreds of books and in all the unpublished theories, the logical starting point might be this:

Who was the single likeliest person who made the final decision to take "executive action" and brazenly assassinate the thirty-fifth president of the United States? Specifically, who, among the many enemies of JFK, met all of the following criteria:

a. Who had the most to gain?
b. Who had the least to lose?
c. Who had the means to do it?
d. Who had the apparatus in place to subsequently cover it up?
e. Who had the kind of narcissistic/sociopathic personality capable of rationalizing the action as acceptable and necessary, together with the resolve and determination to see it through?

Only one person matches the above criteria completely: Lyndon Baines Johnson, the thirty-sixth president of the United States, who succeeded his predecessor by the most unique method possible. The office of the vice president has never been one to which an otherwise successful politician has aspired; it had always been there only as second place for an also-ran candidate, who might aspire to the presidency in a future term. But Johnson knew that at his age, he didn't have any future terms to wait out, and when he realized he could not win the presidential nomination in 1960, he aggressively campaigned for the vice presidency, even though JFK had already picked Senator Stuart Symington for the position. Indeed, it can now be posited that John F. Kennedy's fatal mistake occurred over three years before he died: his agonizing and reluctant decision to accede to the threat of blackmail by Lyndon Johnson and J. Edgar Hoover on July 14, 1960, at the Democratic convention, allowed Johnson to be named as the vice presidential nominee. This action put Johnson next in line to succeed JFK, an essential step in his plot to become president of the United States.

Johnson was uniquely matched to all the criteria noted above, as the most likely person behind JFK's assassination. In the chapters ahead, it will become clear that he met each criterion set forth in subparts a, b, c, and d below. By the last section of this book, it will be clear that subpart "e" also applies, just as certainly as do the first four:

a. **The most to gain.**
   LBJ's lifelong dream—obsession, actually—was to become president of the United States. Each time he voiced this dream, his resolve to achieve it increased, and he mentioned it often to others; one can only speculate how many more times he repeated it to himself, but it probably became a daily mantra.

b. The least to lose.

Consider the alternative to LBJ's *not* taking action: impending indictments, possible prison time, and the permanent loss of his presidential aspirations, which he viewed as his divine and inevitable destiny. He faced a choice with enormous consequences: either proceed with the plan and go to the White House or drop the plan and go to prison, running the risk of still more of his previous crimes coming to the public's attention.

c. The means to do it.

There was no shortage of enemies of JFK who would eagerly participate in the objective in their own limited way. Johnson had been a friend to many of them, and their common wish was bound to surface during their social affairs. The conversations he had with his good friend and neighbor of nearly twenty years, J. Edgar Hoover, might have centered on this plan since the point at which he enlisted Hoover to help force Kennedy to accept him as the vice presidential nominee. His many back channels to the highest officials of the Pentagon and CIA, many of whom were increasingly desirous of replacing JFK as quickly as possible, would provide him with the devices he would need to execute the plan and its immediate cover-up.

d. The apparatus in place to cover it up.

Once he was sworn in as president, the entire federal government was his to run. All other governmental entities, including individual local officeholders such as Dallas Police Captain Will Fritz and the district attorney, Henry Wade, were under his control through the basic and natural deference with which people treated the president of the United States.

e. The kind of narcissistic/psychotic/sociopathic/mendacious personality capable of rationalizing the action as acceptable and necessary, as the means to an ultimate end, as well as the resolve and determination to see it through.

Only someone whose conduct was unconstrained by his conscience could generate an act as heinous as the murder of the president. Lyndon B. Johnson was such a person. He had engaged in numerous crimes during his political career, including stealing elections during his college days and even in the inconsequential "Little Congress" through his initial elevation to the Senate in 1948. Subsequently, he became involved with mobsters and was paid off by them for protecting their illegal activities; furthermore, his involvement with convicted con man Billie Sol Estes, who implicated Johnson in several murders, will be shown, in addition to him having had his own hit man, Malcolm "Mac" Wallace. Johnson managed to corrupt the Texas judicial system such that Wallace was given, incredibly, *a five-year suspended sentence* after being found guilty of first-degree murder. Additionally, two of LBJ's aides in the White House, Bill Moyers and Richard Goodwin, became so concerned about his behavior that they independently consulted psychiatrists to discuss those concerns; both of them would resign in due course. Barr McClellan, who knew LBJ and worked for him as an attorney, called him "psychopathic" and said, "He was willing to kill. And he did." Moreover, McClellan also stated that "his criminal career was capped with the assassination of President Kennedy."[4]

By lowering the threshold for giving LBJ the benefit of the doubt to an extremely circumspect level, it follows that all of those who have testified against him—or who have been thwarted in their efforts to do so, and the scores of assassination witnesses who were ignored (and/or threatened, injured, or killed) because their testimony was not congruent with the "official" version—should be simultaneously and retroactively validated in recognition of their courage and to compensate for almost five decades of abuse and ridicule. The testimony of otherwise ignored witnesses, like Jean Hill, will finally be given appropriate consideration. The solid evidence that has disappeared—the missing photographs of Oswald in Mexico City, the real autopsy photos of JFK that doctors and photographers have stated no longer exist, everything else that was systematically withheld from the Warren Commission—will be introduced as though it still exists and portrays what credible witnesses have stated it portrays. Evidence that has been fabricated will be scrutinized and examined in a way opposite to what was intended by the perpetrators. It also means that other witnesses, despite their own shadowy backgrounds or the fact that they have criminal convictions (like Billie Sol Estes), will be given the courtesy of at least as much credibility as has been extended to Lyndon Johnson all these years. It is only fair that these men and women, who were caught up in the crimes that he orchestrated over a period of many years, be given the same benefit of the doubt that he was granted over his entire lifetime and for four decades beyond. This kind of focused and critical reexamination of the facts is the only conceivable way to get to the truth of the JFK assassination. Much of the case against Johnson relies upon statements and assertions of specific individuals, including one of his mistresses, a lawyer employed by the Austin law firm that handled his political

---

4. McClellan, pp. 3, 5.

business, and his partners in crime or the cover-up, some of whom have not previously been given sufficient attention by other authors. The descriptions of Johnson's behavior contained within are based upon numerous examples cited by historians and others—his peers, friends, neighbors, attorneys, aides, associates, lovers, and a few enemies—together with logical extrapolations reflecting the patterns he established over many years. The stories told by one of the lawyers who worked for him, Barr McClellan, also support this approach because of the compelling case he made regarding the extent of Johnson's criminal history. While Johnson was never convicted for any of his criminal activities, in 1984 a Texas grand jury concluded that he, his aide Cliff Carter, and hit man Mac Wallace were coconspirators to the murder of Henry Marshall.

But for the obvious impossibility of a posthumous indictment, the historical record of Johnson's career has never been put into the correct perspective. Instead of being remembered for the evil, conniving man he was, he is still revered by many of the most learned but ignorant educators, the most influential but predisposed news media, the political world's leaders who refuse to face the enormity of his crimes—in short, in the highest social circles and within government institutions that run the United States of America. His name is on buildings and national parks, the space center near Houston, a big lake in Texas, and a Dallas expressway—all the markings of the beatification of a person being considered for sainthood.

JFK, according to Arthur Schlesinger Jr., once described Johnson's personality as that of a "riverboat gambler."[5] As chronicled in several biographies, his classmates had long ago called him Bull (for bullshit) Johnson.[6] Another of his Texas nicknames was Lyin' Lyndon.[7] JFK once said "that Lyndon was a chronic liar; that he had been making all sorts of assurances to me for years and has lived up to none of them."[8] Robert Kennedy's description of Johnson, which can be heard on the referenced website, was that he was "*mean, bitter, vicious, an animal, in many ways; I think he's got this other side to him that makes his relationships with other human beings very difficult, unless you want to kiss his be-hind all the time.*"[9] The fact is, Johnson had many followers willing to do just that and put up with his boorish and obnoxious behavior for many years, and afterwards, they still didn't regret it. If the reader should become overtaken by a sense of disbelief,

5. Schlesinger, *Robert Kennedy* . . ., p. 219.
6. Caro, *Means of Ascent*, p. 50.
7. McClellan, p. 86.
8. Schlesinger, *Robert Kennedy* . . ., pp. 218–219.
9. Ref. youtube.com: "RFK to LBJ: 'Why did you have my brother killed?'"

that the author has gone off the deep end and no one could have been this bad, it may be helpful to remember, even memorize, the above description of Robert Kennedy's view of Lyndon Johnson.

In the fullness of time, in this case nearly half a century, many irrefutable truths have emerged; it is essential now, for the good of the nation and the world, to look back at the people and events that led to the assassination from a new perspective. Understanding the political and economic contexts, as influenced by the military-intelligence-congressional complex, and the cold war, anti-Communist attitudes then prevalent, mixed with the fervent hatred in some quarters for John F. Kennedy personally, provides the necessary insight into the dynamics that manifested in Dealey Plaza on November 22, 1963, and the many years of cover-up, which still continue. Originally meant to be kept secret for seventy-five years, the slowly unfolding forensic evidence (the ballistic, medical, audio, film, photographic, and other physical materials, and especially the eyewitness testimony from people who would not bow to the pressures exerted by the conspirators) that had been hidden for so many years has slowly leaked out, revealing the unmistakable truth of what happened to John F. Kennedy. Anyone who thoroughly examines these facts and analyzes them objectively, with an open mind, will inevitably conclude at least that a conspiracy existed and a cover-up occurred. Given that premise, a very limited number of men had the power to have possibly carried out these actions. This book shows that only one man had the motive, means, and opportunity to successfully organize the crime of the century, and the corresponding ability to subsequently cover it up. We are only now able to look back at those events from a distance and better understand what happened to us as a country. The horror that was unthinkable then can finally be reconciled with the historical record and an honest but brutal look at the event that shook the world.

PART I

Background

Chapter 1
_____

THE MANIACAL OBSESSION
OF LYNDON B. JOHNSON

I'm just like a fox. I can see the jugular in any man and go for it,
but I always keep myself in rein. I keep myself on a leash, just like you
would an animal.

—LYNDON JOHNSON, DESCRIBING HIMSELF TO A FRIEND.

When he was twelve years old, Lyndon Johnson proclaimed to some friends, "Someday, I'm going to be president of the United States."[1] The other children said they wouldn't vote for him, to which he replied, "I won't need your votes," as if he already knew how to steal elections. As a young man in his early twenties during his college years, he would go to Saturday-night dances dressed in a bright shirt, his hair combed into an elaborate pompadour, where he would strut around and tell anyone who would listen that he was going to be the president of the United States one day—an ambition repeated numerous times to others and no doubt thousands more to himself, as he grew older. In college, he told a fellow student, "Politics is a science, and if you work hard enough at it, you can be president. I'm going to be president."[2] Another time, Lyndon broke up with his girlfriend, Carol Davis, because her father detested the entire Johnson family. Her father forbade her to marry into "that no-account Johnson family," saying, "Everyone in Blanco County knew that Lyndon's grandfather Sam had been 'nothing but an old cattle rustler—one generation after another of shiftless dirt farmers and grubby politicians.'" Johnson retorted, "To hell with your daddy. I wouldn't marry you or anyone in your whole damned family . . . And you can tell your daddy that someday I'll be president of this country."[3]

Eventually, securing the presidency became a deeply ingrained obsession. Given the poverty of his family and his nominal education, he would have to explore every possible way to achieve his goal; he would not need the conventional path as long as he could use other, quasi-constitutional, means.

_____

1. Caro, *The Path*, p. 100.
2. Dugger, p. 122.
3. Ibid., p. 124.

Even when he was a child, qualified observers saw troubling character traits within him that portended the kind of extralegal methods that would characterize his political life. His grandmother on his mother's side, Ruth Baines, regarded him as a disobedient delinquent and had considerable skepticism about Lyndon's future. "More than once," Lyndon's brother, Sam Houston Johnson, recalled, "she told my folks and anyone else who would listen, 'That boy is going to wind up in the penitentiary—just mark my words.'"[4] Lyndon apparently did not disagree with her, saying as he recalled his youth, "I was only a hairsbreadth away from going to jail."[5] This nascent criminality grew stronger until it was LBJ's central attribute.

Despite the realities of his impoverished family, Lyndon always liked to portray them as pillars of their community. J. Evetts Haley, a contemporary Texas historian, in 1964 noted Johnson's "genius of warping time and coincidence to his political purpose," citing as one example his frequent exploitation of the community, Johnson City; Johnson claimed it was named after his family, though it was not.[6] He would often introduce himself as "Lyndon Johnson from Johnson City," his way of implicitly communicating the status accorded to his family for being founders of the town; after he left Texas for Washington, he would use the same technique, yet stretch the lie even further to leave the impression not only that his family founded the town but that they were of some special aristocratic lineage. As Johnson's most prolific biographer Robert Caro confirmed, if anyone asked Johnson directly whether there was a connection, "he would confirm that impression, saying that Johnson City had been founded by his grandfather, a statement that was, of course, not true."[7]

Lyndon had learned this bit of skullduggery from his father, Sam, who had moved his family to Johnson City so he could claim the same thing. He was actually the town drunk; he owed everyone there and was in debt until the day he died.[8] After using up all the credit he could muster in Johnson City, he ventured to other towns in which to charge his purchases; he would open up new accounts and rack up more debt in various stores, until they cut him off. Truman Fawcett, the son of a drugstore owner in Johnson City, said that "he'd save a little cash money and put down some money on his bills here. But he couldn't ever catch up . . . He was a man who didn't pay his bills."[9]

---

4. Caro, *The Path*, p. 102; Dugger, p. 77.
5. Caro, *The Path*, p. 130.
6. Ibid., p. 153; Haley, p. 14.
7. Caro, *The Path*, p. 130.
8. Ibid., p. 90.
9. Ibid., p. 94.

Even many years after Johnson's death, some of his congressional aides during the 1930–1950s still believed the Johnson hyperbole about how his forebears were the town's founders was true: In his oral history recording at the Johnson Library, Horace Busby stated, "Johnson had awfully strong class feelings. They were not of someone from the under class feeling strongly against the upper class; it was the fact that Johnson [felt]—this is my interpretation of it, and this applied when he was president—that there were an awful lot of people from the upper classes elsewhere who did not understand he was from the upper class in Johnson City. *I mean, it was aristocrat against aristocrat*"[10] (emphasis added). This stunning comment, from someone who worked with Johnson so closely for so many years, clearly shows that Johnson's delusions had spread to certain of his credulous subordinates. After all that time with Johnson, Busby was not aware of the poverty, the near starvation of the family, or the filthy house in which LBJ grew up. (A childhood friend of Johnson's told Robert Caro of how he ate dinner once at the Johnson house and was served a few scraps of bread with a little bit of bacon, which was "rancid.")[11] It is instructive as to how so many of Johnson's closest associates during his presidency—men like Marvin Watson and Jack Valenti—had still not fully understood their mentor many years after his death; the reason, of course, was their own credulity in believing anything Johnson said, despite the fact that his compulsive lying about everything, even when he didn't have to lie, was well-known by them and everyone else who knew Johnson.

As for his mother, Rebekah, the regular folks in Johnson City had always felt she was pretentious—uppity, perhaps—and not quite as sophisticated as she liked to portray herself. She felt that her education put her above the menial housework required of a country lady. The inevitable result, of course, was manifested in the description of the Johnson home repeatedly heard by Robert Caro in his interviews with people who knew the family: "Filthy, dirty. It was a *dirty* house!"[12] Lyndon was a precocious tyrant who gave his mother ceaseless demands, turning his mother into his personal servant. He would demand, "Where's my shirt? Where's my britches?"[13] The reason for Rebekah's challenges in keeping a clean and orderly house and her capitulation to Lyndon's demands was that she had inherited genes that had been shaped by two generations before her; she was the third generation of a family that

10. Busby, Horace, Oral History Interview I, April 23, 1981, by Michael L. Gillette [Transcript], Internet copy, LBJ Library. http://www.lbjlib.utexas.edu/johnson/archives. hom/oralhistory.hom/BusbyH/Busby1.pdf
11. Caro, *The Path*, p. 95.
12. Ibid., p. 97.
13. Dallek, p. 44.

had suffered severe, incapacitating depression. Her son Lyndon B. Johnson would be the fourth.[14]

The Onset of Lyndon Johnson's "Great Depression"

Lyndon Johnson was usually brash and aggressive with others, but he began to experience moods, sometimes lasting for several days before he rebounded to his normal self, during which he would become very quiet and hardly say anything to anyone.[15] These episodes of loneliness would plague him for the rest of his life, leading him to rely on others to accompany him during their onset, in some cases having them promise they would stay near him while he slept. Johnson's slips into and out of the depressive phase of his condition were classic examples of manic-depressive cycles.[16] His basic character traits emerged as a child and stayed with him thereafter; another of these was his narcissistic, abnormally self-centered nature. He exacted attention from everyone around him, one way or the other, and according to his classmates, he wanted them to acknowledge his superiority. His tremendous ego had started annoying people by the time he was eleven. The above traits were the initial signs of a person afflicted with what is now referred to as bipolar disorder.[17]

His relationship with and treatment of his staff, now acknowledged in the more honest biographies of him, was often characterized by arrogance, derision, and condescension. For reasons that could only be understood by a person holding a doctoral degree in psychology, they allowed themselves to be manipulated by Johnson in a way that is contrary to the training most self-respecting people get from childhood. The character deficiencies apparently held by all of his subordinates—traits which were obviously instantly detectable by Lyndon Johnson from the first interviews he had with them—allowed them to willingly participate in wholesale unethical, immoral, illegal, or unconstitutional actions, all for the pleasure of their paranoid and delusional boss.

In most cases, Johnson had to work up a violent outburst before he began berating his staff, either to them directly or when he attacked their competence to someone else. In at least one instance—the conversation he had with Bobby in the Oval Office as he quietly told Kennedy that he would

---

14. Hershman, p. 21.
15. Ibid., p. 172.
16. Hershman, pp. 319–320.
17. Ibid., p. 28.

not be selected as the vice presidential nominee—Johnson "urged him to stay at Justice, with its 'outstanding staff.' His own staff, Johnson said, wasn't much. He couldn't really count on Valenti, Jenkins, or Reedy. Moyers was good, but 'his most useful function was rewriting what other people did' . . . Kennedy was appalled. Johnson was bad-mouthing people who were devoting their lives to him."[18]

Dr. Bertram S. Brown, the psychiatrist who had seen a number of presidents and presidential aides, said, "Johnson's humiliation of his employees was a way of exercising his power . . . Johnson was a megalomaniac . . . He was a man of such narcissism that he thought he could do anything."[19] Eventually, Johnson's behavior apparently disintegrated so far that even his top advisers noticed it. According to Anthony Summers, "Two senior aides, Richard Goodwin and Bill Moyers, became so alarmed by the president's state of mind that, secretly and unbeknownst to each other, they turned to psychiatrists for advice."[20] In a letter to *The New York Times*, Richard Goodwin revealed years later, "We were describing a textbook case of paranoid disintegration, the eruption of long-suppressed irrationalities . . . The disintegration could continue, remain constant, or recede depending on the strength of Johnson's resistance."[21] Other Johnson assistants, like former press secretary George Reedy, observing his behavior on a daily basis for an extended period, believed the president was a "manic depressive."[22]

Left unattended and unchecked by the people around him due to the fear of unleashing one of his uncontrollable and violent rages, his condition would culminate in his becoming psychotic in 1966.

Lyndon Learns the Art of Manipulation

In 1923, at age fifteen, before his father fell ill, lost his seat in the legislature, and began a slide into indebtedness, unemployment, and drunkenness that had already cost them their farm, he called Lyndon and asked him to come to Austin so he could buy him a suit. Lyndon saw an opportunity to lay an intricate plan to manipulate his father into buying not just some cheap seersucker suit, but the finest suit in the store. Knowing how his father was highly concerned with appearances, never wanting to look poor, he asked his friend Milton Barnwell to drive him to Austin, not just once, but twice: The

18. Margolis, p. 281.
19. Kessler, *Inside the White House*, p. 32.
20. Summers, *Official and Confidential*, p. 339.
21. Goodwin, Richard N. *President Lyndon Johnson: The War Within. New York Times*, 8–21–1988.
22. Summers, *Official and Confidential*, p. 339.

first trip was to find the suit he wanted, a cream-colored twenty-five-dollar Palm Beach suit that he tried on to ensure it looked good on him. He then told the salesman that when he returned the next day with his father, the salesman must pretend Lyndon hadn't been there and then told him how he must showcase this particular suit and what he should say. The next day, Barnwell drove Lyndon back to Austin, where they met his father at the store; Lyndon's plan worked perfectly since Sam wouldn't dare ask to see a less expensive suit. He didn't appreciate the situation he had been put into, but he couldn't ask the clerk to see cheaper suits, and so he agreed to buy Lyndon the one he wanted.[23] Lyndon's preference for conspicuous clothes was consistent with his lifelong struggle as a manic-depressive. In a school where everyone else wore blue jeans or overalls, he was the only one who showed up daily in slacks, a white shirt, and tie, dress he occasionally augmented with a yellow silk shirt and ascot, or "the only Palm Beach suit and straw boater in town."[24] Lyndon's ability to lay intricate plans to accomplish his long-range objectives had only begun. It would be honed and perfected throughout the next fifty years of his life, even reappearing on the date he selected to be the last day of his life.

Johnson also began learning his skills of persuasion as a boy, following his father around the capitol and mimicking his style of "physical conversation," according to which Sam would rest his hand on the other man's lapel or around his shoulder and put their faces nearly nose to nose as they talked. He copied the way his daddy strutted and schmoozed and blustered with the other politicians in Austin as he began tasting the power of elective office. Men who knew him then recognized his early training, and they commented about it: "He was so much like his father that it was humorous to watch."[25]

But while Lyndon was copying his father's political style, the deepening economic recession would open a chasm between them that would never be healed. As late as 1920, the price of cotton had dropped from forty to eight cents per pound, and the crop itself was decimated by hot weather, yet Sam Johnson tried to keep up appearances; the local paper reported that "Hon. S. E. Johnson and his little son Lyndon, of Stonewall, were among the prominent visitors in Johnson City on Wednesday of this week. Mr. Johnson has one of the largest and best farms in this section of Texas, and has been kept quite busy of late supervising its cultivation."[26] In truth, by Lyndon's twelfth birthday that year, Sam Johnson's farm was on the threshold of

---

23. Caro, *The Path*, p. 104.
24. Hershman, p. 31.
25. Caro, *The Path*, pp. 75–76.
26. Ibid., p. 90.

being foreclosed upon; the "big land deals" and his cars "were nothing but a front."[27]

The disintegration of Sam's career affected Lyndon psychologically; the reports of Lyndon's rejection of his father after Sam had become caught up in the collapse of the agricultural markets in 1920, forcing the sale of the farm in 1922, suggest that he was suddenly now very embarrassed by what followed: the complete collapse of his father's political career in 1923. Sam had turned down big money bribes that year to throw support behind legislation he had proudly sponsored called the "blue-sky bill"; it was intended to protect farmers from being swindled by "high-pressure salesmen" peddling phony oil stocks and was popular among his constituents. Lyndon's sister Josefa used to say to her friends whenever they wanted Sam's permission for something, "Let's get him talking about the Blue Sky Law. Then he'll be in a good mood and he'll say 'all right.'"[28] The virtual collapse of Sam's health followed the loss of the farm and his solvency, leading to bleak years of indebtedness, drunkenness, and the near starvation of his family; all this was seven years before the start of the Great Depression.

Lyndon's rejection of Sam at this point suggests that he saw his father's noble actions regarding the blue-sky law as being the cause of all the family's financial problems and the collapse of his political career. It was a lesson which he clearly never forgot: When the choice involved questions of morality, Lyndon Johnson consistently chose the more pragmatic and profitable, less noble avenue throughout his lifetime.

Lyndon Johnson Goes to College

After his father's political, financial, and physical collapse, Lyndon took off with a couple of other Johnson City boys to make a new life in California; after a few fruitless years there, Johnson decided in 1927 to return home and enroll in college at the Southwest Texas State Teachers College in San Marcos. That was the first year the college would graduate its first fully accredited class. The state considered it a third-class college, and professors were therefore paid less than the scale for high school teachers; it was hard for the school to attract good faculty because of the low pay, and most who taught at San Marcos were there because they couldn't find a job anywhere else, just as the students were there because they couldn't afford to attend anywhere else.[29]

---

27. Ibid., p. 91.
28. Ibid., p. 84.
29. Caro, *The Path*, p. 142.

How intensely Lyndon Johnson's former classmates at San Marcos hated him was stunning; Robert Caro spent several years interviewing people who knew him during those years and concluded: "By the time the researcher completes his work on Lyndon Johnson's college years, he knows that one alumnus had not been exaggerating when he said, 'A lot of people at San Marcos didn't just dislike Lyndon Johnson; they *despised* Lyndon Johnson'"[30] (emphasis added).

When he arrived at San Marcos, he begged his cousin, the captain of the football team, to allow him to stay in a rent-free apartment above the college president's garage, from which he got to know the president.[31] Clearly, the single most important thing Lyndon learned in college was how to control powerful men who were flattered by his exceedingly deferential, sycophantic treatment of them. During his years there, he became more and more skillful at manipulating people, both those in superior positions as well as those below him, through bestowing favors in some cases and trickery, bribery, or outright deceit in others.

In his later years he used the same techniques on other powerful men, politicians who had themselves bullied and blustered their way to the top of their respective careers in the Congress and Senate of the United States. As he learned how and when and to whom to apply this natural and inherited talent, he began to manipulate the faculty and administrative staff of his college, whose president, Cecil Eugene Evans, he found to be particularly vulnerable. Chapter 8 of Caro's first book, titled *Bull Johnson,* vividly describes this talent. Prexy Evans was an aloof man who generally avoided talking to students, except for Lyndon Johnson. He responded strongly to Johnson's sycophancy and gave him a series of jobs, starting with gardening and groundskeeping that culminated in working as his personal assistant.[32] Prexy Evans was the man upon whom Johnson practiced what would become his patented "Johnson treatment." He was excessively deferential to Evans and would run errands for him or his wife without their even asking him to do so. By learning their likes and dislikes, their mannerisms and habits, he was able to become practically a personal servant to them while remaining on the college's payroll. He would go into town early in the morning to retrieve a newspaper so that Evans could read it with his breakfast and accompany Mrs. Evans on shopping trips to carry her packages or groceries. Doing these favors led to quick promotions, including "inside jobs" such as janitorial work, ordinarily given only to athletes. Within five weeks of his arrival at

---

30. Ibid., p. 196.
31. Ibid., pp. 143–145.
32. Ibid., pp. 145–153.

the college, he was working inside the president's office in a newly created position that had never existed before.[33]

Author Caro quoted a Johnson college classmate, Mylton Kennedy, describing Lyndon Johnson's unctuousness: "'Words won't come to describe how Lyndon acted toward the faculty—how kowtowing he was, how suck-assing he was, how brownnosing he was.'"[34] Caro found that many of the people who knew Lyndon Johnson from the San Marcos period intensely disliked him for the same reasons, a feeling as much to do with how he was such a brazen sycophant to those above him as it was about how condescending he was towards his fellow students. Johnson's cringing obsequiousness toward Evans became one of his hallmark character traits that especially manifested around powerful men in superior positions. He knew instinctively that in the San Marcos arena of 1927, the most powerful man in town or on campus was President Evans, and he had to get as close to him as possible in order to target his next quarry. Johnson volunteered to do anything and everything Prexy Evans required, including running errands for him and his wife, flattering him at every opportunity, and generally treated him as though he was the most brilliant, erudite man in the world; his efforts to befriend this lonely, marginally intelligent, and otherwise nondescript man paid off. When he got to Washington, he would use the same techniques to ingratiate himself among the most powerful people in the nation: Speaker of the House, Sam Rayburn; Senator Richard Russell; and President Franklin Roosevelt.[35] Johnson had become a powerful force in San Marcos by the time he departed the campus, even though many of the people he left behind could not stand the man they had nicknamed Bull (for bullshit) Johnson because of his chronic habits of lying and deceit.[36]

The yearbook at San Marcos, the *Pedagog*, contained a section called "The Cat's Claw" that mocked certain students' foibles. In the 1928 edition, Lyndon Johnson was singled out for particularly harsh treatment: a picture of a jackass replaced Lyndon's photo with a caption that said he was a member of the "Sophistry Club . . . Master of the gentle art of spoofing the general public."[37] A humor column in the campus newspaper, the *College Star*, established the following definition: "Bull: Greek philosophy in which Lyndon Johnson has a MB degree." One of his classmates explained, "Master of Bullshit—that's what MB means . . . He was known as the biggest liar on the campus. In private,

---

33. Ibid.
34. Ibid., p. 153.
35. Ibid., p. 199.
36. Ibid., p. 160.
37. Ibid.

when there were no girls around, we called him 'Bullshit Johnson.'"[38] The 1930 edition of the *Pedagog*, released during his senior year, was equally vicious on Johnson and loathsome of his mentor President Evans. Evans wrote that "a number of pages . . . aroused bitter resentment among our students," even though only one student, Lyndon Johnson, resented them. Johnson talked with Evans, and shortly thereafter, Evans ordered his secretary, Tom Nichols, two deans, and several professors to locate every copy they could find and cut out the offending section. By the time they were done, it had been removed from virtually all copies of the yearbook.[39]

The above activity occurred forty-odd years before researchers began looking for glimpses of the Johnson persona at San Marcos; it was as though Lyndon Johnson knew he would eventually receive such scrutiny and needed to act then to shape his reputation and future legacy. He could not allow the assessment of his fellow students to persist and be discovered later by people investigating his past. The destruction of the San Marcos yearbooks was an early marker for measuring the length of his focal point into the future, and represented the starting point of the planning he undertook to become president.

Lyndon Johnson Goes to Washington

After graduating from San Marcos, Johnson spent a year in Houston teaching and coaching at Sam Houston High School, where he liked to talk politics with other teachers and the students on his debate teams. While he was beginning his second year there, a newly elected congressman, Richard Kleberg, gave him a job as an administrative aide. Johnson lived meagerly in a run-down hotel and worked long hours for his congressman, who exercised virtually no power since he had the least seniority of any member.[40] Kleberg was the grandson of the founder of the King Ranch, an enormous two-thousand-square-mile empire that included whole towns within it. As a fabulously rich Texas cowboy, his interest in Washington politics was peripheral at best; he was a playboy and spent more time at the Congressional and Burning Tree golf courses or the polo grounds than inside the Capitol building. He usually spent his morning sleeping off the previous night's poker and bourbon parties and often did not show up to his office in room 258 of the Cannon Building. His detached view of his responsibilities afforded his new aide ample opportunity to fill the

38. Ibid., p. 160.
39. Ibid., p. 198.
40. Ibid., p. 219.

vacuum created by his absence.[41] Lyndon Johnson was thrust into his job as a congressional aide with no training on even the fundamentals of the position; he could not type and he did not know how to dictate a letter, or how to respond to the hundreds of incoming letters seeking assistance from some federal agency or bureau. He had to learn the role on his own, using his wile and whatever tools he could muster from the congressman's office.

Congressman Kleberg delegated to Lyndon Johnson practically all of his own responsibilities; since Kleberg would not even read the mail, Johnson did that too and took whatever action he felt was necessary. Upon learning from other secretaries the way around the federal bureaucracies, he slowly made contacts in key agencies, expanding his telephone list every day until he could at least keep up with the mail, even though his limited dictation skills made him take a long time to accomplish it, having to resort to handwriting the letters he wanted the secretary to type. As his confidence level increased, so did his chutzpah; he began impersonating Congressman Kleberg on the telephone whenever he needed another congressman to do something he felt was particularly important.

Johnson's New Aides

Johnson eventually brought two of the students he had taught in Houston, Gene Latimer and L. E. Jones, to Washington to work as secretaries under him; importing young men from Texas allowed him to exert more control over them than the alternative of simply recruiting Washington-area assistants. To avoid putting them on the district's clerical payroll allotted by Congress—keeping most of that for himself—he secured positions for them in the House Post Office, which paid $130 per month.[42] They were required to work in the post office from 5:00 a.m. to noon; after a thirty-minute lunch, they worked for Lyndon the rest of the day, usually until eight or nine o'clock but often until 11:30 p.m. or later. Latimer, then only eighteen years old, was working eighteen-hour days, barely getting by on his post office salary and the pittance Johnson allowed him from the district's payroll, $91.66 per month. He kept the office open on weekends and would only let Latimer and Jones have free time after 3:00 p.m. on Sundays.[43]

Johnson's demeaning treatment characterized his relationships with his aides, who in most cases nevertheless remained loyal to him. As soon as

41. Ibid.
42. Ibid., p. 230.
43. Ibid., pp. 227–231.

Latimer came into the congressman's office, promptly at twelve-thirty every day after a fast sandwich and drink, Johnson would rip into the mail sacks, barking out instructions to this former debater who so admired his boss. They developed a regimen by which Johnson would tell Latimer in a few words how to reply to each letter: If Johnson said to "butter them up," Latimer knew that meant to lay it on thick; if Lyndon wanted to tell someone how much he liked them, he would say, "You're the greatest guy in the world." Latimer says, "I did get to be a master of laying it on, all right."[44] Johnson trained Latimer to respond to letters with just a few words of instruction—"Say yes. Say no. Tell him we're looking into it. Butter him up"—and Latimer would prepare a letter on his typewriter as though Johnson had written it.[45] Lyndon dictated letters requiring a more detailed response to Jones in another room. Johnson didn't want to distract Latimer, whose "typewriter was supposed never to stop."[46]

As the volume of mail increased with the economic collapse of the Depression, other congressional offices sent mimeographed or *pro forma* responses, or simply didn't reply at all, and fell still further behind. But Congressman Kleberg's office answered every possible letter, because Lyndon Johnson was convinced that doing so would avoid the fate awaiting those congressmen who had lost touch with their districts. Johnson became consumed with the notion that every letter was critical to keeping Kleberg, and thus himself, connected to every constituent in the district. Consequently, he insisted on personal responses to be sent the same day a given letter was received, and on perfection in the typed correspondence; errors would be marked up and the document sent back for retyping. If a response entailed contacting some other department or agency, then that letter had to be sent the same day as well. When his assistants thought they were finished after hours of nonstop typing, Johnson would bring another pile of top-priority letters, the responses to which had to be completed before they left for the night.[47]

In every other congressional office, a constituent's request for assistance would require that statements and justifications be produced before the matter could be referred to the appropriate agency. Requests from the Fourteenth District of Texas were forwarded to the agency that could comply and pursued vigorously, especially requests from veterans for a disability pension, even if the case had been previously heard and denied because of the absence of a connection to a war injury. Johnson would telephone his contacts at the

---

44. Ibid., p. 231.
45. Ibid.
46. Ibid.
47. Ibid., p. 233.

Veterans Administration, and if he was denied, he would procure the veteran a lawyer and file a formal written appeal. Johnson would often accompany the lawyer to the following hearings, but due to his obsession with secrecy, he would request the stenographer to be instructed not to take down his remarks. Latimer would often see the typed minutes of the hearing and see the same sentence, "Mr. Johnson spoke off the record," and know what was coming next—that the decision would be reversed in favor of Johnson's "client." Referring to these outcomes, Latimer said, "It was almost unheard of to get someone 'service-connected' [status] after it had been denied, but the Chief did it. Many times."[48]

Johnson called Latimer "son," and Latimer called him "chief." Latimer admitted he had never called Johnson by his first name and seemed astonished at the very thought he could have been so impertinent.[49] Latimer feared but also idolized Johnson, and acted as though he were completely under Johnson's control. Johnson could convince Latimer to perform any of his requests, that they were simply essential, the right thing to do. If Latimer ever fell out of line, Johnson would make him feel so bad that Latimer claimed he wanted to shoot himself and that it was unforgivable to let Johnson down.[50] He would experience a series of nervous breakdowns and "recurrent, severe bouts of alcoholism." He understood their cause: "'The work broke me,' he says."[51] Despite the extreme pressure exerted by his boss, he invariably returned to Johnson's offices, because he felt he could not do anything else. Gene Latimer became the model for the kind of aide Johnson would value: one who would unconditionally accept whatever orders were given to him without regard to issues of ethics or legality. That is what Latimer meant when he said that Johnson could talk you into *anything* and make you feel it was right.

Latimer was the more malleable of the two clerks working for Johnson in the 1930s. L. E. Jones was much more independent, but Johnson had appealed to his ambition and promised to help him achieve his dreams if he worked hard for him. But Johnson did this in a demeaning way, actually ridiculing the college education that Jones had worked so hard to achieve. Johnson took pleasure in critiquing Jones's letters, slashing across them with his pen, making rejections; Johnson thought they were "too literary": "Is that what they taught you at college, LE? Dumbest goddamned thing I ever read."[52] Jones was a neat, clean, and prim fellow who was disgusted by any kind of crudeness. Nevertheless, Johnson made him take dictation from him while he

---

48. Caro, *The Path* . . ., p. 235.
49. Ibid., p. 237.
50. Ibid.
51. Ibid.
52. Ibid., p. 238.

sat on the toilet; though Jones resisted, Johnson insisted, and he stood in the doorway with his head and nose averted and took dictation. This procedure started with Jones and later became the ultimate form of condescension with which Johnson could treat his subordinates, a powerful way to remove their dignity and assert his authority.[53] Richard Goodwin, a Kennedy aide who continued serving under Johnson when he became president, confirms that Johnson required subordinates and even peers to conduct business while he defecated in the bathroom throughout his career, in the Senate, the vice presidency, and even into the Oval Office.[54] But such repulsive behavior didn't end there; he was often observed by others as he scratched his rear end or crotch, picked his nose in meetings, or pulled his pants down to show his hernia operation when women were present nearby.[55]

Johnson's Condescension to Reporters, Others

Johnson's treatment of his first assistants on Capitol Hill became typical of how he would treat others throughout his career as a congressman, senator, vice president, and as the president. He would employ other methods to demean colleagues, reporters, and politicians, one of which was to call their attention to his manhood; he was apparently endowed with a larger-than-average penis that he referred to as "jumbo" to his friends as a young man.[56] One day, he offered to compare the length of his penis with that of any of the male journalists at the Johnson ranch. "I'll match mine against any of yours," he said.[57] On another occasion, in a moment of exasperation with persistent reporters who wanted him to explain why the United States was at war with Vietnam, he opened his pants, withdrew his penis, and shouted, "This is why!"[58] Evidently, he thought exposing himself would be sufficient to appease his audience, who were so stunned that they walked away and forgot the original question. Johnson also enjoyed taunting reporters, businessmen, and politicians into joining him for a session of skinny-dipping in the White House pool to demonstrate who was superior, if he felt they may have bested him in terms of intelligence, college alma mater, wealth, looks, political savvy, connections, or any other aspect.[59]

---

53. Ibid., p. 239.
54. Goodwin, Richard, pp. 256–258.
55. Caro, *Master* . . ., p. 122.
56. Caro, *The Path* . . ., p. 155.
57. Hershman, p. 211 (ref. Booth Mooney, *LBJ: an Irreverent Chronicle*, New York: Thomas Y. Crowell Col, 1976, p. 73).
58. Dallek, *Flawed* . . ., p. 491.
59. Haley, pp. 234–235.

People in Washington were generally shocked by Johnson's aggressiveness and single-minded intensity. His ironfisted resolve enabled him to achieve his goals regardless of obstacles. Contributing to the manic aggressiveness and fierce ambition were the paranoia, loneliness, and insecurities Johnson tried to hide.[60] Few people perceived his depressive periods, or how sullen and morose he would become, but one of his staff members once observed that "'Lyndon had a side to him. He could get very low. When he got real quiet it was bad,' sometimes 'very bad.'"[61] George Reedy, Johnson's former press secretary, admitted that Johnson's drinking, self-pity, and paranoia reached such depths that his staff often had to hide these tendencies from outsiders, acting as buffers to avoid exposing to the world just how peculiar he was. Reedy noted that during his agonizing depressed days spent holed up in bed, he still drank and spent a lot of time simply looking up at his bedroom ceiling and lashing out at anyone entering the room. Bill Moyers, worried about Johnson's mood, described a similar scene: "'He would just go within himself, just disappear—morose, self-pitying, angry.' While lying in bed with the covers pulled over his head, the President said that he felt he was in a Louisiana swamp, getting sucked under."[62]

Congressman Lyndon Johnson

When the congressman representing Austin and the Tenth Congressional District died on February 22, 1937, the candidates to replace him—senior politicians holding various offices, such as the late congressman Buchanan's trusted manager, C. N. Avery; the district's state senator, Houghton Brownlee; and Austin's mayor, Tom Miller—politely deferred entering the race pending a decision by the widow Buchanan on whether to run or not. Lyndon was virtually unknown in the Tenth District, as Blanco County had been moved into that district only two years before, so he had no base there in 1937. Lyndon sought his father's advice on how to proceed, knowing that his lifetime goal of becoming the president depended upon him winning this seat. Sam advised Lyndon to announce his candidacy as soon as possible, since Mrs. Buchanan was "an old woman . . . too old for a fight."[63] Johnson immediately announced his candidacy, and Mrs. Buchanan bowed out of the race. A special election—not a party primary, but a "sudden death" vote after which the winner would become the congressman regardless of party—was

---

60. Caro, *The Path* . . ., p. 200.
61. Hershman, p. 44.
62. Dallek, *Flawed Giant* . . . p. 255
63. Caro, *The Path* . . ., p. 399.

scheduled with eight names on the ballot, including a number of older, more experienced local politicians who faced off against twenty-eight-year-old Lyndon Johnson (whose campaign would constantly refer to him as being "almost thirty").[64] Johnson quickly assembled a campaign organization determined to have his poster nailed to every fence and telephone pole in the county. He told his boys that he wanted his picture in every paper in the district, so that "you can't wipe your ass on a piece of paper that hasn't got my picture on it."[65] During a long and bitterly fought campaign, he aligned himself with Roosevelt, worked himself sick, and spent, according to Ed Clark, Lyndon's sponsor and fund-raiser for the rest of his political career, between $75,000 and $100,000—the most expensive congressional race conducted in Texas history at that time. While his opponents concentrated on the cities and larger towns, Johnson focused on the most rural parts of the district, driving down long winding country roads, stopping at every general store to politick the owner and any farmers who were around. He correctly figured such a strategy was the only way to win with so many competitors in the race; their division of the "easy votes" in the cities seven ways allowed him to triumph by a margin of over three thousand votes out of about twenty-nine thousand cast.[66]

Johnson's overzealousness during his early years in Congress caused considerable friction with other congressmen; he broke unwritten rules, one of which related to a luncheon every Wednesday that was supposed to include only the members of the Texas delegation: two senators, twenty-one representatives, and Vice President Garner. Once per month, guests could attend; the other three luncheons were supposed to be closed to outside visitors, but Johnson, through his connection with Sam Rayburn, regularly brought guests to them anyway, despite the other members' bitter reactions. Johnson also preemptively announced to thousands of Texans the granting of major projects in congressional districts other than his own, before the member representing the affected district could do so. To his fellow Texas congressmen, including Dick Kleberg, his former employer, Johnson was simply usurping credit for successes he had nothing to do with. They began treating the new congressman with barely checked contempt, their animosity exacerbated by Johnson's overbearing personality, the way he strutted through the House dining room as if he were a famous Hollywood celebrity, smiling and nodding to his fans as he meandered through the tables, talking

---

64. Ibid., p. 403.
65. Ibid., p. 404.
66. Ibid., p. 436.

too loudly to whoever would reciprocate as other congressmen rolled their eyes and muttered under their breaths.[67]

Upon taking his congressional seat, Johnson inherited a major dilemma involving the construction company owned by Herman and George Brown, who would become some of his strongest backers. His predecessor, James P. Buchanan, had approved the start of construction on a huge government project, the Marshall Ford Dam, but the House Rivers and Harbors Committee had never voted on it, nor even held a hearing on its merits. Appropriations were not supposed to be made until a project was authorized; the only "authorization" had been an informal approval from President Roosevelt, who casually told Buchanan "he could have his dam" after Congress recessed for the year. Buchanan then persuaded the comptroller general's office to allow work to begin since he had received Roosevelt's verbal approval and Harold Ickes initiated the necessary order. When Johnson became congressman, the Brown & Root Company had already invested $1.5 million in equipment and preliminary work on the dam; shortly afterward, it was discovered that the federal government did not and under state law could not own the land upon which it was being built. Johnson's first congressional victory, with help from his lawyer-consultant Alvin Wirtz, was pushing Roosevelt to override what had been thought to be insurmountable legal ownership issues through a presidential order. In this manner Johnson repaid Brown & Root for their early support: the Marshall Ford Dam was the company's first major project, and it netted them $2 million.[68]

As soon as the legal issues were resolved and the appropriations resumed, the Browns clamored to make the dam higher, at an additional cost of $17 million, using the argument that the original height was inadequate for effective flood control; why this shortcoming was not considered earlier was never explained. Again using the able Alvin Wirtz's help, the original 190-foot-high dam would no longer be classified as a flood-control but as a power dam. That the flood-control portion of the dam—the additional seventy-eight feet—was not yet built would enable the Bureau of Reclamation to legally pay for it. But a gap remained of over $2 million that Wirtz's legal creativity could not eliminate. Johnson found a more creative lawyer, Abe Fortas, who rewrote the entire plan so that the initial 33 feet over the original 190 was classified as "dual use"—flood control and power generation. As a result, a third agency, the Public Works Administration, would pay for it.[69] The above legal morass would not be the last or most important that

---

67. Ibid., pp. 532–533.
68. Caro, *The Path* . . ., pp. 369–385, 459–462.
69. Ibid., pp. 462–465.

Fortas would be asked to solve, as will be noted below. The resolution to the Marshall Ford Dam cemented Johnson's long and fruitful relationship with the Brown brothers and their company, which would eventually become part of the corporation known as Halliburton.

Johnson inherited a poor staff when he arrived at Congress; two of his assistants were knowledgeable but undependable alcoholics. He immediately sought to correct this situation and looked for young Texas men, mostly recent graduates, especially campus newspaper editors and student leaders from the University of Texas in Austin. His first hire was John Connally, and the others that followed were mostly friends or acquaintances of someone who had already joined Johnson's staff in Austin or Washington. Walter Jenkins, who was invaluable to Johnson's career, came because he had worked in Connally's campaign for student body president. After following John to Washington, he started as a policeman at the Supreme Court and volunteered in Johnson's office after-hours. Johnson would arrange to place men in other government jobs, on other payrolls, where he could evaluate them at arm's length and use them as intelligence sources while admonishing them to avoid becoming known as "Johnson men." Such a practice would allow him to test their willingness to comply with his demands, especially that they work long hours for free as volunteers in his office. Though they worked for agencies such as the Federal Communications Commission (FCC) or the Agriculture Department (USDA)—two of his favorites for placing his people—Johnson made it clear to them that they were beholden to him for those jobs and he expected favors to be returned; they knew that their future careers were tied to his success.

Horace Busby came soon after Walter Jenkins, and later Jake Pickle, George Reedy, Cliff Carter, Bill Moyers, and Malcolm Wallace. Wallace, like Connally, had been president of the student union at UT. Unlike the conservative Connally, however, Wallace was a socialist—in fact, a Marxist. His psychological issues quickly become apparent as his association with his boss developed. Wallace exemplified how Johnson would exploit the weaknesses he perceived in other men; in this case, the results would be deadly for a number of people on the wrong side of Lyndon B. Johnson.

Johnson's World War II "Service"

After Pearl Harbor, Lyndon Johnson decided his political career would benefit from a stint in the navy. He visited Admiral Chester Nimitz, a Hill Country native, who signed the forms necessary to install Johnson as a lieutenant commander, even though he had no training or experience to justify such a position. He originally wanted to be assigned a job in Washington but went to

Undersecretary of the Navy James V. Forrestal to procure orders to conduct an inspection tour of West Coast training programs with his administrative assistant, John Connally, who had enlisted in the Naval Reserve. Johnson's lack of training caused his failure to salute an admiral. His reflection was characteristically self-absorbed: "I did not fully appreciate that my uniform completely concealed my status as a congressman . . . the fact that I looked like any other junior officer and . . . was expected to salute my superiors."[70] Perhaps Johnson felt the admiral had erred in not saluting him, Congressman Lyndon Johnson. Johnson spent several weeks in Los Angeles where one of his financial supporters, who was counsel for Paramount Pictures, arranged for Johnson and John Connally to attend screenings and parties and long sessions with a Hollywood photographer and voice coach to help Johnson improve his speaking style and posing skills; meanwhile, dispatches came in describing the fighting going on in such places as the Bataan Peninsula and the Makassar Straits.[71]

Apparently, the contrast between Johnson's wartime experiences and the battles being waged in faraway places caused his mistress, Alice Glass, to become disillusioned with his character. After five months of politicking and partying on the West Coast, Johnson tried to legitimize his responsibilities by securing an overseas assignment; his secretaries back in Washington had been telling his constituents that though his present location was unknown, he was en route to the war zone in the Pacific. He was finally dispatched with two other congressmen as "observers," a capacity that made them useful to General Douglas MacArthur in relation to his own political necessities; evidently, Johnson subjected MacArthur to his famous treatment at some point, given the bounty he would bring back to Washington.

Johnson arrived early in June in an area of northern Australia that was considered a combat zone. Commander Johnson, like the other observers, accompanied a squadron assigned to bomb an enemy airfield. The mission of June 9 was code-named Tow Nine and involved eleven twin-engine bombers known as Martin B-26A Marauders of the Twenty-second Bombardment Group from Port Moresby, New Guinea. Their target was Lae airdrome, an important Japanese installation on New Guinea's northern coast. At this point, two completely different stories of Johnson's short ride in a Marauder emerge. The first is Johnson's own, which was subsequently reshaped into an account (*The Mission*, by Martin Caidin and Edward Hymoff) that was published in 1964 just as he was preparing his run for the presidency. Caidin was an already-established aviation writer,

---

70. Dugger, p. 239.
71. Caro, *Means*, pp. 24–25.

best known for books on space exploration and WWII in the Pacific; Johnson had doubtlessly heard of his books and apparently commissioned him to create another one.

The second version of Johnson's ride on a Marauder couldn't have differed more from *The Mission*, but considering that it was told by veterans who were actually there, it is the more believable story. The following quotations regarding the story of Johnson's mission, and the Silver Star controversially awarded to him, were taken from the B-26 Marauder Historical Society's website:[72]

> The fact is LBJ never got within sight of Japanese forces. His mission, like so much of his life, was a lie . . . The exact origins of the contrived decoration remain unknown. Major General R. K. Sutherland, MacArthur's chief of staff, made the award in MacArthur's name on June 18, 1942, just nine days after the alleged episode. The following day Brigadier General W. F. Marquat wrote Johnson, filling LBJ's request for a signed copy of the citation. In his cover letter, Marquat stated, "Of course, your outstanding bravery in volunteering for a so-called suicide mission in order to get a first-hand view of what our Army fliers go through has been the subject of much favorable comment since your departure. It is indeed a great government we have when members of the Congress take THOSE chances in order to better serve their fellow men in the legislative bodies. You surely earned your decoration and I am so happy about your having received the award."
>
> Clearly, the perception of Johnson's valor as characterized in General Marguat's letter was not shared by aircrews at the sharp end. Far from the "suicide mission" the general alluded to, 22nd Bomb Group airmen had a far more realistic attitude toward Lae. Records and combat veterans attest that the group lost twice as many aircraft over Rabaul, the naval-air bastion on New Britain, as at Lae. Colonel Leon G. Lewis, USAF (Ret), who flew with Lieutenant Hayes in Shamrock, recalled, "The targets, Lae and Salamaua, were milk runs; on the other hand, Rabaul was a tough mission. We were not aware at the time of Lyndon Johnson's write-up for the Silver Star; they were scarce for aircrews."
>
> The decoration remains a sore point with many 22nd Bomb Group veterans. The Hare's crew chief, retired Master Sergeant W.

H. Harrison, said, "As to the strangeness of LBJ's Silver Star . . . no other crew member aboard 1488 received one." Equally adamant was the Hare's regular gunner Robert Marshal, who said, "We didn't know (LBJ) was awarded the Silver Star until the book came out. We didn't like it. If he got it, then so should everyone else on the mission." In truth, if any decoration was awarded the various observers on the mission, it should have been the Air Medal. Ordinarily presented for five or more missions, it was regarded by aviators as an "I-was-there" award; a means of setting apart those who have performed a combat function. *Award of the Silver Star—even had Johnson's citations been accurate—was an insult to every man who earned the medal.* (emphasis added)

The two leading biographers of Johnson, Robert Caro and Robert Dallek, commented on Johnson's Silver Star in a CNN report, *The Story of LBJ's Silver Star*, by Jamie McIntyre (CNN military affairs correspondent) and Jim Barnett (CNN producer):

Robert Caro: The most you can say about Lyndon Johnson and his Silver Star is that it is surely one of the most undeserved Silver Stars in history. Because [even] if you accept everything that he said, he was still in action for no more than thirteen minutes and only as an observer. Men who flew many missions, brave men, never got a Silver Star . . . I would say that it's an issue of exaggerations. He said that he flew on many missions, not one mission. He said that the crew members, the other members of the Air Force group, were so admiring of him that they called him Raider Johnson. Neither of these things are true.

Robert Dallek: What I concluded was that there was an agreement, a deal made between LBJ and Gen. MacArthur. And the deal was Johnson would get this medal, which somebody later said was the least deserved and most talked about medal in American military history. And MacArthur, in return, had a pledge from Johnson that he would lobby FDR to provide greater resources for the southwest Pacific theater . . . It matters that the record is accurate because it speaks volumes about the man, about his character, about his place in history, about judgments that historians make on him. Is he to be trusted?

When Johnson returned from his war experience, he initially told others that he didn't deserve the medal, claiming that he wouldn't wear it. He even wrote a letter of formal refusal, stating "I cannot in good conscience accept the decoration" and had the letter typed, ready for his signature, but it was filed away, unsigned and never to be mailed.[73] Instead, he arranged to have the Silver Star presented to him in public, several times. He purchased a jeweler's quality battle ribbon emblematic of the Silver Star at a store in Washington and wore it often in public appearances; once at an American Legion post in Fort Worth, he had the commander pin it on him while "a crowd of Legionnaires cheered and Johnson stood before them, head bowed, face somber, hardly able to blink back the tears."[74] To make sure people recognized it, he would place his left hand on his lapel and pull it forward and back, waving it, as he extolled his own heroic and patriotic, death-defying actions during his twenty-minute airplane ride.

Joe M. Kilgore, a Texan who worked for Lyndon Johnson for twenty years, finally realized that Johnson would believe only that which he wanted to, that Johnson often mistook his delusions for truth. Some instances, such as his grandfather's supposed death at the Alamo, were relatively harmless; others, like his belief that he and he alone knew how to beat back the Communists in Vietnam, were highly destructive.[75] According to Kilgore, Johnson went from feigning surprise at receiving the Silver Star, and uttering doubts about whether it was deserved, to complaining that it was "only" the Silver Star; he came to believe he had been shortchanged and should have been granted a superior medal—the Medal of Honor: "He believed it totally."[76] Johnson's propensity to become convinced that the lie was the truth, no matter what, would manifest over and over throughout his career.

The Johnson Recruits—Class of 1948–49

Johnson recruited three of his men during the tumultuous year of 1948, concurrently with the infamous campaign that culminated in his successful theft of the election to the Senate. Johnson met Cliff Carter in 1937 and got to know him further in 1946 when Carter became involved in Olin Teague's congressional campaign. Apparently Carter had impressed Johnson because two years later, as Johnson prepared for his Senate campaign, he called Carter to ask him to be the campaign manager for the Sixth District; thus, their association began in May, 1948. Carter furnished an oral interview explaining how he was appointed to a position of U.S. marshal he not only did not solicit but did not even want:[77]

---

73. Caro, *Means*, p. 51.
74. Ibid., p. 52.
75. Ibid., pp. 52, 53.
76. Ibid.
77. Transcript, Clifton C. Carter Oral History Interview I, 10/1/68, by Dorothy L. Pierce, Internet Copy, LBJ Library, p. 3–5.

Then he won the Democratic nomination and went on to win the election as United States Senator in November, 1948. And on June 8, 1949, he called me one morning—8 o'clock in the morning—and said he wanted to submit my name for nomination as United States Marshal for the Southern District of Texas. I don't think up to that minute I had thought more than sixty seconds in my entire life about a United States Marshal—what a Marshal did—and I thanked him and told him that I was grateful for his consideration, but I really couldn't undertake the job . . . Mr. Johnson said, "Hell, I'm not going to take an answer of no on that. I'll call you back this same time in the morning . . . So, I'll call you back in the morning. I don't want to hear the word no.

Carter found someone else to manage his bottling plant as he took the appointment and went on the government payroll, all while working as a "volunteer" for Johnson, who put his key men on other payrolls to minimize his own; Carter said that Jake Pickle, who was running the overall campaign, told him, "Now, what I ought to do is get you on some company's payroll where you'll be doing this traveling for them and actually attending to this work."[78] Carter refused to allow the campaign to cover his expenses, telling Pickle, "I was doing this because I believed in Mr. Johnson; that I was an amateur and that I wanted to retain my amateur status. I didn't want to be paid for any of it."[79] Carter said that Johnson seemed to him to be planning his presidential candidacy since he first met him in 1937, and specifically "talked to him about that in the 1948 campaign when he was running for the Senate."[80] Johnson had clearly identified useful aspects of Carter's character by then—undoubtedly his 100 percent devotion and willingness to perform any task assigned to him were paramount—and had already decided that he would fit well into his organization. In 1954, Johnson made him the campaign manager for five districts and would rely on him for certain expected future tasks that would require delicate but forceful assertiveness.

Horace Busby and Malcolm Wallace joined the Johnson campaign about the same time as Carter; in fact, it was Carter who brought Wallace to Washington DC, introducing him to Johnson at Johnson's home on 30th Place. Johnson had placed Wallace in the Agriculture Department, and by 1951, Wallace had passed an FBI background check and obtained work as an economist. But as with all the other men installed in government positions by his mentor, Wallace was serving primarily as a Johnson man. Mac Wallace

78. Ibid. p. 6.
79. Ibid.
80. Ibid. p. 43.

and Horace Busby were not only classmates, but fellow radical leftist-socialists and campus activists; both were members of the exclusive Friar Society. They were involved in the same issues during the late 1940s, including the widely reported protests against the firing of the president of the University of Texas, Homer Rainey, a socialist who had been heavily attacked by conservative Texans. When President Rainey was dismissed by the board of regents because of his liberal persuasions, Busby used *The Daily Texan* to organize a campus rally for Rainey. At this rally, the student body president, Malcolm Wallace, led a march to the state capital and then a small group of students to the governor's office, forcing the governor to temporarily leave town. During this period, Busby and Wallace shared the same liberal political beliefs, and both were members in some of the liberal campus clubs and organizations. They also had in common the appearance of both their names in numerous Texas newspapers being read in Washington by Congressman—soon-to-be Senator—Lyndon B. Johnson, who used such news items to recruit men to come to Washington. Busby, as the student editor of the *Texan*, received two letters from Johnson complimenting him on his editorials. When he received an offer from Johnson to come to Washington, he said that John Connally urged him to accept it: "The Congressman is regarded on the Hill, has been regarded almost from the beginning of his career, as having nearly always one of the two or three best staffs in Congress. You don't lose any respect on the House side of Capitol Hill working for Lyndon Johnson, because people just assume that you're good."[81]

Johnson felt that his staff owed him 100 percent loyalty for having the honor of working for him. When any of them went into the military, he expected they would return to work for him, and if they didn't, he took it as a personal insult. Walter Jenkins was the first to return to Johnson's staff; according to Horace Busby, while Johnson was sulking about his employees, he said that he thought Jenkins was okay, but not as good as Connally had been:[82]

> Walter was one of his boys and had gone off in the army and became a major . . . and was back and was working like a dog trying to win the Congressman's approval and he just didn't count. He knew he had a very able assistant, almost a genius assistant, but that still wasn't good enough. Well, what he really wanted was another John Connally . . . He was going to get him another John Connally.

---

81. Busby, Horace, Oral History Interview I, April 23, 1981, by Michael L. Gillette [Transcript], Internet copy, LBJ Library. http://www.lbjlib.utexas.edu/johnson/archives. hom/oralhistory.hom/BusbyH/Busby1.pdf
82. Ibid.

But he [Johnson] kept on sulking. It was clear he was still sulking . . . he was walking around the room and his hands were always poked deep down in his pants pockets, and he was jiggling his keys and change . . . When he was thinking, that was the way he thought. He'd walk around the room looking up at the ceiling and jiggling the change in his pocket. Again, John (Connally), being the most sensitive of the group to these nuances of mood, said, Well, what else is eating on you? Is there something else you want? It took a little coaxing, but he finally came out with it. There was something else he wanted. And he said, "As long as I have been in Washington, I have observed one thing. That the men who go far there, and there's never been an exception to it, they always have some little fellow in their office who sits back in a corner. He doesn't have to have any personality, doesn't have to know how to dress, usually they don't have their tie tied right, a button off their shirt"—typical Johnson, running on at this—"nicotine stains on their fingers, no coat, all like that. But they sit back in the corner, they don't meet any of the people that come in the office. They read and they think and they come up with new ideas, and they make the fellow smart. I've never had one of those, and I want one."

Horace Busby's recollection of Johnson's interest in having his own "little fellow in the corner" makes for interesting conjecture over which of his many congressional aides fit that particular role: Certainly not Connally, probably not Jenkins, and obviously not Wallace; was Busby himself, in the early years, of that genus? Clearly, the original fellow in the corner Johnson brought to Washington, while he was still an aide to Congressman Kleberg, was Gene Latimer.

The import of the last few paragraphs cannot be overstated: Lyndon Johnson had created certain niches for each of his assistants, whether they were on his own payroll or in other government agencies, such as the Congressional Post Office, the Federal Communications Commission, or the Department of Agriculture. One such niche was to mold other men—John Connally, for example—into his own likeness. Another was performing in the role as Johnson's unofficial chief of staff: Walter Jenkins and, after he was discarded, Bill Moyers, though neither had ever held such a title. After Moyers unceremoniously left, Marvin Watson replaced him. The niches he had in mind for Cliff Carter (chief bagman and assistant criminal facilitator) and Malcolm "Mac" Wallace (hit man extraordinaire) were special; there would be no need for successors because they were put in positions from which they could never leave.

When Johnson became a member of Congress, he recognized that the personality traits he had exploited in Prexy Evans were evident in the fearsome Speaker of the House, Sam Rayburn. Most other congressmen or congressional staffers were afraid of him, but Lyndon was determined to become friendly with Sam Rayburn. Lyndon Johnson found that Rayburn reacted much the same to his sycophancy as Prexy Evans had, and began inviting the Speaker to Sunday breakfasts, after which Lady Bird would scoot them into the living room where she stacked all the major Sunday newspapers next to the overstuffed chairs, so they could spend hours reading and commiserating while she cleaned up and washed the dishes. Speaker Rayburn began staying longer and longer as he became closer to the earnest young congressman. Rayburn's friendliness was understood by those who had seen the way Johnson treated him, which was identical to how he treated Prexy Evans back in San Marcos. The other congressional secretaries found one of Johnson's gestures particularly unbelievable: When Johnson met Sam Rayburn in the corridors of the Capitol, he would bend over and kiss him on his bald head.[83]

The traits that Lyndon Johnson exhibited during his youth and in college defined his congressional years: His domination of those below him, combined with obsequiousness toward superiors, together formed an overall art of manipulation that he refined, perfected, and practiced masterfully during his years in the Senate.[84] Johnson always taught his young assistants to read the body language of the people they communicated with: "Watch their hands, watch their eyes," he told them. "Read eyes. No matter what a man is saying to you, it's not as important as what you can read in his eyes . . . The most important thing a man has to tell you is what he's not telling you," he said. "The most important thing he has to say is what he's trying not to say."[85]

A congressional aide with whom Robert Caro talked revealed Lyndon Johnson's ambition to win the political game, to accrue more power, stature, money, and influence. The aide admitted there was nothing whatsoever altruistic about Johnson's motives; he did not care about any of the causes he espoused, certainly not civil rights for minorities, whom he disparaged and ridiculed. The aide felt that the political arena required believing in contemporary issues, regardless of which view one might hold; a man had to believe in *something*. But, Lyndon Johnson "believed in *nothing*, nothing but his own ambition. Everything he did—*everything*—was for his ambition"[86]

---

83. Caro, *The Path* . . ., p. 334.
84. Ibid., p. 335.
85. Caro, *Master of the Senate*, pp. 136–137.
86. Ibid., p. 156; Caro, *The Path* . . ., p. 275.

(emphasis in original). Moreover, the attitude of many people on the Hill toward Johnson was one of antagonism in reaction to the condescension and sycophancy he alternately displayed, depending on whether the person he needed something from was below or above his level. Charles Marsh's daughter, who watched Lyndon unashamedly fawn over her father while he was, "behind his back, sleeping with her mother . . . was reminded 'every time I saw Lyndon' of 'a Uriah Heep from Texas.'" A number of Senate staffers independently used the very same analogy, the very same character, to describe Johnson.[87]

Throughout his years in the House of Representatives, Johnson yearned to take the next step to the Senate, so that he would then be within reach of the presidency. During the four decades of his life to that point, he retained his obsession to become president. Now, in early 1948, at age thirty-nine, he would tell his friend Welly Hopkins, "By God, I'll be President someday!"[88] He knew the 1948 Senate election represented an opportunity that no obstacle could prevent him from realizing: not money, the vagaries of the election process, the rules and controls over handling ballots, or least of all, the absence of a sufficient number of votes. Votes could be bought, counts of ballots adjusted, the process managed to ensure victory. Lyndon Johnson was ready for the Senate.

Stolen Elections

Johnson's storied history of stolen elections dated to his college years and continued while he served as an aide to Congressman Kleberg, when he won a race for the "Little Congress." He stole thousands of votes when he first ran for the Senate in 1941, but unfortunately for him, he had not stolen enough, and thus lost the election. That experience apparently taught him a lesson, because seven years later he stole untold thousands of votes to secure a seat in the United States Senate.

Three days after the balloting, the 1948 election was about to be called for Johnson's opponent, Coke Stevenson, who was leading by 113 votes out of roughly 1 million cast after a long and hard-fought campaign. Suddenly, another ballot box was discovered in the south Texas town of Alice, the home of the Duke of Duval County, George Parr. He was in complete control of

---

87. Caro, *Master of the Senate*, p. 160. (Uriah Heep is a fictional character from the novel *David Copperfield*, written by Charles Dickens. He is remembered for his patronizing obsequiousness, his unbridled ambition and greed, his complete insincerity and his chronic attempts to perpetrate fraud while simultaneously portraying his own "'umbleness.")
88. Caro, *Means*, p. 120.

everything that happened there as well as in several surrounding counties, including Jim Wells County, where Alice was located. Aided by a couple of Mexican pistoleros working as bodyguards, Parr ruled Alice with an iron fist and acted as the county political boss. Johnson pushed him to help Johnson win the election regardless of the risk of returning to the penitentiary. In the process of winning, Johnson stole tens of thousands of votes; the final 202 were merely the last ones needed to put him over the top, going farther than anyone else had ever ventured. Robert Caro wrote that "even in terms of a most elastic political morality—the political morality of 1940s Texas—his methods were immoral."[89]

George Parr had previously favored Coke Stevenson, a former Texas governor, but reportedly switched to Johnson because he had a brother in trouble and needed a politician with more influence and the willingness to use it for illegal purposes. The Stevenson forces attempted to investigate the newly found "Precinct 13" ballots by checking the polling lists inside the boxes with the original ballots, but managed only a fast look at them, memorizing a few of the names, before they were locked away. Recriminations flew, but the Democratic state executive committee upheld LBJ's nomination—and soon thereafter, the last-minute ballots mysteriously disappeared. Johnson's attorneys, Ed Clark and Don Thomas, presented a petition to Judge Roy Archer in Austin, two hundred miles from Jim Wells County, to issue a restraining order to Governor Stevenson so that Johnson would "keep his rightful seat in the United States Senate."

Judge Roy Archer of Austin was securely under Edward Clark's control, whereas Judge Lorenz Broetter of Alice was not.[90] Johnson and Clark's first action was to sign an affidavit that Judge Broetter could not be reached, even though the claim about Judge Broetter's unavailability proved to be a lie. Johnson's lawyers presented the aforementioned petition to Judge Roy Archer in Austin; time was of the essence, as it was reported that "had the action in Judge Archer's chambers been delayed more than an hour, it is highly likely that the Jim Wells Democratic Committee would have met, thrown out Box 13, and restored the electoral decision in Stevenson's favor."[91] Johnson's legal chicanery later prompted an article in the then widely read national magazine *Collier's* which noted that the political maneuvering

> raised a serious question, not alone of honesty and fair play, but also the more serious fact of swearing to a falsehood (that the "resident judge of Jim Wells County . . . cannot be reached in sufficient

89. Caro, *Master of the Senate*, p. 116.
90. McClellan, p. 92; Haley, p. 39.
91. Haley, p. 39.

time," and that therefore "a restraining order without notice to the defendants . . . should be granted') when Johnson knew it was a lie. Just why Judge Archer was beguiled into signing this order in chambers, without notice, thus perverting the vast powers of a District Court to handcuff a victim while ruthless political hijackers mauled and stripped him clean, is a question still unanswered. Maybe it was the legendary Johnson charm and personality. Maybe the decision stemmed from the law of heteronomy rather than the law of Texas. Judge Archer alone has the answer."[92]

In two counties in the area, fires had "accidentally" destroyed poll records: in Duval County, a Parr enterprise employee "had grown nervous over the vast disparity between the election returns and the poll taxes issued—about two to one—and had taken the lists home for safekeeping. There, his wife, in her commendable zeal of housecleaning, had apparently consigned them to the fire. Thus the attempt to get at the actual voting in Duval ended in futility, in complete frustration." In Alice, the poll list turned up missing, after "Commissioner Smith impounded the County's ballot boxes and found them empty. 'Why?' Obviously, it was suggested, the industrious Mexican janitor, ignorant in the premises, must have emptied the boxes and burned the ballots."[93]

Though the Stevenson men only glimpsed the inside of the ballot box, they noticed a number of clues that the ballots were fraudulent: the poll lists for "Box 13" were completed in alphabetical order, and in blue green ink (even though the rest of the lists were completed in black ink); all the signatures were in the same handwriting; and several of the names designated people who were deceased, many of whom had been for several years,* and still other people listed, upon interrogation, claimed they hadn't voted at all.[94] The last man to vote before the 202 were added to the list stated that the election officials were locking the doors immediately after he entered the building. Altogether, evidence that the Johnson campaign perpetrated

---

* The votes recorded on behalf of the deceased led to a joke making the rounds at the bars on Wisconsin Avenue and elegant Georgetown dinner parties (Johnson himself told it often in the Senate cloakroom). The accent mimicked was that of small Mexican American boy in Nuevo Laredo: Manuel was sitting on a curb one day crying when a friend came up and asked him what was wrong. Manuel said, "My father was in town last Saturday, and he did not come to see me." His friend said, "But, Manuel, your father has been dead for ten years. Manuel just sobbed louder, saying, "*Si*, he has been dead for ten years. But he came to town last Saturday to vote for Lyndon Johnson, and he did not come to see me." (Caro, *Means*, p. 399)

92. Ibid. (ref. Gordon Schendel, "Something Is Rotten in the State of Texas," *Colliers*, pp. 13–14, June 9, 1951).
93. Ibid., pp. 46–47.
94. Ibid., pp. 40–42.

voting fraud was overwhelming, going well beyond the Box 13 issue; there
were actually thousands of miscounted or nonexistent votes: "Not eighty-
seven votes 'changed history,' and not two hundred, but thousands, many
thousands," in fact, according to the research done by Robert A. Caro.[95]

For three more weeks the legal wrangling continued, with the Johnson
lawyers manipulating the process to keep the boxes closed, while the Stevenson
men argued that they should be opened and inspected to determine whether
fraudulent votes had been insinuated into the total. Johnson's injunction
effectively kept Coke Stevenson from seeing the poll and tally lists, though
such access was his constitutional legal right. Johnson's ten lawyers, including
John Cofer, Ed Clark, Don Thomas, Alvin Wirtz, and former governor James
V. Allred, fought Stevenson's lawyers. His team, including another former
governor, Dan Moody, then secured their own injunction to keep Johnson's
name from being printed on the ballot for the general election, at least until
October 3, when the ballots had to go to the printer.[96] The federal judge
from the United States District Court, T. Whitfield Davidson, proved to be
an honest and untainted judge, a major frustration for Lyndon Johnson and
Ed Clark. Before the formal start of the trial, Judge Davidson appealed to
Stevenson and Johnson to avoid the taint that would follow them into the
general election if the trial proceeded, suggesting that they agree to put both
names on the ballot along with the Republican candidate, and the voters
would decide whom they wanted to represent them. Stevenson immediately
assented to this plan; meanwhile, a surly Johnson pushed his way out of the
courtroom, uttering simply, "No comment."[97]

Johnson knew that in a general election against Stevenson there was
no way he could win. Without that Senate seat, his chance to pursue his
ultimate goal would disappear and his political career would be over. His
lawyers tried to convince him that conservative voters would split their votes
between Stevenson and the Republican candidate, leaving a wide berth for
him to win. According to Luther Jones, when Lyndon met with his ten widely
respected and learned lawyers to hear them deliver their advice, he "just hit
the goddamned ceiling!"[98] Having ten of the best lawyers money could buy
tell him to accept the judge's compromise was an outrage to him. Behind the
closed doors of the conference room, Johnson raged at his lawyers and lashed
out at the court and judge. That he had taken tremendous risks—to buy
votes, bribe election officials, and agree to future favors demanded by George
Parr for his last-minute "fix"—exacerbated his fury. And he had convinced

95. Caro, *Means*, p. 395.
96. Ibid., p. 366.
97. Ibid., p. 356.
98. Ibid., p. 358.

himself that none of his illegal actions were even pertinent anymore: "This is a free country! I won it fair and square, and you want me to trade it away?"[99] For him to crow about the fairness of his victory after the enormous fraud he had perpetrated (and was desperately trying to hide) vindicates what his aide George Reedy would say about Johnson's veracity: "Whatever Johnson tells you at any given moment he thinks is the truth."[100]

After attempting to stall the hearing of witnesses, John Cofer pleaded with Judge Davidson to dissolve the Stevenson restraining order on the basis that *it* was just a delaying tactic. The judge ignored that request and began hearing the witnesses, one of whom pointed out that the certificate that indicated the vote for Lyndon Johnson was 965 had obviously been changed: the number *9* had originally been a *7*.[101] Witnesses stated that the numbers had been altered to be in Johnson's favor in several other counties as well.[102] Ballot Box 13 was discovered to have been inadvertently lost and then found three days after the election. Johnson's attorneys had already convinced the Democratic Party's executive committee that investigating the votes was "contrary to law," which became the position they adopted in court, where they bizarrely argued that regardless of whether or not Stevenson had been wronged, the law was powerless to right that wrong. The judge rejected this reasoning and asserted there was a legal remedy for every legal wrong, and that there must always be a tribunal wherein the remedy may be determined and subsequently enforced.[103]

The options were closing for Johnson, who feared having a campaign of write-in ballots. Opening the ballot boxes—an obvious danger which the Johnson forces tried to prevent—would have revealed evidence of a much more extensive fraud.[104] The judge decided to appoint three masters in chancery, who were officers of the court with power to subpoena witnesses and evidence, to hold hearings in the three counties and to submit written reports by October 2. This development was not good news for Johnson, who knew that substantial investigations would uncover his criminal activity. What would the judge think of the overall results of all precincts in Duval County, where over 99 percent of registered voters (4,662 out of 4,679) allegedly voted, 99 percent of their votes (4,622 out of 4,662) supporting Johnson while only forty were recorded for Stevenson? What if the investigation

---

99. Ibid.
100. Lasky, *It Didn't Start . . .*, p. 136.
101. Caro, *Means*, pp. 360–362.
102. Ibid.
103. Ibid., p. 363.
104. Ibid., pp. 351–368.

revealed not just 202 fraudulent votes in Box 13, but thousands more; would it not be obvious that Johnson himself was behind it all?[105]

Enter Abe Fortas. When Johnson realized that the attorneys he had employed would fail him, he contacted Fortas—who had helped Johnson circumvent regulatory rules impeding the Marshall Ford Dam a decade before—who promptly flew to Austin. After the lawyers described the dilemma, Fortas said he could envision one possible scenario for Johnson, though it was a very large gamble: The only hope for Johnson was to take the case to a single circuit court judge and ask for a stay of the injunction on jurisdictional grounds, and do so with a weakly presented, unpersuasive plea presented to a judge predisposed to rule against Johnson—essentially the opposite of what any other lawyer would have prescribed. Fortas presented the perfunctory appeal to a Fifth Circuit Court of Appeals judge, who was almost guaranteed to reject it out of hand, on September 24; meanwhile, the rest of the legal team initiated delaying tactics to subvert the investigation by the three masters in chancery. The masters' subpoenas had been issued but practically all of the election officials, upon whom U.S. marshals were supposed to serve the subpoenas, had left town and, in several cases, had gone to Mexico. The marshals also found that much of the evidence had disappeared, including the poll lists from the infamous Box 13. One copy had been taken by an election judge, Luis Salas, in his car and left there while he visited the Baile Espanola bar in Alice, Texas. While he was inside, the car was ransacked; Salas said, "They stole everything." Salas was a former pistolero under George Parr who took the stand to announce that both copies of the poll and tally lists he had been responsible for were gone; the other he had simply "lost." Additionally, Salas denied having told anyone how many votes were reported and the allegation that two hundred more had been added.[106]

The Fortas gamble, if successful, would quickly yield an unfavorable ruling that could be sent immediately to Supreme Court Justice Hugo Black, who could hear the case as a single justice; Fortas thought Justice Black would rule for them, because he knew that Black, a former member of Ku Klux Klan, would ultimately prefer to see Johnson, not Stevenson, in the Senate; Justice Black knew Johnson personally and the two were of like minds. Attorney General Tom Clark, whose son, Ramsey, would eventually be named as Johnson's choice to replace Bobby Kennedy as attorney general, reportedly interceded with Black to assure that it was handled favorably.[107]

---

105. Ibid., pp. 364–365.
106. Ibid., p. 376.
107. Dallek, *Lone Star . . .*, p. 341.

In short order, Justice Black issued "a sweeping order on behalf of Johnson, staying Judge Davidson's temporary injunction and ending the Fort Worth hearing, where the iron curtain tactics of South Texas were on the verge of being proven in federal court."[108] Judge Davidson, in adjourning court, said that "'the United States Supreme Court has altered my opinion, but it hasn't changed my mind' . . . He also remarked that Black's order was unduly hasty 'and probably unlawful,' given that this was not a dispute in a general election, but in a State primary over a party nominee, where even the Senate was without power to act."[109]

The pattern according to which witnesses and evidence alike vanished was manifesting in other counties; clearly, an attempt to stall if not prevent the investigations altogether had been orchestrated. Stevenson's attorney, former governor Moody, made a key mistake by presenting the case as one of fraud on Lyndon Johnson's part—despite clear and convincing evidence of such fraud—without addressing the more fundamental issue of court jurisdiction. Fortas had made jurisdiction *the only* issue to be addressed by the appellate court and beyond there, by Justice Hugo Black, arguing that "election contests were 'irrevocably and incontestably vested'" in Texas state law and should not be supervised by a federal court. Another Johnson lawyer, Alvin J. Wirtz, warned that if the Stevenson injunction was not overturned, no Democratic names would appear on the November ballot, leaving only that of the Republican candidate—an untenable result.[110]

Finally, Supreme Court Justice Hugo Black decided, as predicted by Abe Fortas, that the federal courts had no jurisdiction over the merits or conduct of state elections. Justice Black's response to Moody's contention that the federal courts were the only recourse was that the Senate itself was in the best position to judge the qualifications of its own members.[111] Justice Black's stance was later affirmed by the Supreme Court, which rejected Stevenson's petition for a trial on the merits of the case. The gamble—fueled by the numerous brazen illegalities of the election, wagered on the thinnest slice of esoteric legal theory, and performed in opposition to the will of the voters— paid off, and Lyndon B. Johnson went to the Senate, his springboard onto the presidential election ticket twelve years later. As author and historian J. Evetts Haley put it, Justice Black's ruling "over-rode a distinguished Circuit Federal Judge who had held that the full Court of Appeals should hear Johnson's petition, and had set an immediate date to do so. It peremptorily denied

108. Haley, pp. 47–48.
109. Ibid. (ref. *Fort Worth Star-Telegram*, Sept. 28, 30, 1948).
110. Caro, *Means*, pp. 377–380.
111. Ibid.

justice to Governor Stevenson and nearly half a million Texans who had voted for him. It brazenly abridged the Constitution and the Bill of Rights and the limitations on jurisdiction. But perhaps most terrible of all, it sanctioned corruption as public policy. There is nothing in American history like it."[112] The "celebrated 1948 election"[113] described in Jack Valenti's autobiography must have referred to the party after Justice Black's decision, according to which the young Abe Fortas scored arguably his greatest feat ever: ensuring that his man, Lyndon B. Johnson, became a senator regardless of the will of the people, who had voted overwhelmingly for Johnson's opponent, Coke Stevenson.

Thus ended the effort to decide the 1948 senatorial election case on its merits; had a comprehensive investigation been completed, along with a corresponding airing of the facts, Johnson would have wound up in the Big House instead of the White House. The Davidson-appointed masters were forced to stop their work before the fraud could be completely exposed. But facts that did emerge attest that Lyndon Johnson's election to the Senate was tainted by thousands of fraudulent votes; no one will ever know exactly how many. From that point on, Lyndon Johnson would continue up the senatorial ladder, positioning himself to run twelve years later for the presidency in 1960; his failure at the Los Angeles Convention would be only minor, an anticipated detour until he assumed the next best position as the vice presidential nominee, which formed the only route he could take toward his ultimate goal. In an ideal and perfect world, Johnson never would have become a senator, much less the majority leader of the Senate, but that he did enabled him to exponentially increase his political power; eventually, he would appoint federal judges who were thereafter indebted to him and inclined to listen when he gave them future direction.

Ronnie Dugger, the journalist and author, reported that when he was interviewing Johnson in the White House, Johnson presented a photograph of a car with a 1948 Texas license plate and a small can with a "Precinct 13" label surrounded by five men, including George Parr's cousin, Givens Parr, and Ed Lloyd, the Jim Wells boss. Dugger asked Johnson about the men and occasion, but Johnson said nothing more, offering only a knowing grin.[114] Clearly, that picture reminded Lyndon Johnson of one of his greater triumphs: his blatant theft of the 1948 election through the most conniving, fraudulent scheme ever devised, which not only produced more phony ballots but arguably the most brazen and outrageous judicial miscarriage of justice

112. Haley, pp. 47–48.
113. Valenti, p. 169.
114. Dugger, p. 341.

involving election fraud in history. Knowing that his "victory" was entirely because of a legal technicality over a fuzzy jurisdictional issue and his lawyers' manipulation of the judicial system, rather than a verdict based upon fairness and equity, his grin represented an in-your-face retort to those Texas voters who had the wisdom not to vote for him.

Twenty-nine years later, in 1977—well after he was safely out of Johnson's reach—Luis Salas, the former election judge and pistolero for George Parr, decided to confess his role in the 1948 election fraud. The columnist Hugh Sidey lamented that Johnson was merely one of many politicians "who have come out of the seamy regions of American life and used the devious rituals learned to gain power, but have also held a certain reverence for the system and its goals. Ultimately they may have produced more good than their critics." Sidey also wrote about Salas's belated confession:[115]

> There were indignant headlines last week over the story from Luis Salas, a former election judge and Parr crony, on how L.B.J. made it into the Senate on stolen votes. Salas, now 76 and bent on a spiritual cleansing, claimed to recall a meeting back in 1948 near the town of Alice, Texas, as the votes were being counted. Lyndon was there pleading for 200 more votes, according to Salas, and George Parr ordered them faked and stuffed into ballot box No. 13. Johnson triumphed in that primary election over former Governor Coke Stevenson. The Salas narrative suggested strongly that the protests were smothered because the fix was put in all the way up through Supreme Court Justice Hugo Black and President Harry Truman . . . "Of course, they stole that election," said one former aide. "That's the way they did it down there" . . . As for Lyndon's showing up in Alice to ask for 200 votes, all those old Johnson hands, from John Connally on down, just scoffed. The idea that a man of Johnson's skills would place himself at the scene of the crime was ridiculous. "He was more devious than that," insisted one friend with relish.

Hugh Sidey's diffidence, nearly thirty years after the stolen election, towards Johnson illustrates the way many of his colleagues rationalized his known contradictions with their own desire to maintain cordial relations with him in order to keep their access to the White House. Mr. Sidey acknowledged Johnson's conniving, duplicitous and criminal ways, but seemingly gave him a carte blanche pardon, since after all, he had done some "good things" too, when he wrote:

---

115. Sidey, Hugh, "The Softer They Fall," *Time*, August 15, 1977.

All these twists and turns, the mixing of deceit and truth, the use of corrupt means for noble ends, seem to have inhibited serious assessment of Johnson so far. Around Washington last week there was a thought or two that maybe Johnson, already so suspect, would have less distance to fall than some who had left office on loftier notes.

It was this rationalization of the "noble ends" that had allowed Johnson to become president despite the scandals that nearly drove him out of the vice presidency, and—were it not for the power of his position after November 22, 1963—subsequently avoid impeachment as the president. But it wasn't only journalists who gave Johnson their collective "nod" for him to proceed; it was the entire nation, still in shock at JFK's murder, that kept giving him the "benefit of the doubt." To do otherwise meant that terrible national secrets would have to be exposed and by then the people of the United States were caught up in a new scandal and its aftermath; there was no time to continue dwelling on the previous crisis.

The Kennedy-Johnson ticket won the election of 1960 in eleven states through massive voter fraud, without which the Republican candidate, Richard M. Nixon, would have won the presidency eight years earlier than he eventually did.[116] The voter fraud in the 1960 general election will be explored further in later chapters.

Black Bag Finance and Political Payback

The more honest biographies of Johnson prominently feature his solicitation and extortion of campaign funds and the corresponding political favors and paybacks. In some cases, these stories are obliquely mentioned, then quietly dismissed and ignored as simply the mundane reality of the U.S. political scene. That the actions contained therein were transparently illegal has apparently not tarnished the solid reputation that remains among many of the educators, historians, and contemporary politicians whose judgments determine membership in the pantheon of past presidents.

One such incident came to light years afterward as a result of a SEC lawsuit involving a Gulf Oil lobbyist Claude Wild Jr., who testified about a Gulf Oil commitment to furnish Johnson $50,000 for his personal use; Wild delivered the money, in cash in plain envelopes, to Walter Jenkins, Ed Clark, Cliff Carter, John Connally, or Jesse Kellam.[117] When asked how much money Gulf had contributed, Ed Clark, Lyndon's attorney, responded, "I

---

116. Hersh, S., p. 132.
117. Caro, *Master of the Senate*, p. 406.

knew of about two hundred thousand. And Gulf was only one oil company—and there were non-oil businesses in Texas, too."[118]

In 1956, the columnist Drew Pearson managed to acquire copies of an investigation into Johnson's financial misconduct, including IRS records that showed that George and Herman Brown's company, Brown & Root, paid their employees bonuses with the understanding that they were to immediately deposit them and then send the same amount to one of Johnson's campaign funds.[119] Pearson cited numerous examples of this scheme; for example, an employee named Randolph Mills at the Victoria Gravel Company, a subsidiary of Brown & Root, received a check for $2,500 that he deposited before immediately paying out the same amount to J. Frank Jungman, Lyndon's Houston campaign manager.[120] In another case, Edgar Monteith, a Houston attorney, received several checks in 1941 that he and his partner, A. W. Baring, treated as revenue for their firm and then sent to the Johnson campaign as reimbursement for campaign expenses. Drew Pearson further wrote that "when asked specifically about the matter, Lyndon told the IRS that he 'had never heard of Monteith,' much less of his financial support, though Monteith was the brother of a former Houston mayor."[121]

Still another example of Johnson's illegitimate power can be traced to Brown & Root having been given a contract to build subchasers and destroyers, which was eventually worth $357 million, despite having no experience whatsoever in shipbuilding. After landing the largest navy contract in history, paving the way to expand his construction business into shipbuilding, George Brown observed, "We didn't know the stern from the aft—I mean bow—of the boat."[122] Before Johnson went to Washington to act as Brown & Root's personal emissary and "rainmaker," their company was practically bankrupt and Herman lived with his wife in a tent;[123] shortly after Lyndon went to Washington, thanks to Herman and the Austin attorney, Alvin Wirtz, the contracts began to flow so quickly that the company became highly profitable and one of the largest independent government contractors; in 1962 it was acquired by Halliburton.

At some point during his Senate years, Johnson decided to separate his illegal business transactions into two groups: those he had to manage personally and those he could delegate to his sidekick, Bobby Baker, for

---

118. Ibid., p. 407.
119. Brown, p. 71.
120. Ibid.
121. Ibid., pp. 71–72.
122. Caro, *Master of the Senate*, p. 406.
123. Brown, p. 70.

which he would collect a "skim" that would be too small in nature to occupy his mind and time. Major decisions, such as Brown & Root favors, high-level appointments, awards of defense contracts and legislative initiatives, would be under his control.

Johnson's Connection with the Mob and other Miscreants

Among Johnson's clients were hoodlums and tainted labor leaders who belonged to a group known as the Mafia, the very existence of which was denied by the famed director of the FBI. One of Johnson's longest-term Mob contacts, Jack Halfen, had run a gambling syndicate in Houston while conducting payoffs to the Mob of $100,000 per week before being imprisoned for income tax fraud in 1954. During his trial, Halfen refused to reveal who else he'd been paying off, but he later acknowledged that he'd had business dealings with Lyndon Johnson, stating that over a ten-year period in the 1950s he had given Johnson $500,000 in cash and campaign contributions, and that Johnson, in return, "repeatedly killed anti-rackets legislation, watered down bills that could not be defeated and curbed Congressional investigations of the Mob."[124] Johnson was even given credit for the fact that Tennessee Senator Estes Kefauver, despite holding hearings on organized crime in many cities during the 1950s, never made it to Texas. Johnson continued taking money from mobsters even after he had become president: "During a 1964 cocktail party at Teamster headquarters that [former administrative assistant to Maryland Senator, Daniel Brewster, Jack] Sullivan attended, Brewster and Teamster boss, Jimmy Hoffa, walked off to talk privately on the terrace overlooking Capitol Hill. Afterward, Brewster told Sullivan that Hoffa had asked him to take $100,000 in cash to presidential aide Cliff Carter. The payoff was meant to enlist Johnson's support in blocking Hoffa's prosecution for jury tampering and pension fund fraud, for which Hoffa was ultimately convicted. A few days after the party, Sullivan testified that Teamster lobbyist Sid Zagri came into Senator Brewster's office and gave Brewster a suitcase full of money. Sullivan then accompanied Brewster to Cliff Carter's office and waited in the car as Brewster went into the office with the suitcase and left without it."[125]

Johnson expropriated campaign funds flowing through the Democratic Senatorial Campaign Committee for his own campaigns, those of other senatorial candidates he wanted to control, and in general, for his own personal

---

124. Scheim, p. 247.
125. Ibid. (ref. Sheridan, Walter, *The Fall and Rise of Jimmy Hoffa*, New York: Saturday Review Press, 1972, pp. 380–381).

and unreported use—abuses that were eventually reported in *Life* magazine, ironically in its issue of November 22, 1963, the same day Kennedy was assassinated. The article described a senator who caught Johnson and Baker shortchanging him: "One western candidate was bitter in 1958 when Baker offered him $3,000 in cash; he happened to know that the donor had handed in $25,000 and that $12,000 of it was earmarked for him. 'You're doing all right. You don't need it,' Baker bluntly told him when he protested."[126]

When he was first "elected" to the Senate, Johnson established a close relationship with the twenty-year-old Senate page Bobby Baker, as revealed by Baker himself: "The drawling voice on the telephone said, 'Mr. Baker. I understand you know where the bodies are buried in the Senate. I appreciate it if you'd come by my office and talk to me.'"[127] Baker would become more than an aide or protégé to Johnson; their relationship, as will be seen in later chapters, would become so close that Johnson would say that if he had a son, Bobby Baker would be him. In the same spirit, Baker named two of his children "Lyndon" and "Lynda."[128] Johnson would eventually use him to do much of the dirty work that his financial corruption and connections to the mob entailed. According to a researcher, Peter Dale Scott, "While working for Johnson, Baker became the epitome of Washington wheeler-dealer sleaze. Repeatedly, he fronted for syndicate gamblers Cliff Jones and Ed Levinson in investments that earned super profits for himself and another military–industrial lobbyist, his friend Fred Black Jr. In exchange he intervened to help Jones and Levinson obtain casino contracts with the Intercontinental Hotel system. (Before Fidel Castro's expropriation of privately held property, Jones and Levinson, both associates of Meyer Lansky, owned the casino in the Havana Hilton.)"[129] These investments did not result from Baker's random prescience but from his access to insider knowledge and from financial payoffs through the CEOs of such companies as Mortgage Guaranty Insurance Company of Milwaukee (which sold Baker stock at 50 percent of current market price, for which Baker's original investment of $28,750 increased to $495,000 in 1962).[130] Baker admitted he had advanced knowledge of a favorable Treasury Department ruling that would allow the company to exclude half of its earnings from income taxes, though he quickly explained that he "had no hand or influence in that ruling."[131] Baker would become, along with Walter Jenkins, John Connally, Cliff Carter, and Ed

---

126. *Life* magazine, November 22, 1963, p. 40.
127. Baker, p. 34.
128. Ibid. p. 45.
129. Scott, p. 218.
130. Baker, p. 156.
131. Ibid. p. 157.

Clark, one of the many "bagmen" and intermediaries Johnson would rely upon to obfuscate his relationships with criminals.

Author Peter Dale Scott has pieced together in meticulous detail the extended relationships between men at the lower levels of the hierarchy headed by Lyndon Johnson, the ultimate dispenser of political influence, and his closest associate, Bobby Baker. The next tier in the triangle of influence connected Baker, Clint Murchison, and James Hoffa directly to Carlos Marcello, the Mafia chieftain of New Orleans, and his and Hoffa's longtime lobbyist, Irving Davidson,[132] "a dapper Washington public relations man who did business with government officials in Israel and Latin America."[133] Davidson was deeply involved in Baker's scams, procuring thousands of dollars in "finders fees arrangements for Baker's services: for example, Murchison paid Baker to secure a government contract for a meat-packing company he owned in Haiti, while he worked on defending Jimmy Hoffa."[134] Baker would later intercede for Murchison to reverse a Department of Agriculture ruling prohibiting the importation of unsanitarily processed meat from Haiti to Puerto Rico.[135] Apparently, the prospect of spreading botulism among the citizens of that American territory was insufficient reason to impede the profit taking of Baker's, Johnson's, and Hoover's friend and benefactor, one of the wealthiest of the Dallas oilmen, Clint Murchison.

Johnson's home for twenty years was in a quiet, exclusive neighborhood in Northwest Washington, nestled in the four blocks between Connecticut Avenue and Rock Creek Park at 4921 30th Place.[136] Among his neighbors were J. Edgar Hoover across the street, Fred Black next door, Bobby Baker the next street over, and the king of Washington lobbyists, Irving Davidson, around the block. In 1961, Johnson bought the mansion known as the Elms owned by Washington socialite Pearl Mesta—the "hostess with the mostess '*sic*'" known for her lavish parties featuring artists, entertainers, and Washington political figures, at 4040 52nd Street NW—when he became vice president.[137] Within the next several months, Baker and Black both sold their houses and moved next to the Johnson's so they could be neighbors again: "On one side was [Baker's] friend and business partner Fred Black. On the other side was his longtime mentor, Lyndon B. Johnson."[138]

---

132. Ibid., p. 219.
133. Ibid. (ref. Moldea, Dan E., *The Hoffa Wars*, New York: Paddington Press, 1978).
134. Ibid., p. 221.
135. Scheim, p. 250 (ref. Reid, Ed., *The Grim Reapers: The Anatomy of Organized Crime in America*, New York: Henry Regnery, Bantam, 1970, pp. 140–142).
136. Caro, *Master*, p. 229.
137. Haley, p. 234.
138. North, p. 248 (ref. Rowe, Robert, *The Bobby Baker Story*, New York: Parallax, 1967, pp. 45, 72).

Davidson was connected to everyone in Baker's influence-peddling empire, as well as Jimmy Hoffa and a number of people in organized crime. He once boasted, "I'm a great admirer of Mr. Hoover, and I did have access. We used to have parties before the Redskin games . . . and Hoover always came to them. He was a darned good friend. I lived around the corner from him, three quarters of a block. I'd go over and say hello to him and Clyde Tolson."[139] Irving Davidson was one of the first Washington superlobbyists; his clients ranged from the Coca-Cola Company to the CIA and third world dictators, including the Somozas of Nicaragua, the Duvaliers of Haiti, and the Trujillos of the Dominican Republic.[140] As the registered lobbyist for the Teamsters Union, he was "deeply involved in a Murchison business deal that provided funds for Lyndon Johnson's bagman, Bobby Baker."[141] He represented both Carlos Marcello and Clint Murchison and would also participate in the Teamster Union's effort to prevent Jimmy Hoffa from going to prison, an initiative that eventually led to Hoffa being pardoned by Richard Nixon, another close friend of Davidson. But from 1961 to 1963, Davidson handled illegal bribes and payoffs for Lyndon Johnson with his old neighbors, Bobby Baker and Fred Black, while being simultaneously protected by his other friend and neighbor, J. Edgar Hoover.[142]

The tentacles of these relationships can be traced throughout the United States: to Las Vegas, from Baker to his associates, Eddie Levinson and Ben Siegelbaum, to former FBI agent turned Mafia lawyer Robert Maheu and Johnny Rosselli; to Miami, from Rosselli to Santos Trafficante; and to Dallas, from Murchison, H. L. Hunt, and Mafia boss Joseph Civello, to several policemen, as well as Dallas County Sheriff Bill Decker and Jack Ruby.[143] In neighboring Fort Worth, W. C. Kirkwood hosted Hunt, Murchison, Rayburn, and Lyndon Johnson at his sprawling complex named the Four Deuces.[144] Moreover, several of these men—Rosselli and Jack Ruby in particular—were linked to the Chicago Outfit and Sam Giancana, their lawyer, Sidney Korshak, and finally to the financier, Henry Crown, who happened to be the major stockholder (20 percent) of Fort Worth's General Dynamics Corporation,[145] which will be among the subjects of later chapters.

Johnson's relationship with Carlos Marcello was critical; finances flowing from illegal slot machine profits and bookies using the Marcello racing wire

139. Scott, pp. 233–234.
140. Davis, p. 425.
141. Ibid., p. 426.
142. Ibid., pp. 312, 425–426.
143. Scott, pp. 128, 161.
144. Marrs, p. 292.
145. Scott, p. 155.

services throughout Texas were a major part of the foundation of Johnson's rise to the top of the political empire.[146] The connections these groups had will be traced, in later chapters, to other men, including Meyer Lansky, who was among the few top crime figures never wiretapped or bugged by the FBI, even as Robert Kennedy's Justice Department aggressively pursued Mob figures throughout the United States.[147] The reason for the FBI's reticence had less to do with insufficient cause than it did with the Mob's coercive power over the vulnerable director of the FBI, J. Edgar Hoover.

Johnson's "Rags to Riches" Broadcasting Business

The primary source of Johnson's accumulation of vast personal wealth, beyond his relatively modest income as a congressman and senator, were the radio and television broadcasting stations he had acquired, beginning with the Austin radio station KTBC in 1943 for $17500. In his book *Lone Star Rising: Lyndon Johnson and His Times 1908–1960*, Robert Dallek chronicled how Johnson grew this initial investment into a multimillion-dollar family corporation by the 1950s: He used his position and contacts at the FCC to obtain licenses, additional radio and VHF television stations, approvals for increasing the stations' broadcasting power, and in general, to expand his operation without regulatory interference. During this time, Lyndon was the acknowledged power behind the ascendancy of the radio and television broadcasting businesses, though he consistently denied it and tried to credit their growth to Lady Bird. Likewise, he insisted, and his minions at the FCC complied, that no records of his involvement ever be found in any of the agency's files. His repeated denials of having any influence over the media properties the Johnsons owned were categorically debunked by Robert Caro in *Means of Ascent*.[148]

George Reedy, Johnson's former press secretary who helped perpetuate the myth that it was Lady Bird who ran KTBC-TV, remarked, "Occasionally, the LBJ energy would lead him to intervene in the internal administration of his wife's radio station . . . It really was hers and even in a community-property state he had no right to do so. But no one would seriously have considered stopping him even on occasions when the intervention brought the station close to disaster. That happened frequently . . . his presence shook the entire staff and often brought key personnel to the verge of a mass walkout."[149] Perhaps Mr. Reedy was deluded into thinking Lady Bird

---

146. Davis, p. 518.
147. Scott, p. 144.
148. Caro, *Means of Ascent*, pp. 80–118.
149. Reedy, p. 48.

ran the broadcasting business and simply never knew otherwise. The real story of Johnson's acquisition of KTBC radio—at the time, operating out of a small building with a studio, a control room, and three small offices, essentially bankrupt because of the FCC's continuing resistance to approve its requests for expansion of its weak signal on the high end of the dial—was that Johnson himself had influenced the highest echelons of the FCC to drive the station out of business to prime his coming to its rescue, buying it for a highly discounted price just before its collapse. After months of denying the station's requests for greater broadcasting rights, then denying the application of a syndicate of new owners headed by J. M. West, a prominent Austin businessman and publisher, to purchase the station for $50,000, the FCC, on February 16, 1943, approved the Johnsons' bid to purchase the distressed property. The story was later reported by *Life* magazine's Keith Wheeler and William Lambert in their 1964 series titled "How LBJ's Family Amassed Its Fortune," and more extensively revealed how the business was run primarily by Johnson, quoting men who said they had witnessed "the aggressive personal role" he had played in the acquisition and expansion of the broadcasting holdings:[150]

> For some reason the FCC steadfastly refused to approve the sale. Although West died, the syndicate continued its efforts to buy. Just before Christmas in 1942, 34-year-old Congressman Lyndon Johnson invited a local businessman, E. G. Kingsbery, who was a member of the syndicate, to his Austin office. Kingsbery recalled that during the meeting Johnson reminded him that an appointment to Annapolis for Kingsbery's son, John, had been obtained through L.B.J.'s good offices. Then, according to Kingsbery, Johnson brought up KTBC and said: "Now, E. G., I'm not a lawyer or a newspaperman. I have no means of making a living. At one time I had a second-class teaching license but it has long since expired. I understand you've bought the radio station. I'd like to go in with you or to have the station myself." Kingsbery first put Johnson in telephone contact with the attorney for the syndicate and then advised the congressman to "make his peace" with J. M. West's heirs. "Lyndon told me," said Kingsbery, "he was going up to the West ranch to talk business, and he did and he came away with KTBC."[151]

Unlike J. M. West, the Johnsons had solid connections to the New Dealers running the FCC, including the commissioner himself, Clifford Durr.

150. *Life* magazine, August 21, 1964, p. 62.
151. *Life* magazine, August 21, 1964, pp. 62–63.

Lyndon even had Lady Bird ask for Durr's advice on whether it would be a good investment. He urged her onward, apparently swayed by Lady Bird's concern that Austin needed more liberal political influences to combat such events as the vicious attacks on President Homer Rainey of the University of Texas. KTBC was then called a "sundowner" station because it was limited to daytime broadcasts and therefore not affiliated with any networks; it could not compete with the other Austin stations or the much stronger signals from those based in San Antonio.[152]

Through the help of Johnson's friends—Speaker Sam Rayburn and lobbyist Tommy Corcoran, to whom many of the top officials of the FCC were indebted for their jobs—the FCC shifted its attitude toward KTBC immediately after Lady Bird Johnson submitted her application to buy it.[153] Within months of acquiring the radio station in 1943, the Johnsons applied to the FCC to move the station's frequency to the lower end of the dial (590) and operate twenty-four hours a day, changes that would expand its signal well beyond Austin to thirty-eight surrounding counties. Whereas the previous owners had unsuccessfully tried to accomplish the same improvements for many years, the Johnsons' requests were granted within three weeks. Beforehand, they managed to recruit a popular radio announcer from Dallas, Harfield Weedin, to become manager of their new station, overcoming his reluctance with the promise that the station would be greatly expanded: Lyndon Johnson told him, "Look, the frequency is going to be changed. We're going to go full-time. I have it in the works right now."[154] As soon as the broadcasting changes were approved and implemented, the station was received by listeners much more clearly and until late in the evening. By 1945, approval was obtained from the FCC to increase its power fivefold, from a thousand to five thousand watts, expanding the geographic radius of potential listeners to sixty-three counties.[155] Johnson traveled to New York and called on the president of the CBS radio network, William S. Paley, to ask for an affiliation that would allow Johnson's station to carry the network's famous nationally broadcast shows, an arrangement that would thus attract more advertisers and enable him to charge higher advertising rates. Previous attempts by another Austin radio station, KNOW, to secure a CBS affiliation had been rejected for years on the basis that the network's San Antonio affiliate could be heard in Austin. But after Johnson's visit, Paley and Frank Stanton, the CBS director of research, reexamined the situation and found there was plenty of room for an affiliated station in Austin.[156]

---

152. Caro, *Means of Ascent*, p. 87.
153. Ibid., p. 97.
154. Ibid., p. 99.
155. Ibid., pp. 99–100.
156. Ibid., p. 101.

The turnaround in the FCC's attitude was complete. The *Life* magazine exposé documented the Johnsons' startling success winning FCC approval for everything they wanted, from the time the little radio station was purchased through the conveyance to them of a unique television monopoly in Austin, Texas, that existed until 1972, when the Johnsons sold it for $9 million:[157]

> All of its requests have been acted upon favorably and with dispatch by the agency—beginning with an early application to increase its power and the length of its broadcasting day. The choicest plum of all fell in 1952 when KTBC [TV] was granted the right to broadcast over Channel 7, the only VHF (very high frequency) channel allocated to the Austin area by the FCC. This single outlet contracted to carry programs of all three major TV networks—CBS, ABC and NBC—with whom affiliation is the open sesame to success. True, the FCC also assigned to Austin three prospective UHF (ultra high frequency) channels; but at that time almost no TV receivers existed to pick up a UHF signal. Many sets can receive UHF now, but no one has moved to build a UHF station in Austin. *Since KTBC holds the network contracts, it retains on one VHF channel, an effective telecasting monopoly in a city of 186,000 and its environs.* (emphasis added)[158]

Whereas similar stations in comparable cities charged only $325, in 1964 dollars, as a network base rate for broadcast time, Johnson's television station was charging $575. Such a monopoly did not exist anywhere else in the country. One of the Justice Department's primary duties was, and still is, ferreting out instances of monopoly power under the Sherman Antitrust Act of 1890. Johnson's skills at manipulating people resulted in stunning successes, as illustrated by this bureaucratic dichotomy: He was being granted monopoly power by one federal government agency while holding at bay the one charged with dissolving such power.[159] Bobby Baker described how Johnson coerced an NBC network executive to pay his station the highest rate scale for nationally broadcast commercials: "'But senator,' Johnson was told, 'your market isn't big enough down there. The local affiliate is paid according to its share of the audience. Yours just isn't large enough to qualify.' 'I say it is' Johnson retorted. 'I know how you fellows work—you can do anything you want to. Well, want to!' The network officials thought it over and decided they wanted to."[160]

157. Brown, pp. 69–70.
158. *Life* magazine, August 21, 1964.
159. Ibid.
160. Baker, p. 82.

Johnson's use of political influence to expand his business would cement a lifelong association with Austin attorney Ed Clark, who would become the most powerful attorney in the state. Clark had induced the owner of a statewide chain of grocery stores, and the vendors he purchased from, to advertise on KTBC. In exchange for his patronage, Johnson intervened with the OPA, the wartime government agency that rationed various commodities, to allocate the store an extra 150,000 cases of grapefruit in 1944. Clark also arranged for General Electric to advertise on the station and even sponsored the popular *World News Today* program. His other lawyer friend Alvin Wirtz signed on Humble Oil, which selected KTBC to carry their broadcast of football games. Johnson persuaded the Reconstruction Finance Corporation (RFC) to approve a $1,250,000 loan for the Jaques Power Saw Company so that the latter could advertise on his radio station. It was well-known that the best way to secure some favor from Lyndon was to advertise on his radio station.[161] During 1942, before the Johnsons bought the station, the monthly advertising revenue had been $2,600 per month. After the Johnsons' purchase, the revenue rose almost immediately, and by December 1943 it was $5,645. In 1944, it was $13,500; in 1945, it was $15,300; and in 1946, $22,700 per month. By 1946, revenue totaled $272,500. Lyndon Johnson powered the station's ascendancy, selling not merely the groceries and appliances advertised on his radio but political influence.[162]

During his vice presidency, the above scheme would begin backfiring on him, as will be seen in chapter 4, when his Senate aide and protégé Bobby Baker would coerce kickbacks, channeled through the purchase of advertising time on KTBC in Austin, from an insurance salesman doing business in Maryland, who had no business activities in Texas. Insurance agent Don Reynolds would testify to the other illegal activities he witnessed, including that Baker collected "large amounts of cash, from $10,000 to $13,000 at a time," on behalf of Johnson.[163] Unfortunately for Reynolds, his testimony was taken on November 22, 1963, after which the investigations into Johnson's illegal schemes were quickly scuttled.

Johnson as a Freshman Senator

Soon after Johnson returned to Washington as the newly "elected" Texas senator, he demonstrated both his willingness to give big political paybacks to his financial benefactors and propensity for savagely attacking political

161. Caro, *Means of Ascent*, p. 103.
162. Ibid., pp. 104–105.
163. Mollenhoff, p. 298.

opponents, in his 1949 campaign to oust Leland Olds, the veteran chairman of the Federal Power Commission. Olds's record as chairman was impeccable, and his work was completely in accordance with the congressional standards established for the commission, but because of his effectiveness as a commissioner, he was not liked by certain influential men in Texas who felt he was a threat to their ongoing acquisition of untold fortunes. For this reason, he was to lose his position, meager wealth, home, and financial security. He eventually died as a virtual pauper, all thanks to Lyndon B. Johnson.

The story is still relevant—in fact it is essential to understand Johnson's ruthlessness—because it illustrates Johnson's single-minded determination to ruin people if they did not submit to his will. In this case, Olds didn't accept the unwritten requirement to go easy on Johnson's benefactors—owners and managers of behemoth power companies—who preferred regulatory rules that favored themselves over the interests of ordinary citizens and power consumers. It is ironic that Johnson would take credit throughout his life for how he had fought for those same power companies to electrify the rural parts of his district in the 1930s and 1940s, yet in 1949, when the power companies had finally complied, largely because of the efforts of Leland Olds more than any other man alive, Johnson would savagely attack the real architect of the program.

As a newly elected senator, Lyndon B. Johnson immediately began planning his campaign to oust Leland Olds, whom *The New Republic* had called "the central force and will" of the commission.[164] For months, Johnson devised a project that would ensure Olds would be bushwhacked in a process that Olds had assumed would be a routine approval of his third term on the commission. Once the hearings and subcommittee debate commenced, Olds was unmercifully attacked for his writings twenty-some years earlier, in which he had advanced the idea that public interests were superior to the corporate interests of the power companies. This material was turned against him, and now he was accused of having Communist leanings and running the commission like a "commissar," then purposely given very little time to comply with requests for huge amounts of old records and information. Thus, a man who was in fact a very effective administrator was called "a traitor and a jackass and a crackpot . . . Johnson [would] sneer at him and demand that he answer the question 'yes' or 'no' and stop hedging and dodging."[165] He repeatedly interrupted Olds when he tried to explain his earlier position, "demanding that he either 'repudiate' or 'reassert' them." It was a vicious and brutal attack on a

---

164. Caro, *Master of the Senate*, pp. 232–303.
165. Ibid., p. 232.

man whose exemplary work history provided no substantive reason for having his nomination rejected.

Yet another equally compelling point must be made about Johnson's methodology; he had prepared for months to ambush Olds, ensuring his target would have no warning and no real opportunity to respond. Johnson meticulously planned the attack, selecting members for the subcommittee who would be susceptible to charges of Olds's supposed radicalism, scheduling hearings to make it impossible for Olds to assemble the records he needed for an adequate rebuttal, and conducting the hearings in a way that gave opponents as much time as they wanted while severely restricting Olds's proponents. To avoid completely burning his bridges with liberals who supported Olds, he made sure they attended only the sessions for which most of the other subcommittee members—those he needed to convince of Olds's supposed Communist background—had scheduling conflicts; on these occasions, Johnson appeared much more magnanimous and gracious to his prey. But when pro-Olds witnesses testified, he became impatient and pressed them to quickly wrap up their testimony; he repeatedly pulled out a large stopwatch and stared at it, and made sure they saw it.[166]

Johnson's hearing schedule coincided with a meeting of the International Petroleum Association of America in Fort Worth. When the telegraph came describing how the freshman Texas Senator Lyndon B. Johnson, the subcommittee chairman, had taken on President Truman's veteran nominee for reappointment to the Federal Power Commission and won a unanimous vote, 7–0, for rejection, the eight hundred attendees jumped with jubilation, breaking into wild hoorays and loud rebel yells.[167] During the debate in the full Senate, as Johnson was crucifying Leland Olds, sprinkling his accusations with terms like "Marxist" and "commissar," he would extend his hand to his quarry in the corridor outside the hearing room, saying, "Lee, I hope you understand there's nothing personal in this. We're still friends, aren't we? It's only politics, you know."[168] Many of the ninety-six sitting senators who might have otherwise voted for Olds simply walked out, because they did not want to support a man accused—rightly or wrongly—of being a Communist. When the votes were cast, only sixty-eight senators remained on the floor: Olds's renomination was defeated, fifty-three to fifteen.

Practically all of the leading liberals in Washington, from Eleanor Roosevelt to Tommy "the Cork" Corcoran and Joseph Rauh, felt disgusted and betrayed. Even James Rowe, who had been a Johnson supporter for

166. Ibid., p. 275.
167. Ibid., p. 285.
168. Ibid., p. 303.

years, was stunned: "He grabbed onto the goddamned Commie thing and just ran with it and *ran* with it . . . Ran it into the ground for no reason we could see."[169] (It is little wonder that, only a decade later, the Democrats opted not to select Lyndon B. Johnson as their nominee for president; and when Kennedy chose him to be his running mate, liberals were predictably shocked and angered). President Truman—no great fan of Johnson after this episode—appointed someone who was more acceptable to Johnson and his benefactors: Mon Wallgren, who proceeded to reverse regulatory policies that Olds had worked years to accomplish. In 1952, *Fortune* magazine called Wallgren "quite possibly the least effective chairman, or even member, the FPC has ever had . . . A lazy fellow [and] too preoccupied with politicking to pay proper attention to FPC business."[170]

Exactly three weeks after John F. Kennedy gave Lyndon B. Johnson the nod to become the vice presidential nominee of the Democratic Party, on August 5, 1960, Leland Olds died a broken man. He was destitute, abandoned by his oldest friends, who did not want to be associated with someone publicly labeled a Communist sympathizer; his wife, Maud, never recovered from the attacks. According to their daughter, Zara Olds Chapin, her mother had accompanied her father to the hearings and heard various witnesses attacking him as a commisar, jackass, and crackpot, watching the newly minted senator sneering at him and alternately acting very solicitous, then patronizing, and next obsequious, constantly changing from one mode of attack to another. Zara would lament that her mother "died hating Lyndon Johnson. Until the day she died, she could hardly say his name."[171]

But Lyndon was ecstatic about his success: The fight against Leland Olds had paid off, and from then on he could count on the unanimous support of key Texas power brokers including Ed Clark and even more importantly, the oilmen, with their bottomless money barrels necessary for him to realize his dreams. Their backing made the ambush of Leland Olds worth the cost to him of the support of the liberal wing of his party; he knew such a loss would only be temporary. And he was in the most happy, euphoric mood as any of his aides had ever witnessed. His aide, Warren "Woody" Woodward, wrote to Horace Busby, "It is a real pleasure to be around him when he is feeling this way." Johnson wrote to his poker-playing friend Justice William O. Douglas, "This has been one of the finest years—perhaps the finest—of our lives."[172]

169. Ibid.
170. Ibid., pp. 302–303 (ref. *Fortune*, May 1952).
171. Caro, *Master . . .*, pp. 301–302.
172. Ibid., pp. 299–300.

A few months later, in February 1950, another newly elected senator would begin using similar techniques against many people who had done nothing to deserve such outrageous treatment. Joseph R. "Tailgunner Joe" McCarthy's behavior was likely influenced by what he witnessed during Leland Olds's October 1949 confirmation hearings. McCarthy saw that great power and notoriety could be obtained through public humiliation of government employees who could be portrayed as card-carrying Communists, whether or not they really were. Congressman Richard Nixon (R-CA) evidently noticed this tactic as well. Both McCarthy and Nixon molded their confrontational styles on the grand master of reckless, vicious, and irresponsible accusation: Lyndon B. Johnson. According to one of Johnson's aides, Horace Busby, "McCarthy was scared to death of Johnson. Johnson thought McCarthy would someday come up with a big exposé about Johnson's past association with communists in the thirties, which he had many. McCarthy was too scared of Johnson as a skillful politician ever to bring any of that stuff up. He never did, and wisely so. He could never have made it credible. So he, you know, you couldn't be in Washington in the thirties without knowing people who later turned out to be in some cell."[173] Busby's words leave little doubt about whom McCarthy learned his techniques from.

Johnson's strength was manipulating men and women, a skill he practiced on the president of his college and perfected throughout his career. He was innately talented at forming psychological blueprints of his targets, categorizing their strengths and weaknesses, backgrounds, and characteristics such as intelligence, attitudes, and prejudices. According to author David Halberstam, Johnson "could catalogue the strengths and weaknesses of every man [in Congress]. The strength of a man put him off, but his weaknesses attracted him; it meant a man could be used. Whereas Kennedy had been uneasy in the face of another man's weakness, it embarrassed him and he tended to back off when a man showed frailty, to Johnson there was a smell of blood, more could come of this."[174] Senator Hubert Humphrey, who eventually served as Johnson's vice president, addressed this topic in an oral history interview he did for Joe Frantz and the LBJ Library:

> Johnson was like a psychiatrist. Unbelievable man in terms of sizing up people, what they would do, how they would stand under pressure, what their temperament was. This was his genius. He used to tell me many times, "You've got to study every member of this body to know how they're really going to ultimately act. Everything about

173. Horace Busby, recorded interview by Sheldon H. Stern, Mary 26, 1982, (p. 3), John F. Kennedy Library Oral History Program.
174. Halberstam, p. 446.

them, their family, their background, their attitudes, even watch their moods before you even ask them to vote." He was a master of human relations when it came to that Senate.[175]

Humphrey elaborated upon the above in another oral history conducted by Michael Gillette:

> Johnson always was able to take the measure of a man. He knew those that he could dominate; he knew those that he could outmaneuver. Right off the bat he sized you up. . . . Johnson knew how to woo people. He was a born political lover. It's a most amazing thing . . . what I mean is he knew how to massage the senators. He knew which ones he could just push aside, he knew which ones he could threaten, and above all he knew which ones he'd have to spend time with and nourish along, to bring along, to make sure that they were coming along.[176]

What Humphrey didn't say, though he must surely have known, was that the real key to Johnson's mastery of other people's future actions was his knowledge of their past secrets; and the key to that kind of hidden information was his access to to J. Edgar Hoover's most personal and confidential files.

In later years, Johnson demonstrated his process to two of JFK's famed advisers. Robert Dallek's account references John Kenneth Galbraith's story about how Johnson spent a whole morning with Arthur Schlesinger, examining "every member of the Senate—his drinking habits, his sex habits, his intellectual capacity, reliability, how you manage him. Arthur said, 'Most informative morning I ever spent. Never got a word in edgewise.' Not long afterward, Johnson told Galbraith, 'I've been meeting with your friend, Arthur Schlesinger. Really had a very good meeting. We had a long talk. He's a right smart fellow. But damn fellow talks too much.'"[177] Hubert Humphrey saw that Johnson's efforts culminated in dirt on every sitting U.S. senator: "He knew all the little things that people did. I used to say he had his own private FBI. If you ever knew anybody, if you'd been out on a date, or if you'd had a drink, or if you'd attended a meeting, or you danced with a gal at a nightclub, he knew it! It was just incredible! I don't know how he was able

175. Transcript, Hubert H. Humphrey Oral History Interview I, 8/17/71, by Joe B. Frantz, Internet Copy, LBJ Library.
176. Transcript, Hubert H. Humphrey Oral History Interview III, 6/21/77, by Michael L. Gillette, Internet Copy, LBJ Library.
177. Dallek, *Lone Star* . . ., p. 352 (ref. Arthur Schlesinger Jr. interview, August 3, 1987; Miller, *Lyndon*, p. 247).

to get all that information, but he lived and breathed and walked and talked politics . . . He was just totally immersed in it."[178]

Lyndon Johnson's other great skill stemmed from his Texas upbringing and forms a common trait of many people who live there, especially in the area known as the Hill Country outside of Austin, who often harness country colloquialisms to generate vivid descriptions. For example, instead of saying, "Appearances can be deceptive," a Texan might remark, "Just because a chicken has wings doesn't mean it can fly." Author J. Evetts Haley, himself a native of the Lone Star State and familiar with the art of crafting the perfect Texas idiom, provided other examples, about how Lyndon fit in so well to the political scene in Washington ("He took to the techniques of influence and pressure like a kitten to a warm brick") and how, after Speaker Sam Rayburn had taken Lyndon under his wing, his "career began to glitter like burnished brass."[179] Robert Caro described the Johnsonian lexicon: Instead of calling a special interest group weak, or a House-Senate joint committee a meaningless legislative exercise, Johnson would say the former was "not much stronger than a popcorn fart," and the latter was "as useless as tits on a bull."[180] Johnson's skill was such that he could craft such an expression instantly, on the fly, to describe whatever the situation might require.

A more technical, non-Texan way of summarizing Johnson's treatment of others might be, "The overt manipulation of people through the use of psychoanalytical assessments targeted to his subject's weaknesses, administered simultaneously as he overpowers and seduces his target with verbal entreaties framed in Texas colloquialisms." In his book *Flawed Giant: Lyndon Johnson and His Times*, Robert Dallek portrayed Johnson's trademark:[181]

> Evans and Novak described it as "supplication, accusation, cajolery, exuberance, scorn, tears, complaint, the hint of threat. It was all of these together. It ran the gamut of human emotions. Its velocity was breathtaking, and it was all in one direction. Interjections from the target were rare. Johnson anticipated them before they could be spoken. He moved in close, his face a scant millimeter from his target, his eyes widening and narrowing, his eyebrows rising and falling. From his pockets poured clippings, memos, statistics. Mimicry, humor, and the genius of analogy made 'The Treatment' an almost hypnotic experience and rendered the target stunned and helpless."

178. Transcript, Hubert H. Humphrey Oral History Interview I, 8/17/71, by Joe B. Frantz, Internet Copy, LBJ Library.
179. Haley, pp. 11, 13.
180. Dallek, *Lone Star . . .*, p. 416.
181. Dallek, *Flawed Giant*, pp. 3–6.

Jeff Shesol, author of *Mutual Contempt: Lyndon Johnson, Robert Kennedy, and the Feud That Defined a Decade*, elaborated upon the above:

> Johnson bent his colleagues backward, physically and figuratively, under his enormous frame and by the sheer force of his will. Senator Hubert Humphrey of Minnesota would slink from a room, pleading for a cigarette break, to escape a face-to-face encounter with LBJ. The Johnson Treatment was partly intuitive and partly the product of discreet calculation. LBJ's understanding of a senator's individual vulnerabilities was innate, but he also scripted, rehearsed, and contrived seemingly spontaneous encounters in Capitol corridors. "Johnson knew how to woo people," remembered Humphrey, the frequent object of LBJ's attention. "He was sort of like a cowboy making love . . . He knew how to massage the senators." Johnson knew whom to nurture, whom to threaten, and whom to push aside. The whole chamber seemed subject to his manipulation. "*He played it like an organ*," exclaimed *Times*'s Hugh Sidey. "*Goddamn, it was beautiful! It was just marvelous.*"[182] (emphasis added)

Elements that enhanced Johnson's manipulative abilities were his sense of timing and the seeming spontaneity with which the events he choreographed appeared to his targets. As Robert Dallek wrote, Johnson practiced creating this illusion on his colleagues: "Johnson usually designed his approaches to other senators to seem to be wholly spontaneous—as an accidental encounter in a Senate corridor leading to a private talk. In fact, they were carefully planned . . . *the product of meticulous calculation*"[183] (emphasis added).

As if to verify Johnson's ability to orchestrate events, Harry Blackstone Jr., a radio broadcaster who worked for him at KTBC and whose father was a magician known as the Great Blackstone, was quoted in a newspaper article professing, "I worked quite some time for Lyndon Johnson as broadcast personnel, and I think I learned more about the art of deception from him than I did from my father . . . he was a man who understood the art of misdirection—of making the eye watch 'A' when the dirty work was going on at 'B.'"[184]

During Lyndon Johnson's twelve years as a senator, having risen to become the minority leader after four years and then majority leader after two more, he had acquired almost as much power as the president, and was

---

182. Shesol, pp. 11–12.
183. Dallek, *Lone Star Rising*, pp. 474–475.
184. "Trickster Says LBJ Was Good Model of Deception," *Dallas Times Herald*, May 20, 1989; ref. Twyman, p. 813.

willing to cast aside moral or ethical considerations to attain more. One of the most revealing and troubling insights into this part of Johnson's character appears in Robert Caro's biography: Johnson's hunger was for power "in its most naked form, for power not to improve the lives of others, but to manipulate and dominate them, to bend them to his will . . . it was *a hunger so fierce and consuming that no consideration of morality or ethics, no cost to himself—or to anyone else—could stand before it*" (emphasis added).[185] Becoming the vice president would have represented a step backwards, unless the office was seen as Johnson saw it—merely a stepping stone on his path to the presidency.[186]

Johnson's Vice Presidency

Beginning with his ascension to the Senate and then his position as majority leader, Johnson knew his boyhood dream, the one that he long ago resolved would be kept, was within his grasp. He knew that in order to successfully run for the presidency, he would need to redefine his base, which had always been what he thought was the vast middle class, not wealthy landowners but working class people in Texas. He tried to be a populist candidate, while simultaneously staying grounded on the conservative side of the Democratic Party. He would have to shift toward a more liberal position once he gravitated to a national base; however, those lines had become more and more blurred to him anyway. He was conservative on some issues while taking a very progressive and liberal position on others as he began his makeover. He had started out with a more conservative stance when he first went to Congress but shifted toward the left the more he infused his district with federal funds for New Deal programs, which ultimately paid dividends at the ballot box.

But Johnson's ostensible metamorphosis was diluted even more because of his lack of real convictions—he was driven only by his own need for more power and progress toward his lifelong objective—and a growing tendency to present himself as very conservative when speaking to a like audience, while deftly converting himself to a liberal when the occasion demanded it. His oscillation between political ideologies increased when he "won" his Senate seat and had to appeal to voters throughout the then-largest state in the nation. His psychological need to be universally liked must have caused him extreme frustration, since his actions to appease one group caused such consternation among others. The resulting impasse would come to a

185. Caro, *The Path* . . . p. xix.
186. McClellan, p. 136.

head when he tepidly sought the nomination for president and, to an even greater extent, when he decided to aggressively pursue the vice presidential nomination, which caused the issue to become part of the public debate.

Many Southerners felt betrayed by Lyndon Johnson in the late 1950s and were as dismayed by Kennedy's selection of him as the vice presidential nominee as were the Northern liberals. James J. Kilpatrick, then editor of the *Richmond News Leader*, noted in *Human Events* that "however he may be respected on the Senate floor, [he] is neither liked nor admired below the Potomac. In the South of 1960, as in the South of 1870, a carpetbagger may be bad, but a scalawag is worse." The article continued, "If it had been established that he believed deeply and profoundly both in the need for this (civil rights) legislation and in some constitutional justification for it, his loyalty to personal principle would have won a measure of respect. No such record, and no such dedication, were in evidence. 'South is Betrayed Again by Johnson for the Sake of His Own Ambitions,' cried the Augusta *Herald*. 'He is despised by the people he has betrayed,' claimed the *Shreveport Journal*. 'A political charlatan,' declared the *Nashville Banner*. 'The Southern Benedict Arnold,' alleged the *Jacksonville Times-Union*. In South Carolina, the *Columbia State* termed him 'the Texas Yankee.' In Virginia, the *Richmond Times-Dispatch* bitterly assailed him as 'just another office-hungry Senator.' In Birmingham, *South* magazine called him a 'political polygamist.'"[187]

Despite the rancor from conservative Southerners, Lyndon Johnson had won the enmity of liberals too, as he emasculated the 1957 Civil Rights Act. Thus, when Kennedy announced his selection of Johnson for the vice presidential nomination, civil rights activists like Joe Rauh and Walter Reuther threatened to bring the matter to a floor fight at the convention. To appease them, Johnson promised to support any civil rights legislation proposed by Kennedy, but Johnson would eventually spend most of his time as vice president on advancing his own agenda while undermining Kennedy's: Within weeks of JFK's inauguration, Johnson would pressure the secretary of agriculture to relax regulatory rules so his friend and benefactor Billie Sol Estes could carry out massive financial fraud; collude with military and intelligence officials to subvert Kennedy's Cuban policies; sabotage Kennedy's efforts to secure viable relationships with other countries, notably South Vietnam; continue financially beneficial scams through his numerous contacts in the underworld of mobsters and crooked lobbyists; and extend his own fraudulent schemes with the help of his longtime protégé Bobby Baker.

Lyndon Johnson had learned that power enabled him to control appointments to high-level positions, and the higher his own level, the higher the positions he could control and exploit for his own interests. He exerted

---

187. Kilpatrick, James, *Human Events*, August 25, 1960.

direct control over fundamental government decisions, even as the vice president, which was not previously a very powerful position. Before he became president, he was able to manipulate, cajole, and blackmail John Kennedy into making key appointments that Johnson himself had arranged. One such appointment, to replace John Connally as secretary of the navy—an office he had originally been put into through Johnson, and that he was leaving after one year to run for the governorship of Texas—involved Johnson's old crony Fred Korth, the former president of the Continental National Bank of Fort Worth, Texas; he was given the job of derailing the choice of Boeing Aircraft Corporation as the builder of the new TFX fighter jet, awarding it instead to General Dynamics of Fort Worth, Texas. This event was only one of the Johnson-caused scandals the Kennedy administration would have to defend.

Another example of Johnson-arranged, high-level appointments involved top officials at the Department of Agriculture (DOA), who would become enablers for Johnson's friend and associate Billie Sol Estes. The plethora of confidence schemes and frauds Johnson and Estes conducted would eventually lead to a series of murders (not so carefully disguised as suicides) of men who had obstructed the two of them; these sordid affairs will be detailed in later chapters.

During the early months of the Kennedy administration, Johnson liked to wander around the White House as if he were attending to important business when in fact he was merely snooping around, reading people, and attempting to insinuate himself into current events. Though it seemed innocent enough, Johnson's morning routine was calculated: His chauffer would drop him off at the front of the White House, where he walked through the gates into the entrance, through to the West Wing and out the rear door before going to his own office in the adjacent Executive Office Building (EOB). He may have had many reasons for such an itinerary, but he clearly hoped to learn as much as possible about the latest controversy in the Oval Office.

Horace Busby, in an interview conducted by Michael L. Gillette, attested that:

> Vice President Johnson would disappear out of his EOB offices—well, he didn't disappear, he was gone and you knew where he was gone, most likely was over to the White House—and he was over at the White House wandering around, kind of, you know, your obedient servant just waiting for somebody to say, "Lyndon, would you go down and get the President an apple," or something. It was funny, and these guys, the Kennedy guys, mostly came from the Hill and they'd known him as the awesome majority leader and they were deferential to him, and yet at the same time they didn't want him to mess up anything of theirs, which there had been episodes about that

along the way. And he was over there just kind of exposing himself to serve notice that he was on call. If you need somebody to go to Greenland, I'm here. And so he came back one afternoon, "All right, this is the way they're going to play it." And I don't remember— he had a whole string of paranoid reactions to what he imagined somebody at the White House was setting him up [for], see. Well, this played out that we went to Dakar and word came—what had preceded this, I don't know—word came that we were to go to Spain to a military base there and meet with Spanish government officials. Oh, he just went up the wall. He said, "They got Henry Cabot Lodge's brother there as ambassador," which was true; (inaudible) he hadn't been replaced by the new administration, so we still had a Republican ambassador. And he said, "I can see what they're up to. They want me to come flying in there, and dime to a dollar they'd have Franco out there to meet me" . . . Johnson saw it only as an effort to embarrass him by saying that first crack out of the barrel, you let him go to Washington and he runs off with his natural ally Franco, because he is obviously a Texas fascist and ultra-conservative and all that kind—oh, he was furious.[188]

Lyndon Johnson's ego, despite being bigger than Texas, was nonetheless extremely fragile; he saw not only real slights but imagined ones as well, and never learned to ignore either. He told Clark Clifford of how he seethed over an incident that occurred while he was sitting in the reception area outside the Oval Office waiting to see President Kennedy; Bobby Kennedy walked rapidly through the room and into the Oval Office, without greeting him or even acknowledging his presence.[189] Given that their relationship was built on derisive bitterness and outright animosity toward each other, it is curious that he let such a minor slight bother him. Much has been written about the long-term feud between Johnson and Bobby Kennedy but little about how he really felt about John Kennedy. Many authors mistakenly thought the two basically liked each other yet acknowledged that Kennedy's tolerance of Johnson was tenuous at best, which was evidenced by Johnson's steadily decreasing presence in White House meetings. In the spring of 1960, Peter Lisagor, a *Chicago Daily News* reporter and regular pundit on *Face the Nation*, conversed with Johnson on a plane ride. According to Robert Dallek's account, when Lisagor repeated the conversation to Robert Kennedy,

---

188. Horace Busby, Oral History Interview VIII, April 2, 1989, by Michael L. Gillette [Transcript], Internet copy, LBJ Library.
189. Clifford, pp. 389–390.

"All of the enmity and hostility [Johnson] held for the Kennedys came out." Johnson described Jack as "a little scrawny fellow with rickets" and God knows what other kind of diseases. Johnson predicted that Jack's election would give Joe Kennedy control of the country and would make Bobby Secretary of Labor. When Lisagor finished, four letter words and all, Bobby turned to the window and said: "I knew he hated Jack, but I didn't think he hated him that much." Bobby gave clear expression to his feelings about Lyndon's performance at the CEEO . . . "It brought tensions between Johnson and Kennedy right out on the table and very hard. Everybody was sweating under the armpits . . . what Bobby and the White House saw was a Vice President unable to convince people that his effort to advance black job equality was anything more than a sham." [190]

The hateful relationship between Bobby Kennedy and Lyndon Johnson had many origins, but one in particular would have probably been a major incident in the long litany of examples. It occured in 1959, when Bobby went to Johnson's ranch to discuss LBJ's plans for the 1960 presidential election; he assured RFK that he had no intent to run (despite having the Texas legislature pass enabling legislation to allow him to run for reelection as a senator while simultaneously running for the presidency or vice presidency). He then invited Bobby to go deer hunting with him and handed him a powerful ten-gauge shotgun, without warning him about the recoil it had compared with a rifle, which had little kickback. When Bobby shot it, the force of the recoil knocked him to the ground and the flying gunstock cut his forehead. Lyndon's response was to reach down to help him stand up, saying, "Son, you've got to learn to handle a gun like a man."[191] His failure to warn Kennedy in advance—since he was obviously a novice who had never fired a ten-gauge shotgun—was clearly an attempt to humiliate his guest and show who was the "better man." That shotgun was powerful enough to tear an average whitetail deer in half; no one uses such a gun for anything other than big game or bears, except Lyndon Johnson, who used it as an act of meanness because he doubtlessly knew it would knock Bobby to the ground and in the process possibly injure him when the gunstock flew upward to his face, which in fact it did. After having humiliated and purposely injuring him, it is no surprise that the relationship between them would never recover.

---

190. Dallek, *Flawed Giant*, pp. 33–36.
191. Dallek, Lyndon B. Johnson . . . p. 113.

According to Horace Busby, the bad blood between RFK and LBJ started at least as early as 1953, when Joseph McCarthy introduced three of his new aides, one of whom was Bobby, to Johnson in the Senate cafeteria:

> "Oh, I want you to meet my staff here." And the two, two of the guys stood up to meet the imminent leader; and Bobby didn't stand up. But Joe introduced the two who stood up, and they shook hands with Johnson, and then he said, "And Senator, this is the newest member of our staff, Senator, I mean, Robert Kennedy." Kennedy did not stand up. And when he looked up at Johnson, I was just startled, because it was, it was contempt . . . But it was just almost a tangible thing when he looked up at Johnson. And Johnson said, "Hi, Bobby," and just kind of waved his hand. Bobby made no move either to speak or shake hands or anything.[192]

In those early days, Bobby's emotions and attitudes required no abstruse interpretations, as they were visible if not unmistakable to all; their relationship started sourly and never improved. RFK would later say that "Johnson had this ability 'to eat people up, even people who are considered rather strong figures . . . He's mean, bitter, vicious—an animal in many ways.'"[193] The two had a confrontation at a 1962 White House event, where Johnson asked him, "'Bobby, you do not like me. Your brother likes me. Your sister-in-law likes me. Your daddy likes me. But *you don't like me*. Now, why? Why don't you like me?' A witness to the performance said it 'went on and on for hours.' Finally, Johnson supplied the answer: Bobby thought he had attacked his father at the 1960 convention and had tried to deny Jack the nomination. When Johnson denied both facts, it incensed Bobby, who later complained that *Johnson 'lies all the time. I'm telling you, he just lies continuously, about everything. In every conversation I have with him, he lies. As I've said, he lies even when he doesn't have to'*[194] (emphasis added). JFK agreed on this point, telling Jackie on the evening of November 21, 1963, that Lyndon Johnson was "incapable of telling the truth."[195]

President Kennedy quickly became aware of Johnson's fragile ego, easily hurt feelings, and sensitivity with respect to his schedule. When JFK wanted someone to attend Senegal's independence celebration, he asked McGeorge Bundy, "How about sending Lyndon? . . . feel him out. You know how

192. Horace Busby, recorded interview by Sheldon H. Stern, Mary 26, 1982, (p. 3), John F. Kennedy Library Oral History Program.
193. Guthman, pp. 415, 417. 194. Guthman and Shulman, p. 26 (Interview with Arthur Schlesinger Jr., February 27, 1965).
194. Guthman and Shulman, p. 26 (Interview with Arthur Schlesinger Jr., February 27, 1965).
195. Ibid.

he is—sort of sensitive. He doesn't like to be pushed into anything."[196] Later, he told Bundy, "Since I am going to Paris in May, I wonder if it is a good idea for Johnson to go to Paris. If it is possible for him to go to Rome without going to see the pope, perhaps that would be a better trip. If not, France would be all right . . . it would be best if he . . . not plan to see de Gaulle." When Bundy pointed out that Congressman Rooney, who was planning to go on the trip, would want to see the pope if they went to Rome, Kennedy instructed him to "draft a letter to be sent to Lyndon suggesting the visits to Geneva and Paris."[197] When Johnson initially flatly refused to go on a trip to Vietnam, saying he did not want to become a roving ambassador, Mrs. Lincoln wrote that "Mr. Kennedy, his Irish temper rising a bit, stood his ground. After Mr. Johnson had left the office, Mr. Kennedy said, 'What do you know about that? Lyndon stalked out of here, mad as a hornet, when I asked him to go to Southeast Asia.'"[198]

During his vice presidency, Johnson constantly tried to finagle trips with Kennedy on Air Force One, and had to be repeatedly reminded that, as a matter of security, they should never ride on the same plane. Kennedy consistently refused to share the airplane but always did something to smooth Johnson's ruffled feathers; according to Mrs. Lincoln, "It seemed that that one thing bothered the vice president more than anything else."[199] It probably didn't occur to her that Lyndon simply felt he was being shortchanged, that it was he who should have been riding on Air Force One. Johnson's oversensitivity about how other people treated him, especially any hint of criticism from others, eventually led JFK to say that sending a birthday greeting to Lyndon was like "drafting a state document."[200]

Lyndon constantly complained to the president about the things his brother, Bobby, did to embarrass or humiliate him. JFK's aide Kenneth O'Donnell described the routine he and JFK established to remedy Johnson's ego, according to which JFK would call him in "and denounce me in front of Johnson for whatever the Vice President was beefing about. I would humbly take the blame and promise to correct the situation, and the Vice President would go away somewhat happier."[201] O'Donnell related when RFK had declined Johnson's request to appoint Judge Sarah Hughes to a federal judgeship; Bobby thought Mrs. Hughes, then sixty-five, was too old for such an appointment. Johnson became upset when he learned that she had

---

196. Lincoln, p. 165.
197. Ibid., p. 166.
198. Ibid., p. 167.
199. Ibid., p. 159. 200. Sherrill, p. 50.
200. Sherrill, p. 50.
201. O'Donnell, *Life* magazine, August 7, 1970, p. 48.

been given the judgeship after all; Sam Rayburn had subsequently made the same request, threatening to tie up Justice Department bills in the judiciary committee unless she got the appointment. When Bobby told him that he had declined Johnson on the basis of Mrs. Hughes' age, Rayburn, then almost eighty, glared at the thirty-five-year-old Kennedy. "'Son, everybody looks old to you. Do you want those bills passed, or don't you?' The next day Sarah Hughes was nominated for the federal bench."[202] That Rayburn succeeded where he had failed embarrassed Johnson.

The fighting between Johnson and Bobby Kennedy during the early years of the Kennedy administration led the White House to exclude Johnson from the drafting of the 1963 civil rights bill. Unable to meet with the president even to discuss it, Johnson—still in charge of the Committee on Equal Employment Opportunity—complained behind the scenes about how it was being mismanaged with Congress. He underestimated the importance of the bill's proposed mandate for equal access to public accommodations, and minimized the need to abolish segregation as a means to accomplish economic and education gains. His apparent wariness was no doubt caused by his exclusion from the development of the bill; however, Bobby Kennedy had come to regard Johnson as an obstructionist in the effort. RFK told John Bartlow Martin that *"he [LBJ] very rarely helped when he could help when we were trying to get votes in the Senate. He was against sending any civil rights legislation up."*[203]

The attorney general's attitude about Johnson was more than a reaction simply based upon personal differences, however. The scandals Johnson was associated with in 1961–1963, first related to Billie Sol Estes and then to Bobby Baker, threatened the credibility of the administration to its core, and therefore were jeopardizing the 1964 election. Johnson had convinced himself (correctly, it turns out) that Bobby Kennedy instigated the stories detailing these scandals as a way to remove Johnson from the 1964 ticket. By the late summer of 1963, rumors were rampant that JFK would replace Johnson as vice president, despite the obligatory public denials. JFK's secretary, Evelyn Lincoln, has stated that Kennedy told her he had already decided to drop Johnson and was planning to replace him with another Southerner, Governor Terry Sanford, of North Carolina. Arthur Schlesinger Jr. succinctly described these machinations in his book *Robert Kennedy and His Times*:[204]

> Robert Kennedy was [Johnson's] nemesis. The younger brother had begun by trying to deny him the vice presidential nomination. "He

202. Ibid.
203. Guthman and Shulman, p. 410 (Interview with John Bartlow Martin, May 14, 1964).
204. Schlesinger, *RFK*, p. 673.

repeated that to me over a period of weeks," Pierre Salinger recalled of Johnson's first months in the White House. After the inauguration, said O'Donnell, Johnson felt Robert Kennedy "had taken over his rightful position as the number two man in the government." The Attorney General was the man who humiliated the Vice President at the Committee on Equal Employment Opportunities; who, Johnson assured Hugh Sidey, *Times's* White House correspondent, "bugged him all the time during the time he was Vice President"; who, in the autumn of 1963, Johnson believed, was fomenting the Bobby Baker case in order to deny him re-nomination. "President Kennedy worked so hard at making a place for me, always saying nice things, gave me dignity and standing," Johnson said to Helen Thomas of United Press International after the 1968 election. "But back in the back room they were quoting Bobby, saying I was going to be taken off the ticket."

Lyndon Johnson's Character: A Summation

The abridged history thus far provided, minus the deference ordinarily accorded to those having held the presidential office, details the real persona of Lyndon B. Johnson: he was anything but the magnanimous, good-hearted and public-spirited man often portrayed by other biographers. The thirty-sixth president was cruel, mendacious, narcissistic—concerned only about the pseudolegend he worked an entire lifetime to create, resulting in the false legacy that has persisted today. The character traits assessed previously can be traced throughout the remaining chapters, and the worst—the most narcissistic, megalomaniacal, and criminal—will become ever more predominant.

Johnson's powers of calculation, agreed upon by practically all of his biographers, directly account for how he ingratiated himself into official Washington and the position from which he would springboard into the presidency. William Manchester elegantly and vividly described Lyndon Johnson's overall strategy:[205]

> Johnson approached a strongly fortified position by outflanking it, or burrowing under it, or surprising the defenders from the rear, or raining down obstacles upon them from the sky, or starving them

---

205. Manchester, p. 270.

into submission. Rarely, and then only reluctantly, would he proceed directly from A to B. To him the shortest distance between two points was a tunnel. His supreme talents were those of the man behind the scenes. But his complexities do not even end there, for few men in public life had found less comfort in anonymity. When the circus catch was made, he wanted the fans to note the LBJ brand on the fielder's glove. They noted it. It could not be missed. Yet the feeling persisted that bat, batter, and umpire had been stamped with the same brand—that the play had been set from the start. It was only a feeling. Nothing was ever proved . . . [but] Johnson always managed to be out there in center field at the finish, his mitt outstretched to snag the descending ball.

Many men dream of, and establish complex plans to achieve, becoming president; but no one has ever been more obsessed than Lyndon Johnson, whose desire was so absolute it was in practically all of his thoughts, awakened or not. He considered the presidency his destiny, and nothing—least of all any other person—could stop him. One of the attorneys in Ed Clark's Austin law firm, Barr McClellan, described Johnson's determination as being insuperable, that he would allow *nothing* to stand in the way of his becoming president.[206]

Johnson's ability to deceive people, to make planned events seem spontaneous, and his willingness to take great personal risks to satisfy his need for more power—so thoroughly described by Robert Caro, Robert Dallek, and, before them, by J. Evetts Haley, William Manchester, and others—facilitated his quest to become president. The evidence presented in this book, deeply hidden in most other stories and books about him, shows convincingly that his unique powers over people, especially as president after the assassination, could have only been held by a man in a position to choreograph in macro detail the "crime of the century."

206. McClellan, p. 149.

PART II

The Context of the Times:
Secrets, Scandals, and Scams

Chapter 2

THE INTERNATIONAL SCENE CIRCA 1960–1963

The CIA's growth was like . . . a malignancy which . . . [JFK] was not sure even the White House could control . . . any longer. If the United States ever experiences [an attempt at a coup to overthrow the Government] it will come from the CIA and not the Pentagon. The agency represents a tremendous power and total unaccountability to anyone.

—ARTHUR KROCK, *THE NEW YORK TIMES*, OCTOBER 3, 1963

Allen Dulles, Richard Helms, Carmel Offie and Frank Wisner were the grand masters. If you were in a room with them you were in a room full of people that you had to believe would deservedly end up in hell. I guess I will see them there soon.

—JAMES ANGLETON, CIA CHIEF OF COUNTERINTELLIGENCE

Transitional Government
The Shift of Administrations: Eisenhower to Kennedy

During the 1960 presidential campaign, John F. Kennedy needled Richard Nixon on the Eisenhower administration's ineffectiveness to stabilize Cuba, knowing that he had cornered Nixon because he could not reveal the secret plans then under development to invade Cuba. Kennedy took advantage of Nixon's forced reticence and advocated strongly that the United States openly aid anti-Castro forces inside and outside Cuba—putting himself on the record as an advocate of aggressively helping the exiles in their fight against Fidel Castro while putting the hapless Nixon on the defensive side of the issue—even though he had personally helped develop the plan that Kennedy was advancing. During their last debate, Nixon was forced to argue on national television that the United States was barred by international law from helping Cuban exile groups.[1] Kennedy's campaign rhetoric would come back to bite him within three months of his inauguration.

---

1. Hersh, *The Dark Side*, p. 180.

In his farewell address of January 17, 1961, President Eisenhower had warned the entire nation about what he considered were very dangerous trends associated with the buildup of military powers, which had been going on during the eight years of his administration. He was originally planning to describe the phenomenon as the "military-industrial-congressional complex"; unfortunately, the most critical component of this complex, *congressional*, was dropped from the speech at the last minute, and it was simply referred to as the military-industrial complex:

> We have been compelled to create a permanent armaments industry of vast proportions. Added to this, three and a half million men and women are directly engaged in the defense establishment. We annually spend on military security more than the net income of all United States corporations.
>
> This conjunction of an immense military establishment and a large arms industry is new in the American experience. The total influence—economic, political, even spiritual—is felt in every city, every statehouse, every office of the Federal Government. We recognize the imperative need for this development. Yet we must not fail to comprehend its grave implications. Our toil, resources and livelihood are all involved; so is the very structure of our society. In the councils of government we must guard against the acquisition of unwarranted influence, whether sought or unsought, by the military industrial complex. The potential for the disastrous rise of misplaced power exists and will persist . . . We must never let the weight of this combination endanger our liberties or democratic processes. We should take nothing for granted.

Kennedy had probably taken President Eisenhower's warning more seriously than any of the military or intelligence leaders already in place, or even many of his own appointments in the highest reaches of the executive department. Before long, he had become disappointed by a number of his early appointments; however, he always tried to be supportive of his own men in order to keep them pulling in the same direction as the course he had plotted. On January 19, 1961, in one of his last actions as president, Dwight Eisenhower briefed his successor John F. Kennedy on numerous "items of unfinished business" as part of the presidential transition. As author/historian Richard Reeves described it, there was a built-in wall between them, which impeded the development of any mutual agreements:[2]

> They talked for more than an hour, mostly about national security and foreign affairs. Eisenhower realized quickly what was on Kennedy's mind and he didn't like it. His questions were about the structure of decision making on national security and defense. It was clear to Ike that Kennedy thought his structure was too bureaucratic and slow—with too many debates and decisions outside the President's reach and control. Eisenhower thought Kennedy was naïve, but he was not about to say that, and so he began a long explanation of how and why he had built up what amounted to a military staff apparatus to collect and feed information methodically to the Commander-in-Chief and then coordinate and implement his decisions.

Eisenhower was more interested in the situation in Laos than Vietnam, which he said was the most dangerous trouble spot in Southeast Asia. He mentioned South Vietnam only as a secondary issue since it would be one of the nations that would fall into the Communist side if the United States failed to support the regime in Laos. Kennedy was shocked by what Eisenhower told him. He later told his two aides, Kenneth O'Donnell and David Powers, "There he sat, telling me to get ready to put ground forces into Asia, the thing he himself had been carefully avoiding for the last eight years. And he was very calm about it. I was finding out that things were really just as bad as I had said they were during the campaign."[3] Another of these items was Cuba, and the issue was the plans for an invasion at the Bay of Pigs, "The rebel force that was being trained by the CIA in Guatemala to invade Cuba." O'Donnell and Powers claimed that "Eisenhower urged him to keep on supporting this plan to overthrow Castro."[4]

JFK Confronts the CIA

For the first twenty-five years of its existence, the Central Intelligence Agency was allowed to grow in every way imaginable: the number of people employed; the physical acreage and buildings required to house it, both home and abroad; its reach into other cultures and governments around the world; and its autonomy and independence, uncontrolled by the congressional committees, which dutifully exercised oversight of all other—less dangerous,

2. Reeves, R., p. 22.
3. O'Donnell and Powers, pp. 244–245.
4. Ibid., p. 244.

more easily managed—agencies and departments of the government. Its budget was secret, unauditable, and seemingly unlimited; thus, even the term "budget" was, if not an oxymoron in this context, at least an overstatement.

The CIA was established in 1947, but its mission was not defined until 1949 when Public Law 81-110 was passed; the prevailing attitude in Congress and the other branches of government was that an open-ended license to conduct its shadowy business was necessary in order to match the capabilities of the Soviet Union's secret intelligence agency, the KGB, which operated similarly. Thus, "the Agency" was free to use confidential fiscal and administrative processes to achieve its ends. The act exempted it from having to disclose anything about its organization, functions, officials, titles, salaries, whatever. Given such a broad mandate, it is not surprising that congressional scrutiny was, for practical purposes, nonexistent. The director of central intelligence during most of this period, Allen Dulles, fostered the sense of autonomy and independence throughout all of its sections. Its leaders, including Dulles, Richard Helms, Richard Bissell, James Jesus Angleton, William Colby, and Cord Meyer, were all conscious of one caveat, however: Just as it had been created out of carefully crafted legal language, so too could it be destroyed. In 1961, John F. Kennedy promised to do just that, but it was understood that doing so in his first term would risk his not being reelected, so it would have to wait until his second—presuming that he could have outlived the realization of his promise.

Many historians agree that the real founder of the CIA was Walter Bedell "Beetle" Smith, even though his tenure did not begin until 1950. The Agency he inherited from William J. Donovan had been in a continuing fight with the State Department and the FBI over defining its turf, and the morale within the Agency had been faltering since the end of World War II. Beetle Smith is credited with finally bringing the disparate parts of the CIA together, and with establishing effective command and control throughout the organization. Smith established three branches in the CIA:

- The Office for National Estimates, to develop estimates of other countries' capabilities, pertaining to military defenses, natural resources, etc.
- The Office for Research and Reports (ORR), to monitor and report on economic developments, focused primarily on the Soviet Union and its allied countries
- The Directorate for Intelligence (DDI), to produce intelligence reports

For the last sixty-odd years, the CIA has somehow managed to maintain its reputation despite its checkered past—mostly buried in top secret archives—at a huge, practically unquantifiable cost. Although there were undoubtedly many successful and legal operations in those early years, the unfortunate fact is that its record was replete with numerous instances of its going well outside the charter to obtain knowledge of the world and to take aggressive action to stop threats to the nation. Its global reach enabled it to extend its umbrella over the entire hemisphere and attempt to reshape the world by discreetly manipulating—and worse, forcefully changing—the ideologies of sovereign nations. Even when it operated within its mandate, its history is blemished by deadly mistakes made on the basis of bad intelligence, philosophical flaws and structural failures which, as now well established, have continued into the twenty-first century. Those mistakes have negatively redounded on its reputation, even to the point of exposing itself to baseless and unscrupulous charges from politicians willing to take a swipe at an easy target for narrow and selfish purposes. The errors made and opportunities lost continue to leave the country vulnerable.

The worst of the mistakes were related to its operations within the United States, clearly in violation of its charter. Closely next to that—arguably tied for first place—were the attempts to overthrow foreign governments and assassinate their leaders, essentially putting the United States in charge of how other countries would be run and making murder an official policy of the United States government. Among the worst of those mistakes was an illegal program code-named HTLINGUAL under which the mail for certain individuals and/or organizations was opened, read, and copied before being resealed and delivered.[5] Arguably worse than that was Project MK/ULTRA, the code name for a covert interrogation research program involving the surreptitious use of drugs, as well as hypnosis and other methods, to manipulate people against their conscious will.[6] As noted in later chapters, there were indications that Lee Harvey Oswald was one of the subjects involved with this program.

The 1953 coup that installed the shah of Iran, the 1954 overthrow of the Guatemala government, the assassinations of other heads of state, such as Rafael Trujillo of the Dominican Republic, and the 1961 assassination of Patrice Lumumba of the Democratic Republic of the Congo were all examples of overreaching its originally authorized intelligence mission. In the 1950s it was political suicide to ignore the "international Communist conspiracy," which threatened to take over the world; this was exemplified by the picture flashed across American television sets of Nikita Khrushchev slamming his shoe repeatedly at a meeting of the UN Security Council, while shouting

---

5. Brugioni, pp. 68–69.
6. See "An Interview with Richard Helms," at the CIA website https://www.cia.gov/library/center-for-the-study-of-intelligence/kent-csi/docs/v44i4a07p_0020.htm

"We will bury you!" Neither John Kennedy nor Richard Nixon ignored it; in fact, they actively competed for the strongest position against the young revolutionary Fidel Castro. As noted earlier, Kennedy even took advantage of Nixon's need to be circumspect regarding his own knowledge of a pending attack against the island in an obscure location named the Bay of Pigs.

Another of the CIA's more questionable projects involved the use of Mafia figures against Castro; during 1960, before the presidential election came into full swing, the CIA—acting at the behest of Vice President Nixon (as proxy for President Eisenhower)—recruited ex-FBI agent Robert Maheu, who would later become a top aide to the reclusive billionaire Howard Hughes in Las Vegas, to ask Johnny Rosselli and Sam Giancana for help in murdering Castro. Although the Mafia did not manage to successfully kill Castro with the poison pills they were given by the Agency to accomplish this, that proved to be only the start of an association between the nation's leading intelligence agency and an underworld organization that the head of the Federal Bureau of Investigation claimed did not even exist.[7] Richard Helms would later say that collaborating with the Mafia was "one of the greatest regrets of my life. It was a mistake, a case of poor judgment."[8] He also admitted the CIA's failure "to inform the Warren Commission about the agency's anti-Castro machinations. 'If I had to do it over again, I would've backed up a truck, taken all the documents down, and shoved them onto the Warren Commission's desk.'"[9]

Cuba: America's Playground Becomes America's Nemesis

Until December 1959, the island of Cuba had been considered a playground for wealthy Americans, where gambling and prostitution were legal, the weather was always warm, and the finest rum and cigars in the world were plentiful and cheap. This was a convenient arrangement for the Mafia because it was safely outside the reach of American law enforcement; they had invested millions in building casinos, nightclubs, and brothels that would also keep their fortunes away from the IRS. Of course, to do so, they had paid off the Batista regime under the table, though only for a fraction of the amount of U.S. taxes they would have otherwise had to pay. American corporations owned most of the mining industry as well as the utilities and other businesses that kept the Cuban economy alive.

7. Ibid.
8. Russell, p. 459.
9. Ibid.

Several months before the presidential campaign heated up and Fidel Castro's real agenda became known, he had been welcomed to Washington and applauded by many for his overthrow of the evil dictator Batista. Castro even double-talked his way around a question asked of him by Nixon, on what he thought of the difference between dictatorships and democracy; Castro's curious response was, "Dictatorships are a shameful blot on America, and democracy is more than just a word."[10] During 1960, his revolution against Batista's tyranny morphed into a new form of totalitarianism, becoming merely another socialist dictatorship. In the process, he expropriated hundreds of American-owned facilities, nationalized all industries, did away with the free press, and shut down the bordellos and gambling casinos. The total number of people he tortured or murdered on the way to creating his workers' paradise will never be known, but hundreds of suspected Batista-era agents, policemen, and soldiers were put on public trial for war crimes; most of those convicted were executed by firing squad, and the rest received long prison sentences.

According to Henry Hurt, in *Reasonable Doubt*, a sea change was occurring in the attitudes of Cubans toward the revolution:

> By the end of Castro's first year, the honeymoon with the United States was long over. There was a general sense of horror at Castro's mass executions of former officials, and there were early signs that the new premier had no genuine interest in developing a good relationship with the United States. By the summer of 1960 Castro had seized more than $700 million in U.S. property and was openly dealing with the Soviets. During this metamorphosis, thousands of Cubans, increasingly disenchanted with Castro, were fleeing in waves to the United States. By the end of 1960, 100,000 Cuban refugees were in the United States. They continued to pour in at the rate of 1,700 each week. Finally, on January 3, 1961—just two years after Castro came to power—the United States formally broke diplomatic relations with Cuba. That was the sorry state of affairs between the two countries when, less than three weeks later, John F. Kennedy was sworn in as president.[11]

The Cuban exiles began forming their own coalitions to plan their recapture of Cuba; however, there was no single strong leader until a powerful coalition of several groups was formed for them by the CIA. "It was this coalition,

---

10. Morley, *Our Man in Mexico*, p. 101.
11. Hurt, pp. 324–325 (ref. House Select Committee Report, pp. 148; X HSCA, pp. 6–8; interview with Dominguez, 1984; Phillips, *The Night Watch*, p. 63; Schlesinger, *A Thousand Days*, pp. 204–205, 207; *Public Papers of the Presidents*, 1963, p. 876; Murphy, "Cuba," *The New York Times*, January 4, 1961.

eventually known as the Cuban Revolutionary Council (CRC) that was to coordinate with the CIA the fateful Bay of Pigs invasion."[12]

The Disaster at the Bay of Pigs

Kennedy's narrow victory over Nixon took many of the top officials of the CIA and Pentagon by surprise, but the planning for the secret Cuban invasion proceeded with Kennedy's acquiescence. In short, the plan was to train Cuban exiles, who were recruited and armed by the CIA with aircraft and ships disguised to hide their U.S. ownership. The original beach at which the CIA-trained Cuban brigade would land was known as Zapata; it had an airstrip that was suitable for B-26 bombing operations against Castro's military. Kennedy instructed the CIA to make certain changes in the plan, including moving the beachhead farther west on the island, to the Bahia de Cochinos (Bay of Pigs), which was more lightly populated. There was a reason fewer people lived there, which paralleled the reason why it was uniquely unsuited for such an invasion: The bay featured many dangerous underwater reefs, then unnavigable swamps; the narrow shore was shadowed by a looming mountain range that impeded a quick invasion.

The model used by the CIA was the 1954 Operation Success in Guatemala, which the CIA considered aptly named despite the fact that it had led to a civil war that lasted decades and ended up costing over two hundred thousand lives. The scale would need to be much larger and adapted to the fact that the original version was designed for use in Central America and that Cuba was surrounded by water. The same men who had executed the original plan were named to the new one, which was given the aggressive moniker Operation Zapata after the name of the beach originally planned for the invasion. After its abject failure, the operation would become ignominiously known as the Bay of Pigs fiasco.[13] Some of these same swashbucklers would reemerge over the next few years, as a result of other misadventures, in such places as Miami, New Orleans, Mexico City, and Dallas, Texas: E. Howard Hunt and David Atlee Phillips were two;[14] Bill Harvey and David Morales were others.

Exactly three months after Kennedy took office, on April 17, 1961, the CIA's invasion of Cuba was executed. It was an unmitigated disaster. Getting word of the impending invasion, Castro's army routed the fifteen hundred Cuban exiles that landed at the Bay of Pigs. On the eve of the invasion, JFK

12. Ibid., p. 325.
13. Morley, *Our Man in Mexico*, p. 102.
14. Ibid., pp. 103–106.

cancelled a scheduled second air strike intended to destroy the Cuban air force. The first bombing, carried out two days earlier by eight unmarked WWII B-26s gifted to the Cuban Expeditionary Force, failed after JFK had reduced the number of bombers by half. Kennedy thought a second attempt would more likely implicate the United States, which he had warned the CIA from the beginning would not be done. His cancellation of that mission inevitably led to the disaster when the landing party proceeded into the ambush that awaited them. The plan for the invaders to establish a beachhead and announce the creation of a counterrevolutionary government that would appeal for assistance from the United States and the Organization of American States, while Castro was simultaneously being terminated, came to a halt.[15]

The CIA had begun plotting the assassination of Castro in August 1960, headed by Richard M. Bissell Jr. Moreover, Allen Dulles had gone to see President Eisenhower as early as March 1960 seeking approval to develop a plan to overthrow Castro. The original idea for using Mafia figures to assist the CIA in this plan originated as early as 1960 as well, in a proposal code-named JMARC. Dulles and Bissell briefed president-elect Kennedy on the pending invasion in November 1960; according to Bissell, Kennedy was generally passive, but expressed surprise at the scale of the operation. In March 1961 Kennedy asked the Joint Chiefs of Staff to vet the JMARC project, but they were not given details of the plot to kill Castro. The JCS analyzed the project and reported that if the invaders were given four days of air cover and sufficient support by the people of Trinidad, Cuba, where the invasion was originally designed to occur, and if the invaders were able to join with the guerrillas in the Escambray Mountains, the potential for success was 30 percent. The JCS could not recommend that Kennedy go along with the JMARC project. At a meeting on March 11, 1961, Kennedy rejected Bissell's proposed scheme and told him to revise it to be "less spectacular" and move the landing site away from the town of Trinidad. Kennedy had evidently misunderstood the projections of the report from the JCS, but it is not clear whether the miscommunication was the fault of the information transmitters or of the recipient.[16]

As Allen W. Dulles would later remark, "We felt that when the chips were down, when the crisis arose in reality, any action required for success would be authorized rather than permit the enterprise to fail." In other words, he acknowledged that the new plan was seriously flawed and unlikely to be successful. But the question of whether it would be a complete disaster hung on his belief that Kennedy would order a full-scale invasion when he realized

---

15. Ibid., pp. 108–110.
16. Ibid.

that failure was imminent; Bissell essentially set a trap for Kennedy to force U.S. intervention; however, his quarry refused to take the bait. Bissell met on April 10 with Robert F. Kennedy, telling him that the new plan had a two out of three chance of success. Kennedy agreed to the latest scheme and pressured others to do so as well. On April 14, John Kennedy asked Bissell how many aircraft would be involved; he replied sixteen. Kennedy told him to use only eight. Bissell knew that this would further jeopardize the invasion, yet he accepted the downsizing based on the assumption that Kennedy would later change his mind "when the chips were down."[17]

After the invasion of Cuba commenced, at the United Nations, Cuban foreign minister Raul Roa denounced "this act of imperialistic piracy of the United States." Adlai Stevenson angrily protested this charge and categorically denied U.S. involvement. When he learned that his categorical denial of Roa's charge—and his claim that the attack was the work of Cuban defectors—was a lie, he became incensed at not being briefed earlier on the situation. Author Victor Lasky wrote that Stevenson demanded of Kennedy that there be no more air strikes; it was this gaffe with his own U.N. representative that led to his decision to cancel the second air strike.[18] The consensus of many authors is that the cancellation of the second air strike was due to Stevenson's intimidation of Kennedy from taking measures to ensure the exiles and their CIA-trained leaders could overthrow the Castro regime and restore their country to them. To save face for Adlai Stevenson, Kennedy reneged on a key part of the invasion plan he had previously approved. The man who would lose the most, however, was CIA Deputy Director General Charles Cabell. He had arrived at the Air Operations Center just as the cleanup air strike was about to be launched and decided to routinely alert the White House; to his surprise and chagrin, clearance for the operation was denied. He repeated his request three more times, all of which were denied.[19]

As the above events played out, later that evening Kennedy was caught up in his first big White House reception—a traditional white-tie affair for members of Congress, cabinet members, and their wives. The president and Mrs. Kennedy made their entrance down the grand stairway to the four sets of ruffles and flourishes, followed by "Hail to the Chief," played by the U. S. Marine Corps Band; then, as they mingled with the twelve hundred guests, the band struck up *Mr. Wonderful*, and Jack and Jackie whirled around the East Room, smiling graciously at the applauding guests. One of the old-time servants said it was the most elaborate buffet he had seen in forty years of

---

17. Ibid.
18. Lasky, *JFK—The Man . . .*, pp. 520–521.
19. Ibid.

service. During the course of the dinner, the president was informed that Richard Bissell wished to see him immediately; calls went out to others not already there, including Dean Rusk, General Lemnitzer, and Admiral Arleigh Burke, chief of naval operations. As soon as the guests were whisked out the front door, an intense meeting began in the cabinet room, which lasted into the early-morning hours; Bissell presented the account of a military and intelligence operation already overtaken by disaster. He made a strong case to the president to permit the use of U.S. air power to save the otherwise-doomed invaders. Admiral Burke concurred, but Dean Rusk—not the most innovative thinker there—vigorously dissented, referring to the president's earlier pledge against direct intervention. By the end of the meeting, nothing had changed; Kennedy declined to authorize any further air strikes in the face of certain defeat and loss of the fifteen hundred invaders then under attack.[20]

In a last-ditch effort to persuade the president to reconsider his orders, General Cabell drove to Secretary of State Rusk's hotel, where he again expressed his fears. Despite the hour, 4:00 a.m. of the second day of fighting, Rusk called the president once more, but still the answer was no. Kennedy would never concede that withholding the air strike had caused the failure of the invasion, though the military had pleaded with him, using that very argument. It is easy to see, from different prisms, how Bissell and Cabell could blame Kennedy for the failed mission because he did not act as they assumed he would, yet understand how JFK instinctively knew that he had been sabotaged into not only authorizing the project but being outmaneuvered in its execution. The infuriated president promised to splinter the CIA into a thousand pieces directly in the aftermath of the Bay of Pigs disaster.[21]

Despite the uniformly negative reaction to the Bay of Pigs failure, Kennedy's popularity remained positive; in fact, his Gallup poll approval rating soared to 83 percent as the country rallied to his side.* While JFK publicly took responsibility for the failure of the Bay of Pigs operation, he privately blamed the CIA and the military brass for the debacle and subsequently withdrew any remaining confidence he had given to many of the decision makers who he felt had misled him.[22]

The CIA men, of course, portrayed the debacle quite differently. In their view, JFK had interfered with the operation both in its planning stage

---

* This phenomenon was doubtlessly noted by Lyndon Johnson, as he planned his own eventual presidency: Becoming a "wartime president" was a sure way to establish a legacy as one of the greatest presidents.

20. Lasky, *JFK—The Man . . .*, pp. 522–523.
21. Ibid.
22. Douglass, pp. 14–15.

and again in the middle of its execution. They felt that his changes—to the location of the invasion, the cuts in the number of exiles deployed, and the 50 percent reduction in the number of aircraft authorized for the first bombing raid—and the commitments he broke, including his failure to authorize the second wave of air strikes, were the reasons that the operation failed. This reaction resonated loudly throughout the higher reaches of the military and intelligence communities and beyond, through all tiers of officers and many enlisted men as well. The recriminations echoed through the exile communities in Miami and New Orleans, sharply hostile in a demographic which had previously been favorable to Kennedy's public statements. Now he denied that the United States was involved; this provoked insurrection by the exiles and their counterparts in Cuba and discouraged resistance to Castro. There were many other people who were upset that the invasion failed to remove Castro; chief among them were Mafia heads such as Santos Trafficante and Carlos Marcello, who had invested so much in the casinos and nightclubs, followed by the owners of other businesses large and small that Castro had expropriated. In the months following the Bay of Pigs, JFK attempted to reassert control over his military and intelligence apparatus; he appointed Robert Kennedy to the Special Operations Group (RFK became the "augmented" part of the "SOG augmented") to conduct a critical inquiry of the experience, and by November he would fire the primary original architects: Allen Dulles, Richard Bissell, and General Charles Cabell (who was, coincidentally, the brother of the mayor of Dallas, Texas, Earl Cabell).[23]

Despite the stupendous failure at the Bay of Pigs, the Cuban Revolutionary Council remained a unifying force for the exile community until the Cuban Missile Crisis. Kennedy's concession with the Soviets to drop the idea of invading Cuba caused a reversal in the administration's official policy toward the Cuban exiles, even though there remained, under Bobby Kennedy's direction, renewed efforts to dispatch Castro by one means or another. During 1963, an intense bitterness developed within the community of anti-Castro Cuban exiles toward the man they believed betrayed them, John F. Kennedy; it was a hatred at least as intense as their hatred of Fidel Castro.[24] The CRC, being a creature founded and supported by the CIA, was a conduit for many officials to nourish the hate and give it a firm foundation. Years later, the House Select Committee on Assassinations (HSCA) found that the exiles might have been involved in the assassination, since they "had the motive, based on what they considered President Kennedy's betrayal of their cause,

23. Douglass, p. 116.
24. Hurt, p. 325.

the liberation of Cuba from the Castro regime; the means, since they were trained and practiced in violent acts . . .; and the opportunity, whenever the President . . . appeared at public gatherings, as in Dallas on November 22, 1963."[25] The biggest impact of the failure at the Bay of Pigs was the untenable position it left the Kennedy administration in with its own military and intelligence organizations: They became increasingly isolated from the Joint Chiefs of Staff and the senior CIA officers. The incident occurred so early in their term that the "honeymoon" was over almost before it started, resulting in a breakdown that quickly became a significant impediment in effectively dealing with the smoldering relationships between America and many of its adversaries, especially with the Soviet Union, Cuba, and Vietnam; neither the president nor the "assistant president" (RFK) were widely respected at the Pentagon or in Langley.

That vacuum was filled, somewhat, by the vice president, someone who better "understood" the military mentality not through his own expertise so much as his deference to theirs: He was easier to deal with because of his inclination to let them establish policy, not lead them to a point at odds with their conventional positions. This allegiance to the vice president by the military and intelligence leadership of the country came at the expense of their relationship to the president. Over the course of the next two years, those relationships would continue growing even farther apart and become so well established that it could be argued that in the larger scheme, Lyndon B. Johnson had assumed the mantle of commander in chief. This phenomenon was probably something that Johnson had carefully planned since accepting the vice presidential nomination. Consider that one of his favorite mantras throughout his lifetime was, "Power is where power goes."[26] Another one, even more troubling in retrospect, was, "Behind every success there is a crime."[27]

Operation Mongoose

Although inexperienced in foreign policy, the Kennedys began secretive back-channel communications directly with Soviet Premier Nikita Khrushchev and spent the next eighteen months negotiating foreign policy independently of the existing diplomatic apparatus. Having already been deceived by the CIA and manipulated by the Pentagon, the start of the "back channel"—which will be examined further in the pages ahead—marked the point at which

---

25. Ibid., p. 326 (ref. HSCR, p. 129).
26. Caro, Master . . . p. 1035.
27. Brown, p. 190.

they would find an alternative to the staid and feckless State Department. Bobby Kennedy, just thirty-five years old, within the first six months of JFK's presidency had become the president's legal adviser, political adviser, protector, best friend, and now his primary foreign affairs adviser. This was all on top of his familial responsibility to keep his brother out of personal trouble, which was proving to be a full-time job of itself.

John and Bobby Kennedy were devastated and humiliated by the failures of the Bay of Pigs misadventure and sought revenge on Castro. Four U.S. pilots based in Nicaragua were shot down by Castro's forces. Kennedy had denied any direct U.S. involvement and hoped the pilots were dead; he initially refused to pay their families the military pensions they were due because he was upset about their actions and feared the potential fallout if their involvement was revealed. The families eventually received the pensions after threatening to reveal the real story. But that was only one of a number of duplicitous acts and one of a series of contradictions the Kennedys were involved in during the administration of their government. The Cuba situation would not remain settled for long, either in the USA or in the USSR. Sometime in the fall of 1961,

- the Soviets realized they were failing in Berlin and began quietly pushing it onto the back burner, simultaneously moving Cuba to the front burner as they decided to begin planning the installation of nuclear weapons there;
- the Kennedy administration, with help from the CIA, created a new and aggressive program aimed at overthrowing the Cuban government.

The name Lyndon Johnson will now become, temporarily, more scarce in the narrative because he had been relegated to other noncritical duties to keep him out of town and out of Kennedy's hair. In the thirty-five months of his vice presidency, he visited an average of almost one country every month. Whenever he traveled, he had a constant alcohol buzz, taking dozens of cases of Cutty Sark with him.[28] Braced with whiskey and armored with the euphoric confidence of a manic at the height of his delusion, Johnson ran through the streets of far-off places such as Senegal, passing out souvenir pens and making speeches in English to people who never had the slightest idea of what he was babbling. It is difficult to apportion how much of his ecstatic elation was the result of his mania and how much was the result of his scotch whiskey. During his term as the vice president, he generally had very little to do with anything related to Cuba, though he sided with

---

28. Hershman, p. 117.

General LeMay and the Joint Chiefs regarding the need for an invasion to take out the missiles being installed by the Soviet Union. He had aggressively involved himself with military and intelligence officials regarding Vietnam, and he had made it known to them that he, *Lyndon Johnson*, fundamentally disagreed with Jack Kennedy on that issue, and in fact he agreed with all of the hawks in these organizations that, in order to save Western civilization from the peril of peasants fighting between themselves in a civil war on the other side of the world, the United States should join that war.

The review which follows of John and Robert Kennedy's handling of Cuba, and their efforts to displace Fidel Castro, is essential to the story for two reasons: (1) to understand the explosive relationship between the Kennedys and key military and intelligence officials, especially Bill Harvey; and (2) how their handling of the missile crisis rebounded back to them vis-à-vis the Cuban exiles as well as those same key military and intelligence officials.

After the Bay of Pigs disaster, in November 1961 the president had decided that he could not countenance the ineptitude that he felt was prevalent at the CIA. His solution was to appoint Bobby to another role unrelated to his AG responsibilities: the head of the Special Operations Group—Augmented, which was linked to the National Security Council."[29] The Special Group included, as chairman, Maxwell Taylor, national security adviser McGeorge Bundy, John McCone of the CIA, chairman of the Joint Chiefs Lyman Lemnitzer, Roswell Gilpatric from the Pentagon, and U. Alexis Johnson from the State Department.[30]

A new program, code-named Operation Mongoose, was assigned to counterinsurgency specialist Edward G. Lansdale, which was overseen by the Special Group—Augmented—"SGA." President Kennedy signed the authorization formally establishing Mongoose as a top secret operation on November 30, 1961, "to help Cuba overthrow the Communist regime." Lansdale was given the assignment of developing a program to spark a revolution within Cuba. Shortly afterward, William K. Harvey was put in charge of Task Force W, created by the CIA to execute Operation Mongoose. The task force operated directly under the authority of the SGA, but in many ways, as will be seen shortly, it operated almost autonomously under Harvey and his superiors at Langley, Richard Helms and James Jesus Angleton. It also grew into a very large entity, clearly expedited by the high priority assigned to it by the White House, including four hundred Americans at CIA headquarters and JM/WAVE, its Miami station, plus about two thousand

---

29. Waldron and Hartmann, p. 82.
30. Martin, p. 125.

Cubans and a fleet of speedboats. It also grew in other, more insidious ways as the plans being made to deal with Castro became a blueprint that could be cloned and applied to John F. Kennedy.

William King Harvey was a Hoosier (i.e., Indiana native) with a law degree and a Kentucky wife who liked to drink almost as much as her husband. He started his government career with the FBI, but a combination of his drinking and extramarital activities cost him that job when he stayed out one night and his wife called the bureau the next morning inquiring about his whereabouts, which reportedly did not sit well with J. Edgar Hoover. While his ties with the FBI—and Hoover—may have been erased on paper, others have suggested that they were as strong as ever, that Harvey continued, covertly, reporting to Hoover as his mole within the CIA.[31]

John Kennedy, as many people know, was a fan of Ian Fleming's novels about the superagent 007, the legendary James Bond. Once in a lighthearted comment, JFK referred to Edward Lansdale as America's answer to Bond; Lansdale demurred, saying that would probably be Bill Harvey, whom he would shortly bring to the Oval Office so they could meet. Later, when Lansdale brought Harvey with him to meet the president and his brother, Bobby, in the Oval Office, he turned to him as they were entering the White House and said, "You're not carrying your gun, are you?" His answer was, "Yes, of course." After Lansdale explained to the Secret Service agent that his friend would like to check his firearm, Harvey pulled a revolver from his pants pocket, then, as an afterthought, reached behind his back and pulled out a .38-caliber Detective Special from a holster. In greeting him, Kennedy said, "So you're our James Bond,"[32] but when Harvey conceded that he was really not quite in that league, at least regarding Bond's sexual escapades, he probably did not realize that JFK's own prowess in that area could not be equaled even by the fictional superspy. Bill Harvey was the embodiment of a lot of things, but a "James Bond" would not be the first figure most people would think of, even with his long and storied career in covert operations. His appearance was striking because of his bulging eyes, a result of a thyroid condition he had since birth. He was a huge, obese man with a big round head, a permanently angry-looking facial expression, and a shock of hair surrounding an otherwise bald head. He wheezed and grunted as he talked, and his voice was sometimes compared to the sound of a frog; his belches and other bodily sounds punctuated his utterances but otherwise did not affect his verbal aptitude. Despite his hard-drinking ways, he reveled in the

---

31. Twyman, pp. 459, 624, 668, 734, 769.
32. Martin, pp. 128–129.

world of covert operations, especially those requiring large-scale planning and audacious execution.[33]

JFK's point, of course, referred only to his reputation in the intelligence community, and in that context, it made a little more sense. As noted by Dino A. Brugioni, "It was Harvey, not James Angleton, who fingered Guy Burgess and Donald Maclean as British agents in Washington working for the Soviet Union. He also pointed to Kim Philby as 'the third man' when Burgess and Maclean defected to the Soviet Union."[34] Harvey had a swaggering flamboyance and brashness, but possessed an agile mind with a photographic memory for things he had been involved in; his briefings would last for hours, recited extemporaneously from memory recall.[35] According to Noel Twyman, *"His capacity for planning and carrying out intricate master schemes of a covert, illegal nature was legendary. He knew every detail of his projects"*[36] (emphasis added). Those skills were exactly what Lyndon Johnson would value, as they were similar to his own. There are reasons, as we will see, that Johnson (and/or Hoover or Angleton) would have tapped Harvey at the operational level of his own plan. The communication linkage, of course, connected Harvey to the higher levels through his own direct, daily ties to Angleton. Angleton, in turn, was directly tied to J. Edgar Hoover: A high-level CIA officer (code-named John Scelso) said that "Angleton had 'enormously influential contacts with J. Edgar Hoover,' that he had his own direct line" to Hoover's office[37] (which was doubtlessly put to considerably more use than Hoover's other direct line to Bobby Kennedy).

Moving on to the CIA, Harvey must have seemed to some like an oversized round peg being made to fit into a small square hole. Most of his colleagues in the higher echelons of the CIA, having come from the Ivy League colleges and/or earlier experience in the OSS, were of a decidedly different culture, in terms of physical appearance, mannerisms, and educational background. Dino Brugioni's first impression* of Harvey was illuminating: "In addition to the ubiquitous pistols, he had in his hand a foot-long stiletto. He cleaned his nails and then hurled the stiletto at a target hung on the wall of his office."[38] Not exactly the image one conjures up as being like the dashing ladies' man, "Bond . . . James Bond."

---

* Evidently, this was offered as more evidence of his Indiana upbringing as contrasted with that of many of his Ivy League colleagues, many of whom were born and raised in expensive boarding schools of New York and Connecticut.

33. Brugioni, pp. 66–67; Twyman, p. 430.
34. Ibid.
35. Twyman, p. 430.
36. Ibid.
37. Twyman, p. 385.
38. Brugioni, p. 68.

Harvey earned his reputation as a covert operator in Berlin, 1960–1962, successfully tapping into the main Moscow-Berlin underground communication lines. Using a radar station as a cover, he masterminded the digging of an eighteen-hundred-foot tunnel, twenty-five feet underground from West Berlin to East Berlin.[39] The tunnel was very elaborate, designed to be properly ventilated to avoid overheating the electronic equipment needed to tap the East German telecommunications line. A huge warehouse was built along the border with a basement having a twelve-foot ceiling to accommodate the 3,100 tons of dirt removed from the tunnel. The entire project took eighteen months to complete under the noses of the Vopos, the East German border guards, and produced reams of solid intelligence. The wiretaps worked for almost one year before they were discovered, but the volumes of information they produced took over two more years to process.[40] As David C. Martin noted, "The Russian Army could not have made a military move anywhere in Europe without tipping its hand via the tunnel. When the CIA was set up in 1947, Secretary of State George Marshall was reported to have said, 'I don't care what the CIA does. All I want from them is twenty-four hours' notice of a Soviet attack.' 'Harvey's Hole,' as the tunnel became known, had put the CIA in a position to do just that, and had done it at a time when the Agency had virtually no other assets behind the Iron Curtain."[41]

As good as his career had been, Bill Harvey was not adept at maintaining cordial relations with everyone with whom he worked. This proved to be his undoing when he went to work with Robert F. Kennedy as the head of Task Force W. From their first meeting, a hateful relationship formed that would continue until well after Harvey was fired in January 1963. Harvey questioned Bobby's judgment and considered him to be an amateur. When the author and longtime senior intelligence official Dino Brugioni visited him in his office during the Cuban Missile Crisis to review the results of one operation, he was greeted by a less-than-warm greeting: "What in the hell does a bunch of quacks know about covert operations?"[42]

The Special Group concentrated on covert operations, but there were two other groups related to Cuba that liaised together: One was called the Interdepartmental Committee on Cuba and the other was the Standing Group, which was responsible for longer-range policy objectives. All of these groups reported to Bobby Kennedy. The idea behind these divisions was to

39. Ibid., p. 67.
40. Martin, David C., pp. 76–88.
41. Martin, David C., p. 88.
42. Brugioni, p. 68.

keep each one small enough to be more effective and to minimize the scope of overall knowledge of the participants, except for Bobby, who would be the only one understanding the big picture. Bobby's senior staff included Cyrus Vance, Joseph Califano, and Alexander Haig; his special envoy with the anti-Castro Cubans was Harry [Enrique Ruiz] Williams.[43] Bobby took care to keep his own name out of most of the documents created, but his position as the creator of the Cuban Coordinating Committee (CCC) had left enough evidence to allow his presence to be traced. According to General Al Haig, who was a CCC staffer, "'Bobby Kennedy was running it—hour by hour . . . We were conducting two raids a week at the height of that program against mainland Cuba. People were being killed, sugar mills were being blown up, bridges were demolished. We were using fast boats and mother ships and the United States Army was supporting and training these forces. Cy Vance, the Secretary of the Army, was [presiding] over the State Department, the CIA, and the National Security Council. I was intimately involved. It was wrong-headed, I'm sorry to say. Weekly reports were rendered to Bobby Kennedy—he had a very tight hand on the operation.'"[44] In 1998, General Haig was shown an organizational chart of the numerous Cuban committees at various government agencies. At the top was the president; nowhere on it did the attorney general, Robert Kennedy, appear. "Viewing the chart, Haig chuckled and exclaimed, 'Bobby *was* the President!' as far as Cuban operations were concerned. For emphasis, Haig repeated to the interviewer, 'He *was* the President. Let me repeat, as a reasonably close observer, *he was the president*!' [emphasis in original] Haig said his time on one of those Cuba committees involved the 'impatient prodding of Robert Kennedy and the frequent invocation of the President's name.'"[45]

At the same time that Bobby Kennedy was guiding the CIA—through his new group, the CCC, to conduct clandestine activities, including economic sabotage, raids, the destruction of key electric plants, sugar mills, and oil refineries—he was also forming allies among the Cuban exiles, often bringing them to his Hickory Hill home in Virginia, the Kennedy villa in Palm Beach, or even taking some of them on a ski trip to New Hampshire. The three closest to him were Enrique "Harry" Ruiz-Williams, Manuel Artime, and Rolando Cubela. It was Harry Williams, a former friend of Fidel Castro and Che Guevara, who would be used to recruit Cuban exiles for training, most of which was done either in the Florida Keys, at the CIA's Miami station, or outside of New Orleans, Louisiana, near Lake Pontchartrain—the same

43. Waldron and Hartman, pp. 79–82.
44. Russo, p. 163 (Ref. Al Haig, interview on ABC's *Nightline*, 29 December, 1997).
45. Waldron and Hartman, p. 82.

camp that Lee Harvey Oswald attempted to infiltrate.[46] Bill Harvey had made many of the same contacts during the period he was running his Cuban task force; in fact many of his contacts still hated both Kennedys so much that they would have never cooperated with Bobby in this way. Harvey's attitude regarding Bobby's competence in this field did not change; in fact, he complained to his superiors about Bobby trying to conduct covert operations with little knowledge or experience, while Bobby complained to JFK that not enough covert action was being taken to unseat Castro. Bobby insisted on micromanaging the operations to the extent that he talked directly to the Cuban exile leaders and often met and socialized with a number of them. Harvey violently disagreed with RFK's actions, telling him that someone of his position should not even be known to the covert operatives, much less talk to them and, worse, be seen with them.[47]

By January 1962, Task Force W was already engaged in a wide range of projects, mostly against Cuban ships and aircraft outside Cuba and non-Cuban ships engaged in Cuban trade. Small-time operations came first, things like contaminating shipments of sugar from Cuba and tampering with industrial products imported into the country. The intention was to develop a "strongly motivated political action movement" within Cuba, creating conditions to spark a revolt which would eventually cause the downfall of Castro and his government. Robert Kennedy stated early on that "'no time, money, effort—or manpower . . . be spared.' Mongoose was 'top priority.'"[48] Lansdale quickly developed a plan to incite open revolt among the masses leading to the overthrow of the Communist regime. In late February 1962, Edward Lansdale presented a six-phase plan for effecting political and psychological sabotage through military and intelligence operations, in addition to proposing "attacks on the cadre of the regime, including key leaders." Lansdale noted that a "vital decision" had not yet been made regarding possible U.S. military actions in support of plans to overthrow Fidel Castro. The Lansdale plan included many ideas that appeared to be the result of a "brainstorming session," which were not uncommon in the business field at the time; apparently, the technique was used in the intelligence community as well, given that many of the ideas were clearly "off the wall." The plan called for "nonlethal chemicals to incapacitate sugar workers; 'gangster elements' to attack police officials; defections 'from the top echelon of the Communist gang'; even spearing [*sic*, 'spreading'] word that Castro was the Antichrist and that the Second Coming was imminent—an event to be verified by star

---

46. Russo. pp. 164–167.
47. Brugioni, p. 69.
48. Schlesinger, *Robert Kennedy*, p. 513.

shells sent up from an American submarine off the Cuban coast ('elimination by illumination,' a waspish critic called it)."[49]

At a meeting of the SGA, the scale of Lansdale's Cuba Project was sharply reduced, and Lansdale was directed to develop a detailed plan for an intelligence-gathering program only. On March 1, the SGA confirmed that the immediate objective of the program would be intelligence collection and that all other actions would be inconspicuous and consistent with the United States' overt policy of isolating Castro and neutralizing Cuban influence in the hemisphere. The guidelines were approved by the SGA in mid-March; they specifically noted that "the United States would attempt to 'make maximum use of indigenous resources' in trying to overthrow Fidel Castro but recognize that 'final success will require decisive U.S. military intervention.'" In mid-June 1962, U.S. intelligence received reports of a pending revolt by Cubans against the Castro government, even without sponsorship by the United States. The SGA, upon learning of the reports, requested studies be undertaken to prepare for such a contingency. Lansdale subsequently ordered General Benjamin Harris to develop a contingency action plan designed for that scenario; this contingency plan, disseminated in July, outlined a program for the United States to "support and sustain the rebellion in Cuba through all its resources, including the use of U.S. military force."[50] In July, Edward Lansdale wrote an evaluation of phase 1 of Operation Mongoose, noting some successes, including the infiltration of eleven CIA guerrilla teams into Cuba, one team of which had grown to as many as 250 men. Lansdale warned that "time is running out for the U.S. to make a free choice on Cuba" and outlined four different ways in which the United States could proceed:

a. Cancel operational plans; treat Cuba as a bloc nation; or
b. Exert all possible diplomatic, economic, psychological, and all other pressures except the overt use of military forces;
c. Commit the United States to fully support Cubans to overthrow the Castro regime, including the use of U.S. military force, if the situation required it at the end; or
d. Overthrow the Castro-Communist regime by U.S. military force.

At a meeting of the SGA on August 10, the discussion centered on a course of action for Operation Mongoose following the intelligence collection phase scheduled to conclude in August. The SGA initially chose a plan advanced by

---

49. Ibid.
50. Office of the Secretary of Defense, Memorandum for Special Group-Augmented, July 31, 1962).

John McCone that called for limited actions, including economic sabotage, to force a split between Fidel Castro and "old-line Communists." But President Kennedy rejected that and called for a more ambitious plan aimed expressly at overthrowing Castro. During the meeting, the possibility of assassinating Castro was raised. According to William Harvey, "The question of assassination, particularly of Fidel Castro, was brought up by Secretary McNamara. It was the obvious consensus at that meeting . . . that this is not a subject which has been made a matter of official record."[51]

Kennedy's instructions were formalized in National Security Action Memorandum (NSAM) 181, issued August 23, 1962, yet otherwise based on "option B."[52] Kennedy directed that several additional actions and studies be undertaken "in light of the evidence of new bloc activity in Cuba:" an examination of the pros and cons of a statement warning against the deployment of any nuclear weapons in Cuba; the psychological, political, and military effect of such a deployment; and the military options that might be exercised by the United States to eliminate such a threat. Regarding Operation Mongoose, Kennedy ordered that Plan B Plus, a program aimed at overthrowing Castro without overtly employing the U.S. military, be developed "with all possible speed."[53] A few days after NSAM 181 was signed, Fidel Castro angrily attacked gunboat raids on Cuba in a formal protest to the United Nations, saying that Cuba held the United States responsible for the raid. U.S. officials denied involvement, but the U.S. Coast Guard impounded the two speedboats used in the attack. Although the CIA's Task Force W was behind several harassing attacks, U.S. officials stated they did not sanction this raid; yet it is known that Bill Harvey was by then operating quite independently of Foggy Bottom (as the State Department building is referred to in Washington) and the Pentagon. The CIA also allowed the exile group DRE (Directorio Revolucionario Estudiantil) to base itself in Florida, and had previously trained the group in demolition techniques and donated the speedboats used in the attack.[54]

---

51. Memorandum for Deputy Director (Plans), August 14, 1962; (Alleged Assassination Plots Involving Foreign Leaders, November 20, 1975, p. 147; Document 12, National Security Action Memorandum 181, on Actions and Studies in Response to New Soviet Bloc Activity in Cuba, August 23, 1962; Schlesinger, p. 497).
52. National Security Action Memorandum 181, on Actions and Studies in Response to New Soviet Bloc Activity in Cuba, August 23, 1962; Office of the Secretary of Defense, Memorandum for Special Group-Augmented, July 25, 1962.
53. National Security Action Memorandum 181, on Actions and Studies in Response to New Soviet Bloc Activity in Cuba, August 23, 1962; Recollection of Intelligence Prior to the Discovery of Soviet Missiles and of Penkovsky Affair, n.d.; Chronology of John McCone's Suspicions on the Military Buildup in Cuba Prior to Kennedy's October 22 Speech, November 30, 1962).
54. Memorandum to Robert McCloskey, August 25, 1962; Memorandum from Permanent Mission of Cuba to United Nations, New York, August 25, 1962.

By the summer of 1962, Bill Harvey had grown increasingly angry at Bobby Kennedy's continuing interference in his efforts to build a resistance movement inside Cuba. Bobby couldn't understand why it took so long to get this task done, which Harvey felt was just one of the problems caused by Bobby's inexperience with respect to covert operations. Harvey regarded Bobby's naïveté as a reckless disregard for all of the fundamental precepts of covert operations work. That was bad enough, as it presented a great personal risk to himself on multiple levels; but he sensed that it was the presence of Harry Williams and other exile leaders, anxious to retake control of their homeland, that was the real cause of Bobby's unrelenting pressure to attain results.[55] More than one person in the intelligence division of the CIA was convinced that Bobby had actually been put in charge of Cuban operations for the purpose of dismantling that part of the agency. JFK's famous statement to Mike Mansfield after the Bay of Pigs that "I will tear the CIA into a thousand pieces and scatter it to the wind" had not been forgotten by those who heard it. According to Ray Cline, the deputy director for intelligence, "Both of the Kennedy brothers, and particularly Bobby, felt they had been booby-trapped at the Bay of Pigs, and it became a constant preoccupation, almost an obsession, to right the record somehow."[56]

Harvey had organized three types of operations against Cuba: (1) infiltration of agents, (2) the logistical operations of delivering supplies, and (3) sabotage operations. The last of these was dependent upon the first two, and they required the most lead time to complete. Bobby was only interested in the last one, however, and because he measured success based only on it, he was constantly frustrated. Harvey, for his part, was not happy with this or any other facet of the Kennedy administration's foreign policy; he referred to Bobby as a "fag" and complained that Bobby "was carving a path in the operations so wide that a Mack truck could drive through."[57] Bobby felt that the key to unseating Castro was through the destruction of key industries, through sabotage operations. Harvey had promised the Special Operations Group that this would be done, including some formerly U.S.-owned operations such as the Esso oil refinery in Havana and another at Santiago de Cuba, a nickel-mining operation at Moa Bay, a number of large railroad bridges, and oil and gas storage facilities. His failures at these sabotage attempts soon showed up on the aerial photographs being taken shortly after the operations, infuriating Kennedy. Many times, secondary targets were hit instead of the primary ones; others were missed completely. Harvey became embittered and defensive and often denied the obvious

55. Ibid.
56. Ibid.
57. Ibid., pp. 69–70.

failures. As Dino Brugioni observed firsthand, "Once, while showing him that there was no visible damage to a building that was supposedly bombed, he remarked the damage was all inside."[58] Harvey did not think Kennedy appreciated the great obstacles that had to be overcome; Kennedy did not think Harvey or his operatives were competent to accomplish the objectives. Others who attended meetings between them would report that "there was a chill between Kennedy and Harvey—that Kennedy avoided speaking to Harvey directly and that Harvey avoided eye contact with Kennedy."[59]

The Cuban Missile Crisis

By August 22, 1962, the CIA concluded that photographic images from U-2 overflights showed that SA-2 surface-to-air missile sites were being installed in Cuba. For several weeks after Kennedy was briefed, the military and intelligence agencies watched carefully as more ships arrived in Cuba from the Soviet Union carrying Russian "technicians" and equipment. By mid-September, eight to nine thousand Soviet troops had been delivered to Cuba and hundreds of troops dressed in fatigues were seen in Havana and in convoys along the main highways.[60] Throughout September more U-2 flights were approved to precisely identify the troop movements and site-preparation activities. The Soviets maintained that the arms and military equipment were strictly for Cuba's defensive purposes. In one of their more brazen untruths, a press release stated, "The explosive power of our nuclear weapons is so great and the Soviet Union has such powerful missiles for delivering these nuclear warheads that there is no need to seek sites for them somewhere beyond the borders of the Soviet Union." The Cuban press quickly claimed that Cuba had every reason to ensure its security through help from its friends.[61]

A flurry of political confrontations erupted during early September 1962. A running battle with Republican Senator Homer Capehart of Indiana had started at the end of August when he pressed Kennedy to do something about the Russians "pouring men and equipment into Cuba and the president was doing nothing about it. 'How long will the president examine the situation?'"[62] Kennedy was starting to get pressure from both ends of his own Democratic Party: From the left, Senator J. W. Fulbright had stated that if there were missile bases in Cuba, "I am not sure that our national existence

---

58. Ibid., p. 68, 70.
59. Ibid., p. 106.
60. Ibid., p. 108.
61. Ibid., p. 140.
62. Brugioni, p. 111.

would be substantially in greater danger than is the case today. Nor do I think that such bases would substantially alter the balance of power in the world today. What would substantially alter the balance of power in the world would be precipitate action by the United States resulting in the alienation of Latin America, Asia and Africa."[63] From the right, the well-respected Senator Kenneth Keating of New York pressed the same issues as the hated Senator Capehart had raised, enumerating the key issues that Kennedy had not addressed regarding the Soviet troops being deployed and why they were obviously not "technicians" as the administration had claimed.[64] Although Keating would not reveal the source of his information, it has since become established that it was U.S. Army Col. Philip J. Corso, and his source was a Pentagon Army Intelligence officer who had obtained U-2 photographs from someone at the CIA's National Photographic Interpretation Center (NPIC). Interestingly, Corso wrote about this episode in his 1997 book, *The Day after Roswell*, indicating that, since JFK was in Hyannis at the time, he considered taking the photos to Lyndon Johnson first, but then realized that the scuttlebutt around Washington was that Johnson was to be investigated for the Billie Sol Estes scandal, and his association with Bobby Baker, and that it was unlikely he would still be on the ticket by 1964. Clearly, Senator Keating—realizing that Johnson's career was in jeopardy already and that he could no longer be trusted with releasing this information, even if he would have normally jumped at the chance to sabotage Kennedy—could not go to Johnson, so it was decided to leak the information to a newspaper columnist, Paul Scott. Keating had considered it vital that the information not be kept secret so that the White House couldn't continue ignoring it while the Soviets kept installing missiles. It didn't take long for the news of the Soviet Union's massive installation of nuclear tipped missiles in Cuba to spread to both sides of Capitol Hill, and to both sides of the aisle. The first Democrat to break ranks with Kennedy over the issue was his longtime friend George Smathers of Florida, who backed an invasion of Cuba in conjunction with other countries in the Western Hemisphere. This infuriated the president, but by that time other senators were also calling for a stronger reaction.[65]

Khrushchev had expected to be able to have the missiles installed and the nuclear warheads ready to be deployed before any of it was discovered, presenting the United States with a *fait accompli*, and no realistic way to

---

63. Ibid., p. 72 (ref. Senator J.W. Fulbright, "Some Reflection upon Recent Events and Continuing Problems," Congressional Record, 87th Congress, First session, Senate, June 29, 1961, p. 11704).
64. Brugioni, p. 112.
65. Ibid., p. 113.

undo it. The Kennedy administration, he believed, would "swallow this bitter pill . . . I knew that the United States could knock out some of our installations, but not all of them. If a quarter or even a tenth of our missiles survived—even if only one or two big ones were left—we could still hit New York, and there wouldn't be much of New York left."[66] While Khrushchev felt that he could bluster and intimidate Kennedy into backing down from a confrontation, Ambassador Anatoly Dobrynin did not agree: "Had he asked the embassy beforehand, we could have predicted the violent American reaction to his adventure once it became known . . . Khrushchev wanted to spring a surprise on Washington; it was he who got the surprise in the end when his secret plan was uncovered."[67]

Despite all the braggadocio regarding their military capabilities, the Soviets did not have a viable intercontinental ballistic missile (ICBM), but they did have medium-range (MRBM) and intermediate-range (IRBM) missiles. Their political leaders decided that given the reality of their capabilities, the best place for these missiles would be ninety miles off the coast of the United States, rather than thousands of miles away, where they were then placed. The military leaders were concerned with the enormous logistical problem of maintaining a supply line adequate to make and keep them functional, especially during a confrontation with the United States.[68]

By August, this activity had convinced DCI John McCone that all the Soviet/Cuba activity meant one thing: "If I were Khrushchev, I would put MRBMs in Cuba and I would aim several at Washington and New York and then I would say, 'Mr. President, how would you like looking down the barrels of a shotgun for a while. Now, let's talk about Berlin. Later, we'll bargain about your overseas bases.'"[69] Khrushchev had decided in July that the SA-2 air-defense missiles should be deployed first, so they could shoot down U-2s and prevent detection of the next installations, for medium- and longer-range missiles. The SA-2 missiles were operational by the end of September.[70] Meanwhile, Khrushchev had Ambassador Dobrynin go to Robert Kennedy and attempt to stall him by deceit: He assured Kennedy that there would be no ground-to-ground missiles or any other offensive weapons based in Cuba and that the military buildup was not particularly significant. However, even as those assurances were being given, two ships carrying the first of the MRBMs were on their way to Cuba. Kennedy warned Dobrynin

66. May and Zelikow, p. 678 (ref. Khrushchev, *Khrushchev Remembers*, 1970, p. 494.
67. May and Zelikow, p. 678 (ref. Dobrynin, Anatoly, *In Confidence*, New York: Random House, 1995, pp. 79–80).
68. Brugioni, p. 82.
69. Ibid., p. 96.
70. May and Zelikow, p. 680.

that the United States would continue watching closely but that if offensive missiles were found, there would be grave consequences. Kennedy reported this conversation to the president and Secretaries Rusk and McNamara, but no word of it was referred on to the intelligence community.[71]

As the U-2 flights and other reconnaissance missions continued into October, the military and intelligence community leaders saw the Soviet move into Cuba as a major effort to reverse the balance of power between the superpowers and could not be condoned. On October 16, 1962, Kennedy was given irrefutable U-2 photographic evidence of a Soviet ballistic site in Cuba. On October 17, a total of six U-2 missions over Cuba would be flown, collecting a massive number of photographic images. The images were processed and expedited to Washington for analysis.

Two weeks before the November congressional elections, at 7:00 p.m. on October 22, 1962, the president addressed the nation by television from the Oval Office, saying that the United States now had "unmistakable evidence" that offensive missile sites were being prepared in Cuba, for both MRBMs and IRBMs. This represented, the president said, an explicit threat to the peace and security of the Americas and was directly in contrast to the repeated assurances by Soviet spokesmen that the buildup in Cuba was of a defensive nature. He attacked Foreign Minister Gromyko for misrepresenting their intentions and demanded that the Soviets withdraw or eliminate the missiles. He stated that a "strict quarantine" was being imposed on all offensive military equipment being shipped to Cuba and warned that further actions would be justified if these shipments continued.

The Joint Chiefs of Staff, especially General LeMay, advocated a preemptive air strike and an invasion of the island to destroy all missile installations. General Taylor and Dean Acheson, as a specially invited "old hand" of the newly created ExComm group maintained that U.S. prestige throughout Latin America would be undermined if the missiles were not removed; it was also contended that allowing the missiles would invite the Soviets to make similar moves elsewhere around the world, forcing the United States to have to make other multiple concessions if they let the missiles stand. Acheson went further, saying that the result would be damaging, "across the board—politically, morally, economically, and militarily."[72]

In direct contradiction of his previous consistent and repeated aggressive actions toward Cuba, Robert Kennedy disagreed with the recommendations of the ExComm group. Now, he took the position that a direct military action against Cuba would make the United States "damned in the eyes of

---

71. Ibid., p. 115.
72. Ibid., pp. 240–242.

the world forever." He compared such an action to Japan's attack on Pearl Harbor and argued forcefully against any such provocation, saying that "he did not want his brother to go down in history as the American Tojo."[73] Dean Acheson was appalled that the advice of the president's brother might carry the day; he felt that Bobby's simplistic thinking was akin to clichés and sophomoric analysis. Secretary Rusk, who had invited Acheson to the deliberations, sat quietly throughout them "like a constipated owl," afraid to confront either Kennedy or Acheson. The fear of the military and intelligence leaders regarding Kennedy's argument for acquiescence was that the Soviets would finally achieve a measure of parity and they would then demand additional large concessions in other parts of the world, probably starting with Berlin. Although the message to the president was delicately crafted, the conclusion was unmistakable: "It is generally agreed that the United States cannot tolerate the known presence of offensive nuclear weapons in a country 90 miles from our shore, if our courage and our commitments are ever to be believed by either allies or adversaries."[74]

The normal diplomatic channels had failed to respond effectively to the growing crisis and the president had begun thinking that they were actually impeding communication and negotiation. In fact, John and Bobby Kennedy had become disenchanted with Rusk and with the overall performance of the State Department, often referring to the bureaucratic maze there as "the fudge factory." To the people engaged in evaluating intelligence, it was "the home of 'the gray ladies'—elderly, well-read career women who were regarded as the mainstay of headquarters intelligence, and the 'Jewish lawyers'—scholarly experts in the fields of international law, politics, protocol, and languages, usually preoccupied attending international conferences or writing research papers."[75] To some, the problem seemed to be caused by an overgrown bureaucracy that had become increasingly disconnected from real world events; to others, it was more of a systemic problem related to a culture populated more by scholarly academics than the people with their boots on the ground.

Nikita Khrushchev had begun secret, back-channel direct communication with John Kennedy in September 1961; it had been used by both leaders for one year as a means to communicate directly, around the normal diplomatic channels, and would now play an important part in the settlement of the crisis. In those days, back channels appeared to be extensively used: Another that was operative at the time was JFK's link to Fidel Castro, via William Attwood

73. Ibid., p. 242.
74. Ibid.
75. Brugioni, p. 98.

and Carlos Lechuga at the UN. The ABC News reporter Lisa Howard—before she died of a drug overdose in a similar fashion as Marilyn Monroe and Dorothy Kilgallen—also participated as a direct link between Kennedy and Castro. As we will see, Lyndon Johnson had his own back channels, into both the military establishment and the intelligence community.

The Soviet back channel utilized a KGB agent, Georgi Bolshakov, whom Khrushchev trusted to keep secrets. Their correspondence started with a focus on the dilemma of Berlin, where the two leaders backed away from war but never reached a mutual understanding, much less formal agreement. But for several weeks during June and July of 1961, the situation in Berlin was just as dangerous as the Cuban Missile crisis the following year (even though it was downplayed for public consumption). After JFK met Khrushchev on June 4th in Vienna, where Khrushchev threatened to crush West Berlin, the situation deteriorated to the point that the hawks in JFK's administration—led by former Secretary of State Dean Acheson, the Joint Chiefs of Staff and his own vice president—were advocating the use of tactical nuclear bombs if necessary to "protect" West Berlin. Again, in a shocking act of disunity—only a few months into the beginning of their administration, just weeks after having first challenged the president on his handling of the Bay of Pigs operation in April and then attempting to manipulate the president into taking more aggressive actions in Vietnam in May—the vice president of the United States was actively opposing the president's policies and siding with the hawks who wanted to use the city of Berlin as the "line in the sand" to face down the Soviet Union. It was another hard lesson for John Kennedy as he tried to establish foreign policies which many in his own administration aggressively opposed. Fortunately, Kennedy's determined efforts to find a peaceful outcome to Khrushchev's antagonistic actions caused Berlin to become less and less of an issue, and finally disappear from the radar.[76] Khrushchev's first letter was twenty-six pages long and succeeded in establishing a direct communication link. Kennedy responded by telling Khrushchev, "Whatever our differences, our collaboration to keep the peace is as urgent—if not more urgent—than our collaboration to win the last war."[77] This personal communication between the two leaders would continue sporadically through 1962; paradoxically, it had not been invoked during the period in which Khrushchev was, simultaneously, planning the installation of the missiles in Cuba. Given the apparent duplicity in Khrushchev's use of the back channel, it appears that he was really attempting to deceive Kennedy into believing that the Soviet motives were pure.

---

76. Reeves, pp. 214–222, pp. 273–274.
77. Douglass, p. 25.

Then, in the middle of the crisis, when both leaders were under tremendous pressure by their respective military advisers to take aggressive actions, they would reconnect through their back channel after all of the conventional diplomatic channels had failed to produce a peaceful remedy. It proved to be the key tool that helped Kennedy and Khrushchev find a mutually acceptable solution to the crisis that avoided catastrophic results. On October 23, the Soviet defense minister, after meeting with Khrushchev, placed the Soviet armed forces on a war footing. At about the same time, Khrushchev wrote two letters to Kennedy and sent them through the back channel; the first was received by Kennedy on Friday evening, October 26, and the second the next morning. In the first one, Khrushchev offered to withdraw his missiles in exchange for a pledge from Kennedy to refrain from invading Cuba. The second added another caveat: a demand for a U.S. commitment to remove its missiles from Turkey. "Tit for Tat."[78] The second letter's demand was a much more difficult pill to swallow for Kennedy, since it affected an ally's defenses under a threat. That very morning, a Soviet surface-to-air missile (SAM) had shot down a U-2 reconnaissance plane over Cuba, killing the air force pilot, Major Rudolf Anderson Jr. The Joint Chiefs were pressing for an immediate retaliation to destroy the SAM launch sites. Kennedy held them back, even though he and his brother Robert felt "the noose was tightening on all of us, on Americans, on mankind and the bridges to escape were crumbling."[79]

It was at this point that John Kennedy dispatched Robert to meet secretly with Ambassador Dobrynin to personally convey the president's concerns. His message, according to Khrushchev, was that "the President is in a grave situation . . . and he does not know how to get out of it. We are under very severe stress. In fact we are under pressure from our military to use force against Cuba . . . We want to ask you, Mr. Dobrynin, to pass President Kennedy's message to Chairman Khrushchev through unofficial channels . . . Even though the President himself is very much against starting a war over Cuba, an irreversible chain of events could occur against his will . . . If the situation continues much longer, the President is not sure that the military will not overthrow him and seize power."[80] The back-channel diplomacy, which allowed Kennedy to negotiate directly with Khrushchev, ultimately worked because it allowed Kennedy to circumvent the very bureaucracy (the

---

78. Douglas, p. 26 (ref. State Department volume "Foreign Relations of the United States [FRUS], 1961–1963, Vol. VI: Kennedy–Khrushchev Exchanges," Washington: U.S. Govt. Printing Office, 1996).
79. Ibid. (ref. Robert Kennedy, *Thirteen Days*, p. 97).
80. Ibid., p. 27 (ref. Khrushchev, *Khrushchev Remembers*, pp. 497–498).

Pentagon, the CIA, and the State Department) that had thus far impeded any meaningful progress towards a peaceful resolution.

In a purely logical and theoretical—albeit cold-blooded—sense, LeMay and the Joint Chiefs might have been right in predicting that the Soviets would not have responded; fortunately, we will never know for sure. This game of nuclear chicken being played out between men of highly charged nationalistic fervor could have conceivably turned out in a number of ways, most of them too horrible to imagine. General LeMay was either brilliant and extremely prescient or the exact opposite of those adjectives; regardless, his lack of the more esoteric skills of nuance, grace, and discretion made him a very dangerous man to have held a high-level military position. But he wasn't the only man in Washington to lack those characteristics. Throughout the highly pressurized discussions the Kennedys had with the diplomats, military chiefs and intelligence officers, though they did nothing to encourage Lyndon Johnson's attendance, they had to endure his bullying talk about taking aggressive actions to invade Cuba, as if that course carried no possible risk of retaliatory action by the Cubans or Soviets. While the Kennedys tolerated Johnson's militant manner—even though he did not produce any kind of detailed strategy—they regarded him as a nuisance. Bobby would later say that of the thirteen men in the cabinet room in the ExComm meetings of October 1962, if any of seven of them had been president of the United States, the world would have been blown up; Lyndon Johnson was one of those seven. As we will see in chapter 5, Bobby's purpose in writing *Thirteen Days* was to warn Johnson that "I remember."

When Kennedy responded to a question about whether the premise of a coup d'état in America, as presented in the movie *Seven Days in May*, was realistic, he used an analogy about how many times as a young president he could repeat the disaster of the Bay of Pigs before his own military would remove him from office. He regarded the proposed Nuclear Test Ban Treaty—opposed by most conservatives, the military, and the intelligence communities—as being one such test. He had become pessimistic that it could be done, based upon resistance by not only prominent Republicans but by many within his own party. Senator Everett Dirksen said of Kennedy's efforts, "This has become an exercise not in negotiation but in giveaway." The Joint Chiefs of Staff declared themselves "opposed to a comprehensive ban under almost any terms."[81] When asked about it at a press conference on March 21, 1963, Kennedy replied, "Well, my hopes are dimmed, but nevertheless, I still hope."[82] Ten weeks later, his response had dimmed even

---

81. Douglass, p. 49 (ref. Schlesinger, Arthur, *Thousand Days*, p. 899).
82. Douglass, p. 49 (ref. Public Papers of the Presidents: John F. Kennedy, 1963, p. 107).

more, to the point that he answered essentially the same question with "No, I'm not hopeful, I'm not hopeful . . . We have tried to get an agreement (with the Soviets) on all the rest of it and then come to the question of the number of inspections, but we were unable to get that."[83] However, though not hopeful, he was determined to see it through despite the low chances of doing so successfully. He realized that the testing was not simply escalating the arms race with ever higher destructive potential but the radioactive fallout from these tests was poisoning the world. He took a keen personal interest in this issue and worked directly with Ambassador Averell Harriman, who he had appointed his top negotiator with Moscow, during July 1963. This initiative was being pushed aggressively throughout Kennedy's last summer, the pinnacle of which was his speech on June 10 at American University, when he introduced the topic as the most important one on earth: "World Peace."[84]

The hard-liners in his administration had a quite different take on these events. Although they conceded that the public record was that JFK won the missile crisis by negotiating through strength, it was actually resolved through secret agreements to give Khrushchev what he wanted originally: a promise that the United States would not invade Cuba and the removal of U.S. missiles from Turkey. A week after the missile crisis ended, the Democrats had a successful midterm election, including the election of Ted Kennedy to his first term in the Senate. Lyndon Johnson probably did not understand the situation clearly—Robert Kennedy didn't think so at least—but he would have certainly seen the positive political aspects of this showdown and have come away with the resolve that his own administration would need a similar boost to ensure that his own presidency would be similarly cast.

Post–Missile Crisis Polarization

The resolution of the missile crisis did not deter the Kennedys in their efforts to rid themselves of Castro, but major organizational changes would be made, including the firing of Bill Harvey. Anti-Castro exile groups continued to be funded by the CIA, and provided with arms and oversight under the overall direction of Robert F. Kennedy. While many of the exile groups were gradually assimilated into American society, mostly in Miami, the most militant were consolidated into well-organized and well-trained mercenary groups operated with military precision. In fact, these groups carried on attacks against Cuban and Soviet facilities even while the White

---

83. Ibid.
84. Douglass, pp. 35, 50–51.

House was promising the Soviets that these attacks would be stopped.[85] Fifteen years later, the HSCA examined these groups and found that the most violent and powerful of them, called Alpha 66, had conducted the most daring raids against Castro. Despite Kennedy's appeal to the exiles to stop their attacks, the leader of Alpha 66, Antonio Veciana, "snubbed the President and said that Alpha 66 would continue. If anything, the activities of Alpha 66 were stepped up."[86] The problem was that Veciana and Alpha 66 were not just autonomous, swashbuckling soldiers of fortune operating outside U.S. control. They were acting on instructions from the CIA, specifically under an agent who used the code name Maurice Bishop, who has been identified as none other than David Atlee Phillips.[87] Veciana claimed that "'all the trouble caused by Alpha 66 to disrupt JFK's diplomatic overtures was instigated by Maurice Bishop. At the height of the missile crisis,' Veciana says, 'Bishop told him to step up his raids on Soviet and Cuban vessels. Other examples of such seeming insubordination are reported during this period when certain elements of the CIA appeared to be acting contrary to the policies of the government.'"[88] In September 1963, Veciana met Bishop in the lobby of a downtown Dallas office building and saw him talking to Lee Harvey Oswald. He never asked him about this meeting and didn't recognize Oswald until his face appeared in every newspaper and television news program after his arrest for the murder of Police Officer J. D. Tippit and John F. Kennedy on November 22, 1963.[89]

During the missile crisis, Harvey had planned an invasion into Cuba by sixty people, unbeknownst to anyone else. One of the men who was supposed to go on this mission contacted Bobby, saying, "'We don't mind going, but we want to make sure we're going because *you* think it's worthwhile.' [Bobby said that] 'I checked into it. And nobody knew about it. The CIA didn't. The top officials didn't. We pinned it down to the fellow who was supposed to be in charge [William K. Harvey]. He said we planned it because the military wanted it done. I asked the military, and they never heard of it . . . This other man they put on it was the fellow who'd been the Berlin expert, who had had this great achievement. He ended in disaster by working out this program. Of course, I was furious. I said you were dealing with people's lives—the best of the Cubans. They're the ones who volunteer.

85. Hurt, p. 326.
86. Ibid. (ref. CIA to FBI et al., November 12, 1962 (CIA #F82-0430/106); *Sunday Star*, October 14, 1962; *Washington Post*, October 30, 1962; HSCR, pp. 134–135; *Dallas Morning News*, May 10, 1979; Hinckle and Turner, *The Fish Is Red*, pp. 164–167; Fonzi, "Who Killed JFK?" pp. 180–181).
87. Ibid., pp. 328–335.
88. Ibid., p. 330 (ref. X HSCA, pp. 38–39; Fonzi, "Who Killed JFK?" pp. 176–178).
89. Ibid., p. 330.

And then you're going to go off with a half-assed operation like this. We had a meeting at the Pentagon on it. I've never seen him since.'"[90] Bobby Kennedy never saw William Harvey again because he ordered him removed, and according to author David C. Martin, Richard Helms decided to never allow him to be "near an operation in which the White House was likely to take an active interest. Helms decided to send him to Rome as station chief. The assignment was stunning in its incongruity. The tough-talking, hard-drinking, gun-toting Harvey would be serving in a post whose chief duties were liaison with the Italian intelligence services. Having offended almost every high-ranking national security official in the Kennedy administration, he would now have a chance to offend almost every high-ranking national security official in the Italian government. 'They couldn't have picked a bigger bull for a better china shop,' one CIA officer snorted. The irony cannot have escaped Harvey that it was he, the loyal government servant, and not Rosselli, the mafioso, who was being deported to Italy."[91]

It was in the wake of the October 1962 missile crisis that the Cuba policy was thrown into complete flux. Although Kennedy had forced Khrushchev to back down on the missiles, he had to make certain concessions, one of which was not invading Cuba. This caused Castro to actually emerge in a stronger position vis-à-vis the United States. Although this caused many in the administration to rationalize a peaceful coexistence with Castro, the majority of people in the upper ranks of the CIA and the military could not accept that premise. Kennedy decided to reorganize the CIA's Cuban operations by dumping Harvey and bringing in Edward Lansdale and Desmond FitzGerald under the name of the Special Affairs Staff (SAS), dedicated to Castro's overthrow. It would be overseen by an executive committee of officials from the national security agencies, the ExComm, and very secretly run, with no assistants or deputies to be involved. Bobby was put in charge of the oversight and "came to regard himself as the 'second commander in chief,' forging a new Cuba policy and perhaps his own future presidency."[92]

At this point, Harvey was hardly the only one in the CIA who had irreconcilable differences with the Kennedys. Unlike the circumspect Angleton, who was very careful about to whom he divulged secrets, one of his top aides, Nestor Sanchez, could be more open and candid about the specific gripes of the staff in counterintelligence (CI), accusing the Kennedys of initiating big operations only to pull the rug on them when the tough got going: "'You don't get involved in covert-type operations unless you

90. Guthman and Shulman, p. 378 (Interview with John Bartlow Martin, May 14, 1964).
91. Martin, David C., p. 146.
92. Brugioni, p. 154.

are willing to go the distance.' That type of commitment 'was lacking in the Kennedy administration and it happened twice: the Bay of Pigs and the second one [referring to Operation Mongoose, the secret plan to overthrow Castro that died during the missile crisis]. They backed out of both . . . The buck stops with the President on operations like that. There's no one else. He says yes or no. All the other conspiracies of the agency was running amok, that's baloney . . . God damnit you do it or you don't, and if you don't feel you can do it you either get yourself out, take 'em out, or get someone else.' By the summer of 1963, he felt Kennedy's Cuba policy was not serious. Said Sanchez, 'the waffle was already in there.'"[93]

The top aide to Richard Helms, Sam Halpern, was even more candid about the attitude of the spooks toward their supposed superiors, who they felt were incompetent: "You're dealing with two guys in the White House who made a botch of things at the Bay of Pigs and haven't a clue what it means to run clandestine operations or covert operations or whatever you want to call them; They've got their fingers all over the place trying to make amends, and the more they try to make amends, the worse it gets. Kennedy wouldn't listen. They believe in keeping on doing all this, busy-ness, busy-ness, busy-ness."[94] Sam Halpern's reference to "busy-ness" came from a meeting of the National Security Council in May 1963, at which Kennedy's NSC adviser, McGeorge Bundy, forcefully stated his doubts about the capability of the U.S. government ever overthrowing Castro. "We should face this prospect," he said provocatively to the others present.[95] Defense Secretary McNamara said one option was to "buy off Castro," meaning to discontinue the embargo of the Cuban economy if Castro broke the relationship with the Soviet Union. Bobby Kennedy remarked that something needed to be done even if it would not bring Castro down. Bundy responded, saying, "We can give an impression of busy-ness in Cuba and we can make life difficult for Castro." Halpern was disgusted by what he felt was a prissy word, *busy-ness,* that reflected the weakness of Kennedy's Cuba policy, considering that men had their lives on the line trying to take actions which the White House had demanded. They were actually trying to do exactly what JFK had extolled his countrymen to do, "pay any price, bear any burden" to carry out American policy, in this case, getting rid of Cuban Communism. According to the author Jefferson Morley, "Halpern argued that the deceptiveness of Kennedy's policy virtually justified extra-constitutional correction. 'I'll tell you one thing,' he said, sitting forward in his seat, finger jabbing the air. 'I didn't know that word "busy-

93. Morley, *Our Man in Mexico*, pp. 164–165.
94. Ibid.
95. Ibid., pp. 165–166.

ness." It was never mentioned by Des [FitzGerald] when he came back from that meeting, and it was a good thing he didn't, because you might have had a *Seven Days in May* at that point . . . there might have been a revolt of some kind. I might have led it!'"[96] The intensity of Sam Halpern's comment—made thirty five years after this episode—speaks volumes about how he and many of his colleagues in the upper reaches of the CIA organization felt about the conduct of Cuba policy as practiced by John and Robert Kennedy.

Richard Helms was a very aloof man, some might even have characterized him as smug, but his face evoked a quiet and discreet kind of arrogance; he was not one to use bluff and bluster to express his views. He favored one of the most discreet forms of making his point: His favorite weapon was the newspaper leak, anonymous of course. In his effort to thwart what he considered the Kennedys' amateurish Cuban policies, he gave key information to a Pulitzer Prize–winning reporter for the Knight Ridder newspaper chain in Miami, Hal Hendrix, who used it to write a story called "Backstage with Bobby":[97]

> "There is growing speculation here and in Washington that Attorney General Bobby Kennedy has once again donned an invisible warrior's helmet and is embarking quietly on a new anti-Castro operation with hand-picked Cuban exiles." He highlighted the fact that the Kennedy administration was backing away from the once-prevalent notion that the United States should simply invade Cuba. "No large invasion force is envisioned . . . Instead, in line with the Kennedy Administration's enforcement of the Neutrality Act, hit and run attacks from a base outside the U.S. would be the role of Bobby's Boys."

The Kennedy's campaign to get rid of the Castro problem was doomed from the start, despite all the investments in men, money, material, equipment, and time. Regardless of what Robert Kennedy, in his background role in the Special Operations Group—Augmented, did or didn't do to earn the enmity of Bill Harvey and all of his associates and notwithstanding the contradictory stories of dramatic Cuban exploits, the bottom line is clear: Fidel Castro was not assassinated or removed otherwise in 1963 and in fact remained in power for nearly fifty years thereafter, outliving practically all of his enemies. JFK had promised tens of thousands of Cuban exiles that they would eventually return to their homeland as free men and women without the fear of Castro's prisons, or worse, awaiting their return. Kennedy's resolve to reform Cuba began dissipating in the year following the Cuban Missile Crisis. He had

96. Ibid.
97. Ibid.

taken a number of measures that caused many to believe he had experienced an epiphany with regard to much of the foreign policy he originally inherited from Eisenhower and had initially endeavored to maintain; now, it seemed to many that there was never a sincere and meaningful effort to fulfill all of the commitments which had been made; it appeared to them that they were simply hollow promises made for politically expedient reasons.

Bill Harvey Returns

Robert Kennedy had removed Bill Harvey from his Task Force W immediately after the missile crisis and had him transferred to Rome. But Harvey had unfinished business in the United States and did not remain in Rome for long; it seems that he was actually commuting between Rome and Florida: "He showed up in the spring, summer and fall of 1963 in ominous meetings in the Florida Keys at anti-Castro camps with Johnny Rosselli, David Atlee Phillips and a CIA assassination expert, David Sanchez Morales. Shortly after that, Rosselli met with Guy Banister in New Orleans, and Phillips met with Oswald in Dallas . . . Harvey may have been the chief planner of Kennedy's assassination, working with the CIA's Phillips and Morales and the Mafia's Rosselli, using recruits from the French Mafia whom Harvey contacted while in Italy."[98]

In addition to the meetings in the Keys, there is evidence that Harvey met with Rosselli in Miami and Los Angeles in February 1963, and in Washington DC in June.[99] According to his CIA expense account records, he paid for his own room in the Keys motel as well as someone else's (unnamed, but whose home address was listed as 56510 Wilshire Boulevard, Los Angeles, California, since confirmed to be the Friar's Club, which was like a second home to Rosselli) and even picked up the charges for renting a boat to go to Islamorada (in the Keys) and a dinner one evening at the Fontainebleau Hotel, the favorite haunt of a number of mafiosi, including Sam Giancana and Harvey's fast-lane friend Johnny Rosselli.[100] Their other favorite, the Eden Roc, was also patronized by this group; the entry simply indicated, "For ops hotel room," but didn't include a receipt.[101] Another entry for $1,000 was noted: "Termination payment ZR Rifle/MI." Finally, another entry was for a "First-class plane ticket Miami/Chicago."[102]

---

98. Twyman, pp. 307.
99. Twyman, pp. 440–441.
100. Ibid., pp. 442–443.
101. Ibid., p. 441.
102. Ibid.

For what reason was Bill Harvey back in Florida for so long, and who was his mysterious guest, if not the obvious Johnny Rosselli? And why, after he had been reassigned to Italy specifically to get him off Mongoose and the Castro plot, was he still in contact with him? At this point, the Mafia was no longer involved in plotting against Castro, so what other plots were being hatched by these two? Who had to be flown to and/or from Chicago to Miami, for the sum of $200? (In those days, that probably would have covered a round-trip first-class ticket.) And finally, was there a connection between these meetings and the arrangements, formulated beforehand and publicly announced two days after the meetings had ended, for President Kennedy to visit Dallas in November? It is unlikely that this was all a coincidence, given Harvey's continuing direct connection to Angleton and Angleton's direct lines to Hoover and Vice President Lyndon B. Johnson.

Bill Harvey had teamed up with Johnny Rosselli and the two became fast friends during the CIA's Operation Mongoose, their joint venture with the Mafia in its (original) plan for assassinating Fidel Castro. The two of them made an odd couple because—compared to the standard description of Harvey as being an obese, sloppily dressed, frog-faced man with crude manners—the sharply dressed, tanned, and good-looking ladies' man, Johnny Rosselli, seemed to have come from an entirely different civilization, if not planet. It was Bill Harvey who gave Rosselli the cover he needed to expand the Mafia's influence into many new areas, thanks to his convincing new identification as a U.S. Army colonel. Having complete access to the JM/WAVE headquarters, this world-class (and connected) gangster routinely and often met with a CIA assassin named David Morales, along with Bill Harvey. Another thing the three of them had in common was a vicious hatred of all things Kennedy.

Specifically what actions Rosselli became involved with, beyond the original plan for murdering Castro, will never be known, but his new military identification and these high-level military and intelligence connections suggest a key role in an expanded and redirected assassination scheme. It was just a matter of time, probably during this period in early 1963 when this team met in the Florida Keys, before the subject of the assassination plot against Castro was redirected to Kennedy; a call from Angleton in Washington to his subordinate Harvey in Florida, possibly advising him that a "green light" was being flashed from the White House (i.e., the vice president's suite in the EOB next door) would be the only record of the authorization to Harvey to proceed with the planning, and that bit of evidence, of course, will never be forthcoming. Only a relative handful of CIA operatives would be necessary for this special mission, bypassing many of the others already in place, and few auditable paper trails of their planning would be retained for any possible later discovery. But the dots described earlier from the known records hardly need to be physically connected.

As Noel Twyman established, "Harvey's conceptual notes for *ZR/RIFLE* are a blueprint for the JFK assassination plot, both in concept and detail: First, the employment of French Corsican assassins was planned by Harvey; and evidence shows that French Corsicans were in Dallas on November 22, 1963 and that they were professional assassins. Second, Harvey proposed disinformation schemes to [put the] 'blame on the Soviets' and evidence shows that is exactly what happened to Oswald . . . Third, Harvey was very specific in recruiting only top professional assassins . . . Fourth, Harvey specified rigid controls to keep plots limited to a few participants with strict rules of conversation and no paper trail . . . Finally, Harvey clearly specified the use of phony 201 files in CIA records, backdated and forged, to conceal the identity of participants."[103]

Kennedy's Fear of a Quagmire in Southeast Asia

As the cold war escalated throughout the 1950s, some in the military and intelligence services, and the executive advisers and politicians they influenced, became convinced that the growing Communist menace—if not frozen in its tracks throughout the world—would inevitably pose a threat to the national security of the United States. An official theory to which many of the advisers subscribed postulated that an aggressive Communist power could take over entire continents by snatching up little countries, one at a time; the domino theory became the latest fashionable concept among many of the military, intelligence, and political advisers in the early 1960s. For many people who could not quite understand why the United States was being pulled into the civil war of a small, nonthreatening country on the other side of the world, this theory would provide an answer. It was probably the least profound and baseless conceptual war strategy ever developed, and was debunked by the CIA in June 1964 even before Johnson proceeded to escalate the war. JFK never bought into the theory either; in fact he spent his entire presidency trying to keep his administration from accepting its fatal premise. On the other hand, Lyndon Johnson had no compunction about buying it lock, stock, and barrel, because it fit very well into his plan to be a "wartime president," just like Roosevelt.

The Korean War experience, in which a permanent impasse of sorts had been reached, dividing the country into two quite opposite states, established a precedent of sorts. It also became a kind of mind-set for many

103. Ibid. p. 424.

as an acceptable solution for other trouble spots, such as Southeast Asia. It eventually became the working assumption that South Vietnam could become like South Korea—a strong ally of the United States—irrespective of the pesky issues of its long history of instability and its then current corrupt regime. Yet Kennedy fought against the "groupthink" phenomenon arrayed against him and did so consistently over a two-year period, even though he allowed the number of advisers to increase during his presidency, as he hoped to slow the escalation by the end of his term. Only one of his senior-level advisers, George Ball, held the same strong views as Kennedy. But others, notably Ambassador John Kenneth Galbraith, did as well, and they generally had a better understanding of the pitfalls related to committing U.S. forces to a land war in Southeast Asia.[104]

According to Arthur Schlesinger Jr., John Kennedy's attitudes regarding Vietnam were forged in part by the advice he got from no less a warrior than General Douglas MacArthur, who told him that "it would be a 'mistake' to fight in Southeast Asia. 'He thinks,' the President dictated in a rare *aide-memoire*, 'our line should be Japan, Formosa and the Philippines.'"[105] Robert Kennedy added that MacArthur also said that "we would be foolish to fight on the Asiatic continent and that the future of Southeast Asia should be determined at the diplomatic table."[106] According to Kenneth O'Donnell, "MacArthur was extremely critical of the military advice that the President had been getting from the Pentagon, blaming the military leaders of the previous ten years, who, he said, had advanced the wrong younger officers. 'You were lucky to have that mistake happen in Cuba, where the strategic cost was not too great,' he said about the Bay of Pigs. MacArthur implored the President to avoid a U.S. military build-up in Vietnam, or any other part of the Asian mainland, because he felt that the domino theory was ridiculous in a nuclear age. MacArthur went on to point out that there were domestic problems—the urban crisis, the ghettos, the economy—that should have far more priority than Vietnam. Kennedy came out of the meeting somewhat stunned. That a man like MacArthur should give him such unmilitary advice impressed him enormously."[107] Kennedy had also discussed the issue with General Charles de Gaulle, who told him, "You will sink step by step into a bottomless military and political quagmire, however much you spend in men and money."[108]

---

104. Schlesinger, *Robert Kennedy*, p. 761.
105. Ibid., p. 759.
106. Ibid.
107. O'Donnell and Powers, pp. 13–14; *Life* magazine, August 7, 1970, p. 51.
108. Schlesinger, *Robert Kennedy*, p. 759 (ref. de Gaulle, *Memoirs of Hope: Renewal and Endeavor*, New York, 1971, pp. 255–256).

By the end of 1961, the pressures from the military and most of his advisers to send troops to Vietnam had grown ever stronger, despite Kennedy's view that Ngo Dinh Diem was too much of a tyrant to justify his support. When Ambassador/Professor Galbraith was preparing to return to India, JFK asked him to personally visit Saigon on the way and report back to him; Galbraith's report said in part, "Diem will not reform . . . He cannot. It is politically naïve to expect it. He senses that he cannot let power go because he would be thrown out."[109] Diem could not even conceptualize the idea of democratization; it was incomprehensible to him, at least in a land in which the culture regarded the head of state as "sovereign" and answerable only to God, with whom he directly mediated.[110] Diem's attitude was remarkably similar to that of Lyndon Johnson's after he became president, as will be seen in the last chapter.

Eventually, the pressure from the Pentagon resulted in the Kennedy administration increasing the number of American military personnel in South Vietnam from 685 in January 1960 to 16,732 in October 1963. However, despite this increase in military advisers and material support, Kennedy was still not fully supportive of further increases in troop levels, or of any introduction of combat troops. JFK's position was described clearly at his first ever press conference, when he expressed his wish to create in Vietnam "a peaceful country; an independent country not dominated by either side but concerned with the life of the people within the country."[111] While Kennedy had gone along with increased levels of advisers and equipment, he steadfastly refused to add combat troops. John M. Newman succinctly summed up Kennedy's record in Vietnam:

> *Kennedy turned down combat troops, not when the decision was clouded by ambiguities and contradictions in the reports from the battlefield, but when the battle was unequivocally desperate, when all concerned agreed that Vietnam's fate hung in the balance, and when his principal advisors told him that vital U.S. interests in the region and the world were at stake.*[112]

George Ball had warned Kennedy in 1961, "Within five years we'll have three hundred thousand men in the paddies and jungles and never find them again. That was the French experience. Vietnam is the worst possible terrain both from a physical and political point of view." JFK responded, "George,

---

109. Ibid., p. 763 (ref. Pentagon Papers, Vol. 2, p. 123).
110. Schlesinger, *Robert Kennedy*, p. 763.
111. Newman, pp. 130–138.
112. Newman, p. 138.

you're just crazier than hell. That just isn't going to happen."[113] (According to Schlesinger, that sentence didn't end there; JFK added, "As long as I am President.")[114] Ball turned out to be partially right, of course, even though he *underestimated* by almost half the number of men who would be committed to the paddies and jungles halfway around the world at the peak of the U.S. intervention by JFK's successor. Kennedy's attempts to persuade Ngo Dinh Diem to stop harassing the Buddhists and broaden his government in South Vietnam were unsuccessful. The repressive, often brutal tactics employed by South Vietnam's president Diem jeopardized the anti-Communist cause and complicated JFK's ability to provide continuing support; he began to more strongly resist attempts by his advisers to send additional troops to Vietnam.

General Edward Lansdale, who appeared in a similarly distracting role in the Cuban operations, was originally involved in strategizing the Vietnam situation while attempting to manage it in such a way as to further his own career. Of course, he was not the only one using that tactic at the time, including, arguably, many of the military and intelligence officers advising Kennedy. Lansdale had managed to have himself assigned to a task force under Roswell Gilpatric to develop broad planning for Vietnam. Although he was generally unpopular in Washington, he apparently had a mentor in Walter Rostow, through whom he had managed to get himself nominated to be ambassador to Vietnam. His flamboyance and conniving manner did not impress a number of people at the State Department, and this caused his name to be pulled from the list of candidates; Frederick Nolting was chosen instead, who was a career foreign service officer with no Vietnam experience at all (that was considered to be an asset, since he had no ties to any Vietnamese leaders or generals that might make Diem suspicious of him).[115] According to author John Newman, Lansdale crafted a lengthy plan, listing actionable tasks for handling Vietnam; one of the items included the appointment of a Vietnam task force, but "the real purpose seems to have been for insinuating himself into the government's policy apparatus, putting himself in charge of it."[116] Lansdale figured on being appointed as the operations officer, and being a part of the three-man group accompanying the newly appointed Ambassador Nolting to Vietnam. His own role would have included the responsibility to "supervise and coordinate the activities of every agency carrying out

---

113. Douglass, p. 375 (ref. George W. Ball, *The Past Has Another Pattern: Memoirs*, New York: W.W. Norton, 1982, p. 366).
114. Schlesinger, *Robert Kennedy*, p. 761 (ref. his interview with George Ball).
115. Newman, *JFK and Vietnam*, p. 34.
116. Ibid., p. 36.

operations pursuant to the plan." His own powers would be so vast that he would virtually dictate any changes to Vietnam policy.[117]

In the spring of 1961, as the Bay of Pigs debacle was unfolding in Cuba, the developing crisis in Laos and the quickly deteriorating situation in Vietnam competed for the attention of the president. As the Joint Chiefs continued pressing for the president to take more aggressive actions in Cuba, they also urged him to intervene in Laos and Vietnam. Lansdale and Gilpatric submitted their report on April 29, just days after the Cuban debacle, but the president was not in the mood to make a final decision then; they reissued the task force report on May 1. The revision was to move the military involvement away from solely training roles toward the direction of combat troops. Possibly as a result of this, Lansdale and the Pentagon itself were removed from the task force as Kennedy directed the State Department to take it over and run it.[118] Kennedy told his assistant secretary of state, Roger Hilsman, "The Bay of Pigs has taught me a number of things. One is not to trust generals or the CIA, and the second is that if the American people do not want to use American troops to remove a Communist regime 90 miles away from our coast, how can I ask them to use troops to remove a Communist regime 9,000 miles away?"[119]

In the meantime, Lyndon Johnson stepped in to fill the void left by Kennedy's ever-evolving schism with the military and intelligence chiefs; he did so using a clandestine back channel which he had developed through his decades-long relationship with his military aide Col. Howard Burris, who was connected not only to key people in the Pentagon but in Langley as well. One of the military chiefs, General Curtis LeMay, shared many of Johnson's attitudes, especially about the president, whom he regarded as an indecisive coward and avowed socialist. LeMay thought even less of Bobby, for whom his view was similar to that of J. Edgar Hoover. Burris, LeMay, and Hoover, along with other key people in the military and intelligence organizations of the United States, will be examined further in the next chapter.

Lyndon Johnson Goes to Vietnam, Praises the "Churchill of Asia"

Shortly after the disastrous Bay of Pigs venture, Kennedy decided to rely on his vice president to exercise his famous negotiating skills to intercede on

117. Ibid., p. 37.
118. Newman, *JFK and Vietnam*, p. 56.
119. Marrs, *Crossfire: The Plot That Killed Kennedy*, pp. 306–307.

his behalf with President Diem of South Vietnam, to redirect his autocratic ways into a more democratic rule. That was a mistake John Kennedy came to regret despite his attempt to neuter Johnson's ability to effect substantive changes after his departure. Against his consistent resolve to offer President Diem measured support, while prodding him to abandon the harassment of Buddhists and his other autocratic ways, many of his topmost advisers pushed Kennedy to intercede militarily. He decided to send Vice President Lyndon Johnson to Vietnam in May 1961, expecting him to do some hard bargaining with President Diem. Although he finally prevailed on him to make the trip, he probably wished he hadn't, given the ultimate results.

Johnson was adamantly opposed to making the trip and quickly dug in his heels to avoid it. He had first heard about his new assignment on the radio while he was in New York. According to Air Force Colonel Howard Burris, who had just been appointed Johnson's military representative, "He came back to the White House and told Kennedy he wasn't going to go . . . I remember, I was sitting there against the wall in the NSC meeting listening to all this screaming taking place. Kennedy said he wanted Johnson to go and Johnson just refused. Kennedy said, 'You're going tonight and the Foreign Service and [McGeorge] Bundy will brief you.' [Burris said after that] Johnson went out and just got stoned."[120] Johnson was still in his funk when the plane left Andrews AFB. Kennedy had added a few of his family members to this entourage, including his sister Jean and brother-in-law Stephen Smith, which thoroughly irritated Johnson during the entire trip. Throughout the twenty-plus-hour flight, as he continued drinking and bloviating, Johnson "talked over and over about the fact that he had not been born rich like the Kennedys," and complained that he had not gone to Harvard but to a "little crappy Texas college."

Carl Rowan, a distinguished black journalist who became an assistant secretary of state for public affairs, accompanied Johnson on the trip. Rowan, who later gained fame as a syndicated columnist and television pundit, commented that "Johnson had one of the greatest inferiority complexes I ever saw in a high-level official."[121] He helped Horace Busby write the speech Johnson would give before the Vietnam National Assembly. Rowan said Johnson "was drinking a lot in those days, and the more he drank, the meaner he got, and verbally abused his staff 'in ways I found hard to believe.'"[122] During a press conference, for no apparent reason, Johnson had insulted Rowan by calling him a "dummy." Rowan later called him on it and

120. Newman, *JFK and Vietnam*, pp. 67–68.
121. Ibid., pp. 68–69.
122. Ibid., p. 68.

threatened to take the first plane back to Washington; Johnson responded by telling Rowan that he would not do that again, because he would not be seeing reporters anymore. That promise lasted until noon the next day, when Johnson called Rowan and invited him to bring some reporters to his room, which he did, where they were greeted by Johnson wearing only his underwear. "Hell, bring 'em on in," Johnson said, proceeding to hold "the only press conference that, to my knowledge, a senior American official held in his skivvies."[123]

From Kennedy's perspective, this trip was a mistake, because rather than elicit support for his position, Johnson's efforts were functionally reversed: He recast his own role, to become the advocate not of Kennedy's agenda but of the despotic ruler whom JFK wanted to control. He went well beyond the authority Kennedy had vested in him, even committing the United States to provide equipment (helicopters and armored personnel carriers) without extracting anything about how Diem would finance them. Johnson said that Diem was "tickled as hell," which, considering that Johnson had just handed him everything he wanted, should not have been a surprise. He did this while conceding on positions that the State Department had held for months.[124] Johnson had managed to use his patented "treatment of Diem" to get him on his own side, at Kennedy's expense. He ingratiated himself well when he praised Diem as the "Churchill of Asia" at the reception dinner. As Stanley Karnow put it, it was as if Johnson "were endorsing county sheriffs in a Texas election campaign."[125]

Johnson asked Diem to write two letters to Kennedy, the first one general and the second one stipulating everything he wanted on his "wish list," including his request for an additional hundred thousand men for his army. To get such an approval would implicitly mean additional American troops to train them; the question of asking for combat troops had been discussed as well, and Johnson seemed to have left the two issues dangling when he left for Bermuda to work three days on his report to the White House.[126]

The day after Johnson left on his trip, Kennedy issued NSAM 52, but he modified the earlier draft to delete a provision allowing that a *commitment might result from an NSC decision following the LBJ-Diem talks.*" The result of this is that Johnson thought he had much more authority than he did; in fact, as soon as he was gone, anything he might do or say was without real authority. By ensuring that Johnson would play no role in any decisions after

123. Ibid., p. 71 (ref. Rowan, Carl, *Breaking Barriers*).
124. Ibid., p. 70.
125. Karnow, p. 250.
126. Newman, *JFK and Vietnam*, pp. 76–78.

he had already left on the trip, whatever Johnson might have told Diem would become irrelevant, and anything others, such as the Joint Chiefs, might have been trying to insert would also become moot. During the review process for NSAM 52, the Pentagon's proposal for combat troops was either blocked from the agenda or dealt with and disapproved.[127] While Kennedy technically had the upper hand in this apparent trial balloon of the mission on which he sent Johnson, the fact that Johnson had cobbled together his own agenda for his forced trip around the world still caused major misconceptions in the minds of a lot of people with whom he met. Working secretly behind the scenes in Washington, Edward Lansdale's unseen hand was manipulating, on behalf of the Joint Chiefs and the CIA, to try to get more troops into play (under the guise of their being used only for "training" purposes when they would actually be set up as combat troops). Johnson's aide Colonel Burris confirmed this: "I remember [General Lionel] McGarr saying the troops were for training, but it was really just under the *guise* of training."[128]

Ambassador Nolting evidently was on to Johnson's maneuvering since they had argued over it in Saigon; the ambassador cabled the State Department, attempting to disrupt Johnson and Diem's two-letter scheme. He had been there when Johnson specifically directed Diem to send the second letter before his own return. When Diem tried to have his secretary of state, Thuan, personally take the letter to Washington, Nolting suggested that this be done in mid-June, knowing that Johnson would be returning to Washington on May 24. Nolting had already explained to Chester Bowles what happened during Johnson's visit, and he, in turn, tipped off the White House about the wish list that Thuan would be bringing with him. This ensured that he would receive a cold reception.[129]

Kennedy's use of Johnson on this trip—deliberately entrapping him if he tried to usurp more authority than he had—suggests that he was finally catching on to the agenda shared by a number of his subordinates within the White House and Pentagon. Johnson's recommendation, which he gave to the press, was that the president should not "get bogged down in a land war in Southeast Asia."[130] This was in direct conflict with everything he had said to Diem, and everyone else on the trip, but the president's maneuvers on NSAM 52 had put Johnson into a dilemma between what he really wanted to say, what Kennedy had already done to limit his options, what he knew the Joint Chiefs wanted him to do, and what he wanted Diem

127. Ibid., pp. 84–85.
128. Ibid., p. 73.
129. Ibid., pp. 86–87.
130. Ibid., pp. 88–89.

to request. Diem, anticipating the quandary, had been stalling for time. Johnson also had to consider the reactions of his least favorite group of people, those at the State Department. In the end, he chose to report only the fact that Diem had initially agreed that he would not request combat troops. Johnson neglected to mention that he himself had held out the possibility of adding them under the pretext of using them for training Diem's army.[131]

In the meantime, Johnson had already been lobbied by certain of his old Senate colleagues who were among the most ardent interventionists. Senator Thomas Dodd (the father of the beleaguered Senator Chris Dodd), before he lost his own credibility, had sent Johnson a cable bemoaning how American credibility "was at an all time low in Asia because of the Bay of Pigs fiasco in Cuba."[132] Johnson had elicited this congressional "support" for his own position, not the president's, so of course he was very disappointed that his influence had come to naught. Johnson's report back to Kennedy would be a rebuke of Kennedy's own policies, including what Johnson felt was Kennedy's unfortunate decision to neutralize Laos instead of creating a war there:

> Our [Johnson's] mission arrested the decline of confidence in the United States. It did not—in my judgment—restore any confidence already lost . . . If these men were bankers, I would know—without bothering to ask—that there would be no further extensions on my note.[133]

Johnson's condescending message to Kennedy was essentially telling him that he, the president, was responsible for the continuing collapse of Southeast Asia and that their leaders would not tolerate more of his mistakes; there is no record of how Kennedy reacted to Johnson's impertinence and brazen insubordination. Furthermore, Johnson was implicitly admitting the unsuccessful nature of his own mission to restore the confidence in America, which was tantamount to putting the blame for his own failure back upon Kennedy. His report continued, "The battle against Communism must be joined in Southeast Asia with strength and determination to achieve success there—or the United States, inevitably, must surrender the Pacific and take up our defenses on our own shores"[134] (as if there had been an impending threat of a U.S. invasion by the Viet Minh). Johnson cleverly avoided the

---

131. Ibid., pp. 70–72.
132. Ibid., pp. 92–93.
133. Douglass, pp. 105–106 (ref. Pentagon Papers, Vol. 2, p. 22).
134. Newman, *JFK and Vietnam*, p. 90.

question of additional troops by framing the issue as a choice between U.S. support or complete disengagement: We must decide if we are going to help these countries, or "throw in the towel and pull back our defenses to San Francisco and a 'Fortress of America' concept." Johnson recommended a "clear-cut and strong program of action."[135] The requests on Diem's wish list—cobbled together as requested by Johnson—greatly exceeded anything that Kennedy had expected, especially the request for a hundred-thousand-man increase and $175 million to pay for it. All of the requests were tied to the threat from Laos, and some of the language in Diem's letter bore a striking resemblance to Lansdale's report and General McGarr's expanded version of it. Diem's second letter—written at Lyndon Johnson's specific request—further damaged the already-poor relationship between the president and vice president.

Johnson had gone to Saigon drunk and in one of his famous funks and had evidently remained in an undiplomatic state for most of the time he spent there; he caved on gaining any ground on the negotiating points he was supposed to have restated; he made wild promises to Diem and the national assembly; he foolishly ventured into the issue of combat troops, which he had no business discussing and no authority to change; and finally, when he ran out of provocations and prevarications, he came home disappointed and frustrated.[136] The vice president went before the Senate Foreign Relations Committee on May 25, saying he was very "depressed" about Laos and that nothing would come out of the conference in Geneva. The incredible Senator Dodd lamented that the failure to act decisively now may be the "death knell" for the United States and all of Western civilization.[137]

Lyndon Johnson had sided with the Joint Chiefs of Staff, the CIA, the despotic President Diem, and many of Kennedy's military advisers and cabinet officials against his actual boss, his own president; all of the others whom Johnson was trying to appease were beating their war drums as loudly as they could while Kennedy struggled to get it all under his own control. The pressures were all around Kennedy in the fall of 1961 to send in troops because of the growing number of attacks from the Vietcong. In one month, September 1961, the number of guerrilla attacks in South Vietnam almost tripled from the previous months' totals. The provincial capital of Phuoc Thanh was seized and Diem's appointed chief was beheaded. On November 8, Defense Secretary McNamara, his deputy Roswell Gilpatric, and the Joint Chiefs of Staff all recommended to Kennedy in a memorandum that

135. Ibid., pp. 90–91.
136. Ibid., pp. 96–97.
137. Ibid., pp. 92–93.

we "commit the U.S. to the clear objective of preventing the fall of South Vietnam to Communism and that we support this commitment by the necessary military actions [an initial 8,000 men, followed by six divisions of ground forces, or 'about 205,000 men']."[138] It soon became apparent to Kennedy that Johnson's performance on his special Vietnam mission had cost him greatly, despite the steps Kennedy had taken to pull the rug out from under him as soon as he had left the country. Still, Johnson had given up the administration's long-held positions on a number of issues and had greatly exceeded his authority in the discussions of possible troop deployments, as well as by not setting forth the obligations of Diem's government with any of these issues.[139] Johnson himself was also very frustrated that he had not successfully brought the country squarely into an Indochina war, but he still harbored his own White House aspirations, and he knew that he would handle this war his own way once he was president.

After his rather appalling performance in this episode, he contented himself, like Lansdale, to watch events unfold from the sidelines until he could assume the role of commander in chief. For over two years afterward, Johnson would not be involved in any discussions on Vietnam.[140] This would clearly be at Kennedy's directive, subtly done through a process of omission, by simply not inviting him to strategic meetings on the subject. Johnson's assigned military representative, Howard Burris, said this about Johnson's view of intervention in Vietnam: "*I don't think he had a really deep perception and comprehension of what the whole scene was about.*"[141] According to author John M. Newman, Johnson's views "*were rooted in the superficial politics of Washington, not in the underlying realities of the situation in Vietnam.*"[142]

In other words, Lyndon Johnson was motivated out of a desire to please the military chiefs and the officials in the CIA organization for his own long-term purposes, which he had been developing since at least July 1960. That he had no scintilla of interest in serving the president, as a loyal, effective, and obedient vice president helping JFK pull the bureaucracy in the direction to which he wanted to take it, was evident in all of his actions throughout the period of 1961 to 1963. During his entire tenure as vice president, Lyndon B. Johnson was marching to his own drums, not the president's. Rather than Lyndon Johnson playing a subservient and supportive role under the president, he had come to believe that Kennedy was an inept greenhorn

138. Douglass, pp. 106–107.
139. Newman, *JFK and Vietnam*, pp. 96–97.
140. Ibid., p. 93.
141. Ibid., p. 91.
142. Ibid., p. 92.

who needed the guidance of an experienced and brilliant man like himself. His attitude from the very start was that only he, Lyndon B. Johnson, was equipped to handle the great responsibilities of the presidency.

The Time Bomb of Vietnam

A cursory review of the history of this ancient civilization, which had the misfortune of being thrust into the crosshairs of the political arena of the United States circa 1950–1975, is essential to a full understanding of how Lyndon Johnson became the thirty-sixth president and why he could not be reelected to that position to a second term. Vietnam had fought off many invaders and colonists for most of its long history. It had been under Chinese control for a thousand years before becoming a nation-state for another thousand years. During this period, a number of successive dynasties had ruled over it until it became a colony of France in the nineteenth century. In 1941, a Communist and nationalist liberation movement called the Viet Minh, after its leader Ho Chi Minh, was formed to resist the Japanese invasion and to assert the country's independence from any further colonization. After World War II, the Viet Minh launched a rebellion against the colonial authority governing the colonies of French Indochina (which also included Laos and Cambodia). This led to the defeat of the French in 1954, the Vietnamese having finally thrown off the colonial yoke completely; they had not overcome all of their internal differences, however, so peace was illusory. Ho Chi Minh was more of a Vietnamese nationalist than a Communist, at least in the context of the "international Communist movement" that had captured world headlines in that era. His intent was simply to establish a unified and independent Vietnam in a land that, unfortunately for its inhabitants, would become ground zero in the clash between the international forces of capitalism versus Communism.

Throughout 1961 Kennedy was pressed by some members of his own administration to commit troops to Laos and Vietnam; in addition to Johnson, others who advocated greater support for Diem included Robert McNamara, Dean Rusk, McGeorge Bundy, Walt Rostow, and Roswell Gilpatric. All of these men had impressive credentials coming into the administration, but their ability to think independently and argue against the "groupthink" then dominating the cabinet was impeded by their lack of knowledge about the risks they espoused. Years later, Clark Clifford finally admitted that he privately held strong reservations about Johnson's policies but did not forcefully assert them because he felt he did not understand the issues as much as his colleagues, who apparently did not know anything more than he did but were less introspective about how much they really knew.

Clifford offered the following as a rationale for acceding to Johnson and the other saber-rattlers who were aching for a war:

> I had never considered myself to be an expert on the situation in Vietnam. Many of those who had opposed Ball and me had greater experience and familiarity with the problem, and presented their views with certainty and conviction. Everyone else represented a department or agency of the government, with his own channels of information from the field. My opposition to the buildup had been based to a considerable extent on intuition; I had no firsthand knowledge or sources of information from Southeast Asia to place against the confidence and detailed knowledge of the supporters of the war . . . *When I later took a firsthand look at the situation, I discovered that much of the information from the embassy and the military command in Saigon was either inaccurate or irrelevant. I should have acted earlier on the warning signs, but I did not begin to realize how inaccurate these official reports were until my trip to Southeast Asia in the late summer of 1967. Until then, I was so anxious to find a way out of Vietnam that I accepted them as accurate, and I supported the military requests for more troops as the best way to end the war quickly.*[143] (emphasis added)

Clifford's quasi mea culpa merely begs the further question: How many of the others arguing for committing more American troops, or merely defending the previous actions, in Vietnam privately held the same thoughts during the years of the buildup but were afraid to express them? There are numerous accounts of the fact that Johnson only wanted yes-men around him and how he only wanted to hear good news, and as many stories of how anyone who might have a contrary view would risk being fired. His unctuous secretary of state, Dean Rusk, acknowledged that cabinet members did not disagree openly with him: "At most cabinet meetings Lyndon Johnson asked Bob McNamara and me to comment on Vietnam, and then he would go around the table, asking each cabinet officer, 'Do you have any questions or comments?' Everyone sat silently."[144] Given the obviously uncomfortable position that would put anyone in—at least anyone who had even the slightest streak of integrity left in them—it is troubling that more of his aides and cabinet-level officials did not resign. Eventually, Jack Valenti, McGeorge Bundy, Bill Moyers, and George Ball did leave during 1966, and Robert McNamara a year later (though it's still unclear whether he resigned or was fired), as the

---

143. Clifford, pp. 425–426.
144. Hershman, p. 284 (ref. Dean Rusk, *As I Saw It*, New York: W.W. Norton, 1980, p. 467).

American involvement in Vietnam continued escalating; even after they left, he disparaged them, yet they did not notably fight back.[145]

It may be that some of their attitudes—certainly Johnson's was—were inseparable from their simultaneous efforts, on another track, to push for a military buildup as a means to ensure the financial rewards for the military-industrial complex that Eisenhower had just warned the nation about. The Government Accounting Office found that his friends at Brown & Root "were overcharging by hundreds of millions of dollars beyond what was legitimate for their construction work in Vietnam."[146] As we will see shortly, Johnson's personal investment in Bell Aerospace and General Dynamics might have influenced how the TFX contract for a new-generation fighter plane had been awarded to his favored company. McNamara and Gilpatric were also highly immersed in the political fight to wrest the contract away from Boeing, of Seattle, Washington, in order to pay back political favors to a Texas company that had been floundering until then. A concurrent military escalation at that time would increase the payback dividend of making a new-generation warplane by greatly increasing the number produced. The question of whether political payoffs—significant financial gains for select corporations and individuals—were a major influence in the foreign policy decisions being presented to Kennedy is a disturbing and ironic denouement to his legacy.

In 1962, Johnson's successor as Senate majority leader, Mike Mansfield—a longtime supporter of Diem, to the point of being known popularly in South Vietnam as "Diem's godfather"—reversed his position on the growing U.S. commitment to the support of Diem's government. This reversal caused JFK to ask him to visit Vietnam and give him an independent report on the situation; it was submitted to Kennedy on December 18, 1962, and did not make pleasant reading for the president. The report stated that outside its cities, South Vietnam was "run at least at night by the Vietcong. The government in Saigon is still seeking acceptance by the ordinary people in large areas of the countryside. Out of fear or indifference or hostility the peasants still withhold acquiescence, let alone approval of that government."[147] While Mansfield still supported Diem, he did not have confidence in the government, dominated by Diem's brother Ngo Dinh Nhu, to ever gain popular support. Mansfield warned Kennedy against further escalation of military commitments, saying that to do so would ultimately require "a truly massive commitment of American military personnel and other resources—in short going to war fully ourselves against the

---

145. Ibid.
146. Ibid., p. 216.
147. Douglass, p. 123.

guerrillas—and the establishment of some form of neocolonial rule in South Vietnam."[148] In other words, Mansfield warned Kennedy against *any* additional military support because he knew that it would inexorably lead to greater and greater involvement of the U.S. military and ultimately into the same "unenviable position in Vietnam which was formerly occupied by the French.'"[149]

Stunned into realizing the truth of Mansfield's observations—which aligned with those of his friend Edmund Gullion and adviser John Kenneth Galbraith—by early 1963, he had resolved anew to himself that he would reverse course and begin a withdrawal of the military presence in Vietnam.[150] Kennedy told Mike Mansfield in May 1963 that he now agreed with his thinking "on the need for a complete military withdrawal from Vietnam" but he couldn't do it until after being reelected.[151] After the meeting with Mansfield, Kennedy told Kenneth O'Donnell that "he had made up his mind that after his reelection he would take the risk of unpopularity and make a complete withdrawal of American forces from Vietnam. 'In 1965 I'll be damned everywhere as a Communist appeaser. But I don't care. If I tried to pull out completely now, we would have another Joe McCarthy red scare on our hands, but I can do it after I'm reelected. So we had better make damned sure that I am reelected.'"[152]

During the spring and summer of 1963, conditions in Vietnam continued to deteriorate, precipitated by the government's sudden enforcement of an obsolete law against the public display of religious flags just days before the annual festival honoring Buddha's birthday. The Buddhists flew their flags anyway and defied the order to disperse given to them by the Catholic deputy province chief, who then ordered his troops to fire on the crowd. The ensuing riot left seven dead, including two children crushed by armored vehicles, and fifteen injured. The Diem government lied about the cause, saying a Vietcong agent had thrown a hand grenade into the crowd and that the victims had been crushed in a stampede. The CIA then also lied about the cause, saying that "the weight of evidence [indicates] that government cannon-fire caused the deaths in Hue."[153] This finding ignored the fact that "neither the Saigon government nor the Viet Cong possessed the kind of powerful plastic explosives that decapitated the victims at Hue on May 8. It was only the CIA that had such an explosive, as admitted later by Captain Scott, the U.S. military adviser responsible for the bombing . . . [which was a pattern started eleven years before with] the Agency's use of plastic bombs

148. Ibid.
149. Ibid., p. 124.
150. Ibid.
151. Marrs, p. 307.
152. O'Donnell, *Life* magazine, August 7, 1970, pp. 51–52, op. cit.; *Johnny . . .*, p. 16.
153. Douglass, p. 148.

in Saigon in 1952 to scapegoat the Viet Minh as terrorists . . . Both Kennedy and Diem had been outmaneuvered by the CIA."[154]

Ambassador Nolting said that he thought the crisis had passed and left with his family for a sailing vacation near Greece.[155]

The riots were followed by hunger strikes and mass demonstrations as the public realized how blatantly their government had been lying to them. The crisis was growing to new heights, and government soldiers began using tear gas to control the Buddhist demonstrators. The use of tear gas, or mustard gas, as some suspected, and the severe repression was beginning to pose a very big problem for the United States because of its continued support of the Diem regime. The violence increased daily, and on June 8 Madame Nhu (the outspoken wife of Diem's brother Nhu) exacerbated the tensions by claiming the Buddhists had been infiltrated by Communists. On June 11, Thich Quang Duc became the first monk to burn himself to death, in an ultimate protest, which would be repeated by other monks in the weeks and months ahead. Madame Nhu gleefully called his immolation a "barbecue" and said that if the Buddhists wanted to have another one, "I will be glad to supply the gasoline."[156]

By early 1963, Kennedy was planning to replace Ambassador Nolting with Edmund Gullion, whose diplomatic thinking was more in line with his own. But his secretary of state, Dean Rusk, opposed Gullion, despite his experience as Kennedy's trusted third world ambassador (in Congo), because he considered Gullion's diplomatic style as tilted too far toward ceding greater autonomy to other countries, afraid that anything less would be seen as exerting unfair domination—colonialism—over them.[157] This speaks volumes about Secretary Rusk's worldview as contrasted to Kennedy's; in the same way, Lyndon Johnson was clearly in sync with Rusk. Rusk argued for appointing Kennedy's old Massachusetts political adversary, Republican Henry Cabot Lodge, to take the air out of the Republican right's demands for an escalated war. But in doing this, he assumed that Lodge would act with some modicum of due deference and respect to Kennedy, which was not to be.[158] Instead, Lodge consulted Henry Luce, the archconservative *Time-Life* media magnate, for advice on how to approach his job as U.S. ambassador to South Vietnam.[159] Luce was one of the chief participants of the CIA's

---

154. Ibid. (ref. Ellen Hammer, *A Death in November: America in Vietnam*, Newspaper Hoa Binh's: 1963).

155. Newman, *JFK and Vietnam*, p. 332.

156. Ibid., pp. 333–334.

157. Douglass, pp. 150–151.

158. Ibid., p. 151.

159. Ibid., pp. 163–164.

Operation Mockingbird and had assisted the agency in previous sabotage activities in Vietnam for over ten years. Luce recommended that Lodge start by reading the *Time* articles on Vietnam by staff writer Charles Mohr, which convinced him that he needed to ignore Diem and ride roughshod over the country, imposing his own policies with the full support of the U.S. military and (CIA) intelligence agencies.[160] Unfortunately, he also felt he could ignore Kennedy.

When he appointed Lodge to be his Vietnam ambassador, he joked to his aides Kenny O'Donnell and Dave Powers about his motives: "The idea of getting Lodge mixed up in such a hopeless mess as the one in Vietnam was irresistible."[161] Regrettably, this joke backfired on JFK, costing him more of the little remaining power he had—over the military, the CIA, and many of his own cabinet members and advisers—to control the events that were rapidly unfolding in Saigon. Lodge had grasped primary control over U.S. policy toward Vietnam and would refuse not only to be guided by Kennedy's instructions, but also to even communicate his actions to the president.[162]

Dean Rusk's lackluster performance as secretary of state and his ineffectual foreign policy initiatives were disappointments for Kennedy, according to John Kenneth Galbraith; in August 1963, he had told Galbraith that after the election in November he might replace Rusk with McNamara as his secretary of state; however, he had some concerns about that when he admitted, "But then if I don't have McNamara at Defense to control the generals, I won't have a foreign policy."[163] According to Kennedy's assistant secretary of defense, William Bundy, a growing schism between the president and his military and CIA advisers had resulted in completely dysfunctional relationships; by late summer and into the fall of 1963, he had begun keeping his top CIA and Pentagon advisers out of his discussions on Vietnam.[164] The continual tensions between them led Kennedy to simply keep his thinking on the controversial subjects to himself and to a tight circle of friends. Kennedy had wanted to end the cold war while most of his official advisers wanted to win it, at all costs. By leaving them out of the loop, he had not fooled them; they knew how his sentiments were being shaped by such things as his aggressive support of the nuclear test ban treaty and the comments he made in his peace speech at American University in June.[165]

---

160. Ibid.
161. O'Donnell and Powers, p. 16.
162. Douglass, p. 152.
163. Douglass, p. 121.
164. Ibid., p. 162.
165. Ibid.

In the test-ban talks which followed the missile crisis, the Pentagon and the State Department weren't included in the negotiations; instead, the direct communication link between Washington and Moscow was utilized and a treaty was negotiated to ban nuclear testing, except for underground tests.[166] In the same process the confrontation over Berlin was ended, although it would not be permanently resolved until the wall was brought down almost three decades later.

At the same time that Kennedy was engaged in the test-ban negotiations and attempting to settle the strained relationship with Khrushchev, the Joint Chiefs were pressing for a renewed buildup of strategic forces, arguing for achieving a first-strike capability. On November 2, 1962, they sent a memorandum to Secretary McNamara that stated that such a capability is "feasible and desirable."[167] The previous year he had attended an NSC meeting in which this idea was first broached, and he asked a series of questions about such an attack's likely damage to the USSR and its impact on American citizens, such as how long they would have to remain in fallout shelters afterward. Deputy Secretary of Defense Gilpatric duly noted in his minutes that "finally Kennedy got up and walked right out in the middle of it, and that was the end of it."[168] Against the backdrop of mistrust, paranoia, and mutual derision, Jack Kennedy had begun to form his own ideas as to how to handle the multiple hot spots around the world: Berlin, Cuba, and Vietnam. In almost every aspect, they were positions at odds with those held firmly by the military and intelligence chiefs and of his vice president. In a series of speeches and executive actions, JFK effected changes which, for that era, were regarded by many people—the Joint Chiefs of Staff in particular—as belying a radically left-wing attitude. JFK's biographer Richard Reeves observed, "By moving so swiftly on the Moscow negotiations, Kennedy politically outflanked his own military on the most important military question of the time."[169] Kennedy himself mused about the irony that he and Khrushchev were in essentially the same position within their respective governments; both were trying to prevent nuclear war, but they were both under "severe pressure from [the] hard-line crowd, which interprets every move in that direction as appeasement."[170]

The situation was reported in the newspapers and magazines at the time; the *U.S. News and World Report* of August 5, 1963, contained an article

166. Ibid., p. 53.
167. Ibid., p. 237.
168. Ibid., p. 235.
169. Reeves, Richard, p. 554.
170. Douglas, p. 53 (ref. Cousins, Norman, *Improbable Triumvirate*, pp. 113–114).

headlined "Is U.S. Giving Up in the Arms Race" and referred to "many authorities in the military establishment, who now are silenced . . . [because the] new strategy adds up to a type of intentional and one-sided disarmament."[171] Another article followed in the next edition of the magazine, under the headline "If Peace Does Come—What Happens to Business?"[172]

In his ongoing battles with the Joint Chiefs of Staff, the CIA, and many of his own appointees at the highest levels of the executive department, the schism between the government in its largest context and himself was growing deeper and wider as summer turned into fall. Kennedy was rapidly losing control of his own administration and of the entire government it was supposed to direct. He realized as much when, in September, he discovered that someone had already pulled the plug on the commodity import program that propped up the South Vietnamese economy and might very well trigger a coup against Diem. The head of AID (Agency for International Development), David Bell, made a casual comment that stopped the discussion when he said, "'There's no point in talking about cutting off commodity aid. I've already cut it off' . . . 'You've done what?' said John Kennedy. 'Cut off commodity aid' said Bell. 'Who the hell told you to do that' asked the president. 'No one,' said Bell, 'It's an automatic policy. We do it whenever we have differences with a client government.'"[173]

The CIA had already done what the president had been deliberating, irrespective of the possible ramifications, in order to send a message to the Vietnamese dictator, as well as to the generals waiting in the wings to overthrow him. But the larger point was that it was a message the CIA was sending to the president, who was being told who was really in control of his government.[174] The shock John Kennedy felt this time was nothing compared to what he would later experience when he discovered that his own government had done an end run around him and his administration with the coup d'état in Vietnam and the assassination of Diem and his brother. Only then did he realize how little control he had over the CIA and the combined military organizations symbolized and headed by the Joint Chiefs of Staff.

JFK Attempts to Avoid United States Involvement

On June 10, 1963, Kennedy made his famous Peace Speech for the commencement address he gave to the 1963 graduates and their guests at

---

171. Ibid., p. 37.
172. *U.S. News and World Report*, August 12, 1963.
173. Douglass, pp. 142, 192.
174. Ibid.

American University. This speech came as a surprise to the attendees as well as the news media and his own administration since it was written in the White House, without Pentagon or State Department input or clearance. Kennedy called specifically for a whole new attitude toward the Soviet Union and renewed efforts to achieve world peace. It is the greatest understatement of this book that the Peace Speech was not received well through official Washington, especially the building with the largest footprint ever built, the five-sided one on the Virginia side of the Potomac River named for its polygonal shape; similarly, the views of those on the big campus located about eight miles up the river in Langley were also less than enthusiastic.

The following week Kennedy was brought back to reality; he had received a new proposal by the State Department and the Pentagon to start bombing North Vietnam and to begin mining North Vietnamese ports. This was just another in a long series of proposals for war in Southeast Asia that he had rejected as he attempted to reassert his developing view that the stakes were too high for a continuing increased commitment of U.S. troops. The warnings of such men as de Gaulle and his own advisers John Kenneth Galbraith and Edmund Gullion, Senators Mansfield and Morse, and even Generals Douglas McArthur and David M. Shoup had convinced him that it would be a catastrophic mistake to become any more entangled in Vietnam than was already the case. He struggled furiously with the arguments for and against, but listened intently to these military men who strongly advised against it. Retired General Douglas McArthur had told the president in late April, "Anyone wanting to commit American ground forces to the mainland of Asia should have his head examined."[175] General Shoup would warn him eleven days before he left for Dallas that "unless we were prepared to use a million men in a major drive, we should pull out before the war expanded beyond control."[176]

On August 14, 1963, at Kennedy's insistence, Diem was advised that his present relationship with the United States would be in jeopardy if he did not announce a conciliatory policy toward the Buddhists and other critics of his regime. During this period, Kennedy had begun floating the idea of a gradual withdrawal of American personnel from Vietnam, starting in 1963 and planning for a complete withdrawal by the end of 1965. The plan involved taking the men out in four increments. Despite the disagreement of the Joint Chiefs of Staff, by October 11 he would issue NSAM 263, calling for a thousand-man withdrawal by the end of the year, although the directive

175. Schlesinger, *Thousand Days*, p. 338.
176. Douglass, p. 182.

stated that no formal announcement be made of the implementation of this order. The primary reason for the secrecy was that he was not yet ready to announce his intentions to Diem.

On August 24, 1963, Kennedy was at Hyannis Port, Rusk in New York, McNamara mountain climbing in Wyoming, and McCone vacationing in California when a series of cables came in from Lodge in Saigon regarding the aftermath of the Nhu's crackdown on Buddhists known as the "pagoda raids." Nolting had told Diem that he felt this was a deliberate affront, coming just as a change in ambassadors was being completed, after the appointment of Henry Cabot Lodge. As a proposed response, Roger Hilsman, with Harriman's support, drafted "the single most controversial cable" of the Vietnam War, miring Kennedy in a plot to overthrow Diem and creating a fundamental division in his administration.[177] The cable's genesis remains controversial because Hilsman claims that he sent a copy to Secretary Rusk, and that he strengthened it; however, Rusk denied that he had seen it or had modified it. Unfortunately, Rusk systematically destroyed many records and refused to make his personal records available. The cable was read to Kennedy by Forrestal and then began to be passed around like a hot potato, with different accounts of how it evolved. The cable reflected the desire of Hilsman and Forrestal to depose Diem and had the effect of forcing Kennedy into backing that action, though it went against his own intentions.[178] The germ of this idea became established, and it grew over the next several weeks. The new ambassador, Henry Cabot Lodge, did not think the Diem government was capable of handling itself any better than it had and complained that trying to fix it by getting rid of the Nhus would be regarded by the generals as "a sign of American indecision and delay."[179] Forrestal got Kennedy to endorse the telegram on the basis that all of his advisers had approved the wording for the telegram, which included this phrase: "We wish [to] give Diem reasonable opportunity to remove [the] Nhus, but if he remains obdurate, then we are prepared to accept the obvious implication that we can no longer support Diem." The coldest translation of this statement was that Kennedy had officially endorsed the removal of Diem if he failed to remove the Nhus.[180] The cable was transmitted on Saturday, August 24.

By August of 1963, JFK had managed to keep Lyndon Johnson out of the Vietnam issue for over two years, by simply not inviting him to participate

---

177. Newman, *JFK and Vietnam*, pp. 345–347.
178. Ibid., pp. 348–350.
179. Ibid., pp. 354–355.
180. Douglass, p. 163.

in meetings of his top advisers at the White House. Kennedy's respite from Johnson's presence at his deliberations on Vietnam was about to end, however; it came on a day, August 31, when Kennedy was at Hyannis Port and could not attend the meeting of this group. Taking advantage of that development, Lyndon Johnson, who had not attended these meetings for two years, was there, but he was not happy. He complained about having been left out of Vietnam planning and that he had not known about the "Saturday cable" until Tuesday evening. He said that the generals had failed to organize a coup, so he thought that ties to the Diem government should be reestablished as quickly as possible and then we should get on with fighting the war against the Vietcong. Johnson's comments were "harsh and aggressive" and had a chilling effect on everyone else present.[181] "'We must establish ourselves,' Johnson profoundly announced, 'and stop playing cops and robbers.'"[182] Johnson was simply against Kennedy's conciliatory initiatives intended to democratize Vietnam, and in favor of whatever autocratic measures that might solidify the U.S. presence needed to take control over the country. Lyndon Johnson's 1963 position on Vietnam could not have been more diametrically opposed to John F. Kennedy's; undoubtedly, Johnson would have exploited their differences, using his military and intelligence contacts to muster whatever advantage he could.

Johnson's role had surfaced momentarily, while Kennedy was out of town; when he returned, he told Walter Cronkite, in an interview on September 2, about why he could not continue supporting Diem: "Unless a greater effort is made by the government to win popular support [I don't think] that the war can be won out there. In the final analysis, it is their war. They are the ones who have to win or lose it. We can help them, we can give them equipment, we can send our men out there as advisers . . . but in the final analysis it is their people and their government who have to win or lose this struggle. All we can do is help."[183] Kennedy still hoped that they could persuade Diem to stop the repressive activities of his brother and sister-in-law, and repeatedly tried to get Lodge to keep trying this approach. But Lodge was completely out of step with Kennedy and becoming more aligned with Lyndon Johnson; he had divorced himself from his actual superiors, Dean Rusk, the secretary of state, and the president, when he said, "The best chance of doing it is by the generals taking over the government lock, stock, and barrel . . . I am contemplating no further talks with Diem at this time."[184]

---

181. Newman, *JFK and Vietnam*, pp. 355–356.
182. Ibid., pp. 355–356.
183. O'Donnell, p. 383.
184. Douglass, p. 165.

Henry Cabot Lodge had quickly established himself with the Vietnamese generals through longtime CIA operative Colonel Lucien Conine, who had known them for years. He also aligned himself with those who felt that the sooner the coup, the better. Secretary of State Rusk gave Ambassador Lodge "a free hand as long as the ambassador minimized 'the appearance of collusion with the Generals.' Certain that the 'ship of state' in Vietnam was 'slowly sinking,' Lodge saw a 'drastic change in government' as the only answer to the difficulties in South Vietnam."[185] Diem and Nhu escaped from the palace on a Friday night, eluding the soldiers surrounding it, and were driven by an aide to Cholon. It was there, at the home of a Chinese businessman, where Diem made his last phone call to Henry Cabot Lodge, asking him for the help he had promised in order to protect his "physical safety." Lodge offered to give them asylum and do what he could for them, but declined an offer by his own assistant, Mike Dunn, to go to them and bring them back to the embassy, something that President Kennedy would have wanted them to do. Lodge said to Dunn, "We can't. We just can't get that involved."[186]

On Saturday morning, November 2, Diem and Nhu left the house in Cholon to go to a nearby Catholic church. They had just taken communion when a convoy of two armed jeeps and an armored personnel carrier pulled up in front of the church, sent by General Minh. Based upon what Lodge had told Diem on the phone, he thought they were to be taken to the airport for a flight to another country. Unbeknownst to Diem was the fact that the CIA had no available aircraft capable of flying him far enough away for safe asylum, other than the Boeing 707 that was being held for Ambassador Lodge, of course. Diem and brother Nhu were led to the armored personnel carrier, protesting that it was unseemly for the president to travel in such a fashion when a simple car would do. General Minh's personal bodyguard, Captain Nguyen Van Nhung, a professional assassin who had killed forty people, assisted them as they climbed aboard the vehicle then down the hatch. Major Duong Hieu Nghia shot them point-blank with his submachine gun while Captain Nhung sprayed them with bullets before using a knife on them.[187]

Meanwhile, Back in Washington, DC

As author McMasters described Kennedy's lapse of control leading up to the coup against Diem, "The president seemed ambivalent. Advice from

---

185. McMaster, p. 39.
186. Ibid., p. 209.
187. Ibid., p. 210.

his brother and Taylor almost swayed him, but, at the end of the meeting, Kennedy declared indecisively that he would 'discourage' a coup only if Lodge, on whom he depended to generate Republican support for his policy, shared Taylor's and Robert Kennedy's misgivings. On October 31, McGeorge Bundy instructed Lodge that 'once a coup under responsible leadership has begun . . . it is in the interest of the U.S. government that it should succeed.' Diem's fate was sealed."[188] On Saturday morning, Kennedy held a meeting at the White House with his principal advisers on Vietnam. As the meeting began, the fates of Diem and Nhu were not known, but Michael Forrestal soon walked in with a telegram from Lodge, which said that "Diem and Nhu were both dead, and the coup leaders were claiming their deaths to be suicide."[189] General Maxwell Taylor, seated next to Kennedy in the cabinet room, described Kennedy's reaction: "Kennedy leaped to his feet and rushed from the room with a look of shock and dismay on his face which I had never seen before. He had always insisted that Diem must never suffer more than exile and has been led to believe or had persuaded himself that a change in government could be carried out without bloodshed."[190]

Kennedy had sent Defense Secretary Robert McNamara and Gen. Maxwell Taylor, chairman of the Joint Chiefs and a Kennedy appointee, on a trip to Vietnam in September, and upon their return they advised Kennedy that conditions had improved so impressively that all military personnel could be withdrawn by the end of 1965. Unbeknownst to McNamara and Taylor, their report had been ghostwritten by John and Robert Kennedy and dictated to General Victor Krulak, whose editorial and stenographic team in the Pentagon compiled the raw data being received from McNamara and Taylor. Krulak had been invited to come to the White House to confer with the Kennedys during this trip, and their combined efforts produced a nicely typed report that was bound in a leather cover, flown to Hawaii, and handed to McNamara and Taylor to read on their trip back to Washington.[191] Acting on this new information, Kennedy approved an accelerated withdrawal program,

---

188. McMaster, pp. 40–41 (ref. Bromley K. Smith, Memorandum of Conference between the President, October 29, 1963, 4:20 p.m., Subject: Vietnam, Temporary Box 16, Meetings on Vietnam August–November 1963 (Diem Coup), Papers of Bromley K. Smith, LBJ Library. For confirmation of Harkins's ignorance of coup plans, see Cable, Harkins to Taylor, October 30, 1963, in Gravel, The Papers, Vol. 2, pp. 784–785, and Historical Division of the Joint Secretariat, the Joint Chiefs of Staff and the War in Vietnam, part 1, chap. 7, p. 30).
189. Douglass, pp. 210–211.
190. Ibid. (ref. Maxwell D. Taylor, *Swords and Plowshares*, New York: W.W. Norton, 1972, p. 301).
191. Douglass, p. 187 (ref. Fletcher Prouty, interview by David Ratcliffe, *Understanding Special Operations and Their Impact of the Vietnam War Era*, Santa Cruz, CA: rat haus reality press, 1999, pp. 71–72).

designed to accomplish this complete withdrawal by the end of 1965. A few weeks later, after Kennedy's assassination, amazingly, the same two officials who gave this advice to John Kennedy gave opposite advice to Lyndon Johnson, who had already rescinded the Kennedy plan to withdraw troops just days after his assassination. Instead, the new president, Lyndon Johnson, now decided that a major effort, including American combat troops and a massive clandestine program, was needed to prevent a Communist victory. National Security Action Memorandum (NSAM) 273 went well beyond just canceling the troop withdrawal; it also changed the military objective from "assisting" the Vietnamese to "winning" against the Communists.[192] In fact, as will be seen, the first draft of NSAM 273 was written even before Kennedy left Washington on his fateful, and fatal, trip to Dallas.

As reported by Dick Russell, strange things were afoot by November 21, 1963, at the summit conference on Vietnam in Honolulu. Kennedy's highest-level military advisers, several cabinet members, and Ambassador Lodge attended the meeting. All attendees were provided VIP suites in military quarters, but Lodge turned that down and rented a suite at the Royal Hawaiian Hotel. "There, shortly after lunch on the day before Kennedy's assassination, he was noticed by a reporter for the Honolulu *Star-Bulletin* putting coin after coin into a pay phone in the lobby. The newspaper found this incident worthy of remark, since Lodge had ready access to phones in the privacy of his room or through military circuits."[193] The question this raises—why would Ambassador Lodge need to resort to the use of a pay phone on this date?—can only be answered one of two ways: He was either afraid the hotel room phones were tapped and didn't want to be recorded, or he did not want a paper trail showing to whom he talked—or both of the above. Henry Cabot Lodge had been on his way to Washington to meet with President Kennedy; unbeknownst to him was the fact that JFK had planned to fire him at their meeting on November 24, after his return from Dallas. According to Robert Kennedy, "We were going to try to get rid of Henry Cabot Lodge . . . [it was only a matter of] trying to work out how he could be fired, how we could get rid of him" because he refused to carry out JFK's instructions, or even bother to respond to them; he would not communicate with Kennedy.[194] Given his refusal to communicate with Kennedy, together with the presence of all other high administration officials (except for Johnson) with him there in Hawaii on November 21, the question of whom he had the need to communicate with, using a pay phone in the hotel

192. Marrs, *Crossfire: The Plot That Killed Kennedy*, p. 308.
193. Russell, p. 567 (ref. J. Gary Shaw with Larry R. Harris, *Cover-up*, Cleburne, TX.: self-published, 1976, p. 200.
194. Douglass, pp. 374–375.

lobby on that date to maintain secrecy, raises profound questions as to his alliances and whose agenda he was trying to accomplish, given that it wasn't Kennedy's.

Shortly before his death, Kennedy gave Mike Forrestal odds of a hundred to one that the United States could *not* win in Vietnam. But he also knew that he could not get out before the elections in November 1964, without inviting his own political eclipse . . . He told Forrestal, "I want to start a complete and very profound review of how we got into this country, what we thought we were doing and what we now think we can do . . . I even want to think about whether or not we should be there."[195] Just an hour before he departed for Texas on November 21, 1963, he told Assistant Press Secretary Malcolm Kilduff, "I've just been given a list of the most recent casualties in Vietnam. We're losing too damn many people over there. It's time for us to get out. The Vietnamese aren't fighting for themselves. We're the ones who are doing the fighting . . . After I come back from Texas, that's going to change. There's no reason for us to lose another man over there. Vietnam is not worth another American life."[196] He had also told his friend columnist Charles Bartlett, "We don't have a prayer of staying in Vietnam. We don't have a prayer of prevailing there. Those people hate us. They are going to throw our tails out of there at almost any point. But I can't give up a piece of territory like that to the Communists and then get the American people to reelect me."[197]

Kennedy's friend and personal aide Kenneth O'Donnell said that "he never would have committed U.S. Army combat units and draftees to action against the Viet Cong. Lyndon Johnson's charge in his 1971 memoirs that the Kennedy administration's support of the coup that finally overthrew the Diem-Nhu regime in Saigon was 'a serious blunder which caused deep political confusion' would have astonished Kennedy . . . The killing of Diem and his brother during the coup, after their safe removal from the country had been guaranteed by the military leaders of the revolt, came as a shock to President Kennedy and made him all the more resolved to withdraw from further entanglement in the Vietnam war."[198] Somehow, Lyndon Johnson had managed to portray John F. Kennedy as the architect of the Diem assassination when in fact it was the combination of the intelligence and military forces supported by Johnson which caused it; Lyndon Johnson had managed, in his book at least, to turn the facts around to portray Kennedy as

195. Schlesinger, p. 779 (ref. Brandon, *Anatomy of Error*, p. 30).
196. Douglass, p. 304; Livingstone, p. 503.
197. Ibid., p. 181.
198. O'Donnell, pp. 383–384.

the conniving antagonist and murderer while presenting himself as a friend and benefactor of the unfortunate and misunderstood Ngo Dinh Diem.

If John F. Kennedy was disappointed in some of his cabinet selections by 1962, none of them would have compared to his biggest disappointment: His vice president, whose abject failure to accomplish any of the objectives Kennedy had set for him on his May 1961 trip to Vietnam, was only part of that failed mission. His attempt to curry his own personal favors with President Diem had also impeded Kennedy's goals related to the neutralization of Laos and maintaining stability in Vietnam without introducing U.S. troops. There were many other issues Kennedy was experiencing with Johnson on the home front as well, one of which was his feckless leadership on the Equal Opportunity Commission, which JFK had appointed him to head. The ongoing scandal involving Johnson's involvement with Billie Sol Estes, including his pressure on the Department of Agriculture to accommodate the massive fraud being carried out, which would hit the front pages of practically every newspaper in the country in the spring of 1962, would have certainly given the president some degree of concern, regardless of his public statements to the contrary. The continuation of the scandals surrounding Johnson in 1963, with the name of Bobby Baker replacing Estes's in all the newspapers, would have only increased the presidential anxiety. By October of that year, the Senate investigations threatened to replace Baker's name with that of Johnson and his associates, possibly putting the credibility of his entire administration in jeopardy.

Chapter 3

WASHINGTON AFFAIRS CIRCA 1960–1963

The great enemy of the truth is very often not the lie—deliberate, contrived, and dishonest—but the myth: persistent, persuasive, and unrealistic.

—JOHN F. KENNEDY

The Spy in the White House

John F. Kennedy and his brother Robert, though now venerated by many for their public-spirited idealism and the aggressiveness with which they tackled the great issues of their time, were nonetheless hated viscerally by their enemies for the same qualities. Their political enemies on the right felt that their risk-taking aggressiveness was reckless and their idealism was putting the country at risk of being overcome by its Communist enemies. Their enemies in the Mafia, who felt they had been ambushed by John and Robert, after having helped their father get them elected in 1960, thought they had been used and abused by them. The oilmen of Texas had given at least partial support for the Democratic ticket because of Johnson's presence, but then felt they were being double-crossed as well. Unfortunately for JFK, his decision to allow Lyndon B. Johnson to be his partner put the primary leader of his opposition—the military and the intelligence agencies, the oil barons, the defense contractors, even the Southern segregationists—into the White House.

From the very first days of the Kennedy administration, behind the scenes in the Oval Office, Lyndon Johnson had begun to spy on the president. That story begins with an account of Johnson's daily morning routine; according to JFK's secretary, Evelyn Lincoln,[1]

> [Johnson] started out, from the very beginning, to spend as much time as he possibly could around the White House. There were two

---

1. Lincoln, pp. 149–151.

doors in my office that opened out on the colonnade that led to the South Lawn. Mr. Johnson chose to enter the West Wing through one of the doors of my office. Nearly every morning he would open that door, grunt, and pause for a moment to look around to see what was going on. He would look into the President's office to see if Mr. Kennedy was there, or pause to talk to people who came in and out of my office. If there was nothing to attract his attention, he would amble over to the other door and go out into the hall . . .

One morning he was a little late coming through the door and when he arrived Mr. Kennedy was standing near my desk. They exchanged greetings and Mr. Johnson proceeded on his way to the hall. After Mr. Johnson had gone, Mr. Kennedy turned to me and said, "Does he use this door very often?" "Every day," I replied. "What is he doing in these offices?" Mr. Kennedy asked.

Mrs. Lincoln then talked to Johnson's chauffer and learned that he always let him out near a sidewalk leading to the president's office on the South Lawn. Johnson would then walk up that sidewalk past the windows to the Oval Office and into the door leading to her adjacent office. From there he would then proceed into the hallway leading to the reception room. By taking this meandering route to get to his own office, Johnson left the image—so he thought, anyway—that he was an integral part of Kennedy's team, closely working beside him at all times. There would invariably be reporters or high-level officials in the outer offices who would benefit from such an impression, regardless of what everyone else might have thought about it, including, evidently, even JFK. Johnson's peculiar, habitual actions fed widely based speculation about his possible motive: more than one report of him was ground through the rumor mills of the federal bureaucracy in Washington, which accused the vice president of having a mole in the White House; the mole was usually reported to be a Secret Service agent who was rewarded for solid information on JFK's nonpublic activities and for overhearing private conversations in the West Wing.[2]

There is little doubt that Mrs. Lincoln's suspicion that Johnson was engaged in routine reconnaissance of the Oval Office was shared by other Kennedy aides. According to Kenneth O'Donnell, Johnson also maneuvered Kennedy into allowing him unfettered access to the Oval Office; based upon the nuances of both his and Mrs. Lincoln's statement, this perk could have only been given after Kennedy became conscious of Johnson's actions: "Only two men in the government, Johnson and Bobby Kennedy,

2. Morrow, pp. 125, 145.

were given the special privilege of entering the President's office at any time unseen through the back door from the garden, without following the normal route into the front door and through my [O'Donnell's] office."[3] That special privilege was implicitly given to him after the fact since Johnson started his routine from the first days of the administration, and according to Mrs. Lincoln's account, JFK only became aware of it at a later date. It would appear, in retrospect, that that must have been one huge mistake, rather like giving the keys to the chicken house to a hungry, conniving fox.

Meanwhile, as Johnson was manipulating and sabotaging the president he had sworn to support, John Kennedy mistakenly thought that he had neutralized Johnson by putting him into the vice presidency; he had told an angry Kenneth O'Donnell, when the announcement was being made in Los Angeles, "I'm forty-three years old, and I'm the healthiest candidate for president . . . I'm not going to die in office. So the vice presidency doesn't mean anything . . . I won't be able to live with Lyndon Johnson as the leader of a small Senate majority. Did it occur to you that if Lyndon becomes the vice president, I'll have Mike Mansfield as the Senate leader, somebody I can trust and depend on?"[4] Clearly, John F. Kennedy had finally come to terms with putting a man he deeply distrusted into the vice presidency, not because he thought he could be an effective member of his administration, but to put him into what he considered a dead-end position so that he could achieve his legislative objectives with someone more reliable on Capitol Hill. In fact, as will be seen in chapter 5, Kennedy had been forced into accepting Johnson because he was blackmailed by the aging, duplicitous, and conniving director of the FBI, who was enlisted by Johnson for that very purpose.[5]

Unfortunately for JFK, he had not factored in Johnson's absolute resolve to become president himself, much less how Johnson would undermine his efforts to achieve his objectives on both the domestic and foreign policy agendas.

The Georgetown Crowd, circa 1960

After World War II, a group of people involved in Washington journalism, politics, and covert intelligence began meeting on a regular basis in the long-trendy area of Washington known as Georgetown, thus becoming a

---

3. O'Donnell, Kenneth: *Life* magazine, August 7, 1970, p. 47; *Johnny . . .* , p. 254.
4. Ibid.; *Johnny . . .* , p. 7.
5. Ibid.

group that was referred to as the "Georgetown crowd." Many of them had gone to the same Ivy League universities or worked together; others had been members of the military intelligence agency, OSS (Office of Strategic Services), during the war. Many of the OSS alumni eventually became employed at the highest levels of the Central Intelligence Agency. They strongly supported FDR, yet generally thought that his policies were not radical enough; their views on domestic issues were said to be even more progressive than Roosevelt's. The difference in these distinctions was that they did not believe that American socialists/Communists were a threat to U.S. national security, and they essentially agreed with conservatives with respect to U.S. foreign policy: that the Communists running the Soviet Union and China should not be allowed to take over the smaller, third world countries around the world.

The Alsop brothers—Stewart and Joseph—having returned from service in both of the respective theaters of World War II in 1946, became Georgetown fixtures as well as collaborators in their syndicated newspaper columns and as *Saturday Evening Post* feature writers. Their political influence, based in large part by their ubiquitous presence at Georgetown dinner parties, was directed toward containing Communism in general and Soviet expansionism in particular. Their frame of reference was grounded by a common goal of bringing order to the chaos in countries left ravaged or destroyed by the war. The biggest fruit of their work with key statesmen in Washington was the Marshall Plan; some of the statesmen with whom they collaborated were Averell Harriman, Dean Acheson, Robert Lovett, John McCloy, George Kennan, and Chip Bohlen, who were considered among the original "best and brightest." Joseph Alsop became their leading chronicler, identifying with them in all their causes. Unfortunately, his association with them led him to follow the groupthink attitude into some areas where its simplistic and uncritical application—absent a thorough vetting from an honest debate—produced tragic results.

The Georgetown crowd included Frank Wisner, Richard Bissell, Cord Meyer, Richard Helms, Desmond FitzGerald, Tracy Barnes, Philip Graham, Clark Clifford, Walt Rostow, Eugene Rostow, William Bundy, McGeorge Bundy, William Averell Harriman, John McCloy, Felix Frankfurter, John Sherman Cooper, James Reston, Allen W. Dulles, Paul Nitze, Adlai Stevenson, James Forrestal, William O. Douglas, Dean Acheson, and George Kennan. The legendary CIA master spook James Jesus Angleton and his wife Cicely were also members of this clique, at least until Cicely left him in 1959; Angleton himself became trapped in his own paranoia about this time, which fed his infamous mole hunts, in 1961 with the defection of KGB agent Anatoliy Golitsyn and in 1964, with Yuri Nosenko.

Many of the wives of the married men of this group assumed active participation in it as well, forming another group called the Georgetown Ladies' Social Club, which included women such as Katharine Graham, Pamela Harriman, Polly Wisner, Lorraine Cooper, Evangeline Bruce, Sally Reston, Janet Barnes, Tish Alsop, Cynthia Helms, Marietta FitzGerald, Phyllis Nitze, Annie Bissell, and Mary Pinchot Meyer. The wives of the CIA men—Angleton, Wisner, Barnes, Helms, Fitzgerald, and Meyer—were put in a unique position of access to extremely sensitive and valuable material, and the ladies, though no doubt admonished to be discreet, nevertheless became channels for distribution of certain highly confidential information. Their close connections between the center of the federal government— the executive, legislative, and judicial branches as well as its intelligence apparatus—juxtaposed with the core of the Fourth Estate (also known as the American press, and its constitutional mandate to flush and dispense sensitive information), formed a conundrum that was extremely detrimental to Mary Pinchot Meyer, as we will explore shortly.

An assortment of other politicians also socialized with these people, even some whose diplomatic and social skills would seem to be rather incongruent with the Ivy League background of many of the above names, probably caused by a kind of "moth to a fire" phenomenon—men like Lyndon B. Johnson and Joseph McCarthy, for example. Johnson was a peripheral member of this group, attending many of the same parties and often playing poker with some of the men. Arguably the smartest thing Johnson ever did was to ingratiate himself into the exclusive Georgetown social scene. Despite his hard edges and crudeness, Johnson gained entrée early on with Phil Graham, Joseph Alsop, Drew Pearson, and several other columnists, which gave him direct access to every newspaper in the country; in many cases, the stories to be planted by him were also being pushed simultaneously by the CIA, through the same network of newspapers, journalists, and syndicated columnists.

Although the Georgetown group generally supported Truman's policies, they believed he was not sufficiently proactive regarding national security concerns, specifically his anti-Communist strategy. This caused Frank Wisner and George Kennan to create, with Secretary of Defense James Forrestal's approval, the Office of Special Projects in 1948; it was later renamed the Office of Policy Coordination (OPC), which became the espionage and counterintelligence branch of the Central Intelligence Agency. Frank Wisner was made the original director of OPC, charged with the creation of "propaganda, economic warfare; preventive direct action, including sabotage, anti-sabotage, demolition and evacuation measures; subversion against hostile states, including assistance to underground resistance groups, and support of indigenous anti-Communist elements in threatened countries of the free world."[6] His organization evolved and became the agency's Plans Division in 1951, when Wisner succeeded Allen W. Dulles. In the 1950s, Frank Wisner was intent on establishing direct contacts between the agency and the Fourth Estate—the American press—journalists and book publishers who would willingly assist the CIA to communicate their view on any national or international political or military issue in a favorable light. The principal responsibility of both the OPC and, subsequently, the Plans Division, was the conduct of secret political operations, in contrast to the other agency functions of gathering intelligence and making analysis.

The Beginning of Operation Mockingbird

In 1951, Wisner established Operation Mockingbird, a program to influence the American media. "'Wisner recruited Philip Graham (*Washington Post*) to run the project within the industry,' according to Deborah Davis, in *Katharine the Great*: 'By the early 1950s, Wisner "owned" respected members of *The New York Times, Newsweek, CBS* and other communications vehicles.'"[7] These journalists sometimes wrote articles that were unofficially commissioned by Cord Meyer, based on leaked classified information from the CIA.

As noted earlier, Lyndon Johnson had struggled with recurrent bouts of depression since he was a child, but he was not alone among the men of the Georgetown crowd to have this burden. Phil Graham was one of Wisner's first recruits; he was the publisher of *The Washington Post*, until his own death by a gunshot to the head in 1963 stemming from a long and brutal fight with himself as a manic-depressive. Frank Wisner suffered from the same disease as his friend and collaborator Graham; Wisner became upset in November and December 1956 because of what he felt was the agency's abandonment of Hungarian citizens who had been encouraged by the agency to revolt against Soviet domination. He told friends that he felt that Eisenhower had let Hungary down, pointing out that the agency had spent a great deal of money on Radio Free Europe "to get these people to revolt."[8] In fact, Wisner felt personally betrayed by this behavior, claiming to Clare Boothe Luce that twenty thousand people were killed: "All these people are getting killed and we weren't doing anything, we were ignoring it."[9] The stress and anxiety this produced led to a mental breakdown. Wisner was subsequently treated

---

6. From The Arlington National Cemetery website: http://arlingtoncemetery.net/fgwisner.htm
7. Davis, Deborah, p. 146.
8. From The Arlington National Cemetery website http://www.arlingtoncemetery.net/fgwisner.htm
9. Ibid.

for this condition but could not continue in his previous position. He served for a time in the more relaxed London offices before taking early retirement. Two years after Graham shot himself, so did Wisner; since then, mercifully, pharmaceutical advances have made this disease more manageable.

Philip Graham became the de facto vice chairman of Operation Mockingbird, helping Wisner to recruit other willing journalists. According to Deborah Davis, "By the early 1950s, Wisner had implemented his plan and 'owned' respected members of *The New York Times*, *Newsweek*, *CBS* and other communications vehicles, plus stringers, four to six hundred in all, according to a former CIA analyst. By 1953 the CIA, through Wisner and Graham, had a major influence over 25 major newspapers and wire agencies."[10] Wisner also recruited several members of the Georgetown crowd, including "Richard Bissell, Desmond FitzGerald, Tracy Barnes, and Cord Meyer. Other former members of the OSS such as Arthur Schlesinger worked closely with this group."[11] To make Operation Mockingbird work effectively, Wisner realized that he could not rely only on journalists and publishers like Arthur Hays Sulzberger of *The New York Times*, who shared the Georgetown crowd view of the world. He therefore set out to recruit conservatives like William Paley (CBS), C. D. Jackson, and Henry Luce (of *Time* and *Life* magazines). According to Alex Constantine (*Mockingbird: The Subversion of the Free Press by the CIA*), in the 1950s, "Some 3,000 salaried and contract CIA employees were eventually engaged in propaganda efforts."[12] One of the most important journalists under the control of Operation Mockingbird was Joseph Alsop, whose articles appeared in over three hundred different newspapers. Other journalists willing to promote the views of the Central Intelligence Agency included Stewart Alsop (*New York Herald Tribune*), Ben Bradlee (*Newsweek*), James Reston (*New York Times*), Walter Pincus (*Washington Post*), Herb Gold (*Miami News*), and Charles Bartlett (*Chattanooga Times*).[13]

Many of the same columnists targeted by Wisner and his men were already in the pocket of Lyndon B. Johnson—notably Joseph Alsop—and information in Hoover's "official and confidential" files, which was readily shared with Johnson on request as will be seen shortly,[14] gave him an additional special entrée to these journalists. It was no coincidence that the man who first advanced Johnson's name as a vice presidential candidate in 1960—first to Sam Rayburn and then to the Kennedys—was none other than Johnson's friend Philip Graham. Although we'll never know one way or the other, it

10. Davis, Deborah, p. 139.
11. The Arlington National Cemetery website. [op. cit.]
12. Ibid.
13. Ibid.
14. Summers, *Official and Confidential*, pp. 339–348.

may be that the already-charismatic Phil Graham, in an unusually climactic moment with his charm at full splendor, helped to seduce John F. Kennedy to accept, against his better judgement, Senator Lyndon B. Johnson of Texas as his vice presidential choice. Perhaps Graham even convincingly argued that Johnson would add balance to the ticket precisely where Kennedy would need it most: in the South and West.

In August 1952, the CIA reorganized itself again, merging the Office of Policy Coordination and the Office of Special Operations (the espionage division) into the new Directorate of Plans (DPP). Wisner was put in charge of the new, much-larger organization, and Richard Helms became its chief of operations. The DPP being run by Wisner represented 60 percent of the total personnel within the CIA. About this time Wisner and Dulles were plotting the overthrow of Iran's government, led by Prime Minister Mohammed Mossadegh, who had upset the U.S. government when Iran nationalized their oil industry and carried out radical changes in their agricultural sector, including collective farming and government land ownership. The agency's Operation Ajax succeeded in bringing down Mossadegh's government. The supreme ruler, Mohammad Reza Shah—the shah of Iran—remained until he was overthrown by the fundamentalist Shia clergy, who came to power as a result of widespread concerns about the rapid modernization occurring under the shah. Another reason for the backlash was a deep-seated resentment among the Iranian population about the CIA-backed overthrow of Mossadegh and the residual suspicions about U.S. meddling in their national affairs. The long tail of political backlash was not figured in the calculation of the immediate success in the CIA's sponsorship of this particular coup d'état.

J. Edgar Hoover had continued deep suspicions about the CIA, especially the DPP section, which he referred to as "Wisner's weirdoes" because he felt it had usurped powers that rightfully belonged to "his" bureau. The feud between the CIA and FBI came to a boil when the FBI started carrying out investigations into the past of some of Wisner's top officials; it was soon discovered that a number of them had been active in left-wing politics during the 1930s. Hoover passed this information to his friend, Joseph McCarthy, who started making attacks on some of Wisner's staff. Hoover had also collected details of an affair that Wisner had had with Princess Caradja in Romania during the war; Hoover claimed that the princess was a Soviet agent and fed this information to McCarthy as well.[15] To Joseph McCarthy, for whom the only good Communist was a dead Communist, the nuances of philosophical thought or the socioeconomic-geographic-political environment of respective

---

15. The Arlington National Cemetery website. [op. cit.]

countries did not evoke much interest; he simply wanted as much fodder as he could get, and his pal Hoover was glad to provide it.[16]

J. Edgar Hoover

The truth about J. Edgar Hoover had been well hidden throughout his forty-eight-year term as the head of the FBI. Although many people had long suspected that he was far more enigmatic than he appeared, most of the nation still held him in high esteem, as the ultimate protector of core American values, by the time of his death in 1973. Within two years of that, the truth about him began emerging; a *Time* magazine article in December 1975 would help start the cleansing process:[17]

> He was a brilliant chameleon. But he was also a master con man. That takes intelligence of a certain kind, an astuteness, a shrewdness. He never read anything that would broaden his mind or give depth to his thinking. I never knew him to have an intellectual or educated friend. Neither did Tolson. They lived in their own strange little world.
>
> Sullivan told *Time* that Hoover was so intrigued by stories about expanding life spans through medical rejuvenation that he "ordered FBI officials in Switzerland to send him reports about a Swiss physician's formula for prolonging life." Added Sullivan: "He was a man with the ability to carry on 33 fights at the same time without slackening his pace or confusing one fight with another. He was always fighting—with other Government officials, with the immigration people, with the customs agency, with anyone who criticized him. The fights seemed to stimulate him." The result was an arcane world in which the Washington headquarters, where Hoover reigned so autocratically, was grandiosely referred to in internal FBI memos as the Seat of Government (SOG).

Joseph P. Kennedy had known how to handle J. Edgar Hoover because they were of the same age and shared many friends and values; they were a lot alike. Many of their mutual friends were key Mafia leaders. Ironically, the thirty-five-year-old son of Joseph in 1961 became the attorney general and boss over the sixty-eight-year-old Hoover; Bobby Kennedy had already targeted some of these same friends of his father in his quest to clean up organized crime. The vitriol between Hoover and John and Robert Kennedy was wide, deep, and occasionally stunningly petty: In May 1962, JFK personally ordered that

16. Summers, *Official and Confidential*, pp. 179, 182.
17. *Time*, December 22, 1975 (See http://www.time.com/time/magazine/article/0,9171, 879566-4,00.html#ixzz0XrzvF5NB)

"Hoover's dogs [be] retagged so that his own can be given the top three numbers in the district."[18] "All this meant that Vice President Johnson's beagle, Little Beagle Johnson, slipped to four and J. Edgar Hoover's cairn terriers to five and six."[19]

Those were strange times, indeed: The chief of the FBI—a tyrannical demagogue and bully, unbeknownst to most people at the time (in fact, still a hero to most of the population)—was running an autonomous fiefdom within a federal government agency that he thought virtually belonged to him. Arguably, the worst mistake Joe Kennedy ever made, at least with regard to the long-term safety of his family, was his insistence that Jack, as the newly minted president, appoint his thirty-five-year-old brother, who had never practiced law, to the position of attorney general of the United States. As head of the Justice Department, he would command thirty thousand employees and control a $130 million budget in 1960. Just before he made the announcement, JFK was overheard telling Bobby, "Damn it, Bobby, comb your hair, and don't smile too much or they'll think we're happy about this."[20]

J. Edgar Hoover was not happy with this turn of events. He had been the director of FBI for longer than RFK had been alive, and now "that skinny squealing little liberal shit" was going to be his boss. One of Bobby's first directives was to require the FBI to clear its press releases and speeches with him, and that all press releases would now be coming from the Department of Justice, rather than the FBI.[21] By 1960, Hoover felt that he owned the bureau and could do whatever he wished. According to Anthony Summers, "Edgar 'lived like an Oriental potentate.' Edgar declared that he would eat ice cream only out of a round package—so it was flown in and kept in a freezer in the basement of the Justice Department. He wanted sides of beef from Colorado—they were flown in, too, all for free . . . Hoover had a heated toilet seat invented in the FBI laboratory. When he decided it was either a quarter of an inch too high or too low, it had to be redone."[22]

Once Bobby Kennedy brought some of his children along with him to the office, and they all decided to "visit the Director's office at a time when Hoover himself had stepped out briefly. The safe was open, Robert Kennedy Jr. recollects with no small glee, and he and his siblings jumped in and started pulling out documents by the handful. Just then Hoover himself appeared,

---

18. North, p. 190.
19. Ibid., p. 271 (ref. *New York Times*, May 19, 1962).
20. Wolfe, p. 358.
21. Ibid.; Hersh, Burton, p. 219.
22. Summers, *Official and Confidential*, p. 223.

and the younger Kennedy has still not quite gotten over the tantrum the enraged FBI Director mounted."[23]

The November 1957 raid at the home of the mobster Joseph "Joe the Barber" Barbara, in Apalachin, New York, brought the reality of the Mafia's existence directly to the front pages of every newspaper in the country. This meeting, which was portrayed in the movie *The Godfather*, was attended by roughly one hundred Mafia crime bosses from the United States, Canada, and Italy. Local police became concerned when they noticed numerous expensive cars with license plates from around the country; the local police alerted the state police, who together raided the meeting, causing mafiosi to flee into the woods and the surrounding area of the Apalachin estate. Over sixty underworld bosses were detained and indicted because of the disastrous meeting. The incident was most notable for the complete absence of any FBI agents, since their august leader had told them there was no such thing as organized crime syndicates.

Hoover's many contradictions are much more widely known today than when the news media were still keeping them secret, which is to say, the period of his entire lifetime, ending May 2, 1972. But it is now widely known that, according to Anthony Summers's account, "Mr. G-Man" J. Edgar Hoover was a closet homosexual and cross-dressing transvestite in his private life.[24] He was also closely associated with a number of leading Mafia gangsters from time spent at the racetracks and the month-long free annual vacations at the La Jolla, California, resort owned by Texas oilman Clint Murchison. Hoover was indebted to Murchison and Sid Richardson for all their favors but was simultaneously being blackmailed by them and their guests from the Mafia, as a result of the well-known "secret" among many of them of the pictures their colleague Meyer Lansky had of Hoover "in some kind of gay situation with Clyde Tolson. Lansky was the guy who controlled the pictures, and he had made his deal with Hoover—to lay off. That was the reason, they said, that for a long time they had nothing to fear from the FBI."[25] Other people, including Gordon Novel, a CIA electronics expert, stated that James Angleton had shown him similar pictures, specifically of Edgar "giving Clyde Tolson a blow job."[26] Lewis and Susan Rosenstiel—philanthropists and owners of Schenley Distillers, and among the wealthiest people alive in the late 1950s—said they witnessed Edgar in full drag at a party in 1958 at the Plaza Hotel. "He was wearing a fluffy black dress, very fluffy, with flounces,

23. Hersh, Burton, p. 219.
24. Summers, *Official and Confidential*, p. 254–255.
25. Summers, *Official and Confidential*, p. 242.
26. Ibid., p. 244.

and lace stockings and high heels, and a black curly wig. He had makeup on, and false eyelashes. It was a very short skirt, and he was sitting there in the living room of the suite with his legs crossed. Roy introduced him to me as 'Mary' and he replied, 'good evening,' brusque, like the first time I'd met him. It was obvious he wasn't a woman, you could see where he shaved. It was Hoover. You've never seen anything like it. I couldn't believe it, that I should see the head of the FBI dressed as a woman."[27]

Edgar the "blackmail*ee*" meanwhile was, on a much grander scale, "a master blackmail*er*" himself according to one of his closest colleagues, William Sullivan.[28] He used his huge cache of official and confidential files to blackmail anyone whom he deemed necessary, including congressmen, senators, high-level officials in every department or agency up to and including a succession of presidents, from Roosevelt to Nixon[29] (but no doubt excluding his namesake, Herbert Hoover, who appointed him initially to his position). In most cases, his blackmailing of presidents was related to forcing them to allow him to continue in his position, and it was done through innuendo and hints that he would drop about having knowledge of certain indiscretions.

At the beginning of the Kennedy administration, knowing about his twelve-year-old son Steven born by Johnson's mistress, Madeleine Brown, Hoover had used this information to seek Johnson's help in getting a mandatory retirement waiver from Kennedy: "At one of their trysts at Austin's Driskill Hotel, said Brown, he confided that he had 'a big problem.' 'Hoover,' he told her, 'wants me to try to influence Kennedy to keep him on as FBI director. He knows about you and Steven, and he's calling in his marker." Johnson's solution, Brown said, was to push her into a paper marriage hastily organized by Jesse Kellam, the confidante who had introduced them years earlier: "It was done to stop any gossip, and it worked, especially later, when he moved into the White House."[30]

But their friendship superseded any real animus or actual blackmail threats, as evidenced by his continuing amicable relationship with Hoover and the complete access he had to any of Hoover's files he requested. Evidently, Johnson and Hoover ultimately reached an understanding because the official and confidential files on LBJ, when finally opened after Hoover's death, contained little information on Johnson's secrets, corruption scandals, or his mistress. According to *The Washington Post*,

---

27. Ibid., p. 254.
28. Ibid., p. 12.
29. Ibid., p. 336.
30. Ibid., p. 336.

"Tapes and memos once existed concerning Johnson's backdoor activities. Some of this embarrassing material was removed from the files and sent to him at the White House."[31]

The Kennedys, both John and Robert, felt that J. Edgar Hoover was dangerous. Unfortunately, they underestimated how dangerous he was generally, but more importantly, how dangerous he was to them. Bobby later told Anthony Lewis, "It was a danger that we could control, that we were on top of, that we could deal with at the appropriate times. That's the way we looked at it. In the interests of the administration and in the interests of the country, it was well that we had control over it. There wasn't anything that he could do. We were giving him direction. And there wasn't anybody he could go to or anything he could do with the information or the material. So it was fine. He served our interests."[32] That view is debatable, given all of the blackmail material Hoover had already collected on both of them, including records Hoover kept on an incident in the Chicago FBI office, when the special agent in charge asked Kennedy if he would like to listen to some sensitive tapes. According to William Sullivan, "Kennedy should have refused, should have asked to have transcripts sent through the usual channels. Instead, he sat down and listened to the tapes, and by doing so compromised himself. After listening to the tapes for just a moment or two, Kennedy had to realize that they were the result of unauthorized taps. But he kept listening, which to Hoover implied tacit approval. Never a man to let an opportunity go by, Hoover insisted on and got sworn affidavits from every agent present stating that Kennedy had listened to the tapes and had not questioned their legality."[33]

These stories depict a vicious and vulnerable man, who was contemptuous of both JFK and RFK and desperate to protect his own turf, fully aware that the Kennedys were intent on its destruction. Knowing Hoover as well as anyone outside the highest levels of the FBI possibly could, Lyndon Johnson no doubt knew that he would immediately have Hoover's cooperation when the plan he was devising was ready for execution; he never doubted that Hoover would cooperate in the cover-up.

Rich Texas Oilmen, and Their Mobster Friends

In the early 1960s, Texas accounted for over half of the proven oil reserves in the United States, and six Texas companies controlled 80 percent of it.

31. Ibid., p. 337.
32. Guthman, p. 134.
33. Sullivan, pp. 55–56

Oilmen had known since the 1960 election that Kennedy was threatening to eliminate their favorite law, called the "oil depletion allowance," which allowed them to retain 27.5 percent of their oil revenue tax-free; its loss, according to *World Petroleum* magazine, stood to cost the industry as much as $280 million in annual profits.[34] The original rationale for such an allowance was that the product that their investments yielded was a finite resource that would require continual investments in exploration and recovery in order to extend the flow of raw material; the more the companies produced, the less was available. Recognition of this depletion of the asset was intended as an incentive for finding and recovering more oil fields. (How this particular commodity was materially different from other forms of mining, or commercial ocean fishing, or even farming, was never fully explained, other than perhaps the oilmen having better lobbyists than the others.) Some of the oilmen had partly supported the Kennedy-Johnson ticket during the 1960 election (others had supported Nixon) because of Johnson's promise that they would not push for elimination of the oil depletion allowance; nevertheless, John F. Kennedy had doubts about its fairness and efficacy, and in early 1963 attacked this tax loophole.

The oilmen were mostly former "wildcat" operators who had gained their fortune almost overnight, and they realized all too well that they could lose it just as quickly. One of the richest of the oilmen, Clint Murchison of Dallas, owned the Del Charro, the resort hotel located in southern California where he treated his friend J. Edgar Hoover and his partner Clyde Tolson to a month's vacation every year, near the racetrack he also owned, the Del-Mar. Another of Murchison's friends, Sid Richardson, went there at the same time, and other guests who would pop in during the month or so of Hoover's stay included Richard Nixon, John Connally, Lyndon Johnson, and such mafiosi as Meyer Lanksky, Santos Trafficante, Johnny Rosselli of Los Angeles, Sam Giancana of Chicago, and Carlos Marcello of New Orleans.[35] Murchison, like Estes and Johnson, was also involved with Jimmy Hoffa and the Teamsters and Mafia don Frank Costello, a good friend of Sam Giancana and former business associate of Joseph P. Kennedy.[36] According to Anthony Summers, "The Del Charro was small, and in its comparative privacy Edgar rubbed shoulders with a bevy of white-collar crooks. Those welcomed at the hotel in the fifties included Ed Levinson, John Drew, and Ray Ryan, all notorious names to rackets investigators.

---

34. Russell, p. 587 (ref. James Hepburn, *Farewell America*, pp. 234–238).
35. Hack, *Puppetmaster—The secret Life of J. Edgar Hoover*, p. 285.
36. Davis, *Mafia Kingfish*, pp. 128–140.

Drew once departed leaving a valuable antique, a bottle of pre-Prohibition whiskey, as a present for Edgar."[37] During these weeks spent at the racetrack and the resort with some of the most notorious criminals in the country, it can be assumed that they commiserated endlessly about the sorry state of affairs with the Kennedys in charge. Furthermore, it isn't a stretch to speculate in how many ways such a powerful group could envision ending the administration's term of office.

The core of the Texas base, called the 8F Group for the suite at the Lamar Hotel in Houston where they met, was primarily Texas oilmen: H. L. Hunt, Clint Murchison, and Sid Richardson were among this group, but it included others from various industries—men like George and Herman Brown, owners of the Brown & Root Corporation, a major construction company and the single largest benefactor of Lyndon Johnson, as well as Johnson's chief lawyer and bagman, Edward A. Clark. All of these men were extreme right-wing anti-Communists of the John Birch Society genre willing to fund like-minded groups. But more importantly, they were businessmen who wanted to make money regardless of the niceties of due process, the integrity of the competitive bidding process or the constraints of ethical conduct; they needed their own like-minded man in Congress. Johnson knew that these men would be willing to pay a considerable amount of money in bribes and kickbacks in order to get profitable government contracts; he would become their indispensable Washington asset, a man who would become uniquely positioned to control their fortunes and, indeed, their continued existence. The oilmen, especially, were growing desperate over the issue of Kennedy's determined intent to eliminate the depletion allowance. In their view, considering the cost to them of its elimination, any expense to save it was worth the investment.

The material presented in later chapters indicates that Johnson collected many hundreds of thousands of dollars from these sources, practically all of it unrestricted insofar as how it would be spent; he alone determined how much would go to other politicians in Washington or elsewhere who would subordinate their interests to his and how much he would divert to his own personal wealth accumulation. Even as other politicians of lesser note (Senator Thomas Dodd of Connecticut, for example) would be censured for illegally converting campaign funds to their personal use, Lyndon Johnson—the most prolific campaign fund abuse practitioner in history, bar none—would escape such scrutiny, doubtlessly because too many others were indebted to him and/or justifiably afraid of him.

---

37. Summers, *Official* . . . p. 232.

The Mafia Connections and Cuban Exiles

In his official capacity as the attorney general, Robert F. Kennedy had undertaken a war with organized crime, extending the work he had begun in 1956 as an investigator for his brother's Senate committee examining the issue. On the morning of November 22, 1963, RFK was conducting a conference to review the progress and establish the priorities for the ongoing battle. His top four targets were Sam Giancana of Chicago, Santos Trafficante of Florida, labor boss Jimmy Hoffa, and Carlos Marcello of New Orleans. Marcello was already being tried in New Orleans at that moment, and Kennedy was hopeful that the trial would lead to a permanent deportation since Marcello had snuck back into the country after Bobby had had him unceremoniously thrown out in 1961, without the formality of deportation. At Marcello's side, acting as a strategist in his case, was David Ferrie, who, it has now been established, was another CIA contract employee.[38]*

Bobby's aggressive efforts to get rid of Marcello must have been an embarrassment to Lyndon Johnson, who had long worked in behalf of the interest of many mafiosi, Carlos Marcello in particular. His ties to Marcello went back to the early 1950s, when one of Marcello's lieutenants, Jack Halfen, agreed to set aside a percentage of profits to help LBJ fund his senatorial campaigns. This would prove to be a good investment: In exchange for such contributions, Johnson consistently impeded antiracketeering legislation throughout his governmental service,[39] and once he became president, the Justice Department's organized crime operation was suspended; Johnson ordered all FBI bugging of the Mafia to cease. FBI Special Agent William F. Roemer Jr., who had been spearheading the attack on the Mob in Chicago, concluded "If you judge a man by his acts, here was a man [LBJ] who did more to hinder the government agency fighting crime than any other president or leader in our history."[40] According to author John H. Davis, "It has been estimated that the Marcello-Halfen group funneled at least $50,000 a year of the Marcello's gambling profits alone to Lyndon Johnson, and, in return, Johnson helped kill in committee all anti-rackets legislation that could have harmed the interests of Carlos Marcello and Jack Halfen. It was safe to say, then, that thanks partly to the influence of Vice President Lyndon Johnson, Carlos Marcello was able to operate freely in Dallas in 1963."[41] Jack Halfen was in prison by 1964, but he had kept eight hundred feet of home movies

---

* Ferrie's involvement in setting up Oswald is detailed in chapter 6.
38. Russell, p. 574.
39. Mahoney, p. 384, 388.
40. Roemer, p. 218.
41. Davis, *Mafia Kingfish*, p. 139.

showing him and his wife partying with the Johnsons at their ranch, and he need only give the nod to have it given over to RFK along with whatever other information he might wish to contribute to Bobby's already-extensive files on Johnson's Halfen-Marcello activities.[42] Jack Halfen was later given a full pardon for his transgressions by President Lyndon Johnson in 1966.

Yet despite the intensity of Kennedy's drive to eradicate organized crime throughout the country, the FBI, which reported to him, somehow avoided ever wiretapping Meyer Lansky, Carlos Marcello, or Santos Trafficante, the only three high-level crime figures who were not tapped.[43] The reason for Lansky's excusal was due to the secrets he had used to control Hoover for over a decade already. In the cases of Marcello and Trafficante, the reason could only be that, despite RFK's pursuit of mobsters in general, the CIA gave both men necessary cover and protection by involving them in the plan to assassinate Fidel Castro.[44] Lyndon Johnson's (and J. Edgar Hoover's) longtime relationship with Marcello, through his lieutenants in Texas discussed elsewhere, was another reason for the absence of wiretaps in his case.

In his unofficial role as JFK's overseer of the CIA, Robert F. Kennedy was the driving force in the continuing initiative to put Castro out of business in 1963. The Kennedys knew that Cuba would become a major political liability in the 1964 election unless Castro was removed and the Communist menace eradicated for good in the Western Hemisphere. According to authors Lamar Waldron and Thom Hartmann, Bobby Kennedy was the creator of a top secret plan to solve what was really a political problem, for an invasion of Cuba that was scheduled for December 1, 1963. RFK was acting directly on behalf of the president—not in his capacity as the attorney general—but through a back channel to Cuban leaders Manuel Artime, Harry Williams, and others to a high-level Cuban officer, Juan Almeida. Bobby worked directly with these Cuban leaders through the Army Secretary's Office with Cyrus Vance, Joseph Califano, and Al Haig.[45] Califano and Haig have both written accounts that confirm this, and even speak of the intensity to which Bobby worked to get rid of Castro: Califano wrote that "as Robert Kennedy pressed for tougher actions, I thought: he is obsessed with Castro; he is pursuing a total war with Castro."[46] According to Al Haig, "'Bobby Kennedy was running' the covert Cuban operations 'hour by hour. I was part of it, as deputy to Joe Califano and military assistant to General Vance . . . people were being killed . . . and the United States Army was supporting and training these forces . . . Cy

42. Ibid., p. 273.
43. Ibid., p. 144.
44. Scott, p. 227.
45. Waldron, pp. 82–91.
46. Ibid. (ref. Califano, Joseph A., *Inside*, New York: Public Affairs, 2004, pp. 118, 122).

Vance, the Secretary of the Army, was [presiding] over the State Department, the CIA, and the National Security Council. I was intimately involved . . . weekly reports were rendered to Bobby Kennedy—he had a very tight hand on the operation.'"[47] In this capacity, Colonel Haig "wrote a July 19, 1963 memo suggesting 'a concerted effort to create circumstances leading to US action to reestablish a non-Communist Cuba and expel the Soviet presence, including [US] military action and invasion if necessary.'"[48]

Califano also explained the political pressure on the Kennedys that caused their intense actions directed at Castro: "President Kennedy had to do something about Cuba and Castro, because even though the Soviet missiles had been removed, thousands of 'Russian troops remained on the island.'"[49] Another unidentified source quoted by Lamar Waldron characterized Bobby's attitude in this operation as "'hard-nosed' and 'determined' but also 'rash and arrogant and frequently wrong.' He felt that Bobby's 'Cuba policy wasn't dictated by concern for democracy as much as realism and resentment toward Castro over the Bay of Pigs defeat.'"[50]

The CIA's plan to assassinate Fidel Castro, which emanated from the Eisenhower administration's 1960 planning, under Vice President Richard Nixon's tutelage, had involved Sam Giancana and Johnny Rosselli. In 1960, ex–FBI agent Robert Maheu, who later became a top aide to the reclusive billionaire Howard Hughes in Las Vegas, recruited Johnny Rosselli on behalf of the CIA to assist them in killing Fidel Castro. Rosselli introduced Maheu to Sam Giancana (a.k.a. Sam Gold) and Santos Trafficante (who was called Joe), the Florida Mob boss who had also been the most powerful of the mafiosi running casinos and bordellos in prerevolutionary Cuba; they were given six poison pills to murder Castro. For several months, attempts were made, unsuccessfully, to put the pills in Castro's food. Beginning in the later part of 1961, after the Bay of Pigs fiasco, the methods were adjusted to other, more distant, forms of attack, including the training of sniper teams, using a secret CIA base in the Florida Keys. The man in charge of this operation, Task Force W, was the legendary Bill Harvey, who hated both Kennedy brothers with a passion. They didn't think too much of him either, and as time went on, the hatred between them grew exponentially, as their disagreements over the best way to handle Cuba careened out of control.

47. Ibid., p. 84 (ref. Haig, Alexander M. Jr., *Inner Circles: How America Changed the World: A Memoir.* New York: Warner Books, 1991, p. 111).
48. Ibid. (ref. Army document, 7-19063, Memo from Alexander Haig to Captain Zumwalt, Califano Papers, Record no. 198-10004-10005, declassified October 7, 1997).
49. Ibid., p. 83 (ref. Califano, *Inside*, pp. 118–122).
50. Ibid., p. 85.

As noted in the previous chapter, Johnny Rosselli had become a friend of Bill Harvey, meeting him in his Washington home as well as in Miami, at JM/WAVE headquarters with David Morales. Morales was the chief of operations in Miami and was in direct contact with Maurice Bishop, the cover name for David Atlee Phillips,[51] who became the handler of both Lee Harvey Oswald and Carlos Bringuier. Bringuier was the head of the militant group DRE (Directorio Revolucionario Estudiantil) who engaged in a street fight with Oswald in New Orleans in August 1963. It appears that this fight was staged by one or both of them, given their mutual handler, to establish Oswald's bona fides as a radical Communist and supporter of Fidel Castro. Clearly this was an early part of the conspiracy to kill Kennedy, as the operational planner (Bill Harvey) maneuvered Oswald into a vulnerable position: regardless of which option was later chosen—JFK killed by a lone nut, a maladjusted, delusional Communist, or an international Communist conspiracy traceable to Cuba—Oswald would have a definite trail to either.

Noel Twyman pieced together the relationships between the CIA men at JM/WAVE[52] and Rosselli, Giancana, Marcello, Trafficante, David Ferrie, and Jack Ruby, and then described Rosselli's ultimate demise, which was connected to these relationships: "Years later, Rosselli would start talking and reveal to columnist Jack Anderson that Ruby was 'one of our boys and had been ordered to kill Oswald.' Shortly after his discussion with Anderson, and just after he testified in closed session to the Church Committee, Rosselli was murdered in the late summer of 1976; his body was found cut into pieces and stuffed in an oil drum that floated to the surface in a Florida intercoastal waterway."[53]

Within three weeks of Kennedy's murder, a team of FBI agents had uncovered evidence connecting all of the above names in an apparent conspiracy to assassinate the president, putting the team "in a position to crack the case wide open if it had only pursued the evidence. Then, suddenly, on December 18, 1963, all FBI investigations ceased. No mention of David Ferrie or Carlos Marcello was made to the Warren Commission in its supplemental report of January 13, 1964."[54] Hoover obviously realized, only three weeks after the assassination, that if he did not put an immediate stop to any further investigation of the murder of the president, then he and Johnson would run the risk of one of his own investigators finding out about the real plot.

---

51. Twyman, pp. 355–356.
52. Ibid., p. 386.
53. Ibid., p. 257.
54. Ibid., p. 772.

JFK's Legendary Sex Life

JFK's predilection for sexual relations with a wide variety of young women is essential to the understanding of his vulnerability to other high-ranking government and military officials. Unfortunately, it became such a major part of his character that he allowed it to become a direct threat to his fitness for office, at least in the opinion of many men within the federal government bureaucracy, military establishment, and the intelligence community. If it had not involved a series of high-risk affairs with suspected spies, it might not have risen to the level that threatened his life. But it did involve very high-risk liaisons with the wrong women.

J. Edgar Hoover, of course, had known all about Kennedy's affairs with numerous women, and he had made sure that both JFK and RFK knew that he knew all about them. Hoover's agents had documentation on JFK liaisons with as many as thirty-two women during his presidency.[55] Although most of the president's sexual conquests were with women who posed no national security threats—girls from the office, like Fiddle (Priscella Wear) and Faddle (Jill Cowen), secretaries who did little typing,[56] for example—there were several others who posed a serious threat. Those included women who were suspected spies, such as Ellen Rometsch, Maria Novotny, and Suzie Chang; Judith Campbell, the mobster's moll; and finally, the glamorous Marilyn Monroe, who had threatened, only days before her own demise, to hold a press conference to reveal the details of her intimate affairs with the president and the attorney general, as well as the secrets of the international affairs that she had learned. Since Hoover's knowledge of these affairs can be seen as Lyndon Johnson's as well, a logically extended presumption can be made that he would have shared these secrets with a select few others—men whose support he would need for his planned coup—who might need to be convinced of the need to replace Kennedy because of these "treasons."

As president, John F. Kennedy became very compromised as a result of his personal obsessions. Most of the innumerable affairs he had conducted—even the noontime skinny-dipping sessions with young female secretaries like Fiddle and Faddle, which were often attended by his brothers Bobby and Teddy, but to the exclusion of practically everyone else—were successfully kept out of the public domain and therefore did not pose a threat to his presidency.[57] In the interest of brevity, we will consider further only JFK's relationships with Marilyn Monroe, Mary Pinchot Meyer, Judith Exner,

---

55. Scott, p. 227.
56. Kessler, *In the President's . . .* , p. 13.
57. Hersh, Seymour M, *The Dark Side*, pp. 236–238.

and Ellen Rometsch, all of which, in their own ways, were potential time bombs that had to be contained. The high-risk affairs of both the Kennedy brothers with the Hollywood star Marilyn Monroe were also obliquely connected to still another potentially explosive threat: the intrepid celebrity-gossip journalist and television personality Dorothy Kilgallen; Ms. Kilgallen had published references to Marilyn Monroe's lover, who she wrote was "a handsome gentleman who is a bigger name than Joe DiMaggio in his heyday." On August 1, 1962, three days before Monroe died, Kilgallen had even called Bobby Kennedy at the Justice Department to try to verify the rumors.[58] Dorothy Kilgallen's inquisitiveness would eventually prove to be a deadly curse, but not before both Marilyn Monroe and John F. Kennedy were themselves dead.

Altogether, four of the people involved in JFK's affairs—Kennedy himself; Dorothy Kilgallen, who had never met any of the others, yet became exposed to them through her work; Mary Meyer; and Marilyn Monroe—would eventually die of unnatural causes. Judith Campbell (later Exner), considering her other boyfriends, was lucky to escape with her life; Rometsch, then used to a glamorous life, swinging with the most powerful men in the world, would be thrown out of the country and consigned to a life in one of the bleakest of countries, East Germany.

For the president and his attorney general brother, there were obvious risks of having been involved with a famous Hollywood sex symbol. Unfortunately for all concerned, this one was a lady whose hold on rationality was tenuous at best: The most glamorous movie star of all time was now threatening to expose her affairs by conducting a news conference to announce her experiences with both of the Kennedys and to disclose her knowledge of major national secrets. But the special nature of Kennedy's affairs with Marilyn Monroe and Mary Meyer requires additional consideration, as presented below. Marilyn was murdered fifteen months before JFK was assassinated; Mary Meyer was killed eleven months afterwards. Kilgallen would die the year after Meyer. The three women did not know each other, but they had one thing in common: They were all *women who knew too much*. Their knowledge of Kennedy's secrets (in Kilgallen's case, secrets obtained about Lyndon Johnson from Jack Ruby) might have been the cause of their murders. For the Meyer affair, it was the disturbing circumstances surrounding the murder of an ex-wife of a top CIA official, a man who despised John F. Kennedy since their childhood days.

---

58. Wolfe, p. 447.

Mary Pinchot Meyer

Mary Meyer's long-term affair with JFK would have been known to Hoover and Johnson, though she was not yet the national security threat presented by the others. That would come later, after JFK's assassination, when Mary Meyer had learned more than she should have about the conspiracy and her ex-husband's involvement in it. It is the context of her intimate relationship with the president before he was assassinated that must be understood in order to assess the implications of what later happened to her. To appreciate how close they were, it is necessary to start with her past and juxtapose events of their lifelines into a single thread.

Mary Pinchot Meyer was unlike any of the other women in John F. Kennedy's life. She was someone he was intimate with in more than just a physical way; she connected with him on an intellectual level to a much greater degree than did any other woman, arguably including even his wife, Jacqueline.[59] Among all his other lovers, according to James Jesus Angleton, who had reason to know, the president was in love with Mary Meyer: "They had something very important."[60] They had met as teenagers at a dance she attended at Choate, where he was a student. By the mid-1950s, Mary had married Cord Meyer, and the couple lived with their two sons in a large home in the Virginia suburbs, next door to Hickory Hill, at the time John and Jackie's home before he became president, after which it was taken over by Bobby. In 1955, the Meyers' pet dog was run over and killed. For some reason, Cord Meyer interpreted this as a threat related to his work and soon thereafter sought other employment, planning to leave the CIA. The following year, their son Michael was run over and killed at exactly the same spot. Cord considered that as a major reinforcement of the point: He could never leave the CIA.

Mary had already come to hate her husband's job, and the death of their son destroyed what was left of their marriage; Mary divorced him, and Cord subsequently became a covert-operations agent in London. Mary moved to Georgetown to live in an apartment and art studio in the converted garage of her sister, Antoinette Pinchot Bradlee, and her husband Ben Bradlee. In the fall of 1961, Mary began visiting the White House, at first to attend various social events and private parties. JFK had attempted to have an affair with her; however, she put him off until January 1962, when she changed her mind. Another CIA official, Bill Walton—a very good friend of both JFK and Mary Meyer—would often

---

59. Burleigh (unless otherwise noted, all material on the background of Mary Meyer was summarized from this book in its entirety).
60. Trento, p. 280.

escort her to White House social events as a pretext to getting her inside while seeking to avoid creating suspicions as to her real purpose, especially when Jacqueline was there.

Before long, Mary and JFK had allegedly—there is no proof of it—begun to take marijuana together, and later other rumors suggested they had experimented with other more powerful drugs. Angleton, a friend of Cord Meyer who was also fond of Mary, was concerned that she had become too entangled with Kennedy to remain unaffected by it. It may just be a coincidence that, concurrently with his affair with Mary Pinchot Meyer and their rumored use of drugs together, Kennedy had become less tolerant of the CIA's intelligence breakdowns and the Pentagon's aggressive provocations for military actions, especially in Vietnam.

His Peace Speech in June 1963 represented a sea change in his attitudes: Previously, during the campaign, he had accused Eisenhower of not being tough enough on fighting Communism; now, in 1963, he began seeking more peaceful overtures to Russia, Cuba, and Vietnam, and less confrontational actions in the world's trouble spots. This shift toward peaceful coexistence was not well received in all parts of Washington DC, especially on the other, Virginia, side of the Potomac River. The fact was that Mary Meyer was regarded as a serious threat to the national security by many very high level men in the CIA. In her case, that didn't happen *before* the assassination; for her, the risk of her revealing her own secrets came ten months *after* the assassination, just as the whitewash represented by the Warren Commission Report was being released. But the fuse which ultimately led to the firing of point-blank gunshots to her head and upper body—hallmarks of a professional hit—was lit well before her death.

Early in 1963, as Phil Graham's mental state continued deteriorating, he went (uninvited) to a newsmen's convention in Phoenix, took over the dais, "grabbed the microphone and drunkenly announced to the crowd, many of whom knew him, that he was going to tell them exactly who in Washington was sleeping with whom, beginning with President Kennedy. His favorite, screamed Phil, was now Mary Meyer, who had been married to CIA official Cord Meyer and was the sister of Ben Bradlee's wife, Tony." One of the newsmen immediately called President Kennedy, who then called Katherine Graham to advise her of what happened and offered to help; however, she was too angry at Kennedy to accept. Phil's assistant, James Truitt, took the phone and asked Kennedy to have a military jet take Leslie Farber, Phil's doctor, to Phoenix immediately, which he did.[61] This episode may have had something to do with Bradlee's transfer of Truitt to Tokyo shortly thereafter.

---

61. Davis, Deborah, p. 165.

In any event, this unfortunate incident came very close to being an explosive news story in every newspaper in the country, were it not for some very quick actions to shut Phil up and make sure none of the newsmen would report it. Katherine Graham flew to Phoenix in the chartered Gulfstream jet that had taken Phil there earlier to retrieve him and have him committed to a very expensive psychiatric hospital, Chestnut Lodge in Rockville, Maryland. On August 3, 1963—the fifteenth anniversary of the Washington Post Company, the umbrella corporation for the newspaper and other properties—Phil Graham called Katherine and asked her to come pick him up so they could spend the weekend together at their farm. Once there, Phil shot himself in the head.[62]

Marilyn Monroe

As to the Monroe affair, JFK's vulnerabilities stem from the even more troubling nature of the questions surrounding her death and Bobby's alleged involvement, at least his presence in her apartment shortly before her death.[63] There were a number of men in Washington DC who were watching Marilyn Monroe in more ways than simply having a prurient interest in her movies, her scantily dressed photographs on calendars, and the completely nude photos of her being passed discreetly among friends. These men regarded her as an extremely dangerous person, a threat to the national security of America. From another prism, Jack and Robert Kennedy also regarded her as dangerous. But the danger she presented to them involved their ability to continue to stay in office, given what would happen if their enemies caught wind of what was going on. In fact, their biggest enemy, J. Edgar Hoover, knew all about their secret lives, thanks to the wiretaps and bugging devices he had had installed in her house.

John F. Kennedy's affair with Marilyn Monroe was an open secret in Hollywood, having started as early as 1956, when they were both on European trips. They spent many evenings together during the 1960 convention and, after a dinner on one such evening, were seen "the next morning emerging from a shower at the (Peter) Lawford beach house."[64] The affair began before the election and continued well after he went to the White House. Hoover had warned Jack about exposing his affairs with Judith Campbell and Marilyn Monroe, so he had resigned himself to give up both, no doubt because there were many others to replace them.

---

62. Ibid., p. 171.
63. Wolfe, pp. 454–464.
64. Ibid., pp. 346–347.

Author Donald H. Wolfe, in *The Last Days of Marilyn Monroe*, made a compelling case that Robert F. Kennedy was not only the last visitor of Marilyn Monroe before she died but was actually involved in it in some way. To be sure, other authors, including Donald Spoto in his book *Marilyn Monroe*, disagree vehemently with such a conclusion. A more likely scenario was presented by researcher Stephen Pegues in 1997, who wrote that it was a Giancana hit man, Gianola Tortorello, and two other men who broke into Monroe's home and forced a Nembutal suppository into her rectum;[65] this would explain the lack of the same chemical in her stomach, as reported in her autopsy. Giancana, like his mafioso brethren, were all outraged at what they considered as a double cross by Joseph Kennedy, who had promised them freedom from prosecution. His son Bobby apparently did not get that memo; the death of Marilyn Monroe, under this hypothesis, was a message for all three of the Kennedy men from the underworld about the dangers of reneging on promises.

It is not our purpose here to settle that case; however, it is clear that whatever involvement Bobby may have had would have been known to his nemesis, J. Edgar Hoover; he wouldn't hesitate a moment to use the secret scandals known only to the handful of people who had access to the FBI reports to keep Bobby Kennedy rattled and under complete control. RFK had found out about Hoover's channels when he ordered the FBI to confiscate the records of her telephone calls from General Telephone within hours of her death. He knew that Hoover knew all about the outgoing and incoming telephone calls, not just the precise times of each call but the taped conversations as well. Since August 4, 1962, J. Edgar Hoover possessed information on both Kennedy brothers that was so potentially damaging that it could end their political careers. From then on, they were held hostage by Hoover, who would continue to use this advantage in the days and weeks following November 22, 1963, to gain total control over the investigation of JFK's assassination.[66] When RFK tried to use his most trusted men in the Justice Department's criminal division, Jack Miller and Robert Peloquin, to inject themselves into the investigation, they were shunned by the FBI on the orders of the director. He would also withhold reports from his field agents to the Justice Department, thus precluding Kennedy's awareness of the information they had gathered about Oswald's New Orleans connections to CIA and Mafia figures like David Ferrie and Carlos Marcello.[67]

---

65. Pegues, p. 119.
66. Davis, pp. 242–243.
67. Ibid.

For the last fifteen months of their administration, both John and Robert Kennedy were rendered impotent by their own FBI head. Robert Kennedy's seeming reticence about vigorously pursuing the murderers of his brother was, ironically—at least in part—due to his own vulnerability within the federal law enforcement bureaucracy because his authority as attorney general had been trumped by J. Edgar Hoover.

Judith Campbell

At roughly the same time that JFK was sexually involved with Marilyn Monroe, he was carrying on another high-risk affair with Judith Campbell.[68] She, in turn, was in a simultaneous, long-term intimate relationship with the boss of the Chicago Mob, Sam Giancana—the same Sam Giancana that JFK's father had leaned on for financial and arm-twisting kinds of support in the election that got him elected president, and the same Sam Giancana who had become the target of his brother Robert for over five years, along with all the other mobsters who, coincidentally, were arm's-length business associates of their father, Joseph P. Kennedy Sr. Judith Campbell (later known as Judith Exner) was a gorgeous California socialite and twenty-five years old when she was introduced to JFK by Frank Sinatra in early 1960. One month later they became lovers. A month after that, JFK asked Campbell to carry a satchel containing at least $250,000 ("for the [presidential primary] campaign") to Giancana, who was also recently introduced to Campbell by Sinatra. She became a conduit between Kennedy and Giancana during the primaries and remained so during the general election and the Kennedy administration. She carried money and documents on the elimination of Castro from JFK to Giancana and arranged meetings between the two. Throughout her years with JFK, Campbell was under intense FBI surveillance because of her association with Giancana. The surveillance revealed to the FBI her relationship with JFK. Hoover chose not to make this information public at least in part because revealing it would indicate the extent of his illegal bugging and would damage his and the FBI's reputations.[69]

During the FBI's surveillance of her Fontaine Avenue apartment, Agent William Carter observed two men as they broke into her place and then fleeing fifteen minutes later. They traced the getaway car to Mr. I. B. Hale, of Fort Worth, Texas, and identified the two men as his sons, Bobby

---

68. Hersh, Seymour M, *The Dark Side* . . . , pp. 294–325.
69. Ibid., pp. 306–314.

and Billy. Mr. Hale was in charge of security for the General Dynamics Corporation. This break-in, apparently for the purpose of placing a wiretap on her telephone, was not reported to local police. The questions it raises suggest that someone in a position to know of her relationships with JFK and Sam Giancana was attempting to obtain information that would help in their efforts related to winning—or keeping—the TFX contract.[70]

By the fall of 1962, Campbell was out of JFK's life. The FBI surveillance and JFK's waning passion for her (he'd brought another woman to their bed much to Campbell's dismay) left her heartbroken. Exner (Campbell) claimed to have gotten pregnant from JFK during their last sexual encounter. According to Exner, JFK told her not to keep the baby and to seek help from Giancana, who had also become her lover, in terminating the pregnancy.[71] It was probably fortuitous that Kennedy's affair with Campbell was over when it was, and that the affairs he and his brother Bobby had with Marilyn Monroe were also coming to an end at the same time, even though the reason was due to the death of the other party. Had they become tangled up with the numerous scandals which broke—or were on the precipice of imploding—the following year, it would have probably been impossible for the Kennedy administration to have survived. On the other hand, John might have personally survived, since there would have been fewer issues to have enraged his enemies.

The British Sex Scandal

In early 1963, the British government became embroiled in its own sex scandal that led to the resignation of John Profumo, the minister of war, after he admitted that he had lied to the House of Commons. This scandal went well beyond mere naughtiness with prostitutes, because one of the girls, Christine Keeler, was having a simultaneous affair with Yevgeny Ivanov, a Soviet naval attaché. Ivanov found this out first and had Keeler and four other prostitutes ask questions of Profumo about British nuclear policy. The British tabloids had picked up this story, and it was making front-page news for months until the entire Macmillan government was brought down by it.

John F. Kennedy was fascinated by the British scandal. Ben Bradlee reported in *Conversations with Kennedy*, "Kennedy had devoured every word written about the Profumo case . . . It combined so many of the things that interested him: low doings in high places, the British nobility, sex, and

---

70. Ibid., pp. 317–318.
71. Ibid., p. 323.

spying. Someone in the State Department had apparently sent him an early cable on the Profumo case from David Bruce, the American ambassador to Great Britain. Kennedy . . . ordered all further cables from Bruce on that subject sent to him immediately."[72]

The real cause of his anxiety over the British scandal, however, had been related to his own intimate knowledge of his similar conduct with women from the same clique involved in the Profumo scandal. In fact, the story came within a hair's breadth of morphing into an American scandal on June 23, 1963. The front-page headline that day in the *New York Journal American* was "High U.S. Aide Implicated in V-Girl Scandal," and the story referred to a "man who holds a 'very high' elective office." Though it did not name the president, it came close enough to propel Bobby into high gear, calling the reporters into his office. Threatening to bring an antitrust suit against the Hearst organization, he forced them to drop the story.[73]

It was later determined that the rumors inundating the news in mid-June 1963 were being fed by none other than J. Edgar Hoover, apparently prompted by his reaction to the president's Peace Speech of June 10 at American University, followed a week later by the installation of a hotline between the White House and the Kremlin.[74] Days after that, "there was a flurry of veiled hints linking the President to the Profumo story, such as the Drew Pearson-Jack Anderson column for June 29: 'Britishers who read American criticisms of Profumo throw back the question 'what high American official was involved with Marilyn Monroe?'"[75]

In addition to his affairs with women he shared with the Mafia, JFK had been serviced in New York by at least three call girls from Communist countries. Two of these women, Maria Novotny (Czech) and Suzy Chang (Chinese), were also involved with John Profumo, the British minister of war, getting answers to questions about British nuclear policy being fed to them by a Soviet naval attaché.

After the story was deleted in subsequent editions of the *New York Journal American*, Bobby telephoned JFK in the middle of his dinner with Harold Macmillan to let him know that the story had been squelched. While Bobby was successful in getting the story stopped in the United States, that didn't happen in the UK. Minister Harold Macmillan eventually resigned, and his government was shortly voted out of office.

---

72. Ibid., p. 391.
73. Summers, *Official and Confidential*, p. 307.
74. Scott, pp. 228–229.
75. Ibid.

Ellen Rometsch

The third Communist call girl, beautiful German-born Ellen Rometsch, became one of the White House pool party girls. As a youth and young adult, she was a member of the Communist Party. Bobby Baker had made sure that LBJ knew all about JFK's affair with her, and he, of course, tipped off his friend, Hoover. In fact, as demonstrated below, it appears that Lyndon Johnson was the instigator of Baker's involvement in helping to procure women for Kennedy. From the time of their first association, in 1948, Baker would do anything and everything that Johnson told him to do and, Johnson—whose primary skill was in using men's weaknesses to gain an advantage over them—would not have hesitated to exploit any such opportunity.

When the FBI learned of the Rometsch-Kennedy connection, they began to investigate her as a possible spy, and JFK—aware of the potentially disastrous results if it were to become public—had Bobby Kennedy arrange to immediately deport her to Germany and paid her to keep her mouth shut. He enlisted the help of several friends to pay her the hush money, raising the funds in his behalf despite the fact that donors could not deduct the contributions or expect any acknowledgment from him. Hoover cooperated with RFK in this instance—not to help protect the president—to protect the vice president, who he feared could be connected to a Baker prostitute if the ongoing investigations led to a public disclosure.[76]

Rometsch was stunningly attractive, an Elizabeth Taylor look-alike. One of Jack Kennedy's friends, Bill Thompson, had discovered her at the Quorum Club and asked Baker about her. Baker told him, "She was a very lovely, beautiful party girl . . . who always wore beautiful clothes. She had good manners, and she was very accommodating. I must have had fifty friends who went with her, and not one of them ever complained. She was a real joy to be with."[77] The *Life* magazine article of November 22, 1963, edition, noted earlier, described what went on frequently within the Q, as it was called by some of the regular girls: "Sometimes she . . . [did] other dances which required no costume whatsoever. Once, perhaps because it was a hot summer night, the idea caught on and the other girl guests either decided independently or were persuaded to peel as well. That time the girls grew playful and finished the party pouring champagne over one another."[78]

In helping Baker to set up the Q, Lyndon Johnson knew that he would have to keep the operation at arm's-length distance from himself

76. North, p. 193.
77. Ibid., p. 389.
78. *Life*, November 22, 1963, p. 92.

because the primary unstated purpose of the club was to provide a source of dirt on others, which he could use for multiple other future purposes. It would have originally been intended by him, in the 1950s, to target other congressmen. But by 1961, the focus of these nighttime enterprises would be moved to the other end of Pennsylvania Avenue, to the White House, to gather dirt on the president; if through Hoover's resources he could get enough dirt on JFK without exposing himself, he might have been able to assume the presidency through the impeachment process. Beginning in that year, immediately after the election, Bobby Baker and Fred Black acquired another business associate, a New York lawyer and newly minted lobbyist named Myron "Mickey" Weiner, who would eventually work so closely with Baker that the office secretary Margaret M. Broome stated that it was not inaccurate to say Weiner "made Baker's office his 'second office.'"[79] By then, his non-Capitol regular office/apartment at 1028 Connecticut Avenue was apparently used mostly for parties, according to his own testimony later given to a Senate investigatory hearing: "Weiner said that Carole Tyler . . . came to Weiner's apartment on some occasions along with [Bobby] Baker and the female secretary of a U.S. Senator."[80] Another source referred to as Ms. E admitted prostitution services, on one occasion accompanied by Ellen Rometsch; she also "went to parties in Myron Weiner's suite." In an attempt at face-saving for himself, he admitted keeping "the names and addresses of 'a few girls' in the event one of his customer's desired female company while in town." Apparently contradicting himself, he went on to state that he used the services of party girls, including Rometsch, but denied he ever secured their services for anyone else.[81]

On July 3, 1963, Hoover told the Kennedys that Rometsch was alleged to be from East Germany and to have formerly worked for Walter Ulbricht, the Communist leader of East Germany. He went on to say that the FBI suspected that she was a spy.[82] RFK also realized that Bobby Baker, who had arranged these sessions, not only had tapes and photographs of JFK's sexual activities involving Rometsch, but also knew about earlier trysts with Maria Novotny and Suzy Chang, both of whom were from Communist countries and had been named as part of the spy ring that had trapped John Profumo, the British war minister. Bobby knew that Johnson, through his connections

---

79. U.S. Senate Committee on rules and Administration. *Construction of the District of Columbia Stadium and Matters Related Thereto.* Washington, DC: U.S. Government Printing Office, 1965, pt. 12, p. 1101.
80. Ibid. (also see pt. 4, p. 550).
81. Ibid.
82. North., pp. 398–399.

with both Bobby Baker and Hoover, would have also known all about these vulnerabilities of his brother and would not hesitate to use the knowledge to his own advantage. RFK became convinced that if these stories were published, his brother might be forced to resign.[83]

Hoover, of course, knew all about JFK's involvement with Ellen Rometsch when JFK was still sleeping with her. Apparently, the president agreed with the other fifty customers that Baker had referred to, and wanted to keep her on. By the time Baker started dropping her name, in reaction to the pressure that Bobby was putting on him, Hoover had already directed his FBI agents to question Rometsch about her time in East Germany. They came to the conclusion that she was probably a Soviet spy. When Hoover then passed this information on to the Kennedys, Robert Kennedy arranged to give her $50,000 and have her sent back to Germany. She was satisfied with this arrangement for a short time, but then wanted to return to the United States to marry her boyfriend. The Kennedys now had to raise more money to keep her in Germany, and happy and content to remain there. For that, JFK decided to recruit his old pal Grant Stockdale to help raise additional money.[84]

By this time, AG Kennedy knew that the lid was very close to blowing, and he had to do everything he could to keep that from happening. There was pressure from the Republicans to have Rometsch returned to Washington to be interviewed, an idea that caused AG Kennedy to appeal to Hoover's sense of patriotism to stop, in the interests of the presidency itself. After discussing it with Hoover by telephone in the morning, he met with him the same afternoon to force him to persuade the Senate leadership to abort the Senate investigation of this story, because it was "contrary to the national interest." He also told him to let it be known that other leading members of Congress would be drawn into this scandal, and so it was also contrary to the interests of Congress.[85]

The Fallout from the White House Sexcapades

Although the attitude of journalists in the 1960s toward the private lives of politicians was generally more benign, when the situation did rise to a level at which it could not be kept from the public, the ensuing scandal was generally much greater than might now be the case. As noted earlier, such a scandal brought down the British government. John F. Kennedy had been intimate

83. Ibid., pp. 404–406.
84. Ibid., p. 409.
85. Ibid., pp. 403–404.

with some of the same women who were involved in the British scandal, so by the fall of 1963, the festering animosities threatened the continued existence of the Kennedy administration.

Seymour Hersh interviewed four former Secret Service agents who reported that they saw a president obsessed with sex, willing to take enormous risks to gratify that obsession, a president who came late many times to the Oval Office and who was not readily available for hours during the day. According to a Secret Service agent who was on the Kennedy presidential detail, "When she (Jackie) was there, it was no fun. He just had headaches. You really saw him droop because he wasn't getting laid. He was like a rooster getting hit with a water hose."[86] Secret Service agents were frustrated by the many unknown women who were brought to the president for one-night stands. The women were not searched before meeting the president. The agents feared that one of these women would blackmail or even kill JFK. This was not the only way the agents felt derelict in their duty; they also allowed crimes to go unreported. When traveling, local officials would often bring call girls and hookers (often more than one at a time) to the president. The agents, rather than arresting the president or his aides, friends, and supporters for procuring prostitutes, would say nothing. There were many budding Hollywood starlets brought to the White House for their services with it made clear that sex with the president could help a career, but news of the affair would end it.[87]

Long after his death, incredible rumors and credible stories emerged of JFK's love life with beautiful women of many backgrounds: Audrey Hepburn, Jayne Mansfield, Gene Tierney, Marlene Dietrich, Kim Novak, Janet Leigh, and Rhonda Flemming were among the Hollywood set; Angie Dickinson was also widely rumored to have shared a bed not only with Elvis Presley but with the president as well (presumably at different times). However, she may not have been totally satisfied by that rendezvous since she reportedly said JFK's brutal lovemaking style was "the best twenty seconds of my life." His German spy lover, Inga Arvad, later confided to columnist Arthur Krock that "Jack was a poor lover—a 'boy, not a man, who was intent upon ejaculation and not a woman's pleasure.'"[88] That lament is curiously similar to one supposedly made by his wife, as reported in the book *Grace and Power* by Sally Smith: "Jackie said JFK was a flop as a lover. She told a friend he 'just goes too fast and falls asleep.'"

86. Hersh, Seymour, p. 238.
87. Ibid., pp. 229–230, 237.
88. Kessler, *The Sins of the Father*, p. 264.

JFK's poolside cavorting may have been a factor in his death: In September 1963, while frolicking poolside with another of his sexual partners (possibly Fiddle or Faddle, the secretaries from the White House staff who were evidently hired on the basis of skills other than the usual filing, typing, and shorthand variety), JFK tore a groin muscle. To relieve pain and promote healing, he had to wear a stiff shoulder-to-groin brace that locked his body in a rigid stationary posture. It was far more constraining than his usual back brace, which he also continued to wear. The two braces made it impossible for JFK to bend in reflex when he was struck in the neck by a bullet fired by the assassins in Dealey Plaza. The president's back remained erect for the last, fatal, shot, allowing his head to stay in a relatively stable, upright position (Hersch, *The Dark Side of Camelot*, p. 12).

Lest the reader conclude that the reason for this journey "into the weeds" of the lurid bedroom antics of the president and his brother, the "assistant president," with beautiful women was merely a prurient detour, it is the undeniable direct connection between the brothers' risky behavior and what several other men thought of them that formed a critical mass that eventually exploded in Dallas (and possibly again five years later in Los Angeles and Memphis, but that's a subject for other books). Those other men, representing the highest levels of the military, intelligence, and law enforcement agencies of the government—led all along, since even before their 1961 inauguration, by the vice president of the United States—decided that the Kennedys' activities were tantamount to a serious national security risk and amounted to "consorting with the enemy." These men had the power to eliminate this risk and came to believe that JFK's liaisons were nothing other than treasonous acts that had to be dealt with accordingly.

The Cast of Spooks—Key CIA Men

In addition to Bill Harvey, who was described at length in the previous chapter, there were a number of men of the CIA who deserve a few words in order to properly set the context into which the nation, and the world, was thrust during the early 1960s as the cold war reached a boil.

Allen Dulles, Director of Central Intelligence

Allen Dulles, previously a member of the OSS before coming to the CIA at its inception, took over from Walter Bedell "Beetle" Smith when Eisenhower appointed Smith to become secretary of state in 1953. Dulles served until November 1961, when he was fired by President Kennedy for the failures of the Bay of Pigs fiasco. Due to his background, Dulles was mostly interested in covert operations and proceeded quickly to take the agency into the uncharted waters of overthrowing governments unfriendly to the United States. During his tenure as DCI, he initiated coups in Iran in 1953 and Costa Rica and Guatemala in 1954, which were considered successful because they accomplished the goal, irrespective of the later consequences. The operations not considered successful included those of Indonesia and Tibet in 1958, Vietnam from 1954 through 1964, and Operation Mongoose against Cuba in 1961–1962. Considering this record and later developments in these countries, in retrospect it is hard to consider any of this work a success. John F. Kennedy certainly had his doubts, which led to him firing Dulles, along with Gen. Charles Cabell, ostensibly for their parts in the failure of the Bay of Pigs invasion. These firings were widely considered to be the first step in his longer-term plan to break up the CIA, carrying out his vow "to splinter the CIA in a thousand pieces and scatter it to the winds."[89]

The Guatemala operation was owned by Allen Dulles, who did not approve of the small group of advisers to President Jacobo Arbenz who were seeking socialist remedies for the rural poverty afflicting much of the population of their country. When the Arbenz government moved to expropriate 174,000 acres from United Fruit Company, Dulles decided to take action despite the strong objections of the State Department. Called Operation Success, it cost about $3 million and lasted eight months. The overthrow of a small country's democratically elected government in 1954, due to a perception held by a few people in Washington that somehow Guatemala was a threat to the security of the United States, led to a civil war that lasted decades and cost over two hundred thousand lives.[90] Dulles considered Operation Success a success, at least compared with his multiple failures to stop the spread of Communism in Europe, because it turned around the socialistic direction of the Guatemalan government. This was the first covert operation for a young David Atlee Phillips, who received a Distinguished Intelligence Medal for his creation of a "completely notional situation" (i.e., hypothetical) that led to the Guatemalan government being deluded into thinking it was in far worse shape than it actually was, leading to its early surrender.

The final, black irony of Allen Dulles's career was his appointment, by the new president Lyndon B. Johnson, to serve on the commission charged with certifying the integrity of the investigation into John Kennedy's assassination, though his real mission there was to help protect secrets. That project, of course, would be considered a definite success.

Unfortunately, the fallout from the many illegal operations allowed by Dulles would continue for at least two decades; it could be argued that the

89. Douglass, pp. 14–15.
90. Morley, *Our Man in Mexico*, pp. 65–72.

biggest fallout occurred just one decade after Dulles ascended to his position as DCI, an event generally referred to as "the crime of the century." Many of the same men involved in the Guatemala coup, for example, would turn up in Dallas on November 22, 1963, including E. Howard Hunt, Edward Lansdale, Tracy Barnes, Grayston Lynch, "Rip" Robertson, David Sanchez Morales, and David Atlee Phillips. Others who were not there, yet were figuratively only one step removed, included Bill Harvey, Frank Wisner, Cord Meyer, James Angleton, Richard Helms, and Allen Dulles.

The Enigmatic James Jesus Angleton

The head of the CIA's counterintelligence branch for twenty years, through 1974, Angleton was known widely as the "poet-spy," whose literary journal, *Furioso*, published the works of Ezra Pound, e. e. cummings, and Archibald MacLeish. He also enjoyed growing orchids and has been memorialized in more than one movie for these avocations. Toward the end of his career, he would sit before a congressional committee and say that "it is inconceivable that a secret intelligence arm of the government has to comply with all the overt orders of the government."[91] To say that Angleton was a complex man, full of contradictions, would be an understatement; perhaps his pursuit of artful things and delicate flowers was meant to balance his senses.

Like many of his peers, Angleton was in the Office of Strategic Services (OSS), the World War II predecessor to the CIA. For Angleton, the cold war was an extension of WWII, morphed into an anti-Communist crusade with his double agents engaged in an underground battle against the international Communist peril. Angleton became involved as a supervisor of a CIA assassination unit in the 1950s, headed by Army Colonel Boris Pash. This unit was designed especially for the killing of suspected double agents, according to the statement of E. Howard Hunt. According to Mark Lane, "Pash's assassination unit was assigned to James Jesus Angleton."[92] Angleton also had a long association with a number of Mob figures, from his days in Italy with the OSS and later through a number of connections with Meyer Lansky.[93] After his retirement, he told an investigator that he knew which Mob figures had killed Sam Giancana and blamed the Church Committee for causing his death, as well as Johnny Rosselli's, by demanding testimony on topics about which the Mafia's code of silence (omerta) required absolute

---

91. Ibid., p. 164.
92. Lane, *Plausible Denial*, p. 164.
93. Scott, p. 195 (ref. McCoy, "Politics of Heroin," pp. 59, 62; *Saturday Evening Post*, May 20, 1967).

secrecy.[94] In his oversight of the CIA's counterintelligence division, the program of international mail interception had tracked Lee Harvey Oswald from his visit to the Soviet Union and tracked him during his trip to Mexico City.[95]

David Martin's book *Wilderness of Mirrors* thoroughly described the myriad of deceptions and disinformation the CIA has employed since its inception. But it was Angleton who originally coined the phrase Martin used for the book title, an excellent and succinct description of Angleton's life. Unfortunately, his increasingly obsessive, ultimately unsuccessful hunt for "moles" (KGB double agents) within the CIA led him to collect thousands of files on CIA employees and others whom he suspected. His files closely resembled (and no doubt were somewhat redundant of) the files being collected by his friend J. Edgar Hoover, labeled "official and confidential" and "personal," a shameful collection of rumors, innuendos, and fabrications.

Angleton's paranoia about moles under every chair, and his habit of labeling anyone who disagreed with him as a spy, intimidated the agency to the extent that recruitment of agents had to be suspended. By talking in riddles and conducting his domain as if he were the only person alive who really understood the world of counterintelligence—together with the huge files he kept on all CIA officers and key political figures—he had successfully intimidated his superiors from taking action against him for decades, before being removed by William Colby in 1974. By then, he had already removed many of the files he maintained, including everything he had on John F. Kennedy. For all his paranoia about moles within the CIA, he had been mesmerized by the defector Anatoli Golytsin, who manipulated him. He was also naïve about Harold "Kim" Philby, a high-ranking officer of the British Intelligence Service MI-6 who, it turned out, was actually a doubled master Soviet KGB agent; Angleton himself, "the hunter of moles," had confided many of the nation's secrets to Kim Philby during their weekly lunches together at Harvey's or La Nicoise restaurants.[96]

Theodore "Ted" Shackley, the Linguistics Major

Ted Shackley had a background in linguistics at the University of Maryland, which was his entrée into the world of spooks not far from College Park, across the Potomac River in Langley, Virginia. Before that, he served in

---

94. Ibid.
95. Brugioni, pp. 68–69.
96. Kessler, *The CIA…* pp. 54–56.

the army's counterintelligence division, where he became involved with the recruitment of Polish agents. Upon joining the CIA, he became involved in numerous "black operations" and became known as the Blond Ghost for his refusal to be photographed. Others believe that this appellation referred to a mysterious series of deaths that occurred shortly after he was posted in various stations; he had worked under Bill Harvey since 1953. About the same time as Operation Mongoose was launched, Shackley was named the station chief of the Miami station, known under its code name JM/WAVE. He was responsible for the CIA officers who were supervising approximately two thousand Cuban exiles and agents still living underground in Cuba, as well as their own navy fleet, comprised mostly of agile speedboats, built with heavy hulls and large, powerful engines.

David Atlee Phillips, a.k.a. Maurice Bishop

Shackley's second in command of JM/WAVE was David Atlee Phillips, who was identified under his code name Maurice Bishop. Phillips's first duty as a CIA operative was during the insurrection he induced; his role in that operation was to create a blitz of propaganda to persuade the Guatemalan government that it was in far worse shape than it was in reality. He received a Distinguished Intelligence Medal for his role in deluding an entire government of their fatal deficiencies, which led to the Guatemalan government not mounting an effective defense when the revolution began.

Phillips was involved in directing Oswald to some degree, certainly by the time Oswald had returned to Dallas, where he was seen meeting with Phillips by Antonio Veciana. There are two possibilities as to what this involvement was:[97]

- Preparing a number of witness sightings and paper trails purposely implicating Oswald in advance of his mission, including the trip to Mexico, for the purpose of connecting Kennedy's assassination directly, and quickly, to Cuba and the Soviet Union, as a means to trigger an invasion of Cuba, at the risk of Soviet retaliation.
- Creating the above sightings and paper trails for some other mission being set up for Oswald but being usurped later by superiors in Washington (i.e., Angleton) and/or Miami (Harvey) for the mission to kill Kennedy.

The second possibility was the most likely, involving a simulated assassination being set up as the pretext to indirectly force Kennedy into an invasion of Cuba.

---

97. Scott, pp. 313–386.

That plan was hijacked along the way and recast as an actual assassination, but Oswald's role remained the same: the patsy of the operation. This attempt ultimately failed, of course, because after Kennedy was assassinated, it became Lyndon Johnson's choice; his preference all along was to avoid a confrontation with the Soviet Union, as some in the Pentagon (e.g., LeMay, Willoughby) would have preferred. Johnson probably did not favor this because it might result in leveling Washington DC, taking him out with it, thereby ruining his opportunity to be the greatest U.S. president of all time.

David Atlee Phillips said before he died that fringe elements of U.S. intelligence may have been involved in the conspiracy.[98] According to his nephew Shawn Phillips, as David neared death, Shawn's father, James Phillips, contacted his brother David after a six-year estrangement caused by their inability to converse about some of David's secrets. James had already concluded that David "was seriously involved" in the JFK assassination; Shawn wrote, "Finally, as David was dying of irreversible lung cancer, he called Jim and there was apparently no reconciliation between them, as Jim asked David pointedly, 'Were you in Dallas on that day'? David said, 'Yes', and Jim hung the phone up."[99]

David Sanchez Morales, the Big Indian

David Sanchez Morales worked closely with David Atlee Phillips and Bill Harvey. He was also very close to Johnny Rosselli and John Martino. Thanks to his successful work on a number of black bag operations, he developed a reputation as the best CIA assassin in Latin America. Morales was an important figure at the Havana station between 1958 and 1960, working under the cover of an advertising agency headed by David A. Phillips. He was involved in setting up the JM/WAVE CIA station in Miami and planning the Bay of Pigs invasion, and before that, he participated in Operation Phoenix, in Laos and Vietnam, a program that involved widespread destruction of entire villages and the inhabitants thereof, and eventually led to the My Lai massacre.

Morales was a big, muscular man of very dark complexion, nicknamed El Indio (the Indian). Several witnesses on Dealey Plaza, most of whom were not called to testify before the Warren Commission, described a man fitting Morales's description. These witnesses saw such a man at the windows of the sixth floor of the Texas School Book Depository shortly before Kennedy's motorcade passed by, as well as minutes after the shooting, fleeing from the

98. Twyman, p. 285.
99. http://www.jfkmurdersolved.com/phillips.htm

back of the building with two other men in a station wagon. Under the influence of alcohol, he had hinted to close friends that he had been involved in the Kennedy assassination, saying, "'Well, we took care of that son of a bitch, didn't we?'"[100]

Morales was a close associate of David Phillips, who was second in charge at JM/WAVE. He was a very active CIA asset, showing up in Guatemala in 1954, Venezuela during 1955–1958, Havana in 1960, Peru during 1965–1966, Laos in 1966, Bolivia in 1967, and Chile in 1973. Wherever the action was, Morales could be found close by. Morales died on May 8, 1978, from a sudden heart attack under mysterious circumstances; his death occurred just days before he was scheduled to testify for the House Select Committee of Assassinations.

Antonio Veciana, of Alpha 66

Veciana was the head of Alpha 66, by far the most violent of the several exile groups that were committed to murdering Fidel Castro and returning Cuba to its rightful owners. It was also the group most hateful of both Kennedys, and many within it had sworn to kill them both if they did not make good on their empty promises to return Cuba and oust Castro.

Veciana was recruited in Havana in 1960 by his CIA contact, Maurice Bishop (generally thought to be David A. Phillips, though Veciana was very coy about that and never admitted it), who tutored him in such guerrilla methods as psychological warfare, organization of cells, counterfeiting Cuban currency, maritime sabotage, and political assassination.[101] What is known is that the CIA agent working under the Maurice Bishop code name was involved in the attacks on Soviet ships coming into Havana, and that Veciana said that Bishop had told him it was his intention to cause trouble between Kennedy and the Russians so that JFK would be forced to violate his pledge to Khrushchev not to invade Cuba; furthermore, Bishop had told him that Kennedy was inexperienced and surrounded by others who could not properly run the country and that their mission was to force Kennedy into removing Castro's regime.[102] Once, in Dallas, he met Bishop at the Southland Center; Bishop was accompanied by a stranger whom, after the assassination, he recognized as Lee Harvey Oswald. Veciana was adamantly certain that the stranger was either Oswald or his "double."[103]

---

100. Fonzi, *The Last Investigation*, p. 390.
101. DiEugenio, *Destiny Betrayed*, p. 236.
102. Ibid., p. 237.
103. Ibid.

George de Mohrenschildt, Oswald's Mysterious Friend

George de Mohrenschildt was a well-connected oil geologist and happened also to be a relative of Jacqueline Kennedy. A well-educated world traveler, he was probably the least likely person to become Oswald's best friend in Dallas; yet that is exactly what he did, assisting him in finding a job and relocating to New Orleans and then back to Dallas. He had begun writing and talking in the second half of the 1970s. Writers Willem Oltems and Edward Epstein were after de Mohrenschildt for more of his story, and so was HSCA investigator Gaeton Fonzi. Within hours of Fonzi's calling upon de Mohrenschildt and leaving a card with his daughter, the man who had admitted talking about Oswald with the Dallas CIA representative was dead of a shotgun blast, allegedly self-inflicted. De Mohrenschildt's death paradoxically played a role in the HSCA receiving its needed renewal with the new Congress. De Mohrenschildt's role in setting up Oswald will be explored further in chapter 6.

George Joannides: A Varied, Virtual Mole

Many CIA secrets associated with the Kennedy assassination are still being protected from public scrutiny despite the 1992 passage of JFK Assassination Records Collection Act. Most of the agency's files on Joannides, the chief of psychological warfare at the agency's JM/WAVE station in Miami at the time, are a case in point. In 1963, he was in charge of leading the so-called DRE (Revolutionary Cuban Student Directorate). He provided them with up to $50,000 per month of agency funds, instilling in the process a military-style discipline and obeisance to his leadership; he was rated highly for his abilities in this regard, as noted in his job evaluation done in July 1963.[104]

A week after Joannides's performance review, Lee Harvey Oswald had a confrontation with members of the DRE in New Orleans as he distributed his "free Cuba" pamphlets on a street corner, setting off a string of encounters between the supposedly pro-Castro ex-marine and the anti-Castro exiles. The DRE sent a member to Oswald's house posing as a Castro supporter and subsequently challenged him to a radio debate. They made a tape of the debate, which was sent to Joannides. Because his files are still being withheld, it is still unknown what role Joannides had with the encounters between his DRE agents and Oswald. What is known is that within an hour of Oswald's arrest on November 22, 1963, the leaders of the group he supervised—the DRE in Miami—went public with their documentation of

104. Morley, *Our Man . . .* , pp. 170–171.

Oswald's involvement in support of Castro, providing the press information that would help shape the image just being formed by millions of Americans about the person who stood accused of killing the president.[105]

Joannides's career was one of perpetual "virtual denials." The Warren Commission was not informed about Joannides's connection to the DRE and the men Oswald had confronted in New Orleans. Likewise, the House Select Committee on Assassinations (HSCA) was not informed of his previous duties when he was brought out of retirement and appointed as their liaison to the CIA. That connection was not uncovered for another twenty years, in 1998; Joannides had died seven years earlier, still holding his secrets. The former general counsel to the committee, Bob Blakey, was outraged at this news and maintained that this action constituted obstruction of Congress.[106]

Researcher-author Jefferson Morley filed a suit against the CIA in December 2003, seeking records of Joannides's activities in 1963 and 1978.[107] A year later he was given about 150 pages of heavily redacted and incomplete records from Joannides's personnel file. The Agency informed Morley that the remaining records about Joannides's actions *"will not be released in any form. These JFK assassination records are still considered secret in the name of national security"*[108] (emphasis added).

The records that the CIA did release are troubling. They show that Joannides traveled to New Orleans in connection with his CIA duties in 1963–1964 and that he was cleared for two highly sensitive operations in December 1962 and June 1963 but do not state any details regarding his assignments in those operations. The CIA was legally required to make these records public with the passage of the 1992 JFK Assassination Records Collection Act.[109] As the world awaits the release of legally mandated information, the CIA continues openly defying and obstructing Congress. In the meantime, the status of Mr. Morley's continuing lawsuit with the CIA remains a topic of discussion on the Internet.*

Edward Lansdale: The Ugly American

Like many of his colleagues, Edward Lansdale had been in the OSS during World War II; after that he served in the army and then the air force. Before

---

*Among internet sites following it are the Mary Ferrell website and the Future of Freedom website.
105. Ibid.
106. Ibid.
107. Morley, Jefferson, *The George Joannides Coverup* (JFKLancer.com).
108. Ibid.
109. Ibid.

his service in the war, he had been an advertising executive and was—as most people drawn to that vocation are—rather flamboyant and gifted in people skills, at least with those who were malleable and vulnerable to his devices. Lansdale was a highly skilled political manipulator, whose character became ignominiously caricaturized as Colonel Hillindale in the novel *The Ugly American*.[110] He had become a self-styled "expert" on Vietnam and was sent by the CIA to help the South Vietnamese government, becoming a personal friend of President Ngo Dinh Diem in the process. Lansdale had been there in March–May 1954 at the battle of Dien Bien Phu; the peace conference in Switzerland which produced the Geneva Accords provided him a blueprint of how he and the CIA could wrest control of the government of the newly partitioned area south of the 17th parallel.

The Accords defined how the French and Viet Minh were to disengage, and for one year the population could choose which part of the partitioned Vietnam in which they wanted to live. Lansdale went to work to give incentives to people living in the more populous north, including most of the Catholic population, to move to the southern section. He developed a plan which used many of the eclectic ideas one might expect from a man with his background as an advertising executive: made-up disinformation and paid-off fortune-tellers, using the well-developed indigenous rumor mill, to sell the population on the merits of living south of the 17th parallel. One of the rumors fed to the villagers was that the Viet Minh had made a deal to allow Chinese troops into the north again and they were already beginning to rape the women and pillage the villages there. "Black leaflets" were distributed to warn people how to conduct themselves when the Viet Minh took over, and a description of how a program of "monetary reform" would commence, which had the effect of immediately halving the value of the currency. The leaflets, booklets, and rumors scared nine hundred thousand people enough to move south. Lansdale and his team had succeeded—through clever disinformation and psychological warfare tactics with a population which strongly believed in astrology, superstition, and soothsayers—in their ruse to sabotage the Viet Minh. An almanac was even printed and sold in the marketplaces which predicted great fortunes for those who decided to live in the south, whereas those in the north could expect only the bleakest existence. All of this caused great confusion just before the elections held as stipulated by the Geneva Accords. The result of Lansdale's efforts was a successful birth of the Republic of South Vietnam, with Diem at the helm, deeply grateful to Edward Lansdale for the gift.

---

110. Newman, p. 27.

Lansdale's real goal, however, was to become the ambassador to South Vietnam, in spite of the fact that he was not well liked by many people in the State Department; the sentiment was bilateral, and for that reason, his goal was not realistic. Within six days of his inauguration, President Kennedy reviewed a report from Lansdale that was "an extremely vivid and well-written account of a place that was going to hell in a hack."[111] He wrote it in a way that denigrated the performance of Ambassador Durbrow, which successfully convinced Kennedy to relieve the ambassador of his duties. After his command performance at the White House on January 28, Lansdale "returned to his office 'jubilant,' and boasted, 'I'm going back to Vietnam in a higher assignment.'"[112] He had worked closely with Diem in his efforts to depose Durbrow and take over as ambassador, liaising with his military and intelligence contacts, particularly his friend General Lionel McGarr (MAAG chief in Saigon) and William Colby, CIA station chief in Saigon.

In the State Department, Dean Rusk had been informed by his assistant for Far Eastern affairs, J. Graham Parsons, that Lansdale was too much of a maverick, who resented officials coming from foreign service training and was therefore not "a team player." Rusk also learned of Lansdale's covert credentials for the first time; all of this cost Lansdale any consideration of being named as the ambassador.[113] Much of the discussion within the State Department regarding Lansdale remains classified or has disappeared, and the result is a "murky trail . . . typical of the life of Lansdale, who would probably turn in his grave if any question about him could be easily answered."[114] It appears now that Edward Lansdale had deluded himself into thinking he knew more about Vietnam than did anyone else, either there or in Washington, and set out to get Ambassador Durbrow thrown out and himself installed in his position. After failing at that, he wrote a report urging a large U.S. troop commitment to Vietnam, effectively taking sides against JFK's stated objectives; the timing of this report indicates that it was done in conjunction with Lyndon Johnson's visit to Vietnam, which further suggests that the document's message was heavily influenced by Johnson.

Cord Meyer: One of the Blue Bloods of the CIA

Cord Meyer had always despised John F. Kennedy. Meyer had come from a long line of Yankee blue bloods listed in the New York Social Register who were accustomed to regal treatment and regular coverage in the society

111. Newman, p. 3 (ref. Rusk memo to JFK from first week of Feb., 1961, JFK Library).
112. Ibid., p. 27 (ref. author's interview with Air Force Colonel Fletcher Prouty, June 26, 1991).
113. Ibid.
114. Ibid., p. 34.

pages; they were presumed to be of higher intellect, greater erudition, and altogether more worthy of the respect and adulation of those poor souls beneath their station. He had been trained from an early age to treat the *nouveau riche* with a subtle disdain, or outright condescension, depending upon how far down the totem pole from his own lofty position in mainstream society he might deem someone to be. Those having been born of wealth and privilege for multiple generations were presumed to have a higher claim on the world's opportunities than that of the class who had only made their way across the ocean in the last generation or two, whose grueling passage was made in the lower, smellier decks of the ocean liners. The Kennedys were among the latter group, despite the rapidity with which their bank accounts had caught up and surpassed many families whose ancestors had crossed the ocean on the *Mayflower*. Cord Meyer started out with a low regard for the immigrant's son John F. Kennedy, and in the course of life's events, his disdain would develop into a loathing contempt. In between the two, of course, was his wife, Mary Pinchot Meyer, whose murder along the Potomac River in October 1964 has now been conclusively shown to have been orchestrated by top CIA officials Cord Meyer and Wistar Janney in the 2012 book *Mary's Mosaic*, by Peter Janney, the son of Wistar Janney.

Young Cord was given a classically liberal education at Yale, where he was a member of the Scroll and Key Society, and became an advocate of world government as a means for solving all the world's problems. In 1945, he took his young bride, Mary Pinchot Meyer, with him to San Francisco for the United Nations planning conference. John F. Kennedy also attended this conference and recognized Mary from having dated her during their prep school days; something happened between them in San Francisco during that conference, which years later, caused Kennedy to decline giving Cord Meyer a political appointment. He explained to Charles Bartlett, a mutual friend of theirs, that he could not support Meyer "due to some incident that occurred at the UN conference in San Francisco in 1945, there was no possibility." This incident was widely believed to have been an attempt by JFK to seduce Cord's new wife (it is not clear whether it was successful or not); regardless, Cord developed a visceral hatred for Kennedy from that day on.[115]

After the formation of the United Nations, Meyer established the United World Federalists, an organization that promoted the idea of a world without nuclear weapons. Cord Meyer had been shocked by the atom bombs dropped on Hiroshima and Nagasaki. After the war, Meyer commissioned a film by Pare Lorentz called *The Beginning or the End*. Meyer wanted this film to be the definitive statement about the dangers of the atomic age. In the left versus right wings, which later developed within the CIA, there is little doubt

---

115. Burleigh, p. 48.

which side Cord Meyer would inhabit. That Cord viewed the "Agency" in a third-person context, as though he had little control over its past, present, or future direction—despite his own influence over it—was evident up to his dying day, when someone asked him who he thought was behind the murder of his ex-wife; his response to that question was, "The same sons of bitches that killed John F. Kennedy."[116]

Richard Helms: Chief Dissembler

The largest question about Helms's possible involvement surfaced in 1975 when the Church Committee began looking into the CIA's ZR/RIFLE program, which he had a direct hand in creating. Helms testified about two members of that team—WI/ROGUE and QJ/WIN—who seemed to appear in advance of JFK's assassination and then disappear back into the woodwork a few months afterward; it also revealed how Bill Harvey reported directly to Helms as well as his nominal boss, Angleton. A February 19, 1962, memo from Helms to Bill Harvey had authorized Harvey to hire the assassin known as QJ/WIN for the ZR/RIFLE operation.[117] The testimony indicated that WI/ROGUE was "an essentially stateless soldier of fortune, a forger and former bank robber," but the "principal agent" was QJ/WIN, whom Richard Helms described thusly: "If you need somebody to carry out murder, I guess you had a man who might be prepared to carry it out."[118] Documents would surface that proved not only that Dick Helms and Des FitzGerald ran ZR/RIFLE, but that Bobby Kennedy had authorized the plots, which were run by Bill Harvey; in the end, only Bill Harvey acknowledged his role in the assassination attempts against Castro.[119]

The attention given to these mysterious Europeans led several researchers—including Steve Rivele, Bernard Fensterwald Jr., and Jim Lesar, among others—to attempt to find out more about them. Noel Twyman analyzed the disparate facts and concluded that the names associated with the codes WI/ROGUE and QJ/WIN—who suddenly vanished from the CIA payroll in February 1964—were possibly Lucien Sarti and Jean Soutre (a.k.a. Michel Mertz and Michel Roux), respectively. An extensive description of the basis of this conclusion is presented in chapter 20 of his book, *Bloody Treason*.[120] He also described the expulsion of Soutre the day following the assassination and confirmed his presence in Dallas on November 22, 1963. According to author Gus Russo, QJ/WIN was named as Jose Mankel by

116. Ibid.
117. Russo, p. 432.
118. Twyman, pp. 393–394 (ref. The Church Committee Report, p. 182).
119. Ibid., pp. 432–433.
120. Ibid., pp. 387–427.

the contract agent code-named WI/ROGUE, David Dzitzichwili, who was described by the CIA as a man who "learns quickly and carries out any assignment without regard for the danger . . . in a word, he can rationalize all actions."[121] Mankel was described as a mercenary from Cologne, Germany, and as a man without scruples, "a man who would do anything—including assassination";[122] he was to become the link between Bill Harvey, Guy Banister, and David Ferrie in New Orleans; the leaders of the Cuban exiles; Johnny Rosselli, whom he worked with on the Castro assassination attempts; and the French assassins commissioned to be one of the three teams in Dealey Plaza.

The Cast of Military Men

In contrast to the "great generals" of the World War II era, men like Douglas MacArthur and George Patton, there were others who thought of themselves as "great" but whose unfamiliarity with the great lessons of world history and a general absence of an appreciation of the nuances of the cultural milieu in other parts of the globe caused them to be lesser figures. In the previous chapter, it was observed that, in fact, MacArthur himself was critical of the military advice that President Kennedy had received from the Pentagon in reference to Southeast Asia; he blamed the previous generation of military leaders, who, he said, had advanced the wrong younger officers. One of the key elements leading up to the assassination of Kennedy, and the willingness of certain high-level military officers to participate in a coup d'état to remove him and allow Lyndon Johnson to replace him, was this very phenomenon. A few representative examples, though not nearly complete, will serve to make the point.

General Curtis LeMay—The Mad Bomber

The best way to describe the air force representative to the Joint Chiefs of Staff, appointed to advise the president of the most sophisticated and thoughtful military views on the state of the world, is to present a portion of a column printed by *The Washington Post*, July 19, 1961, by the nationally syndicated columnist Marquis Childs:

> *At a Georgetown dinner party recently, the wife of a leading senator sat next to Gen. Curtis LeMay, chief of staff of the Air Force. He told her a nuclear war was inevitable. It would begin in December and be all over*

121. Russo, pp. 62; 525 [fn #52] (Ref. Church Committee Interim Report, 46).
122. Ibid. p. 62.

by the first of the year. In that interval, every major American city—
Washington, New York, Philadelphia, Detroit, Chicago, Los Angeles—
would be reduced to rubble. Similarly, the principal cities of the Soviet
Union would be destroyed. The lady, as she tells it, asked if there were
any place where she could take her children and grandchildren to safety;
the general would, of course, at the first alert be inside the top-secret
underground hideout near Washington from which the retaliatory
strike would be directed. He told her that certain unpopulated areas in
the far west would be safest.

If ever there were a rogue general capable of pulling off a coup, it would
have been General LeMay: A stereotypical ultra-right-wing reactionary, he
was a belligerent, cigar-chomping cold warrior undaunted by the messy
"collateral damages" of human suffering and destruction of property that
are a necessary by-product of war, cataclysmic though they may be.*,123
LeMay was like Lyndon Johnson in many ways: Petulant and often childish
when he didn't get his way, LeMay would light a cigar and blow smoke in
the direction of anyone challenging his position. To show utter disgust, he
would walk into the private Joint Chiefs of Staff toilet, leave the door open,
urinate or break wind loudly, and flush the commode a number of times as
he finished cleaning himself up. He would then walk calmly back into the
meeting pretending that nothing had happened. When angry with individual
staff members, he would resort to sarcasm; if that failed, he would direct his
wrath to the entire staff.[124]

Time magazine, in its May 25, 1962 issue, described LeMay leaving
Capitol Hill a few days before that, after testifying there about the new air
force budget: "Scowling ferociously, Air Force Chief of Staff Curtis LeMay,
55, wanted the Senate Appropriations subcommittee to get one thing
straight. 'I object to having the term "bomber man" applied to me,' he said,
even as he was urging Congress to lay out $491 million for the long-range

---

* It was General LeMay who was satirized on the big screen in 1964, caricaturized as General
Jack D. Ripper in the classic movie *Dr. Strangelove*, about a general who became enamored
with the concept of first strike nuclear bombing capability, which then morphed into an
inevitability before, by logical extension, an essential necessity, "sooner rather than later,"
when it would become too late for practical use. The concept evolves, during the movie, to
its ultimate manifestation, reflected in the second part of the movie's title: *How I Learned to
Stop Worrying and Love the Bomb*. Another character, Major TJ "King" Kong (played by Slim
Pickens), in forcing the bomb bay doors of a B-52 open, releases one of the nuclear bombs;
Kong is mounted on top of it like a rodeo cowboy and rides it into oblivion, whooping and
hollering as the bomb falls out at fifty thousand feet, into a climactic explosion. Although not
overtly sexual, the innuendo abounds.
123. Brugioni, Dino A., *Eyeball to eyeball*, p. 262.
124. Ibid.

RS-70 bomber, $320 million more than the administration wanted. 'I will use the most effective weapons system that will do the job. If that's kiddie cars, I'll use kiddie cars.'" General LeMay talked openly about a preemptive attack in which one hundred million people would be killed. He persistently recommended taking aggressive action regarding an attack on Cuba in order to overthrow Castro, beginning with the Bay of Pigs invasion and continually through the period of the Cuban Missile Crisis, as Kennedy continually resisted his recommendations. LeMay was a proponent of the concept of "nuclear first strike," saying that we should give the Russians the "Sunday punch" before they did it to us. In the 1950s, under Eisenhower, LeMay had the authority to order a nuclear strike without presidential authorization if the president could not be contacted. Kennedy made it clear that that authority was no longer applicable. According to David Talbot, "Years after he left the air force, in an oral history for the Johnson Library, LeMay was still venting in remarkably savage terms, calling the Kennedy crowd "ruthless,' 'vindictive,' morally debased vermin whom LBJ should have 'stepped on' when he took over the White House, 'like the cockroaches they were.'" Kennedy did not have warm feelings for LeMay either, of course: "I don't want that man near me again," he once spat out, after walking out on one of the general's briefings. "A prick like LeMay—Kennedy didn't trust him as far as he could throw a marble pillar," said Charles Daly, one of Kennedy's White House political aides.[125]

Like LeMay, most of the other military chiefs resented the Kennedys, McNamara, and their "whiz kids" academics who had no experience in military affairs. On the other hand, Kennedy questioned the general knowledge of the military chiefs, and he was skeptical of their judgment of the potential international fallout from the military actions they recommended. Kennedy had accepted some of their recommendations during the Bay of Pigs debacle, only to realize later how ill-conceived the overall planning had been. Both sides of this divide seemed to try to be more condescending to the other side; neither had the least respect for the other. The military commanders were accustomed to presidents who let them do their thing, with minimal meddling in their sphere of operations.

One of LeMay's close friends was Charles "Babe" Baron, a general in the Illinois National Guard and an associate of Meyer Lansky and Chicago political boss Jake Arvey. It was determined, by the House Select Committee in 1978, that committee investigators confirmed that "Baron was visiting LeMay the following week [after the assassination]."[126] According to Peter

125. Talbot, pp. 67–68.
126. Scott, p. 199.

Dale Scott, Babe Baron was a "constant companion" of Johnny Rosselli and an even closer friend of Patrick Hoy, who worked for Henry Crown, an Illinois financier and part owner of General Dynamics of Fort Worth, Texas,[127] one of the primary beneficiaries of Johnson's presidency.* Both of them were also close associates of Sidney Korshak, a lawyer who worked for the Chicago Mob who was described by senior Justice Department officials as one of "the most powerful members of the underworld." When Johnson appointed the Warren Commission, he chose as panel commissioners John McCloy, Allen Dulles, Gerald Ford, among others, to serve on it because he knew they would be controllable, as will be explored in later chapters. They, in turn, selected Lee Rankin as chief counsel and Albert E. Jenner Jr.—the personal attorney for General Dynamics's largest stockholder, Henry Crown—to be an assistant counsel. Jenner was put in charge of, among other things, investigating whether Oswald and/or Ruby had past associations or were part of a wider conspiracy. According to famed columnist Drew Pearson, the key people controlling the Mob in Chicago during the 1950s included Henry Crown and Walter Annenberg. The circle of ties from Johnson and Hoover to the top of the commission, through its key staff members, and back to the people closest to the Chicago Mob, would be complete.[128]

General Charles Willoughby (Retired)—General MacArthur's "Little Fascist"

General Willoughby's birth name was actually Adolf Tscheppe-Weidenbach when he was born in Heidelberg, Germany, in 1892. When JFK was assassinated, Willoughby was seventy-one years old and long retired, but he was still very much actively involved on the far-right fringes of the political spectrum, including the John Birch Society and the American friends of the Anti-Bolshevik Bloc of Nations (the ABN) and other anti-Communist extremist organizations in Europe, Japan, and Korea. Willoughby had a reputation for being autocratic and arrogant; he spoke in a German accent but was fluent in four languages. He became the chief of intelligence in the Pacific for General MacArthur, who referred to him as "my little fascist," though he was six feet three inches tall and weighed 220 pounds.[129]

---

*Henry's son Lester Crown, now eighty-four, lost $1 billion (20 percent of his net worth) in the crashing economy of 2008–09; the family fortune is now down to $4 billion (*Forbes* magazine: The Forbes 400, October 19, 2009) p. 124.

127. Ibid., p. 179.
128. Pearson, *Diaries*, p. 470.
129. Twyman, pp. 570–572 (ref. Bruce Cumings, *The Origins of the Korean War, Vol. II—The Roaring of the Cataract, 1947–1950* (Princeton: Princeton University Press, 1990, p. 104).

One of his European links was to the OAS, the French terrorist organization intent on assassinating Charles de Gaulle; this connected him also to Jean Soutre (or Souetre), the French terrorist who showed up in Dallas at the time of the JFK assassination. Willoughby earned his moniker "my little fascist" because he was an avowed racist and fanatical supporter of extreme right-wing causes. In this vein, Willoughby had once written of Italian dictator Mussolini, "Historical judgment, freed from the emotional haze of the moment, will credit Mussolini with wiping out a memory of defeat by re-establishing the traditional military supremacy of the white race."[130] In the United States, he was closely associated with General Edwin Walker, H. L. Hunt, and the Dallas Chapter of the John Birch Society. Willoughby had admired Francisco Franco since the 1920s. In his later years, Willoughby would publish the racist *Foreign Intelligence Digest* newspaper and worked closely with H. L. Hunt on the extreme right-wing organization *International Committee for the Defense of Christian Culture*. It was connected to the John Birch Society and the Minutemen.

The author Bruce Cumings wrote of him, "Willoughby was a profound racist and anti-Semite who saw the Soviet bloc as 'the historical continuity of 'Mongoloid-PanSlavism.' He once wrote that 'when the teeming millions of the Orient and the tropics got their hands on magazine rifles, Kipling's white man was on the way out.' He deplored Asian wars in which 'illiterate Chinese coolies' wiped out American draftees, given that 'the white man is an expensive and limited commodity.' . . . His 'intelligence digest' recommended all through the 1960's that 'weapons of mass destruction,' unspecified, be used against the Vietnamese people. It is hard to find something nice to balance this account. Willoughby was a thoroughly loathsome persona whose entire world view consisted of piles of ethnic stereotypes; he was apparently capable of anything."[131] Willoughby was a close associate of H. L. Hunt, and both were leaders in a worldwide, extreme right-wing network with connections to a number of like-minded organizations, including the John Birch Society and the Minutemen in the United States; similar groups in Europe, including the CIA-front corporation Permindex in Italy and the French OAS, put them in direct association with professional French and Corsican assassins.

Willoughby railed against the liberal Eastern establishment internationalists recruited from Ivy League universities to run the CIA and the State Department (people like Cord Meyer, James Angleton, Dean Acheson, Alger Hiss, and Averell Harriman), who were considered to be

---

130. See The Education Forum: http://educationforum.ipbhost.com/index.php?showtopic=9198
131. Twyman, pp. 570–572 (ref. Cumings, op. cit.).

among the evil one-worlders intent on surrendering the sovereignty of the United States to the United Nations (a continuing argument fifty years later). He eventually became involved with the "red smear" campaigns of Senator Joseph McCarthy and Richard Nixon, through names supplied by his friend J. Edgar Hoover. It has been suggested that the catalyst for Willoughby's interest in the plot to kill Kennedy might have been, ironically, the destruction of the CIA and the men who he felt were selling out the interests of the United States, the same men who linked the intelligence failure in not predicting the entry into the Korean War of the Chinese, to the humiliating retreat of American forces when the Chinese crossed the Yalu River[132]—a theme that became the battle cry of the John Birchers who ached to expand that war too.

General LeMay felt that Kennedy's handling of the Bay of Pigs showed him to be a coward; during the Cuban Missile Crisis, he advocated a massive surprise air strike and was infuriated when Kennedy reached a peaceful end to the crisis, especially when he found out it meant taking missiles out of Turkey.

General Thomas Power, USAF

General Power had the distinction of being called by his superior LeMay a "sadist." He is credited along with LeMay for inspiring the defense concept of "mutually assured destruction" (MAD), though neither of them was an advocate of equivalency of defense: Their position was more toward dominance, overwhelming superiority, and continual preparedness for a massive first-strike capability. General Power is perhaps most well-known for unilaterally elevating the security level of the Strategic Air Command, at the height of the missile crisis, to DEFCON-2, only one step away from active nuclear war, which left JFK flabbergasted when he realized how limited his power was as the president. It effectively put the SAC in command of one thousand five hundred strategic bombers on constant alert—two hundred in the air at all times—and all carrying nuclear weapons. This put practically the entire population on wartime alert, which created enormous pressure on President Kennedy to take aggressive actions to appease the military while trying to calm the nation.

General Edwin Walker (Retired)

General Edwin Walker had been fired, or pressed to resign, from his military career after he had begun distributing John Birch Society propaganda to

---

132. Ibid., pp. 573–574.

enlisted men on a military base in Germany. He was quoted by a military newspaper, the *Overseas Weekly*, as saying that Harry S. Truman, Eleanor Roosevelt, and Dean Acheson were "pink," apparently meaning they were not far from Red as the Communists were described. Secretary of Defense Robert McNamara relieved Walker of his command, while an inquiry was conducted, and in October Walker was reassigned to Hawaii to become assistant chief of staff for training and operations in the Pacific. Walker opted to resign instead of discontinuing his political activities. He entered the race for governor of Texas, but finished last among Democratic candidates in their primary election in May won by John Connally.

Walker organized protests in September 1962 against the use of federal troops to enforce the enrollment of African American James Meredith at the racially segregated University of Mississippi. His appearance helped to incite a major riot on the campus in which two people were killed. He was arrested on four federal charges; upon his return to Dallas, he was met by a crowd of a few hundred supporters. In January 1963, a federal grand jury declined to indict him, and the charges were dropped. Because his name was in the news, Lee Harvey Oswald supposedly took notice and decided to do something about this "fascist" and allegedly took a shot at him on April 10, 1963, with a rifle he had purchased a few weeks before from Klein's Sporting Goods in Chicago. Two weeks after this—one day after JFK's plans to visit Texas were announced—it appears, perhaps coincidentally, Oswald's handlers decided he should be moved to New Orleans for additional training, by rabid anti-Communists, in order to strengthen his pro-Communist credentials.

Linkages

Beyond the obvious linkages noted earlier between individuals and groups such as the Suite 8F and Georgetown society (e.g., Allen Dulles and John McCloy, who were closely aligned with both), there were many interconnections between the aforementioned parties, which will become more evident as the story line progresses through the following chapters. One illustration of this was the direct telephone line between J. Edgar Hoover and James J. Angleton. Another was the thick solid connection between Angleton and Bill Harvey. A dotted line linked Hoover to Harvey, who had left the FBI to join the CIA in the early 1950s, though the evidence suggests that such a transition was meant to provide Hoover with a mole within the CIA, of which he was jealous to the point of paranoia because of what he felt was its intrusion into his turf. It has also been suggested that Guy Banister in New Orleans was actually working undercover for

Hoover.[133] It is also important to note the close associations between Willoughby and Edward Lansdale, who was also very close to H. L. Hunt and Clint Murchison; he was purportedly the recipient of large sums of money from them for various covert operations.

By the same token, General LeMay had many friends and associates of like minds across the "org charts" of the military, some of whom were clearly visible in his position as the air force representative on the Joint Chiefs of Staff, but other links were even stronger, yet not represented by any visible lines: for example, his links through General Willoughby to H. L. Hunt. Anyone connected to H. L. Hunt was linked to the men in Suite 8F, specifically including Ed Clark, Johnson's chief lawyer and financial bagman. Links from all of these would run underground, to the Mafia as noted elsewhere, directly back to Lyndon Johnson's right-hand man, Bobby Baker, and of course, to Lyndon B. Johnson himself. Johnson and Baker's friend, neighbor, and business associate Fred Black was a longtime friend and associate of Johnny Rosselli. Black was one of the most influential lobbyists in those days, but he was also connected to other mobsters and Las Vegas interests such as Ed Levinson and Benjamin Siegelbaum. Baker and Black were majority owners of Serve U Corp which, through Johnson's political influence to appoint government contracts, was given exclusive vending machine contracts to such companies as North American Aviation, Northrop and Space Technologies.[134] Fred Black's income in the late 1950s and early 1960s was about half a million dollars per year, though he "rarely had the money to pay his taxes when due."[135]

John J. McCloy—of whom Harold Ickes once said, "He is more or less inclined to be a Fascist"[136]—later picked by Johnson to serve on the Warren Commission, was a longtime close friend and associate of H. L. Hunt, Clint Murchison, and Sid Richardson.[137] The link between H. L. Hunt, who thought his wealth and power would protect him against anything, and Lyndon Johnson would be reflected—hours after JFK's assassination—in his decision, at the urging of someone high up in the FBI, to come to Washington and his subsequent statement that he was going there "to help Lyndon."

Hunt was also connected directly to both Jack Ruby and Lee Harvey Oswald: A mysterious note signed by Oswald (and authenticated by three handwriting experts) addressed to "Mr. Hunt" and asking for information

---

133. Ibid., p. 769.
134. Hancock, pp. 208–311.
135. Baker, p. 170.
136. DiEugenio, "A Comprehensive Review of *Reclaiming History*"(Part 8) on the CTKA website: http://www.ctka.net/2008/bugliosi_8_review.html
137. Brown, M., p. 186.

"concerding [*sic*] my position" surfaced in 1975, copies of which were sent anonymously to three separate researchers, from someone in Mexico.[138] It is noteworthy to observe that Hunt had a big hacienda in a remote area of northern Mexico, near Atilano de la Garza, where he spent considerable time, including the period after his return from Washington in December 1963. The provenance of this mysterious note, if it could be established with certainty, might itself be a Rosetta stone to solving the Kennedy assassination: Could it have been someone from Hunt's own family—considering that he was married three times, simultaneously since he had never divorced, and fathered fourteen children, perhaps someone who felt shortchanged by his will—or a longtime servant or other associate, who discovered this note after his death, and then sent copies of it anonymously to three researchers on August 18, 1975? (Hunt had died nine months earlier on November 29, 1974.) According to a statement made by Johnson's longtime mistress, Madeleine Brown, there was also a direct link between Jack Ruby and Oswald, whom she had seen at the Carousel Club. Furthermore, she stated in her book that "John Curington, H. L. Hunt's assistant, has admitted to me that he saw Ruby, Oswald, George De Mohrenschildt and H. L. Hunt together on various occasions."[139] There have been other reports of sightings of H. L. Hunt together with Ruby, including one the day before the assassination.[140]

As the story unfolds in subsequent chapters, other linkages between men involved in the conspiracy and specific actions that were clearly related to it will become apparent. As an example, a direct and obviously sinister connection will be shown between the aforementioned Major General Charles Willoughby (retired)—through one of the rabid anti-Communist organizations he supported (the Anti-Bolshevik Bloc of Nations—the ABN)—and a man by the name of Spas T. Raikin. Raikin was the peculiar representative of the Traveler's Aid Society who greeted the Oswalds when they returned to the United States in June 1962; he also happened to be a ranking officer (secretary general) of the ABN.[141] Likewise, shortly after the Oswalds arrived in Fort Worth, they would become friends with a number of people involved in the White Russian community, who generally shared the extreme anti-Communist ideology. One in particular, George De Mohrenschildt, would become a friend and benefactor of Oswald, a relationship that would otherwise have been unlikely to have developed without some external guidance. Interestingly, when Oswald left Texas for

---

138. Summers, *The Kennedy Conspiracy*, p. 465.
139. Brown, M., p. 96.
140. Twyman, p. 273.
141. Ibid., p. 570.

New Orleans, he immediately became involved—not with left-wing radicals, as one might assume from his faux background formulated immediately after the assassination—with a host of people and organizations having the same, extreme right-wing, anti-Communist agenda. It is this complex mix of characters, and their interrelationships to each other, that led to the perfect storm of people and elements that were the prerequisites of a widely based conspiracy. In the chapters that follow, traces of this tangled web of relationships will emerge that will compound and further define how the core group was organized, financed, and deployed to assassinate John F. Kennedy.

Chapter 4

UNSOLVED MURDERS AND OTHER LINGERING LBJ SCANDALS

Every time I came into John Kennedy's presence, I felt like a goddamn raven hovering over his shoulder. Away from the Oval Office, it was even worse. The Vice-Presidency is filled with trips around the world, chauffeurs, men saluting, people clapping, chairmanships of councils, but in the end, it is nothing. I detested every minute of it.[1]

—LYNDON B. JOHNSON

Guilty by His Associations

As early as 1950, Lyndon Johnson had begun populating the different federal agencies with men whom he could control; he did so by appointing men who would be beholden to him and who would understand implicitly the terms of their service: they worked first for Lyndon Johnson and secondarily to the department or agency upon whose payroll their names appeared. The Labor Department, the Federal Communications Commission, and the Department of Agriculture were his favorite spots to plant his own men, the most notable being one Malcolm Wallace, who would become one of his most trusted personal aides despite being a convicted murderer and sexual abuser of his own daughter. Wallace had been placed in a decision-making position as an economist at the Department of Agriculture through Johnson,[2] but his more important function was working behind the scenes as a facilitator for Johnson and anyone else Johnson designated for special treatment.

---

1. Schlesinger, *RFK* . . . , p. 670, Kearns Goodwin, p. 164 (Johnson's analogy about the raven begets the question, "What would Freud have said about that?").
2. Mollenhoff, p. 107.

By the time Johnson became vice president, he had succeeded installing people in select positions throughout the USDA bureaucracy, to ensure that his influence was as wide and deep as possible. According to Gerry Patrick Hemming (a CIA contract agent deeply involved in Operation Mongoose, among other things), the USDA was a repository for CIA agents around the world,[3] because of the perfect cover it provided for its agents to embed themselves into offices and operations under the guise of being agricultural workers, agronomy scientists, or weather specialists; whatever masquerade might be necessary to suit the need was readily accommodated. Johnson had placed Wallace in the Department of Agriculture as early as 1950. He resigned after his arrest in 1952, as requested by Johnson, to keep his name from being associated with Johnson. As we will review shortly, Wallace was then on trial for first-degree murder. Billie Sol Estes would eventually testify that a number of other people were later murdered by this same Mac Wallace.

Lyndon Johnson and Robert Kennedy hated each other with a passion. J. Edgar Hoover also hated Robert Kennedy, possibly even more than Johnson did, and Kennedy reciprocated at the same level.[4] To ease the tension between his "best and brightest" men and Johnson, and to get him out of town and out of the way, JFK sent Johnson on numerous missions abroad, visiting twenty-six countries in all. He had no interest whatsoever in other cultures, but he did receive his due adulation when he traveled abroad, until, at least, he learned that Robert Kennedy had told the Scandinavian heads of state that "Johnson did not speak for the government" when he visited their country. Johnson commiserated often with John Connally about his situation; the two of them had been close since the early 1940s and had been associated with Fort Worth gamblers, who in turn were colleagues of Jack Ruby. W. C. Kirkwood—the father of Pat Kirkwood, in whose nightclub the Secret Service men had been entertained the night before and into the early-morning hours on the day of the assassination—was well connected to oilmen, including Sid Richardson, H. L. Hunt, and Clint Murchison, all of whom he would often entertain at his sprawling complex named the Four Deuces in Fort Worth, many times with Lyndon Johnson as the guest of honor.[5] Connally was also Sid Richardson's attorney and a lobbyist for the oil industry. As the new secretary of the navy, he had the power to issue lucrative contracts to Texas oil companies. When he resigned to become governor of Texas, he was replaced by another one of Johnson's Texan friends, Fred

---

3. Twyman, pp. 656–658 (interview with Gerry Patrick Hemming).
4. Mahoney, pp. 304–305.
5. Marrs, p. 292.

Korth, until his forced resignation in October 1963 as a result of another Johnson-backed corruption scandal—the award of the TFX contract to General Dynamics. Other associates of the Dallas, Houston, and Fort Worth oilmen and club owners included Charles and Earl Cabell; Charles went on to become the deputy director of the CIA, before eventually being fired by Kennedy after the Bay of Pigs, and Earl was the mayor of Dallas at the time of the Kennedy assassination.

Clint Murchison and Lyndon Johnson had been feeding off each other for many years, Murchison providing practically unlimited financial support and Johnson providing practically unlimited political influence and legislative favors. Johnson's rapid rise in power, especially after he was in the Senate, was directly related to his ability to raise money and dole it out to other politicians, who would thereafter be in his debt. Early on, wealthy Texans realized that, through Johnson, they could increase their leverage in the Senate beyond that which would come from only the two senators they were allotted. Murchison considered Lyndon Johnson his personal agent in Washington, knowing that he was in a position of enormous influence for the Senate at large, and the entire Capitol for that matter. His primary interest, and that of the other Texas oilmen, was in Johnson's ability to protect their 27.5 percent oil depletion allowance, a direct tax credit that allowed them to continue saving hundreds of millions of dollars from their federal taxes— revenue lost from the government coffers that would have to be made up for by other taxpayers.

Johnson's most important fund-raisers during this time were Tommy Corcoran, George and Herman Brown, John Connally—who gathered cash from Sid Richardson and H. L. Hunt—and Ed Clark, who funneled money from Clint Murchison, among others.[6] Johnson received payoffs not only from men like Murchison, but also from Teamster leader Jimmy Hoffa, another enemy of Robert Kennedy.[7] For years, men came into Johnson's office and handed him envelopes stuffed with cash. John Connally and Ed Clark spoke freely to Robert Caro about taking envelopes stuffed with cash to Washington inside the breast pockets of their suit jackets; they stated that the amounts were much larger than about which Claude Wild Jr. testified.[8] As noted in chapter 1, Wild had testified that "the commitment was that Gulf Oil would furnish $50,000 (annually) to Senator Johnson for his use." Yet Wild did not go to work for Gulf until 1959, and the payments started years before then. Connally stated, "I handled inordinate amounts of cash," and

6. Caro, *Master*, p. 407.
7. Zirbel, p. 118.
8. Caro, *Master*, p. 407.

Clark said, about the Gulf Oil payments, "I knew about that fifty thousand. I knew about two hundred thousand."[9] That was only one company, and Ed Clark was the cash courier for many other companies, including Brown & Root and the Humble Oil Company; he handled money transfers from many of the individual oilmen as well, even, on occasion, George R. Brown.[10] Clark said all contributions were made in cash and given to Lyndon to disburse however he pleased, to himself, to his own campaigns, or to those of other favored senators. Ed Clark, Jesse Kellam, John Connally, and Tommy "the Cork" Corcoran all admitted to being involved in collecting cash campaign contributions in Johnson's behalf. If Johnson decided that help needed to be extended to a particular senator, he would pass the word through his network, and shortly thereafter, the cash would be delivered to him. "All we knew was that Lyndon asked for it, and we gave it,' Tommy ("The Cork") Corcoran was to say."[11]

Johnson's involvement with the infamous Billie Sol Estes resulted from his need to have someone in Washington pave the way for his complex frauds against the federal government. Of course, he needed someone very highly placed in order to accomplish his deceit—someone who could literally rewrite the rules of the Agriculture Department's cotton allotments program for example—and that kind of influence would not come cheap. Johnson's "hatchet man," Clifton Carter, had introduced Estes to Johnson in the mid-1950s, and he, in turn, introduced his mistress, Madeleine Brown, to Estes at a Democratic social function in Austin. According to her account, "Billie Sol had promised Lyndon a $500,000 contribution, but had been slow in sending it. Lyndon called before dawn one morning, 'Where the hell is that cash" he bellowed from our suite at the Driskill. 'Lyndon, do you know what time it is?' Billie Sol replied. 'Hell, I didn't call you to find out what time it is! I called you to find out where the hell that cash is. I want you to get out to the fucking airport and get that goddamn cash on its way *now*!'"[12] (emphasis in original). As will be noted in a later chapter, during the course of their volatile relationship, Johnson had reportedly accepted $10 million altogether from Billie Sol Estes alone.

All of the information concerning the collection and disbursement of millions of dollars of "campaign contributions" came not from any investigation into Lyndon Johnson's illegal activities though; those hearings had come to an abrupt close shortly after he became president. The startling information coming to light in 1975 about Johnson started accidentally, as a

9. Ibid.
10. Ibid.
11. Ibid., p. 408.
12. Brown, M., p. 102.

result of a Securities and Exchange Commission lawsuit against the Gulf Oil Corporation; this came about not because the federal bureaucracy breathed any life into the earlier investigations into Lyndon Johnson, but two years after his death, as part of the investigation into his successor's much-smaller-scale scandal named Watergate.[13] In a historical irony, the wheels of justice—grinding ever so slowly—aiming to bring down Richard Nixon for arguably much smaller transgressions and abuses of power, accidentally uncovered some of the slightest of Lyndon Johnson's criminal acts, and then over two years after his death. But the alleged "campaign donations" weren't the only source of funds Johnson was tapping, as will be seen shortly.

The TFX Scandal

The largest military contract ever, in 1960, was still being negotiated as the Eisenhower administration wound down. The air force had initiated the plan for a successor to its F-105 tactical fighter, which became known as the TFX/ F-111 project. The air force proposal was for a supersonic swing-wing fighter designated the TFX. The procurement program had been initiated during 1960, but the final design and bidding process had just begun. The assumption of the military officials involved with it was that the Boeing Company was clearly in first position to win the contract because of its superior design for the fighter jet fleet. The budget called for an expenditure of $7 billion, so other, less-experienced companies were interested in competing for the bid. The awarding of this contract became a gift for the new administration to dispense. The new vice president, Lyndon Johnson, immediately saw it as a choice plum that could be used as a "payoff" for his financial backers. Unfortunately for it, the Boeing Corporation was located in the wrong states—Washington and Kansas—and was not a significant contributor to Johnson's money machine.[14] It was Johnson himself, pressuring McNamara and Kennedy, who manipulated the award of this contract to General Dynamics Corporation of Fort Worth, Texas.[15] As noted previously, the person having the greatest ownership stake in General Dynamics (20 percent) was Henry Crown, a major Democratic Party fund-raiser and financier in Chicago, who had numerous Mob connections, from Los Angeles and Las Vegas to New Orleans, Miami, and Dallas.[16] Crown was also a close associate of Sidney Korshak, a lawyer who worked for the Chicago Mob and was described by

---

13. Caro, *Master*, p. 406.
14. See Spartacus Educational website: http://www.spartacus.schoolnet.co.uk/JFKkorth.htm
15. Baker, p. 112.
16. Scott, p. 155.

senior Justice Department officials as one of "the most powerful members of the underworld."[17]

In January 1961, immediately upon assuming office as the secretary of defense, Robert McNamara changed the TFX from an air force program to a joint air force–navy project and announced a new round of studies, purportedly for the purpose of economizing the acquisitions and combining them into a single airframe. The companies that were bidding on it were to be given new technical specifications. On October 1, 1961, the two services sent the companies the requests for proposals (RFPs) on the TFX, with instructions to submit the bids by December 1, 1961. There were a total of six bids, three of which were submitted by individual companies: the Lockheed Aircraft Corporation, the North American Aviation Corporation, and the Boeing Company. The other three bids represented joint ventures: Republic Aviation and Chance Vought, General Dynamics Corporation and Grumman Aircraft, and McDonnell Aircraft and Douglas Aircraft. Of all these defense firms, the one benefiting most from the transfer of power from Eisenhower to Kennedy and Johnson was General Dynamics, whose main aircraft plant was located in Fort Worth, Texas. After Kennedy's assassination, it gained even more, its stock rising from $23.75 on November 22 to $25.13 on November 26, and by February 1964 it was up over $30.[18]

Before he ran for governor of Texas, John Connally had been named as the secretary of the navy by JFK, with Lyndon Johnson's backing. When he left the position to return to Texas, he was replaced by another Texan, Fred Korth, the former president of the Continental National Bank of Fort Worth, Texas, again after strong lobbying by Lyndon Johnson. Fred Korth was a member of the exclusive Suite 8F Group discussed in chapter 3, and for many years was a director of Bell Aerospace Corporation of Fort Worth and a longtime friend of Lyndon B. Johnson. Before joining the administration, Korth used his political influence in Washington to promote General Dynamics contracts. As the former president of Continental National Bank, which had loaned General Dynamics millions of dollars, he knew in 1962 that in the two previous years, it had lost over $170 million and was close to bankruptcy if it did not get the TFX contract. The deputy secretary of defense in 1962 was Roswell Gilpatric, who was previously chief counsel for General Dynamics and strongly supported their bid for the contract.[19]

An air force evaluation indicated that General Dynamics's bid was almost $400 million *more* than the one from Boeing; moreover, Defense Department

---

17. Scheim, pp. 241–242.
18. Mollenhoff, pp. 390–391.
19. Ibid.

memos suggested that Boeing's design was "operationally superior." "Three times the Pentagon's Source Selection Board found that Boeing's bid was better and cheaper than that of General Dynamics and three times the bids were sent back for fresh submissions by the two bidders and fresh reviews. On the fourth round, the military still held that Boeing was better but found *at last* that the General Dynamics bid was also acceptable"[20] (emphasis added). Against these recommendations, McNamara threw his support to General Dynamics because "Boeing had from the very beginning consistently chosen more technically risky tradeoffs in an effort to achieve operational features which exceeded the required performance characteristics." It cannot be said that McNamara was slow to learn how to speak in bureaucratic double-talk to rationalize otherwise unconvincing arguments during his years in Washington DC.

On October 24, 1962, Seth Kantor reported in the *Fort Worth Press* that "General Dynamics of Fort Worth will get the multibillion-dollar defense contract to build the supersonic TFX Air Force and Navy fighter plane, the *Fort Worth Press* learned today from top Government sources." Korth later told the McClellan committee that investigated the granting of the TFX contract to General Dynamics "that because of his peculiar position he had deliberately refrained from taking a directing hand in this decision (within the Navy) until the last possible moment."[21]

A few weeks before the assassination, General Dynamics was the subject of still another congressional investigation, to look into charges of "influence peddling" regarding the Pentagon's controversial award of the TFX fighter-bomber, later known as the F-111. Before the investigation was stopped, immediately after Kennedy's assassination, it had turned up the fact that one of the key participants in the selection of General Dynamics was Deputy Defense Secretary Roswell Gilpatric, another Texan and friend of Lyndon Johnson, who was General Dynamics's special counsel before joining the administration in 1961. It also discovered that Fred Korth's old employer, the Continental National Bank of Fort Worth, was the principal money source for the General Dynamics plant. Shortly after this was discovered, Korth was forced to resign on November 1, 1963. But nothing was done to reverse the flawed decision, and on December 12, 1963, the new president, Lyndon Johnson, visited Fort Worth to attend the celebration at the General Dynamics plant. Congressman James Wright, the Texas Democrat who later had to resign his position as Speaker of the House

20. The Education Forum, Controversial Issues in History, JFK Assassination Debate: TFX Scandal and the JFK assassination [Quoted by Frederic M. Scherer, The Weapons Acquisition Process: Economic Incentives, 1964, p. 37].
21. See Spartacus Educational website: http://www.spartacus.schoolnet.co.uk/JFKkorth.htm

because of his own conflicts of interest, introduced Johnson as the "greatest Texan of them all." He explained that Johnson was responsible for obtaining the TFX contract.

During Senator McClellan's Permanent Investigations Committee hearings into the contract, Senator Sam Ervin asked Robert McNamara "whether or not there was any connection whatever between your selection of General Dynamics, and the fact that the Vice President of the United States happens to be a resident of the state in which that company has one of its principal, if not its principal office." McNamara tearfully responded, "Last night when I got home at midnight, after preparing for today's hearing, my wife told me that my own 12-year-old son had asked how long it would take for his father to prove his honesty."[22]

McClellan's Senate committee never issued a report on the TFX scandal. In fact, it stopped meeting after the assassination of JFK and after the new president Lyndon Johnson began pressuring Senator McClellan to quietly bring the matter to a close before anything was concluded that might prove to be too embarrassing.[23] At that point, even honorable men serving in Congress agreed implicitly with that decision, in the face of the certain constitutional crisis that would have resulted in the impeachment of the new president for any criminal action. Also, the probability that such a report would have condemned Kennedy—as well as Johnson, Korth, Gilpatric, and McNamara—would further explain why the entire matter was permanently shelved. Having McNamara's imprint on the TFX matter may explain Johnson's power over him. A common tactic LBJ used to increase his leverage over others was to have them become implicated in his corrupt activities, making them even more beholden to him.

On June 26, 1963, Clark R. Mollenhoff interviewed Robert McNamara about his role in awarding the TFX contract to General Dynamics. McNamara claimed that Johnson had applied no political pressure on him concerning the contract. He admitted that he knew all about Fred Korth's business relationship with General Dynamics and Bell Aerospace. He also revealed he was aware of Roswell Gilpatric's role "as a lawyer for General Dynamics just prior to coming into government, the role of Gilpatric's law firm in continuing to represent General Dynamics, and the amount of money Gilpatric had received from the law firm since becoming Deputy Defense Secretary." McNamara maintained that he was convinced that this did not influence the decision made by Korth and Gilpatric.[24]

---

22. Ibid.
23. Baker, p. 112.
24. Mollenhoff, p. 376.

Johnson's role in these events was confirmed when Don B. Reynolds testified on November 22, 1963, in a secret session of the Senate Rules Committee. Reynolds told the committee of seeing a suitcase full of money that Bobby Baker had described as a "$100,000 payoff to Johnson for his role in securing the Fort Worth TFX contract."[25] The thread of this plot becomes woven into other similar Johnson-Baker scams below and will reappear shortly. As the U.S. Congress pondered the crescendo of scandals in the fall of 1963, after John F. Kennedy's assassination, the various investigations into Lyndon Johnson's conduct would be closed down, one at a time, until a few months later, they had all been scrapped forever even though none of them had ever been satisfactorily resolved. Lyndon Johnson had benefited once again from the same "benefit of the doubt" that had always been given to him.

Billie Sol Estes and his Friends

Billie Sol Estes had moved to the small town of Pecos, Texas, in 1946 and set up a small business selling irrigation pumps that used cheap natural gas instead of the more expensive electricity formerly used. He also sold anhydrous ammonia as a fertilizer; both of these business lines were profitable, and he soon became a wealthy businessman. Over the next few years he developed other sideline businesses that involved less tangible property but higher risks and even higher profits. One involved his specious claims about growing and storing cotton, which never really existed, and then using the invisible cotton and the (largely) nonexistent fertilizer storage tanks as collateral for bank loans. The story of the crash of the Estes empire was a long time in coming, but when it did, it was an explosive journalistic moment. In a lengthy cover-page article on May 25, 1962, *Time* magazine described Estes as "a bundle of contradictions and paradoxes who makes Dr. Jekyll seem almost wholesome."

Estes held himself out as a person of high morals and was very active in his church as a lay preacher, assisting the regular pastor as needed, often delivering sermons on Sunday mornings. As evidence of his morality, he liked to tell people that he never smoked, drank, gambled, or swore, and he considered dancing immoral. But while Billie could qualify as a paragon of virtue on Sundays in church, on the other days of the week, his modus operandi was that of a cutthroat, ruthless businessman who did not hesitate to use his skills of fraud and deceit on a massive scale to ruin competitors and amass a personal fortune.[26] The multiple frauds that the sanctimonious Estes

---

25. Lasky, *It Didn't Start* . . . , pp. 135–137.
26. *Time* magazine, May 25, 1962.

had been committing for over fifteen years, all while trying to portray himself as beyond reproach, were beginning to be exposed by the end of 1960. As the new Kennedy-Johnson administration was taking form in Washington in January 1961, Estes had been put under increasing pressure by USDA officials and their Texas inspector, Henry Marshall, who had questioned some of the allotments that Estes had applied to certain untillable and/or submerged lands and other government-expropriated acreages. In the short-term context at least, no other single person gained more from the election of the Kennedy-Johnson team than Billie Sol Estes, who had established solid connections to the "second man" on that team. The 1962 cover article in *Time* contained this vivid description of Billie Sol:[27]

> The Amarillo Daily News called him "probably the biggest wheeler and dealer in all of West Texas." He conveyed an impression that he wielded a lot of political influence beyond the boundaries of Pecos and even beyond Texas. He liked to flash a card indicating that he had donated $100,000 to the Democratic Party during the 1960 campaign. He displayed on the walls of his office photos, some fondly signed, of President Kennedy, Vice President Johnson, Harry Truman, Adlai Stevenson, John McClellan and other Democratic political notables. He boasted of his friendships with politicians, including Texas' Democratic Senator Ralph Yarborough.
>
> But for all his aura of wealth and power, Billie Sol remained a somewhat ridiculous figure; the inner bumpkin kept showing through. One acquaintance recalls him as "the kind of man whose lapels always seem a little too wide." He sported a diamond stickpin that seemed garish even in Texas. He was constantly bumbling into grotesque situations. Invited to Governor Clement's second inaugural in 1955, he was the only guest to show up in the ornate regalia of a Tennessee colonel. In 1956, he made a fool of himself by trying to persuade the president of a Pecos bank to help finance a wacky scheme to help Adlai Stevenson win the election. Under the Estes plan, large schools of parakeets, trained to say "I like Adlai" in unison, would fly over U.S. cities. When the banker tried to tell Estes that parakeets could not be trained to say "I like Adlai," much less say it in unison, Estes got purple-angry, accused the banker of being anti-Stevenson, and stomped out.

Billie Sol Estes, having started out the son of a dirt-poor farmer whose mother sold hand-churned butter to help pay the mortgage, had the singular ambition

---

27. Ibid.

from his earliest years of becoming as rich as the Murchison family of Dallas, the most famous of the Texas oil millionaires.[28] He had his own theories about how he would accomplish that goal, one of which was to ingratiate himself with key or influential people, putting them in his debt by one means or another. His favorite means was by handing out presents—a car, fancy shoes, or clothes, even cash—for which the recipient would implicitly understand that he was now obliged to return the favor at some point. Estes preferred to control that point, to ensure a profit on his investment was realized, and maximized. He practiced this theory especially on politicians, and from his earliest days of business, his biggest "score" was Senator Lyndon B. Johnson,[29] who perhaps had met his match when it came to the political games of "pay for play" and the timeless quid pro quo, referred to in Texas colloquialism as "You scratch my back and I'll scratch yours." One of Estes's novel ideas was that the value of the creditor's interest in the debtor was determined by the size of the debt, the more the debt, the greater the creditor's interest in the solvency of the debtor; when a debt got big enough, the creditor acquired an interest in the very survival of the debtor. He liked to say, "If you get into anybody far enough, you've got yourself a partner." In Estes's case, he certainly got far enough into Commercial Solvents, a New York chemical manufacturer, which did become a sort of partner. It was this partnership that enabled Estes to get into big-time wheeling and dealing that became his trademark.[30]

Despite the energy he invested in his business and his continual creation of new ventures and new ways to defraud the government, the public, and other businesses, his schemes were eventually found to be like a house of cards built on quicksand: He wound up not only broke but hopelessly in the red, $12 million by his own figures, closer to $20 million by those of Texas Attorney General Wilson.[31]

Enigmatic Affairs, Political Intrigue, and Murder . . . At the Department of Agriculture?

Billie Sol's legal troubles began in 1957 after Congress passed legislation to support artificial (nonmarket driven) price supports for cotton farmers. In exchange for the government's price subsidy, the Department of Agriculture (USDA) was directed to establish rules to control the production of cotton through allotments that stipulated how much each farmer could plant. The

28. Ibid.
29. Ibid.
30. Ibid.
31. Ibid.

existing land that had been used for cotton production was "grandfathered" into the program; however, strict controls were established to prohibit cotton from being grown on other acreage. In accordance with this legislation, the USDA promulgated strict rules to administer cotton production and empowered its field agents to enforce the rules. These simple rules would eventually catch up with Billie Sol Estes, but not before at least four men were murdered. As will be seen shortly, Estes would eventually finger his old friend Lyndon B. Johnson—the man whom he had gone to for assistance in perpetrating his swindles in 1957—as the man who ordered those murders.

To understand the context and why Johnson was in the unique position to be the culprit behind the Estes allegations, it is necessary to review how the two of them got to be business associates in the first place, and how it came to be that Johnson's political influence came to bear on Billie Sol Estes's various business interests. This "partnership" started in 1957, when Johnson began acting as Estes's business agent in Washington, getting favorable rulings through the men whom he had had the foresight to assist in getting placed within various federal agencies. In the process, Johnson invested in one of the vendors which supplied fertilizer to Estes, Commercial Solvents, which was suspected of having gangster connections.[32] Johnson had also assisted Estes in establishing contacts within the Agricultural Department to facilitate his business transactions in a number of areas. As the Senate majority leader, his political influence was without peer, and he had perfected, by then, his use of the famed "Johnson treatment" in arranging for personal favors at many federal agencies, including the FCC, to facilitate favorable decisions in his own behalf for his radio and television stations. When he became vice president, he unleashed his famed "Johnson treatment" on the new secretary of agriculture, Orville Freeman, as a means of directly influencing the internal policies of the department at its very topmost hierarchal level; this ensured that his friend and collaborator Billie Sol Estes could continue his fraud against the government, which had been so profitable for both of them.

The relationship between Johnson and Estes was not just an arm's-length business arrangement between an official of the U.S. government and a "shady character." Billie Sol's involvement—and his reciprocal "campaign contributions"—was extended to a warm personal friendship with Johnson and a number of his aides, particularly Walter Jenkins and Cliff Carter.[33] According to author Haley, "The Vice President's letters reflected warm pleasure over Billie's visit 'with Lady Bird and me' in their Washington mansion; his enjoyment of Billie's favorite gift, the famed Pecos cantaloupes;

32. North, p. 122.
33. Haley, p. 115.

holiday roses at the Christmas season and his interest in helping promote Billie Sol's religious and denominational zeal through the Department of State, 'in behalf of the churches' in Tanganyika; and so on."[34] Estes had told an associate that he spent $100,000 a year on a "situation" in Washington but never explained what that was, being mindful of Johnson's order to him to keep his name out of it. He did admit that he was going to build a ten-thousand-bushel grain storage elevator at Hereford, Texas, and give an eighth interest to Vice President Johnson.[35]

Estes had visited Johnson's home in Washington at least twice: In January of 1961 he was there for the inaugural parties, and he visited again in January 1962.[36] In those days, campaign funds collected by politicians were not closely monitored, as they were presumed to be handled in accordance with prudent fiduciary standards by completely honest men; obviously, there were weaknesses in that paradigm that inevitably resulted in massive abuses. It will never be known how much money was involved, because Johnson had placed himself as the central Democratic banker—the "decider" of how much money the Democratic Party would disburse to senatorial candidates, and to whom—the extent his personal fortune benefited from his role will likewise remain a mystery. One incident which reflects that situation was reported in the May 25, 1962, issue of *Time*: "Still not adequately explained are three checks totaling $145,015.14 that Estes drew on a bank account in Pecos last January and then cashed in Austin just before taking off on a trip to Washington, D.C."[37] It was apparently the Estes contribution to "Assistant Secretary of Labor Jerry Holleman, before his forced resignation due to his acceptance of gifts from Estes,[38] he had asked Estes and other Texans to ante up for a big dinner party given by Labor Secretary Arthur Goldberg last January for Lyndon Johnson."[39] Eventually, Johnson nominated Abe Fortas to replace Goldberg on the Supreme Court; however he served there while continuing to give counsel to the president, which was unprecedented then and never repeated since. He later tried to elevate Fortas to be chief justice, but that backfired when his financial dealings were given greater scrutiny and his nomination was withdrawn.

Johnson supported Kennedy's choice of Orville Freeman as the secretary of agriculture and volunteered to help Freeman find top-level USDA officers (though the unsuspecting Freeman had no idea of the real motives of Johnson,

34. Ibid., pp. 115–116.
35. North, p. 170.
36. Ibid., p. 124.
37. *Time* magazine, May 25, 1962.
38. Lincoln, p. 181.
39. *Time* magazine, May 25, 1962.

at least initially). The highest level of the "Johnson men" in the USDA included Assistant Secretary of Agriculture James T. Ralph and his assistant William E. Morris, both of whom were ultimately fired for having accepted gifts from Estes, along with a dozen other employees of the USDA, who had also been recipients of Billie Sol's generosity.[40] Another "Johnson man," Red Jacobs, was also later removed from his position. Still another man Johnson had placed in the USDA was Jack Puterbaugh (who was, months later, involved in assisting Johnson plan Kennedy's Dallas trip, including many changes in the motorcade to drop standard protection measures).[41] Puterbaugh, before being assigned to work with Johnson and Carter to liaise with the Dallas Police Department and the Secret Service on motorcade planning, had been employed by the Democratic National Committee.

On January 17, 1961, two days before Johnson took his solemn oath of office, he had a small party at his home in Washington, which was attended by, among others, Cliff Carter, Mac Wallace, and Billie Sol Estes.[42] Johnson moved this group to the back patio, despite the cold January weather, to assure absolute privacy in their discussion of what to do about Henry Marshall, knowing that unless he could be brought under control, Johnson's entire career could end in disaster. Marshall had already refused a Johnson-arranged promotion to the USDA Washington headquarters, and it was feared that he was about to go public with his investigation. Vice President Johnson, according to Estes, finally said, "Get rid of him," and Malcolm "Mac" Wallace was given the assignment. As reported by Barr McClellan, it was agreed that Wallace would be sent to meet with Marshall again to try once more to make him understand that he had to back off in his investigatory zeal, even if it meant a financial payoff to him, but if he still wouldn't cooperate, then it was understood by all that to avoid the risk of Henry Marshall pursuing his case against the Estes fraud, he must be removed.[43]

The decision on handling Henry Marshall was only one facet that Johnson was developing in his counterattack. During the ten-day period after the inauguration, he focused on other ways around the dilemma being experienced by his friend Billie Sol, looking for a way to subvert the regulations in a more routine business manner that would not raise too many flags. He needed the Agriculture Department to adopt a method that put the decision-making authority in the hands of local officials—who might be more malleable and vulnerable than those in Washington—to allow them to

40. Mollenhoff, p. 107.
41. Twyman, pp. 844–845.
42. McClellan, pp. 156–157.
43. Ibid.

make exceptions to the rules on their own. Pursuing this idea further, the newly sworn vice president wrote the newly sworn cabinet secretary Orville Freeman on January 31, 1961, in support of Estes and asked him to intervene in the matter. The secretary responded to Johnson on February 17 (tardily, by Johnson's reckoning) by pointing out that "there have been some abuses of the law in this regard . . . [which] had the effect of an outright sale of the pooled allotment by the displaced owner under subterfuge practices," which were not consistent with the law.[44] Johnson replied to Freeman, asking for a personal meeting, undoubtedly as a means for Lyndon to apply the Johnson treatment to his new colleague, who evidently did not previously have the benefit of the experience and had not been properly schooled on how Washington really worked.

Johnson's cajoling of the new cabinet secretary, Orville Freeman, was quite effective in bringing him into the loop very quickly. The best evidence of that were the results: Shortly after these contacts, changes were made in the rules to make them a little more flexible. Freeman was just learning how to move a bureaucracy, but when he did respond, the effect was tantamount to giving Estes a fast track through the USDA regulations. The new secretary Freeman—apparently wanting to show that he was a "team player" after being given a lesson in political expediency by the master himself—agreed to certain changes in the rules. The net effect of the revisions was to allow them to be liberally interpreted by local officials: The local county committee was given the authority to consider exceptions as long as the petitioner appeared before it with all applicable documents and answered all pertinent questions bearing on the transfer. However, the new rules were given even more flexibility through an exception that allowed the committee to "waive appearance" if it "unduly inconvenienced the applicant," or "because of illness or other good cause."[45] On top of all that, Freeman's letter to Johnson explaining this windfall stated that he felt "'sure that the State Committee' would 'be reasonable in passing judgment,' should the applicant fail to appear under the 'conditions enumerated.'"[46]

Estes regarded this as manna from heaven and expected it would eliminate any further need to observe the rules as long as he got dispensation from the local committees, which would not present the "king of Pecos" any problem.*

---

* According to author Haley, former Pecos City manager L. A. Patterson was quoted in the June 11, 1962, *Corpus Christi Caller-Times* as saying, "You have to remember that Billie Sol was like a god in this town. It was freely reported that anyone opposed to him might just as well pack up their [sic] bags and leave town."

44. Haley, 117–127.
45. Ibid., pp. 117–118.
46. Ibid., p. 118.

Unfortunately, the Estes empire was basically a classic pyramid scheme that would soon begin crumbling anyway, despite the estimated annual income of $5,000,000 to $7,000,000 he was banking at the time.[47] In addition to the normal kickbacks, campaign contributions, and other payments Johnson received from Estes, it was also reported that Mrs. Johnson was a "heavy investor" in Commercial Solvents, which furnished the fertilizer being sold by Estes in conjunction with his many other "services."[48] Even though Orville Freeman approved, in September 1961, a $42,000 fine against Estes for the illegal cotton allotments, in November he appointed Estes to the National Cotton Advisory Board.[49],* "Freeman's explanation: Estes had originally been appointed to the board in July 1961, and in November the department had merely 'reconstituted' the old board. Seven months after that, Freeman was still claiming there was 'no evidence' that Billie Sol Estes had received special favors from the Department of Agriculture."[50] Freeman explained that he considered all of this merely a "lawyer's quarrel." The USDA finally got around to fining Estes $554,162 for his numerous violations.[51]

Freeman's magnanimous attitude toward Billie Sol Estes extended to helping him keep his capital costs down by keeping his fidelity bond—set at $700,000 in 1960—at the same level, despite having reported losses with the Internal Revenue Service each year. In fact, he reported no income at all to the IRS despite his bragging to everyone else about being worth $12 million. An attempt was made to increase the bond on January 18, 1962, but Estes protested, and one week later, thanks to Johnson's influence with Undersecretary Murphy, the increase was rescinded.[52] "Freeman explained the department's generosity to Estes by saying that he had filed a financial statement showing a net worth of $12 million to prove that he was a good risk. But that financial statement was grossly inflated, and could not have passed a reasonably careful scrutiny" (not to mention the contradictory tax filings he made).[53]

The delays the Agriculture Department continued having in its investigation led Texas Attorney General Wilson to begin his own

---

* According to author J. Evetts Haley, "At one time a Texan was ready to take the stand and swear that he had seen Billie Sol buy a $395 suit and two pairs of $245 alligator shoes for Orville Freeman, paying in $100 bills . . . Freeman was a little too high to touch." (Haley, p. 128)

47. Ibid., p. 122.
48. Ibid., pp. 116–117.
49. Mollenhoff, p. 107.
50. North, p. 145 (ref. *New York Times*, May 8, 1962).
51. *Time* magazine, May 25, 1962.
52. North, pp. 124, 126.
53. *Time* magazine, May 25, 1962.

investigation; the first investigative reports soon produced the news stories on the front pages of local newspapers. One of the early items reported on involved employees of Dallas's famed Neiman-Marcus luxury department store, who stated that Estes had bought expensive clothing for three officials of the U.S. Agriculture Department. On one occasion, Estes took Assistant Secretary James T. Ralph and Ralph's assistant, William E. Morris, into the menswear department of the downtown store; the two USDA employees selected more than $1,000 worth of clothing, which Estes paid for. In October, he went back, this time with Emery E. Jacobs, deputy administrator of the USDA's Commodity Stabilization Service. Jacobs selected $1,433.20 worth of clothing; Estes went into the fitting room with him; "when they came out, Jacobs proceeded to pay the entire bill himself—with cash."[54]

According to information presented by the author Larry Hancock, "Billie Sol Estes told Wilson C. Tucker, deputy director of the Agriculture Department's cotton division, on 1st August, 1961, that he threatened to 'embarrass the Kennedy administration if the investigation were not halted.'" Tucker went on to testify, "Estes stated that this pooled cotton allotment matter had caused the death of one person and then asked me if I knew Henry Marshall." As Tucker pointed out, this was six months before questions about Marshall's death had been raised publicly.[55] There were many other reports of Estes using his connection with Lyndon Johnson as leverage against uncooperative people, two of which were reported in newspapers of the day:

- Robert E. Manuel, minority (Republican) counsel to the House subcommittee investigating the Estes matter, grew impatient with the cover-up being done and "leaked" a USDA report detailing the fraud. He also revealed that Estes had pressured a department employee, Carl J. Miller, by "invoking the names and influence of Lyndon B. Johnson and the late Sam Rayburn. Manuel's "whistle-blower" reward for advancing a measure of truth into the House deliberations was being fired immediately afterward.
- One of Estes's creditors, Frank Cain of Pacific Finance, swore under oath that when he told Estes that the FBI was investigating him, Estes retorted, "I can stop all that. I will get Lyndon Johnson on the phone," and that night Estes added, "I've got that investigation stopped."[56]

In the early part of 1962, stories were beginning to appear in Texas newspapers about the vice president's involvement with Estes, including a report that

---

54. Ibid.
55. See John Simkin's "The Education Forum, Controversial Issues in History, JFK Online Seminars: Malcolm Wallace, Parts 1 and 2.
56. Haley, p. 128 (ref. *San Angelo Standard-Times*, April 21, 1962).

Johnson had lent Estes $5 million; CBS News had picked up on this story, so Johnson contacted Hoover for help from the FBI in squashing it by having his agents talk to the editor. "Hoover promised to 'get started on it right away.' Johnson and Hoover then discussed how best this could be done, the vice president inquiring 'what to do on these things except to call DeLoach.' (an Assistant Director of the FBI.) 'That was the thing to do,' Hoover replied, and DeLoach apparently defanged the editor. Johnson also agreed that in the future, 'he would have his assistant, Walter Jenkins, get in touch with Mr. DeLoach in such instances.'"[57] Hoover had known for a long time about his secrets, including "the ballot-rigging of 1948 that had brought him to the Senate, and he had an inside track (through his friend Clint Murchison) on the corruption that made Johnson rich. Two years earlier—responding to an appeal for help from Johnson—Edgar had used FBI clout to squash press interest in the Billie Sol Estes fraud scandal."[58]

Johnson had effectively, with Hoover's acquiescence, set up a permanent procedure to efficiently shut down whatever future incidents that might crop up, without having to be bothered with them himself: His man, Jenkins, would contact Hoover's man, DeLoach, and the entire resources of the FBI would be unleashed on anyone not toeing the line in behalf of Lyndon B. Johnson. When Republican Congressman Bill Cramer (FL) started to prepare impeachment proceedings against Johnson's associations with Estes, Jenkins contacted DeLoach to send agents to interview/intimidate Cramer; soon, Hoover would report back that "we have already checked into the story told by Cramer and found it false; Cramer himself is a loud mouth."[59] There were many, *many* other instances of Johnson's use of Hoover to block investigations that came dangerously close to involving himself. Another such case occurred in the spring of 1962, when the editors of *Farm & Ranch* magazine published allegations of Johnson's connections with Billie Sol Estes; he had Hoover send FBI agents to interview the editors as a way to (successfully, it turned out) intimidate them from continuing to look into the scandal. Hoover's cooperation in helping Johnson like this only encouraged him to take advantage of this tool, which he would continue doing from then on, throughout the remainder of the Kennedy administration and then throughout his own presidency.[60] This outrageous and illegal misallocation of federal law enforcement practices would reach its zenith at the 1964 Democratic National Convention.

---

57. North, p. 142 (ref. Theoharis, Athan G., and John Sutart Cox, *The Boss*, Philadelphia: Temple University Press, 1988, pp. 346–347 (hardcover edn.).
58. Summers, *Official and Confidential . . .* , p. 336.
59. North, p. 129.
60. Ibid., pp. 142–143.

In August 1962, the press reported that "the name of Vice President Johnson . . . figured in testimony before two congressional subcommittees investigating the Billie Sol Estes case. Spokesmen for Johnson immediately denied that he ever sought favors for Estes. The Senate Investigations subcommittee made public an Agriculture Department memorandum that said Johnson discussed the disputed Estes cotton allotments with Undersecretary of Agriculture Charles S. Murphy . . . LBJ telephones Agriculture Department employee [John E.] Bagwell [author of the memo], ostensibly to obtain a copy of his 4/10/62 memo to Secretary of Agriculture Freeman regarding Estes and LBJ."[61] As noted by author North, "Such a call makes little sense considering the Vice President's inside contacts with Hoover . . . More likely, Johnson is either seeking to learn just what Estes has told Bagwell or simply intimidate the official, or both. Note also that the subcommittee had made public copies of the report prior to Johnson's call."[62]

The original connection between Estes and Johnson was through Estes's anhydrous ammonia fertilizer business, including the related handling of the mobile tanks for the distribution and storage of the material. At first, this business involved chattel mortgages on the mobile tanks; however, the fraud involved the placement of real mortgages on nonexistent tanks, thousands of them, in Texas, Louisiana, Oklahoma, and other states throughout the South and West. Closely tied into these operations was the supplier of the anhydrous ammonia, Commercial Solvents Corporation, in which Johnson was invested; it was carrying huge credits in Estes's deals as he was trying to force out competitors. Other financial backers included Walter E. Heller and Company of Chicago.[63] According to author Haley, "Ward Jackson, a high official with Commercial Solvents, attended a business conference with the President, Vice-President and Cabinet Members in Washington in February, 1961, and enjoyed the special services of Clifford Carter and a visit with Vice-President Johnson himself. The fact that he wrote Estes that he had discussed, 'in general the situation in Texas and in the overall business area,' with Vice President Johnson served to heighten the Texas suspicion of them all—Johnson, Commercial Solvents and Billie Sol."[64]

By 1958—as he took huge losses by selling product substantially less than its cost in order to drive competitors out of business so he could garner monopolistic market control—Estes had gotten behind in his anhydrous ammonia bills from Commercial Solvents, and he owed it over $550,000. He went to New York and sold officers of the firm on a complex deal, by

---

61. *New York Times*, August 17, 1962.
62. North, pp. 176–177.
63. Haley, p. 116.
64. Ibid.

which, in exchange for Commercial Solvents' deferring the payment of the debt and lending Estes an additional $350,000 (a credit of $125,000 for future purchases of anhydrous ammonia and $225,000 as start-up capital for a new Estes enterprise: the grain-storage business), Estes promised to pay off the debt in installments over a five-year span. The installments would comprise 100 percent of the fees he received for storing grain.[65] Billie Sol Estes's amazing success in his visit with Commercial Solvents, having gone there to meet with their executives "with his hat in his hand," as a man who owed them over half a million dollars, had witnessed one of his business maxims being validated: He often said, "If you get into anybody's pocket deeply enough, you've got yourself a partner." The result of his New York trip couldn't have been better for Billie Sol Estes. As a result of this meeting, Commercial Solvents agreed to completely refinance his existing debt, ship him all the anhydrous ammonia he wanted, and provide financing for another fraudulent business scheme.

Still another scam that he came up with was the matter of fraudulently transferred "cotton allotments." Estes discovered that the only obstacle to growing more cotton and making more money was a set of pesky USDA rules that imposed strict acreage controls. One of the rules stated that the acreage allotment remained with the land and could not otherwise be sold or applied to other acreage; the only exception to the rule pertained to land taken by the government through eminent domain, in which case the cotton allotment could be transferred to other land bought by the farmer within three years. These transfers had to be approved by the Department of Agriculture, and in Texas they were reviewed by USDA agent Henry Marshall, who noticed that Estes was suddenly involved in hundreds of requests for exceptions to the rule.

Estes had quickly seen all the loopholes in the law—some real, some by virtue of his loose "interpretation" of it—and lost no time in exploiting them, aided by his close association with Lyndon Johnson and all of the bureaucrats he controlled. He had previously bought cotton allotments for land submerged under water, planning to have them transferred to other land he had not yet purchased.[66] He also went to farmers across the South who had lost cotton land by eminent domain, much of it the result of the construction of the interstate highway system during that period, soliciting them to purchase land from him. The plan was for a farmer to buy a certain tract of land, then place their cotton allotment on it, and finally lease it back to Estes for $50 per acre. The farmer's land contract called for four installments

65. *Time* Magazine, May 25, 1962.
66. Morrow, p. 124.

to Estes, but it was quietly understood that the farmer would fail to make even the first payment, which would allow Estes to foreclose, taking back the land as well as the newly created cotton allotment with it. The farmer benefited by having been paid in advance for leasing the land back to Estes. The final result was that Estes still owned the land, but it now was an acreage upon which cotton could be grown.[67]

Regrettably for himself, Henry Marshall evidently did not get the memo liberalizing the rules, as he continued to pressure Estes to comply with the old rules, disapproving his creative use of the new loopholes put in place just for him. Since the new rules relied on local officials to accede to the shortcuts, but didn't require that they be waived completely, they could be applied on a discretionary basis. The arguably overjealous Henry Marshall—who had not appreciated the threats already made against him—was not about to use discretion to sidestep the rules he had been enforcing and, if anything, resolved only to more vigorously use them to prevent the obvious fraud that Estes was committing. He proceeded to mount a personal campaign against the Estes cotton scam, traveling around West Texas to visit county agricultural committees, explaining the methods used by Estes to circumvent the rules, demonstrating a sample Estes-type contract, and alerting the local office managers to watch for such fraudulent applications.[68] The word that Henry Marshall was proving to be a thorn in the sides of Estes and Johnson would quickly spread and cause considerable consternation in both; Ed Clark was also very concerned about how things were shaping up and appealed to Johnson to take firm action immediately to head off worse problems later.

Lyndon Johnson's Tirade with His Pilots (and the Resulting Airplane Crash That Took Their Lives)

Only a few weeks into the new administration, in early February 1961, it became apparent that the initial meeting between Mac Wallace and Henry Marshall had not been successful—evidently, Marshall was too honest and incapable of accepting either bribes or threats—and the situation continued to spiral out of control. Johnson's actions at this point can only be described as hysterical.* Estes was insisting on another meeting, and Ed Clark pressed Johnson to fly to Pecos to meet with him again to come up with a plan to

---

*A comparison to his other major meltdowns throughout his career is difficult, since other firsthand observers to these episodes were not usually willing to risk his wrath by making a contemporaneous record of them; however, there was one such account, which will be revealed in chapter 9, "The Aftermath."

67. Day, pp. 132–133.
68. *Time* magazine, May 25, 1962.

contain the potential calamity if Marshall was not immediately stopped from his ongoing "persecution" of Billie Sol.[69]

So, on a day in which Johnson was apparently having a particularly serious manic/irritability attack, only one month after the newly minted Kennedy-Johnson administration took office, he would lose any remaining rationality in a screaming fit that he had by telephone to his pilots, who had stayed over in Austin and who had the audacity to attempt to talk Lyndon out of a flight that day—Friday, February 17, 1961—because of "below minimum" weather conditions. In a hysterical blind rage, on a cold, foggy, and overcast evening in south Texas, after hearing Ed Clark tell him he had to meet again with Estes, Johnson called for his airplane to pick him up and expected immediate obedience. He had trained all his other minions to obey his every command— *who were these men to think they did not have the same duty to pay proper homage to him, the vice president of the United States?* Of all the accounts noted within these pages of Lyndon Johnson's narcissism, arrogance, and condescension toward the people who worked for him, this incident was clearly the most egregious. His reckless disregard for the safety of the pilots, when their caution impinged on his need to pursue his own criminal conduct, illustrates his abject arrogance better than any words could possibly convey.

Pilot Harold Teague was advised by the Austin airport against making the flight.[70] When Teague complained and tried to refuse to make the flight because of the extremely dangerous weather conditions and the lack of ground control instruments at the landing strip, "Johnson is said to have exploded, venting his profanity upon the pilot, demanding to know 'what do you think I'm paying you for?' and again ordering him to 'get that plane' to the ranch."[71] Yet Lyndon B. Johnson would not—could not—let some yokel trying to observe standard minimum visibility aircraft safety rules override him, the vice president of the United States. Johnson had never seen a rule that couldn't be bent or broken at his whim; we can be sure that he told the pilots something like, "To *hell* with those rules, who do you work for, the Austin airport manager or me? Get that *goddamn* airplane over here now!" This kind of reaction can be surmised not only from everything we know already about the real Lyndon Johnson, but from the actual results in the official records, as reported through newspaper accounts of the time describing the tragic aftermath.

Johnson ordered the pilots into the air to pick him up under threat of losing their jobs. Teague finally agreed and nervously called his wife to tell

---

69. McClellan, pp. 157–158.
70. Haley, p. 249.
71. Ibid., pp. 249–250.

her they had been ordered to make the flight, before whispering to her that he loved her and asked her to remember that. Minutes later, as "Johnson's Convair roared into the murky night, flying above the hilly terrain . . . hopelessly groping down for lights they could not see, had at last flown into a cedar-covered hill."[72] As the pilots searched for the runway through the fog, having no radio beams with which to locate it, they flew lower and lower until the plane crashed into a rocky hillside near the boss's ranch. The two pilots were killed instantly, paying the ultimate cost of disobeying flight rules—not because they decided to do that but because Lyndon B. Johnson insisted on it—as a result of extremely high-risk maneuvers. It was not the first, nor would it be the last, time that men paid with their lives to satisfy the whims of Lyndon B. Johnson; the irony would be that, had he been on board the aircraft, those same flight rules would have remained inviolate.* This single incident speaks volumes about the numerous flaws—apparent from his earliest years, based upon his grandmother's prescient comments noted earlier—in the character of Lyndon B. Johnson.

In a still-unexplained mystery, it took three days for the accident to be reported. The news on Monday, February 20, 1961, got out that the plane was "overdue" from a trip originating only sixty miles away in Austin the previous Friday. The papers did reassure readers that their beloved vice president was safe. He took time out of his busy schedule to visit the crash site and attend their funerals, appearing "appropriately distressed" according to newspaper accounts at the time.[73] While the deaths of the two pilots could arguably be blamed upon themselves (i.e., they ultimately agreed to make the flight and assume the risk of crashing), there were a number of other deaths which would begin occurring a few months later for which blame sharing could not be argued, starting with that of Henry Marshall in June 1961.

The Murderous Mac Wallace

The allegations concerning murders instigated by Lyndon B. Johnson in the pages that follow allow us to get a little closer to an honest evaluation of how the darker elements of his being—in his lifelong quest to become

---

* The airplane, a Convair 240, was the subject of still another Johnson scam, although quite incidental to the rest of this story. It seems that the plane was not owned by Johnson, merely borrowed from John W. Mecom, a Houston oilman, for the 1960 campaign but never returned. The building of the airport with its six-thousand-foot runway and navigational lights is yet another story of how he had already managed to make significant improvements to his ranch at the taxpayers' expense (see Haley, pp. 250–252).
72. Ibid.
73. McClellan, p. 157.

president—led him to direct the murders that others have stated he initiated. Given the weight of the evidence presented, it is not unreasonable to make the charges; it could be argued that continuing to keep them swept under the rug, as they have been for over fifty years, is—and has been—a perverse and outrageous miscarriage of justice for which the country is still burdened.

The man who would eventually become Lyndon Johnson's hit man, Malcolm "Mac" Wallace, was born in Mount Pleasant, Texas, in October 1921. He joined the marines when he turned eighteen, later serving on the aircraft carrier USS *Lexington*. Within a year, he fell from a ladder and injured his back, resulting in a medical discharge in September 1940. The following year, Wallace became a student at the University of Texas in Austin and was subsequently elected president of the student union. He became involved in left-wing student groups and, in October 1944, led a student protest in support of Homer P. Rainey, the university president who had been fired because of his socialist leanings; this "movement" failed in its mission to reinstate Rainey. Lyndon Johnson, who read all the Austin newspapers regularly, would have known all about this "rebel with a cause." Wallace graduated six years later and married Mary Andre DuBose Barton, the daughter of a Methodist preacher. He then went to graduate school at Columbia, where he started working on his doctorate while teaching economics at other universities. At about this time, he met, through his college friend Cliff Carter, Edward Clark, who would later introduce him to Lyndon Johnson. Johnson helped him to get a job as an economist at the United States Department of Agriculture. Although former friends and colleagues considered Mac Wallace as a gifted scholar, he had an explosive temper and had been involved in physical violence.[74]

The First Murder: John Douglas Kinser

In 1949, two brothers from Austin, Texas, Winston and John (Douglas) Kinser, both veterans of World War II, decided to lease a section of the floodplain along the Colorado River, across from downtown Austin, to make a "chip and putt" golf course. Winston, the older brother, already had a profitable liquor store, but he was trying to help his brother get himself established and settled down. They had used up most of their savings in making improvements to the lot. When they first got started, the land was a dump, nothing but trash among tangled brush, cast-off refrigerators, tires,

---

74. Much of the information on Malcolm Wallace was obtained from John Simkin's website Education Forum to which other researchers contribute. In this instance, researcher/author Larry Hancock provided valuable information regarding Wallace and his connections to Lyndon Johnson. Ref.: http://educationforum.ipbhost.com/index.php?showtopic=2326

and other debris. As the two brothers personally cleared the area, Winston designed the par-3 course around the small hills and valleys and trees at the site, and the two of them built the course with very little outside assistance. After the course opened, Winston returned to tending the liquor store he owned downtown and Doug ran the golf course.[75]

Doug had also been an amateur actor, playing in Austin's local theaters, and had been a carefree bachelor, enjoying the company of many young ladies around Austin. Unfortunately for him, one of the young ladies with whom he had become involved was Mac Wallace's wife, Mary Andre, and to complicate matters further, another one was Lyndon Johnson's sister, Josefa; on increasing occasions, he was enjoying a ménage à trois with both Mary Andre and Josefa at the same time. As if that weren't enough, even more unfortunate for Kinser was the fact that Mac Wallace, the jealous husband of Mary Andre, was also having a simultaneous affair with Josefa, which at least doubled his level of jealousy toward the unwitting Doug Kinser.[76]

In her younger years, Josefa had been an intelligent and vivacious girl who enjoyed her social life to its limits. Like her brothers, Lyndon and Sam Houston, she had a long history of fun-loving, uncontrolled wildness. Hers was of a kind that was openly gender-neutral, however. Like her brothers in many ways, she was even more uninhibited, in that she experimented liberally, and openly, on both the hetero and homo dimensions of her sexuality. In 1948, she had been deeply involved in helping with Lyndon's Senate campaign and later moved to Washington DC, which greatly expanded her horizons and nightlife experiences while further diminishing any residual inhibitions that might have previously constrained her activities. By 1950, at age thirty-eight, she had been married and divorced twice and was then working in Hattie Valdez's brothel in Austin, Texas. Josefa was a longtime abuser of alcohol and had more recently begun using hard drugs as well. She had a well-earned reputation for being promiscuous. She had become friends and lovers with fellow thespians Doug Kinser and Mary Andre Wallace and particularly enjoyed their experiments with threesomes, which provided her the ultimate erotic pleasure, given her bisexual predilections. Their rendezvous sites even included encounters in Austin's Zilker Park, which caused complaints from ordinary folks in the park, who, perhaps inadvertently, witnessed some of their public displays of affection, leading the police to increase the park's police surveillance.[77]

---

75. Akers, Dianne King, *Austin American-Statesman*: June 19, 2000, Lifestyle Section, p. E1.
76. Haley, pp. 106-109; McClellan, pp. 104–115; Brown, M. p. 79.
77. The information regarding Josefa, Mac Wallace, his wife Mary Andre, and Doug Kinser, unless otherwise specifically noted, comes from J. Evetts Haley (pp. 106–109) and Barr McClellan (pp. 104–115) and John Simkin's Education Forum or Spartacus Educational websites.

Josefa was also known for using information about her famous brother as an entrée to expand her social life; she openly disclosed personal information and stories about Lyndon, especially when she was high; the higher she was, the more lurid the stories became. Lyndon was acutely aware of her loose lips and feared that she might have already disclosed some illegal activities about himself to Kinser, specifically certain activities he had engaged in during his race for the Senate. In the early 1950s, well before the sexual revolution of the late 1960s and 1970s, this kind of sexual scandal had the potential of ending Lyndon's political career. Johnson also had a rather myopic, puritanical, and paranoid view of his sister's amorality; his demands for prudence were, of course, at odds with his own conduct, but he felt he could at least be discreet if not secretive, while concluding that she could not be either. To him, if his sister's wild behavior became public knowledge, it would put his own political career at risk; he could allow nothing like this to interfere with his obsession to become president of the United States. Johnson must have come to fear that his sister's wild behavior posed too high a risk for his own personal objectives: He could not risk having his entire career jeopardized by his high-risk, freewheeling sister and her boyfriends and girlfriends. Something had to be done to fix the problem, and fix it quickly.

Meanwhile, Doug Kinser had been pressing Josefa to enlist Lyndon's help in getting a loan to pay off and consolidate business debts and to fund start-up operational expenses for the new pitch and putt golf course he and his brother were in the process of opening. Josefa had broached the subject with Lyndon; however, he inferred from it that the request was a not-so-subtle blackmail attempt. The more Johnson and his Austin partner Ed Clark found out what was going on, the more upset and angry they became. Clark was worried as much or perhaps more than Lyndon over what both saw as an emerging scandal that threatened Lyndon's political career and therefore the future of Clark's own business of brokering LBJ's influence and siphoning from the cash flow pouring into his fund-raising operations. Johnson's political fortunes were the basis of both of their amazingly high-flying careers, and the threat posed to both of them by the "love triangle" developing in Austin in the summer and fall of 1951 was simply unacceptable. Johnson was determined to achieve his goal and would let nothing get in his way. As described fully by Barr McClellan, a former attorney in Ed Clark's law firm, the relationship between Clark and Johnson became so close as to make them almost inseparable; there was only one circumstance that would cause their relationship to be terminated, and that was if it became necessary in order to protect Lyndon's political future; it was tacitly agreed that, if Lyndon Johnson ever became directly threatened because of the crimes he had facilitated, Ed Clark would become the final fall guy.[78] This made it all the more critical for both of them to abide by other maneuvers to keep themselves several steps removed from the criminal acts, to ensure that there were two to three more men in between themselves and the operations which they might initiate.

Mac Wallace had long been upset with his wife's acting out her sexual fantasies—starting within days of their marriage. She was, likewise, not happy to find that he was comparatively rather prudish and not interested in exploring the outer edges of marital bliss. Practically as soon as they tied the knot, their marriage entered the rocky stage usually reached by people discovering "irreconcilable differences" after at least several months or a few years of frustration. When Ed Clark called Malcolm Wallace in October 1951 regarding the emerging rumors about his wife having a lesbian affair with Lyndon Johnson's sister and the simultaneous straight affair with Kinser—and their activities as a threesome—he was hardly surprised by then. His anger had already been festering for four years and had caused her to seek a divorce several times for his abusive behavior. Clark told Mac that he needed to do something immediately to stop this scandal before it got any worse, risking Lyndon Johnson's family reputation because of Josefa's involvement. Clark told him that he, Mac Wallace, the distraught husband of this lesbian tramp, was in the unique position of being able to end this nightmare quickly; hell, even if he was caught, reasoned the estimable lawyer, it would be easy to persuade a jury of a man's natural rights to control his deranged wife, especially in south-central Texas, circa 1951. Clark told him that he had discussed it with Lyndon, who also promised him his support and urged him to terminate Kinser and thereby contain their problem.

Mac Wallace took an immediate vacation from his job at the Department of Agriculture in Washington—which he had gotten as a result of LBJ's influence—and drove to Dallas to obtain a gun from an FBI agent friend of his, Joe Schott. He then drove on to Austin, spending several days talking to Mary Andre and separately to her mother, Mrs. Roberta D. Barton, trying to persuade Andre to become a more conventional wife. Mrs. Barton told Texas Ranger Clint Peoples that Mac had told her, "'She was a homosexual and a whore. He said that Andre had slept with men and women both since he had been married to her.' Addressing Mrs. Barton, Wallace accused Andre of having 'had an affair with a man and [he] asked me who it was.' Wallace stated that he would get the man's name."[79] The next day Wallace took his two children to Dallas for a visit with their grandparents. On the evening of

---

78. McClellan, p. 108.
79. Day, p. 81.

October 21, he brought them back to their maternal grandmother in Austin. Mrs. Barton tells what happened on the morning of October 22:[80]

> Mac talked to me and explained to me that he had told Andre that in spite of everything he was going to leave his insurance to her, and that he wanted her to invest it in my real estate. That if anything happened to him that he wanted Andre and I to know that. I told him that nothing was going to happen to him and he kinda laughed it off and said that you could never tell.

Right after that conversation, Wallace got into his blue Pontiac with the unusual (for South Texas) Virginia license plates and proceeded to drive into Austin and south on Lamar across the Colorado River to West Riverside Drive and the Butler Park pitch and putt golf course. Despite the presence of several golfers close by, he then proceeded into Doug Kinser's golf shop and began shooting him point-blank multiple times. In June 2000, the murder scene was summarized on the fiftieth anniversary of the golf course, in the *Austin American-Statesman*:[81]

> Midafternoon on Oct. 22, 1951, a man entered the clubhouse where Douglas Kinser was working and shot him five times, killing him. Shortly after, according to newspaper reports, police picked up Malcolm E. "Mac" Wallace, a former student body president of the University of Texas. Evidence included witnesses, a bloody shirt and spent cartridge found in Wallace's car, the fact that the blood on the shirt and blood at the scene matched, and paraffin test evidence that Wallace had recently fired a gun.
>
> Wallace, an economist with the U.S. Department of Agriculture, was found guilty of murder with malice Feb. 27, 1952. But he was given an astounding five-year suspended sentence. There were rumors then, and there are rumors now, about Wallace's motives, *about his connection to men of high influence, about why a man convicted of first-degree murder was virtually let off.* (emphasis added)

A customer heard the shots and saw Wallace running out of the shop and to his car, which led to Wallace's arrest. Had he not neglected to remove or switch its Virginia license plates with a stolen set before making the hit, he might have escaped entirely. The police were looking for his distinctive car almost immediately, and he was arrested shortly thereafter. The sloppiness of

---

80. Day, p. 81.
81. Akers, op. cit. (This June 2000 article appeared on the occasion of the fiftieth anniversary of the pitch and putt golf course.)

his MO would be repeated many times in later years, but would not cause him undue worry since he knew he had effectively been given a "license to kill." As promised, Ed Clark arranged for bail immediately through business friends M. E. Ruby and Bill Carroll (whose wife was then hired as a lawyer by Clark). Also, Clark arranged for his criminal attorney, John Cofer, to represent Wallace. Clark's many years of political and judicial corruption ensured that both the district attorney and the presiding judge were under his control.[82] Ed Clark and Lyndon Johnson were in absolute control over the entire proceeding; they had reassured Wallace that he would be protected, and his confidence in their ability to protect him would be apparent throughout the trial. On February 1, 1952, Wallace resigned from his government job at the request of Johnson, in order to put some distance between the two; his trial began seventeen days later. Wallace did not testify as his attorneys knew that would not be necessary. Johnson recognized that he would be able to use his friend Wallace in the future if he could help him to keep out of prison now. He therefore took time out from his Senate duties back in Washington and rented a room near the courthouse; to avoid appearing personally interested in the outcome, he did not attend the trial but had runners keep him updated constantly on the testimony and trial proceedings.

The Trial That Left a City in Shock

The trial commenced with two of Ed Clark's best criminal lawyers, John Cofer and Polk Shelton, first interviewing the potential jurors. They emphasized one concern throughout these sessions, which was each juror's attitude toward the "suspended sentence laws," as though that was to be of utmost importance in their deliberations on Wallace's guilt or innocence of first-degree murder. Indeed, that issue did take precedence over everything else at the end of the trial. They presented no evidence of extenuating circumstances or other rationales to defend Wallace, nor did they allow him to testify. The reason for this lackluster defense and tepid prosecution was that both sides were skating around the underlying scandal because both were so instructed by Johnson: The lack of a motive being presented was due to the need to keep the Johnson family name out of the proceeding.[83] Cofer filed a one-page motion for an instructed verdict, based upon the premise that the state had no solid evidence to find him guilty. District Attorney Robert Long likewise conducted a very perfunctory prosecution and never attempted to

---

82. McClellan, pp. 109–111.
83. Pegues, p. 34.

rebut Cofer's motion. The jury took only two hours to find Wallace guilty "of murder with malice aforethought." Prosecutor Long apparently could not wait to get out of the courtroom, even leaving as the verdict was still being read.[84] A contemporaneous account of the final moments of the trial, as reported in the local newspaper, revealed the leavening of tension as the verdict was read:[85]

> Thirty-year-old "Mac" Wallace stared intently at each of the 12 jurors as they filed into the still-as-a-tomb courtroom. As the solemn-faced men, weary from nine days of confinement and strain, took their seats in the jury box for the last time, bright sunlight flashed from Wallace's dark, horn rimmed glasses. If there was tension within him when Court Clerk Pearl Smith cleared her throat to read the verdict, Wallace kept it out of sight. No trace of feeling crossed his face as the clerk read the verdict of the jury: guilty of murder with malice in the October gun slaying of Golf Professional "Doug" Kinser. Still no expression when the sentence was read: five years in the State Penitentiary. Then came the recommendation—suspended sentence—and for a fleeting moment Wallace's mask broke. *A faint smile played about the corners of his mouth.* . . . [emphasis added, to point out the obvious: *as he thought to himself, 'By god, they—Johnson and Clark—did it!—ed.*]. Judge Charles O. Betts had warned that there would be no demonstration of any kind when the verdict was read. There was none; only a low "hum" in the half-filled courtroom.

It is clear from this contemporaneous newspaper description that the reason Mac Wallace was so ambivalent about his situation during the entire course of the trial was that he had been assured that the "fix" was in and that there was nothing to worry about. During the deliberations, eleven of the jurors had been insisting on a guilty verdict, but one juror insisted on an acquittal verdict and threatened to cause a hung jury. A compromise was reached wherein the jury would return a guilty verdict but recommend the sentence be suspended, probably because the other jurors assumed that the judge would overrule such an absurd result and at least lock the man up for several years. According to author Day, the judge did not have that discretion: "Presiding Judge Charles O. Betts of the 98th District Court had no choice, under law, but to accept the jury's recommendation. Judge Betts announced a sentence of five years' imprisonment, then immediately suspended the sentence and put Wallace on five years' probation instead. What the sentence meant was that Wallace

---

84. Haley, pp. 107–109.
85. The *Austin American-Statesman*, February 27, 1952.

would not go to prison unless he committed a felony or misdemeanor during the next five years. At the end of that period he could appear at court to swear that he had not broken the law and the verdict would be set aside."[86]

Researcher/author Glen Sample stated that someone who had been one of the former jury members on the Malcolm Wallace murder trial had confirmed that they were all threatened:

> He had carried with him a burden of guilt because of the outcome of the trial, but explained that the jury members, each one, had been threatened. Describing the period of time during the trial, he said that one evening during dinner, he and his wife were interrupted by two well dressed men who knocked at his door. As he responded to the callers, he noticed that one of them held a shotgun in his hands. After cocking the gun, the visitor pointed the weapon at the man and pulled the trigger. Click. The weapon was empty. "This gun could just as easily have been loaded" warned the visitor. "Be very careful about your decision" And then the men were gone. *These kinds of men were plentiful, and Johnson had the knack of finding them and keeping them loyal.*[87] (emphasis added)

Thirty-five years after the crime, in a March 31, 1986, *Dallas Times Herald* interview, Mr. D. L. Johnson admitted being the juror who forced the others to recommend the verdict and suspended sentence. He admitted being a cousin and good friend of one of Wallace's defense attorneys; it had been juror D. L. Johnson whom District Attorney Bob Long had referred to when he later stated, "I lost it because I let a sinker get on the jury. He worked for the telephone company. I didn't like him because he had a little moustache (this was 1952), but I was down to three challenges and let him get on."[88] Prosecutor Long claimed to be as perplexed by the situation as Ranger Peoples; Long was to say that it was unlike any other case he had ever handled in all his fifty years of law enforcement experience.[89] According to Bill Adler of the *Texas Observer*, several of the jurors telephoned Kinser's parents to apologize for being a part of the suspended sentence, but said they went along with it only because threats had been made against their families.

Much additional information eventually became known, ironically, because of Lyndon Johnson's efforts to secure classified security for his murderous protégé. A full decade after Douglas Kinser's murder, a Naval Intelligence security investigation conducted in 1961 uncovered significant

---

86. Day, p. 82.
87. The Education Forum, "Death Bed Confession: LBJ" Blog #5.
88. Day, p. 82.
89. Ibid.

additional information about the circumstances of the murder that had been suppressed at the original trial. The investigation came about as a result of Johnson's continued patronage of Malcolm Wallace, specifically his requests for the placement of Wallace in positions of trust within the defense industry; it was clearly an obligation that he felt toward Wallace to repay him for all the favors received. The worst part of this paradox was that, despite the ONI's unanimous decision against granting Wallace a security clearance, Johnson overruled the denial and forced them to grant him his classified status. This was simply a continuation of Johnson's actions begun ten years earlier to protect this murderer, his own personal hit man, thus giving him a "license to kill." Researcher/author Larry Hancock, writing on the Education Forum, described and excerpted additional background information that provides context to the situation—a condensed summary of which appears below—regarding Malcolm Wallace and the murder of Douglas Kinser:[90]

> The defense attorneys were very concerned about the possible appearance on the stand of Wallace's wife and mother-in-law. Both were sworn in as witnesses, the wife by the defense and the mother-in-law by the prosecution. However, the wife's testimony had been limited by the defense to that of character witness and if she had been called the prosecution could only cross examine on points raised with her by the defense. The prosecution had not challenged this position. In addition, after both were sworn in, defense requested and was granted a private conference with the mother-in-law. In the end, neither relative was called to the stand nor was Malcolm Wallace himself. The Naval Intelligence investigators contacted the two prosecution investigators, Texas Ranger Clint Peoples, the prosecutor and other sources including Wallace's wife Andre, who acknowledged having a sexual relationship with Douglas Kinser. The prosecutor went even further, revealing for the first time an association between Kinser and Josefa Johnson, Lyndon Johnson's sister.

The Naval Intelligence investigators—*ten years after the fact, just as Wallace was suddenly becoming active again in a whole series of murders*—finally uncovered facts that were hidden in the 1951 trial because of the efforts of Lyndon Johnson and his legal team of Ed Clark, Don Thomas, and John Cofer. Among these revelations, as discovered and described by Larry Hancock,[91] were the following:

90. See http://educationforum.ipbhost.com/index.php?showtopic=2326
91. Ibid.

- Andre Wallace was a self-acknowledged bisexual; Malcolm had figured this out shortly after their marriage. Her lesbianism and a history of "deviant" sexual activities with both women and men had been documented in 1951 by the Austin police and Ranger Clint Peoples.

- Malcolm Wallace was violently opposed to Andre's first pregnancy and tried to force her into an abortion. This caused her to leave him in New York, where he was doing graduate work at Columbia University, and return to Austin to stay with her mother.

- In the summer of 1950, she separated from Malcolm when she became pregnant for the second time and returned to live with her mother in Austin. While she was staying in Austin, she met Douglas Kinser and began an affair with him.

- Another incident in 1950 occurred when Wallace went to Austin and told Andre that he wanted her to take him to the golf course and point out Kinser so he could "bash his face in." Wallace then told her that if she came back to Virginia with him, he would forget about the episode. Andre returned to Virginia to live with Malcolm, but while there he beat her, sending her to the hospital.

- Andre's mother gave a detailed description of a visit from Malcolm Wallace upon his arrival in Austin from Washington in October 1951, immediately before the murder of Kinser. She described Wallace calling Andre a sexual pervert, of how she slept with other men and women since their marriage, of how she continually embarrassed him.

- The prosecutor in 1951, District Attorney Bob Long, told the naval investigators that the original investigation had turned up an individual who had tried to date Andre and, when she rejected him (or her), Malcolm Wallace—by then a "Johnson man" in Washington DC—received a letter detailing her affair with a local man in Austin.

Furthermore, Hancock established that the naval investigators found some other strange aspects to the case concerning what they referred to as potential political ramifications. They concluded that someone had gotten to District Attorney Long and convinced (or bribed) him to keep information out of the trial and away from the media. Prosecutor Long obviously knew all along that Doug Kinser had been conducting simultaneous affairs with Andre Wallace and Josefa Johnson—literally, simultaneously (a la ménage à trois)—and that Wallace had dated Josefa himself while living in Washington DC, which revealed that Mac Wallace's jealousy had a dual basis. Long even had an investigator interview Josefa and confirm the association. Long made it very clear that he understood the potential political impact on Johnson and implied he took great care to keep the information from coming out in order to protect Lyndon Johnson.

Long said, "And of course, the anti-Johnson people here. Boy, in twenty-four hours it'd have been everywhere."

Josefa apparently thought that Kinser was only seeing her because he wanted to use her influence with Lyndon to get a small business loan for his pitch and putt. She told the investigator she broke off with Kinser and that "Lyndon wouldn't listen to me anyway." District Attorney Long had all the evidence he needed, but he failed to introduce any of it in court; he presented only the basic facts used to charge Wallace in the first place and made only a perfunctory effort to prosecute the case. In the process, he allowed a violent and brutal murderer to walk out of the courtroom with only a five-year suspended sentence for "murder with malice." He did it because Lyndon Johnson insisted on it and had the political muscle to force him to cooperate. Johnson admitted to his longtime mistress, Madeleine Brown, that he helped get Wallace off the hook, saying, "Hell, I've got friends in Austin who owe me favors. I'm going to call in my markers for Wallace's trial. Madeleine, I can't have this bullshit embarrassing my family."[92] Clearly, there was more behind his actions than the embarrassment that Josefa's involvement with him might have caused.

In addition to DA Long's belated acknowledgment of holding back evidence that might reveal Lyndon Johnson's involvement, the naval investigators found that both of Wallace's lawyers had a long legal association with LBJ himself. Lead counsel Cofer had represented Johnson during his election fraud in the 1948 senatorial vote during the Box 13 election scandal and would later represent Johnson's crime partner Billie Sol Estes; in that future trial a decade later, Cofer also did a good job of limiting testimony—including keeping Estes himself off the stand—but that time, he bent rules to ensure his client was convicted so that he would not embarrass the boss, Lyndon Johnson.

Even more importantly, the investigators interviewed Detective Lee, formerly with the Austin Police Department, who reported that when Wallace was arrested, he told the investigators that "he was working for Mr. Johnson and (that's why) he had to get back to Washington."[93] Wallace's ex-wife Virginia Ledgerwood also described Wallace talking about knowing both Lyndon and Lady Bird Johnson. Moreover, it was found that Horace Busby, a longtime aide and speechwriter to Lyndon Johnson, not only knew Wallace but was a friend, a "fellow traveler," and fellow student leader at the University of Texas.

92. Brown, M., p. 79.
93. op. cit. See Education Forum, Malcolm Wallace Part 2...

The Last Christmas Present for Josefa Johnson

The objective of shutting down the Austin imbroglio to eliminate the threat presented by the trio of lovers was accomplished with the murder of Doug Kinser. It had the dual advantage of getting the attention of Josefa sufficiently to make her a more cooperative, obedient, and restrained sister for Lyndon. It didn't require an interpreter to understand the consequences of not complying with Lyndon's demand for her to fade into the background and stop embarrassing him, for a while, at least; it bought her another decade of life. However, the mortal days of Josefa Johnson were numbered. After she divorced her husband Willard White, she had adopted a son, Rodney, in 1948 during the time before she married Jim Moss of Fredericksburg, Texas. According to some reports, the boy was actually the son of Josefa and Lyndon's brother, Sam Houston Johnson. She had gained ten more years of life after the 1951 "Kinser incident," but her inability to completely reform herself, and stop embarrassing Lyndon, may have cut her life short. The Fredericksburg, Texas, newspaper carried the story a few days after Christmas 1961, under the headline, "Sister of LBJ, Mrs. Moss, Dies." The article stated that she "died Sunday night of a cerebral hemorrhage. She was forty-nine. Mrs. Moss died in her sleep after spending the evening with the entire Johnson clan around the Christmas tree at the LBJ ranch east of Fredericksburg."

The article was short on substantive information about the Christmas party and who the other guests might have been, although rumors suggested that Malcolm Wallace was one of the other guests. Shortly after leaving the party and returning to her home, Josefa died mysteriously in the early-morning hours of December 25, 1961. In a final deference to the wishes of her brother, the vice president of the United States, it was decided that—in direct contradiction of the laws of the State of Texas—no autopsy or inquest or other investigation was necessary. Moreover, stunningly, the death certificate was executed by a doctor who never even examined the body. Josefa Johnson was embalmed the same day, apparently her last Christmas present; she was quickly buried the following morning.[94] Like most Johnson operations, the story was wiped clean and quickly put to bed with very few traces remaining of her life. There is scarcely a word about her in the more than thirty-five million records stored in Lyndon's own library-museum (though it looks more like the mausoleum of a giant) in Austin, Texas. In her case, the mystery of her sudden death, on what is normally a joyous day, deepens; it is unlikely that anyone will ever understand what really happened to her and why her

---

94. Brown, Walt, "The Sordid Story of Mac Wallace," *JFK/Deep Politics Quarterly*, July 1998.

own brother—evidently, since no one else there would have had the power—decided that her death needed no investigation, contrary to Texas law and ordinary standards of decency. But "decency" had no meaning or place at the LBJ Ranch, other than what might have been left of it with his long-suffering wife, Lady Bird; her doubts and conflicts about Lyndon's methods were quietly suppressed by her for many years. By December 1961, Johnson was clearly very frustrated by what had been happening all year with his criminal partner Estes but decided that he couldn't have him killed because that would certainly have been traced back to himself.

In December 1961, Johnson and Estes were still buddies in crime, acting in concert to prevent any investigation of their collusion. But Johnson had spent a lot of time browbeating Estes on the need to keep quiet, lest he end up like the others; at that time the reference would only have been to Henry Marshall, but Josefa's mysterious death—regardless of how and why she died—might have been useful as a timely reminder by Lyndon to Billie Sol to wise up. Within four or five months of that, he would have a few other names to add to the list. Whether Johnson gave the final order to Mac Wallace that evening, of course, will never be known for sure, but it would conform to a criminal pattern already put into place by Johnson in his quest for more power as well as his long-term concerns about his fear that his sister posed too great a risk to his own political career. But for some reason, known only to himself and a friend of his named Kyle Brown, Billie Sol Estes in 1984 included her name on his list of eight people who he personally knew died on the orders of Lyndon B. Johnson. By the time Estes made his startling assertions, he had served his time and had little to gain by divulging this information.

Mac Wallace's "Other Employment"

With Clark and Johnson's help, Mac Wallace was soon employed with one of the Texas-based military suppliers, Luscombe Aircraft Corporation, which was soon absorbed by the conglomerate known as Ling-Temco-Vaught, or LTV, a company in which Johnson had financial as well as political interests. This company would subsequently become a beneficiary of the federal government's largesse through military contracts after Johnson became president. In this capacity, Wallace worked directly for D. H. Byrd, an executive and later chief executive of LTV as well as the owner of the Texas School Book Depository building, where Wallace would leave a fingerprint on November 22, 1963.[95]

---

95. McClellan, pp. 323–332: Exhibits G, H, and I.

Wallace still managed to secure top secret clearances, thanks again to Lyndon Johnson, despite his conviction for first-degree murder ("murder with malice aforethought") and his numerous contacts with Marxists. His new wife had a greater moralistic view of life and personal conduct, which caused her to later complain to authorities about an incestuous affair Wallace was having with their nine-year-old daughter at her divorce proceeding. Neither did his arrests on public drunkenness charges jeopardize his ability to keep his security clearances. In an internal memorandum of the Screening Board of the Office of Naval Intelligence dated September 27, 1962, these facts, together with a summary of his guilty verdict in the murder of Doug Kinser, the incident of his having "incestuous relations with his nine year old daughter in 1959," and his public drunkenness conviction in February 1961 when "he found difficulty, extreme difficulty in walking—his breath was strong of alcohol—his speech slow and uneven," were all spelled out as the basis for the panel's decision.[96] The panel of naval officers who reviewed his application *unanimously denied it*, stating the following:

> *This case needs little rationalizing. Applicant's conviction of murder with malice; his abnormal sexual behavior and his omissions on his current Personnel Security Questionnaire indicate that the granting of access authorization is not in the national interest.*[97]

Yet in another astonishing turnaround concerning Lyndon Johnson's protégé, Malcolm "Mac" Wallace had been given the security clearances as requested, *despite the unanimous objections* by the military officers at the Office of Naval Intelligence, which must have produced a few surprised and quizzical looks on the faces of those officers the morning that the news broke. Texas Ranger Clint Peoples had also opposed the security clearances, saying he "considered applicant a bad security risk and would not trust him in any capacity. He characterized applicant as a pervert."[98] But the word was out that "higher-ups" in Washington were behind it, and he therefore understood why his objection was ignored.[99] Ranger Captain Peoples obviously understood exactly what was happening by this time, but he had insufficient proof, or the required political clout, to do anything about it.

It was not the first time Ranger Peoples had run into Wallace; as noted earlier, he had worked on the Kinser case in 1952 and knew that some very strong strings were pulled all the way from Washington DC in behalf of

---

96. A copy of the ONI memorandum is included in McClellan's *Blood, Money . . .* , after p. 332 in "Pictures and Documents" (Item 22).
97. Ibid.
98. Ibid.
99. McClellan, p. 114.

Wallace to effectively set him free after having been convicted of first-degree murder. According to his biographer James M. Day, Ranger Clint Peoples was aware "that Wallace had friendly connections with Lyndon B. Johnson's family and several high-ranking state officials. As Peoples expressed it, 'I knew that I had to put every bit that I had into the investigation because the smell of politics was all around there.'"[100] It is obviously a tremendous understatement to say that Wallace "had friendly connections with LBJ's family." The connection was (aside from his having sex with Lyndon's sister Josefa and being a welcome guest for Lady Bird) directly to Lyndon himself. It goes without saying, but being someone's hit man is about as "close and personal" as one can get.

Sam Smithwick: Another "Texas Suicide?"

The Duke of Duval, George Parr, who was mentioned in chapter 1, had delivered the necessary 201 votes Johnson had requested to secure the 1948 senatorial election. There were a number of oddities noted about these votes, delivered in Box 13: They were delivered seventy-two hours after the election was over; the polling list, before it was destroyed, showed that many of the people on it had been dead for some time; the voters nevertheless obediently got into line in alphabetical order; and all signed their names in the same pen and handwriting, a stunning display of obedience—or corruption.

In 1952, Sam Smithwick, a deputy sheriff working for George Parr, the political boss of Alice, Texas, was in the state prison in Huntsville, convicted of the murder of a local radio announcer who had criticized the Parr regime. He had grown weary of the situation he found himself in, after having been pressed to murder Bill Mason, the radio commentator who had begun attacking George Parr. Until then, Parr had been pretty much invincible in Duval, Nueces, and Jim Wells counties; his influence was felt in fifteen other counties, through alliances with other political bosses. It was in Parr's territory that the famous Box 13 voter fraud occurred, the result of which was the illegitimate election of Lyndon Johnson to the U.S. Senate. According to author Day, the biographer of Ranger Clint Peoples, "During the 1950's, national magazine and news media articles accused him of ruling by threats, economic boycotts, and maintaining a private army of *pistoleros* who posed as deputy sheriffs."[101] Moreover, Ranger Peoples learned additional details about just how deep George Parr's hold on the area was, including the fact that he got a share of the profits not only from gambling and prostitution,

100. Day, pp. 81–82.
101. Ibid., p. 94.

but even from the sales of alcohol in Duval County, receiving a nickel from every bottle of beer sold.[102] By now, Smithwick was unhappy with his fate because he had assumed that Parr would have intervened somehow and saved him from prison for the murder of the radio announcer. He figured that if he "came clean" about his involvement and knowledge of the Box 13 voter fraud affair engineered by Lyndon Johnson and executed by George Parr, he might qualify for an early parole. He was ready to talk, and he wrote to the man Johnson had "defeated," Coke Stevenson, offering to testify about the election fraud.

Unfortunately, word got out of this astounding news that threatened Lyndon Johnson's career, and before long, Ed Clark got wind of it. Barr McClellan, who long worked in Clark's Austin law firm and knew him and the other key men there, traced the tentacles of Johnson and Clark to their man on the Texas Board of Prisons, one Hubert Hardison "Pete" Coffield, who "had the access needed to get rid of Smithwick for good."[103] The method involved a Texas tradition, involving a few well-compensated key guards. The "tradition" simply involved the direction to these "death rangers" to eliminate a specific inmate, usually by methods disguised as those of a "suicide," with the understanding that they would be protected from any recriminations. In this case, it was Smithwick who got the tag and, shortly thereafter, was found hanging from the steel bars of the jail cell. Although it was routinely handled as a suicide by the prison officials, few people actually believed that, including Governor Allan Shivers, who was convinced that Lyndon B. Johnson was behind it.[104] As reported by Robert Dallek, Governor Shivers actually accused Johnson of having Smithwick murdered.[105]

In those days, however, the guards were well protected. There were no attorneys jumping into the fray, and the public just did not care too much about justice for a convicted prisoner. Ed Clark anticipated that it would quickly wind down, and he was correct. Since the action was so well "executed," there was no proof of a crime; therefore, there was no crime to investigate.[106] Given the totality of the evidence—including specifically that Texas Governor Allan Shivers had been convinced of Johnson's involvement—the inescapable conclusion was that Lyndon B. Johnson had been behind the murder of Sam Smithwick.

---

102. Ibid.
103. McClellan, pp. 103–104
104. Ibid.
105. Dallek, p. 347.
106. McClellan, pp. 103–104.

Dale Disappears, or Dies . . . Because She Saw "the Hug"?

Sam Smithwick's name was not on the list eventually supplied by Billie Sol Estes of eight people who he knew were victims of Lyndon Johnson; Estes knew there had been possibly ten others but did not know the circumstances of the other murders and therefore omitted them from his list. Yet, according to the credible Madeleine Brown and others, there were indeed more victims of Johnson's malevolent devices. For example, there is the case of the missing maid. Dale Turner had been employed for over a decade by Madeleine Brown and had become what she referred to as a "surrogate mother" for Lyndon's own son, Steven Mark, born to Madeleine in December 1950. Months after becoming vice president in 1961, in a visit to San Antonio where he had planned to meet Madeleine at the posh Menger Hotel, they exchanged an affectionate hug as his eyes caught son Steven with Dale inside the suite. Unfortunately for her, there was a very brief but meaningful eye contact between them. He had always been paranoid about their affair becoming public; now he told Madeline that he would need to have Jerome Ragsdale (one of his lawyers and business managers) replace her immediately. Madeleine objected strongly to this, explaining to him that Dale was more than just an employee, that she had become part of their family. He told her that he would think about it but then decided, after a long quarrel with her, that the maid would have to go and that Madeleine should "tell Dale goodbye."[107] A few days later, Dale requested a little time off for personal business. That was the last time Madeleine or anyone else ever saw Dale Turner, except of course for whoever was responsible for her disappearance and certain death.[108] The disappearance of Dale Turner occurred shortly before the 1961 Christmas death of Lyndon's sister. Clearly, 1961 and 1962 were watershed years of Lyndon Johnson's crime sprees; Apparently, once started, it became easier to rationalize to himself and therefore easier to give the orders to fellow sociopath Mac Wallace to execute. It is more than likely that, among the reasons that Johnson decided Dale Turner was expendable, a secondary consideration was that it would reinforce with clarity his admonitions to Madeleine to "keep her mouth shut" in the same way that the same lesson—during the same time period—would also be applied to Billie Sol Estes, as will be considered below.

The Murder of an Uncooperative Department of Agriculture Agent, Henry Marshall

On June 3, 1961, Henry Marshall—the Department of Agriculture inspector in Bryan, Texas, who, as previously described, was quietly investigating the

---

107. Brown, pp. 134–136.
108. Ibid.

Billie Sol Estes scams unbeknownst to almost anyone other than his superiors and the principals—was found dead in a remote area of his farm. Despite the fact that he had been beaten on his head and upper body, forcefully poisoned with carbon monoxide, and shot five times with a rifle, his death was immediately ruled a suicide by the local sheriff, at whose insistence the coroner concurred. No one who knew him well thought that was possible (the fact that the sheriff and coroner ruled as they did indicates the depth of the Johnson-Clark political power throughout Texas).[109] It was reported that "Justice of the Peace Leo Farmer, who [originally] pronounced [a] suicide verdict without ordering an autopsy, said tonight, 'I just don't have nothing to say now.'"[110] In the same contemporaneous article, it was said that Marshall had been shot in the back.[111]

Those who knew of his involvement in investigating the cotton allotment and fertilizer tank scams being run by Billie Sol Estes suspected a connection between his dogged determination to solve those crimes and his untimely death. A year later, after the mysterious and similar deaths of four other Estes associates, his body was exhumed because Captain Clint Peoples of the Texas Rangers had also suspected that his death was more likely a homicide, with political connections to Washington DC, and began an investigation to find out.[112] By May 21, 1962, Captain Peoples had convinced District Judge John M. Barron to call a grand jury. On that day, the body of Henry Marshall was exhumed, and shortly thereafter, a report was submitted by the medical examiner, Dr. Joseph Jachimczyk, which concluded that his death was the result of five gunshot wounds, three of which were deemed to be "rapidly incapacitating." He also found a large bruise on the left side of the head and a 15 percent carbon monoxide level, which he estimated was probably 30 percent at the time of death. He concluded that one cannot say "'on a purely scientific basis that a verdict of suicide is absolutely impossible in this case; most improbable, but not impossible.' He changed the official record of the cause of death to be a 'possible suicide, probable homicide.'"[113] It was reported that the medical examiner "'firmly believed it was not suicide,' but for some reason was reluctant to pronounce it murder."[114] On July 13, 1962, Captain Peoples rendered his own report, stating that "it would have been utterly impossible for Mr. Marshall to have taken his own life."[115] He

---

109. Haley, p. 118–124; McClellan pp. 49–61
110. North, p. 148 (ref. *New York Times*, May 23, 1962).
111. Ibid.
112. Day, pp. 132–133 (*Op. Cit.*).
113. Day, pp. 132–133.
114. Haley, p. 135.
115. Day, pp. 132–133.

enumerated a thirteen-point list of issues to support that assertion, among them were the following:[116]

- Marshall would have had to dispose of the materials used to administer the carbon monoxide, which were never found.
- He had received a severe blow to the left side of his head, causing his eye to protrude.
- His blood was found on all sides of the truck, which also had a large dent in one of the doors not previously noted by family members.
- In order to have shot himself five times with the bolt-action rifle, he would have had to hold it at arm's length away from him and work the bolt to reload after each shot, taking it down each time and ejecting the shell; yet Marshall had difficulty, due to a prior injury, in even straightening out his right arm, making it necessary to use his left arm.

Ranger Peoples further stated that Marshall's investigation of the cotton program and his "reluctance to approve many shady aspects, without a doubt, created animosity among people who were attempting to accomplish their goals. From the findings of this investigation it is my personal opinion that it would have been beneficial to a vast number of shady operators for Mr. Henry Marshall to have been disposed of."[117] Captain Peoples suspected all along that it was Billie Sol Estes's political friend in Washington, Lyndon Johnson, whom he had also suspected of complicity in the murder of Doug Kinser ten years before. Almost immediately after Ranger Peoples submitted his report, Senator McClellan's subcommittee considered the same evidence. As reported in *Time* magazine on July 20, 1962, "Said the Senator [McClellan] sternly: 'I don't think it takes many deductions to reach the irrevocable conclusion that no man committed suicide with a weapon like this. He would have had to place the gun in an awkward position, pull the trigger and then work the bolt, while wounded, four more times.'"

From all the other evidence presented, including the testimony of a witness who testified under oath about a stranger who stopped at his service station asking for directions to Marshall's farm—whose description closely matched that of Mac Wallace—it is clear that Mac Wallace visited Marshall at his ranch that day and became angry at Marshall's resistance to stopping his investigation. He then proceeded to beat him with an object, possibly a pistol, and then attempted to rig a plastic pipe to the exhaust of Marshall's truck to simulate a suicide. He evidently heard a truck approaching the scene

---

116. Ibid.
117. Ibid.

and decided to shoot him with Marshall's own rifle. Five shots were then fired from this bolt-action rifle, all of them from the same angle into his body, of which three would have been immediately fatal.

Ranger Peoples's lack of success in getting an indictment from the grand jury was due to the fact that three or four members of the grand jury were related to Sheriff Howard Stegall.[118] The same sheriff who originally deemed the bizarre death of Henry Marshall a "suicide" had gone out of his way to assist Lyndon Johnson in undermining the grand jury's stated mission to investigate the death of Henry Marshall: Instead of being randomly selected as normal procedure required, he handpicked the grand jury to ensure the outcome would not put Johnson, Estes, or anyone else in jeopardy. The Stegall clan was not only well represented around Franklin, Texas, but in the White House as well: Glynn Stegall and his wife Mildred were among Johnson's sycophantic staff members. This was reflected in Robert Caro's account: "Glynn Stegall, whose hands would shake as Lyndon Johnson humiliated him in front of this wife." Lyndon Johnson's tentacles—extended through his obedient staff—reached deeply into every geographic region of Texas and enabled him to assert his influence through many others, always forcefully yet invisibly.

Years later, in 1979, Ranger Peoples had occasion to discuss the case with Billie Sol Estes as he escorted him to a federal prison at El Paso. Peoples explained to Estes that he was frustrated at not having been able to solve this crime, and Estes confirmed that Marshall had been murdered and suggested that Peoples might not be looking in the right direction. Estes then said, "'Well, you know I cannot say too much because I am in the penitentiary. However, you should be looking at the people that had the most to lose.' 'Should I have been looking in the direction of Washington?' Peoples asked, and Estes replied, 'You are now very definitely on the right track.'"[119] As we shall see, five years later, in 1984, Billie Sol Estes elaborated further, identifying the man behind this and a number of other murders as President Lyndon B. Johnson. But at the time of the inquest, in 1962, USDA Inspector Henry Marshall had already been dead almost ten months. Within a few days of Estes's arrest, a number of other men who had the misfortune of having dealt with Estes—and vicariously, through him, with Lyndon B. Johnson—would also turn up dead through similar means, all at the hand of the same Mac Wallace. These deaths, set up to look like suicides, will be reviewed shortly. The official investigation into the Estes scandals and the related murders would come close to being solved in July 1962, as the Senate Investigations Subcommittee, chaired by Senator John McClellan

---

118. Pegues, 103.
119. Day, p. 135.

of Arkansas, revealed that several times Marshall had warned Agriculture Department officials that he suspected Billie Sol's wholesale cotton allotment transfers were illegal. Leonard C. Williams, a former assistant to Marshall, testified that his boss had first warned his staff in 1960 that Estes's deals were fishy and were being investigated.[120]

Why had the Agriculture Department delayed acting on it for two years, until May 1962? By then, there had been two suspicious deaths and the scandal had finally made headlines in newspapers across the country, beginning in March 1962. One of the reasons might have been related to Secretary Freeman's *laisse faire* attitude about conflict of interest issues confronting his Agriculture Department. The July 20 issue of *Time* magazine quoted him as saying "the Estes affair had been 'ballooned out of all proportion.' There was 'no evidence,' he insisted, that Estes had received special favors from the Agriculture Department."[121] W. Lewis David, Marshall's onetime boss in Texas, also answered that question when he told the committee he had approved Estes's operations—with Marshall's reluctant consent—*under a Washington directive that such dealings were to be okayed if the applicant merely certified that the transaction was bona fide.* These were the "new rules" that, as we noted earlier, Lyndon Johnson, acting in behalf of his friend Billie Sol Estes, had asked Agriculture Secretary Freeman to have written in order to gut the existing guidelines, effectively neutralizing the governmental regulatory apparatus as it pertained to this particular issue.

The singular purpose of Johnson's actions—requesting, successfully, that a government agency rewrite its procedures in order to better facilitate massive fraud to be conducted against itself—was to open the door for Estes to continue conducting that massive fraud, which he was already perpetrating. Johnson's motives could only have been prompted by kickbacks from Estes and the financial gains he would make through his investments in the Commercial Solvents Company, which was an active participant in the Estes frauds. The only reason Johnson would have gone to the lengths he did to help Estes was for his own financial gain—up to $10 million total, as will be documented shortly—which was well beyond the norm for "constituent service." For the first year, Estes had managed to hold Ranger Peoples at bay; the second year of ever-increasing fraudulent activity can be attributed to the new "Johnson rules" but, more importantly, the disappearance from the scene of Inspector Henry Marshall and the inhibiting effect that his murder had on anyone else who might have wanted to stop the continuing fraud.

---

120. *Time* magazine, July 20, 1962.
121. Ibid.

Directly as a result of Johnson's intervention—the use of his influence to further a criminal enterprise—the regulatory apparatus that Congress had set up to administer a system of price supports in exchange for the rationing of cotton farming was essentially dismantled by simply rewriting the administrative rules. When Henry Marshall would not yield and continued to try to enforce the old rules and ignore the newly created loopholes— because he knew that Estes was engaging in fraud—he was killed, much like Johnson's and Hoover's Mob friends would handle a problem of this kind. When Johnson realized the inevitable consequences if this scandal was not contained and the fact that his position as vice president and his entire political career was now in jeopardy, according to Barr McClellan, he summoned Ed Clark to his ranch, and the two of them began putting the "meat on the skeleton." They were now ready to start the high-level planning for executing Johnson's plan for the assassination of JFK: the financing and contracting with professional killers, through CIA contacts, complete with multiple options for a massive cover-up once the act was accomplished.

The Murders Continue
George Krutilek

Within a year of Henry Marshall's death, as the publicity on the Billie Sol Estes scams finally became front-page news in all the nation's newspapers during March 1962, the FBI finally stepped up their investigation of Estes as well. On April 2, 1962, two FBI agents interrogated forty-nine-year-old George Krutilek, a CPA, who was Estes's chief accountant. Krutilek was killed immediately after the FBI interview; by the time his body was found two days later, in the desert close to El Paso, his body had already decomposed significantly. He had not been seen or heard from during the period after the secret grilling by the FBI and when his body was found. A hose had been hooked to his vehicle's exhaust pipe to make it look like a suicide, but an El Paso pathologist said that was not the cause of death. A severe bruise on his head did not persuade the coroner that there might have been more to his death than it being just another "Texas suicide," but that is what he classified it for the legal record.[122] According to the previously cited contemporaneous article in *Time* magazine, "A few days after the Estes scandal broke, Krutilek was found dead in his car with the windows up and a rubber hose leading from the exhaust to the interior of the car. But an autopsy revealed no trace of carbon monoxide in his lungs, and local authorities ruled that he had died of a heart attack."[123] Evidently, the severe bruise on

---

122. Haley, p. 137.
123. *Time* magazine, July 20, 1962.

his head and the obvious staging of a suicide were unpersuasive to the local authorities. Or, more likely, rather than the contradictory evidence, it was really "someone else" who was more persuasive to the local authorities.

Harold Orr, Howard Pratt, and Coleman Wade

Harold Eugene Orr had been president of the Superior Manufacturing Company of Amarillo, Texas. Orr had been involved in Estes's financial affairs and was arrested with Estes, convicted for his role in the frauds, and given a ten-year federal prison sentence. On February 28, 1964, after his conviction and sentencing, as he was about to commence serving his prison term, he went out to his garage supposedly to change the exhaust pipe on his car. His body was found a few hours later under the car, with tools scattered around him (tools that were reported to be not suitable for the job he was supposedly working on). His death was ruled "accidental by carbon monoxide." It was reported that he was finally preparing to reveal more about the Estes frauds to the authorities to get a lighter sentence. A few weeks later, Howard Pratt, the Chicago office manager of Commercial Solvents, the vendor supplying the fertilizer for Billie Sol Estes, was also found dead in his car, another victim of carbon monoxide poisoning according to his death certificate.

Coleman Wade was a building contractor from Oklahoma who had contracted with Billie Sol Estes to build many of Estes's storage facilities. In early 1963, Wade was flying home from Pecos, Texas, in his private plane when it mysteriously crashed outside of Kermit, Texas, its occupants instantly killed. "Government investigators swept in and instead of expeditiously cleaning up the wreckage in their routine way, kept the area roped off for days."[124] Wade was a friend of Billie Sol's pilot, who, it was reported, was nearly scared to death because of the ominous overtones of the airplane crash.

Madeleine Brown admitted Lyndon Johnson's involvement in these murders when she wrote, "Had Marshall and the others not been killed, Lyndon would have been forced out of office right then, but the rest of us had no idea what was really going on. I was beginning to learn."[125]

Billie Sol's Empire Continues to Crumble

As two separate investigations into Marshall's death continued in the latter half of 1961, Estes got word that an audit of his business transaction was

---

124. Ibid., p. 141.
125. Brown, M., p. 79.

about to begin. By the end of the year, Estes would reveal his close ties to Lyndon Johnson to many people in the Department of Agriculture, as a result of his protestations of the continuing investigations and the cancellation of the 1961 allotments which had been promised him previously. One week after the cancellation of the allotments, Estes's promise to take the matter up with Johnson paid off; not only was the allotment cancellation reversed, but Charles S. Murphy, the undersecretary of agriculture, even named Estes to the Cotton Advisory Board, a position which allowed him to give his expert advice on matters pertaining to the administration of the entire regulatory framework of the USDA's cotton program. This was also about the same time that Estes financed the Johnson gala, through the three checks totaling $145,015 noted earlier.[126]

What brought down the Estes empire? Not the government, despite the determined efforts of Henry Marshall and others who tried to trap him as he repeatedly changed his deceptive financial schemes.[127] In fact, through Lyndon Johnson's efforts, the Agriculture Department practically gave Billie Sol carte blanche to proceed full-bore into his entrepreneurial enterprises. Nor did the major newspapers of the day pursue this story of fraud and political corruption either, even though they had the first opportunity to carry the stories. The big dailies finally started covering it, but only as a secondary story after it got its start in the presses of the little town of Pecos, Texas.

The first real hero in this sordid affair was a local dentist, Dr. John Dunn (the second, coming on to the scene later as the investigation turned to the murders of men connected with the Estes scams, was Texas Ranger Captain Clint Peoples). Dr. Dunn had acquired some of the security agreements and began printing details of the loans, allegedly including one by Johnson himself to Estes.[128] Dr. Dunn appealed to numerous law enforcement agencies to take up Marshall's investigation, and after providing his analysis of Estes's massive frauds to congressmen, senators, and major newspapers, he could find no other way to bring public attention to the scandal, so he bought his own newspaper. The *Pecos Independent and Enterprise* was only a biweekly local newspaper, but he published three articles in it to expose the truth about the sanctimonious local legend, Billie Sol Estes, who claimed that he "never took a drink, smoked, or cursed."[129]

A single cataclysmic event led to the downfall of Billie Sol Estes, and came closer than most people realized to bringing down at least the vice

126. Ibid., pp. 168–169.
127. Ibid., p. 155.
128. Haley, p. 123; McClellan, p. 169.
129. *Time* magazine, May 25, 1962.

president of the United States, if not more than a few others in Congress and a variety of federal agencies, including the Department of Agriculture. The cataclysmic event was the Great Pecos Texas School Board Election of 1961, as reported several months later by *Time* magazine:[130]

> Estes was widely feared in Pecos because of his seeming wealth and power. But he was not widely liked. When he ran for a place on the local school board last year, he lost to a write-in candidate. That humiliating defeat led to Estes' downfall. The local paper, the twice-weekly *Independent*, had opposed him for the school board post. To get revenge, Estes set up a rival paper. Upshot: the *Independent* investigated and printed the first exposure of Billie Sol's tank-mortgage fraud.

It took a lot of courage for Dr. Dunn to publish his stories of the massive fraud being conducted under the guise of a man previously portrayed as "the leading churchman, the financial genius and the 'most promising' citizen of the city of Pecos."[131] For his efforts to bring his fellow Texas citizens the truth of the Estes empire, he was threatened, condemned, barred from practice at the local hospital by the city council, and hounded out of town. Dr. Dunn's articles appeared in the newspaper between February 12 and March 1, 1962, including many details of select transactions involving fifteen thousand alleged tanks for his county alone and loans totaling $34,000,000 in several Texas counties, most of it on fictitious tanks.[132] Those articles were picked up by other larger newspapers in the area, then the statewide papers, and finally, through the wire services, they began appearing in the national press. During the remaining four weeks of March 1962, the scandal grew by the day until, within a few weeks, Billie Sol Estes, local Pecos legend, was in jail. On Friday, March 30, 1962, the *Independent* published with a banner headline saying "Federal Charge Jails Estes." The article, written by Oscar Griffin, said that Estes was arrested by FBI agents at 6:00 p.m., March 29, 1962, and booked into the Reeves County Jail about 10:00 p.m. because of failure to raise a $500,000 bond.

As Dr. Dunn's newspaper published follow-up articles after the first three, the other town newspaper, the *Daily News,* began publishing articles of a generally defensive nature, backing Estes's business practices. One example of this was a story carried in the *Daily News* of April 29 stating that C. H. Mosley declared that he alone, and not Agriculture Department

130. Ibid.
131. Haley, p. 127.
132. Ibid., p. 120.

officials in Washington, made decisions concerning grain storage by Billie Sol Estes. (Obviously the department's new rules, described earlier, granting local officials more autonomy—which Lyndon Johnson had pushed the department to adopt—had recently been received by Mosley.) He also said that no favoritism had been shown to Estes and the government had suffered no loss, and is threatened with none, on the entire grain operation. After that, the rumors, counter rumors, and unfounded gossip sent Pecos into a tailspin, with the town divided into two camps, either for or against Billie Sol Estes. Dr. Dunn was destroyed professionally and financially through a particularly well-orchestrated and sophisticated public relations campaign designed to portray *him* as the wrongdoer.[133] The organizers of the campaign against Dr. Dunn operated secretly behind the scenes and were never revealed, but the methods used were well beyond the resources and skills of Estes. There were, however, many connections, to the Austin law firm of Ed Clark and his Washington benefactor, Lyndon B. Johnson.

A number of FBI agents were assigned the task of investigating Dr. Dunn, who suddenly began receiving numerous calls from Washington, inquiring specifically about the alleged connections between Estes and Johnson. As reported by J. Evetts Haley, "The agent in charge admits[ed] that they 'had the green light' from Washington, which meant from Bobby Kennedy and his brother."[134] As would happen again later, when the Bobby Baker case broke wide open in the summer of 1963, there were strong indications as early as May 1962 that the Kennedys were preparing to replace Johnson in 1964. The aforementioned news articles, leading up to the major cover story previously cited in *Time* magazine, as well as other stories in *The New York Times*, *The Washington Post*, *Life* magazine, and untold hundreds of other major newspapers and magazines around the country, were causing too much political blowback for the Kennedys; their only problem was how to handle the delicate matter of announcing such a decision without repercussions from Johnson and his friend Hoover.[135]

Johnson went into hiding for the entire month, winding up at Clint Murchison's resort and racetrack in California, along with J. Edgar Hoover.[136] Johnson refused to take any calls from Estes, who then unsuccessfully attempted to get a loan from Jimmy Hoffa. The pyramid was in full collapse by then. It was at this point that Johnson began trying to deny any involvement with Estes, distancing himself from his close associate in a fashion similar to that

133. Ibid., p. 124.
134. Ibid., p. 144.
135. Ibid.
136. McClellan, p. 169.

he would use with Bobby Baker some eighteen months later, in the middle of his growing scandal. According to an article in *The New York Times*, "Vice President Johnson has told friends privately that he had never had any dealings or communications with Mr. Estes. Mr. Johnson also has said privately that he met Mr. Estes only once . . . The Vice President said he wouldn't know Mr. Estes if he saw him again. It was learned at the Department of Agriculture that when Mr. Estes' empire collapsed, Mr. Johnson telephoned [Freeman]. He is said to have told Mr. Freeman that he had never heard of Mr. Estes except on the one occasion at his home."[137] It is likely that Johnson believed his own words, despite the lack of any element of truth.

Intimidation of Whistle-Blowers

A midlevel manager in the Agriculture Department, N. Battle Hales, openly charged that the department had shown favoritism toward Estes; Hales had caught on to the Estes scam and was one of the—apparently few—incorruptible staff who thought that Estes should be investigated. For this, he had been suddenly downgraded and shifted to other clerical work, but no one seemed to know where; before he left, he had dropped hints that his outspoken comments caused him to be shunted off to another job in the department and denied further access to the Estes files. Hales's treatment by Agriculture Department officials led to one of the most unseemly and outrageous assaults on a worker by a federal agency in the annals of human resource management.

In April 1962, a government secretary, Ms. Mary Kimbrough Jones, an employee at the USDA for eleven years, insisted on finding her superior N. Battle Hales and demanded to talk to him; soon, a "doctor" showed up and blocked her exit and shortly had her dragged off to the DC General Hospital as a mental patient. She was stripped of her clothing there and given only a pajama top, then, according to Hales, "left hungry and alone in a room 'with just a mattress on the floor and possibly a sheet' . . . Later, in defense, attendants said that 'there was no *misuse* of Mary in any way [emphasis in original]. But when they shut her up they said she 'became hysterical,' and when one Dr. Lee Buchanan, 'of the department's health unit,' was sent to check on her, he reported that 'she screamed and yelled; [and] that he could not deal with her rationally.' After such a 'rational' approach? She was then determined to be 'a very sick girl, in need of treatment for mental disease' and hence 'dangerous to herself and others because of her mental condition.'"[138] Hales's real crime

---

137. North, pp. 150–151. (ref. *The New York Times*, May 29, 1962).
138. Haley, pp. 129–131.

was that he was a commited Kennedy supporter, determined to help Bobby Kennedy clean up America; it soon became apparent that Lyndon Johnson did not like government workers whom he could not count on to do his bidding over either of the Kennedys. His career was effectively over as soon as Lyndon Johnson determined that he had chosen the wrong side.[139]

Senator John J. Williams of Delaware, who was, as legend had it, "the conscience of the Senate," found out about the plight of Ms. Jones and protested that she was railroaded to a mental institution because she knew too much' about the Estes case; he charged that she was 'guilty of nothing other than refusing to cooperate in covering up the corruption . . .' and that Dr. Buchanan had 'arbitrarily ordered' her committed to a 'mental institution.'"[140] Her own doctor said that "he had at no time ever detected anything which would even raise the slightest question as to Miss Jones' sanity."[141] This was not the only time we will encounter the use of such tyrannical methods to control people who would not accede to Lyndon Johnson. The depth of his troubles no doubt caused Johnson extreme frustration, and it is likely that it was during this time, with these key participants, that Johnson's resolve to proceed with his plan was firmed and the specific actions began taking shape. The man who replaced Battle Hales at the Department of Agriculture, Jack Puterbaugh, was handpicked by Lyndon Johnson for that assignment; Puterbaugh would later be put on the payroll of the Democratic National Committee.[142] In November 1963, he would be sent to Dallas to assist in planning the motorcade and making the numerous last-minute changes in the sequence of vehicles, as described in chapter 7. He would ride in the pilot car to ensure that all other logistical details were adhered to, moments before the remaining vehicles followed that car through the streets of Dallas.

It was reported in June 1962, after an assistant state attorney general had obtained the telephone company records, that many calls had been made from Billie Sol Estes's telephones to Lyndon Johnson and/or Cliff Carter during March 1961: "Three calls had been made to Cliff Carter . . . He indicated one call had gone to an unlisted number in Washington . . . One call had been placed from an Estes telephone March 28 to a 'Mr. Carter' at Arlington, VA . . . Mr. Estes had talked six minutes to 'Mr. Carter.' . . . Two calls had been made from Mr. Estes' telephones in Pecos to Henry Marshall."[143] Johnson had

139. Pegues, p. 123.
140. Haley, pp. 129–131.
141. Ibid. (ref. *San Angelo Standard-Times*, May 15, 1962).
142. Pegues, p. 84.
143. North, pp. 157–158. (ref. The *New York Times*, June 24, 1962).

obviously trained his aide to obfuscate, as evidenced by his statement in that report: "Clifton C. Carter, a staff assistant to Vice President Johnson, said today he had received two or three telephone calls from Billie Sol Estes earlier this year, including one the day before Mr. Estes was arrested. 'I told him I knew nothing about it.' Mr. Carter said. He said Mr. Estes had asked him to call back if he found out anything. 'But I did not call back,' Mr. Carter said. 'I have no unlisted phone and I have never had one. My phone has always been listed in the Washington directory since I've been here.'"[144] What he did not say was that his boss, Lyndon Johnson, did have an unlisted telephone number.

In the meantime, Estes struggled to contain the damage, meeting with the chief executives of the companies that were involved in his deals—Commercial Solvents, Walter E. Heller and Company of Chicago, and Pacific Finance, during the latter part of March. On Thursday, March 29, 1962, Estes and three associates were charged with fraud. During the next few weeks, as Estes scrambled to put a defensive plan together with his lawyers, the extreme reactions of his mentor became more and more obvious to him. First, his chief accountant was interviewed by the FBI a few days after this, on April 2; he was then immediately killed, and his body found two days later. There were many panicked calls between Washington DC, and Austin and Pecos, Texas, in the next few weeks as Estes, Clark, and Johnson grappled with the now-explosive scandal that threatened to bring down the vice president, who was now being closely watched by John and Robert Kennedy. Any effort of Johnson's to see his friend and collaborator Billie Sol directly would only hasten the implosion, so he needed some alternate way to personally visit with his unscrupulous business associate and regain control of a volatile situation. In fact, Johnson was stuck in Washington and being monitored by his nemesis, Bobby Kennedy, who Johnson imagined was somehow behind the whole crumbling affair. Fortune smiled on Lyndon shortly thereafter, when one of his friends, Mayor Tom Miller of Austin, died.

On April 30, 1962, Vice President Johnson flew down to Austin for the funeral in a military jet. But before returning to Washington, the jet was ordered to be flown on a side trip to Midland, Texas, where it was parked away from the terminal and closely guarded by the Secret Service. Johnson never left the plane, but two men were escorted to it and stayed for one hour before the airplane took off again for Dallas, where, unfortunately for Lyndon, it made the news because the aircraft skidded off the runway on its landing, causing the hapless Johnson to have to return to Washington by commercial flight. When reporters tried to get the Midland airport records of the stopover, they were told that the records of that day's flights had been sealed by government order.[145]

---

144. Ibid.
145. Ibid., pp. 145–146.

238 • LBJ: THE MASTERMIND OF THE JFK ASSASSINATION

The two men surreptitiously visiting Johnson's airplane that evening were Billie Sol Estes and one of his lawyers.[146] There was, of course, no record made of the discussions between Johnson and Estes at this secret meeting, but it is safe to assume that Johnson would have been anxious to assure that his friend Billie Sol would keep his mouth shut and make sure that Johnson's name would be kept out of the growing scandal. The facts of the overall situation at this time suggest that the discussion might have touched on the following:

- *The need for Estes to keep quiet.* His refusal to talk about any of his activities, in fact, caused the investigations to practically come to a halt. Billie Sol Estes later claimed that Johnson had promised him that "if I wouldn't talk, I would not go to jail."[147] Given their mutual secrets, Estes had to consider also that his own life could be endangered if he crossed Johnson.

- *Getting Estes a good lawyer.* Lyndon Johnson's special criminal lawyer, John Cofer, who had represented him in the election fraud scandal in 1948, and who had gotten his hit man, Mac Wallace, out of jail in 1952, was assigned to Estes. Cofer was an attorney employed by Ed Clark's law firm in Austin, who was, behind the scenes, managing the entire defense effort on behalf of Lyndon Johnson, including the PR campaign aimed at discrediting Dr. Dunn.[148] It was undoubtedly John Cofer who met with Johnson and Estes on the airplane in Midland.

- *Keeping his closest associates silent as well.* One of them had already been eliminated, just four weeks previous to this meeting. George Krutilek had been murdered immediately after talking to the FBI on April 2, 1962, and others would follow, partly for the purpose of simply reminding Estes of the need to keep quiet. Krutilek had been Estes's chief accountant, the one man besides Estes who could have unraveled the immense fraud that had developed over several years. The body of George Krutilek was proof enough to Estes that Johnson was serious, and if he fell out of line, the same fate would await him.

By May 1962, the pressure on Estes had continued mounting, but he continued to resist talking about any of it. Although he thought that his connections and his lawyer would get him an acquittal, Johnson, Clark, and Cofer knew they could not let that happen because the gregarious Billie Sol might then lose his incentive not to talk, and of course, he knew way too

---

146. Ibid.
147. See http://www.billiesolestes.com/billie.php
148. McClellan, p. 173.

much to risk that. If he were convicted and spent at least a few years in prison, he would not only learn how not to talk, but, as a convict, his word would also lack the credibility that would otherwise be the case in the future.[149]

At this point, the FBI (briefly and inexplicably, given Johnson's close relationship with Hoover) turned its investigation toward Vice President Johnson. It wanted to know the circumstances of the 1961 airplane crash on his ranch (sixteen months prior), including the three separate transfers of ownership of the plane that took place during the week *after* the crash. The investigators had evidently been routinely assigned by their supervisors to look into these issues that ran so closely into Johnson's turf; if J. Edgar Hoover had been aware of it beforehand, it is unlikely the investigation would have taken this turn against his old friend and neighbor of nineteen years.

Clark assigned one of his firm's top attorneys, Don Thomas, to handle the FBI's inquiry because it was Thomas who had erred, in his haste to cover up Johnson's under-the-table theft of the airplane through a purchase contract (that had been intended only as a pro forma document "for the record" by the supposed seller—oilman John W. Mecom—who was merely loaning it to Johnson) that had required him to procure the hull insurance. In order to correct the records for the insurance claim (which was undoubtedly still another fraud, given the ambiguous ownership issues which were then uncovered), the ownership needed to be transferred into one of Johnson's entities. Thomas had initially assigned it to the "campaign funds" laundering company Brazos-Tenth Street Corporation, which was not then publicly known or even talked about. According to Haley, "When the campaign was over and Mecom demanded the return of his plane, Lyndon replied that he wanted to buy it. Mecom protested vigorously, reminding Lyndon that there was really no agreement to sell, [it was] just a campaign trick for Lyndon's protection. Lyndon is said to have retorted that they had signed a contract, that he was standing on his option, and that he was going to buy the plane. And he did."[150] Don Thomas was in the middle of his FBI deposition "when a phone call conveniently interrupted. The agents were ordered to leave. The testimony was suspended, never to be completed."[151] Whether the interview was cancelled directly by Director Hoover or any of his assistants, there was little doubt about the true origin of the order to suspend the investigation.

On May 7, 1962, Secretary Freeman, now coming under pressure from his own people in the Agriculture Department, admitted that Henry

149. Ibid.
150. Haley, pp. 251–252.
151. McClellan, pp. 173–174.

Marshall had been a "key figure" in the investigation of the affairs of Billie Sol Estes, specifically in the fraudulent cotton allotments.[152] Secretary Freeman admitted that the murder case was cloudy since many of the facts died with Marshall. In addition to acknowledging Marshall's work, the department confirmed its significance by assessing a fine of $544,162.71 against Estes for the fraudulent allotments.[153] At his press conference, a reporter asked Freeman if he knew Estes personally. The secretary shrugged helplessly and admitted that he had met Estes once, briefly "when Estes was paying one of many visits to Agriculture Department headquarters in Washington. Said Freeman, 'I might recognize him in pictures.' Then he mustered up a bit of bitter humor: 'I'm sure I'll never forget the name.' The newsmen laughed."[154]

By now, President Kennedy was following the case closely, even taking administration credit for having broken it. Texas Attorney General Wilson reacted to this claim, arguing that the Agriculture Department had not even cooperated with their investigation and accused it of having a "defensive attitude," further claiming that it even refused to reveal why certain department officials believed he (Marshall) had been murdered.[155] According to a report in *The New York Times*, on June 20, 1962, the Estes attorney from Ed Clark's law firm, John Cofer, "charged that . . . the president and attorney general had made it impossible for the grand jury to be unbiased" because they had already pronounced Estes guilty before he was tried.[156] As noted by author Mark North, "The schism between LBJ and President Kennedy can only be growing with rhetoric such as this."[157] Bobby Baker gave some insight into the widening chasm between the president and vice president in 1962: "I was leaving the Oval Office after the conference with the President [when] JFK said to me in a hearty and jovial manner, 'Bobby, how about this damned Texas tycoon, what's his name? Billie Sol Estes? Is he a pal of yours?' I sensed that the President was on a fishing expedition, attempting to find out what I might know of any connections between his vice-president and the Texas wheeler-dealer who'd just been charged with any number of crimes."[158]

The New York Times reported on June 25, 1962, that the previous day "'Billie Sol Estes appeared in Texas District Court today and in a surprise

152. Day, p. 132.
153. Haley, p. 134.
154. *Time* magazine, May 25, 1962.
155. Haley, p. 135.
156. *The New York Times*, June 21, 1962.
157. North, p. 156.
158. Baker, p. 117.

move demanded an immediate trial on charges of stealing $827,577 in fertilizer tank deals. Mr. Estes appeared almost jovial in court. Mr. Estes' demand for a quick trial, made through his lawyer John Cofer, surprised Atty. General Will Wilson of Texas. *Mr. Estes . . . cannot be summoned to Washington to testify before a Congressional committee if he is being tried in Pecos, his hometown.*' As LBJ's friend, Cofer's plan is clearly to prevent Estes from testifying in Washington. In conjunction with that goal, he will also prevent Estes from testifying during his trials in Texas. By use of this tactic, connections to federal officials such as Johnson can be concealed."[159] (emphasis in original)

Billie Sol Estes Tries to Cleanse His Conscience

On April 3, 1962, the day after George Krutilek died, Estes was indicted by a federal grand jury on fifty-seven counts of fraud. The same attorney who had helped Lyndon Johnson through the 1948 voter fraud scandal and who was able (with inside help from the judge and a tainted jury) to keep convicted murderer Mac Wallace out of jail was named as Estes's lawyer: John Cofer, who worked in the Austin law firm of Ed Clark. This clearly illustrates—again—Billie Sol Estes's connection to Lyndon Johnson, through his longtime personal lawyer and adviser, Ed Clark; it also validates much of what Barr McClellan wrote about the criminal activities of Johnson leading up to the ultimate crime: the murder of JFK. An article in the *Texas Observer* in 1986 described some of the background of the investigations into the Estes frauds from over twenty-five years before that time:[160]

> In Washington, the House Intergovernmental Relations subcommittee was holding hearings on Billie Sol's cotton allotments. Among those testifying was Carl J. Miller, the Agriculture Department official responsible for allowing the Estes grain storage bond to remain at $700,000 instead of raising it to $1 million (as normal procedure would have required). Miller said he'd been visited by Estes, who mentioned names of the politically powerful to whom he was connected [i.e., Lyndon B. Johnson—ed.]. Meanwhile, the Robertson County grand jury heard testimony from a Hearne gas station attendant named Nolan Griffin, who said that reading about the case in the newspapers had reminded him of a fellow who stopped by the station to ask directions around the time Marshall died, a year earlier. The

---

159. Ibid., p. 158.
160. Adler, Bill, 'The Killing of Henry Marshall,' *The Texas Observer*, November 7, 1986.

man asked Griffin where the county seat was and then he asked where "the Marshall place" was, Griffin told the grand jury. The following day, the man returned to the station and told Griffin, "You gave me the wrong Marshall, but that's all right. I got my deer lease." Griffin said the man drove a 1958 or '59 Plymouth or Dodge station wagon [matching Wallace's car]. He said the man wore dark-rimmed glasses, had dark hair and a scarred, dark face. A Texas Ranger artist, Thadd Johnson, drew a facial sketch of the fellow, dubbed "Mr. X," which was circulated in newspapers across the state and country.

By the middle of August, the police had a lead in West Texas. On August 21, Texas Ranger Captain Clint Peoples flew with Griffin to Odessa, where a man said to resemble the composite drawing was interrogated by Peoples and positively identified by Griffin, according to a sworn statement Griffin made the following week. The lead, however, proved unfounded: the man, whose name was not released and has since been lost to time, was "checked out and completely cleared" by the Rangers after passing a polygraph test. A few days after Griffin returned home, he received an eerie, anonymous phone call warning him to keep an eye on his children and to watch what he said, Griffin recalled recently. Shortly after that, Griffin said, Hearne Police Chief Perkins visited him at work one morning and told him Bryan Russ, the county attorney, wanted to see him right away. Griffin waited for his boss to return and rushed over to Russ's office, where he found Russ sitting with Sheriff Howard Stegall (who, as noted above, had already gone out of his way to accommodate a number of requests from Lyndon Johnson, through the Stegall connection in the White House). "While I was talking to Howard," Griffin, now a Hearne city councilman, told the *Observer*, "he handed me a pen and Bryan shoved a paper under me and asked me to sign it. I didn't know what it was, didn't read it or anything. They were my friends and I just did what they asked me to. A minute or so later, they got up, shook my hand, and I left." What Griffin did, he now says, was unwittingly sign an affidavit stating that he positively identified the Odessa man on August 21, 1962. This meant, of course, that the testimony he gave the grand jury was effectively discredited, giving added weight to the local authorities and to the FBI's suicide theory. "I never positively identified the man. All I did was sign my name when they shoved the thing under me." The affidavit states: "I told the Rangers on that day that this was the man and I knew it on that date and I know it now. I cannot identify any other person for I am positive that this is the man."

Shortly after this happened, Nolan Griffin received a telephone call from a man with an intimidating voice who warned Griffin that he knew where he lived and that he knew all about his family, including his children. He then told Griffin to back off if he knew what was good for his family, then hung up the telephone. Griffin later heard that Lyndon Johnson had flown into Bryan at least twice during this period with Cliff Carter to meet Billie Sol Estes.[161] These incidents are included here to illustrate the lengths to which Johnson and Clark would go in order to sabotage the investigation and divert attention away from the real perpetrator of the murder, Malcolm Wallace, who Captain Peoples was convinced was the murderer of Henry Marshall. As Peoples's biographer James M. Day wrote, "As Peoples thinks back, *he believes he questioned the person involved in murdering Henry Marshall*, but, without concrete evidence, he will not be able to prove anything. It rankles him."[162] The following excerpts from Billie Sol Estes's website provide additional insight into his promise to help Captain Peoples, before the threats of prosecution (read, persecution) from the Justice Department and his own acknowledgment regarding his associations with Lyndon Johnson:[163]

> Billie Sol Estes was released from prison in December, 1983. Three months later he appeared before the Robertson County grand jury. He confessed that Henry Marshall was murdered because it was feared he would "blow the whistle" on the cotton allotment scam. Billie Sol Estes claimed that Marshall was murdered on the orders of Lyndon B. Johnson, who was afraid that his own role in this scam would become public knowledge. According to Estes, Clifton C. Carter, Johnson's long-term aide, had ordered Marshall to approve 138 cotton allotment transfers. Billie Sol Estes told the grand jury that he had a meeting with Johnson and Carter about Henry Marshall. Johnson suggested that Marshall be promoted out of Texas. Estes agreed and replied: "Let's transfer him, let's get him out of here. Get him a better job. Make him an assistant secretary of agriculture." However, Marshall rejected the idea of being promoted in order to keep him quiet. Estes, Johnson and Carter had another meeting on 17th January, 1961, to discuss what to do about Henry Marshall. Also at the meeting was Mac Wallace. After it was pointed out that Marshall had refused promotion to Washington, Johnson said: "It looks like we'll just have to get rid of him." Wallace, who Estes described as a hitman, was given the assignment.

---

161. Pegues, p. 105.
162. Day, p. 135.
163. See http://www.billiesolestes.com/billie.php

After having served a total of ten years in prison, Estes was anxious to "stay clean" and avoid a return. Clint Peoples of the Texas Rangers had remained in contact with him and convinced Estes to testify before the Robertson County grand jury when he was released in 1984. The grand jury agreed that Henry Marshall had been murdered and heard Estes testify that Lyndon B. Johnson, Mac Wallace, Cliff Carter, and Estes himself had met several times to discuss the investigation being carried out by Henry Marshall. According to Estes's testimony, Johnson gave Mac Wallace the assignment of getting rid of Marshall.[164] Unfortunately, though the grand jury found this testimony persuasive of Johnson's guilt as being behind Marshall's death, there was little they could do since all parties to those meetings were dead, except for the witness who wished to confess his own complicity. The grand jury did agree to change the cause of death listed on Henry Marshall's death certificate from "suicide" to "death by gunshot." The grand jury investigation ended with this finding since the perpetrator was no longer available for prosecution; unfortunately for posterity, and the historical record, this finding did not seem to blemish the thirty-sixth president's reputation. Other testimony in the grand jury hearings stated that Lyndon Johnson approved the murder because he feared that Henry Marshall would give Attorney General Robert F. Kennedy evidence concerning cotton allotments incriminating Johnson. Unfortunately, the grand jury's actions were anticlimactic and did not get widespread publicity since, by 1984, there was no one left to prosecute. The protectors of presidential legacies, namely, the historians who have a vested interest in portraying only the approved conventional wisdom proffered by the selfsame historians, have also attempted to avoid this particular news item.

The fact that former president Johnson had already been dead for more than a decade, putting him yet again beyond the reach of the law, allowed him one more final "benefit of the doubt." Despite the stunning news of his complicity in Henry Marshall's murder, the fact that he was never found officially guilty of this or any other murder caused his standings of "presidential greatness" among historians to never waver, as though none of his criminal activities had caused a single blemish on his reputation as a great president. After he left Washington, he knew his own death would be the final "pass" he needed to cement his standing as one of the United States' greatest presidents and that no amount of evidence of his clear criminal conduct would ever change that since he could no longer be prosecuted for his crimes, making it seem, in the record, that they never happened. But for that very record, we shall attempt to do just that.

---

164. McClellan, pp. 156–158.

Billie Sol Estes asserted that all of these murders were committed by Mac Wallace at the behest of Lyndon Johnson, for the purpose of protecting Johnson's political career so that he, in turn, could continue protecting Estes and Wallace. These revelations are contained in a series of letters between Estes's lawyer, Doug Caddy, and Stephen Trott, an assistant attorney general in the Department of Justice. A witness to the meeting between Estes and Carter—in which they talked extensively of all the "old times" with Johnson, including, according to Estes, *up to seventeen murders*—was named: one Kyle Brown, then living in Brady, Texas. Twenty-two years later, author Harrison Livingstone spoke to Kyle Brown, who confirmed everything Estes had said.[165] According to Larry Hancock, "Billie Sol Estes . . . related that he had been personally told of Johnson's involvement in Kennedy's assassination by none other than his long time associate, Cliff Carter. Estes related being told that a convicted murderer named Malcolm Wallace had also been involved . . . Carter has named a third party [Tom Bowden], who had heard the tape and has verified Estes' description of the content to researchers. Bowden has not provided any detail on the tape other than to affirm it does contain what Estes has maintained and can be taken to implicate Lyndon Johnson as a murderer. Brown's words to Lyle Sardie included the statement: '*They prove that Johnson was a cold-blooded killer.*'"[166]

The witness Kyle Brown is on record as stating that as a young man he often carried cash between Estes and Carter—cash destined for Lyndon Johnson. The cash involved amounts from $50,000 to $100,000 dollars in the 1950s. Brown had been closely associated with Cliff Carter when he managed Johnson's political network in Texas and administered both Texas patronage privileges and politics (in his oral history Carter identified his primary responsibilities for the vice president as the political and patronage areas), and it is clear that Estes's affairs involved both of these areas. Estes invited both Carter and Brown to an impromptu meeting in 1971; Brown listened to Carter say that he regretted assisting Johnson in the criminal activities including murder. Brown described Carter as remorseful, very sad, and very much "down," apparently attempting to clear his conscience, but was simultaneously also warning Estes that Johnson was becoming more and more paranoid.[167]

This cursory examination of the Estes affair is sufficient for the reader to grasp the essence of the unfolding events in the period 1961 through the end of 1962, by which time, through Johnson's control, the scandal had receded enough to be off the front pages of newspapers and no longer the crisis to Lyndon Johnson's political career that it had been just months before. At this

---

165. Livingstone, *Killing the Truth*, p. 248.
166. Hancock, p. 405.
167. op. cit. See Education Forum, Malcolm Wallace Part 2.

point, the efforts of Johnson and Ed Clark seemed to have paid off, and they felt that the crisis was over. But it still left many questions in the minds of a lot of journalists and Washington politicians about the troubling details of the "Billie Sol Estes affair," to say nothing of the American public. That it left the murky relationship of Johnson with Billie Sol Estes on the back shelf was all that Johnson could hope for at the time. Estes had clearly been threatened by Johnson to keep quiet, and for as long as Johnson remained alive, he obeyed that ultimatum; he continued his silence for eleven more years after Johnson died. But Texas Ranger Clint Peoples, who knew more than anyone else about the long and tumultuous relationship between Billie Sol and Lyndon, was convinced that Johnson was behind the murder of Henry Marshall.

Many links between Estes and Johnson remained, even as the story disappeared from the newspapers and magazines in the latter part of 1962. By August, Johnson had arranged for the scandal to be put on the back burner indefinitely by having his friend and associate Morris Jaffe purchase the Estes bankruptcy estate for $7 million. "With his trial set to begin in a few days, Estes' assets and legal fate are now in the hands of men close to Vice President Johnson."[168] Among the tidbits of anecdotal (hearsay) information—at an earlier time, it could have been called "admittable circumstantial evidence"— was a report on April 25, 1984, in *The Dallas Morning News* that Vice President Johnson or his staff had written over twenty letters to Billie Sol Estes in the period during which they conspired to conduct and/or protect the scandal. The letters to Estes evoke a tone of complete deference to Estes, soliciting his requests with pleas such as "Please call me when we can be of service." But there were no traces of the illegal activities, which were carefully confined to face-to-face meetings or telephone calls from public telephones. In better days, a notable example of their friendly linkage, which Estes had cherished, was Johnson's personalized photographic portrait, which had hung prominently in Estes's Pecos home, inscribed, "To Billie Sol Estes with warm regards and best wishes. *Lyndon B. Johnson.*"[169]

As long as the money flowed into his coffers and Billie Sol kept out of trouble—then kept his mouth shut when trouble came—Johnson continued to be his "dear friend." When Johnson was dead for over eleven years, Estes— coached to do so by Captain Peoples—finally made what he thought was an honest effort to tell the truth, though he did ask for a number of concessions, including immunity from prosecution and having his parole restrictions lifted. On August 9, 1984, Estes's lawyer Douglas Caddy wrote to Stephen S. Trott at the U.S. Department of Justice. In the letter Caddy acknowledged

168. North, p. 203.
169. Haley, p. 115.

that Estes, Lyndon B. Johnson, Mac Wallace, and Cliff Carter had been involved in many more murders; Henry Marshall was only the first: George Krutilek, Harold Orr, Ike Rogers, Coleman Wade, Josefa Johnson, John (Doug) Kinser, and John F. Kennedy were also on the list furnished by Estes. Caddy added, "Mr. Estes is willing to testify that LBJ ordered these killings, and that he transmitted his orders through Cliff Carter to Mac Wallace, who executed the murders."[170] The Department of Justice responded with a letter from Stephen Trott, dated September 13, 1984, which made it very clear that if any errors were found in Estes's testimony, "the promise not to use any statements against Mr. Estes will be null and void and the government will not be bound by any other representations or agreements it makes."

Estes might have concluded from this letter that, to continue this process any further, he was running the risk of the Justice Department finding a way to impeach his testimony and put him back in prison. It was after these threats that he decided his efforts to "come clean" were foolish if it meant cutting his own throat. The negotiations fell apart immediately thereafter, and from then on, Billie Sol Estes's lips were sealed, and he began his "circumspect" period that would prevail for the next twenty years. A careful reading of Stephen Trott's September 13, 1984, letter indicates all the conditions that might prompt further criminal action against Estes. It is possible that Billie Sol Estes read that letter as a threat of more jail time for him if he chose to press the matter any further, though his attorney Douglas Caddy has stated to this author that "Trott's letter was a standard U.S. Department of Justice communication used under such circumstances . . . Why Estes' backed out has remained a mystery. U.S. Marshal Clint Peoples told me afterwards that he thought Estes backed out because one of his family members might have ended up being implicated in the dealings with LBJ had the disclosure project proceeded."

Twenty years after all of this, Estes published, in France, the book *JFK, the Last Standing Man.** In an interview with journalist Pete Kendall about Lyndon Johnson's criminal actions, Estes said, *"He (Johnson) told me if I wouldn't talk,*

---

* In 2005, Billie Sol Estes lent his support to the work of a French investigative reporter, William Reymond, who eventually produced both a book and a video presenting the Johnson/Carter/Wallace conspiracy story in considerable detail, with corroboration from individuals (including Kyle Brown, a former associate of both Carter and Estes) who had heard Carter describing the conspiracy on tape as well as in person. Unfortunately, this long-awaited confirmation was undermined by the later release of a book under Estes's own name, which presented a much larger conspiracy scenario and recanted on some points which he had related to Caddy, the Justice Department, and Reymond. As Larry Hancock recounted to me, the Estes book and the material in it left many researchers, who had been deeply involved investigating the Johnson/Carter/Wallace conspiracy, very much "up in the air." Despite contacts with Estes himself, no resolution was ever obtained with the issues created by the appearance of his book.
170. These letters are available on the Internet; one such site is at: 'http://home.earthlink.net/~sixthfloor/estes.htm'

I would not go to jail." Estes has had no contact with LBJ's other longtime associates, he said, since the book's publication. "About all of them are dead, really. I think I'm about the last one standing." That's partly why, he said, he wasn't interested in doing a book sooner. "I've been accused of being dumb," he said, "but I'm not stupid."[171]

Clearly, Estes's checkered past causes anyone to be skeptical about his general credibility; therefore the veracity of his statements regarding Johnson's involvement is open to debate. Yet one man—a man whose impeccable credentials and highly regarded reputation among Texas law enforcement officials, a man who knew Estes for more than two decades and was responsible for his finally being arraigned—Texas Ranger Captain Clint Peoples, felt that Estes's unique knowledge of Johnson's history of criminal conduct was the key to solving the "crime of the century." Captain Peoples made the judgment that Estes was then a convincing witness who should be listened to; clearly, Peoples considered the man's character at that point in time and felt that it justified giving him an equal measure, at least, of the "benefit of the doubt" so long extended to Lyndon B. Johnson. After working on his own time for many years to break the Wallace murders open, and tie him directly into the Kennedy assassination as well, as he was about to announce his findings, his car was broadsided by a large truck, immediately killing him. According to Madeleine Brown, who had gotten to know him and had furnished information to him regarding Mac Wallace, "His wrists showed marks (that apparently were caused) from handcuffs."[172] Captain Peoples knew too much and was still a threat to certain people and institutions as late as 1992. The statements made by Billie Sol Estes, therefore, are vindicated not by the author but by the estimable Ranger Captain Clint Peoples, whose intimate knowledge of the people and events related to this sorry chapter of American history more than offset any sway of doubt about the veracity of Estes. Interestingly, and perhaps coincidentally, both of Johnson's key assistants in carrying out the darker dealings he determined were necessary died in mysterious ways two years before Johnson, in 1971: Mac Wallace died on January 9, 1971, when his late-model car mysteriously lost its steering capability at an inopportune time and ran off the road a few miles south of Pittsburg, Texas. The "accident" was also facilitated by the "stuffed" tailpipe, which caused carbon monoxide to seep into the interior of the car. At the time, Wallace was working for L&G Oil, in Longview, Texas, and had reportedly pressured Ed Clark for more money, based upon his past deeds.*

---

* According to information furnished by a researcher who wishes to remain anomyous, both Ed Clark and Lyndon Johnson were "silent partners" in L&G Oil at the time of the 1963 "accident" that claimed the life of Mac Wallace.
171. See http://www.billiesolestes.com/billie.php
172. Brown, p. 85.

Cliff Carter died of pneumonia in September of that year when, apparently, no penicillin could be located anywhere in Washington DC.[173] Twenty-one years later, the former Texas Ranger who became a U.S. marshal, Clint Peoples, told a friend of his on June 19, 1992, that he had documentary evidence (a fingerprint) that Mac Wallace was involved in JFK's assassination at the Texas School Book Depository building—four days before he was killed in the mysterious automobile accident.[174]

Johnson went to great lengths to ensure that no audit trails would exist that might allow an investigator to establish any connection with himself to any of these murders. One such method he adopted was to avoid ever sending Wallace on commercial airlines, thus ensuring that his name was not on airline passenger manifests. Douglas Caddy, the onetime attorney for Billie Sol Estes, confirmed to this author that Estes stated to him that Johnson would always arrange transportation on military aircraft for these deadly trips:

> In 1984 I was administering grants from the Moody Foundation of Galveston, Texas to several tax-exempt organizations. A trustee of the foundation wanted to give a grant to Abilene Christian University that would partially be used to underwrite a book to be written by Billie Sol Estes about his first hand knowledge of Lyndon B. Johnson. In order to get the background information necessary so that the grant might be approved, the trustee asked me to visit Billie Sol Estes in Abilene, which I did. At that time Billie Sol Estes outlined to me the proposed contents of his book, which dealt, among other topics, with murders commissioned by LBJ. He indicated that LBJ over the years employed Malcolm Wallace as a stone cold killer to murder certain individuals who posed a threat to LBJ's political ambitions. Billie Sol Estes told me that Johnson arranged at times for Malcolm Wallace to use a U.S. military plane to transport him to the location where the victim would be found. The pilots of the plane had no idea of the purpose of the trip, only that they were to provide transportation. Once Malcolm Wallace completed his assignment, he would reboard the military plane for the return trip. The Moody Foundation trustee was eager to get the grant approved so that Billie Sol Estes could write his historical account of LBJ but Abilene Christian University withdrew its interest in the grant after Billie Sol Estes testified before a Robertson County, Texas, grand jury about the roles of LBJ and Malcolm Wallace in the murder of Henry Marshall.[175]

---

173. Jones, Penn Jr., p. 30.
174. Ibid.
175. Letter dated January 26, 2011. from Douglas Caddy to author.

The *modus operandi* of Johnson and his hit team from the first murder to the last contained a common thread of characteristics (akin to crime scene DNA) that can be reduced to this: There was a single murderer of all the victims noted earlier, from Doug Kinser on through all the rest before JFK, and that was Mac Wallace: He consistently acted hurriedly and carelessly in all of these cases, just as he did in the first murder in which he was found guilty by a jury, yet let off the hook through the political muscle of Lyndon B. Johnson. The evidence left by the killer of Henry Marshall—the furtive attempt to try to make his death look like suicide by carbon monoxide poisoning—was also consistent with the murders of others connected to the Estes scandal. Also, the crime scene in Marshall's murder closely resembled that in Kinser's: signs of a struggle, multiple gunshot wounds; all indications that the murder was sloppily planned and carelessly executed.

Bobby Baker and Friends

The biggest threat facing LBJ throughout the summer and fall of 1963—greater than the Billie Sol Estes affair, which had been mostly contained at long last—was the ongoing Senate investigation of Johnson's loyal aide and protégé, a man he often referred to as his "son": Bobby Baker. ("I have two daughters," Johnson used to say. "If I had a son, this would be the boy.")[176] Baker had worked in the Senate since 1943, when he was a fourteen-year-old page. From Lyndon's election to the Senate in 1948, he knew that Johnson would be the key to his success, and Johnson likewise knew that he could train this boy and make him his protégé. If there was ever a question about how to handle a delicate problem, or an obstinate senator, Bobby would learn it from his mentor and boss. He came to be called the "one hundred and first senator" and was the closest person in Washington to Lyndon Johnson. Bobby even bought two houses (first on 30th Place, then on 52nd Street) next to Johnson's in order to be as close as possible at all times to him. In the same block on 30th Place lived J. Edgar Hoover and the superlobbyist Fred Black, a very close associate and friend of Johnny Rosselli over many years.*

Baker was hired by Johnson in 1955 as the secretary to the Senate majority leader. After the 1960 elections, Baker retained his position as Senate secretary under the wing of Senator Bob Kerr. In only eight years, while his

---

* Years later, Black would phone Rosselli in Miami from Los Angeles, warning him to get out of Miami the night before Rosselli was murdered on July 28, 1976. Obviously, and unfortunately for him, he ignored Fred Black's "insider information" and stayed in Miami; his old friend Trafficante was not pleased with his secret testimony to the Senate Intelligence Committee, and shortly after that his dismembered body was found in an oil drum in Miami's Biscayne Bay. Rosselli had last been seen "on a boat owned by a Trafficante associate."
176. Ibid.

salary doubled to $19,600, he reported (probably understated) his net worth as $2,166,866, which had grown from about $10,000 at the start. Despite his $20,000 salary, Baker had ownership interests in nine different corporations, including his own vending company, a travel agency, and one of the first high-rise hotels in Ocean City, Maryland, the Carousel. As the finishing touches were being put on the Carousel in the spring of 1962, the worst northeaster storm in history pounded the East Coast, from the mid-Atlantic northward to New England, destroying or heavily damaging thousands of homes, hotels, and/or other businesses; the damages to the Carousel were heavy as well, causing Baker and his partners to have to increase their already-sizeable investment even more. Baker had to tap some of his friends for more funds at that time: "I went to the best friend I ever had around the Capitol . . . Vice President [Johnson]."[177]

Baker had also talked a friend, Alfred Novak, his wife, and brother into investing in the hotel and used the leverage of their money to build it. But they were more conservative than Baker and became very concerned when he kept expanding the building to include fancy restaurants and a nightclub. "The Novaks found themselves tied up in a scary three-way partnership which had $75,000 invested in real estate and its names on some $584,000 in mortgages and notes"[178] (in 1962 money; the 2010 equivalents would be $469,000 and $3,650,000 respectively). Alfred Novak was afraid of losing his shirt and began complaining to Baker about his concerns. "On the morning of March 3, 1962, Mrs. Novak found him dead in the garage, the car engine running and the door open only a few inches."[179] It may only be a coincidence that this method of what was assumed to be a suicide was strikingly similar to one of the methods used in a series of murders of men involved in the Billie Sol Estes case committed during virtually the same time period. To strengthen his financial position, Baker arranged for additional loans from his friends Eddie Levinson, a Las Vegas hotel/casino man, and Benjy Siegelbaum, a Miami investor and gambler, to bail out Novak's estate and finish the Carousel. When the hotel finally opened on July 22, 1962, the guest of honor at the grand opening— amid "a bevy of lush and scantily dressed beauties as hostesses"—was none other than Vice President Lyndon Johnson.[180]

Although Johnson claimed to have only attended this for a few minutes before returning to Washington, his account was not credible, considering the news reports of it: "Bob Baker went into the hotel business with a

---

177. North, p. 138. (ref. Robert Rowe, *The Bobby Baker Story*, New York: Parallax Publishing Co., 1967, p. 145.
178. *Life* magazine, November 22, 1963, p. 96.
179. Ibid.
180. Haley, p. 75; *Life* magazine, November 22, 1963, p. 96.

50-state splash that opened his [motel/casino], six miles north of Ocean City . . . Guests watched the limousine arrival of Vice President Johnson"[181] According to North, "Given the obvious closeness of Baker to Johnson, it is safe to assume at this point that the aide well knows of the Vice President's dislike for the Kennedys. It is not known whether Levinson and/or Siegelbaum are present at this gala event, but their absence would be surprising."[182] Johnson's prevarication about how long he was there was no doubt intended to obscure the question of whom he met and partied with at the gala event. He must have enjoyed his trip to Ocean City, since he made a second appearance there three months later, in October; one of the party girls who was also there was the lovely Ellen Rometsch, who "was said to have organized a ring of Government girls to provide party fun."[183]

In addition to his close relationship with Lyndon Johnson, with whom he skimmed money through favors made and traded, influence peddling, and governmental job appointments, Baker had managed to ingratiate himself into the government bureaucracy that controlled the awarding of contracts for many areas of governmental commerce. This enabled him to award routine contracts and broker deals for companies interested in doing business with the government. One of the businesses that Baker so successfully ran on the side was his vending company, Serv-U Corporation, which allowed him to place his equipment and snacks and sodas into factories doing business with the government. It was this company that became his downfall, all because a competitor wanted a piece of the action. But before he formed his own company, he had extracted fees from other vending companies for being awarded contracts for such businesses.

An example of Baker's control over routine government contracts occurred in 1962, when Ralph L. Hill, owner of the Capitol Vending Company, came to Baker to get a contract to place vending machines on government-controlled property. For a fee of $5,600, Baker gave Hill such a contract with Melpar Inc., a subsidiary of North American Aviation. Hill did not realize that this fee would have to be paid annually, so when it came up for renewal in 1963, Baker wanted another $5,600. Hill complained that the fee was too high, and Baker then tried to force Hill to sell him his company, but Hill refused. Baker wanted to squeeze Hill out of the Melpar contract so his own company, Serv-U Corp., could take it over. Baker then threatened to cancel Hill's contract, causing a fierce argument between the two.[184] Ralph Hill also knew Speaker McCormack, whom he appealed to several times,

---

181. *New York Times*, October 24, 1963.
182. North, p. 161.
183. Ibid., pp. 215–216.
184. Mellenhoff, p. 296.

asking him to get Vice President Johnson to force Baker off his back. Johnson apparently did not take Hill's early threats seriously enough, and Baker failed to respond to these entreaties; the feud escalated into personal threats between other congressmen on both sides of the rotunda, many of whom had become the subjects of Baker's own "confidential files"—another tactic learned from the master—through their appearances at another of Baker's businesses: the Quorum Club. There were many other facets of the Bobby Baker enterprises that require elucidation, in order to fully understand the context and strength of the case against Lyndon B. Johnson, as it existed on the morning of November 22, 1963.

Other Bobby Baker Ventures

The Quorum Club was a private club started by Lyndon Johnson and Bobby Baker on the second floor of the Carroll Arms Hotel on Capitol Hill. Its "membership was comprised of senators, congressmen, lobbyists, Capitol Hill staffers, and other well-connecteds who wanted to enjoy their drinks, meals, poker games, and shared secrets in private accommodations," according to Baker.[185] He is either being credulous, facetious, or coy here, because, unbeknownst to the partygoers, they only thought they were sharing secrets; in fact, the FBI had bugged the lounge, and Baker himself was even making his own tapes of the conversations at certain tables. This was not a unique situation, however, as Baker's (and Johnson's) friend Fred Black Jr., a major defense lobbyist, "kept a hotel suite at the Sheraton-Carlton in Washington where he and his friends . . . repaired to conduct business . . . or entertain ladies. Though we did not know it then, that suite was bugged by the FBI."[186]

Baker got to know all the good-looking young women working at the Senate, and a few high-class prostitutes as well, to provide entertainment for the politicians at the Quorum Club. The Quorum provided Hoover (and therefore, Johnson) much information for his files on the sexual activities of politicians; it also reaped even more valuable evidence about other chicanery being practiced by those same men, such as their acceptance of bribes for their influence in getting legislation passed that benefited certain companies willing to pay for it. In addition to the Quorum, another party place was owned by Baker, a town house on Capitol Hill that he rented to his secretary and mistress, Carole Tyler (she would eventually die in a plane crash, ironically on the beach directly in front of the Carousel).

---

185. Baker, *Wheeling*, pp. 78–80.
186. Ibid., p. 170.

Baker, Black, and Hoover all passed information to LBJ regarding many politicians, the use of which explains how Johnson managed to survive other scandals, such as the aforementioned TFX and Billie Sol Estes episodes, that might have forced anyone else to have already resigned.[187] The Serv-U Corporation was set up with financing arranged by Senator Kerr; other investors were solicited, including Baker's lawyer, Ernest Tucker, and his friends Eddie Levinson and Benjamin B. Siegelbaum. By 1963, the business was grossing millions annually, functioning as a near monopoly on soft drink, candy, and cigarette sales from machines installed at sites where companies were performing defense-related work that depended on government contracts.[188] It had been awarded the lion's share of business at three major aerospace companies; at North American Aviation alone, it raked in $2.5 million annually from the California plants.[189] Baker had done business with Jimmy Hoffa and a number of Mob figures in Las Vegas, Chicago, and New Orleans through Eddie Levinson. He was also involved with Clint Murchison in a meatpacking plant in Haiti that was kicking back thousands to Baker.[190] In two cases, the slaughterhouse in Haiti failed USDA inspections because of poor sanitary practices, but after a trip to the Dominican Republic with Johnson, Baker's leverage with the Department of Agriculture expanded, and he managed to help get the meatpacking operation approved despite the hygienic issues. The Haitians became dissatisfied with the product, and Murchison's other lobbyist, Irving Davidson, brokered a new deal to allow the meat to be sold in the United States. Baker's cut of a half cent per pound continued under the newer, more lucrative deal.[191] As described by Peter Dale Scott, "While working for Johnson, Baker became the epitome of Washington wheeler-dealer sleaze. Repeatedly, he fronted for syndicate gamblers Cliff Jones and Ed Levinson, in investments which earned super-profits for himself and another military-industrial lobbyist, his friend Fred Black Jr. In exchange he intervened to help Jones and Levinson obtain casino contracts with the Intercontinental hotel system."[192] On August 21, 1963, Vice President Lyndon Johnson met with Bobby Baker and Fred Black and a senior executive from North American Aviation in his Executive Office Building. Normally, he would take the necessary precautions and avoid meeting with his cronies in his official offices, since doing so would be

---

187. Ibid.
188. Ibid.
189. North, p. 121.
190. Russell, p. 523.
191. Hancock, p. 316.
192. Scott, p. 218.

recorded in the office's daily log. It is not clear why Johnson had let down his guard on this occasion but the danger this posed to Johnson, if any of these three were foolish enough to confront him, could potentially expose him to blackmail.[193]

The luck and the political influence and the resulting financial successes enjoyed by Bobby Baker during his years on Capitol Hill, as the "son" and protégé of Lyndon Johnson, began unraveling in early September 1963. With a little help from information supplied to him by Robert Kennedy, Senator John J. Williams of Delaware initiated an investigation into Baker's activities as part of his desire to eliminate political corruption on Capitol Hill. Kennedy's motive was to force Lyndon Johnson off the ticket in 1964 by getting this story into the press well ahead of the start of the campaign. Baker had been surrounded by unsavory characters and activities, which caused Kennedy to worry that this story would blow up in the middle of the 1964 campaign, becoming a major scandal for the entire administration, jeopardizing not only the reelection of JFK but the Democratic majority in Congress. Clearly, Johnson's days in the Kennedy administration were numbered; in order to have him removed and for the dust created by the skirmish to have time to settle, his "retirement" would have to be announced within the first four or five months of 1964, which would have left his remaining time as vice president no more than about six months. Such a chain of events would have, of course, eliminated any possibility of his lifetime obsession ever being satisfied.

Senator Williams already had a reputation as the Sherlock Holmes of Capitol Hill for his previous work; during a fifteen-year period his investigations resulted in over 200 indictments and 125 convictions. Williams was a humble, self-effacing man, beyond reproach, tenaciously dedicated to performing his duties as a public servant and intent on cleaning up the inner bureaucracy of the federal government by exposing bribery, sales of political influence, conflicts of interest, and all other sins of a government he did not quite trust. During his service in the Senate, he was rightly referred to as "the conscience of the Senate." Senator Williams became the prime mover in bringing about the investigation of Baker, during which he leaked information to his primary media contact: Clark Mollenhoff of the *Des Moines Register*, who wrote a series of stories about Baker's business activities. He had observed firsthand the activities of Bobby Baker and quickly found that his suspicions of a conflict of interest with his Serv-U Corporation were valid indeed. Fellow committee member Senator Hugh Scott of Pennsylvania

---

193. Hancock, p. 319.

joined Williams in his campaign, prompting a cataclysmic implosion that rocked the entire Senate: Lyndon Johnson had attempted to stop Scott by threatening to make public information about his relationship with certain lobbyists and told Scott that he would use his influence to close down the Philadelphia Navy Yard unless he backed off. When Scott refused, the lid blew off in the full Senate, causing Barry Goldwater to demand an official Senate investigation. In the meantime, Johnson knew that Robert Kennedy had been passing information about the Baker case to Senator Williams to assist him in investigating Baker. This was revealed in interviews that Burkett Van Kirk, chief counsel for the Republicans on the Rules Committee, gave to Seymour Hersh for his book, *The Dark Side of Camelot*. Bobby even assigned a Justice Department lawyer to serve as an intermediary to the minority (Republican) staff to supply them with documents about Johnson and his financial dealings with Baker. As Seymour Hersh reported, "There was no doubt about Bobby's motive in providing this information to the Republicans, Van Kirk said: 'To get rid of Johnson. To dump him. I am as sure of that as I am that the sun comes up in the East.'"[194] Van Kirk also told Hersh, "There's no doubt in my mind . . . that Reynold's testimony would have gotten Johnson out of the vice presidency."[195]

Johnson knew what the Kennedys were up to, and he tried to get them to back off by having Hoover confront them about JFK's involvement with Ellen Rometsch. Rometsch was one of the party girls who had frolicked with him at the nude pool parties in the White House. Since she had been furnished to Kennedy in the first place by Bobby Baker, from the Quorum Club, both Baker and Johnson (ergo, Hoover as well) had enough information about her background to enable any of them to threaten both John and Robert Kennedy with blackmail. Although Johnson tried to distance himself from Baker, even to the extent of denying that they had ever had close business dealings, it was widely known that Baker was Johnson's protégé and would inevitably be linked to Lyndon (by then, it was already being reported that the Bakers had even named their one-year-old son Lyndon, obviously in tribute to the man who once said of Baker, "If I had a son, this would be him"; Cliff Carter had probably felt a bit jealous of this attention since he had also named a son after Lyndon).

When the Baker scandal broke, Fortas was immediately appointed as his counsel, and having spoken with Fortas only four times in the previous six months, Johnson and Fortas talked by telephone almost daily during October, from a few minutes to an hour and, when he returned to

194. Hersh, *The Dark Side* . . . , p. 407.
195. Ibid., p. 447.

Washington, had Fortas visit him twice, on October 14 and 21. Johnson also visited Fortas in his home for two hours, driven there by Mrs. Johnson in a borrowed car.[196] After October 29, Johnson returned to his ranch to begin the detailed planning for the Dallas segment of Kennedy's trip to Texas. Back in Washington, with Johnson out of town, JFK began planning his political strategies for the 1964 campaign with his top political advisers: his brother Bobby, John Bailey, Ted Sorenson, Steve Smith, Larry O'Brien, Kenny O'Donnell, and others, none of whom were amenable to Lyndon Johnson's continued presence around the White House.[197] Something apparently happened at that point to allay Johnson's worries about the Baker scandal and the continuing Senate investigations about it, because the number of calls between himself and Fortas declined;[198] after the assassination, Fortas was replaced as counsel to Baker by another of Johnson's lawyers, and Fortas was then put back to work directly under Johnson, working full-time on shutting down both congressional investigations.

The news of the emerging scandals began showing up more regularly in *The New York Times* during September 1963 and continued throughout October, including linkages of Baker to Johnson, Davidson, and Murchison and stories about another associate, Ed Levinson, and his Las Vegas skimming operation.[199] The Long Island tabloid *Newsday* printed an article on October 29, 1963, titled "Baker Scandal Quiz Opens Today," beginning with these words: "Already liberally spiced with sex, scandal, and intrigue, the tantalizing case of Robert G. (Bobby) Baker comes under official scrutiny today. And what everyone wants to know is: Who is going to get caught?" The article included the following: "A report, from those who claim 'inside information,' is that *the Justice Department started an investigation of Baker as a means of embarrassing Johnson and eliminating him from the Democratic ticket next year . . .*" (emphasis added). The November 8 issue of *Life* magazine featured a cover page with a picture of Bobby Baker at a masquerade party with a bold headline: "CAPITAL BUZZES OVER STORIES OF MISCONDUCT IN HIGH PLACES: THE BOBBY BAKER BOMBSHELL." The article (p. 36) asked the rhetorical question, "How had a simple, hardworking majority secretary, earning $19,612 a year, struck it so rich in so short a time?"

Johnson and Hoover knew they had to tread carefully around the breaking news stories and rumors that were quickly spreading about Capitol Hill's sex scandal because it was so closely related to the concurrent Bobby Baker

196. Hancock, pp. 319–321.
197. Lincoln, p. 199.
198. Hancock, pp. 319–321.
199. Scott, p. 220.

financial scandals, which included Johnson's procurement and acceptance of a $100,000 payoff for the TFX contract and numerous other related financial payoff schemes developed over many years.[200] Bobby Kennedy, meanwhile, had to turn to Hoover—in desperation—for his help in quashing the Rometsch story, to avoid it bringing down the entire administration. Hoover's intense hatred of both Kennedy brothers put him into a quandary over how far he could go to help them, but he thought he could use their anxiety as his "ace in the hole" to obtain another waiver from the mandatory retirement rule. As Burton Hersh noted,

> According to Justice Department insiders . . . Hoover had been tapping his attorney general's line, and he had heard Bobby laughingly assure his friends that, as big a pain in the ass as the Director had become, it really would not matter for a whole lot longer because he was on his way out. At worst, he would be seventy in 1965 and Jack would dump him then. . . . Hoover—to whom his position and his existence were interchangeable—panicked. The stage was set for that very grim executive-mansion lunch. Watching both autocrats, Courtney Evans could imagine a head-on collision that would obliterate them both. "I figured I had one mission," Evans maintains with all the conviction his ninety years can muster. Just keep the Kennedys from firing J. Edgar Hoover. I thought that was a blow they'd never recover from politically. Hoover had such connections on the Hill, such a reputation for having all the gossip in Washington stored away. . . .
>
> Both Kennedy brothers had to consider the successive updates the Director kept sending over to Bobby relating to Judith Campbell (Exner) and Sam Giancana. Along with the fact that, on Robert Kennedy's orders, the late Marilyn Monroe's telephone records had been confiscated by the FBI . . . Hoover's grip on the brothers was getting tighter every day.[201]

Bobby Kennedy decided to stop any investigation into the Rometsch affair by having her deported and then tried to stop the Senate from investigating the "sex angle" of the multifaceted Bobby Baker scandals any further. His actions immediately hit the newspapers (e.g., the headline on October 28, 1963, of the *Des Moines Register* was "U.S. Expels Girl Linked to Officials— Is Sent to Germany after FBI Probe"), and this article was subsequently read

---

200. Lasky, *It Didn't Start* . . . , pp. 135–137.
201. Hersh, Burton, *Bobby and J. Edgar* . . . , pp. 206–209.

into the Congressional Record. Although RFK thereafter tried to steer the investigation away from the "sex angle," he continued for a time to feed Senator Williams information on the financial frauds being committed and was conducting his own investigation on Baker for tax evasion.[202] He couldn't go to Johnson for help, so he went to J. Edgar Hoover, hat in hand. This put the director in the position of added leverage with Bobby, to be used as an IOU and as a guarantee of his extended tenure. Hoover reluctantly agreed to Bobby's request of him to meet with Senators Mansfield and Dirksen to ask them to limit the Senate's investigation; doing so for Bobby wasn't appealing to him, but Hoover decided that he would go along with it since it would also benefit his friend Lyndon B. Johnson.

Bobby had "put together the information regarding all the girls and the members of Congress and the Senate who had been associated with the girls—and it got to be large numbers in both ways," he told Anthony Lewis. Hoover used this information in a secret meeting with Senate Majority Leader Mansfield and Senate Minority Leader Dirksen on October 28, 1963, at Mansfield's apartment.[203] Bobby's plan worked very well, because by that afternoon, the Senate's plans to discuss Rometsch had been canceled. As noted by Richard Mahoney, "There was no more private discussion, much less public debate, of the Rometsch affair by the 'world's greatest deliberative body.' But Hoover had a high price for his service: assurance from both the attorney general and the president (with whom he lunched on October 31) that he would be confirmed in his position as director. Further, he exacted from Bobby approval for four new wiretaps on Martin Luther King Jr., a man both Kennedys, but particularly Bobby, had come to admire and respect."[204] Being so compromised, RFK would also have to discontinue feeding Senator Williams information on the financial side of Baker's activities, information that he had planted in order to force Johnson off the ticket in 1964.

Although Hoover agreed to get the discussion of the Rometsch scandal stopped on Capitol Hill, he decided to have the dirty laundry put into the journalistic record; he leaked pieces of the more embarrassing lascivious details to Clark Mollenhoff of the *Des Moines Register* about a Washington party girl cavorting with "members of the Senate" and high executive branch officials.[205] *Life* magazine, in a story written days before the assassination, published an article in its November 22, 1963, edition about Bobby Baker's Quorum Club and its reputation as a rendezvous hot spot among Washington's

---

202. Scott, p. 220.
203. Summers, *Official and Confidential*, pp. 312–313.
204. Mahoney, p. 278. (citing Guthman and Shulman, p. 130).
205. Summers, *Official.*, p. 311.

elite, some of their clerical help, and additional support from the city's most elite call girls. The secrets of both Lyndon Johnson and John F. Kennedy had begun to unravel during October and November 1963 and spilled over on the very day of JFK's assassination. Bobby Baker's troubles were far from over, but Lyndon Johnson's predicament of being intertwined with Baker was growing inexorably into as complex and unsettled a mess as he had ever been in, which is saying a lot. Unless his long-planned executive action—the assassination of John F. Kennedy—was performed soon, a potentially destructive, ongoing controversy ultimately culminating in possible prison terms for both of them was now almost inevitable. The man Johnson had proudly taught, his surrogate son to whom he had become a mentor, would become, by the end of 1963, "just an employee around here."[206]

Baker Scandal Status Quo: November 21–22, 1963

By the autumn of 1963, the rumors of Lyndon Johnson's many entanglements with the Billie Sol Estes case and the TFX payoff were still percolating. The latest scandal was referred to generally under the name of its chief architect, Bobby Baker, and must have been seen by Johnson as the biggest threat of them all, especially since Baker was no longer communicating with Johnson—or vice versa. JFK's secretary, Evelyn Lincoln, said that Bobby Kennedy was also investigating Bobby Baker for tax evasion and fraud. This is where the matter was on November 19, 1963: The president had discussed the Baker investigation with his secretary and told her that his running mate in 1964 would not be Lyndon Johnson, two days before the president left for Texas. Jack Kennedy knew that if he kept Johnson on the ticket, he would be like a time bomb that could go off at any time. Doing so could lead to certain defeat in 1964. He and his brother Bobby decided to agree to Hoover's terms to try to stop the Bobby Baker investigation and help cover it up. Unfortunately for them, it was too late; the unraveling had already gone too far.

Insurance salesman Don Reynolds had come forward with information that Lyndon Johnson had been involved in receiving kickbacks from a life insurance contract that Reynolds had sold him through their mutual friend Bobby Baker. He also had intimate knowledge of other financial bribery and extortion involving Baker, including Baker's skimming "commissions" from other transactions such as those involving Ralph Hill of Capitol Vending and Matthew McCloskey, a major construction contractor who benefited from the largesse of Baker's ties to many government officials on the take.

---

206. Hersh, Burton, *Bobby and J. Edgar*, p. 57.

McCloskey had been the contractor who built, among other things, the Rayburn House Office Building and was then building the new stadium in DC which would later be renamed RFK Stadium. Among other charges, Reynolds would testify that McCloskey had bribed Baker to get the stadium contract and then managed to increase the cost of it from $6 million to $20 million in his statement to the investigating subcommittee of the Senate Rules Committee on November 22, 1963.[207] The question about how much of the "cost overruns" would be kicked back to Baker and Lyndon Johnson was never established before Johnson's efforts to close down this investigation were complete. Reynolds had initially been a reluctant witness, and he was under pressure to either "forget" the answers or take the Fifth Amendment and refuse to talk. He was warned that he was tampering with the reputations of "big men" and that it could only cause him trouble if he talked.[208] Despite this pressure, Reynolds was determined to cooperate; some of his determination was supplied by his wife, who was tired of life in the "fast lane," the weekend parties in New York and Miami, and the "fast buck" attitude in the crowd her husband was now involved with—Bobby Baker, Fred Black Jr., and Tommy Webb in particular.[209]

Although it was to be a closed session, Johnson knew that Williams would leak the committee's findings to the press, which he undoubtedly saw as a Hobson's choice for himself: He had to proceed as planned and Kennedy had to die on November 22. After that, it would be too late to contain the problem presented by the new witness, Mr. Reynolds. He knew by this time that he could cover up this story only after becoming the president of the United States, his lifetime goal that was now within his grasp. While Johnson knew that he would be taking a big risk with the assassination, and then trying to deftly cover it up, it would be much more manageable when he was president, since he would then have complete power to control the vast resources of the federal government and comparable power over even local governments, especially in Texas.

Reynolds told Chairman B. Everett Jordan and his committee on November 22, 1963, that Johnson had demanded kickbacks in the commissions Reynolds was to receive for the two $100,000 life insurance policies he sold to Johnson in 1957 and 1961. This included a $585 Magnavox stereo. Reynolds also had to pay for $1,200 worth of advertising on KTBC, Johnson's television station in Austin. Reynolds had paperwork for this transaction, including a delivery receipt that indicated the stereo had been sent to the

207. Mollenhoff, *Despoilers*, p. 296.
208. Ibid., p. 294.
209. Ibid., p. 294.

home of Johnson. Reynolds also told the Senate Rules Committee of seeing a suitcase full of money that Bobby Baker had described as a "$100,000 payoff to Johnson for his role in securing the Fort Worth TFX contract."[210] About 1:30 p.m. in Washington—as JFK was being shot to death in Dallas—he was still testifying and producing records to substantiate his story. He said that he purchased the stereo at wholesale, through a friend, but its normal retail price was $900. It was a set that Mrs. Johnson selected from a catalogue that Reynolds said was sent to her by Bobby Baker. Lady Bird wanted the stereo for a musical, so he had to send it by airfreight to Baltimore Friendship Airport, where it was picked up by a Senate delivery truck, which brought it directly to Johnson's home.[211] He also said that he tried to resist the kickback, which he felt was illegal, but both Bobby Baker and Walter Jenkins called him and told him to pay it. To the committee, Reynolds denied that it was a "kickback" (which would have been illegal and might have subjected him to prosecution); instead, he said it was a "shakedown," an "after the fact" demand put to him as a veiled threat. He asked Jenkins if he would allow him (Reynolds) to resell the advertising time on KTBC, since he really had no use for it since his marketing area was one thousand five hundred miles away from Austin, Texas. He said Jenkins consented to his request.[212]

As his testimony came to an end at about 2:30 p.m. Washington time (1:30 p.m. Dallas), a secretary burst into the room, sobbing hysterically that "President Kennedy has been killed!" . . . "Reynolds was stunned. If President Kennedy was dead, then Lyndon Johnson, the man about whom he had been talking, was President of the United States . . . Reynolds reached for the documents on the committee table which confirmed his story of the gift stereo set and the television advertising contract. He quietly pulled the documents toward him. 'I guess you won't need these,' Reynolds said soberly. 'Giving testimony involving the Vice President is one thing, but when it involves the President himself, that is something else. You can just forget that I ever said anything if you want to.' Counsel Van Kirk replied that Reynolds should not concern himself with the problem of what should be done with the evidence. 'The documents on this matter are now the records of the Rules Committee,' Van Kirk said. 'The decision on whether we will use them is a matter that the Committee will have to decide. None of us can do anything about it."[213] Johnson's continuing efforts to stop the Senate investigations are described in chapter 9, "The Aftermath."

210. Lasky, *It Didn't Start . . .*, pp. 135–137.
211. Mollenhoff, *Despoilers*, p. 298.
212. Ibid., p. 298.
213. Ibid., p. 299.

This is where the unfolding scandals of Bobby Baker rested, along with all of the many direct connections from them back to Lyndon B. Johnson, when the thirty-fifth president of the United States was shot down in the streets of Dallas, Texas, by assassins acting—albeit well removed, through many layers of plausible deniability—under the authority of his successor, the thirty-sixth president. They were guaranteed protection against prosecution, and by all accounts, that promise was fulfilled.

PART III
The Preassassination Conspiracy

Chapter 5

THE MASTERMIND SECURES
THE VICE PRESIDENCY

I'm forty-three years old. I'm not going to die in office. So the vice presidency doesn't mean anything.[1]

—JOHN F. KENNEDY TO KENNY O'DONNELL

One out of every four presidents has died in office. I'm a gambling man, darling, and this is the only chance I got.[2]

—LYNDON B. JOHNSON TO CLARE BOOTHE LUCE

LBJ's Route to the Presidency

John Kennedy, like Lyndon Johnson, was very much aware of the presidential death cycle, which started in 1840 and remained unbroken: Every twenty years, the president elected—Harrison, Lincoln, Garfield, McKinley, Harding, and Franklin D. Roosevelt—had died in office. Kennedy had laughed at the freakish statistic: "That was one tradition . . . that he intended to break."*[3] Unfortunately for him, his forced selection of Johnson as his vice presidential nominee was the very decision that would cause the cycle to continue.

Lyndon Johnson had a lifelong, obsessive dream to become the president of the United States, yet he realized that his chances of winning a national election as a Southerner running for the presidency were practically nil. He had repeatedly stated his intention to become president numerous times, beginning when he was a child following his father around the Texas legislature and repeated throughout his high school and college days. Knowing the available time to achieve that dream was very limited, and that between John and Robert Kennedy, it would be unlikely that he could even

---

*Ronald Reagan, the president elected at the next cycle, 1980, managed to break the pattern, but just barely.

1. O'Donnell, Kenneth, *Life* magazine, August 7, 1970, p. 47; *Johnny . . .*, p. 7.
2. Summers, *Official and Confidential*, p. 273.
3. Manchester, p. 141.

mount an effective campaign before he was sixty-eight years old (and well
beyond his life expectancy based on family history), LBJ had an overwhelming
motive to fulfill his lifetime goal. As the new president, Johnson knew he
would have the power to control the subsequent investigation; he would use
it immediately to derail attempts to find the truth into a well-coordinated,
intensive cover-up.

Lyndon Johnson had begun actively planning for his ascension in 1941,
when even though he still lacked sufficient personal funds and was desperate
to accumulate wealth, he actually turned down what amounted to a gift
of approximately three quarters of a million dollars. His benefactors, led
by Charles Marsh, Sid Richardson, and Herman Brown, had offered him
essentially a free stake in an oil company. Johnson turned it down, saying that
he couldn't be a successful politician if he was considered to be an "oilman."[4]
The problem with the logic of that is that being an oilman in Texas would
not have adversely affected his success as a politician; it would have probably
helped, not hindered, his Texas political career. It was because his eyes were
focused not on the immediate goals so much as on his ultimate goal, to
prepare for being a candidate for the presidency and therefore the need to
appeal to a national electorate. He was also thinking in terms of acquiring
businesses that he could claim were run by his wife, even though it was
none other than himself who would have actual control. The broadcasting
business—specifically radio station KTBC, which was near bankruptcy
largely because of Johnson's influence with the FCC as discussed elsewhere
when he bought it at a discount—matched his requirements for securing the
financial wherewithal he needed; it miraculously turned around immediately
when he bought it, becoming extremely profitable. Having "Johnson men"
throughout the government bureaucracy, including the FCC in getting
approvals for expanding its license multiple times over the years, would pay
huge dividends to Johnson during his tenure.

Beginning with his ascension to the Senate as the result of the stolen
election in 1948 (detailed in chapter 1) and then in his position as majority
leader, Johnson knew that his boyhood dream, the one that he long ago resolved
would be kept, was within his grasp. He knew that in order to successfully
run for the presidency, he would need to redefine his base, which had always
been what he thought was the vast middle class, not wealthy landowners,
but the working-class people in Texas. He tried to be a "populist" type of
candidate, while simultaneously trying to stay grounded on the conservative
side of the Texas Democratic Party. In order to appeal to a national base, he
sought ways to blur the normal political lines: He portrayed himself—on the

4. Caro, *Master of the Senate*, p. 111.

same issue—as a conservative when meeting with conservative people and liberal when meeting with liberals.

He took every opportunity to publicize himself, cultivating (mostly superficial) friendships with others in Congress; even more important, he sought out newspaper and magazine journalists to get his name before voters on a national scale. By 1952 he was forty-four years old and still a first-term senator having only four years' tenure and little influence among the older, more experienced senators with whom he worked, but he considered himself ready to begin more definite planning for his career goal. In January of that year he was given the opportunity to be interviewed for an article in *Nation's Business* magazine. Alfred Steinberg had planned to write about four senators though, and that outraged Johnson. He moved his chair closer to Steinberg, close enough that his face was only inches away from his quarry; then he grabbed one of Steinberg's lapels and asked him, why not do a story on him alone? Then he said, after looking around to make sure they were alone, why not write a story on Johnson's potential run for the presidential nomination: "President! That's the angle you want to write about me."[5]

Senate Majority Leader, 1956–1959

In one sense, Johnson had campaigned for the presidency for much of his lifetime and with increasing resolve for at least two decades, ever since the 1941 incident mentioned above, when he turned down an offer to a Texas oilman because it might interfere with his future presidential aspirations. Yet in another, more direct sense, his was arguably the shortest campaign of any candidate in memory: He announced his candidacy only five days before the 1960 Democratic National Convention commenced. The reasons for this dichotomy were rooted in Johnson's disease: According to the assessment of author Hershman, his bouts with manic euphoria caused him to be deluded about his own talent, intelligence, social status, and powers—his own were those usually associated with divinities—but all of this could turn quickly to severe depression; he alternately worried that his health would give out and his death would mean he could never get to be president, and that would trigger a vicious cycle of hopeless depression, which convinced half of his mind that he couldn't run because he could not withstand his depressive periods. His utter fear of the agony of ego-crushing rejection caused him to refuse to enter the political campaigning that had taken him so far previously.[6] A preview of the 1960 campaign occurred in

---

5. Caro, *Master of the Senate*, p. 463–464.
6. Hershman, pp. 104–105.

1956: He convinced himself that the Northern labor block would flock to his support despite his repeated efforts against civil rights laws and join with his Southern base to take the nomination away from Stevenson at the last minute, as some kind of dark horse "people's candidate." This "plan" was revealed at a surprise announcement on August 13, 1956, the first day of the 1956 Democratic National Convention, when he announced his candidacy for the presidency of the United States.[7] Most of the delegates there were flabbergasted, and not particularly impressed. Johnson had lost his first attempt to run for the presidency in 1956. There were many reasons for this, but the primary one was his lack of a national base and the corollary image of him being a regional, Southern, and Western man, beholden only to the interests of the population of that area and not appealing to the more urban Midwestern and Eastern electorate. After the failed candidacy of 1956, he knew that he would—he must—make his move in 1960 if he was to have any chance of fulfilling his dream.

Ironically, despite his reputation for hard work, efficiency, and masterfully running the Senate, his own legislative record was weak. As Robert Sherrill noted, "Forget the stereotypes the newspapers and weekly news magazines used to make of Johnson—the legislator possessed, the architect of government—and look back over his career for yourself. After twenty-three years in Congress, Johnson left not one progressive piece of legislation with his name on it, not one piece of legislation that measurably advanced the nation beyond the stage in which he discovered it at the time he entered Congress in 1937."[8] Even after the recession of 1957–1958 resulted in a huge Democratic congressional victory with 62 Democratic senators versus 34 Republicans and 282 Democratic congressmen versus 158 Republicans, Johnson accomplished little. He "settled down into his customary cautious posture, agreeing that there must be no 'reckless spending' and permitting Senator Harry F. Byrd, of whom he never lost his freshman's fear, to torpedo a Senate-approved workman's compensation measure by surrendering in a House-Senate conference committee. This was only symptomatic of the leadership's malaise."[9] After engineering a cutback in a bill introduced in the Senate in 1959 calling for a ten-year $600-million-per-year expenditure to assist cities with infrastructure assistance, to a one-year $900-million bill, and then passing the antilabor Landrum-Griffin Act, a younger Texas congressman observed that "in the final analysis, the largest Democratic majority in Congress since 1936 out-did the Republican 80th Congress

---

7. Ibid.
8. Sherrill, p. 19.
9. Ibid., p. 67.

[which passed the Taft-Hartley Act] in passing anti-labor and in not passing pro-people legislation."[10]

Johnson's handpicked biographer Doris Kearns-Goodwin dutifully repeated his thoughts, attitudes, and opinions, one of which was the observation that "the qualities the Senate rewarded were not adapted to the institutional process of presidential nomination nor, probably, to that of presidential election, *for it was unlikely that Johnson could have moved from majority leader to election as president on his own*"[11] (emphasis added). The essential truth of that statement would have been derived directly from Johnson, and it must have been his overriding, perplexing thought as he considered how he would attain his prized, single-minded goal to become president. If it appeared to many that he gave up trying to win the 1960 nomination before the election season had even started, the idea sprung more from substantive reality than ephemeral thought. After his aborted effort to run for president in 1956, Johnson decided that if his boyhood promise was to be fulfilled, it must be done in 1960. If not, it was likely that "waiting his turn" would mean he wouldn't have another chance until 1968, when he would be sixty years old and probably near the end of his life expectancy, given his family history and considering his 1955 heart attack. Then there was the likelihood of RFK being positioned to succeed his brother in that year. He knew that this would be his last realistic chance to take the office he felt was his ultimate destiny.

Preparing for the 1960 Presidential Election

Johnson wanted to be in a position to run for president or vice president in 1960, but at the same time, afraid of the risk of losing, he did not want to have to forfeit his senatorial position, the term of which was expiring in 1960. He began planning for this dilemma in 1958, when he went to Texas State Senator Dorsey Hardeman, a leading conservative legislator, to sponsor a new bill to allow him to simultaneously run for president or vice president and the Senate at the same time.[12] This suggests that he was fully intent to enter the race in some capacity regardless of the pretense of his seeming ambivalence leading up to the 1960 convention. The other most active potential candidates, John Kennedy and Hubert Humphrey, were planning their own runs, and Johnson hoped they would beat each other up in their primary battles, leaving the convention deadlocked and providing

---

10. Ibid., p. 68.
11. Kearns, p. 396.
12. Haley, p. 191.

his entrée as a "dark horse" candidate to win the nomination in the smoky back rooms without having to dirty his hands trying to beat Kennedy in the primary states. In case he was unable to win the nomination—which he had always regarded as unlikely anyway—he would position himself as the leading candidate for the vice presidential nomination. As previously noted, Bobby Kennedy visited him in 1959 on his ranch, for the express purpose of finding out what his plans were in 1960; Johnson denied planning to run for president even as he was then working through Senator Hardeman to pass enabling legislation to allow him to run simultaneously for two positions.

In 1960, the Democratic Party "pros" in most states selected their favored nominee for the presidency; there were only seven states that held full "primary" elections where registered party voters were allowed to select the candidate. Illinois had a "write-in preferential primary" event, where 34,000 people wrote in JFK's name, compared with only 8,000 for the former governor, Adlai Stevenson—and only 442 named Lyndon Johnson.[13] The seven primary states were all relatively small states: New Hampshire and a couple of others like Oregon and Maryland were solidly in Kennedy's camp, so the primary race came down to two hotly contested states: Wisconsin and West Virginia. While Kennedy won the first of these, Wisconsin, the press claimed that it was a moral victory for Hubert Humphrey because the victory wasn't as high as the margins that had been predicted. During these primary elections, while Kennedy was campaigning in Oregon, a reporter asked him, "What would you have done when the U-2 plane was shot down over Russia? How would you, what message would you have sent to Chairman Khrushchev?" And he said, "I would have apologized."

This report was not received well back on Capitol Hill, and many of Johnson's fellow senators began pressing him to enter the fray because they feared Kennedy becoming president. Horace Busby said that they would come up to Johnson in the Capitol corridors, alarmed at Kennedy's response to the U-2 controversy:

> This must have sent a chill down the spine of all of those people in, the elders of the Senate. They began coming to Johnson—I was present once or twice—and they were saying, "You have got to make this race for your country. We've got to have an alternative to Kennedy. We cannot have him as president. He's weak; he's inexperienced. A remark like that by a president, or an action like that by a president would tilt the balances of power."[14]

13. Lincoln, p. 44.
14. Horace Busby, recorded interview by Sheldon H. Stern, Mary 26, 1982, (p. 4), John F. Kennedy Library Oral History Program.

Despite this groundswell of support in Congress, Johnson steadfastly refused to enter the campaign while Congress was still in session. His plan was to take a Shermanesque position and decline for the time being, hoping that people would see his martyr side and assume that such dogfights were beneath his dignity. His alternate strategy—because he could not stand the possibility of rejection in the primary battles—was to stay in Washington and attempt to show the world what a hard worker he was. He wanted people to understand that his responsibilities were too enormous and that he couldn't leave the Senate because someone had to "mind the store," unlike the "boy wonder" Kennedy, whom he kept calling the "absentee senator" in his statements to the press. Somehow, Johnson was able to finagle an endorsement from the controversial Harlem Congressman Adam Clayton Powell through some kind of horse-trading deal, which raised a few eyebrows: According to Evelyn Lincoln, "Not everyone seemed to believe he did so on a popular demand from his Harlem constituents."[15] Instead of entering any of the state primary elections, Johnson sat out all of them, thinking that while his opponents were splitting the delegates in the primary states, he could do an end run at the smoke-filled rooms of a deadlocked convention, garnering enough votes from nonprimary states and horse-trading with the runner-up candidates to take the convention through the back door. In his last-ditch effort to win the presidential nomination, he planned to derail the Kennedy candidacy in the days before, and during, the convention through personal attacks—made through his surrogate John Connally—alluding to the then secret fact that John Kennedy suffered from the incurable Addison's disease, which RFK said was "malicious and false."[16] Johnson's knowledge of JFK's secret disease could have only come directly from the "personal and confidential" files of J. Edgar Hoover.

It was assumed that Humphrey would win West Virginia, because of a perception that Kennedy's liberal East Coast and Catholic background would not work in that state. But the pundits did not anticipate Joseph Kennedy's willingness to buy that election, committing at least $2 million (over $20 million in today's dollars) and possibly twice that, to ensure the critical victory in West Virginia.[17] The paymasters included JFK's brothers, Bobby and Teddy Kennedy, who focused on the county sheriffs as being in local control of all election workers, some of whom pocketed up to $50,000 of Kennedy money to throw the election.[18] The man in charge of Harrison County, Victor Gabriel, was too honest to accept any more than he calculated

15. Ibid., p. 43.
16. Haley, p. 196.
17. Hersh, *The Dark Side . . .*, pp. 90, 95.
18. Ibid., p. 93.

his expenses to be and indicated that he only needed $5,000 to accomplish the goals for his county. At the victory party in Charleston, Bobby couldn't understand this thinking and pulled him aside to show him the ledger in which he recorded the amount given to other county chairmen, such as the $40,000 given to Sid Christie in McDowell County, and how all the others were accepting much larger sums than Gabriel had. However, Gabriel still couldn't understand how such sums could be spent beyond the amount he had accepted, so he declined taking any more money for his efforts. Mr. Gabriel was obviously not a typical 1960 West Virginia Democrat campaign worker.[19] The archbishop of Boston, Richard Cardinal Cushing, later revealed to Humphrey that he had met with Joe Kennedy to come up with a plan to counter West Virginia's anti-Catholicism. Their plan was to bribe Protestant churches, especially those in black communities: "We decided which church and preacher would get two hundred dollars or one hundred dollars or five hundred dollars."[20] Joe Kennedy also involved his Mafia friends in helping to raise funds for the West Virginia primary. He promised Paul "Skinny" D'Amato, who ran certain Atlantic City and Nevada nightclubs, that Jack would reverse a deportation order against Mafia boss Joey Adonis if he was elected. Against his father's wishes, Bobby refused to do this and even had D'Amato indicted for income tax evasion.[21]

Johnson had, with Bobby Baker's assistance, total control over the Democratic Senate Campaign Committee. All funds collected by this committee were doled out to senators for their respective campaigns in whatever manner Johnson determined was appropriate. As it happened, most of these funds were showing up only in the states where Johnson had his greatest hopes for gaining convention delegates; Kennedy protested this result, to no avail.[22] One month before the convention, the polls were showing Kennedy with 620 convention delegates, Johnson 510, Symington 140, Humphrey 100, and Adlai Stevenson 75, with 761 needed to win.[23] Johnson thought that he might have a chance to stop Kennedy on the first ballot and peel away enough votes from him and others on the second and third ballots to win the nomination.

Johnson fought his entire presidential campaign in the corridors of the Capitol. Having purloined Kennedy's medical records with help from his friend Hoover, coupled with stories of JFK's philandering, he set out to run an entirely negative campaign against his primary challenger. The other notable

19. Ibid., pp. 97–98.
20. Ibid., p. 100.
21. Ibid.
22. Lincoln, p. 53.
23. Ibid., p. 55.

part of his campaign was his use of blackmail against his fellow Democratic delegates. According to author Anthony Summers, in his interviews with Evelyn Lincoln, she stated that "sexual blackmail . . . had long been part of Lyndon Johnson's modus operandi—abetted by Edgar. 'J. Edgar Hoover' . . . gave Johnson the information about various congressmen and senators so that Johnson could go to X senator and say, 'How about this little deal you have with this woman?' and so forth. That's how he kept them in line. He used his IOUs with them as what he hoped was his road to the presidency. He had this trivia to use, because he had Hoover in his corner."[24] With Hoover's help, Johnson was able to keep his presidential campaign confined to the smoke-filled back rooms, almost entirely in Washington DC and Los Angeles. As the foremost political pro of the age, he apparently expected to be able to control enough votes to deny Kennedy a first-ballot win without even leaving town. Johnson's 1960 presidential campaign strategy was arguably not just the oddest attempt by any presidential candidate in history, it can also be said to have been the shortest and most negative, since there was very little that could be called positive, or even considered by anyone as a normal campaign. In any case, it was wholly ineffective, at least in terms of an attempt to get the Democratic nomination for president in 1960.

His strategy of relying on his Senate cronies, instead of going out to hustle delegates, had taken him as far as it could; he must have seen the futility in that before he arrived in Los Angeles with his wife and daughters.[25] One sign that he did was that, since Kennedy's win in West Virginia, Johnson grew very irritable and extremely temperamental, blasting his "volunteers" for things he thought they should have done. "'He barked at aides, cursed, slammed down telephones,' recalled [his] aide, Bobby Baker. 'He refused to go and thank his exhausted campaign workers.'"[26] It was reported that Johnson's mood would swing from one extreme to another—from being docile and quiet to lashing out to everyone around him—and that his staff could never predict how long one mood would last before it would swing back to the other side.[27]

Johnson and his friend the Speaker of the House Sam Rayburn decided one way they might coerce senators and representatives to vote for him was by not adjourning Congress *sine die* just before the convention. By keeping Congress open for three weeks after the convention before adjourning it the end of August, they thought they could force them to vote for him in order to get pending legislation passed. This idea was roundly criticized on both

---

24. Summers, Official p. 272
25. Hersh, *The Dark Side . . .*, p. 91.
26. Ibid. p. 271
27. Lincoln, p. 65.

sides of the aisle of both houses because of the usual hot and humid summer days, which hit Washington particularly hard that year. It was not something that John F. Kennedy came to appreciate either, when he returned to the Hill for three weeks instead of starting his campaign for the presidency.[28]

The 1960 Democratic Convention

For the previous six years of the Eisenhower era, the second most powerful man in America was Lyndon Johnson, the Senate majority leader. He had grown to love the power he wielded and was eager to ascend to the number one position, as though it should automatically be his right. But he recognized that his base was only regional—only his own state actually, and only fractionally there—and he was not psychologically prepared to launch a serious national campaign. His efforts to mount such a campaign were as perfunctory as they were futile; he had decided he would have to gain office in another way. As the leader of the party, he believed the other contenders would eventually be shown to be lightweight junior senators who were not quite ready for the Oval Office. Although he had marshaled the assistance of some very powerful men—from Joseph Alsop the columnist, to the publisher of *The Washington Post* Philip Graham, to Speaker of the House Sam Rayburn and the king of all lobbyists Tommy Corcoran—to help him win the nomination, that was not nearly enough to stop the momentum that Kennedy had built up from his primary election victories and preconvention campaigning across the country. Johnson would take excursions into key states while campaigning only in a negative context, at every stop brutally attacking John Kennedy and his father.[29]

Even before the convention, Johnson had John Connally circulate rumors about Kennedy's health problems and the story of how JFK's father had bought the West Virginia primary, but they refused to do stories on them when he did not produce the proof.[30] Connally even held a press conference on the Fourth of July at which he and India Edwards, the former head of the women's division of the Democratic National Committee, charged that "Mr. Kennedy is a very sick man. He has Addison's disease," implying that he might not live much longer.[31] Coincidentally, just weeks before this incident, the offices of two of Kennedy's doctors, Eugene Cohen and Janet Travell,

28. Ibid., p. 71.
29. Kearns, p. 42.
30. Haley, p. 194.
31. Lincoln, p. 70.

were broken into and ransacked for medical records;[32] the burglars were never caught, possibly because—as Robert Kennedy thought—they were on J. Edgar Hoover's payroll.[33] That such "black bag" operations were routinely committed by the FBI at Hoover's direction is now common knowledge; former FBI agent M. Wesley Swearingen, in his book, described his own involvement in these exploits, sometimes doing two such jobs in the course of one day, altogether totaling in the hundreds.[34] This is the only realistic explanation of how the information about Kennedy's rare disease, a closely held family secret, would have become known to Johnson and his minions. It was probably with partial reference to this incident that Johnson reportedly told some reporter friends over drinks, "J. Edgar Hoover has Jack Kennedy by the balls.[35]

The sudden turnaround of Johnson's passive and perfunctory presidential campaign into an aggressively negative, "take no prisoners" pursuit of the vice presidential nomination was marked by Connally's statements about Kennedy's illness on July 4, 1960, followed by Johnson's announcement on July 5.

The acid-tongued conservative Texas author J. Evetts Haley in 1964 summed up Johnson's dilemma of 1960: "For the anti-Southerners, he was still a Southerner in spite of all he had done to deny it; with the Southerners he was a copperhead and a traitor . . . His strange combination of Texans ranged from high party faithful to such veteran oil figures as H.L Hunt and the parvenu tycoon, Morris Jaffe, who gathered to beat the drums, carry the money bags and mingle with such case-hardened New Deal Johnson friends as Oscar Chapman, Dean Acheson, Tommy Corcoran and Benny Cohen."[36] When Kennedy "rolled to victory on the first roll call and the Convention erupted into turmoil, 'the Texas delegation sat stunned, still and grim.' Upon the motion to make his nomination unanimous, only one Texas hand was seen to go up while the entire delegation held their seats. As the ovation ran on, Rayburn and Connally finally rose, Connally turning and nodding to the delegates behind him, who grudgingly got up, except for Governor Price Daniel, who angrily kept his place."[37]

Johnson watched the proceedings from his hotel room—the little speeches given by the person from each state delegation—and as Kennedy got closer to victory and Johnson got closer to defeat, the realization of his pending loss must have been galling for the majority leader, even though he

---

32. Mahoney, p. 126.
33. Reeves, pp. 273–274.
34. Swearingen, pp. 11–13.
35. Reeves, p. 288.
36. Haley, pp. 195–196.
37. Ibid., p. 197.

knew the story wouldn't end there regardless of who won the presidential nomination. As Evelyn Lincoln noted, that "probably explains why he never went out to his Convention Hall headquarters to thank his loyal supporters for the work they had done, even in defeat."[38] Speaker Sam Rayburn sat in Convention Hall, sadly watching the balloting—an unmarked tally sheet in his hand. Later, in Kennedy's private hideaway retreat on North Rossmore Street, someone asked him if Johnson had come to the arena to congratulate him. His response was, "If he did, I didn't see him."[39]

At this juncture, one must ask the following question: Did Lyndon Johnson really ever believe he would be in the running for the presidential nomination in 1960? He had been counseled by Rayburn and Russell for years that, as a Southerner, he had little chance to run for national office because the only opportunity for that was on the presidential–vice presidential ticket; there was no intermediate transition from a state to a national ticket, and the odds were against a Southerner, at that time, to wage a successful campaign.[40] According to a man who was later befriended by Johnson (given the "treatment" as we saw in the previous chapter), Orville Freeman made a revealing statement in an oral history interview for Johnson's library that has not previously been given the attention that it deserves: Freeman said that longtime Johnson associate Jim Rowe had asked Johnson in late 1959 if he was planning to run for the presidency in 1960, because if not, Rowe wanted to join Humphrey's campaign. "*Johnson had told Rowe quite emphatically that under no circumstances would he be a candidate for President. And it was at that point that Rowe went to work with Humphrey. So we didn't even consider Johnson in the picture at all, and of course I never felt that he had any chance to get enough votes in the convention, so we just never took it seriously*"[41] (emphasis added). This insightful comment has been ignored by every one of the many Johnson biographers who have consistently chosen to overlook the way he forced himself onto Kennedy's ticket in 1960, as we shall now begin to explore. If in fact he had planned a serious run for the presidency, why would he have allowed his friend and associate Jim Rowe to sign on to Hubert Humphrey's campaign? But it wasn't just Jim Rowe he dissuaded. In 1960, he would tell most of his aides and associates that he was not interested in the presidency, without revealing the reason: his fear of rejection, fueled by his paranoia and cylical depressive episodes. Those who knew him the closest, however, knew otherwise: John Connally, according to Horace Busby, "*says*

38. Lincoln, p. 86.
39. Ibid., p. 89.
40. Caro, *Master* . . ., p. 473.
41. Orville Freeman, Oral History Interview I, February 14, 1969, by T. H. Baker [Transcript], Internet copy, LBJ Library.

he never has another thought, another waking thought except to lust after the office"[42](emphasis added).

Horace Busby was among the majority of aides and associates who felt that Johnson didn't want to run for the presidency because he was afraid of becoming president, which of course is the way that Johnson would want it to be; he could never have admitted to them or anyone else that he was afraid of losing the election because that would forever end his chance of running again. Busby said that finally, John Connally proceeded to organize a campaign, "with or without the Senator. And so by January, that effort was trying to get off the ground. It's pretty handicapping when you don't have a candidate, but [laughter] nonetheless we were trying. So from January, you know, on through for quite a long time we were active, some of us were actively engaged basically trying to counter Kennedy. And so you became specialists in anti-Kennedy information and all like that [*sic*]. But you couldn't talk about it around Johnson, you just didn't talk about it. Well, the major candidates by then were all senators. He couldn't let a word pass his lips about anybody, and that's not the way he felt. He maintained the position he was the leader, and he couldn't go out and engage in a partisan campaign, and he did not finally, in fact, announce that he was a candidate until three days before the convention began." (The interviewer corrected that to "a week before, though the precise number of days was five.)[43] Johnson's columnist friend Drew Pearson said in an oral history interview that he "was for Lyndon in that race . . . [but] I wasn't too optimistic . . . There were several troubles. Number one, he figured his work in the Senate was more important than going out to campaign, and he didn't do hardly any campaigning. He stayed in Washington and he didn't go out to corral delegates. He was given warnings by Senator Earl Clements of Kentucky, who was one of his unofficial campaign managers, that he had to get out, but he stayed around here."[44] Pearson attended the Democratic convention in Los Angeles and talked to Senator Johnson and to some of his colleagues and staff, concluding that "it was pretty much a hopeless case. He had no chance of stopping Kennedy even on a deadlock."[45]

It is unlikely that Johnson ever seriously entertained the idea that he could realistically win the Democratic nomination for president in 1960, much less successfully run for the office against Richard Nixon if he did win the nomination. Given the strong possibility that he might be rejected at either

---

42. Horace Busby, recorded interview by Sheldon H. Stern, Mary 26, 1982, (p. 4), John F. Kennedy Library Oral History Program.
43. Ibid.
44. Transcript, Drew Pearson Oral History Interview I, 4/10/69, by Joe B. Frantz, Internet Copy, LBJ Library.
45. Ibid.

of two levels—that, even if he won the nomination, the possibility of losing to Richard Nixon in November in a grand finale loss—he would have worried that the looming damage to his ego was probably more than he could bear. This was not the first time Johnson had experienced such a case of nerves as he prepared for an election run; in other cases, he had gotten himself into such an anxious and stressful state that he became physically ill as election day neared. The totality of the evidence set forth below indicates that he was not prepared to conduct such a dangerous and debilitating endeavor. Yet he still wanted to be president, he considered it his destiny. His eyes were set all along on another route to the presidency, one that would require a stint in the only other constitutional office that might provide the necessary transition from being a Southerner to a nationally recognized, highly experienced man ready to assume the presidency in a heartbeat, though at a somewhat later date.

His misgivings—demonstrated repeatedly during the months (arguably, twenty-four months) leading up to the convention, as he refused the pressure and demands from his staff and colleagues to enter the race—are one clue that he had clearly conceived of his alternate strategy, in the seemingly inevitable event that he would lose the presidential nomination, well before his last-minute announcement on July 5, 1960. It would have necessarily been in the back of his mind throughout that period, as the anchor which allowed him to withstand the pressure, while—to himself at least—keeping his hat in the ring for what he knew was a 1960 move that was essential to the fulfillment of his destiny. That is clearly the most veritable explanation of his behavior throughout the 1958–1960 period, from the time he lobbied the Texas legislature to pass "Lyndon's law" allowing him to run for national office concurrently with running for reelection as the senior Texas Senator.

He must have instinctively decided that losing the presidential nomination to Kennedy might actually be the surest way for him to achieve his lifetime goal, because the "Kennedy-Johnson" team would have a much better chance to win in November than a "Johnson-Anyone Else" team; the fulfillment of his dream could then be managed after that. It would then be only a matter of time, and the effective management of the inherent risk, but he evidently knew that by "calling in his markers" with all of his longtime cronies in high places, the risks would be minimized. This route would also satisfy his biggest concern: his fear of being roundly rejected by voters in far-off states where he was an unknown.

The Vice Presidential Nomination

As he maneuvered for the vice presidential nomination after losing the presidential nomination to Kennedy, Lyndon Johnson tried to portray his Texas base as solid and essential to the general election even though, as we shall shortly see, Kennedy had no intention of naming him to the ticket at that point in time; he wasn't even on Kennedy's long list, much less the short one. Johnson's plan for his ten-day run for the presidency was simply a way to insert himself on to the list of possible nominees, even though he did not expect to win the presidential nomination on the second or third ballot, never mind the first. By the time he appeared in Los Angeles on Sunday, July 10, his subsequent actions indicate that he had already decided on an alternate plan to assume the presidency.

The "master of the Senate" was now used to being a very powerful man, and almost no one would have expected him to give up that power to become the vice presidential nominee; no one except for him, because he had figured out that getting into that office was the only conceivable way that he could position himself to become president at a later time. Of course, he never really wanted the position of vice president for its own sake; none of the many men who ever held it had sought it out as their objective, that would have been comparable to a major league baseball team seeking to merely come in second in the World Series. But Johnson's situation—reflected by his virtual absence from the campaign until July 5—was different from any other candidate who had become their party's candidate for vice president. He joined the campaign late for the very purpose of becoming a "spoiler" in order to force his way on to the top of Kennedy's list of vice presidential candidates. This required a deft touch, since he did not want to appear too eager for the offer; that would have run the risk of giving away bargaining chips that he would need to obtain the broadest powers possible as vice president. But his ambivalence about becoming the vice presidential nominee was a ruse. After all, he had been the force behind a change in the Texas law that allowed him to simultaneously run for his Senate seat and the presidency or vice presidency, months before the convention, though he never proceeded to mount an effective campaign for the presidential nomination. After going to those lengths to pave the way to run for two offices at once, he did not bother to even declare his candidacy until July 5, only five days before the start of the convention. Compared with his tepid presidential campaign, his campaign for the vice presidential nomination was stunningly hard-fought, viciously aggressive, meticulously planned, and ultimately successful.

In the weeks before the convention, John Kennedy had narrowed the list of potential vice presidential nominees to two senators: Stuart Symington of Missouri or Henry "Scoop" Jackson of Washington. Johnson had enlisted several influential men—his mentors Speaker Sam Rayburn and Senator Richard Russell of Georgia, as well as *Washington Post* publisher Philip Graham, the mighty lobbyist Tommy "the Cork" Corcoran, and the acerbic columnist Joseph Alsop—to assist him in lobbying Kennedy, yet Lyndon Johnson was still not on Kennedy's list when he won the presidential nomination on the first ballot. Immediately after Kennedy had secured the nomination, Johnson learned that the Knight Newspaper chain was planning a midnight edition saying that JFK was considering three men for the vice presidential spot—none of whom had the initials LBJ.[46] This news would have caused him to enlist every one of his "men" to pull every string at their disposal to put his name on the top of Kennedy's list.

Seymour Hersh interviewed several men involved in the decision Kennedy faced regarding the vice presidential nominee, including Hyman Raskin, who had worked as a strategist and campaign aide for Kennedy for two years before the convention and had an intimate knowledge of the events leading to the selection of Johnson as the vice presidential nominee. According to Raskin, Johnson asked for a meeting with JFK immediately after Kennedy had been nominated. At that point, Raskin stated emphatically that "Johnson was not being given the slightest bit of consideration by any of the Kennedys."[47] According to Clark Clifford, Kennedy had already decided on Senator Symington when he received a call from Evelyn Lincoln asking him to meet with Kennedy in his private rented residence; Kennedy had complimentary things to say about Symington when the two met that evening, stressing the dignified way he conducted himself (implicitly contrasting his demeanor with Johnson's), and he then asked Clifford to convey his offer of the vice presidential nomination to Symingon. "'Find out if Stuart will accept and let me know right away.' This was an unequivocal proposal from the candidate."[48] When Clifford took the offer to Symington, after he had deliberated with his family—and against their wishes, their consensus was against accepting it—the senator told Clifford, "You can tell Jack I will accept his offer."[49]

Three of Johnson's men—Graham, Corcoran, and Rayburn—first took the case to John Kennedy that he, Johnson, should be given the vice presidential nomination. Rayburn himself took a lot of convincing, but when Johnson explained that he wanted it because it would put him next in line for the presidency, Rayburn became completely in favor of it. There are many stories about how Rayburn came to change his mind, but one thing was consistent through all of them: Rayburn hated the Kennedys, not just John and Bobby, but their father as well. "The speaker snapped at Corcoran. 'No, I won't go along with it.' He said. 'I wouldn't trust Joe Kennedy across the street. He'll double-cross us sure as hell.'"[50] Rayburn had originally been

46. Summers, *Official* p. 271.
47. Hersh, *The Dark Side* . . ., p. 124.
48. Clifford, p. 317.
49. Ibid., p. 318.
50. Shesol, p. 45.

flatly against Johnson's acceptance of such an offer, but Johnson met with him when it became obvious that he would not be the presidential nominee, and they talked long into the wee hours of the following morning. The next morning, "To the shocked Texans who gathered in Johnson's suite, Rayburn shrugged his shoulders. 'I'm a damn sight smarter than I was last night,' he said sheepishly."[51] According to author J. Evetts Haley's contemporaneous account, Johnson and Rayburn issued an ultimatum to Bobby Kennedy: a threat to create a fight on the convention floor over the vice presidential nomination, regardless of the party disunity that would result.[52]

According to Seymour M. Hersh, Kennedy was supposed to stop by the campaign's command post that evening to acknowledge and thank his loyal staff, before going on to the convention hall; but something had happened to change his plans, and he didn't make an appearance in either of these places until moments before his speech to the delegates. Hyman Raskin said that he was told that Kennedy was running late, but he later determined that the real reason Kennedy didn't appear was because he had received a stunning telephone call from either Johnson or Rayburn. The call was made just a few hours before Kennedy was to give his acceptance speech, and it was made after the three Johnson men (Graham, Corcoran, and Rayburn) had made their case to Kennedy; the call was made because Kennedy had not responded favorably to their entreaty. Clearly, Johnson himself was behind it, whether the call was from him or Rayburn; Johnson knew that this was his one last chance to get his name on the 1960 Democratic ticket. Immediately after JFK's speech, Bobby Kennedy called Raskin; he was very upset and simply wanted to tell him to cancel a scheduled meeting JFK had with party leaders (from which Johnson and Rayburn had been excluded). When the party leaders heard about this, it set off gossip and speculation about what was going on, but Bobby told Raskin the only thing he could say to them was that "you don't know" what was going on. Raskin worried all night about what had happened, unable to sleep; he assumed that it might have been related to the scheduled meeting for which Johnson had been excluded, which he thought might have "backfired." By the next day, he was surprised to find that Johnson—who had not only been excluded from the list of possible vice presidential nominees, but even excluded from the meeting of party leaders—was now the big news of the convention, having been named as the vice presidential nominee.[53]

---

51. Ibid.
52. Haley, p. 198.
53. Hersh, *The Dark Side* . . ., p. 125.

The Offer JFK Could Not Refuse

The phone call the previous evening from Johnson or Rayburn was apparently an ultimatum delivered to Kennedy, and a request for a meeting, either late that night or early the next morning. Raskin wrote that the short list of running mates was "precipitously and totally discarded" when Kennedy met with Johnson and Rayburn, at which he was given "an offer he could not refuse."[54] JFK's personal secretary, Evelyn Lincoln, was also aware of what happened. She told Anthony Summers that Hoover had been involved in the plot to install LBJ as JFK's running mate. Lincoln believed it was Hoover's evidence of JFK's womanizing that was being used to blackmail him to put LBJ on the ticket. She stated that Johnson "had been using all the information Hoover could find on Kennedy—during the campaign, even before the convention. And Hoover was in on the pressure on Kennedy at the convention . . . about womanizing, and things in Joe Kennedy's background, and anything he could dig up. Johnson was using that clout. Kennedy was angry, because they had boxed him into a corner."[55] One piece of information in Hoover's files which might have been used related to an affair he had fifteen years earlier with Inga Arvad, a woman who had been close to Hitler just before that (having shared a box seat at the 1936 Olympic games with the führer)[56] which would have especially upset the Jewish constituency.[57] Still another might have been an offer that was then being made to Johnson by one of Kennedy's former lovers, Alicia Darr, of documentation of her long-term affair with JFK, and rumors of an abortion, for a fee of $150,000.[58] This transaction was being brokered by Myron "Mickey" Weiner, the New Jersey attorney who would thereafter become associated closely with Bobby Baker, even spending so much time in his Capitol Hill office that office secretaries would say he was on Baker's staff. Weiner took the offer to Bobby Baker in the early part of 1960 for transmittal to Lyndon Johnson; Baker saw it as blackmail and took it instead to Kennedy, who had to realize that this was merely a part of Johnson's larger, but almost invisible, campaign against him.[59]

According to Anthony Summers, "Former Secretary of State Dean Rusk would later say: 'Hoover passed along gossip to the President he served, and that practice could raise questions in a President's mind. What did Hoover

---

54. Ibid. p. 123.
55. Summers, *Official and Confidential*, pp. 271–273.
56. Pegues, p. 47.
57. Summers, *Official and Confidential*, pp. 271–273.
58. Hersh, S. p. 116.
59. U.S. Senate Committee on rules and Administration. *Construction of the District of Columbia Stadium and Matters Related Thereto*. Washington, DC: U.S. Government Printing Office, 1965, pt. 12, p. 1101.

know about him? In theoretical terms, that put Hoover in the position of a veiled blackmailer.'"[60] The combination of Hoover's extensive files of compromising information on Kennedy's numerous sexual affairs and health records, including his history of Addison's disease, together with Lyndon Johnson's propensity for using brazen and brutal force to achieve his ends, put enormous pressure on JFK to accede to LBJ's demands.

By the next morning, Clifford took another call from Evelyn Lincoln, asking him to come to Kennedy's room. This time, Kennedy's mood was much more subdued and weary, as though he had not slept well the night before. He then explained to Clifford that he regrettably had to withdraw the offer of the vice presidential nomination he had just proffered the evening before to Senator Symington; he admitted that the reason for this was that "'during the night I have been persuaded that I cannot win without Lyndon on the ticket. I have offered the Vice Presidency to him— and he has accepted. Tell Stuart that I am sorry.' Kennedy added that no one in his whole family liked Lyndon Johnson; there had been a 'family ruckus' about his selection, [but] he saw no alternative, no matter how painful the choice."[61] After a day of chaotic rumors and commotion—at the start of which, Johnson was not on JFK's lists, either the long one or the short one—his was the only name left; Lyndon B. Johnson stepped before the cameras and announced that "Jack Kennedy has asked me to serve. I accept."[62]

All hell broke loose at the Biltmore when word got out that Bull Johnson had bulled his way onto Kennedy's ticket. Suddenly, Pierre Salinger was besieged by calls from reporters wanting a confirmation of a story being prepared by John S. Knight, of Knight Newspapers, revealing how Johnson had forced Kennedy to nominate him as his vice presidential nominee. Salinger simply issued a perfunctory denial, which resulted in a telephone call from the beleaguered staff and aides of the irate Johnson. An hour after he had released the original statement, he was awakened by a call, "from Bill Moyers of Senator Johnson's staff. He said the speaker, Mr. Rayburn wanted to speak to me, Mr. Rayburn got on the phone and it was evident that he was highly agitated. He wanted, first, a complete denial of the story under Senator Kennedy's name and, second, he wanted me to awaken Senator Kennedy and have him call John S. Knight and tell the latter of the story's falsity. Mr. Rayburn said Senator Johnson was extremely disturbed about the story and wanted it nipped in the bud before it got wide circulation. George Reedy,

---

60. Summers, *Official and Confidential.*, p. 260.
61. Clifford. p. 318.
62. Summers, *Official and Confidential.*, p. 271.

who was Senator Johnson's Press Secretary, had located Knight and told me where Knight could be reached."[63]

Johnson's fear of being exposed for these tactics—for how he had brutally forced Kennedy to accept him as his vice presidential nominee—can only be related to how he feared such news would surely be interpreted when he assumed the presidency later: People might begin to connect this incident with future incongruities regarding how he had in fact hated being vice president and was not only ineffectual in it but actually acted contrary to Kennedy's many agendas, even sabotaged him; all of this had not yet happened, of course, in 1960, but he did not want his actions at the convention known because he knew they would look bad later. What he did want known was the lie, the fiction that Johnson was the first and only name Kennedy had wanted as his running mate. This lie was repeated by Johnson so many times that he—and the sycophants he had around him—actually came to believe it. Thankfully, for the true historical record, even though the story was practically ignored for over four decades, Pierre Salinger decided to include the truthful account in his 1966 book.

Thursday morning, July 14, began, according to Bobby Kennedy, "'the most indecisive time we ever had,' a period hopelessly snarled by confusion, miscommunication, and murky, mixed intentions."[64] The "murky, mixed intentions" apparently referred to the fact that Johnson had let it be known that, although he expected to be first offered the position out of due deference, he would not accept it, allowing Kennedy to then offer it to Symington as a second choice. Kennedy decided to go talk to Johnson because, until he had done so, he still "could not truly believe that the majority leader—despite assurances—would willingly accept such a profound diminution of power. According to Bobby, JFK went to Johnson's suite simply 'to talk to him about it.' 'I didn't really offer the nomination to Lyndon Johnson,' John Kennedy told reporter Charles Bartlett a few days later, off the record. 'I just held it out to here'—he poised his hand two or three inches from his pocket, implying that Johnson snatched the opportunity."[65] Bartlett then reported that Johnson then seized the offer and "held fast to it through uncertain hours of shocked reaction within the Kennedy camp." Johnson had cast his line with the expertise of an experienced fly fisherman and held his quarry throughout the ensuing reaction by party liberals; in the meantime, he simply told others that he assumed "that Jack Kennedy's offer at the morning conference was as firm as it could be."[66]

---

63. Salinger, p. 44.
64. Shesol, p. 48.
65. Ibid., p. 50.
66. Ibid. (quoting Bobby Baker).

After John Kennedy's visit with Johnson, Kennedy returned to his room, where Robert Kennedy was waiting, "and he said, 'You just won't believe it.' I said, 'What?' and he said, 'He wants it,' and I said, 'Oh, my God!' He said, 'Now what do we do?' . . . We both promised each other that we'd never tell what happened—but we spent the rest of the day alternating between thinking it was good and thinking that it wasn't good that he'd offered him the Vice Presidency, and how could he get out of it."[67] All of Kennedy's consultants and advisers were chagrined at the news, and there followed many hours of intense discussions and indecision. Evelyn Lincoln later "told of finding Bobby and Jack deep in conversation . . . 'I went in and listened. They were very upset and trying to figure out how they could get around it, but they didn't know how they could do it.' She did not hear any mention then of a specific threat from Johnson, Lincoln said. But she added, 'Jack knew that Hoover and LBJ would just fill the air with womanizing.'"[68] RFK later said, "We changed our minds eight times during the course of it. Finally . . . we decided by about two o'clock that we'd try to get him out of there and not have him because Jack thought he would be unpleasant with him, associated with him, and if he could get him to withdraw and still be happy, that would be fine."[69]

When word leaked out that an offer had been extended to Johnson, and that he had accepted it, the liberals went ballistic: "Salinger was outraged; O'Donnell denounced the choice of Johnson as a 'disaster' and told JFK it was 'the worst mistake' he ever made. 'In your first move after the nomination, you go against all the people who supported you,' he said. O'Donnell, JFK's liaison to labor, 'was so furious that I could hardly talk. I thought of the promises we had made to the labor leaders and the civil rights groups . . . I felt that we had been double-crossed.' . . . Walter Reuther, President of the United Auto Workers (UAW) union, 'exploded in a profane fury.'"[70] He and the other labor leaders had never forgiven Johnson for his vote for the Taft-Hartley bill, which was considered anti-labor because it allowed for states to elect to make union membership optional for individual workers (it was also known as the "right to work" law). Bobby complained to Johnson's advocates that they (the Kennedys) were in danger of losing control of the convention because of the growing labor revolt.[71] Many liberals, such as Joseph Rauh, were still upset with Johnson because of the way he had

---

67. Schlesinger, *Robert Kennedy and His Times*, p. 224.
68. Hersh, p. 129.
68. Schlesinger, *Robert Kennedy and His Times*, p. 224–225.
70. Shesol, pp. 51, 57.
71. Ibid., p. 52.

attacked and humiliated Leland Olds in 1949, causing his nomination for reappointment to the Federal Power Commission chairmanship to be rejected; they remembered how Johnson had practically destroyed the man and had never forgiven him for it (coincidentally, exactly three weeks later in fact, on August 5, 1960, Leland Olds died, a broken man, with probably more suppressed outrage about his party's vice presidential nominee than anyone else alive on that date).*

The furor at the offer to Johnson caused Jack and Robert Kennedy to try to undo the damage. Bobby went three times to Johnson's suite to discuss the situation, the first to feel him out further; then he subsequently returned to propose that Johnson become chairman of the national committee instead. The first time was at about 1:30 p.m., after calling him, which allowed Johnson to stall for time, saying, "'Whatever it is, I don't want to see him.' Phil Graham . . . was tugged into a separate bedroom by an insistent LBJ. Johnson and Graham sat on the bed with Lady Bird, 'about as composed,' Graham recorded, 'as three Mexican jumping beans.' Johnson said that Bobby Kennedy was making a final offer of the vice presidency. It was time for a final decision."[72] But as Kennedy spoke to him, Johnson became extremely upset; Bobby later described the way Johnson responded:

> He is one of the greatest sad-looking people in the world—you know, he can turn that on. I thought he'd burst into tears . . . I mean, it was my feeling at that time, although I've seen him afterwards look so sad I don't know whether it was just an act . . . But he just shook and tears came into his eyes, and he said, "I want to be Vice President, and, if the President will have me, I'll join him in making a fight for it." So it was that kind of a conversation. I said, "Well, then that's fine. He wants you to be Vice President if you want to be Vice President."[73]

After the first visit, things settled down until Bill Moyers discovered that Bobby was back in Johnson's suite for another visit. In a room down the hall, a group of Southern governors were meeting to discuss with Phil Graham and Sam Rayburn the question of who should be on the list to give seconding speeches for LBJ's nomination. Moyers burst into the room, exclaiming, "Graham, my God, Bobby is in the room!"[74] Moyers dragged Graham by

---

*A few senators paid tribute to Leland Olds; JFK was one, who stated, "'Developments such as the St. Lawrence Waterway and power projects are a permanent memorial to him.' There was no comment from the Democratic vice presidential nominee." (Ref. Caro, *Master . . .*, p. 303.)

72. Ibid.

73. Schlesinger, *Robert Kennedy and His Times*, p. 225–226.

74. Shesol, p. 54.

the arm to Johnson's suite, and upon entering, they saw complete bedlam; Johnson was in a state of near panic as he screamed to Graham that Bobby was trying to get him back off the ticket. "'Call Jack Kennedy and straighten out this mess!' Rayburn barked at Graham. Graham dialed the extension to Kennedy's suite, saying, 'Bobby is down here and is telling the speaker and Lyndon that there is opposition and that Lyndon should withdraw.' 'Oh,' Jack replied serenely, 'that's all right; Bobby's been out of touch and doesn't know what's happening.' . . . According to Graham, Bobby took the phone, listened a moment to JFK, and said, 'Well, it's too late now,' before half slamming down the receiver.'"[75]

As Bobby was trying to get Johnson to remove himself from the ticket, John Kennedy had received a call from Clark Clifford, who told him that his indecision was disastrous, and that he had to take him now. After Bobby's last visit, the moods of everyone in the Johnson suite turned into hysterical anger, as though Johnson's own mood had infected the psyches of the group; Johnson himself was livid, Lady Bird was crying uncontrollably; Graham and Corcoran listened as Rayburn screamed about how this was a typical Kennedy double cross. As Jeff Shesol described it, however, Johnson "did not blame John Kennedy as the agent of his stinging repudiation; the villain, Johnson believed, was Bobby Kennedy—Bobby, who opposed Johnson from the beginning; Bobby, who sided with labor against him; Bobby, who ruthlessly tried to humiliate him. In Baker's recollection it was Bobby, not Jack, whom Johnson denounced as 'that little shit-ass' and a score of epithets more coarse."[76]

JFK did tell Raskin why he had changed his mind: "You know we had never considered Lyndon, but I was left with no choice. He and Sam Rayburn made it damn clear to me that Lyndon had to be the candidate. Those bastards were trying to frame me. They threatened me with problems and I don't need more problems."[77] His explanation to others, such as Kenneth O'Donnell, who asked him why, was, "Are we going to spend the whole campaign apologizing for Lyndon Johnson and trying to explain why he voted against everything you ever stood for," was to angrily defend his decision, saying, "I'm forty-three years old, and I'm the healthiest candidate for President in the United States. You've traveled with me enough to know that. I'm not going to die in office. So the Vice Presidency doesn't mean anything. I'm thinking of something else, the leadership in the Senate. If

---

75. Ibid.
76. Ibid., pp. 55–56.
77. Hersh, S., p. 126.

we win, it will be by a small margin and I won't be able to live with Lyndon Johnson as the leader of a small Senate majority. Did it occur to you that if Lyndon Johnson becomes the Vice President I'll have Mike Mansfield as the Senate leader, somebody I can trust and depend on?"[78] Referring to Johnson and Rayburn's decision to hold Congress open during August, Kennedy continued, "If Johnson and Rayburn leave here mad at me, they'll ruin me in Congress next month. Then I'll be the laughingstock of the country. Nixon will say I haven't any power in my own party, and I'll lose the election before Labor Day. So I've got to make peace now with Johnson and Rayburn, and offering Lyndon the Vice Presidency, whether he accepts it or not, is one way of keeping him friendly until Congress adjourns."[79]

JFK's explanation to O'Donnell about why he chose Johnson was apparently one of the "rationalizations" that Bobby had referred to when he said they spent so many hours "snarled by confusion, miscommunication, and murky, mixed intentions . . . we spent the rest of the day alternating between thinking it was good and thinking that it wasn't good." Getting Johnson out of the Senate, therefore, was clearly one of the good reasons, one that they would use to justify the decision to their friends and associates, obviously practiced enough to seem convincing to them. Unfortunately for them both, especially John—and possibly Robert as well, but that is the subject for another book—they should have spent a little more time listing the cons of having Lyndon "Bull" Johnson anywhere near the White House, in a position to assume the presidency in the only other way that a person can achieve that high office without having been specifically elected to it.

The truth about all the various rumors concerning Kennedy's selection of Johnson as his vice presidential nominee has taken almost as long to emerge as the truth about his assassination. These accounts by credible witnesses—Clark Clifford, Hyman Raskin, Evelyn Lincoln, and even Bobby Kennedy—confirm that Johnson called Kennedy just before he was to give his acceptance speech to deliver his threats and inform him of the extensive damning information he had collected from FBI's dossier on Kennedy. This is the only logical explanation of how he had come from not being seriously considered at all to being given the offer though it had already been given to Stuart Symington. Lyndon Johnson's attempt to become vice president under John F. Kennedy was all part of his carefully designed plan to become president himself, and this was the single most critical component of it.

Robert Kennedy would later tell his friend Charles Spalding, "Charlie, we really weren't at our best this time . . . we were all too tired." To his friend

---

78. O'Donnell, Kenneth, *Life* magazine, August 7, 1970, p. 47; *Johnny . . .*, pp. 7, 193.
79. Ibid.

Charles Bartlett, he said, "Yesterday was the best day of my life . . . and today was the worst day." And to John Seigenthaler, he said, "We were right at eight, ten and two and wrong at four."[80] John F. Kennedy's fatal mistake was made after an agonizing day of deliberation with his brother Bobby, when he grudgingly accepted the blackmail threats of Johnson and Hoover. By allowing Lyndon Johnson to become the vice presidential candidate, John F. Kennedy unwittingly signed his own death warrant. In later years, after both Kennedys were dead, Johnson would claim to his favored authors, historians, and associates—the ones who accepted practically everything Johnson said at face value, not realizing their own credulity in doing so— that he was always Kennedy's first choice, thus explaining why there were so many conflicting stories and misrepresentations about the widely reported drama that unfolded at the Biltmore Hotel, validated by many of the other participants.

Although the more persevering and intellectually honest historians would eventually record the truth, the above story made it into a number of biographies Lyndon Johnson persuaded people to write. Merle Miller tried to make the case that Johnson very reluctantly accepted Kennedy's offer, as though he had been the first and only choice, and had even initially declined it.[81] Others, like Doris Kearns and George Reedy, completely ignored the stunning events in Los Angeles[82] that caused Kennedy to make a last-minute, 180-degree about-face to name Johnson, who had never seriously been considered, to the ticket, requiring him to uninvite his actual preference, Senator Stuart Symington. The truth was, Johnson had alienated so many of the liberal senators; in 1959 and 1960, party liberals "had undermined Johnson's effectiveness as Leader. 'Johnson felt he had lost control,' [Eliot] Janeway says. 'He had lost emotional control of the Senate. And he was very bitter against a good third of the Democratic caucus.' Theodore F. Green of Rhode Island told Tommy Corcoran that 'Lyndon was finished as an effective majority leader . . . If he went back, Green said, they might give him the title again but they wouldn't follow him.'"[83] Eliot Janeway stated that Johnson "was very anxious to get out of the majority leadership. *Johnson would have paid for the vice presidency*"[84] (emphasis added).

A few days after the decision had been made, Pierre Salinger asked Kennedy why. Kennedy's last words on the subject were, "The whole story will never be known. And it's just as well that it won't be."[85] Salinger then added, "I cannot

---

80. Shesol, p. 227.
81. Miller, p. 258.
82. Kearns-Goodwin, pp. 160–161; Reedy, p. 129.
83. Dallek, Lone Star . . . p. 577.
84. Ibid., p. 576.
85. Salinger, p. 46.

explain the cryptic remark. I can only report that JFK made it."[86] Although he did not say categorically that he thought Johnson had blackmailed Kennedy to get onto the ticket in his 1966 book, *With Kennedy,* anyone coming away with such an impression from reading between the lines could be forgiven for coming to such a conclusion through the use of basic deductive reasoning. That cryptic remark as he called it was far more revealing than most other entire accounts of Johnson's selection, including Phil Graham's self-serving account[87] of how he practically single-handedly engineered the decision. It also no doubt helps explain why Pierre Salinger was the first of Kennedy's aides—all of whom Johnson had begged to stay on with him, separately telling each one, "I need you more than he did"—to leave the White House, in March 1964. Salinger's dislike of Johnson probably stemmed from the 1960 campaign, when he was trying to give him advice on how to increase his appeal to voters; Johnson interrupted him to make his own suggestion, which was to present himself as another "Matt Dillion," the favorite television Western hero of the time: "You know . . . big, six-foot-three, good looking—a tall, tough Texan coming down the street." Pierre Salinger, despite his 1966 book in which he thanked Johnson for his "many kindnesses,"[88] clearly knew he did not want to be around the new president any longer than necessary; he proved it by leaving as quickly as he could.

More than one person familiar with what really happened said, "The full story of how Kennedy selected Johnson as vice president will never be told." One was Myer Feldman, a special counsel to President Kennedy, who asked him what the true story was and received this response: "Well, you know, I don't think anybody will ever know."[89] The fact that this answer was adopted by both JFK and RFK, and used as a pro forma, boilerplate response, after both promised each other to never reveal the truth, suggests that the secret they were trying to contain was a major sore point. That the rationale for selecting the vice presidential nominee of their party had to be kept a secret for all time indicates as clearly as anything could that they acceded to a forced request against their will. It is axiomatic that the wrong person was selected if he was chosen for illegitimate reasons. The next logical progression, given his criminal past and the precarious position he was in by November 1963—that he would have had nothing to lose and everything to gain from JFK's murder—leads to an inescapable conclusion, which shall be held in abeyance for a few more chapters.

---

86. Ibid.
87. *Life* magazine, June 18, 1965, p. 90.
88. Salinger, p. 340.
89. Dallek, *Lone Star* . . ., p. 578.

The 1960 Campaign

Johnson's tainted victory in winning the vice presidential nomination did not make him jubilant. In fact, he became depressed immediately afterward. He became so upset that Lynda Bird could not be found in time to join the family on the convention platform, playing her role as a smiling member of the happy Johnson family, that Lyndon launched into a public rage which embarrassed "Uncle" Sam Rayburn, who had witnessed such outbursts before. Johnson knew that he had succeeded in getting into the office that he would use as a springboard into the Oval Office, yet the stress that that success produced would fuel even stronger swings from euphoric mania to irritable and depressive mania.

The infamous "rump session" of Congress required that all senators and representatives return to Washington for three weeks beginning August 8. Johnson had managed to alienate practically everyone on Capitol Hill because of that dubious idea, not the least of whom was his own new leader, John F. Kennedy, who said, "Why Mr. Johnson, the masterminded Majority Leader, would ever dream up a scheme like this is beyond me. Even if he is the Democratic nominee, what can it possibly gain? The Republicans will do everything in their power to embarrass the Democrats."[90] Throughout the strange three-week rump session held in the middle of a very hot and humid Washington August, Kennedy struggled to get the national campaign kicked off, holding strategy meetings, planning schedules, and making all other campaign decisions ordinary to the general election, which was always expected to be a very close contest. The Democratic congressmen were trying to make the best of a very difficult situation created by their esteemed senator and his friend, the Speaker; Johnson, of course, was simultaneously rerunning for his Senate seat and the vice presidency, not willing to sacrifice one for the risk of losing the other. They had hoped that if the majority leader could get some worthwhile legislation passed, at least it could be made into a productive session; those hopes were dashed from the start, and practically nothing came of the legislative circus other than extreme frustration on the part of everyone having to participate in it.

In order to get some semblance of order, Kennedy requested the sergeant at arms to provide a suite of offices near the Senate floor where he could meet with staff members and leaders and hold conferences. He was able to assign JFK a small suite, with a desk in one corner and a refrigerator and sink in another to store soft drinks for visitors, along with a small conference room. This suite was, ironically, directly across the hall from Johnson's main (one

---

90. Lincoln, p. 72.

of three) Senate office, a huge space he had remodeled with garish green and gold drapes and ankle-deep carpeting, which reporters had taken to calling the "Taj Mahal," or the "Nookie Room," which was filled with the latest telephonic push-button gadgetry, the finest furniture and accessories, the largest conference room facilities of any Senate office suite, and of course, Johnson's own personal adjoining "throne room" so he didn't have far to go when he had to find a toilet, usually taking an aide with him to complete his dictation. Everything in his suite was of the finest linen or leather, all stamped with his cattle brand, "LBJ." Kennedy tried his best to ignore this contrast, but it became difficult because of all the well-wishers dropping by the crowded little suite across the hall from the majority leader/vice presidential nominee's big suite. It was also difficult because Lyndon would constantly come over to offer his suggestions for the campaign and, sometimes, would storm off in a huff when he couldn't get his way or had to wait to see JFK on some matter he considered more important than whatever else was going on. The "final blow," according to Mrs. Lincoln, was when the two bills which Kennedy had pushed the hardest—for increasing the minimum wage and funding aid to schools—were defeated; the only good thing about this strange congressional episode was that it finally ended before fistfights broke out on the floor of both houses.[91]

As Johnson started his dual campaigns—on the Kennedy-Johnson presidential and vice presidential offices, while simultaneously running for his third term as a senator, thanks to the passage of the new Texas law he had pressed for to enable him to do that—he was left in a dilemma over the conflicts in the party's Texas platform and the national platform; the contrasts between the two reflected the differences between his old Southern base and the national base to which he aspired. They were stunningly polar opposites:

- The national platform called for greater federal concentration of power, while the state platform denounced the "growing and menacing power in central government."
- The national platform endorsed sit-in demonstrations, and the state called for the "enforcement of laws designed to protect private property from physical occupation."
- The national platform called for the closing of the oil depletion allowance, while the state platform demanded the "retention of the present oil and gas depletions allowance."

---

91. Ibid., pp. 104–118.

- The national platform called for federal aid to education; the state platform opposed it.
- The national platform called for school desegregation; the state platform pledged local operation and control of schools.
- The national platform called for medical care for the aged; the state platform deplored socialistic medical measures.
- The national platform called for legislation repealing the state right-to-work laws, while the state endorsed the existing Taft-Hartley right-to-work law as essential to free enterprise.[92]

Lyndon Johnson, accustomed to playing both sides of the political spectrum, managed to position himself as firmly behind both the national and the Texas state Democratic platforms in the 1960 elections despite the diametrically opposite positions. The Texas state platform was essentially a "state's rights" position written by a conservative, Johnson-controlled committee; the national platform was written by a committee so liberal that the socialist pundit Norman Thomas called it "utopian."[93] In a stroke of sheer hypocrisy, according to Victor Lasky, "in Las Vegas, Johnson assailed the Republicans as a party of 'two faces.' One face, in the North, was that of Governor Rockefeller 'who rewrites the Republican platform' to appeal to Liberals. The other, in the South, was that of Senator Goldwater assuring the people of conservative government."[94] Shortly after this paradoxical gaffe, he was in New York, to accept the nomination of the Liberal Party, which threw a third platform into the mix (Johnson, struggling for something smart to say, came up with "you are against the sweatshop and I am against the sweatshop").[95]

Throughout the campaign, Johnson was wound very tight as he attacked Nixon and likened attacks on Kennedy's Catholicism to the prejudice against the South he confronted. He was greeted by hecklers with signs declaring "LBJ is a Friend of Socialism."[96] He was even worried about whether the ticket would carry Texas, an eventuality that would cost him any chance of ever running again on a future ticket. This was undoubtedly a factor in what would later be shown to be massive election fraud, as we will shortly review in more detail. His anxiety about possibly losing Texas caused him to fly off the handle with everyone trying to help him; practically anything that went wrong caused him to launch into a tirade with his staff—a tight schedule, crowds he considered as too small or unresponsive, a podium that didn't meet his specifications.

92. Haley, pp. 202–203 (ref. Victor Lasky, *JFK: The Man and the Myth*, pp. 402, 409).
93. Ibid.
94. Lasky, *JFK—The Man*, p. 436.
95. Ibid., pp. 436–437.
96. Dallek, p. 586.

According to Robert Dallek's account, "When Johnson tried to bully Kennedy into rushing to make an appointment with Sam Rayburn, Jack told him, 'I believe you're cracking up. If you do, where do you want me to send it?'"[97] His longtime supporter Jim Rowe was so upset with him that he called him a "Mogul emperor."[98] A very ugly incident in Dallas four days before the election occurred when Lyndon confronted a group of angry protestors at the Adolphus Hotel as Lyndon and Lady Bird crossed the street and made their way to the elevator. As they inched along, Lyndon told the police to leave, saying, "If the time has come when I can't walk through the lobby of a hotel in Dallas with my lady without a police escort, I want to know it."[99] Seeing all the photographers and reporters recording the event, Johnson milked it for all it was worth: People who were there said it could have been done in five minutes, but they took thirty minutes as they soaked up all the publicity, exploiting the incident to criticize Republicans for being extremists.[100]

While Kennedy was trying to ignore—even minimize—Johnson's part in the campaign, on September 14, William S. White wrote of a new issue that Johnson had stumbled onto in Jacksonville, Florida, when he snapped, "I wasn't the Vice President who presided over the communization of Cuba."[101] White wrote that "the Democrats believe they have got hold of something— the charge that a Republican administration permitted a pro-Communist bridgehead to rise within 90 miles of the American coastline—which well might hit the Republicans with violent impact in November." By October 6, Kennedy made a major address in Cincinnati slamming Nixon's involvement in managing the Cuban "problem," charging that "as a result the Communists took over Cuba with virtually no opposition from the United States."[102] This was the first time Kennedy had expressed any interest in Cuba; his previous visits there were purely social—nightclubs, golfing, and sailing.

Kennedy had been given classified information by a Castro supporter in the State Department, William Wieland, who "unbeknownst to the CIA, [Cuban exile leader Mario Garcia] Kohly,* and Nixon, introduced the Cuban Revolutionary Council's leftist leaders to Kennedy at the time of

---

*Kohly was the conservative exile leader and a prominent Cuban businessman, a distinguished statesman who represented a large number of American interests in Cuba and was favored by Nixon to replace Castro; Kennedy switched support to a more leftist group (the CRC) led by Manuel Artime, to avoid being associated with a right-wing group.
97. Ibid., p. 587.
98. Ibid.
99. Ibid., pp. 587–588.
100. Ibid.
101. Lasky, *JFK—The Man*, p. 445.
102. Ibid.

the Democratic National Convention. The CRC leaders gave the presidential nominee what details they had on the planned Cuban invasion."[103] Kennedy wanted to contrast his aggressive approach to the Cuba issue to an image of Nixon as a typical politician who made promises that he reneged on, so he had his aide "Richard Goodwin—an abrasive, pockmarked, twenty-eight year old former clerk for Supreme Court Justice Felix Frankfurter, and recently hired Kennedy political writer—[release] a story to *The New York Times* on the day before the last political debate . . . The release of [the] story was a great political coup. Kennedy knew that Nixon, abiding by security restrictions he could not disavow, was bound to limit his debate discussions to the official government line: there was to be no U.S. intervention in Cuban affairs."[104] This gave Kennedy a major advantage over Nixon in this debate, further boosting his position in the polls. The result of suddenly making Cuba the focus of the 1960 presidential campaign would play out over many years, with tragic and fatal consequences for many participants; John F. Kennedy would be among those.

Kennedy must have heard the joke that circulated during the 1960 presidential campaign, especially in the bars and parties around Austin, Boston, and Washington, that had Kennedy telling Johnson, "Lyndon, when we get elected I'm going to dig a tunnel to the Vatican," to which Lyndon replied, "That's OK with me, as long as Brown & Root gets the contract."[105] JFK's knowledge of Johnson's corrupt past, using his senatorial office as a branch office of the company he had so long championed, was implied in the joke, as was the general public knowledge of Johnson's murky past.

Johnson Ascends to the Vice Presidency

The *Chicago Tribune* described the eventual voting irregularities in Cook County: "The election of November 8 was characterized by such gross and palpable fraud as to justify the conclusion that [Richard Nixon] was deprived of victory." In one place 100 votes were cast before the polls even opened; in another precinct 71 votes were cast by people giving false names; 34 others voted twice and "residents of Chicago flophouses were hauled in to vote the names of absent or dead voters."[106] The Daley machine in Chicago, with the assistance of the Giancana Mob, manufactured 10,000 additional votes mostly from people who were deceased, allowing the Democrats to offset

103. Morrow, pp. 32–33.
104. Ibid., p. 33.
105. Dugger, pp. 286–287.
106. Lasky, *JFK—The Man*, p. 495.

losses downstate and win statewide by 8,585 votes.[107] The fraud was much grander in the state of Texas where "a minimum of 100,000 votes tallied for the Kennedy-Johnson ticket never existed in the first place. Yet despite all this, the ticket finally carried Texas by a slim margin of 46,000 votes."[108] In one Texas precinct, there were 86 total voters receiving ballots, yet the number cast was 171: Nixon got 24 and Kennedy got 147. This pattern was repeated all over Texas: "Tens of thousands of ballots disappeared overnight . . . in one county which voted Nixon over Kennedy, 458 to 350, 182 ballots were declared void at the 'discretion of the judges.' But in the other, 68 to 1 for Kennedy, not a single ballot was declared void."[109]

Although it might be argued that Illinois wasn't essential anyway, without it, Kennedy would have had a plurality of only seven electoral votes over Nixon, which would have caused more unpledged electors in certain Southern states to switch their votes to Senator Harry F. Byrd, of Virginia, as fourteen of them eventually did anyway. That would have thrown the election into the House of Representatives and opened the possibility of a more aggressive investigation of voter fraud in up to eleven states. As it was, the complaints filed by the Republicans were stymied by the Justice Department, which was due to get a new attorney general.[110] Richard Nixon was unusually magnanimous in defeat; despite knowing of the many irregularities, he refused to challenge the results and even asked *The New York Herald Tribune* newspaper to cancel the remainder of their series because "our country can't afford the agony of a constitutional crisis."[111]

There was no victory celebration in the Johnson's hotel suite at the Driskill Hotel in Austin on election night even though it was apparent shortly after midnight that the Kennedy-Johnson ticket had won in what might charitably be called a close election. Johnson must have been particularly shocked and disappointed at the closeness of the Texas victory, especially considering that 100,000 bogus votes were required to do it, as noted earlier. After the victory was declared, the Johnson "party" left their suite and walked across Seventh Street to an all-night café to get a bite to eat. "There was no jubilation. Lyndon looked as if he'd lost his last friend on earth," one of his secretaries, who was appalled by LBJ's rude behavior, recalled.[112]

---

107. Lasky, *It Didn't Start . . .*, pp. 47–48 (citing *Chicago Tribune*, Dec. 11, 1960).
108. Ibid., p. 49 (citing *New York Herald-Tribune*).
109. Lasky, *JFK—The Man*, p. 495.
110. Dallek, *Flawed Giant*, p. 39.
111. Lasky, *It Didn't Start*, pp. 50–51.
112. Ibid., p. 60 (ref. Merle Miller, *Lyndon: An Oral Biography*, New York: G.P. Putnam's Sons, 1980).

As author Victor Lasky noted, "At seven the next morning . . . Liz Carpenter walked into the living room of the suite. It was littered with coffee cups and cigarette butts, souvenirs of last night's nervousness. There, amid the rubbish, Johnson sat alone, staring at the television. His unhappiness at winning the vice presidency was palpable. Of his many political victories, this was the least welcome."[113] The reason for his despondency was the growing realization that the power he had come to enjoy as the majority leader would be forfeited. He knew the vice presidential position would lack any autonomous power at all—only that which would be delegated to him by the president, or worse, his brother Bobby, who was already being recognized as the "assistant president." Considering how hard—viciously hard—he had fought for the vice presidential nomination, and knowing in advance the diminution in power from his previous position as majority leader, the picture of him, ascribed to his secretary and Liz Carpenter, as being dejected about having won the election is of more than passing interest; it reveals his internal conflict over losing real power in exchange for attaining a position having no power other than that which might be delegated to him by the president. Unless, of course, the new president should die in office, in which case he would automatically become the most powerful man in the nation. It was arguably that possibility which provided him the resolve to go forward with his plan to become president through the only constitutional framework possible, given his lack of a national base and a very limited amount of time to accomplish it through the more customary channel.

After the election, he turned his attention to the ways that he could retain some of his old powers while seeking the broadest powers he could wrangle from the president for his new position. He had previously infused a number of positions he held with greater power than what existed before he held them, and he expected to do the same with this one. He had friends in the press to help instill this idea in the public mind-set, including Tom Wicker of the *New York Times*, who wrote, "The restless and able Mr. Johnson is obviously unwilling to become a ceremonial nonentity."[114] Johnson came up with a two-pronged approach to retain his old powers and simultaneously assume more power:

• With help from his old friend and Senate secretary Bobby Baker, he would get his Senate colleagues to rally around the idea of keeping him on as leader of the Democratic Caucus. Baker was "astonished and horrified" at the prospect of such an audacious scheme, so contrary to the traditions and

---

113. Ibid.
114. Ibid.

prerogatives of the Senate and a breach of the constitutional separation of powers. He asked Baker to "sound out" his colleagues on the idea, but he found the reaction was cold at best, and even broaching it "fueled apprehensions about the continued pressure of Johnson's heavy hand."[115] When the caucus had their organizational meeting on January 3, 1961, they acknowledged Johnson's accomplishments and elected Mike Mansfield as the new leader. Then Mansfield thanked his colleagues and proposed that Johnson be invited to act as coleader and be invited to chair future meetings. Five men rose to denounce the motion on general principles, having tired of being subjected to the "Johnson treatment," and strongly objected on constitutional grounds. The caucus finally gave in to Mansfield's threat to resign and voted 46 to 17 to uphold the motion, but it was hardly a victory. "Mortified, Johnson darted from the caucus room to which he would never return as vice president. Moments later, Johnson stalked the Taj Mahal in a paranoid rage. 'Those bastards sandbagged me,' he fumed to Bobby Baker. 'They'd plotted to humiliate me, all those goddamn red-hots and troublemakers . . . Hell, we didn't pull any big surprise on 'em! But no, they had to humiliate me in public.' Over drinks, Baker spoke soothing words, but LBJ was inconsolable. 'Now I know the difference between a caucus and a cactus,' Johnson reportedly groused. 'In a cactus all the pricks are on the outside.'"[116]

• He then attempted to redefine the executive authority of the vice presidential role, seeking help from Nicholas Katzenbach, the new assistant attorney general, who sent him a long memo which found that "the office was endowed with more executive authority than generally presumed. A supervisory role, Katzenbach concluded, was not at all improper. Soon thereafter, a Johnson aide drafted an executive order granting the vice president 'general supervision' of a broad span of government activities, including the National Aeronautics and Space Administration (NASA). Reports, plans, and proposals traditionally sent to the president would go instead to Lyndon Johnson . . . [Johnson] approved it . . . and forwarded it to the president. John Kennedy was astonished and bemused. He ignored the order. And Lyndon Johnson, now twice rebuffed, did not press the issue."[117]

Although Kennedy did not approve the draft order presented to him by Johnson, he did go out of his way to accommodate most of Johnson's requests for special privileges. One of the most important of these would

---

115. Ibid., p. 62.
116. Ibid., p. 63.
117. Ibid., p. 64.

be the authority to control all patronage appointments in Texas, something usually reserved for the party's representatives in the Senate, in this case Ralph Yarborough. Johnson was so jealous of Yarborough and so mean-spirited toward him that he did everything in his power to remind Yarborough just who was in charge of the state of Texas and took every opportunity to deny him any of the perquisites of power that he, Lyndon B. Johnson, took for granted. He had even blocked his fellow Texas senator from being permitted to be a delegate to the 1960 convention.[118] But Kennedy did disapprove another request from Johnson, to have his office located close to the Oval Office in the West Wing; he was assigned an office across the street in the Executive Office Building instead. However, that did not stop his pretending to be at JFK's right hand; as noted in chapter 3, Johnson had made his presence in the West Wing known, as he portrayed himself as being on the inside track of the Oval Office. His actions all during this period were directed to subverting JFK's agenda from the very start of the inauguration of the Kennedy-Johnson "team." Having failed in his audacious attempts to increase his power as the vice president, he would spend the next three years chomping at the bit. Those three years were dedicated to taking the overseas trips he hated, chairing the Commission on Equal Employment Opportunity, whose objectives he carefully thwarted, and engaging in his continuing feuds with Ralph Yarborough and Bobby Kennedy.

The Marginalized Johnson Causes Friction

Johnson had felt from the start that Robert Kennedy, having failed to kick him off the ticket in Los Angeles, was intent on making him the most impotent vice president of all time: "'He repeated that to me over a period of weeks,' Pierre Salinger recalled of Johnson's first months in the White House. After the inauguration, said [Ken] O'Donnell, Johnson felt Robert Kennedy 'had taken over his rightful position as the number two man in the government.'"[119]

Of his chairmanship of the Equal Employment Opportunity Committee, Arthur Schlesinger wrote, "Robert Kennedy and the successive Secretaries of Labor, Arthur Goldberg and Willard Wirtz, came to feel that the committee was badly run and that it was Johnson's fault. 'There wasn't any problem about making it an effective organization,' Bobby Kennedy said later, 'just if the Vice President gave it some direction. It was mostly a public relations operation. I mean . . . a lot of it was public relations. Secondly there wasn't

118. Lincoln, p. 124.
119. Schlesinger, *Robert Kennedy . . .*, p. 673.

any adequate follow-up. Thirdly, the head of the staff . . . Hobart Taylor, whom I have contempt for because I thought he was so ineffective.'"[120] In a conversation between Bobby and John Kennedy regarding Johnson's ineffectual handling of the EEO committee, JFK said, "That man can't run this committee. Can you think of anything more deplorable than him trying to run the United States? That's why he can't ever be President of the United States."[121] JFK and RFK both had relied on Johnson to use his position as chairman of the Committee on Equal Employment Opportunity to increase employment of minorities in all federal government jobs, and for two years had heard nothing but Johnson's routine, perfunctory assurances that this was happening. At a meeting of this committee on May 29, 1963, Robert Kennedy found that out of two thousand such jobs in Birmingham, Alabama, only fifteen were filled by blacks; he verbally attacked James Webb, head of the NASA and a Johnson protégé. According to Arthur Schlesinger, the meeting was a memorable one for those present: "And then finally, after completely humiliating Webb and making the Vice President look like a fraud . . . he walked out."[122]

Both of the Kennedys, unaware of Johnson's schemes against them, had misunderstood his ineffectiveness on the EEO Committee; they assumed that he was merely incompetent. They had still not realized that he had no interest in advancing their civil rights agenda because, evidently—looking at it retrospectively, with the benefit of the historical record—he needed to save that for his own program, which was still being planned. In May and June of 1963, as President Kennedy prepared for the introduction of a civil rights bill, he asked Burke Marshall, at the Department of Justice, to discuss it with Vice President Johnson. The meeting he had was related to the drafting of the legislation as well as the development of a strategy for getting the bill through Congress. Marshall said that Kennedy's intent at the time was to make the bill as broad and all-encompassing as possible, including separate titles for voting rights, equal employment, and elimination of discrimination in public restaurants, hotels, and other public accommodations. But Johnson only wanted to talk about "economic problems" and how the public works programs of the '30s were so effective. His interest seemed to be limited to only improving the economic situation of Negroes. According to Burke's oral history interview, his general impression of Johnson's interest in civil rights legislation, only six months before he ascended to the presidency, was one of "diffidence." He said that Johnson specifically questioned the broader

---

120. Ibid., pp. 336–337.
121. Guthman, p. 153.
122. Schlesinger, p. 361.

approach being pushed by Kennedy and said that "*he was very dubious that we could get it passed.*" Marshall also stated that Johnson's view was that "*the President ought to hold it back until he thoroughly discussed it at least with the Congressional leaders.*"[123] (Emphasis supplied.)

According to John Kenneth Galbraith, who became a friend of Johnson after having been a friend of JFK, "They each had their own agenda. LBJ didn't urge a strong public program on Kennedy, and Kennedy was quite content to leave Lyndon to his own senate role, his own legislative role, and his own life. They were not close."[124] Perhaps in finally agreeing to allow Johnson to run as his vice presidential nominee, Kennedy had assumed that he would at least help him get legislation through Congress; after all, that is the rationale he used to explain the decision to the many people who questioned the move. The most likely explanation for this conundrum is that JFK had finally tuned out Johnson, becoming too weary of his boorish and crude behavior to even try to persuade him to use his legendary congressional skills.

Johnson's EEO Committee had succumbed to bickering from the very start because of his conflicted interests in securing real progress as well as his mismanagement involving the people he had appointed to it. One of these appointments involved Jerry R. Holleman, a Texan whom Johnson had placed into a high-level position as an assistant secretary of labor. He was assigned to work closely with the EEO Committee, though the question of how much "work" he did and whether he was pulling in the direction the Kennedys wished is another matter. Within months, it became apparent that Mr. Holleman's primary qualification for the job was his willingness to expedite whatever fraudulent requests might come through for Johnson's friend Billie Sol Estes. To smooth the way, Estes had given Holleman the customary bribes; that information became public eventually as the investigation got under way and came dangerously close to directly implicating Johnson before the murders of Estes's associates frightened witnesses into keeping their mouths shut. By then, testimony had clearly tracked the money Estes paid Holleman for personal luxury items; his forced resignation soon followed.[125] He wasn't out of work too long, however, before Johnson's longtime friend Morris Jaffe of San Antonio hired him; Jaffe was also the beneficiary of Estes's bankruptcy, coming along just in time to buy up the Estes's properties (presumably excluding the nonexistent grain silos and elevators) for pennies

123. Transcript, Burke Marshall Oral History Interview I, 10/28/68, by T. H. Baker, Internet copy, LBJ Library, pp. 6–7.
124. John Kenneth Galbraith, interviewed by Vicki Daitch, September 12, 2002. Oral History Program, JFK Library.
125. Lincoln, pp. 181–182; Haley, pp. 133–134.

on the dollar.

As the most powerful Senate majority leader ever, Johnson had enjoyed the perquisites of the office more than any majority leader before him. His carefully crafted ability to persuade men into taking actions that would normally be anathema to them was based on his exercise of that power, tempered with his own conniving personality and skills, together with his access to whatever secrets each of them might prefer to keep hidden. But as vice president, Johnson had lost most of his influence on Capitol Hill; as one observer noted, "Lyndon has no chits to call in anymore."[126] President Kennedy was angered by Johnson's apparent abdication of his commitments to help facilitate the passage of the administration's legislative agenda: "'He thought that Lyndon ought to be up there really beating their heads in,' as presidential aide Ralph Dungan recalled. Ted Sorensen, who was responsible for JFK's legislative effort, said that 'we expected him [LBJ] to be a major voice in not only shaping but delivering and selling the program, and he did very little, if any, of that.' Johnson's tentative, halfhearted advice disappointed Kennedy. His respect for LBJ began to wane."[127]

Robert Kennedy's respect for LBJ was never great enough for it to ever wane. During the Cuban missile crisis, his utter contempt for Lyndon Johnson would become firmly established; the president himself would stop consulting Johnson altogether on anything of substance.[128] Johnson rarely attended ExComm meetings but quickly sided with the hawks of the Pentagon and the unctuous Dean Rusk at the State Department, who felt an attack on Cuba was warranted to take out the missiles, regardless of the risks of unleashing a retaliatory attack by the Soviets. As noted by author Jeff Shesol, "'Lyndon Johnson never made any suggestions or recommendations as to what we should do at the time of the Cuban missile crisis,' Robert Kennedy complained later. 'He was displeased with what we were doing although he never made it clear what he would do.' According to Bobby, as the nuclear confrontation reached its climax the following Saturday, Johnson did no more than indicate displeasure with the president's policy. 'He was shaking his head, mad,' Bobby recalled."[129] According to Adam Walinsky, the purpose of RFK's book, *Thirteen Days*, was "to contrast the cool, rational, deliberate decision-making of the Kennedy cabinet with the muddled, reactive nature of Johnson's Vietnam policy by 1967."[130]

Johnson's attempt to show the public that he was a team player,

126. Shesol, p. 99.
127. Ibid.
128. Ibid., p. 92.
129. Ibid., p. 94.
130. Ibid., p. 98.

despite his chronic disagreements with Kennedy, caused him to hide his disdain from reporters, but not necessarily his columnist friends like Walter Winchell. According to Schlesinger, "There was never a whiff of discord, complaint or self-pity to newspapermen or even to old friends on the Hill. *This unprecedented self-discipline exacted a growing psychic cost.* By 1963 the Vice-President faded astonishingly into the background. Evelyn Lincoln calculated that in 1961 he had spent ten hours and nineteen minutes in private conferences with the President, in 1963 one hour and fifty-three minutes. At meetings in the Cabinet Room he became an almost spectral presence. As the President's 'sureness and independence increased,' Mrs. Lincoln noted, 'the Vice President became more apprehensive and anxious to please.' Bill Moyers, who had worked for him in the Senate and was now deputy director of the Peace Corps, thought that his self-confidence was trickling away. He was, said Moyers, '*a man without a purpose . . . a great horse in a very small corral*' . . . Daniel Patrick Moynihan remembered looking into the Vice President's eyes and thinking, '*This is a bull castrated very late in life*'"[131] (emphasis added).

As for Lyndon Johnson's surprising attitude about the office that he had worked so hard to achieve, having even resorted to blackmailing Kennedy to get it, he now desperately feared the thought of losing it, even though he hated it: "I detested every minute of it," he would say of his time as vice president.[132] This is an absolutely stunning comment and begs the question: If he hated it so much, why did he force Kennedy to take him in the first place and why did he fear the Kennedy's efforts to bump him off the ticket the following year? Perhaps that best explains a comment Johnson once made, "Every time I came into John Kennedy's presence, I felt like a goddamn raven hovering over his shoulder."[133] There is only one possible explanation for this anomaly: Clearly, Johnson loathed every minute of his time as vice president, yet he feared losing it because he knew it would mean the end of his career, and worse, if he were to face prison time, it would mean his legacy would be disgraced forever. But he kept on sloughing through those times because he knew secrets that very few others knew and had known all along that the vice presidency was only a temporary position. He had to have known that he would soon be thankful for an end to his suffering and humiliation because by Thanksgiving Day 1963, his lifetime goal of becoming president would be achieved. Retribution against the Kennedys would then be his, and Bobby

---

131. Schlesinger, *Robert Kennedy* . . ., p. 671 (quoting Bill Moyers in a television interview with David Susskind, October 13, 1974, and Daniel Patrick Moynihan, *Playboy*, March 1977).
132. Kearns, p. 164.
133. Ibid.

would be the one to suffer.

The problem for Johnson was actually worse than simply losing his power base and suddenly becoming ineffectual. He saw that his rightful position as the second in command was overridden from the start by his nemesis, the president's brother, Robert F. Kennedy. "'Johnson,' wrote O'Donnell, 'blamed his fallen prestige on Bobby Kennedy.' 'His complaints against Bobby Kennedy,' said Bobby Baker, 'were frequent and may have bordered on the paranoiac.' No affection contaminated the relationship between the Vice President and the Attorney General. It was a pure case of mutual dislike. 'Maybe it was just a matter of chemistry,' Johnson said in retrospect."[134] Within six months of the beginning of JFK's term, the news magazine, *U.S. News & World Report*, "proclaimed Bobby the 'number-two man in Washington . . . second only to the president in power and influence.' He was the 'assistant president.'"[135] Robert Kennedy's rise in Washington was as rapid as Lyndon Johnson's decline. His loss of power and prestige affected him much more than he had figured on, and he didn't like it. His presence wasn't missed at important meetings until the last minute, when JFK might occasionally remember to invite him belatedly. These slights greatly hurt the fragile but inflated ego of Johnson, who had trouble trying to pretend to stay busy, and usually did so with a simulated flair that evoked his old days as the "master of the Senate."[136] The reality was that John Kennedy simply stopped consulting Johnson on anything of importance and rarely invited him to meetings on substantive subjects.[137] Despite his loss of power to Robert Kennedy during those years, or maybe because of it, Johnson "still derided Bobby quite loudly as a 'snot-nosed little son-of-a-bitch.' Bobby Kennedy, Johnson once told Bobby Baker, was laughably underprepared to lead the nation's law enforcement effort and was sure to politicize the Justice Department."[138]

Johnson had been humiliated by the Senate's rejection of his bid to become chairman of the Democratic Caucus and became more and more ambivalent toward Congress. He regarded his actual, constitutional role as the Senate's presiding officer as beneath his dignity and an inconvenience, an obligation he would fulfill as minimally as possible. He received a daily call from his protégé Bobby Baker, who would fill him in on the latest gossip

---

134. Schlesinger, *Robert Kennedy . . .*, p. 671 (ref. O'Donnell and Powers, *Johnny*, p. 6; Baker, *Wheeling and Dealing*, p. 126; Lyndon B. Johnson, *The Vantage Point*, New York, 1971, p. 539).
135. Shesol, p. 74.
136. Ibid., p. 76.
137. Ibid., p. 92.
138. Ibid., p. 66.
139. Shesol, p. 98.

about his former Senate colleagues.[139] Little else aroused his interest beyond tending to his remaining Texas constituency. During meetings with legislative leaders, he was described as "vacant and gray . . . discontented and tired."[140] His behavior all throughout this period suggests that he was preoccupied with other things on his agenda that only a few of his closest cronies knew anything about. He seemed to withdraw more and more from participating in anything substantial, as though he either didn't have time for the most important initiatives of the administration in which he served and/or that he didn't want to make progress on the White House agenda; perhaps he simply preferred to defer them to a later date, when he could then "pull all the plugs" to whip up Congress into passage of the biggest set of progressive social legislation in the history of the world. Such speculation, though difficult to prove, somehow fills some gaps in this fascinating puzzle.

Throughout his tenure as vice president, as the shock of having lost practically all his power settled in, and as all the "Harvards" and "Bostons" began taking over the reins of power, Johnson receded more and more into the background. The worst part for him was the constant humiliation he felt from the Eastern boys who had taken to calling him "Colonel Cornpone" and the "hayseed hick" behind his back;[141] in his mind, he had become the most powerful man in Washington in the 1950s because he knew a lot more about running the nation than did all of these "whiz kids" from Harvard combined. Johnson disagreed strongly with Kennedy's efforts toward détente with the Soviet Union; when the president authorized the sale of wheat—at a time when the United States had 1.2 billion bushels in storage and another one billion new bushels then being harvested, while subsidizing American wheat farmers to the tune of fifty-five cents per bushel over the world market price[142]—to the Soviets, who had experienced massive crop failures because of drought, Lyndon Johnson objected. Kennedy told Arthur Schlesinger, on October 11, 1963, "The Vice President . . . thinks that this is the worst foreign policy mistake we have made in this administration."[143] Despite the general cold war animosity toward the Soviet Union at that time, the public understood the issues better than the vice president and generally approved of the sale. According to a contemporaneous account in *Life* magazine, "The government's change of heart reflected the hardheaded attitude of a Midwest farmer who said, 'I'm in favor of selling the Reds anything they can't shoot

140. Ibid.
141. Shesol, pp. 60, 142;
142. *Life* magazine, October 11, 1963, p. 31.
143. Schlesinger, Robert Kennedy . . ., p. 644.
144. *Life* magazine, October 11, 1963, p. 31.

back."[144]

Lyndon Johnson's disagreement with Kennedy's Russian wheat sale was no different than his position on many other issues throughout the nearly three-year term of JFK's administration; he was either overtly against the Kennedy position or cunningly attempting to undermine it, as has been demonstrated in the case of Kennedy's policies toward both South Vietnam and Cuba. Johnson was simply marching to his own drum the entire period while trying to present himself as Kennedy's biggest supporter; this is reflected in the number of times his biographers noted that he never publicly said unkind things about JFK. In reality, by early 1963, Johnson could not count on John F. Kennedy's help anymore; his relationship with JFK, RFK, and the rest of the Kennedy administration was at an all-time low, thanks to his negligible efforts to support his nominal boss. He had purposely done nothing to help JFK pass legislation through Congress, an objective that had made his appointment to the vice presidency three years before more palatable to Kennedy. Unfortunately, Johnson's role so far had been the opposite of Kennedy's expectation; if anything, LBJ had done everything he could to thwart JFK's agenda.

The Kennedys Discover Pretext to Remove LBJ

In addition to being very frustrated by Johnson's ineptitude, John Kennedy was afraid that the Baker and Estes scandals would blow up during the 1964 campaign, jeopardizing his own reelection chances. He had discussed this with Bobby on many occasions, and despite RFK's repeated and expected denials, the decision to replace Johnson had been made; it was only necessary to be able to justify it, to him or anyone else. Bobby had been procuring information on Johnson's Mafia ties, specifically with his own nemesis, Carlos Marcello. A former Justice Department official has stated that on November 21, 1963, "Robert Kennedy had a thick investigative file on his desk on the Marcello-LBJ connection. In the 1950s, Marcello's Texas 'political fixer' Jack Halfen had arranged to siphon off a percentage of the mobster's racing wire and slot machine profits for LBJ's Senate campaigns. In exchange, according to journalist Michael Dorman in his book *Payoff*, LBJ had helped kill certain antiracketeering legislation in committee."[145] According to author David E. Scheim, referencing Dorman's research, "Halfen disclosed that a gambling network controlled by organized crime 'had given $500,000 in cash and campaign contributions to Johnson over a ten-year period while Johnson

145. Russell, p. 523 (ref. Davis, *Mafia Kingfish*, pp. 272–273); North, p. 371.
146. Scheim, p. 247 (ref. Michael Dorman, "LBJ and the Racketeers," *Ramparts*, May 1968, pp. 27–28).

was in the Senate.'"[146] Jack Halfen had been serving his second year of a ten-year sentence in 1961 when Bobby Kennedy sent one of his investigators to interview him after Halfen had hinted that he might be willing to reveal incriminating information about Johnson. It would take thirty-seven years—until 1998—for the FBI records relating to all of this to be released; when they were, thirty-seven of the forty names on Halfen's list were blacked out, leaving only three close friends of Johnson: Tom Clark (father of Ramsey and a former U.S. Attorney General and Supreme Court Justice), U.S. Congressman Albert Thomas (who would be caught winking at Johnson immediately after he was sworn in on Air Force One), and a former Texas deputy sheriff named Jake Colca.[147]

Yet another author, John H. Davis, in *Mafia Kingfish : Carlos Marcello and the Assassination of John F. Kennedy*, also documented Johnson's connections to the underworld through his close friend and neighbor, the lobbyist I. Irving Davidson, who had long, extensive contacts with a number of mafia figures, including Carlos Marcello: "It had been principally Davidson who had provided Marcello with most of his entrees into the agencies of the federal government, including the CIA, for which Davidson acted as a lobbyist on Capitol Hill, and into the worlds of Washington politics, international big business, and high finance . . . it was through Davidson that Marcello had been able to extend the reach of his influence to the oil-rich Murchisons of Dallas, to certain embarrassing members of President Lyndon Johnson's camp, men such as Bobby Baker and Billie Sol Estes, . . . Davidson's endless collection of people in high places, people who could possibly fill a key position in Carlos Marcello's invisible government, also included none other than FBI Director J. Edgar Hoover, who in turn was a good friend of Davidson's and Marcello's friend Clint Murchison."[148] The tentacles of Johnson's arm's length reach into the underworld—through his close associations with such men as Bobby Baker, Mickey Weiner, Fred Black, Billie Sol Estes, Cliff Carter, and Irving Davidson—and led ultimately to Carlos Marcello, the head of the mafia in New Orleans.

In due course, it became well known that John F. Kennedy followed all news of Johnson's legal entanglements, and he would specifically take much interest in the investigation of the Billie Sol Estes and Bobby Baker cases, with all of their connections to Johnson.[149] This was confirmed in the early days of the administration, in a newspaper that Johnson had always read closely. *The*

---

147. Russo, pp. 283–284.
148. Davis, *Mafia Kingfish* p. 312.
149. Dallek, *Flawed Giant*, p. 39.

Dallas Morning News carried a headline in 1961 titled, "JFK Takes Interest in Henry Marshall Death."[150] Over three decades later, according to author Gus Russo's sources, "In 1998, a high government official, on condition of anonymity, confirmed that Robert Kennedy had in fact instructed his Justice Department to initiate a 'criminal investigation of Lyndon Johnson.'"[151] By the time of the trip to Texas, Bobby Kennedy had information documenting Johnson's long criminal history on many fronts: Bobby Baker, Billie Sol Estes, and Jack Halfen, the legendary go-between who connected Lyndon Johnson directly to Carlos Marcello.[152]

It is likely that both John and Robert Kennedy had read the November 22, 1963, edition (distributed a few days before that date) of *Life* magazine, then the leading weekly *People*-type magazine, which had a cover page read by millions with a banner headline titled, "The Bobby Baker Case: U.S. Senate writhes as nation focuses on a mess involving one of its own . . . SCANDAL GROWS AND GROWS IN WASHINGTON." The article noted how the ambitious young man from Pickens, South Carolina, had begun his career in the Senate as a page then rose to higher and higher levels, brought along all the way by his mentor, Lyndon B. Johnson. The description of how Baker's influence had grown as a result of Johnson's tutelage included the following: "Like a young Sabu herding bewildered elephants, he was adept at settling freshman senators into their strange surrounds and thereby incurring debts of gratitude that were payable on future call. Later, as Baker grew in stature, he became adroit at shepherding stray solons tamely into the Establishment's fold. 'You get along if you go along,' was his standard counsel, and senators listened."[153] The Establishment was, of course, that group of about forty senators aligned closely with their majority leader, Lyndon B. Johnson. The article then went on to note the closeness of the Johnson-Baker connection: "'He always spoke of LBJ as 'The Leader,' a man who knows Baker well said recently. 'He even tried to be Johnson. He copied Johnson's clothes and mannerisms. When he came into the Senate chamber, he'd take the Johnson stance, smooth his sideburns, brace his shoulders and scowl up at the balcony—the whole bit. The only thing wrong with his act was that he was six inches too short.'"[154]

Moreover, the *Life* cover page article was undoubtedly read thoroughly by millions when that entire weekend became a national period of mourning, as they turned away from their televisions for a brief respite, trying to find out

---

150. Ibid.
151. Russo, p. 284.
152. Ibid., p. 283.
153. *Life* magazine, November 22, 1963, p. 40.
154. Ibid.

as much as they could about the previously ignored vice president. It is not an overstatement to say that practically everyone in America cancelled at least some of their previous plans and devoted their attention to the aftershock, the cortege and funeral of JFK, the shooting of Oswald and Tippit, and all the other information exploding out of Dallas and Washington that weekend of televised, commercial-free news coverage. The article these millions of people were reading that weekend was very revealing of this man who was so close to the new president; it went on to describe him and his tremendous influence. One incident described the power the vice president still wielded in the Senate even after he left it in 1961; it involved Johnson's instruction to Baker to reject what should have been the routine appointment of North Dakota Senator Quentin Burdick to the Judiciary Committee, who eagerly awaited the announcement. Baker discreetly passed the lie that Burdick had changed his mind about it, and the committee picked Ed Long of Missouri instead. The reason for this, according to this timely issue of the most popular U.S. magazine at that time, now being read by millions, was, "Burdick was a Kennedy supporter and therefore didn't belong to the Establishment—a combination Lyndon Johnson wasn't likely to forgive. So Bobby Baker shivved Burdick."[155] The time that the above-mentioned incident occurred, in January 1961, was exactly when the Kennedy-Johnson team was being inaugurated. So much for having a vice president who was a "team player" and who actually supported—by his deeds as well as his mouth—the president whom he was supposed to serve.

In addition to the published article noted above, in the November 22, 1963 edition of *Life* magazine, another breaking news story was being prepared by the same publication which was expected to end Johnson's political life, at the very least removing him from the 1964 ticket, but in all likelihood, forcing him to resign before that and probably result in his criminal indictment. According to an assistant to *Life* magazine's executive editor in 1963, James Wagenvoord, then twenty-seven years old, this article was pulled at the last minute and never published. In early November 2009, he contacted John Simkin, whose widely read Web site at the Education Forum subsequently published the following (edited) statement:

> Beginning in late summer 1963 [*Life*] magazine, based upon information fed from Bobby Kennedy and the Justice Department, had been developing a major newsbreak piece concerning Johnson and Bobby Baker. *On publication Johnson would have been finished and off the '64 ticket ([the] reason the material was fed to us) and*

---

155. Ibid.

would probably have been facing prison time. At the time *Life* magazine was arguably the most important general news source in the United States. The top management of Time, Inc. was closely allied with the USA's various intelligence agencies and we were used . . . by the Kennedy Justice Department as a conduit to the public . . . The LBJ/Baker piece was in the final editing stages and was scheduled to break in the issue of the magazine due out the week of November 24 (most likely one of the next scheduled editions, November 29th or December 6th, distributed four or five days earlier than those dates). It had been prepared in relative secrecy by a small special editorial team. *On Kennedy's death, research files and all numbered copies of the nearly print-ready draft were gathered up by my boss (he had been the top editor on the team) and shredded.* The issue that was to expose LBJ instead featured the Zapruder film. Based upon our success in syndicating the Zapruder film I became Chief of *Time/ Life* editorial services and remained in that job until 1968 (emphasis added).

Wagenvoord later added the following: "It was stated flatly that this was to be the end of LBJ on the '64 ticket. *Life* had already run two Baker pieces, the first a general survey bad guy picture essay detailing the opening of the Carousel Hotel and his generally [*sic*] sleaziness"; and "I had seen Department of Justice couriers coming in and out of the offices and knew that a lot of material was being fed directly to the magazine from the department."[156]

This late report about Bobby Kennedy supplying information to *Life* implicating Johnson, for the purpose of forcing him out of the administration, validates much of the other information included in this book; it also goes further, with respect to vindicating the charges, that *Life* immediately reversed its plan to publish incriminating information about Johnson and, instead, actively suppressed that information. Although the owner and chief executive of *Life* and *Time* magazines (Henry Luce and C. D. Jackson respectively) were ultraconservatives and disliked both John Kennedy and Lyndon Johnson, their interest before November 22, 1963, would have been to harm the administration any way it could, and revealing the Johnson scandals would have done that. After JFK's assassination, they quickly realized that subjecting the nation to the ordeal of a possible impeachment and trial of Johnson, on the heels of the assassination of Kennedy, could potentially lead to ever-increasing instability that might be enormously destructive to the country. Their previous dislike of both Kennedy and Johnson then morphed

156. See http://educationforum.ipbhost.com/index.php?showtopic=14966&st=0

into reverence for the former and tepid support for the latter as a means of averting the constitutional crisis that might otherwise unfold. Any lingering suspicion of Johnson's criminal past—or his possible involvement in Kennedy's murder—would also undoubtedly be shelved for the same reason.

Furthermore, and no doubt in cooperation with the CIA in its continuation of Operation Mockingbird, *Life* magazine then arranged to purchase all of the rights to the Zapruder film, not for the purpose of using it to enlighten the public about the assassination, but to participate with the CIA in hiding the fact that Kennedy's fatal head shot came from the front. The fact that the film was kept from the public for twelve years, and then found to have been tampered with (as documented in chapter 9), speaks volumes about the real purpose behind the manipulation of evidence. It also corroborates the charges made in later chapters regarding Johnson's and Hoover's direct involvement in evidence tampering.

Lyndon Johnson's November Dilemma

The Baker scandal was looming as a major roadblock to Lyndon Johnson's political career and therefore his dream of becoming president. He knew all about Bobby Kennedy feeding information to Senator Williams and to the *Life* magazine reporters right out of the Justice Department; there was very little that his chief collaborator, J. Edgar Hoover, didn't know about, especially in Washington and at the Department of Justice. The situation for Johnson had now become so desperate that his nemesis, Bobby Kennedy, had even begun working to help his protégé, Bobby Baker, to avoid incriminating himself. According to Drew Pearson, Kennedy called Baker, telling him, "'Get off the phone. You shouldn't be talking' warned Kennedy cryptically. In view of the Justice Department's recent [1966] revelation that wire taps and electronic devices were used to monitor some of Baker's conversations, the warning is highly significant."[157] Clearly, by the fall of 1963, Kennedy had begun using every tool at his disposal to move the subject of the Justice Department investigation away from Johnson's enablers and underlings and directly at the vice president himself. Johnson had replaced Baker as the real subject of Robert F. Kennedy's investigations. RFK had even begun using IRS investigators in order to use Johnson's legal problems as leverage to force him off the ticket if he, as expected, attempted to fight the Kennedys in order to hold on to his position. One of these investigators, Walt Perry, told author Gus Russo in 1992 that Billie Sol Estes had "funneled $10 million in bribes

---

157. Pearson, Drew. *Issues in Baker Trial*, January 7, 1967.

to Johnson and that Bobby Kennedy had contacted Estes in prison, making him an offer: 'If you testify against Johnson, you're out [of prison].' Billie declined the offer, saying, 'If I testified against him [Johnson], I'd be dead within twenty-four hours.'"[158]

All of the talk around Washington about Lyndon Johnson being knocked off the Democratic ticket in 1964 was not only known to him but was his central concern. The Kennedys denied it publicly, but behind the scenes, the decision had been made to replace Johnson. Colonel Burris, Johnson's military aide, said in 1992, "He was really down. 1963 was the beginning of the end for Johnson. He was cut out; they were not giving him anything, and the message was basically: 'We don't want you and we don't want your opinion.' He knew that he was going to be thrown off the ticket and that was going to be the end for him."[159] As further confirmation of the above, JFK's personal secretary, Evelyn Lincoln, wrote that JFK had revealed to her, shortly before he left for Texas, that he had grown weary of Johnson and his precarious legal issues, which threatened the entire administration:

> As Mr. Kennedy sat in the rocker in my office, his head resting on its back, he placed his left leg across his right knee. He rocked slightly as he talked. In a slow pensive voice he said to me, "You know if I am re-elected in sixty-four, I am going to spend more and more time toward making government service an honorable career. I would like to tailor the executive and legislative branches of government so that they can keep up with the tremendous strides and progress being made in other fields." . . . "I am going to advocate changing some of the outmoded rules and regulations in the Congress, such as the seniority rule."
>
> "To do this I will need as a running mate in sixty-four a man who believes as I do. I am going to Texas, because I have made a commitment. I can't patch up those warring factions. This is for them to do, but I will go because I have told them I would. And it is too early to make an announcement about another running mate— that will perhaps wait until the convention."
>
> I was fascinated by this conversation and wrote it down verbatim in my diary. I was extremely proud of the man with whom I was associated. I was also glad that I could be a part of the goals and ambitions he was striving for in the future.

---

158. Russo, p. 283.
159. Russo, p. 284 (Ref. John Newman interview with Howard Burris, 21 November, 1992.

He had talked and I had just listened, but I did venture one question. We had not seen Mr. Johnson since he left for Texas in late October. Now I asked, "Who is your choice as a running-mate?" He looked straight ahead, and without hesitating he replied, "at this time I am thinking about Governor Terry Sanford of North Carolina. But it will not be Lyndon."[160]

Johnson was clearly headed toward being dropped from the Democratic ticket the next year, if he even made it that far; the continuing Senate investigations fueled by leaks he knew were coming directly from Bobby Kennedy made criminal prosecution before then a certainty. It was becoming clearer by the day that his future would turn on the question of his resolve to execute his long-planned "executive action." The Hobson's choice before him was really the final catalyst that gave Johnson the will to proceed with the plan he had originally crafted in 1958–59 and affirmed in July 1960 at the Los Angeles Democratic Convention. If he had harbored any doubts about his ability and resolve to execute his plan, he kept reminding himself that this was the only way his childhood dream would ever be fulfilled, and he had promised himself that it would be fulfilled for about one half century. To ensure sufficient levels of plausible deniability up and down the hierarchy of conspirators, he and his key men at the top had ensured that all planning was tightly compartmentalized, starting broadly with his own functions (for example, manipulating the Dallas motorcade) and those of the FBI, CIA/ Mob, and Secret Service. Each participant had a narrowly defined scope of "need to know" knowledge.

If he did not grasp this opportunity, it meant that he would remain, for a time, a passive actor in a job he detested, continuing his battle with RFK on a daily basis, and hoping that his legal problems would somehow go away, which he knew was impossible since it was RFK who was feeding the dirt on him to the Senate investigators. The Bobby Baker hearings would inevitably produce one scandalous story after another. The reporters would have a field day, linking the stories of sex, bribery, and financial wheeling and dealing on the taxpayers' dime that were all part of the overall mosaic of criminal activity he had created and expanded upon for decades. If he surrendered now, his future looked bleak indeed: prison, the length of term variable depending upon the depth of the ongoing inquiries, which were already teetering on the edge of going completely out of control. The destiny that he had always envisioned for himself—that of a great leader revered by his subjects—would come to naught. He would be remembered only for being the first vice

---

160. Lincoln, pp. 204–205.

president to be sentenced to the penitentiary for illegal campaign-funding activities, influence peddling, bribery, tax fraud, extortion, and—if the investigators were persistent and thorough enough, as Henry Marshall had been before his untimely demise—for his own involvement with a number of murders in his home state.

In Lyndon Johnson's view, that was really no choice at all. Why would he willingly capitulate to the vagaries of the natural course of history? He had never done so before, given the opportunity to force his will on the course of events affecting his life. To the contrary, he had a long history of bending rules as necessary to advance the long and gradual fulfillment of his destiny. All the rigged elections, the brazen conflicts of interest, the selling of his political influence to the highest bidder, the awarding of government contracts not to the most qualified contractor, but to the one willing to "pay to play," the use of his political power to appoint "Johnson men" into various bureaucracies to fulfill his demands and to short-circuit regulatory rules to his benefit, and numerous other illegal acts up to and including multiple murders—all of these acts could have still been proven in 1963, and if justice had been served, instead of becoming president, his future would be as it had been predicted by his prescient grandmother: his last decade of life would have been spent in a penitentiary. Lyndon Johnson knew, at this time and at his age, that he had one single opportunity to dramatically change the course of history; he knew that powerful people were willing to help get him quickly propelled into the presidency, where he could then reverse the course of events that would otherwise befall him. He had resolved to himself, long ago, that his "rightful" place, the position that he had been actively planning to acquire for over twenty years, was now within his grasp. To not take advantage of the opportunity—after all the planning, the logistics of putting all operatives in place, the "national security" imperatives that had been understood by key people at CIA and the Joint Chiefs of Staff of the Pentagon, the backing of others in the FBI and Secret Service and key Dallas officials, the work and support of his sponsors and oilmen financiers, the agreed cover-up strategy already in place—would, at this stage, be unthinkable.

Throughout his obligatory stint as the vice president, Lyndon Johnson had begun planning his own legacy, which would be based upon the lofty, but unmet, goals of JFK. Even as head of the administration's Equal Opportunity Commission, he had stalled three years on any meaningful civil rights initiatives knowing that shelving them until he was president meant that he could pull them off the shelf when he was in the Oval Office, providing him an instant legacy. If he pulled it off, he would go down in history as one of the greatest presidents, bringing forth the civil rights agenda that he had stymied under Kennedy, pending his ascension. He had even decided on a name for his agenda: the Great Society. It was a continuum of Roosevelt's New Deal, Truman's Fair Deal, and his unwitting predecessor's New Frontier. Unfortunately for Kennedy, who Johnson always thought was too young, inexperienced, and ineffectual for the presidency, his program never really took off because of constant opposition from Congress. Johnson saw to that, but that would all change once he moved into the Oval Office. His success in getting Kennedy's stalled civil rights legislation would guarantee the support of black Americans for two hundred years, as he later predicted.[161] He would ensure greatness also by becoming a wartime president, just like FDR and Truman.

By November 21, 1963, Vice President Lyndon B. Johnson was caught in a web of legal and political troubles that threatened to remove him from politics forever. The Senate investigations had reached the point of no return; the only way to change the course was for him to become president. Johnson sensed that he had no viable alternative other than to proceed according to the plan to assassinate John F. Kennedy.

---

161. Kessler, *Inside the White House*, p. 33.

Chapter 6

THE CONSPIRATORS

A mansion has many rooms . . . I'm not privy to who struck John.
—JAMES JESUS ANGLETON

We have not been told the truth about Oswald.
—SENATOR RICHARD RUSSELL

The Originator

The scenario presented in the following pages is based upon the premise that elements of the various intelligence agencies, along with other key "rogue" officials of the government and the Mafia protected from discovery through the invocation of the customary government secrecy devices, conspired to kill the thirty-fifth president of the United States, John F. Kennedy. Though it can be said that this is merely this author's opinion, it cannot be said that the assertions are without considerable support. The accumulated totality of evidence cited throughout the narrative to this point and into the remaining chapters with even more compelling evidence meets the "clear and convincing" threshold for what should be the equivalent of a grand jury indictment of first-degree murder, as a posthumous verdict. It should be considered that the only reason Lyndon Johnson was able to avoid justice during his lifetime of crime and corruption was because of his own obfuscatory ability, with the help of bribery, blackmail, and his many enablers.

The crime could have only been accomplished with at least the acquiescence and foreknowledge of the only man capable of choreographing the massive cover-up which was immediately launched. It is axiomatic that since the cover-up started even before the shots were fired, the order for JFK's assassination could only have come from his successor, Lyndon B. Johnson. No other possible candidate for the key man of the assassination—not Santos Trafficante, Carlos Marcello, or Sam Giancana; not H. L. Hunt or Clint Murchison; not James Angleton, Bill Harvey, or David Morales; not Curtis LeMay, Charles Willoughby, or John McCloy; not even J. Edgar Hoover; and certainly not Lee Harvey Oswald—had the motive, the means, the opportunity, the demonstrated pattern of previous criminal, even murderous conduct and the overall demented resolve to see it through. Only one man met all of the criteria required for the murder of John F. Kennedy: Lyndon B. Johnson.

The "Executive Action" Organization: Highest Levels of the Hierarchy

By the fall of 1963, John F. Kennedy had come to the realization that he couldn't control key men in his own military: the CIA, the State Department, J. Edgar Hoover or his FBI empire, the Congress, the Cuban exiles, and worst of all, even his own vice president. He had used up much of his bully pulpit influence with his support for the Nuclear Test Ban Treaty with the Soviets; his sway with big business was shattered after his pressure against U.S. Steel's attempt to raise prices. Many were alarmed at his decision to sidestep the Federal Reserve and print silver certificates, and his support for the abolition of the oil depletion allowance outraged the oil barons. There were a lot of very influential men, in 1963, who had one thing in common: they thought that they knew better than Kennedy did about what was needed to win the cold war with Russia, the festering imbroglio with Cuba, and the nascent conflict in Vietnam. As the nation teetered closer to wars on several fronts, the darkness of a deadly conspiracy was beginning to coalesesce in Washington DC, fronted by a politician to whom the Kennedys had bowed. They were forced by his unscrupulous blackmail to place him in his position of trust and subsequently made to endure his petulant, overbearing, and boorish personality. In exchange for their accommodations to him, he became a saboteur of their most critical programs and finally an albatross that, they determined, had to be cast off within months in order to salvage their chances for reelection.

As Johnson became less and less interested in his vice presidential duties, he enlisted the help of several key men he knew he could count on to assist him in his plan. Through the vicarious use of their authority over the vast independent bureaucracies they controlled, he would gain the ultimate control over the men they selected to follow the necessary orders; most of them would not even know the real objective, of course. For those who he determined to be in the loop, most would be operating under the illusion that the plan was only for a single part, a simulated assassination,* at least until phase 2, the postassassination cover-up. Later, it would become apparent even to them

---

* This is consistent with a number of theories by researchers (for example, see Twyman, p. 760) that the entire phase 1 of the plot was designed such that most participants believed they would be participating in a fake assassination attempt for training purposes by the Secret Service; in most cases the standard covert operations devices—e.g., "need to know," "plausible denial," etc., in phase 1; "secrecy oaths" in phase 2 would be sufficient to ensure silence. Where it didn't, other, more final, methods were available.

The Conspirators • 319

that it was a multiple-part, carefully prepared and coordinated plan involving elements of the Mafia, the Cuban exile community, international professional assassins, and renegades from the intelligence community who were involved with all three sets of assassination teams.

The top level of his secret "task force" would have to comprise only men who shared his hatred of the Kennedys enough to act on it, with full knowledge of the risks and implications of being caught. It was imperative that all the "renegades" picked for this assignment were the best and could be trusted to keep the secret. Some were recruited for planning a simulated assassination that the Secret Service was supposedly planning as a pretext for the removal of all protection when the motorcade arrived in Dealey Plaza. These men could be trusted to "sign on" to phase 2 without a missed step. It was also understood that certain men of the Dallas Police force would have to be called in as necessary, and the three key men—Chief Curry, Captain Fritz, and Sheriff Decker—would need to be extensively investigated beforehand in order to get any negative information on them to force their cooperation in the event they resisted. While there was apparently little dirt found on Captain Fritz or Chief Curry,* there were some issues in Sheriff Decker's past that would compromise his ability to withstand Johnson's demands. According to author Peter Dale Scott, Bill Decker was described in 1946 Congressional transcripts of a political corruption investigation as "an old-time bootlegger" and "a payoff man with Bennie Binion" (owner of the University Club across the street from Jack Ruby's Carousel Club as well as the Golden Horseshoe in Las Vegas) and once "served as a character witness for Dallas mafioso Joseph Civello"). In the absence of dirt, they would simply be coerced into cooperation through the force of Lyndon Johnson's "persuasiveness," which they knew Curry would be susceptible to since he seemed to be overly anxious to accommodate all of Johnson's requests, as will also be seen in chapter 8. It was also a given that he, LBJ himself, might need to make some postassassination calls to the local officials in the event that his assistant, Cliff Carter, failed to "close the deal."

His longtime neighbor on Thirtieth Place next to Rock Creek Park in Washington DC, and a friend before and after that, J. Edgar Hoover, would be enlisted to help in a myriad of ways, possibly before but at least starting immediately after the event; he knew intuitively that Hoover could be relied on to handle the postevent phase after given enough cues to manage the investigation according to Johnson's direction. Hoover's unique abilities for

---

* Curry's vanity would prove to be helpful in phase 2, when he showed up in practically every one of the Stoughton photographs on Air Force One after the assassination, even as the "investigation" commenced back at headquarters.

dissembling, evidence tampering, stealing, and fabrication of evidence would eventually be manifested in numerous traces of his manipulation of his own staff in Dallas, New Orleans, and Washington DC, much of which would emerge over the ensuing four decades.[1]

Hoover knew that if Kennedy was reelected in 1964, his ability to retain his directorship would be in jeopardy. While he had plenty of dirt on both Kennedys, he knew that they also knew about many of his own secrets. Hoover also realized that if he were removed from his position, he would lose his power to conceal those secrets; if the real story of the legendary director got out, his reputation as the greatest crime fighter of all time would be lost, and the new FBI building he had envisioned, with his name boldly engraved over the entrance, would never materialize. Any question about whether Hoover's motivations were consonant with Johnson's would be answered within the first days and weeks after the assassination, as he stopped the investigation at all the key points, after he pronounced Oswald was the "lone nut," New Orleans and Mexico City in particular.[2]

Other high-level and like-minded officials of the government, who Johnson knew were either personally beholden to him or whose own hatred of John and/or Robert Kennedy was at least as great as his own, had been recruited one by one to handle key aspects of the plan. A variety of inducements would be applied, depending upon their vulnerabilities as determined by Johnson as only he could tabulate based upon their individual weaknesses. He instinctively knew who could be trusted to know the broadest parts of the true mission, a number which had to be minimized. For everyone else farther down in the hierarchy, a successively smaller span of knowledge of the entire plan would be maintained; most would become unwitting participants simply because they were overtly forced to or were misled by a superior into unwittingly taking an action that facilitated the series of acts which culminated in the assassination. For example, the need to control the Secret Service—to provide for a complete breakdown of all the normal security elements during a motorcade—would only need the actions of one man at the top: the head of the Secret Service, James Rowley, who was a good friend of Johnson as well as Hoover, his former boss.[3]

Besides Hoover, other key men in the FBI, including his male concubine, Clyde Tolson, and Bill Roemer, have been reported by others to have facilitated the assassination. In Roemer's case, according to author and former FBI agent M. Wesley Swearingen, it is not clear as to whether it was due to his active

---

1. For example, see Swearingen, pp. 97–100 (additional references to follow in chapter 9).
2. Ibid.
3. Palamara, p. 53.
4. Swearingen, pp. 248–252.

complicity, his blind allegiance and acts of omission, or simply his chronic incompetence.[4] Hoover had a pathological need to control everything in any matter in which he became involved, and he knew whom he could trust to carry out even the most questionable orders without objection. By the same token, Rowley knew the men in his agency whom he could trust to carry out his orders, even the most bizarre of them, which would all but abandon the president in Dealey Plaza. Many of the orders that reached down to the field agents would even seem rather innocuous, relating to some fuzzy request supposedly coming from JFK himself about his desire to get "closer to the public," or that he preferred having the bubble top off the limousine when in fact he had always been very cooperative with all of their recommendations and never questioned the presence of motorcycle escorts.[5]

Covert Operations as Applied to LBJ's "Executive Action Plan"

The scenario that follows is based upon speculative but reasoned opinion of the dynamics involved in the "behind the scenes" plan originally developed at the macro level by Lyndon B. Johnson and carefully deployed through his numerous contacts throughout governmental and social associations documented in the other chapters of this book. But it is not conjecture to state, for instance, that he had long established personal relationships with the parties noted, and that these parties had their own long-term associations with the other people to whom they are linked and so on down the hierarchal "flowchart." The underlying facts of the mutual hatred of John and/or Robert Kennedy by each of these named individuals are documented as well, throughout this book and its cited sources. The viciousness of this hatred—for example, by Bill Harvey, Carlos Marcello, Jimmy Hoffa, David Atlee Phillips, David Ferrie, David Morales, and many others—has been demonstrated as well. Finally, the attributes noted for the individuals, here and in other references contained in other chapters, are also well established: For example, that Lyndon Johnson himself was an accomplished planner of complex scenarios, whereby the subjects of them never suspected their own manipulation, has been shown in several places already. Likewise, Bill Harvey and David Ferrie were similarly gifted, in their case at a "micro" level, involving the logistical movements of men and equipment. The venomous nature of H. L. Hunt's and Clint Murchison's attitudes toward Kennedy has been proven—if not, consider Hunt's statement that there was "no way left to get these traitors out of our

---

5. See Palamara, Vincent M., *Boring Is Interesting*. http://www.maryferrell.org/mffweb/ archive/viewer/showDoc.do?absPageId=519589
6. Scheim, p. 69 (ref. Joachim Joesten, *The Case Against Lyndon Johnson in the Assassination of President Kennedy*, Munich: Dreischstr. 5, Selbstveriag, 1967, p. 9).

government except by shooting them out."⁶ Their financial wherewithal to finance the operation need not be documented; that is a "given."

Johnson, through a handful of key men noted throughout the narrative, had already ensured that all planning would be "compartmentalized" in a way to avoid any one person having any more responsibility for a single aspect than absolutely necessary, all the way up and down the line. He knew enough about how his friends at the CIA worked their "black bag jobs"—and in the initial planning had discussed the point in depth with them—to know that he had to emulate their secret methods. This meant that the precept of "plausible deniability," combining outright lying with the absence of paper trails or any other physical evidence of illegal conduct, would become the guideline. It would mean there could never be the slightest hint of an explicit order to assassinate the president or other such physical record anywhere up or down the line that could be traced back to its source. All involved would understand that they would support the mission: obey their superiors, never question their authority, accept even the oddest orders strictly "by the book," and understand that the precept "need to know" was the primary governing rule. In turn, they would be assured that they had nothing to fear from any law enforcement agency: federal, state, or local. Johnson's man Mac Wallace was one who understood all of this; it had worked well for him twelve years earlier after his first murder, and he had remained a free man, gainfully employed since then in well-paying classified jobs with defense industry companies even after an untold number of more murders.

Clint Murchison wasn't the only rich Texas oilman close to Johnson and Hoover. H. L. Hunt's top aide, John Curington, revealed that Hunt's and Hoover's close relationship went back to the early 1950s when they were poker-playing friends who shared right-wing political views and a visceral hatred of both Kennedys as well as Martin Luther King Jr. Another member of this group was retired army general Charles Willoughby who was connected to a worldwide right-wing anti-Communist organization, as described fully in chapter 3. One of his still-active contacts in the army was his former boss, General John Magruder, who ran the strategic services unit of military intelligence. According to Gerry Patrick Hemming who was involved in the periphery of the assassination (tagged as another "patsy" had there been a need to exercise the plan B option), Magruder's linkage to Willoughby was only one of the interconnections of renegades from the military back to H. L. Hunt and J. Edgar Hoover; still another name mentioned by Hemming as part of the cabal was Charles Siragusa, the top agent in the Federal Bureau of Narcotics whom he claimed was a lower-level "mastermind" in charge of the hit team(s): "Narcotics is the only way to be on top of intell around the world because you've got everybody on your payroll and anything that moves you know about."[7] These military connections would become most useful in phase 2, when it became critical to initiate the many facets of the cover-up, especially invoking the top-secret, clandestine autopsy procedures.

Johnson's "executive action plan" was devised such that plausible deniability would become the watchword from the top down, through the middle-level planners such as Bill Harvey and David Ferrie, to the bottom feeders, such as Jack Ruby, the actual shooters, and of course, the unwitting Lee Harvey Oswald. The basic tenets of covert intelligence, including the uppermost plausible deniability, were closely enforced by all participants. Dick Russell said that Hemming also told him that Felipe Vidal Santiago "had dealt directly with the Hunts in Dallas but *'they did not want to know about operational plans.'*"[8] Colonel William Bishop, a CIA hit man, corroborated the story of Richard Case Nagell and explained many of the linkages between the Texas oilmen described earlier and certain military officers and intelligence operatives involved in the cabal. One of these was Bill Harvey, who would become the key "pivot" man in the center of the entire enterprise, the glue that held it all together; Harvey has been discussed previously and will become more and more the focal point of phase 1, the preassassination part of the conspiracy. Bishop also connected the Mafia to the conspiracy, primarily through Carlos Marcello, as well as having provided the linkage to Jimmy Hoffa who contributed financially to the shared objectives.[9]

Edward Clark, through his longtime association with Johnson as his "legal consultant/campaign finance manager/partner in crime," had arranged for funding to be collected from all of the parties who wanted Kennedy dead.[10] Through Clark, his main money and influence broker, Johnson indirectly tapped this source of funds to finance his "executive action plan." Clint Murchison and H. L. Hunt were the major underwriters of the expenses of the operation: the French sharpshooters, the Mob hit men, the renegades from the CIA as well as the expenses for the equipment and logistics of moving men and guns into position and paying off the right politicians and police officials to expedite the plan. The understandings between Clark and Murchison, as with H. L. Hunt, would be agreed to over drinks and dinner at the Lamar Hotel in Houston, the Driskill Hotel in Austin, or the Dallas Petroleum Club, with phrases from old Texas colloquialisms, such

---

7. Twyman, pp. 667–668, 777–781.
8. Ibid., p. 624.
9. Ibid., pp. 622–624.
10. McClellan, pp. 180–183.

as "I got a dog that hunts" (i.e., my man Lyndon is going to deliver). Barr McClellan described the understanding: "Not a word was said about crimes. The code was clear. The more obscure and clouded a gentleman's proposal was, the more terrible the plan. Murchison knew that. He knew no one could be incriminated. He knew he would hear more, later, about the delivery of the goods. He knew a payoff would be expected."[11]

Everyone in these groups was expected to contribute, not only for the financial and planning needs, but for symbolic purposes as well; it was a way to ensure that everyone would have a chip in the game as a reminder to be discreet. Sharing the legal peril was the best way to keep mouths sealed. Johnson himself threw in his own chip: Malcolm Wallace, furnished with Secret Service credentials, was there not as a shooter but as a supervisor who would ensure that the planted evidence included shells that matched the Mannlicher-Carcano, which would be found in the "sniper's lair" and the rifle would be stashed along the stairwell on the fifth floor. The other rifle, the precision German Mauser actually used and inadvertently found by other unsuspecting officers, was supposed to be hidden among the boxes so that it could be snuck out later by a policeman on the payroll. The shells Wallace planted had indeed been shot from the planted Mannlicher-Carcano to tie them back to the gun; others had created false records purportedly showing that Oswald had ordered it from a Chicago gun dealer through a magazine ad and having it allegedly mailed to a post office box leased by him. One of the bullets shot from one of those shells—pristine, because it had been fired into a barrel filled with water—would wind up on a hospital gurney at Parkland Hospital, placed there by none other than Jack Ruby shortly after the assassination.[12]

The authorities for the general tactical planning would emanate from Johnson through his back channel conduits to the military and intelligence network they helped establish, as described elsewhere, and from there through multiple channels to men given a very limited span of knowledge. Discreet instructions to destroy evidence of bureau connections to Oswald would be delivered, and requests to begin collecting the necessary funds to finance the operation would be communicated to his friends Clint Murchison and H. L. Hunt. Instructions would flow through to Bill Harvey to begin the complex plans for a three-pronged operation using entirely separate teams to ensure adequate redundancy. Harvey knew immediately, instinctively, that they would be composed of professionals from Corsica, his friends in the American Mafia, and the CIA operatives he had worked with for years,

---

11. Ibid., p. 263.
12. Marrs, pp. 366–367.

including a group of men in New Orleans associated with the Cuban exiles, all of whom he knew shared his passionate hatred of Kennedy. The other operatives would represent the chips from the groups Harvey would line up. The Marcello-Trafficante Mob would contribute their best planner, the odd-looking homosexual pilot from New Orleans named David Ferrie, who would not only place and set up the "patsy," and his immediate handler Ruby, but help recruit other men to take shots from the west end of the Texas School Book Depository Building (opposite the infamous "sniper's nest" of the TSBD). Ferrie, like Harvey and Johnson himself, had a natural planning ability as well as a latent hatred of Kennedy and a wish to see him dead.[13] Among his plans was to be nowhere near Dallas on November 22; in fact, he was sitting alongside Carlos Marcello in a federal courthouse in New Orleans at the time of the assassination. But shortly thereafter, as we shall see, he hurriedly fled New Orleans and drove through a stormy night with two friends to position himself in Houston, ready to fly men to Mexico. These participants would assure not only that JFK's bodily protection would disappear at the right time to allow a synchronized multi attack on him, but that the conspiracy to assassinate him would immediately morph into a second conspiracy to cover up the crime and convince the American people that he was shot by a "lone nut." Angleton had groomed the hapless Oswald for many years as someone who could be portrayed to be a social misfit and a confused "silly communist" who had already demonstrated his traitorous character by defecting to the Soviet Union.

In return for all their efforts, Johnson assured the oilmen they would get their extensions of their oil depletion allowance, and the military, industrial, and intelligence people got the war they had been promised. A lot of other men got a lot of money for their work and assurances that they would be protected forever from prosecution, under the single caveat that they must keep their lips sealed, forever. Some of the shooters made it to freedom while others died in the mysterious crash of an airplane in the Gulf of Mexico, off Corpus Christi. And Lyndon Johnson would not only step up to the succession plate but be in a position to force the congressional leaders of his own party to shut down both congressional investigations into his own activitities, which had already gotten too far along; had they proceeded, the evidence already collected was enough for RFK's Justice Department to push for an indictment that would have led to near-certain imprisonment. Thanks to his manipulative skills and his deeply embedded tentacles into the pockets of many politicians on Capitol Hill, he had already created enough IOUs to

---

13. Summers, *The Kennedy Conspiracy* . . ., pp. 246–245, 367–368; Garrison, pp. 176–181; Scheim, pp. 218.

ensure that he would be saved from any further embarrassing investigations. He had already developed a legislative agenda comprising pent-up House and Senate bills that were ready for passage as a memorial to the fallen president. The credit, of course, would not go to him; it would be given to the new president of the United States, Lyndon B. Johnson.

Despite the careful measures taken by Bill Harvey and his lieutenants to keep the planning secret, such an audacious and treasonous action would present the potential for inherently risky leaks, which might endanger its execution. One in particular occurred in October 1963 in France, involving Eugene B. Dinkin who discovered the plot as he routinely processed messages between the plotters. He then made the mistake of informing his superiors "that a conspiracy was in the making for the 'military' of the United States, perhaps combined with an 'ultra right wing economic group.'"[14] His discovery—and the extreme retribution it caused to him personally—will be explored shortly, but it is noteworthy here because it proves conclusively that the use of military communications and intelligence assets played a critical role in the preplanning of the operation and was therefore an essential element of a very sophisticated and widely based covert operation involving those very U.S. assets for the purpose of a domestic coup d'état. This is regarded as the single most important of the enumerated instances in which the plot surfaced before Dallas, though, as we shall see, it is by no means the only one.

The Georgetown Crowd Meets the Suite 8F Group

The general political tilt of the members of the Georgetown crowd has been described in earlier chapters; their primary interest lay in international affairs and the contemporary anti-Communist fervor. It was probably due to their notion of privileged erudition that they saw, paradoxically, in Lyndon Johnson the leadership qualities and a willingness to adapt that had the makings for being in their minds a "good president." Certainly, he had known how to "talk their talk," an ability he could skillfully exercise with whomever he wished. His friendship with his fellow manic Philip Graham, often over numerous drinks with their charm and charisma at full splendor, eventually brought him broad support from this group as he mounted his short-lived candidacy for president in 1960. As previously noted, when it became apparent before the convention that Kennedy would get the nomination, Phil Graham, the "chairman" of this group, became actively involved in lobbying Kennedy.[15] He and Sam Rayburn set out to try to convince JFK that Johnson was his best choice for vice president.

---

14. Twyman, pp. 522–525.
15. Davis, Deborah, p. 157.

Johnson's primary source of support, however, was not the Georgetown crowd but the Texas-based wealthy businessmen, attorneys, and politicians referred to as the Suite 8F Group. That both of these groups somehow thought that Johnson represented their own views—on questions of political and social issues, economic theory, and tax policy—speaks volumes about Johnson's ability to portray himself differently to diverse audiences. Johnson was uniquely able to bring seemingly disparate and unconnected groups together to assist him in his plans to become president. Not every member of these groups was involved of course, only those who had to be recruited for specific purposes, as described elsewhere. People from all of these groups had their own reasons to distrust and hate John F. Kennedy, as described in other previous chapters; they had only one thing in common: all were convinced that the plan was not only essential to the "security" of the nation, but it was also, in their view, the ultimate patriotic act that they could perform. Their common goal was the destruction of international communism, but beyond that they were counting on Johnson to fulfill their respective lists of objectives while keeping them safe from prosecution. They knew that, as long as Johnson remained free, so too would they be. The highest-level co-conspirators would discreetly sign on others who they knew could be relied upon to fill out their respective rosters. The men they would select were professionals in their field, thoroughly trained or schooled in their chosen specialties, men who had access to every conceivable tool they would need. The nucleus of CIA men at the top knew precisely who could be trusted implicitly to devise the operational planning that would ensure success. Their recruitment of men like Bill Harvey, David Morales, David Atlee Phillips, and over a dozen others lower in the hierarchy would proceed over a period of many months.

The "Johnson plan" would be based upon the concept that the operational and tactical plans would be carefully kept away from the highest level planners; Johnson and Angleton, possibly Hoover and LeMay as well, consistent with the precepts of "plausible deniability" and interagency secrecy protocols, would protect others throughout the hierarchical chain.

James Jesus Angleton, the CIA counterintelligence master, probably signed on after he found out about Kennedy's secret negotiations, through Lisa Howard and Jean Daniel, to achieve a peaceful coexistence with Cuba. This would have caused many others at Langley similar concern given that such negotiations, if successful, would be exactly opposite their long-held objective of returning capitalism to Cuba. But even more than that, their biggest concern was Kennedy's intent to dissolve the CIA early in his next term if he were reelected. Angleton had been behind Oswald and the other Soviet infiltrators all along and was the "puppet master" who had the other handlers move him back to Fort Worth then Dallas and New Orleans, originally for the purpose of being involved in a fake (and failed) assassination of Kennedy intended to be used as the basis for an invasion of Cuba. But when all of the anti-Kennedy forces described throughout these pages came together as a "critical mass," and it was made clear to them that Johnson was behind the mission and would protect them, the middle-level planners morphed the original plan into the more diabolical scheme to assassinate Kennedy.

The first associate Angleton would involve was Harvey; everyone at Langley knew he hated both Kennedys with a passion, especially Bobby whom he felt was a bull-headed amateur and had no business being in charge of clandestine activities. Harvey would then enlist others with whom he had worked closely in Operation Mongoose, starting with David Phillips and others he knew to be born renegades and fellow haters of the Kennedys: men such as David Morales, Rip Robertson, and Carl Jenkins. It was Harvey who posted David Morales in Miami in 1961 as chief of covert operations for JM/WAVE, with the objective of destabilizing Castro by whatever means they could. Morales was a cold-blooded killer who had been involved in all of the deepest black ops situations which called for someone's elimination. Harvey had no problem recruiting those men, but others were very resistant, at least initially, because even they were afraid of some of the men already part of the operation, such as Morales. The anti-Castro exiles, with whom Harvey and Morales had shared many other missions, were easy to recruit even though they had only the vaguest idea of their single compartment of the entire operation since they had only been told what they "needed to know." According to E. Howard Hunt, "The Cuban paramilitary group consisted of Antonio Veciana, ruthless leader of Alpha 66 and a well-known Kennedy hater, whose CIA handler was none other than David Atlee Phillips; David Morales, admitted CIA executioner with a list of bodies dating back to 1954 when he and Hunt worked to overthrow the Guatemala government. Morales was part of the ground team and was at the meetings at which the 'Big Event' (Kennedy's killing) was discussed and organized. Morales died mysteriously just before he was to testify before the House Select Committee on Assassinations in 1978."[16]

Researcher/author John Newman, in an appendix he added in 2008, after thirteen years of further reflection to his 1995 book *Oswald and the CIA*, argued persuasively that the only person who could have possibly set up Oswald was Angleton:[17]

16. Hunt, E. H., *American Spy*, pp. 126–47.
17. Newman, *Oswald and the CIA*, (2008) pp. 636–637.

The person who designed this plot had to have access to all of the information on Oswald at CIA HQS. The person who designed this plot had to have the authority to alter how information on Oswald was kept at CIA HQS. The person who designed this plot had to have access to project *TUMBLEWEED*, the sensitive joint agency operation against the KGB assassin, Valery Kostikov. The person who designed this plot had the authority to instigate a counterintelligence operation in the Cuban affairs staff (SAS) at CIA HQS. In my view, there is only one person whose hands fit into these gloves: James Jesus Angleton, Chief of CIA's Counterintelligence Staff . . . In my view, whoever Oswald's direct handler or handlers were, we must now seriously consider the possibility that Angleton was probably their general manager. No one else in the Agency had the access, the authority, and the diabolically ingenious mind to manage this sophisticated plot. No one else had the means necessary to plant the WWIII virus in Oswald's files and keep it dormant for six weeks until the president's assassination . . . The only person who could ensure that a national security cover-up of an apparent counterintelligence nightmare was the head of counterintelligence.

The mission would be run by men who were experts at covert intelligence work, operatives whose experience included assassinations of leaders in Central and South America and Africa. They learned their espionage, counterespionage, and assassination skills during the early cold war, just as the CIA was coming into being, and were dedicated to preventing the spread of communism throughout the world, but especially in the Western Hemisphere. The key participants were rogue government officials using their cover and the tools available to them. There were men with intelligence backgrounds as well as exiles from Cuba. Many of the operatives involved in setting up Oswald were told that the operation was to fake an assassination for the purpose of scaring Kennedy into taking forceful action against Castro. Most were so hateful of JFK that they would not have flinched at being involved in his assassination even if they knew it was to be real. They were convinced that John Kennedy had betrayed them in the Bay of Pigs incursion and that he now stood in the way of having their homeland returned to them. There were others who represented men who had lost millions when Fidel Castro had expropriated their investments in valuable properties and businesses. Others were part of what J. Edgar Hoover had always resisted acknowledging even existed: the "Mafia" network of organized crime.

The Three-Pronged Plan

To ensure absolute confidence that the assassination of John Kennedy would succeed, the plotters agreed early on that operational redundancy was key. Too many things could go wrong with a single plan, even if there were multiple shooters from two or three directions. In that situation, discovery of one operative beforehand, even one of a low-level handler, could give it away and lead to the exposure of the entire operation, which could only lead to disastrous results for everyone connected with it. Even short of that kind of calamity, if something went wrong with the logistics of putting the shooters or their equipment in place, the objective might not be successful. The men at the top, schooled in "black bag operations" for decades, knew that it would be necessary to run three parallel operations, each one nearly autonomous from the others. It was finally settled that they would be set up according to this loosely defined plan:

• *Team 1*: The first would be a team deployed in the Texas School Book Depository, to include the "patsy," a decoy assassin set up to believe that he was helping to carry out a simulated assassin only; he would take a shot with an old Italian rifle not nearly capable of the precision necessary to shoot a moving target, hitting the pavement in front of the limousine. He would then be served up to satisfy the public need for a quick closure, with plenty of phony evidence generously planted to support the frame-up, but be killed upon capture. The handlers of this naive vagabond, the wannabe spy Lee Harvey Oswald, knew him to be highly malleable, and a background would be fabricated for him that would ensure his guilt would be well established. A "double" had been employed for several months to help create false trails of Oswald's connections to Dallas-area people and businesses; another would be sent to Mexico and Cuba for the creation of a "plan B" in case it became necessary to show a "communist conspiracy" as being behind the assassination.

   Fortunately, Oswald had already been used in a rather transparent operation to insert him into the Soviet Union as a spy, which would now help to establish his credentials as a dedicated Communist for either plan and ensure his continued unwitting cooperation. CIA agent David Phillips (a.k.a. Maurice Bishop) and his operatives were already working closely with Cuban exiles in Miami and New Orleans who would be employed to help embellish his Communist credentials; all of this was more background for getting him set up as the "assassin" with two optional trails for later selection by the new president: A for the "lone nut" canard, B for the international Communist conspirator hoax.

   The expensive precision rifle found on the sixth floor of the book depository (a 7.65 Mauser)—before the Mannlicher-Carcano allegedly used by Oswald was discovered on a lower floor—was put there for use by one of the sharpshooters (either Morales himself or someone under his direction). This rifle—clearly identified correctly by Deputies Boone, Weitzman, and Craig before the first two were forced to recant their original statements—was later snuck out of the building by someone on the Dallas Police Department. Men matching the descriptions of both Mac Wallace and David Morales were seen in the windows of the Texas School Book Depository Building. Lyndon Johnson's personal hit man, Malcolm Wallace, was there simply to help frame Oswald at the scene. He was Johnson's "chip," it being understood that each of the sponsors had to contribute someone just to keep everyone honest afterward.

- *Team 2:* The second team would consist of professional French and/or Corsican assassins equipped with the best rifles available at the time. Their sharpshooters would be positioned on the "grassy knoll" at the south end of the Triple Overpass, near concrete sewer ventilation/access structures, which directly faced traffic coming down Elm Street beginning just past the Houston Street intersection. It appears that at least one rifle was equipped with frangible bullets that would explode on impact, ensuring that any shots taken with it would be fatal. Author Twyman showed that Bill Harvey and David Sanchez Morales had connections to the Antoine Guerini Mob headquartered in Marseilles, France. Moreover, he reported that Christian David had been initially offered a contract to murder Kennedy, but he turned it down, after which the offer was then given to Lucien Sarti who, with two accomplices, accepted it.[18] It appears that he may have been using the pseudonym "John Marty." Unfortunately for himself, as described shortly in detail, an elisted man named Eugene Dinkin was innocently caught up in those connections when he discovered secret communications between Harvey and/or Trafficante and the French Mafia Corsicans.

- *Team 3:* The third team would be comprised of hit men from the Mob, courtesy of Carlos Marcello, Santos Trafficante, Sam Giancana, and others, intent on cutting off the "head" of the serpent, which was out to destroy their livelihoods. They would operate from buildings across Houston Street, the least obvious location: the Dal-Tex Building and/or the County Records Building. Their shooters would also utilize expensive, high-quality modern rifles with finely tuned telescopic sights; their shots would be relatively easy, and their locations would help assure their quick escape as the attention of the few police officers would be focused on the first two locations. Johnny Rosselli would play a double role in the assassination, having assisted in recruiting the French Mob as well as the Mafia shooters.

---

18. Twyman, pp. 424–427.

One of the objectives of Bill Harvey and others from the military or intelligence agencies in the assassination was to trigger an invasion of Cuba. To achieve that, the planners at the operational level needed trails that would lead there when Oswald was killed at the scene or upon his arrest as he attempted to escape arrest. The idea was that the country would quickly get behind an invasion of Cuba once the trail of the assassin led back there, implicating Castro in the murder. The ensuing attack and invasion of Cuba would not only solve the "Castro problem" but it would return the island to the many people who had lost their property to Castro, including the many Americans and U.S.-owned corporations, which lost their factories, mines, plantations, casinos, bordellos, and factories, many of which had been headquartered in Washington DC.

In the event "plan B" had been invoked, Oswald's multiple IDs, wallets, sightings, and travel records were planted in the appropriate places; this created the necessary trails and would have enabled the government investigators to quickly establish a Cuban connection in order to assure this result. In fact, within hours of the assassination, news of Oswald's associations with the Fair Play for Cuba group came from Miami and New Orleans, which quickly led to evidence of his trip to Mexico. It appears that this news was found so quickly because certain of the co-conspirators were growing anxious to put the investigation onto this track; however, the trail itself was one of the reasons this plan had to be discarded early on when Oswald was not killed immediately.

The Designated "Patsy": Lee Harvey Oswald

The state of the U.S. culture in 1963 was influenced by the shadowy mystique of international espionage: James Bond spy novels, a weekly spy television show called *I Led Three Lives*, and a book and movie entitled *The Manchurian Candidate*. In that book, a candidate for the U.S. presidency is assassinated and the vice presidential candidate succeeds to the presidency amidst mass hysteria of the population, allowing the demagogic new president to rule over America, but on behalf of the Communists. Though it was sold in the "fiction" section, the book was based upon real attempts by the CIA to develop a behavior control research project code-named MK-ULTRA. Lee Harvey Oswald, who loved novels, television shows, and movies about spies, would have had many opportunities to see this movie at Dallas theaters as it was playing in the winter of 1962–1963, just before his move to New Orleans in the spring of 1963. If so, he no doubt realized that the movie might even have been made about experiences very similar to his own.

---

19. Newman, *Oswald and the CIA . . .*, p. 162.

Oswald's "defection" to the Soviet Union in 1959, his return under the most expeditious circumstances despite his having (supposedly)[19] renounced his citizenship, and his continuing involvement with the CIA in Dallas and New Orleans make it likely that his connections to the plot of the book and movie were more substantive than his being merely a fan of the genre. In fact, it is now clear, despite the CIA's attempts to keep the covers on its association with Oswald, that he was being groomed for his role in the assassination by a number of "handlers"; it is logical to presume that he was subjected to an assortment of the latest techniques compiled by the psychological warfare unit. James Douglass, in *JFK and the Unspeakable*, best described the reality of Oswald's life and how he had been manipulated from the time he was a teenager to the point where he was readied for his ultimate and final assignment:

> Lee Harvey Oswald, a young man on assignment in Russia for American intelligence . . . [whose life] trajectory . . . would end up meeting Kennedy's in Dallas, was guided not by the heavens or fate or even, as the Warren Report would have it, by a disturbed psyche. Oswald was guided by intelligence handlers. Lee Harvey Oswald was a pawn in the game. He was a minor piece in the deadly game Kennedy wanted to end. Oswald was being moved square by square across a giant board stretching from Atsugi to Moscow to Minsk to Dallas. For the sake of victory in the Cold War, the hands moving Oswald were prepared to sacrifice him and any other piece on the board. However, there was one player, John Kennedy, who no longer believed in the game and was threatening to turn over the board.[20]

The obvious question raised by this assessment is, "Why was Oswald so malleable as to allow himself to be used in this way, since it clearly wasn't for pecuniary gain?" The answer begins with Oswald's fatherless childhood and his early life with a cold and distant mother and siblings much older than himself. His brother, Robert, provided an interesting insight to Lee's early years. Appearing on PBS's Frontline show November 20, 2003, Robert said,

> Lee's fantasy life, to me, became apparent in the 1948, 1949, 1950 period. "I Led Three Lives"—he became really engrossed in that particular TV show, and he was still watching it when I left to go in the Marine Corps in 1952. . . . . he just liked the atmosphere

---

20. Douglass, pp. 40–41.

that you could do anything that you wanted to do, that you could imagine you could do. . . . The fact that he could put on a facade and pretended [sic] to be somebody he wasn't—to me, it gets down to what happened later on. That was a training ground [for] his imagination."

His fantasies apparently extended to the books he read, including various Ian Fleming novels about James Bond's exploits. According to the FBI's investigation of his New Orleans library records and the testimony of an acquaintance of his and Marina's, Katherine Ford, he tended to like books "about how to be a spy." It is ironic that Oswald shared one thing in common with Lyndon Johnson, destined to become the new president of the United States: a determined obsession with fulfilling the fantasies which he dreamt about as a child. In Lee's case, there is significant evidence that despite his young age, he had already achieved some success in his plan to become a spy, beginning with his recruitment initially by the ONI, subsequently with the CIA's initial mission to the Soviet Union, and finally, most recently in 1962, when he became an FBI informant.[21]

Oswald's History in the Intelligence Business

Despite the forty-plus years of CIA roadblocks and lies under oath by Richard Helms, James Angleton, Allen Dulles, and others, the general consensus among serious researchers is that Lee Harvey Oswald was in fact trained by the Office of Naval Intelligence (ONI), under the direction of the CIA, beginning in 1957 as a young enlistee in the Marine Corps. In 1989, Jim Marrs helped to establish, after years of obfuscation by the CIA, that Lee Harvey Oswald was recruited early on during his Marine Corps service, initially by the ONI, to become trained specifically for a future spy mission to the USSR.

Marrs showed that Oswald's service in the Marine Corps was riddled with inexplicable events; chief among them was how his supposed self-study of the Russian language led to his becoming so proficient—in such a linguistically dissimilar language than his native tongue—that some Russians stated that he spoke like a locally indigenous citizen, this despite his long-term documented learning disabilities. Men who knew him during his period at the Atsugi base in Japan—the largest CIA installation in the world at the time—have stated that Oswald worked for U.S. intelligence, beginning with the Office of Naval Intelligence (ONI). Marrs documented how Oswald travelled relatively easily

---

21. Ford: Portrait . . ., pp. 49–52.

in his journeys both to and from the Soviet Union, including getting passports and visas issued as rapidly as possible (a routine procedure for documentation done for intelligence agencies). Marrs also established that the Minox camera found by the Dallas police was quickly changed on the FBI's records as being merely a "Minox light meter." Detective Gus Rose apparently didn't get the memo, however, telling the *Dallas Morning News*, "[The FBI] were calling it a light meter, I know that. But I know a camera when I see it . . . The thing we got at Irving out of Oswald's seabag was a Minox camera. No question about it. They tried to get me to change the records because it wasn't a light meter. I don't know why they wanted it changed, but they must have had some motive for it." Moreover, reporter Earl Golz determined that the serial number on the camera had not even been available for sale in the United States in 1963. In 1979, the lie started to unravel when the FBI released a number of photographs which they admitted were taken with Oswald's Minox camera.[22]

After volunteering for the Marines, Oswald was assigned to Atsugi Air Force Base in Japan, which was also the largest CIA facility in the world outside of the United States. Oswald had a top secret clearance and access to the CIA's U-2 spy planes, which flew spy missions and photographed military facilities over the Soviet Union and China.[23] One of Oswald's roommates from the Marine Corps was James Botelho, who later became a California judge. Botelho stated that Oswald was not a Communist or a Marxist and was in fact, anti-Soviet. After the assassination, a cursory investigation of Oswald's background was made in which two civilians visited him but took no written statements, made no recordings, and only asked a few perfunctory questions regarding Oswald's background. Judge Botelho said it was "a cover-investigation so that it could be said there had been an investigation . . . Oswald, it was said, was the only Marine ever to defect from his country to another country, a Communist country, during peacetime. That was a major event. When the Marine Corps and American intelligence decided not to probe the reasons for the 'defection,' I knew then what I know now: Oswald was on an assignment in Russia for American intelligence."[24]

As a fatherless boy with a loveless mother and an absent brother, Oswald began disassociating himself from the daily monotony and boredom that had started to become the norm. He had been tapped by someone he had known since he was an adolescent, David Ferrie, when in 1956 he joined the Civil Air Patrol in an effort to begin acting out his boyhood dreams of being

---

22. Marrs, *Crossfire*, pp. 189–191.
23. Melanson, *Spy Saga: Lee Harvey Oswald and U. S. Intelligence*, pp. 7–10.
24. Marrs, p. 110 (citing Mark Lane's interview with James Botelho).

a spy and living his life on the outer boundaries of reality. He found more enjoyment in pretending that his role in life would be much more than the other people he came into contact with in the "real world." His fascination with *I Led Three Lives* may have started out as a diversion—but it grew into an obsession.

Although he did not live long enough to stand trial, and his CIA, ONI, and FBI files were laundered in the days just before and after the assassination, there were still numerous trails that end at their doorsteps: Oswald's advanced language training in Japan and California, his early "honorable" separation from the Marine Corps (subsequently changed to dishonorable), the financial help and expedited passport and travel visas he was able to secure, his trip via Helsinki (apparently by military aircraft since there was no commercial flight available at that time) for his debriefings, his contacts with CIA personnel as he entered and exited the Soviet Union and his contact with a number of CIA operatives, including his Dallas handler George de Mohrenschildt, and his New Orleans handlers (Clay Shaw, Guy Banister, and David Ferrie) are all chronicled in meticulous detail by Philip H. Melanson.[25]

Oswald tried to leave home and join the Marine Corps, as his brother had done, but found that the marines were not interested in sixteen-year-olds as recruits. After waiting a year, he joined the marines and wound up in Japan where he became involved with the top secret air force spy plane called the U-2. While he was there, his interests in the intelligence field caught the attention of the Office of Naval Intelligence (ONI), which subsequently referred his name to the appropriate counterintelligence officials in the Central Intelligence Agency (CIA). Oswald had been given very special treatment to facilitate his desire for intelligence work, including the assignment of a very attractive female tutor to help him learn Russian on a fast-track basis. He was given extra leave so he could spend more time with her, mostly in bars in the area around the Atsugi Air Force Base, which was one of the biggest CIA installations outside the United States due to its use as the base of the supersecret long-range U-2 reconnaissance plane from which it flew missions over both the Soviet Union and China. Near the end of his term of service, Oswald was given an early "hardship" discharge in September 1959, which intended to help establish that he was no longer associated with the U.S. military; he would request asylum in Russia on the basis of his disillusionment with life in the capitalist world. He had inserted himself into Russia by way of a mysterious journey through Finland where he was first given infiltration instructions and briefings by the CIA. Similarly, when he left Russia, he was given expedited service for a new passport and then subsequently debriefed

---

25. Melanson, *Spy Saga: Lee Harvey Oswald and U.S. Intelligence.*

in Helsinki. Moreover, using Philip Melanson's and John Newman's original research as the basis for the charge, it is also reasonable to state that it appears that Oswald furnished too much information to the Soviets regarding the U-2, which helped them to shoot down the spy plane piloted by Francis Gary Powers on May Day 1960, six months after Oswald's arrival.

When Oswald and his family were welcomed back into the country, they were met on arrival by a representative of the Travelers' Aid Society, who also happened to represent the rabid anticommunist organization, "American Friends of the Anti-Bolshevik Nations" (ABN), Spas T. Raikin[26] (the latter association was kept from the public by the Warren Commission).* Oswald was then given advance funds to resettle and was shortly befriended in Fort Worth by the unlikeliest of new friends, the urbane, well-educated (and CIA connected) George de Mohrenschildt who assisted him in getting employment at Jaggars-Chiles-Stovall in Dallas, a company doing top secret work for the U.S. Army, including processing reconnaissance photographs of Cuba, among other things.

Somewhere along the line, Oswald had obviously caught the attention of a lot of highly placed people. But at least one man had known all about Oswald well before his staged "defection" to the Soviet Union; James Jesus Angleton was his chief "handler" all along.[27] Evidence provided by Gerry Hemming indicated that Angleton had "discovered" Oswald while he was serving in Japan and had secretly recruited him (unbeknownst to the entire CIA hierarchy at Langley) to go to the Soviet Union in the first place, "dangling" him as an ex-Marine malcontent, ready to divulge top secret U.S. military information.[28] According to John Newman, Oswald was only one of twelve to seventeen other infiltrators,[29] and according to Victor Marchetti, a former CIA officer, in his book *The CIA and the Cult of Intelligence*, the program originally "involved three dozen, maybe forty young men who were made to appear disenchanted, poor, American youths who had become turned off and wanted to see what communism was all about. Some of these people lasted only a few weeks. They were sent into the Soviet Union, or into Eastern Europe, with the specific intention the Soviets would pick them up and 'double' them if they suspected them of being U.S. agents, or recruit

---

* Recall that in chapter 3, Major General Charles Willoughby was identified as a strong supporter of the ABN; the name of its founder, Yaroslaw Stetzko, was on the masthead of Willoughby's Foreign Intelligence Digest. Twyman, pp. 570–571 (ref. Russell, *The Man* . . . p. 254).
26. Warren Report, p. 713.
27. Russell, *On the Trail* . . ., p. 214.
28. Twyman, p. 720.
29. Newman, *Oswald and the CIA* . . ., pp. 171, 172.

them as KGB agents. They were trained at various naval installations both here and abroad but the operation was being run out of Nag's Head, North Carolina." (The reference to North Carolina begs the question of whether Lee Harvey Oswald's 10:45 p.m. telephone call after he was arrested to a "John Hurt" in that state had anything to do with the naval installation located there).

It was likely that the shoot-down of the U-2 incident caused Angleton to facilitate Oswald's quick reentry into the United States in 1962 for the express purpose of using him as a "patsy" for the original plan to simulate an assassination of Kennedy as a pretext for an invasion of Cuba. What apparently occurred was that the original plan evolved and eventually morphed into an amalgamated, and real, assassination plot; Oswald's role simply morphed with it, but he was never apprised of the change in plans, where he became the sacrificial lamb as the "lone nut" shooter of the president in a general plot originally initiated by Lyndon B. Johnson, which was extended, modified, and customized by Bill Harvey and given life by James Jesus Angleton. Given that Angleton's files were not accessible to anyone else at Langley and that he destroyed many of them in the weeks before he was fired in 1974, the answer to this piece of the puzzle will probably forever remain lost in the *Wilderness of Mirrors* of Langley Virginia.

The pilot of the U-2 shot down over Soviet territory, Gary Powers, raised the question about whether the shoot-down of his aircraft might have been the result of information the Soviets obtained from Oswald. Yet in 1962, when Oswald returned to the U.S. embassy in Moscow, he was welcomed back, given his passport and entry visas for his family, and even a loan to return to the country he had supposedly betrayed. Despite Oswald's supposed "defection," the CIA professed to have no interest in him. It maintained that it did not contact him or attempt to debrief him, and it did not place him on a watch list.* The Agency was simultaneously spinning an oddly solicitous and forgiving view of Oswald's record and reputation on the one hand while implicitly confessing to a prima facie case of their own dereliction of duty on the other. A larger picture of the potential uses the Agency might have for Oswald was slowly emerging despite the cloud of purposely created ambiguity into which he had been placed.

There were indications in 1964 that the Warren Commission was fully aware of possible connections between Oswald and the CIA and FBI. Two Warren Commission staff lawyers, W. David Slawson and William T.

---

* A former CIA officer, Donald Benzlea, has conceded that he read a debriefing document on Oswald in 1962. His statement is available on youtube.com as "The CIA Debriefing of Oswald."

Coleman, wrote a report, which was withheld from the public until 1975, that portrayed Oswald as possibly having been manipulated by some of the exiles *(or, by extension, their CIA handlers—ed.)* into a position as the alleged killer of JFK for the very purpose of blaming the assassination on Castro, thus creating a basis for his overthrow.[30] The CIA's lies about having no connection to Oswald's handlers—Guy Banister, Clay Shaw, and David Ferrie—were revealed by a former high-ranking CIA staff officer, Victor Marchetti, who said in an interview with Anthony Summers, he "'observed consternation on the part of then CIA Director Richard Helms and other senior officials when Ferrie's name was first publicly linked with the assassination in 1967.' Marchetti claimed he asked a colleague about this and was told that 'Ferrie had been a contract agent to the Agency in the early sixties and had been involved in some of the Cuban activities.'"[31]

Enter George de Mohrenschildt

Shortly after Oswald's return to Fort Worth, Texas, they were welcomed by a local White Russian community, which was decidedly anticommunist in their world view. One of the leaders of this group was George de Mohrenschildt, a highly educated geologist and world traveler who was known as "the Baron" by his friends, a group which included several men owning the oil companies with which he consulted. De Mohrenschildt was very well connected in Dallas, directly to men like H. L. Hunt, Sid Richardson, and Clint Murchison; according to an army intelligence report on a Haitian named Clemard Joseph Charles and his association with de Mohrenschildt, the latter was also known to be a friend and business associate of Vice President Lyndon B. Johnson; according to researcher Horne, "An excerpt from another attached document reads: "He [Charles] is traveling with a business associate whom I understand is somehow associated with Vice President Johnson. Mr. Charles has an appointment with Mr. Johnson."[32]

Years later, de Mohrenschildt would admit that he was the initial CIA "handler" for Oswald. This, he said, started in late 1961 in a meeting with CIA agent J. Walton Moore who told him about "an ex-American Marine who had worked in an electronics factory in Minsk for the past year and in whom there was 'interest.'" This ex-marine would be returning to the Dallas area, de Mohrenschildt said, well before Oswald had done anything to indicate such an intent. Several months later, in the summer of 1962,

---

30. Hurt,. p. 326 (ref. Coleman and Slawson, "Oswald's Foreign Activities," pp. 110–11).
31. Summers, *The Kennedy Conspiracy*, p. 233.
32. Horne, p. 1491.

de Mohrenschildt said he was handed Oswald's address by "one of Moore's associates," who requested him to meet Oswald. Later, Moore gave "the Baron" the nod to befriend Oswald, with the understanding that this was a favor to the CIA. De Mohrenschildt later said that "I would never have contacted Oswald in a million years if Moore had not sanctioned it . . . Too much was at stake."[33] De Mohrenschildt had even checked with Moore before proceeding to become involved with Oswald and got his response: "Yes, he's okay. He's just a harmless lunatic."[34]

On October 7, 1962, de Mohrenschildt urged Oswald to move from Fort Worth to Dallas. Oswald didn't need much convincing it seems; the next day, he did just that, taking a new job arranged for him by the Baron at a graphic arts company, Jaggars-Chiles-Stovall (JCS), cleverly described by the Warren Commission simply as a "commercial advertising photography firm."[35] Their description of the firm deftly avoided the fact that it had contracts with the U.S. Army Map Service and was cleared for top secret work, including the current project, which involved photography of Cuba from altitudes of seventy to ninety thousand feet, taken from U-2 flights in preparation for President Kennedy's showdown with Cuba. The JCS part in the process was to set the type for place-names to go on the recon maps; the actual maps were not in their shop, but the place-names would have been valuable to a Soviet spy trying to find out what was being photographed and how valuable the intelligence was which was being lost.[36] Oswald was given full access to all the information being processed through that company; security was so casual that anyone wanting a Coke from the machine had to pass a "restricted security" area to reach it. On one occasion, "Oswald overheard two employees as they tried to identify the Cyrillic type of Russian place names. Oswald, displaying his fluency in Russian, offered his help." The Warren Commission decided to soft-pedal Oswald's association with the Jaggars-Chiles-Stovall firm, for multiple reasons:[37]

- It would raise embarrassing questions regarding how he managed to walk off his previous job giving no advance notice and then immediately become employed by a company working with the army in highly classified document processing;
- The matter of his being a former defector, who had famously offered to give the Soviet Union the military secrets he had, which were directly

33. Douglass, p. 46.
34. Marrs, p. 200.
35. Warren Report, p. 403.
36. Hurt, p. 219.
37. Ibid.

related to the secret U-2 airplane and its capabilities and missions;
* That his employment there defied the normal security barriers, which would have kept a person of his background from obtaining a job requiring top secret clearances;
* That Jaggars-Chiles-Stovall was connected directly to the CIA and its agent in the Domestic Contacts Division, J. Walter Moore and he, in turn, was using George de Mohrenschildt on contract and that among his duties was being the 'Babysitter/Handler" for none other than Lee Harvey Oswald.

In March 1963, through help of the CIA, de Mohrenschildt received a Haitian government contract and shortly departed for Haiti, never seeing Oswald again. He and his wife maintained that Oswald had been a scapegoat for the assassination, and it appears they had been unwitting "babysitters" for the Oswalds, without foreknowledge of the fate that awaited the "baby." The Warren Report's euphemistic description of de Mohrenschildt's intelligence connections is worthy of note: "a highly individualistic person of varied interests." Unfortunately for him, three hours after he revealed that the CIA had sanctioned his contact with Oswald, George de Mohrenschildt was found shot to death in his daughter's house in Manalapan, Florida.[38]

According to the official story, on March 12, 1963, Oswald purchased a mail-order rifle from Klein's Sporting Goods in Chicago, which was then shipped to "A. Hidell" at a post office box owned by Lee H. Oswald. Doing this by mail guaranteed that a paper trail would be recorded when, at that time, a rifle could be purchased from any gun store in Texas without a permit and no record of the transfer would be maintained. Interestingly, the commission's own exhibit 2585 stated that "Oswald did not indicate on his application that others, including an 'A. Hidell,' would receive mail through the box . . ." According to the post office's standard practices, any such mail should be returned to the sender. The *current* United States Postal Service Domestic Mail Manual, section 508.4.3.1 a (2) reads, "Other adult persons who receive mail in the Post Office box of an individual box customer must be listed on PS Form 1093 and must present two forms of valid identification to the Post Office." The regulation in effect in 1963 was not materially different than this.

When he was arrested at the theater on November 22, Oswald carried a fake Selective Service card with the name of A. J. Hidell and an expired U.S. Department of Defense card. On April 10, Oswald allegedly attempted to kill General Walker with this same rifle as he worked on his taxes. The shooting incident was witnessed by a fourteen-year-old boy, Walter Coleman,

---

38. Marrs, p. 200.

who stated that he saw at least two men involved in this incident; other men testified that they saw other suspicious activity in the area a few days before that involving more than one man. The Warren Commission was anxious to accept all factors pointing to Oswald's guilt, in order to portray him as a man capable of such violence, but chose to ignore all exculpatory evidence pointing to others, of which there was plenty.[39] Two weeks after this, Oswald's rabidly anti-Communist "handlers" decided he should be moved to New Orleans for additional training to strengthen his pro-Communist *bona fides*.

Oswald in New Orleans

On April 24, 1963, the same day that the *Dallas Times Herald* reported that President Kennedy was planning to visit Dallas and other Texas cities, Oswald left Dallas and went to New Orleans where he proceeded to make contact with a number of people, none of whom were Communists nor friends of Castro, Cuba, or the Soviet Union. In fact, they were uniformly antagonistic to all of the above. He quickly found a job at the Reily Coffee Company, owned by William B. Reily, a supporter of the CIA-sponsored Cuban Revolutionary Council.[40] The Reily Coffee Company and its owner had a long association with the CIA going back to at least 1949 and was located at the center of the U.S. intelligence community in New Orleans, close to the offices of the CIA, FBI, ONI, and the Secret Service. Another nearby office was that of the detective agency owned by former FBI agent William Guy Banister.[41]

In 1963, Banister's private investigation firm, Guy Banister Associates, had its offices in the Newman Building, located at 544 Camp Street in New Orleans. David Ferrie worked part-time as a private investigator for Banister and part-time for Carlos Marcello, doing whatever was necessary to assist the head of the New Orleans Mob; in fact, as we shall see, he was well alibied on November 22, 1963, sitting alongside Marcello at the end of his deportation trial. During the summer of 1963, unbeknownst to the Warren Commission, Ferrie, Banister, and Lee Harvey Oswald were often together at Banister's office, which was only a block away from the coffee company where Oswald worked. Oswald even stamped "544 Camp Street" on pro-Castro brochures he handed out.

David Ferrie was, among other things, a fanatical right-wing extremist who hated Fidel Castro with the same intensity as he hated John F. Kennedy;

---

39. Twyman, pp. 338–341.
40. Summers, *Not in Your Lifetime*, pp. 220–221.
41. Garrison, pp. 29–30.

Ferrie had connections to both the CIA and the Mafia. Guy Banister, a former FBI agent and former New Orleans assistant police chief, was also a fanatical right-wing extremist and anti-Castroite who also had CIA connections. Banister had set up two CIA backed anti-Castro organizations—the Cuban Revolutionary Democratic Front and the Friends of a Democratic Cuba; he was also an active member of several militant anti-Communist organizations including the John Birch Society, the Minutemen, and the Anti-Communist League of the Caribbean. It is likely that Oswald had reacquainted himself with Ferrie soon after he arrived in New Orleans since he had known him since 1955 when they were both in the Civil Air Patrol squadron in Dallas (a unit which had been started by D. H. Byrd, who also happened to own the Texas School Book Depository Building).

The enigmatic Oswald—supposedly a radical leftist having left a community of ultraright White Russians in Dallas—had gone to New Orleans and immediately become involved with still more right-wing zealots, including Shaw, Ferrie, and Banister. Despite all of his "real" associations with right wingers, he then set out to create at least a paper trail to left wingers, becoming a member of the pro-Castro Fair Play for Cuba Committee. The portrayal of Oswald as a pro-Communist, pro-Castro activist attempting to infiltrate right-wing circles is less believable than that he was merely "playing a role," which was carefully designed to appeal to his delusion of himself as a professional spy; it is doubtful that the youthful Oswald could have presumed that he could fool his old friend Ferrie and the even older, presumably wiser Banister, least of all their leader Clay Shaw, all of whom had extensive intelligence backgrounds and extreme right-wing political views. The only realistic explanation for his portrayal as being pro-Castro was that this is exactly how Ferrie and Banister decided he should be developed in the role that they were preparing for him. The role he was being groomed for required that he have a "legend," which was essentially a continuation of his original cover as a Communist sympathizer, which had originally been created for him when he defected to the Soviet Union in 1959. It is known that Bill Harvey had been meeting with Banister in Miami[42] in 1962 through early 1963, and it is reasonable to speculate as to the nature of their discussions. This started just before Oswald returned from the Soviet Union and was running parallel to the time (referenced in chapter 2) in which Harvey was involved in ominous meetings in the Florida Keys, at anti-Castro camps with Johnny Rosselli, David Atlee Phillips, and David Sanchez Morales. The plan Harvey was devising, with help from Angleton, involved setting Lee Harvey Oswald up for later use as an expendable fall guy a "patsy," in a plan that

42. Twyman, p. 706.

was only then being created. They delighted in linking Oswald to the FBI, through a variety of clues left behind, which they knew would force Hoover's hand in the cover-up phase.

Banister had started grooming Oswald shortly after his arrival in New Orleans in the spring of 1963, according to a fellow FBI agent and business associate Ivan Nitschke.[43] The manager of a parking garage across the street from Banister's office, Adrian Alba, had a contract to look after FBI cars and would later testify that Oswald was handed "a good-sized envelop" from an FBI agent in one of those cars. He stated that "Lee Oswald went across the sidewalk. He bent down as if to look in the window and was handed [the envelop] . . . He turned and bent as if to hold the envelop to his abdomen, and I think he put it under his shirt. Oswald then went back into the building, and the car drove off . . . Oswald met the car again a couple of days later and talked briefly with the driver . . . Apparently Oswald is being utilized by the New Orleans field office through Banister's agency to help them infiltrate the Cuban exile community as a way of ferreting out pro-Castroites."[44] At the same time, Oswald was being managed by the CIA through David Ferrie, also a Marcello functionary, completing a circle that connects all three of the main entities, which were then planning the JFK assassination.

The presence of the closely knit intelligence community in New Orleans in 1963 was among the largest in the country, second only to Miami. In both cities, they shared the same focus, and that was vengeance toward Cuba, its Communist leaders, and its continued occupation by thousands of Russian soldiers.

Oswald Himself Helps Advance the Imposter Illusion

Oswald was seen by many people in Clinton, Louisiana, during a civil rights voter registration line as a lone white male standing in a long line amongst all the black people for whom the drive was organized. This was only one event in a string of evidence that Oswald, while in New Orleans for almost six months in 1963, associated with millionaire Clay Shaw, director of the New Orleans Trade Mart, a prominent business leader with CIA connections. The day after Martin Luther King's famous "I have a dream" speech, August 29, 1963, Oswald, accompanied by David Ferrie and Clay Shaw, traveled to Clinton, a small Louisiana town about 120 miles northwest of New Orleans, near the Mississippi border.[45] The odd sight of Oswald standing in line for

43. North, p. 276 (Ref. Summers, *Conspiracy*, p. 345).
44. Ibid., p. 277.
45. Baker, Judyth, p. 467.

about ninety minutes with a line of black country folks, trucked there for the first of a series of major "voter registration drives" sponsored by the Congress of Racial Equality, ensured that numerous people witnessed his appearance. An additional oddity of the situation that many people noticed was that two men waited for Oswald in a new black Cadillac sedan: one was a tall, gray-haired handsome man known as Clay Shaw, or Clay Bertrand depending upon the circumstances. The other man was a very strange-looking character with glaring stare and no hair, other than the moplike wig he wore, and painted eyebrows. His name was David Ferrie, a friend and renowned homosexual, like Clay Shaw/Bertrand.[46]

Clinton is thirty miles west of Kentwood, Clay Shaw's hometown, where he was born and buried. He spent many years growing up in the university town of Hammond, just thirty-four miles south of Kentwood, and Hammond was only a few miles from Lake Pontchartrain, the site of one of the CIA's secret training camps used for the training of anti-Castro insurgents prior and subsequent to the Bay of Pigs invasion. This camp was set up on land owned by a man named Bill McLaney, an old business friend of Jack Ruby's. Moreover, another old Ruby friend, Lewis McWillie, was the manager of Meyer Lansky's Havana casino resort, the Tropicana, when Ruby visited him in 1959 at a time during which they were both involved in smuggling firearms to Cuba; they were still tightly connected in 1963 when McWillie worked for Lansky at the Thunderbird Hotel in Las Vegas and received seven telephone calls from Ruby in that year. Through this connection, Ruby was also involved with Johnny Rosselli, with whom he met twice in October 1963, and Santos Trafficante.[47] According to Peter Dale Scott, Ruby's contacts with mob figures, "far from being meager and easily enumerated, are so manifold as to defy enumeration . . . Ruby was in contact, up to the very hours before the assassination, with establishment figures who in turn interfaced with the intelligence-mob connection."[48]

All of this explains Ruby's comment to a friend in his jail cell after the assassination: "They're going to find out about Cuba. They're going to find out about the guns, find out about New Orleans, and find out about everything."[49] Ruby was wrong, of course. The Warren Commission and the House Select Committee fifteen years later steered clear of getting too close to Ruby's connections to Cuba, to gunrunning and narcotics smuggling, and all his other long history of illegal activities for fear of discovering more

46. Garrison, pp. 122–125; DiEugenio, pp. 32–36.
47. Scott, p. 180; Scheim, p. 225 (ref. Malone, William Scott, "The Secret Life of Jack Ruby" *New Times*, January 23, 1978).
48. Scott, p. 198.
49. Scott, p. 179 (Ref. Blakey and Billings, *The Plot*, p. 302; Summers, *Conspiracy*, 460–61).

information than it could handle.

The Clinton appearance occurred shortly after the FBI had conducted a raid on a building at the Lake Pontchartrain site, July 31, 1963. In that raid they confiscated ammunition, dynamite, bomb casings, fuses, and fuel explosives. These were being collected for the purpose of bombing oil refineries in Cuba. The FBI had been tipped off to this violation of the Neutrality Act and acted on the president's orders. They also captured some key players in the movement but, oddly, released them without filing charges. In this appearance in Clinton, the real Oswald appeared, not his "double" who made a number of other appearances in New Orleans and Dallas. This indicated that Oswald himself was enlisted in the effort to obfuscate his background while creating another "thread on the web." Judyth Vary Baker, who persuasively claims to have been Oswald's lover during the summer of 1963 in New Orleans, stated that the purpose of the trip to Clinton was for the group to meet up with a convoy of patients who were being transported to the hospital. One of the patients was a Cuban man of the same age and physique as Fidel Castro; he had been selected to become a "guinea pig" for testing an injection of cancer cells which she had helped to develop. She had purportedly worked at the Ochsner Clinic in New Orleans on this project with others, including David Ferrie and Dr. Mary Sherman, to develop a "galloping" form of cancer intended for Castro. The Cadillac was parked near the courthouse where the registration line had formed, next to a pay telephone so they could await a call informing them of when to expect the convoy. In the meantime, Oswald became upset that a black lady, who was a college graduate, had been rejected for registration due to her having failed a "literacy test." As the group awaited the telephone call, Lee made a bet with Shaw and Ferrie that he could register to vote simply because he was white, even though he did not live in the district, simply if he said he was just moving there to get a job at the mental hospital. He failed, though, for that very reason, and left as the Registrar said "Forget about a job there, you belong in a mental hospital."[50]

Oswald Leaves New Orleans for Good

As noted in chapter 2, Antonio Veciana tied David Phillips (known to him as his code name, Maurice Bishop) directly to Lee Harvey Oswald when he saw the two engaged in a conversation in Dallas in late August or early September 1963. The primary function of David Atlee Phillips's *operation AMSPELL* was to oversee one of the most bitterly anti-Kennedy Cuban

---

50. Baker, Judyth, pp. 468–469.

exile groups, known as the Directorio Revolucionario Estudiantil (DRE). Whether this was actually Oswald or his look-alike double has never been resolved.

The Agency's tolerance of what would otherwise clearly be treasonous acts was extended further for Oswald. When he applied for a new passport in New Orleans on June 24, 1963, he was favored with the issuance of a new one overnight, despite the fact that he had stated that his destination, again, was the Soviet Union.[51] On September 17, 1963, when Oswald went to the Mexican consulate in New Orleans to apply for and receive a tourist permit (No. 24085), the person in line immediately in front of him—the person who received permit No. 24084, was William Gaudet, a longtime CIA contact agent.[52]

Oswald in Mexico and the Dissembling of the FBI, the CIA, and Lyndon B. Johnson

Immediately after the assassination, it would become clear to Johnson that Oswald had to be set up as a "patsy" because the photographs received from the CIA in Mexico City clearly showed that the man purported to be Oswald at the Soviet Embassy was, in fact, an imposter. In telephone calls Saturday morning, beginning less than twenty-four hours after the assassination, Johnson and Hoover discussed the early results of FBI investigations into the death of President Kennedy. The first of these, recorded at 10:01 a.m. on November 23, appears to have been mysteriously erased, but a transcript of the call survived the erasure. In it, Hoover told Johnson that tapes of Oswald contacting the Soviet Embassy in Mexico City didn't match the voice of the living Oswald. Hoover said, "*It appears that there is a second person who was at the Soviet Embassy down there.*" (The text of this transcript is contained in chapter 7). As John Newman observed, this impersonation of Oswald "had to be suppressed in order to maintain the lone nut façade called for in the Katzenbach directive . . . there was a darker purpose, however, for the suppression. As long as the tapes survived, the story in them was undermined by the fact that Oswald's voice was not on them. *The cover-up of the Mexico tapes began three hours after Hoover told Johnson that the voice on them was not Oswald's. If this dark detail became widely known, LBJ would not be able to play the WW III trump card on leaders like Senator Russell and Chief Justice Warren. It is virtually certain that the order to concoct a cover story saying the tapes were erased before the assassination*

---

51. Melanson. p. 21.
52. Newman, *Oswald and the CIA*, pp. 346–47.
53. Newman, *Oswald and the CIA*, p. 633.

came from the White House."[53] (Emphasis added.)

An FBI memo was sent to both the White House and the Secret Service as a follow-up to the telephone call between Hoover and Johnson to confirm to them that the alleged assassin had been impersonated in phone calls to the Soviet Embassy in Mexico City; this was a clear indication that, not only was there a conspiracy in the assassination, but a significant effort had been made to "set up" Oswald as a killer. As documented by author Scott, among others, the inescapable point of this FBI memo was that in fact, Oswald was the "patsy" which he claimed to be:

> The CIA advised that on October 1, 1963, an extremely sensitive source had reported that an individual identified himself as Lee Oswald, who contacted the Soviet Embassy in Mexico City inquiring as to any messages. Special Agents of this Bureau, who have conversed with Oswald in Dallas, Texas, have observed photographs of the individual referred to above, and have listened to a recording of his voice. These special agents are of the opinion that the above-referred-to individual was not Lee Harvey Oswald.[54]

Ordinarily, the fact that the only suspect under investigation in a major crime had been impersonated shortly before the crime would cause an all-out intensive investigation of the circumstances and be considered exculpatory evidence of the suspect's innocence. Even more stunning was the fact that in one of the recordings, a man impersonating Oswald had referred to a meeting with a Soviet official well known to the CIA and FBI, Valery Kostikov, who had already been under investigation because of his involvement with a unit of the KGB, which specialized in assassinations, "Department 13." This otherwise inexplicable impersonation takes on an entirely new meaning in the context of the Oswald impersonator attempting to make it appear that Oswald was a hired killer, one hired by the Soviet Union to assassinate the president of the United States. In this scenario, Lyndon Johnson's later comment was probably about right. It was a prescription for World War III. It was that realization that apparently caused him to decide to go with the "lone nut" scenario, probably out of fear that such a war would put his own life in jeopardy.

Author Jefferson Morley, working closely with Michael Scott—the son of Winston Scott, who in 1963 was the CIA's station chief of Mexico City, found that Oswald was linked to four CIA coded operations: *AMSPELL, LIERODE, LIENVOY,* and *LIEMPTY,* the last two of which Win Scott

---

54. Scott, *Deep Politics*, pp. 41–42.
55. Morley, p. 169.

oversaw; the first two were overseen by David Atlee Phillips.[55] Oswald's file in Washington was held within the Counterintelligence Division, by the Special Investigations Group, and any questions about him were answered by men and women who reported to the legendary James Jesus Angleton.[56] One of the men who reported to Angleton at that time was Bill Harvey, RFK's bitter enemy; David Atlee Phillips and David Morales were others. Harvey, Phillips, and Morales were all deeply involved with Operation Mongoose and the most militant Cuban exiles affiliated with Alpha 66, including Antonio Veciana, examined in chapter 2.

Author Morley also established that the higher-ups at CIA headquarters in Langley purposely kept Win Scott "out of the loop" when he inquired about Oswald as a result of his trip to Mexico and omitted the latest information they had obtained from the FBI. Their response to his inquiry, which was not handled in the normal, routine manner as might be expected, was prepared with the assistance of three people from Angleton's office and given the final approval of Richard Helms' highest-level assistant, Tom Karamessines. The "latest information" they cabled back to Win Scott was that, after having spent over two years in the Soviet Union, "he and his Soviet wife have exit permits and Dept. of State had given approval for their travel with infant child to USA."[57] The CIA failed to inform their own man in Mexico City of the reports they had received from the FBI filed by agent Hosty advising of Oswald's move to New Orleans or of his subsequent clashes with the DRE in New Orleans. The record showed that both had been in the Oswald "201" file when the response to Scott's cable was being drafted; in fact, the latter report had just been placed into the Oswald file less than a week before that.[58]

When Jefferson Morley and John Newman interviewed former CIA administrator Jane Roman in 1995 regarding the above incident, she acknowledged that the handling of this cable was very unusual, that it was "indicative of some sort of operational interest in Oswald's file . . . a keen interest in Oswald held very closely on the need-to-know basis." She could not explain her own behavior in the incident thirty-two years earlier, other than admit that "I'm signing off on something I know isn't true."[59]
As Morley noted:

> This trifecta of intelligence jargon suggested the sort of activity usually associated with a covert operation . . . "a keen interest" in Oswald meant that one or more persons involved in anti-Castro

56. Ibid.
57. Morley, p. 192.
58. Ibid., p. 195.
59. Ibid.

operations were focused on the man who would be accused of killing Kennedy. A likely candidate was Dave Phillips, who said under oath that he was interested in Oswald in the first week of October 1963. If the chain of command in anti-Castro operations was functioning, his man in Miami, George Joannides, had reported back in August on *AMSPELL*'s efforts to discredit Oswald's one-man chapter of the Fair Play for Cuba Committee in New Orleans. Phillips certainly knew that Oswald had been in contact with the Cubans in Mexico City on September 27. And he had visited Washington after Oswald's presence was detected and before the misleading October 10, 1963, cable was drafted. But if, as Phillips would claim, Oswald was a mere "blip," why would senior officers at headquarters handle information about him on a 'need-to-know' basis?[60]

The puzzle left by the CIA's highest-level management in their less-than-forthcoming response to their own Mexico City station chief was not the end of this ongoing (to this day*) tale of nondisclosure of information pertaining to the (alleged) president's assassin. When Win Scott continued his efforts to find out more about the mysterious man who had contacted the Cuban embassy in Mexico City, he asked for a photo of Oswald to compare it to pictures of the man they photographed at the embassy; he never received a reply to that request.

Because of the structural barriers constructed by James Jesus Angleton to isolate his files from the rest of the Agency's, and the nature of those files, it is unlikely that the missing pieces of this part of the puzzle will ever be known.[61] Most of the people who might have known about them are now dead. Angleton's command and communications channels were designed to bypass CIA stations, so duplicate files were not routinely kept elsewhere. And as author Morley has noted, "Whatever Angleton's interest in Oswald, no trace of it remains. After Angleton was forced out of his job in late 1974, the CIA destroyed all of his files on Kennedy's assassination."[62] In light of the situation, which had been clearly laid out for pinning the assassination on Oswald as a Communist acting on behalf of the Cuban and USSR governments, it appears that the plan was foiled when Oswald was captured instead of being killed. After being interrogated, and having his voice recorded and publicly broadcast, it became impossible to contend that the voice on the tapes was his. The tapes were apparently flown up

*See chapter 2, regarding Jefferson Morley's continuing lawsuit against the CIA. Also, *The George Joannides Coverup* (JFKLancer.com).
60. Ibid., p. 197.
61. Ibid., p. 201.
62. Ibid., p. 201.

from the CIA's Mexico City station on the evening of November 22.

By November 25, FBI memos made no more mention of tapes, only the transcripts. The CIA then maintained for years that the tapes were routinely recycled prior to the assassination and that no tapes were ever sent. This lie was eventually laid to rest through overwhelming contradictory evidence including several FBI memos, a call from Hoover to LBJ, which appears to have been suspiciously erased (but not before a transcript was made of it, which will be examined shortly), and even the word of two Warren Commission staffers who said they listened to the tapes during their visit to Mexico City in April 1964. The CIA has always maintained that the tapes had been routinely destroyed according to Agency procedures, leaving only transcripts as evidence. Yet Hoover, in his conversation with Johnson, inadvertently revealed that the tapes were available after the assassination, long enough for some of his agents to have listened to them. The Lopez Report referenced a memorandum from FBI's Belmont to Tolson on November 23, 1963, which stated,[63]

> Inasmuch as the Dallas Agents who listened to the tape of the conversation allegedly of Oswald from the Cuban Embassy to the Russian Embassy in Mexico and [who] examined the photographs of the visitor to the Embassy in Mexico and were of the opinion that neither the tape nor the photograph pertained to Oswald, . . .

Even after the destruction of the tapes story was announced, the tapes were still not destroyed; it appears that the CIA's Mexico City station chief, Winfield Scott, hid the original copy, evidently with at least the acquiescence of James Jesus Angleton. Win Scott hid the tapes in his safe because he had been upset by disinformation being put out by Langley, blaming the confusion on the Mexico City station's errors regarding Oswald's alleged appearance, including the bungled photographic and audio tape recording. Scott even went further than that; he bought copies of the tape from Oswald's radio debate so that he could compare the voice on the audio tape in his file to that of the radio debate recording, of course finding that there was no match.[64]

In his biography of Win Scott, Jefferson Morley discovered that years later, two days after Scott died in 1971 in Mexico City, his widow Janet Scott had a visitor: James Jesus Angleton. She did not exactly like or trust him and asked him sarcastically, "Why did it take so long for you to come?" After the normal pleasantries, he told her he wanted to be sure she collected

63. Scott, *Deep Politics*, pp. 41–42.
64. Newman, p. 635.

everything which he was entitled to, implicitly leaving a vague threat about the need for her cooperation in collecting agency materials. She gave him permission to go through Win's private study the next day. Included in the material taken was his personal correspondence and financial records and a 220-page manuscript he had been working on entitled *It Came to Little*. He also took a stack of reel-to-reel tape boxes, the biggest of which was "a stack of tapes three or four inches thick . . . marked 'Oswald.'"[65] Fifteen years after that, his son Michael Scott requested the return of his father's manuscript. It was immediately obvious that Win Scott's story had displeased his longtime friends in the CIA, both Angleton and the recently named DCI, Richard Helms. Over half of it had been redacted, leaving only the first thirty-five years of his life leading up to when he joined the Agency. Nothing was left about any of the three decades he had spent with the Agency.[66]

While many of the sightings of Oswald in Mexico were clearly of an imposter, he apparently did make the trip and visit the Soviet and Cuban embassies and was recorded on wiretaps and was photographed. The CIA claimed that they did not have photographs of the real Oswald entering or leaving either embassy until the House Assassinations Committee found three officials who saw a picture and two more had heard about it.[67] "The way Joseph B. Smith remembered it, according to a committee interview with him, 'the discovery of the picture was supposed to have greatly pleased President Johnson and made Mexico City station chief Win Scott 'his number one boy.' He [Smith] said the story was that someone remembered seeing Oswald's face somewhere in the photo coverage of the Cuban or Russian embassy, went back through the files and found the picture. Smith said he heard that story certainly more than once, at least, when he got to Mexico City and perhaps when he first got into WH [Western Hemisphere Division]."[68] The only reasonable explanation for Johnson being happy with the discovery of the one photograph, which showed Oswald instead of the imposter, was that he thought that would eliminate all the talk of Oswald being set up as a patsy and therefore he could be portrayed as just a "lone nut." The truth of this particular obscure piece of the historical record has emerged despite the morass of double-talk from the men in charge of the bogus investigation conducted under J. Edgar Hoover, its acceptance by the subservient commission, and the overall approval of Lyndon B. Johnson who ordered and controlled the specious "inquiry" in the first place.

65. Morley, pp. 6–7.
66. Ibid., p. 15.
67. Russell, p. 495.
68. Ibid.

David Phillips lied under oath many years later when he stated that the CIA had no photos of Oswald because the surveillance cameras were broken on the day of his visit. One explanation for this is that all materials which actually connected Oswald to Mexico had (supposedly) been destroyed because they were suddenly unnecessary. The last-minute changes in plans were caused by the two-day delay in Oswald's scheduled execution, which inadvertently resulted in his photo and voice becoming well known. The scramble to change the "official story" suddenly required that the focus be kept away from Cuba, Russia, or Mexico and squarely on Dallas, home of the "lone nut." Whatever the original intent of his handlers in creating the numerous preassassination "sightings" might have been, suddenly that avenue came to a dead end, and the story was now to be that he was acting entirely on his own in his deranged plot to kill the president. Clearly, Oswald could not be portrayed to have been involved with anyone else, certainly not set up by offshore enemies in an international Communist conspiracy.

Another Unexplained "Oswald" Appearance

In September 1963, three men showed up at the apartment of Sylvia Odio, the daughter of one of Castro's political prisoners who had organized a Dallas chapter of JURE (Junta Revoluncionaria), an anti-Castro Cuban exile organization founded by her father in Miami. Two of the men were Latinos, either Cuban or Mexican. The third was American, introduced to her as "Leon."* The following day, the spokesman for the trio, "Leopoldo" told Ms. Odio by telephone that "Leon" was an ex-marine, a crack rifle shot, and someone who believed not only that Castro should be killed but Kennedy too because of his betrayal at the Bay of Pigs. She didn't see or hear anything else from them for two months but immediately after the assassination when she and her sister saw the pictures of Lee Harvey Oswald being broadcast on television, they were both shocked and astonished to see that this was the same person who had been introduced to them that night in September.[69]

If this man had indeed been Lee Harvey Oswald, as the Odios claimed, then her report was obviously clear evidence of a conspiracy; if it was an Oswald look-alike who appeared at her door, it was still prima facie evidence that he was being set up as the "patsy" which he claimed to be. According to Judyth Baker's account, Oswald was flown from the Houma-Terrebonne airport in Louisiana to Austin Texas to deliver files from a "Mr. Le Corque" to Lyndon Johnson's attorneys there, and to receive an

---

* In New Orleans, Oswald had also been introduced to others by Banister as "Leon."
69. Ibid., pp. 72–73.

envelope stuffed with cash. Clay Shaw also gave Oswald a zippered bag with two thermoses containing the deadly cancer cells which would be delivered to Mexico City. He went into the city of Austin with the Latinos who met them with a rental car and later, alone by then, decided spontaneously to go to the Selective Service office there to complain about his discharge from the Marine Corps having been changed to "dishonorable." She believed that he did it to create an alibi and to confuse the timelines for his whereabouts, already suspicious of being set up as a "patsy." When he returned to meet with the Latinos he had met at the airport, they left for the airport and flew on to Dallas. He then accompanied the two Latinos to visit Sylvia Odio, being introduced to her as "Leon Oswald." Afterwards, he was flown back to Houston, where he boarded a bus to Laredo. All of this was accomplished in the same timeframe that the Warren Commission claimed Oswald was riding in a bus from New Orleans to Houston, before boarding the one to Laredo.[70]

Ms. Odio had made a very impressive, compelling, and convincing witness, one who had placed a potential bombshell at the commission's door, which caused the members some trepidation since her testimony was in direct conflict with their planned conclusions. Toward the end of the Warren Commission's term, J. Edgar Hoover moved to quell the commission's dilemma when he claimed to have found the three men in California and therefore Oswald could not have been at Ms. Odio's apartment; they were subsequently questioned and exonerated, but by then the report was at the printers and the commission had been adjourned.

Like many of the details surrounding the events leading up to the assassination, these reports now seem intertwined, twisted, ragged, and tangled. That is the inevitable result of their having been created through a very complex web of covert intelligence operatives laying the groundwork for an assassination and an evidence trail that would lead in multiple directions away from its real center. On this particular thread of the web, we can see the commission deftly balancing the need for demonstrating its effectiveness and thoroughness against a major piece of conflicting evidence. Had it not been for Hoover's eleventh-hour announcement, they would have had great difficulty getting past her testimony, and it is as difficult now as it was then for the commission to ignore her testimony. J. Edgar Hoover's ability to step in at exactly the right moment to redirect the course of the commission's deliberations was invaluable to the new president Lyndon B. Johnson and his effort to put a lid on the entire affair weeks before the 1964 presidential election.

---

70. Baker, Judyth, pp. 496–498.

More Appearances of an Oswald Impersonator

On May 29, 1963, a man using the name Osborne showed up at a New Orleans printing company to place an order for several hundred "Hands off Cuba" handbills. The same man who the owner of the printing company, Douglas Jones, described as a "husky-type" man who had the "appearance of a laborer" showed up again a week later, paying the bill in cash. The FBI questioned both Jones and his secretary about this incident; neither of them could identify the picture of Oswald as having been the man in question. This was highly exculpatory evidence of a conspiracy, which the FBI tried to hide.[71] When the Secret Service began looking into the incident, "FBI Washington immediately contacted the FBI's liaison with James J. Rowley to request that Rowley have his agent stand down. That same day, December 12, Rice received instructions from Secret Service headquarters in Washington to drop his investigation into the matter. He was informed, in effect, that he was poaching in an area of the investigation that was exclusively the FBI's domain. [John] Rice [the Secret Service agent in New Orleans] was clearly dumbfounded."[72] Rice was apparently not aware that the investigation had long since been closed down; in fact, "Hoover fired off a memo to the General Investigative Division saying, 'Wrap up investigation; seems to me we have the basic facts now'" on Tuesday, November 26, 1963, the day after Kennedy's funeral and requested the report be "completed here at Seat of Government" by Friday, November 29, despite his knowledge of the many loose ends still unresolved.[73]

There were several other incidents which show that Oswald was being systematically impersonated during the weeks leading up to the assassination, all while the real Lee was verified to be with his wife and Ruth Paine, their landlady. A very detailed account of these incidents was developed by Jim Marrs, partly with previous documentation by others as noted therein, including names, dates, and citations to sworn testimony before the Warren Commission; the following is a consolidated summary of this original compelling research:[74]

- On April 1, 1963, a former immigration inspector interviewed "Lee Harvey Oswald" in a jail cell in New Orleans because he claimed to be a Cuban alien, which the inspector found to be untrue;

---

71. McKnight, p. 16.
72. Ibid.
73. Ibid., p. 20.
74. Marrs, pp. 539–550.

- On September 25, 1963, an official with the Selective Service system in Austin, Texas, reported that a Harvey Oswald visited her to get his military discharge changed from "other than honorable" to "honorable";
- On November 7, 1963, a man drove up in a blue/white two-tone Ford with his wife to a furniture store that still had a "Guns" sign in the window from its previous tenant. The man waved his wife into the store to look at furniture and indicated he needed to find a gun store for a repair and was referred to the Irving Sports Shop where he left a rifle that he would never reclaim. He had written the name Oswald on the claim ticket.[75]
- On November 8, 1963, a man claiming to be Oswald attempted to cash a check for $189 in a small Irving grocery store;
- On November 9, 1963, a man named Oswald bragged to a car dealer in Dallas that he would be coming into a large amount of money in a few weeks. He produced a driver's license and then test drove a new car at speeds up to 70 mph and recklessly weaving through traffic on the Stemmons Expressway. The salesman, Al Bogard, told one of the other salesmen that he drove like a "madman." Of course, the real Oswald did not drive and did not have a driver's license, yet the salesmen identified him as Oswald.
- For several days beginning November 10, 1963, a man named Lee Oswald began showing up at the Sports Drome Rifle Range in Dallas to practice shooting his rifle. "Thirteen year old Sterling Wood was shooting with his father when the two noticed an unusual flame spouting from the rifle of the man next to them. The father told the boy it was okay; the rifle was only an Italian carbine, and the man was an excellent shot. When Dr. Wood looked over at his neighbor's target, he saw that most of the hits were in the bull's-eye. The few that missed were outside it by an inch or two. After watching this for a while, Sterling walked over to the man and asked if it was a 6.5 Italian carbine with a four-power scope. The man replied that it was. Garland Slack had talked briefly to this mysterious marksman on November 10 at the same range. Exactly one week later the man burned himself into Slack's memory. While on the next firing slot, he began shooting at Slack's target. And hitting it. All three witnesses later identified the rifleman as Lee Oswald. Sterling was also right about the rifle."[76]

Regardless of the recollections of these witnesses whose sightings of Oswald were brief and several weeks old by the time of their testimony, the real Oswald was not in the places they stated; he was either at work or home.

---

75. DiEugenio, pp. 55–56.
76. DiEugenio, pp. 55–56 (referencing Popkin, *The Second Oswald*, p. 86 and Meagher, *Accessories*, p. 370–372).

In all of these cases, the Warren Commission concluded that Oswald could not have been present and thus used that as an excuse to summarily dismiss the claims. Evidently, the absence of a real investigative process, or even simple, logical curiosity—or perhaps it was simply the continued prodding of Johnson, Hoover, and their minions—caused this "blue ribbon committee" to ignore these important leads and therefore the obvious, unanswered, question: who *was* pretending to be Oswald and why?

The Oswald Setup Continues from New Orleans, November 22, 1963

As the operatives in Dallas prepared for their work, the New Orleans Mafia chief Carlos Marcello's final day on trial was proceeding. One of the CIA contract agents with whom he had planned JFK's assassination, David Ferrie, attended the trial with him and was there when Judge Herbert Christenberry read a note that had just been handed to him by the bailiff announcing the news from Dallas. After a brief recess, the trial continued, ending with the acquittal of Marcello. Immediately afterward, Ferrie set out on a road trip to Houston, driving all night through a violent thunderstorm with two young male companions. Early the next day, November 23, he went to the Winterland Skating Rink, taking calls and calling others on a payphone.[77] One of the calls was to Marcello's headquarters back in New Orleans.[78]

Dick Russell reported that "when he [Ferrie] returned to New Orleans, he learned from Marcello's attorney, G. Wray Gill, that his own library card had apparently been found on Lee Harvey Oswald after the alleged assassin's arrest."[79] Ferrie panicked on this news and went to Dallas, frantically searching for anyone knowing the whereabouts of his library card, including Oswald's former landlady, his neighbor, and several former members of the Civil Air Patrol where Ferrie and Oswald had first met.[80] Russell also interviewed a friend of Ferrie's, Raymond Broshears, who provided many details of Ferrie's unique personality that explain some of these actions. Broshears stated that Ferrie was convinced that Kennedy was a Communist and that he believed that the United States would soon be at war with the USSR because of the continuing struggles between the superpowers over Cuba; he was also convinced that the Soviet nuclear bombs and missiles were still in Cuba, which would lead to an all-out atomic holocaust within the United States.[81]

---

77. Russell, p. 574.
78. Ibid.
79. Russell, p. 575.
80. Ibid.
81. Ibid., pp. 574–575.

According to Broshears, the reason Ferrie suddenly took the trip to Texas was that he "was to meet a plane. He was going to fly these people on to Mexico, and eventually to South Africa, which did not have an extradition treaty with the United States. They had left from some little airfield between Dallas and Fort Worth, and David had a twin-engine plane ready for them, and that was the purpose of his mad dash through a driving rainstorm from New Orleans. But the plane crashed off the coast of Texas near Corpus Christi. That was what David was told in the telephone booth that day. Apparently they had decided to try to make it to Mexico on their own. They did not."[82]

Other Evidence of the Oswald Frame-up

On January 22, 1964, as it met in executive session, "the Warren Commission heard from both Dallas District Attorney Henry Wade and Texas attorney general Waggoner Carr that Oswald had been an FBI informant since September, 1962, that he had a federal government voucher for $200 at the time of his arrest, and that FBI Agent James Hosty's name and phone number were in his address book."[83] Yet when the FBI originally supplied it with a list of the names in Oswald's notebook, Hosty's name had been omitted.[84] The transcript of that meeting revealed a great amount of concern that this information would cause them problems if it were ever made public:

LEE RANKIN:	*"If that was true and it ever came out . . . then you would have people think that there was a conspiracy to accomplish this assassination.*
HALE BOGGS:	*You are so right.*
ALLEN DULLES:	*Oh, terrible.*
HALE BOGGS:	*The implications of this are fantastic.*
EARL WARREN:	*Terrific.*
LEE RANKIN:	*I am confident that the FBI will never admit it, and I presume their records will never show it.*

J. Edgar Hoover testified to the commission that Oswald had never been employed by the FBI, just as Richard Helms did when he denied that the CIA had ever employed Oswald. This was only one instance, which would later prompt Majority Leader Hale Boggs, a member of the Warren Commission,

---

82. Ibid., pp. 575–576.
83. Scott, p. 242 (ref. Curt Gentry in *J. Edgar Hoover*).
84. Ibid.

to say, "Hoover lied his eyes out to the Commission, on Oswald, on Ruby, on their friends, the bullets, the gun, you name it . . ."[85]

During the course of the Warren Commission's and FBI's "investigation" of Oswald, his former superior, Marine Corps Lieutenant John E. Donavan, testified to the commission that Oswald "had the access to the location of all bases in the west coast area, all radio frequencies for all squadrons, all tactical call signs, and the relative strength of all squadrons, number and type of aircraft in a squadron, who was the commanding officer, the authentication code of entering and exiting the ADIZ, which stands for Air Defense Identification Zone. He knew the range of our radar. He knew the range of our radio. And he knew the range of the surrounding units' radio and radar."[86] But the Warren Commission carefully avoided asking any questions related to Oswald's U-2 knowledge.

Donavan was puzzled by the lack of interest of the Warren Commission on the subject of Oswald's connection to the top secret U-2. He asked a fellow witness who also knew of this connection whether the lawyers had asked him anything about it, and he said they had not. He then asked one of the commission lawyers about it and the lawyer said, "We asked you exactly what we wanted to know from you and we asked you everything we wanted for now and that is all. And if there is anything else we want to ask you, we will."[87] The frame-up of evidence implicating Oswald also included the planting of Commission Exhibit 399—the "magic bullet," which matched Oswald's rifle—the planting of the weapon and the matching shells near the so-called "sniper's nest" in the Book Depository. The true evidence in this and many other cited books—that ballistics evidence and medical records were subsequently tampered with in order to support the lone gunman theory—further tie together the many unresolved aspects which the Warren Commission had left dangling.

While the preassassination Oswald setup events are at first glance more intriguing, because they are inherently part of the assassination plot, the post-assassination cover-up activities also served to frame Oswald for the murder and to hide his connections to the intelligence community. It is the continuity of the frame-up, beginning months before the assassination and immediately continuing for days, weeks, and months (arguably years and decades) afterward, that tie the two phases together. One of the most important traces of the frame-up was the connection to the planted Cuban conspiracy, which was aborted in the days after the assassination. It continued to be the single

85. Summers, *Official and Confidential*, p. 314.
86. Warren Commission Hearings: Vol. VIII, p. 298.
87. Newman, *Oswald and the CIA*, p. 45.

most important point for several days because Lyndon Johnson used it in his enlistment of "volunteers" to serve on the Warren Commission, including Earl Warren himself who may have been cornered into participating in the cover-up on the basis of the perceived need to mask traces to an international conspiracy. It succeeded at that but in the process aided in the cover-up of the real conspiracy, which was of a domestic design by powerful men directly associated with the very law enforcement and intelligence agencies from which the commission depended for its information.

Traces of the Conspiracy Surface—Before Dallas

Eugene B. Dinkin

Exactly one month before JFK was assassinated, a cryptographic code operator working for the U.S. Army Ordnance in Metz, France, tried to alert his superiors—all the way up to Robert F. Kennedy—that John F. Kennedy would be assassinated in November, in Texas. An FBI report dated April 9, 1964, confirmed that Eugene B. Dinkin, entrusted with the military's highest Crypto clearance, predicted "that a conspiracy was in the making for the 'military' of the United States, perhaps combined with an 'ultra right wing economic group'"[88] He discovered the plot as he routinely processed messages between the plotters (i.e., Bill Harvey and/or Guy Banister and *QJ/WIN*, a hit man of French origin, associated with the Antoine Guerini Mob headquartered in Marseilles, France. A number of known hit men were part of this gang, some known variously as Carlos Rigal, Victor Michael Mertz, Michel Roux, Lucien Sarti, or Jean Soutre).

His mistake was letting certain of his superiors know about his discovery and that he was preparing to leak this information despite his sworn oath of secrecy; evidently, he felt that there was a higher duty owed to his country than to knowingly participate, by omission, in the murder of the president. Dinkin heard through the grapevine that he was going to be locked up as a psychotic and decided to go AWOL, taking a train to Geneva, Switzerland, where he found reporters in the pressroom of the United Nations office to whom he told his story. From there he went on to Luxembourg where he reported it to several embassies and finally on to Germany where he reported it to *Overseas Weekly* where he was talked into turning himself in. At that point, the grapevine rumor came true. His reward for trying to save the president's life was to be committed to a psychiatric hospital. By December 5, 1963, he had been brought back to Washington DC. and put into

---

88. Twyman, pp. 522–525.

Walter Reed Hospital where he was given strong drugs and electric shock treatment.[89] He was forced to admit that he was only looking for attention; whenever he said otherwise, he was given an electric shock. "Dinkin said that he feigned cooperation and professed understanding of his unfortunate mental condition being 'schizo-assassination prognostication.'"[90] Dinkin discussed his treatment with his mother, who then wrote Robert Kennedy on December 20, 1963, stating, among other things, that "Col. Dickson and Lt. Col. Black came into the orderly room of his company and phoned psychiatrist Col Hutson and gave him a direct order to find him psychologically unfit to handle security information, and to write a paranoiac evaluation. He claims this to be a frame up."[91]

In a civil action lawsuit in 1975, Dinkin stated that the information he intercepted revealed that "*blame would then be placed upon a Communist or Negro, who would be designated the assassin*; and believing that the conspiracy was being engineered by elements of the military, I did speculate that a military coup might ensue. I did request of the Attorney General that he dispatch a representative of the Justice Department to Metz, France to discuss this warning."[92]

Either Angleton's tentacles reached deeply enough to intercept Dinkin's letter to Robert F. Kennedy or military superiors familiar with Johnson's plan caught it; it is possible that RFK simply ignored it after being reassured that Dinkin was a nut. In any event, it got Richard Helms's attention who alerted a number of others in a classified memo, which stated, "All aspects of this story were known, as reported above, by U.S. military authorities and have been reported by military attaché cable through military channels."[93]

The CIA was coincidentally running its Operation MK/ULTRA (owned by Allen Dulles and operated by Richard Helms) at the same time, which involved psychological warfare, mind control, and hypnosis with a little LSD experimentation mixed in; the evidence presented by author Twyman indicates that Dinkin was quickly swept into that program as soon as he was institutionalized.[94] It was within this same program that Oswald was possibly groomed for his adventures in the Soviet Union and beyond.

---

89. Twyman, pp. 522–525.
90. Ibid., p. 526.
91. Ibid., p. 528.
92. Ibid.
93. Ibid., p. 525.
94. Ibid., p. 527.

Abraham Bolden, Secret Service Agent

Mr. Bolden was the first black Secret Service agent in the United States, recruited personally by John F. Kennedy when the two met in Chicago during the 1960 campaign. He was also harassed repeatedly during his tenure, some of which was spent with the White House detail traveling with Kennedy around the country. Bolden was working in the Chicago office of the Secret Service three weeks before Kennedy's Texas trip when a threat was received in connection with a planned trip to see a football game; the threat involved a four-man Cuban hit squad armed with high-powered rifles. Presumably as a result of this threat, the trip was cancelled.

As he wrote in 2008,[95] the information was not communicated to the Dallas's office. Neither was it provided to the Warren Commission; he attempted to personally correct that oversight, however, before he could tell his story, he was forced back to Chicago under the pretext of his being needed for an investigation; the real purpose was to "frame" him for allegedly stolen Secret Service files. This gambit was successful for the government agents' intent on shutting him up and keeping the secrets, but to do so required sending an innocent man to prison for seven years. His book is very persuasive that he was indeed "setup."

M. Wesley Swearingen, FBI Agent

Mr. Swearingen was an FBI agent, also in Chicago, who got caught up in the preassassination rumors of the pending presidential ambush. He had found out, from a Cuban exile informant named Ramon in 1962, that plans were being put together in different cities which JFK would probably travel to—Chicago, Miami, and Dallas, possibly others—for teams to shoot at the president. "The different teams will make sure that Kennedy is killed, without it looking like a Mafia hit, that's where the CIA comes in, and then the patsy, who takes the first shot, will be killed. It is a very simple plan. The idea is to make it look like there was just one assassin. We practiced this in Florida when Castro was the target. The problem was that we couldn't get close to Castro because his security knows who we are. Shooting Kennedy will be much easier than shooting Castro."[96] Ramon was one of the few exiles left who liked Kennedy and had divulged this information to Swearingen because he had already scared another Cuban—purportedly a hit man working for Castro—into leaving with a

95. Bolden, pp. 41–60.
96. Swearingen, p. 58.

threat that he would spread the word that he was an informant for the CIA and the FBI.[97] Ramon passed on additional details to Swearingen, which confirmed that Bill Harvey was involved in this plan, including how he had been sacked by Hoover for not maintaining contact with his office, that he was "big, red faced, heavy set. He drinks a lot. He hates both of the Kennedys." He also knew about Guy Banister's involvement with a potential patsy who was a real "nutcase" though he didn't know his name. Swearingen had known Banister himself, having worked for him when he was the SAC of Chicago and wasn't surprised that he had become involved in the plot. He continued, "Knowing what Ramon had told me, I could see the assassination coming a year before it happened, but my superiors did not believe the CIA could carry out such a dastardly deed as to kill the president of the United States."[98]

Swearingen said that he told his SAIC, Bill Roemer, the story he had gotten from Ramon, but he thought Ramon was a "nutcase" He then decided to tell Supervisor Joseph Culkin "and then write an office memo to the SAC under the caption 'Chicago Mob and the CIA Plan to assassinate President Kennedy. Miscellaneous File 62-0.'" Culkin's response was "Is that your joke for the day, Ivan?" The nickname Ivan referred to how Swearingen dressed up like a Russian to keep warm during Chicago's cold winters. His reward for filing this report was getting a transfer to Paintsville, Kentucky, then to London, Kentucky, and later from that outpost to New York City. On the day Kennedy was assassinated, he was in a training class in Washington when Inspector W. Mark Felt (later identified as the anonymous character "Deep Throat" of Watergate infamy) ran in and yelled, "President Kennedy has just been shot in Dallas!" He volunteered to go immediately to Dallas, telling Felt that he had "reason to believe Kennedy's shooting may involve a conspiracy between the CIA, the Mafia and some Cuban exiles. I can be there in a few hours. If you pick other agents from around the country they will have to dictate leads on their cases, go home, pack, make reservation, say good-bye to their kids, and then fly to Dallas. This whole In-service class could be in Dallas before dinner this evening. Felt responded, 'That's okay. We'll handle it. You go home and take care of the work you've neglected for the past two weeks.' The Inspector turned on his right heel and walked away."[99]

97. Ibid., p. 62.
98. Ibid., pp. 65–67.
99. Ibid., pp. 75–77.

Rose Cheramie

Rose Cheramie was found unconscious by the side of the road at Eunice, Louisiana, on November 20, 1963. Lieutenant Francis Frudge of the Louisiana State Police took her to the state hospital. On the way to the hospital, Cheramie said that she had been thrown out of a car by two gangsters, either Cuban or Italian, who she believed worked for Jack Ruby as they drove from Florida to Dallas. She claimed that the men were involved in a plot to kill John F. Kennedy. Cheramie added that Kennedy would be killed in Dallas within a few days. She told the same story to doctors and nurses who treated her at the hospital. As she appeared to be under the influence of drugs, her story was ignored.[100]

Following the assassination, Cheramie was interviewed by the police. She claimed that Lee Harvey Oswald had visited Ruby's nightclub. In fact, she believed the two men were having a homosexual relationship. The word spread around the hospital that she had predicted Kennedy's murder in advance. Dr. Wayne Owen, who had been interning from LSU at the time, later told the *Madison Capital Times* that he and other interns were told of the plot in advance of the assassination. Moreover, Cheramie even predicted the role of her former boss Jack Ruby when she told one of the interns "that one of the men involved in the plot was a man named Jack Rubinstein," Ruby's former name, which some people still called him.[101]

Richard Case Nagell

The plain, unvarnished, and undeniable truth regarding Richard Case Nagell is that he shot up a bank in El Paso so that he would be arrested and be in jail on the day that the JFK assassination occurred so that he couldn't be accused of being a part of the conspiracy. The only thing he got wrong about that was the date of the assassination, which he thought would come in September or October. He did this in order to avoid being connected with the crime, figuring that a couple of years in jail beat being locked away for the rest of his life. The facts are widely available even though the FBI tried repeatedly to obfuscate and bury his testimony and destroy his credibility by questioning his mental capacity to testify. Dick Russell, in his book *The Man Who Knew Too Much*, tells the story of Nagell, a man who, two months before Kennedy's assassination, walked into the bank, pulled out a Colt .45 caliber pistol, fired two shots into the

---

100. Hancock, pp. 460–470 (Ref. HSCA and U.S. Customs reports).
101. Ibid.

ceiling, and then calmly walked back outside and sat on the curb waiting to be arrested. When later questioned by the FBI, he would only say that "I would rather be arrested than commit murder and treason."[102]

Nagell had been an army counterintelligence officer in the late 1950s who had been advised that "in the event I was apprehended, killed or compromised during the performance of my illegal Field Operations Intelligence (FOI) duties, the Department of the Army would publicly disclaim any knowledge of or connection with such duties, exercising its right of plausible denial."[103]

While he was stationed in Japan in the late 1950s, Nagell worked side by side with Lee Harvey Oswald, both of whom were being trained in counterintelligence under an operation having the code name "Hidell," which Oswald would later use as part of his alias, "Alek James Hidell."[104] Continuing his role as a double agent, Nagell began working with Soviet intelligence in Mexico City, reporting back to the CIA and working under Desmond FitzGerald; he was assigned the task of monitoring Oswald after he had returned from Russia. He became aware of the fact that Oswald was involved with two Cuban exiles in what he saw was a "large operation to kill JFK." The Cubans were known by their covert names, "Angel and Leopoldo," and were working closely with the notorious CIA-financed group of exiles known as "Alpha 66," which was also directed by CIA Agent David Atlee Phillips.[105]

Author Russell described his interviews with an ex-CIA operative named Colonel Bill Bishop who agreed to tell him certain information regarding the assassination "up to the point where it does not create personal jeopardy, legally or otherwise." Colonel Bishop admitted that "we had a *coup d'état* on November 22, 1963." He stated that he had met Lee Harvey Oswald, Richard Case Nagell, and Rolando Masferrer in the exile training camp near Lake Pontchartrain. He claimed that Oswald was in the camp, trying to get involved with the Cuban exiles, having been sent there by Clay Shaw (a.k.a Bertrand). Bishop didn't think much of Oswald's performance as a sharpshooter, saying, "There's no way in hell he could have fired three shots in that space of time, with that accuracy, with that weapon."[106] He said that Nagell was associated with the notorious Alpha 66 group and their "Operation 40," the ultrasecret CIA "hit squad" set up before the Bay of Pigs invasion. This group was described as the "elite troops of the old

---

102. Russell, p. 45.
103. Ibid., p. 104.
104. Ibid.
105. Ibid., pp. 294, 331.
106. Russell, p. 508.

guard within the exile movement," who made an effective alliance with CIA right-wingers against CIA liberals and made up of assassins-for-hire, Mob henchmen, and informers. One of the missions which Phillips had sent Alpha 66 was to attack Russian ships in Cuban ports in an attempt to draw JFK into a war with Cuba.[107]

According to Colonel Bishop, as reported in Russell's book, Nagell was involved as a CIA contract agent in intelligence and was working with the anti-Castro exiles, trying to find out about things "he had no business knowing."[108] Colonel Bishop said that he called Bill Colby, whom he knew from training at Fort Benning, to find out more about Nagell. Colby didn't know Nagell, so Bishop had assigned one of the Cubans to follow him several months before Nagell showed up in the El Paso bank. By that time, Bishop was no longer involved in the operation, but he found out that there was still a Cuban following Nagell when he went to El Paso, though he didn't know if it was the same Cuban he had assigned earlier to do that. In the process of acquiring too much knowledge—information well beyond his "need to know"—Nagell violated the basic precept of his trade and decided he had to take the action he did to avoid becoming caught up in the assassination.

In his doubled counterespionage role, the Soviets ordered Nagell to convince Oswald that he was being set up by Angel and Leopoldo as the "patsy" of the assassination. According to Russell, the KGB had learned of the plot and wanted to avoid becoming scapegoats themselves; their strategy was to destroy the plan by eliminating the designated "patsy." Nagell met with Oswald in New Orleans and gave him the warning; however, Oswald was not responsive. Rather than carry out the order to kill Oswald if he wouldn't quit his role in the assassination, he decided to send a registered letter to J. Edgar Hoover explaining the plot to kill the president. His letter, dated September 17, 1963, detailed his knowledge of the plan, which he thought might occur as early as the following week, in Washington DC, but it was unclear, and he used the word "probably" to indicate that the date and setting were not finalized. About the same time, Oswald was considering a move to the Baltimore-Washington area and had written to the Communist Party and to the Socialist Workers Party in New York inquiring how he might get in contact with their representatives. These letters would also provide a record of his attempt to establish his communist bona fides for any future investigators to ponder.

Bishop stated that he was involved in obtaining funding from the "'Syndicate out of New Orleans, for Alpha 66. At that point in time, Rolando

107. Ibid.
108. Ibid.

Masferrer was the key bagman, for lack of a better term, for Alpha 66. Primarily the funding came through the Syndicate, because of Masferrer's connections with those people back in Cuba. He had ties with Santos Trafficante, Jr., and other criminal elements . . . He also had different ties with Jimmy Hoffa."[109] Russell quotes Colonel Bishop as saying, "Hoffa gave Masferrer $50,000 expense money to partially set up the assassination team. I didn't realize until later that's what the money was for. I didn't see the money, but I heard that from reliable sources . . . It was later, not too long before the assassination, that Masferrer made the statement—more than once, not only to me but to others—that Kennedy was gonna be hit. But hell, I had heard that before, from any number of people, I didn't pay no mind to it. I mean, it wasn't unusual for Jimmy Hoffa or Trafficante to come up with X number of dollars to support the exiles' operation, okay?"[110]

On October 31, 1995, the Assassination Records Review Board (ARRB) sent a registered letter notifying Nagell that he was to be interviewed to obtain his sworn testimony. One day after the letter was mailed, Nagell was found dead in his apartment, the victim of an apparent heart attack. Until then, he had no history of heart problems and claimed to be in good health. Russell discussed this with the Los Angeles coroner Gary Kellerman to find out if a heart attack could be induced. Kellerman's reply is pertinent to not only Nagell's death but a number of other similar deaths of key witnesses as well. "I'm not sure what chemical you have to use, but I've heard of it. From what I understand, it's a chemical that gets into the system and then it's gone. You can't find it."[111]

Dick Russell had gotten to know Nagell better than anyone and knew from his conversations with him that if "an official government body ever took him seriously," as was now finally the case, *"he would probably cooperate"*[112] (emphasis in original).

James Wilcott

Fifteen years after the assassination, James Wilcott, a former CIA finance officer, testified before the U.S. House of Representatives Select Committee on Assassinations that he had handled the funding for a CIA project in which Oswald had been recruited as a CIA spy.[113] In his testimony to the HSCA, Wilcott said Oswald served the CIA specifically as a double agent in the Soviet Union who afterward came under suspicion by the Agency. He was uniquely

---

109. Ibid., pp. 510–511.
110. Ibid., pp.512–514.
111. Ibid., p. 452.
112. Ibid., p. 447.
113. Garrison, *On the Trail of the Assassins*, p. 49.

qualified to testify openly and honestly about Oswald because he and his wife Elsie had resigned from the Agency in 1966 directly as a result of their horror of how the Agency was implicated in the JFK assassination. "Because we became convinced that what CIA was doing couldn't be reconciled to basic principles of democracy or basic principles of humanism."[114]

Wilcott worked in the finance branch of the Tokyo CIA Station at the time of the assassination and knew several agents who had found out the truth of what happened: *the CIA was involved in the assassination*. He didn't believe them at first until one of them told him the cryptonym under which Oswald had drawn funds when he returned from Russia to the United States. "It was a cryptonym that I was familiar with. It must have been at least two or there times that I had remembered it, and it did ring a bell . . . It was common knowledge in the Tokyo CIA station that Oswald worked for the agency."[115]

Trouble in Miami

John F. Kennedy had gone to Miami a few weeks before his trip to Dallas; shortly before the trip to Miami, a police informant had uncovered the existence of a plot to kill him either there or in some other unspecified city. The plan was to shoot him "from an office window with a high-powered rifle."[116] The Miami Police turned this information over to the FBI and the Secret Service, yet this information was never given to the Secret Service agents who were responsible for the Dallas trip. On his trip to Miami, the plan for a motorcade was scrapped, and he was whisked into and out of town by helicopter from the airport. The informant had taped Joseph A. Milteer as he made this prediction; he concluded by saying that "[an investigation] wouldn't leave any stone unturned there . . . They will pick up somebody within hours afterward . . . just to throw the public off."[117]

Normally, this kind of threat would not have simply been discarded as soon as the first presidential trip after that had been finished, at least not until it was fully investigated and the perpetrators brought to justice. Until the plot had been dealt with completely, it would have been treated only as the beginning, and from then on the FBI and the Secret Service would have been on maximum alert. Of all the powerful men positioned throughout these

---

114. Douglass, p. 146 (ref. James Bl Wilcott's Testimony before the House Select Committee on Assassination, March 22, 1978, p. 48, JFK Record Number 180-10116-10096).
115. Ibid. (Ref. Bob Loomis, *Ex-CIA Couple Tell of Disillusion*, Oakland Tribune September 18, 1978, p. B14. Also Warren Hinckle, *Couple Talks about Oswald and the CIA*, San Francisco Chronicle (September 12, 1978).
116. Marrs, Crossfire, p. 265.
117. Ibid.

organizations, from the White House down to the FBI's local offices, who would have pulled them off the job? Why would that have been done?

Gunmen Spotted in Dealey Plaza, November 20, 1963

During a routine patrol in Dealey Plaza on Wednesday morning, two police officers noticed several men standing behind the wooden fence on the grassy knoll, engaged in a mock target practice, aiming their rifles over the fence in the direction of the plaza. The police ran toward the fence, but the men on the knoll saw them coming and quickly departed in a car which had been parked nearby. The officers did not think too much of the incident until after the assassination two days later, when they reported it to the FBI. Though it was acknowledged in a cursory report, the incident was not reported in their major investigation reports used by the Warren Commission. The original report remained buried for fifteen years until it was released as a result of a Freedom of Information Act request.[118] Evidently, someone decided that this particular police report was detrimental to the overall mission, which was meant to prove exactly the opposite of what this report suggested was going on in Dealey Plaza in the days just before the assassination.

---

118. Davis, *Mafia Kingfish* . . . pp. 175–176

PART IV

The November 22, 1963, Coup d'état

Chapter 7

THE HIT AND THE AFTERSHOCK: ANOMALIES ABOUND

Washington's word to me was that it would hurt foreign relations if I alleged conspiracy whether I could prove it or not. I was just to charge Oswald with plain murder and go for the death penalty. Johnson had Cliff Carter call me three or four times that weekend.

—DALLAS DISTRICT ATTORNEY HENRY WADE

The thing I am concerned about, and so is [Deputy Attorney General Nicholas] Katzenbach, is having something issued so we can convince the public that Oswald is the real assassin.

—FBI DIRECTOR J. EDGAR HOOVER*

JFK's Trip to Texas

Before the ill-fated Dallas trip, as the president took a number of actions to begin a U.S. withdrawal from Vietnam, he himself was being eased out of control by high officials in the Pentagon and the CIA. These officials had gradually become very alarmed by information they had begun receiving about Kennedy's secret life and his turn toward peaceful coexistence with enemies of the United States. Some of it would have come from Hoover's wiretaps and bugs placed in Marilyn Monroe's room so that all of their personal activities would have been recorded, including her knowledge of state secrets; then there was the matter of her unfortunate demise, under mysterious circumstances, which was doubtlessly monitored as well by Hoover. JFK's record-breaking promiscuity threatened to become public, with a little help from the "personal and confidential" FBI files available to Hoover and, therefore, Lyndon Johnson. In all, Kennedy's problems in the autumn of 1963 were as bad as they had ever been, and it would be hard to imagine that they could get any worse; they were surpassed only by those confronted by Lyndon Johnson.

---

* To Johnson aide Walter Jenkins two hours after Oswald was murdered by Jack Ruby.

It is clear that John Kennedy never wanted to go to Texas in the first place, but he had been repeatedly pressed by Johnson to make the trip as an early campaign stop. Because of the flurry of investigations into Johnson's involvement with the Bobby Baker scandal, JFK had already come to a decision to replace Johnson with Senator Terry Sanford of North Carolina, according to Evelyn Lincoln. A week before the Texas trip, on Air Force One as they returned from Florida, Kennedy told his friend Senator Smathers that he didn't even want to go to Texas, a comment that Smathers went to the trouble of recording on video:[1]

> **Sen. George Smathers, U.S. Congress 1946–1968:** I came back to Washington with the President. He was laying down. They had a bed in the Air Force One for him to lie on. So he said, "Gee, I really hate to go to Texas. I got to go to Texas next week and it's just a pain in the rear end and I just don't want to go. I wish I could get out of it." And I said, "Well, what's the problem?"
>
> He said, "Well, you know how Lyndon is." Lyndon was Vice President. "Lyndon wants to ride with me, but John Connolly is the governor and he wants to ride and I think that protocol says that he's supposed to ride and Johnson wants Jackie to ride with him." And Connolly was, at that time, a little bit jealous of Lyndon and Lyndon was a little jealous of him, so it's all these fights were going on. He said, "I just don't want to go down in that mess. I hate to go. I wish I could think of a way to get out of it."

Hearing this from his close friend Senator Smathers, it is hard to believe those who have said that it was Kennedy who wanted to go to Texas and that Johnson didn't want him to go.

> In the aftermath of the assassination, Johnson exploded with rage at the fiction—so often repeated—that the trip was his idea, that he had dragged a reluctant president to Dallas and to his death. "That's a great myth," Johnson complained privately. "I didn't force him to come to Texas. Hell, he wanted to come out there himself!" But LBJ was not about to interrupt Kennedy's long wake by protesting his own innocence. He was powerless to silence Dungan, O'Donnell, Schlesinger, Sorensen, or any of the other agents of his humiliation.[2]

---

1. PBS: American Experience: http://www.pbs.org/wgbh/americanexperience/films/kennedys/player/ (at 1:44:30 of the video) Transcript: http://www.pbs.org/wgbh/amex/presidents/35_kennedy/filmmore/filmscript.html
2. Shesol, p. 138.

According to Arthur Schlesinger Jr., Bobby Kennedy said JFK blamed Johnson for not being able to stop the infighting going on between himself and his protégé, John Connally, with Senator Ralph Yarborough. Kennedy was irritated with Johnson because of his intransigence on many fronts, not least of which was the political situation in Texas; he just didn't feel that Johnson wanted to do anything to patch up the growing discord in his own home state.[3] Another person close to JFK was his personal secretary, Evelyn Lincoln, who agreed that Kennedy did not relish the idea of the Texas trip but went anyway because he had made the commitment to do so; she wrote, "Reluctantly, Mr. Kennedy agreed to go to Texas. Advance reports from our own staff and from many other people gave us cause to worry about the tense climate in Texas—and, most especially, in Dallas. Dallas was removed and then put back on the planned itinerary several times. Our own advance man urged that the motorcade not take the route through the underpass and past the Book Depository, but he was overruled."[4]

The preponderance of the evidence shows that Johnson and Connally pressed Kennedy for over one year to make this trip, a trip that JFK tried to put off until finally he was boxed in by a commitment that he couldn't break. Theodore Sorensen confirmed this on video, saying Kennedy "was implored to come to Texas, where two factions of the Democratic Party were at each other's throats."[5] (This begs the question, was this political schism provoked or perpetuated to ensure Kennedy's cooperation with making the trip because of his known interest in getting the matter settled?) Kennedy pretended to look forward to making the trip, but his best friends and closest associates knew otherwise. On the trip, he had to continue begging both men to get along, to ride together in the various motorcades, and to try to make up, all to no avail. It was a trip into a one-party Democratic state, but a territory his vice president could not control despite his best efforts of playing both sides of the spectrum: he had been a conservative to conservatives and a liberal to liberals, yet not well liked by either. Many in Texas had figured this out already, and Johnson feared losing both sides by his pandering to the other as he continued talking out of both sides of his mouth. The conservative side of the Democratic Party had already begun splintering off to the Republicans, and the liberals had been attracted more and more to the Yarborough wing, putting him more in jeopardy of losing his hold on his own party.

---

3. Schlesinger, *Robert Kennedy*, p. 654.
4. Lincoln, pp. 198–199.
5. See youtube.com (http://www.youtube.com/watch?v=z54HP5WdGPY).

October to November 20, 1963

John Connally went to Washington DC on October 4, 1963, to finalize plans for the president's trip to Texas. Johnson and Connally had to convince Kennedy to proceed with the trip since some of his staff had warned him not to make the trip because the risks were too great compared to the dubious political rewards. Two weeks later, Johnson left for his Texas ranch to begin planning a "Texas welcome" for Kennedy's trip. For over one month, he supposedly spent his time doing nothing other than planning for Kennedy's trip, including the mundane planning of logistics for the president's Dallas appearances and motorcade. In fact, these details were largely delegated to the same White House staff that routinely performed that function. By this point, his lieutenants in the special operation would have finished all of the critical tasks and had signed on all the necessary plotters; financing had been arranged with help from H. L. Hunt and Clint Murchison; the equipment was ready; the shooters and false Secret Service agents were trained and ready, provided their official looking credentials; and his own part of the elaborate plan was ready to be executed by mid-November. His personal involvement would focus only on the one event that would become the start of his presidency—the planning of the motorcade and the breakdown of security by every agency having a piece of that responsibility—eliminating Kennedy's protection by Secret Service, the FBI, the Dallas Police, and the Dallas County Sheriff. Within Dealey Plaza, there would be no official security officers of any of these organizations, only a dozen or so unofficial "security officers" having IDs that purported to show that they were official. The handoff to the assassins, by now operating almost independently of Johnson, would be completed at the corner of Main and Houston streets.

Johnson's involvement in the choice of venues for Kennedy's speech was simple: it had to be the Trade Mart because the motorcade route to that location would allow a trip down Main Street, with a little dogleg turn up Houston Street to Elm Street, past the Texas School Book Depository building. That meant that he would need to override the predominant thinking that the Women's Building at the fairgrounds would be the better choice from a security standpoint because it had only three entrances compared with over fifty at the Trade Mart; the Trade Mart also had catwalks above the stage that would provide cover for someone attempting to assassinate the president. Gerald Behn, special agent in charge of the White House Secret Service detail, was against the choice of the Trade Mart for all those reasons; he was in agreement with Jerry Bruno, the president's political-advance man, who testified to the HSCA that he believed the Women's Building was the final choice; this was only one of a number of statements which indicated that the site was changed after the original selection. Bruno had prepared an itinerary on November 7, which indicated that the *Women's Building* was the destination. He had done that because, based upon his experience and observations, he knew that Behn customarily had the final authority to make that decision.[6]

The confusion caused by Johnson's insistence on the Trade Mart as the luncheon site continued for months, even many years afterward. Secret Service Chief Rowley, arguably a key operator in the conspiracy, told the Warren Commission that presidential aide Kenneth O'Donnell was to blame for the choice of the Trade Mart, which was not true. Jerry Bruno told HSCA investigators on December 13, 1977, that he, Behn, and Ken O'Donnell wanted the Women's Building. Contradicting Bruno, Behn told the HSCA in executive session on March 15, 1978, "O'Donnell simply informed Behn that the Trade Mart was the final selection and ordered him to secure it."[7] Behn claimed during his HSCA staff interview that he recalled that O'Donnell's announcement favoring the Trade Mart "was made between the 5th and the 9th of November," yet security meetings were held between November 13 and 15, 1963, during which this decision had not been revealed. Behn got word that the local agents claimed that they could secure the Trade Mart, "and we were going with that."[8] John Connally later made the same claim that Rowley and Behn had made, that O'Donnell had wanted the Trade Mart. Since Ken O'Donnell had passed away in September 1977, it appeared that these statements were an attempt to place blame on a dead man.

As previously noted, Johnson's own man, who he had placed in the USDA, Jack Puterbaugh, was sent to Dallas ostensibly by the Democratic National Committee to ensure that Johnson's key interests were met; he was put in charge of motorcade political protocol and had recommended the Trade Mart for the luncheon site. In addition to Puterbaugh, Johnson's people included Cliff Carter, John Connally, Bill Moyers, and Betty Harris, all of whom were following Johnson's orders on exactly how the motorcade would be planned.[9] It is clear that Puterbaugh and Johnson's other men, and woman, were all insisting on the Trade Mart site; in fact, Connally was becoming rather strident about it. Further complicating the issue, Secret Service Agent Winston Lawson claimed that the decision in favor of the Trade Mart was Jerry Bruno's when in fact, Bruno had never wavered from his recommendation for the Women's Building.[10] Agent Lawson testified

6. HSCA, Vol. 11, p. 517.
7. Palamara, Vincent M., *Survivor's Guilt*.
8. Ibid., p. 518.
9. Ibid., p. 520.
10. HSCA, Vol. 11, p. 517.

that "all he knew was that the decision about the motorcade was made in Washington, and that he assumed that it was made by the White House."[11] In his summary report to the HSCA, Lawson stated that it was Jack Puterbaugh who "recommended the Trade Mart" for the noontime Kennedy luncheon.

According to Bruno, the decision had been made by his going through Bill Moyers, who had deferred it to Johnson and Connally; Bruno made the following entry in his journal, noting that the feud had become bitter by this point:

> November 15—The White House announced that the Trade Mart had been approved. I met with O'Donnell and Moyers who said that Connally was unbearable and on the verge of canceling the trip. They decided they had to let the Governor have his way.[12]

Moyers' assistant, Betty Harris, testified that Secret Service Agent Lawson "seemed concerned primarily about . . . the time factor and only secondarily about the security factors."[13] It is odd that Connally was so insistent upon the selection of the Trade Mart, which was a prerequisite for the zigzag tour of Dealey Plaza, over the Women's Building favored by all the security people and Kennedy's aides. Given the obvious contravention of normal secret service standards for motorcades, it suggests the unseen hand of his mentor, Lyndon Johnson. When practically everyone who would ordinarily make that kind of decision is on one side and Johnson was really the only one—other than his assistants and longtime cronics— on the other side favoring the site uniformly rejected by the staff, there can be only one logical conclusion about how the Trade Mart came to be selected. One needs only to reread Jerry Bruno's comment about Connally's demeanor. As we have seen throughout this book, such a reaction is exactly what occurred whenever one of Johnson's stooges was acting on his behalf: they mimicked the very same reaction they had seen from Johnson himself. To have delegated any of these last-minute matters might have jeopardized the entire plan since he knew his word would be absolute; anyone else's would not carry sufficient authority to ensure that orders would be followed. From there, the orders of the chief of the Secret Service, James Rowley, and assistant chief, Floyd Boring, would carry down to every field officer as needed; they would be obeyed without question. The chief of the Dallas Police would similarly dictate the requisite orders to his men, expecting them to be fulfilled completely.

---

11. Ibid.
12. Ibid., p. 520.
13. Ibid., p. 521.

The orders of both would turn toward a neutral "omission" rather than an active "commission," which would further shield them from scrutiny. Likewise, Sheriff Decker's odd orders, detailed shortly, for his men to merely watch the motorcade as observers would similarly be followed to a tee, except for one deputy named Roger Craig.

Johnson knew that there were hundreds or thousands of essential details that he personally needed to anticipate, in addition to those being managed by the other planners. Among the many other points which he would need to factor in to his planning, which would explain all of the following actions he doubtlessly anticipated:

- Order Secret Service Agent Kellerman to take JFK's body before it could be autopsied.
- Order other agents to clean the presidential limousine and have it flown back to Washington immediately, essentially destroying and removing the "crime scene" from the scene of the crime.
- Subsequently order the Secret Service to have the limousine flown to Detroit and then Cincinnati to have it thoroughly cleaned and repaired and subsequently rebuilt (as though there were a budgetary issue that prevented its replacement with a new vehicle, Rowley's denials of the same notwithstanding).
- Switch airplanes. This would ensure Jackie's presence and assure the nation of the continuity of government, that LBJ's firm hand was on the rudder and the world was safe.
- Insist on holding the plane for Jackie to arrive with the body of JFK, thus ensuring that Jackie would unwittingly assist Kellerman in absconding with JFK's body. The larger objective was to ensure that the autopsy was conducted under the control of his designated military men (it would not be unreasonable to suspect that they had been chosen well in advance, for aptitudes—or vulnerabilities—other than their forensic pathology skills or experience, which were practically nonexistent).
- Take over JFK's quarters on Air Force One, immediately making the necessary calls from his desk telephone, knowing they wouldn't be recorded until the plane was airborne (and subsequently causing many of those that were recorded to be erased or lost).
- Be sworn in before leaving Dallas. To set this up, he would first need to call Bobby Kennedy to put the question to him not so much for his permission but to be able to say later that he did so and that Bobby agreed with it. He would also need to remember to offer him condolences for the loss of his brother.
- Lie to Kenneth O'Donnell and others about having been told that he should be sworn in, as quickly as possible, by RFK.

- Make the call, personally, to get Judge Sarah Hughes to Love Field for the swearing ceremony.
- Ensure that the presidential photographer was on hand to record the event for posterity (even though he accidentally made a photograph of Johnson exchanging winks with Congressman Thomas, a photograph which survived despite the disappearance of the negative for that particular photograph).

The key to the assassination, according to Johnson's plan, concerned the orders to the Dallas Police and Sheriff's Departments to end their protection of the JFK motorcade at the corner of Main and Houston, under the disinformation that the Secret Service would take over at that point. Johnson would be in daily contact with his Washington staff, both the official one and the rogue group that was already finalizing the operational plans for the assassination. The real team in charge of Dealey Plaza that day had fake Secret Service identification, which they would successfully use to ward off any efforts by real policemen to investigate the source of the shooting.[14] Johnson had specifically instructed Rowley and Boring that they were to advise the Dallas officials to end their protection at the intersection of Main and Houston streets; these orders were passed on to Agent Winston C. Lawson, as verified later through Sheriff Decker and Police Chief Curry.

- Chief Curry told his officers to end supervision of Friday's crowd at Houston and Main, a block short of the ambush, on the ground that traffic would begin to thin out there. In fact, the real reason, he later revealed in his book, was that he was simply following the orders of the Secret Service. "The Dallas Police Department carefully carried out the security plans which were laid out by Mr. Lawson, the Secret Service representative from Washington, D.C." In his book, *JFK Assassination File*, he added that, "in the midst of comprehensive security it seems a freak of history that this short stretch of Elm Street would be the assassination site, and that the Texas Book Depository Building was virtually ignored in the security plans for the motorcade."[15]
- Sheriff Decker held a meeting at 10:30 a.m. on November 22 with all of his deputies, about hundred men altogether, including the plainclothes men and detectives. This was unusual given that his message to them was that they "were to take no part whatsoever in the security of that

---

14. Twyman, pp. 762–769.
15. Douglass, p. 270 (ref. Manchester, p. 33; Jesse Curry, *JFK Assassination File*, p. 21).

[presidential] motorcade." Rather, their assignment for that day was "to stand out in front of the building, 505 Main Street, and represent the Sheriff's Office."[16]

The fact that Dealey Plaza had been selected as the scene for the crime of the century was due to the phantom organizer's realization that it was the perfect location for multiple snipers. The tall buildings, the overpass, the fencing at the grassy knoll, and the "manhole" covers over the drainage pipes made it the best location for their operation. Their selection of the "zig and zag" turns onto Houston Street and then the hairpin 120-degree turn to Elm Street ensured the car would be going very slowly. All of this was recognized four days earlier by Agents Lawson and Sorrels as they made a "dry run" through the motorcade route in downtown Dallas with Chief Curry, and Sorrels remarked, "'Hell, we'd be sitting ducks'; The other two concurred and shrugged," as they drove away, filing the thought away for good.[17]

Johnson's focus of planning the motorcade was minimal security throughout but especially at Dealey Plaza where it would disappear almost completely. The motorcycle escorts would need to be minimized, and the men told to ride well behind JFK's limousine; the Secret Service would be instructed to keep any agents off the rear of the car—they would all ride in the "Queen Mary," the 1956 Cadillac convertible once used by Eisenhower. Johnson's own car, a rented Lincoln convertible, would follow that car, safely back at least two to three car lengths. He had still not managed to have Governor Connally switch places with Senator Yarborough, who he had hoped might "inadvertently" be put in the line of fire even though the shooters had been told to avoid hitting anyone other than JFK if at all possible. He had even urged President Kennedy to allow Jackie to ride with himself and Lady Bird, an idea JFK quickly rebuffed.

The operation would require the focused use of "need to know" in order to survive the inevitable investigations that would surely follow. Most of the orders would also be couched in terms of ambiguities and secretively cast within the Secret Service as being a "simulated assassination" for training purposes to many of the agents, even though that would be denied to investigators. Later, orders would be issued to all agents to never discuss any aspect of these plans with anyone, for all time. Some of Johnson's instructions, given at the highest levels of the Secret Service hierarchy had filtered down through the ranks and would later be revealed by Dallas Patrolman B. J.

---

16. Ibid. (ref. Roger Craig, *When They Kill a President*, p. 5).
17. Manchester, p. 32.

Martin, one of the motorcyclists in the motorcade. Martin would later recall, for example, that the Secret Service instructed them, at Love Field, that there would be no forward escorts, only one at each rear fender and that they were to stay behind the rear wheels of the car at all times. As Dallas Police Chief Curry would later acknowledge to the Warren Commission, there were many more motorcycles lined up to be with the president's car, consistent with the routine practice for presidential motorcades, but the Secret Service had told him at the last minute to drop some of them. "We actually had two on each side but we wanted four on each side and they asked us to drop out some of them and back down the motorcade, along the motorcade, which we did."[18]

All of the orders to "stand down" were to be presented to subordinates downstream as coming directly from JFK, who was allegedly irritated by the noise of the motorcycles and the presence of Secret Service agents who "came between him and the people." (These were among the most publicized lies perpetrated upon the Warren Commission by the Secret Service and the Dallas Police and have been conclusively debunked by later testimony.)[19] In fact, Kennedy was very accommodating to Secret Service recommendations and requests and had not ordered any changes in security, either in the November 22 motorcade or generally. This inconsistency may not have been entirely the fault of the Secret Service, after all; it is not beyond reason to posit that someone else, someone with the clout necessary to do so, had cleverly plotted the dissolution of any semblance of security for the president. Such a person who was uniquely placed, whose orders would not be questioned—who could have made certain specific requests, such as keeping Secret Service agents off the rear bumper of the Lincoln and/or eliminating some of the most critical motorcycle escorts—could also portray them as having come from the president himself. A simple explanation, such as "the president wants to be closer to 'the people'" or "the president does not like the noise from the motorcycles," would suffice from a person of high-enough stature who had the implicit authority to convey such an order, especially if he had also been serving as the chief organizer and planner of the motorcade. A simple, casually uttered directive given to his own staff people—all of whom had been trained since their first day on the job to obey him regardless of their own doubts—would achieve the desired results. That Johnson could, and would, interject himself in such a way is completely in keeping with his manipulative behavior, as amply demonstrated throughout this book.

18. Fetzer, Weldon, *Murder in Dealey Plaza*, p. 155.
19. See, for example, Palamara, Vincent M., *Survivor's Guilt*.

November 21, 1963

At this point, during the evening of November 21, on the way from Houston to Fort Worth, Johnson had undoubtedly known that the plan by then was on autopilot. The operatives, tools, and tactical plans were in place; the designated "patsy" had been deluded into believing his entrée into the covert spy world was imminent—still oblivious to the real agenda; and the planning was subject only to any last-minute decision from him, and him alone, to abort the mission. Johnson knew enough of the details—the microlevel points developed by his rogue managers like Harvey, Morales, and Ferrie—of his grand plan to know that every contingency had been accounted for. As he flew into Fort Worth Thursday evening with the presidential party and then slipped out after arriving at the Texas Hotel to take a midnight trip in a private limousine the thirty-some miles over to the party in Dallas at Clint Murchison's home, his confidence grew that the plan would work; it would not only work, but it would keep him out of prison and ensure his chance to become the great president that would fulfill his destiny. When he arrived at the Murchison mansion, his mentality would be simple, along the lines of, "Proceed as planned. It's now or never."

The purpose of the "Murchison Party" was to allow the principals of the enterprise—the key sponsors and facilitators or their representatives as being a "congruency of interests"—one last chance to gauge the operational readiness of its disparate facets. It was essential that its success be practically guaranteed; otherwise, they would all be put in legal jeopardy. Conducting it as a "party" honoring fellow plotter J. Edgar Hoover required the presence of a number of other randomly selected individuals, all of whom had vague personal or political connections to the principals; but it was merely a veil that hid the real intent of the meeting if word had leaked out that such a meeting occurred. But only when the most important of these principals—the one most critical to a successful execution—was present would they separate themselves from the others and meet in executive session "behind closed doors."

Lyndon Johnson arrived very late at Clint Murchison's mansion, but he felt he owed it to some of his best friends to attend since it was a party honoring their mutual friend, J. Edgar Hoover. The only thing liberal at the Murchison home in Dallas that evening was as a measure of how the drinks flowed. Also attending were John J. McCloy, Richard Nixon, H. L. Hunt, John Curington, George Brown, former Texas Congressman Bruce Alger, and Hoover's lover, Clyde Tolson. Critics who have attempted to deny that this party actually occurred have argued that:

- Johnson would have arrived very late, well after midnight, thus making his appearance implausible; perhaps they were unaware that Johnson generally kept very late hours, often getting only three or four hours of sleep per night. It is acknowledged that he might not have arrived at the "party" until 1:00 a.m. or later. However, that does not make his appearance impossible; therefore, that argument is specious.

- Clint Murchison had suffered a debilitating stroke which rendered him immobile and therefore could not have made this appearance in one of his own houses. That argument is simply not valid as Murchison's biographer (his former secretary) Earnestine Van Buren showed in her book *Clint*. He was completely mobile and traveled frequently at least through 1965; from then until his death in 1969, he was increasingly less mobile and more confined to his home at Glad Oaks.

- And finally, it is suggested that J. Edgar Hoover could not have attended because he was back in his office late the next morning and because he always used FBI agents to chauffer him around. This is the least persuasive counterargument because it assumes that Hoover would not fly back to Washington until the next day; of course, he had access to the best aircraft of the FBI fleet (e.g., a business jet like the Jetstar) that could have been parked at Addison airport, a mile or two from Murchison's estate on Preston Road at Keller Springs, and could have flown him back to Washington before 6:00 a.m. And even Hoover might have relaxed his standards to allow Clint's chauffer to pick him up and later return him to the airport, as it appears was the case. It should also be noted that Hoover's calendar was completely open; no entries made on the day before the assassination, Thursday, November 21, 1963.

This party and meeting was first reported by Penn Jones Jr. in his book *Forgive My Grief* and confirmed by Harrison Livingstone in his 1993 book *Killing the Truth*.[20] Lyndon's mistress Madeline Brown wrote her own book, *Texas in the Morning*, in 1997, in which she recounts many details of her long-term relationship with Johnson, including gifts of a home, expensive jewelry, automobiles, and a full-length mink coat. Several other authors, including James Fetzer, Jim Marrs, and Noel Twyman, interviewed Ms. Brown and found her to be a very credible person despite the circumstances of her relationship with Johnson. She may have been guilty of embellishment and exaggeration of basic truths, but she had no reason to make up such a charge out of thin air, and her description of the event has been affirmed over the years by others who were there.

---

20. Livingstone, *Killing the Truth* . . . , pp. 483–487.

Ms. Brown remembered the tension before Johnson's arrival. "There was a real atmosphere of uneasiness at that party. It was a social gathering, but as soon as Johnson arrived, at a very late hour, the men who were still there (it is not clear exactly which men had remained and attended that meeting) immediately convened in private in Murchison's office, suddenly leaving the ladies where they were sitting or standing." She recalled,[21]

> Tension filled the room upon his arrival. The group immediately went behind closed doors. A short time later Lyndon, anxious and red-faced, re-appeared. I knew how secretly Lyndon operated. Therefore I said nothing . . . not even that I was happy to see him. Squeezing my hand so hard, it felt crushed from the pressure, he spoke with a grating whisper, a quiet growl, into my ear, not a love message, but one I'll always remember: "After tomorrow those goddamn Kennedys will never embarrass me again—that's no threat—that's a promise."

November 22, 1963

As Lyndon Johnson awoke, his first thought was probably what he knew he had to do: meet with Kennedy to try one more time to get the seating arrangements for the motorcade changed; he didn't want to jeopardize his friend John Connally's life. He wanted to offer Ralph Yarborough the opportunity to ride in the president's car instead, an act he probably thought he could sell on the basis of it being a rather magnanimous gesture. Of course, he knew that was a lie, but somehow he was able to see it the way he thought Kennedy should see it, absent the knowledge of the unfolding plot. Johnson was very good, as we have seen, about convincing even himself that something was true which he knew to be a lie.

As he showered and dressed for his meeting, he undoubtedly reflected on what he knew would happen this day; he would become president, finally after all the years of hard work and planning. He had always been driven by his ruthless lust for power. But now that had become secondary to another one, which he had spent months trying to quash, unable to force it off the Senate calendar, he now had the urgent need to take the necessary action to make the Senate leadership dispense with their investigations so he could stay out of prison. His problems had mushroomed over the last year to the point that it was doubtful he could now even be reelected in his own state. In fact, as he

---

21. Brown, M., p. 166 (also, ref. youtube.com: "LBJ's Mistress Blows Whistle on JFK Assassination").

drank his morning coffee, he would have noticed news articles appearing in all the major Texas newspapers that morning that cited a statewide poll showing that the Kennedy-Johnson popularity was trailing Barry Goldwater by 52 to 48 percent. The same poll also showed that Senator Ralph Yarborough had become virtually unbeatable. When Yarborough was questioned by a reporter about it, he had responded vigorously, beating the table, and roaring, "Let the bastards run somebody against me! I want the bastards to run somebody against me, so I can beat the living hell out of 'em!" (Ralph's enthusiasm for a confrontation speaks volumes about the Texas chasm.) That's how he and his liberal supporters felt, eager for a showdown.[22] There was also a risk, at this point in time hours before the assassination, that liberals would take over the state Democratic convention, pushing aside the Connally-Johnson forces, which would further undermine his political position.[23]

There was another headline story Johnson would have also seen in the *Dallas Morning News*: "Nixon Predicts Kennedy May Drop Johnson." Many of the reporters covering the event, no doubt even some of those who would participate in the motorcade itself, would have heard the macabre joke making the rounds, "JFK is safe in Texas, because 'You-Know-Who' is Vice President."[24] Jokes like that had always irked the thin-skinned Johnson.

When Johnson met with JFK in his Texas Hotel suite that morning, he found that Kennedy was not impressed with his attempt at magnanimity, so he had to modify his approach, and suddenly he was demanding that the motorcade seating arrangements be changed; this led quickly to back and forth shouting between the two men that was overheard by the hotel staff outside in the hallway. Johnson wanted Governor Connally to ride with him and wanted Senator Yarborough, his longtime political enemy, to ride with JFK in the presidential limousine, which he continued pointing out, was an unusually generous gesture on his part to his long-term enemy.[25] The hotel servants were in and out of the suite and heard Yarborough's name mentioned several times; their impressions were consistent—that Kennedy felt the senator was not being treated fairly by Johnson and Connally and their staffs and that he expressed himself emphatically. Kennedy refused to change those arrangements and ordered Johnson to "make up" with Yarborough for the good of the party and the 1964 elections. The hotel staff and caterers also said that Johnson had tried to control his famous temper in JFK's presence, but that when he exited, "he left that suite like a pistol," said one, Max

---

22. Sherrill, p. 107.
23. Ibid.
24. Trask, *Pictures* . . . p. 417.
25. Zirbel, pp. 190–191.

Peck, who watched him lurch down the corridor, "long legs pumping and looking furious."[26] Jackie asked JFK what the argument was about, and he said, "That's just Lyndon. He's having a bad day."[27] Kennedy had also told his wife that Johnson is "incapable of telling the truth."[28]

William Manchester only hinted at the sinister implications of this argument between JFK and Johnson, and this story was one which was so damning of Johnson's conduct that much of it, and a number of other stories related to Johnson's conduct, was cut back or eliminated entirely from his book at Jacqueline Kennedy's request—to avoid further worsening the relationship of Johnson and Bobby Kennedy—and put under seal for one hundred years. The stories that remained in the book still enraged Johnson to such an extent that he sought out Jim Bishop to write a more empathetic version, one without all the anti-Johnson bias. The real story which Manchester was forced to suppress will not be released by the Kennedy Library until the year 2067; in and of itself, that speaks volumes about the secrets that had to be hidden for a hundred years.

Mysterious Multiple Breakdowns in Presidential Security Begin in Dallas

The evening before the Dallas motorcade, a number of Secret Service agents, in yet another violation of rules, had spent the night at a Fort Worth club called The Cellar, until about 4:00 a.m., clearly taking their sworn duties to protect the president rather lightly. Apparently, this had become the norm; as former Secret Service Agent Abraham Bolden stated to James W. Douglass, "'The Secret Service agents around Kennedy were joking in a more sinister direction—that they would step out of the way if an assassin aimed a shot at the president.' In Dallas, the Secret Service would step out of the way not just individually but collectively."[29]

When the motorcade began forming at Love Field at about 11:30 a.m. pending the arrival of the president and vice president and the other dignitaries, the Secret Service detail began to abandon any semblance of protection of JFK, going beyond the cuts already made, as described previously. One of the most stunning examples of this was the further cutback in placement of motorcycle escorts around the presidential limousine, from six to each side or the minimal four down to two to a side, and only riding in tandem behind

---

26. Manchester, p. 82.
27. Ibid., pp. 82–83.
28. Ibid.
29. Douglass, p. 142.

the vehicle. In contrast to the day before in Houston, six motorcycles flanked each side of the presidential limousine the entire way; in the downtown area, this was increased to twelve motorcycles to each side (twenty-four total). By the time the limousine began its way down Elm Street, even the four remaining motorcycles would draw back. In accordance with a police escort plan developed only the day before, DPD Captain Perdue Lawrence assigned a total of eight motorcycle officers, four on each side: Hargis, Martin, McLain, and Courson were to ride on the left side and Jackson, Chaney, Haygood, and Baker were assigned to the right side.[30]

According to one of the motorcycle officers, as they were getting into position at Love Field, Secret Service escorts accompanying Lyndon B. Johnson instructed them that only two motorcycles were to flank each side of the rear bumper of the limousine.[31] One of the last-minute changes involved modifying the "normal" format where instead of a motorcycle at each wheel of the limousine (front and back) both cycles would remain behind the rear wheels. A partial list of "last-minute" changes would include the following:

- Captain Perdue Lawrence testified that the Secret Service told them to stay to the rear of the limousine; his understanding was that this was due to JFK's "desires";[32]
- DPD Assistant Chief Charles Batchelor testified that the orders he received were to place four motorcycles on either side (eight total) . . . immediately to the rear of the president's vehicle;[33]
- SAIC Lawson overruled that plan because he felt that having four cycles on each side flanking the rear wheels would be too many in that configuration; he changed the number to two per side;[34]
- Motorcycle Officer M. L. Baker testified that there was a last-minute change made at Love Field to stay well to the rear of the limousine;[35]
- Motorcycle Officer B. J. Martin stated that "they instructed us that they didn't want anyone riding past the President's car and that we were to ride to the rear, to the rear of his car, about the rear bumper."[36]
- Another standard procedure that was cast aside was to have one of his military aides (A. F. Brigadier General Godfrey McHugh, Navy Captain Tazewell Shepard, or Army Major General Ted Clifton) riding with him; when space did not permit, they would ride in the follow-up vehicle; in

---

30. WCH 20, p. 489.
31. Hill, p. 113.
32. WCH 7, p. 580–581.
33. WCH 21, p. 571.
34. Ibid.
35. WCH 3, p. 244.
36. WCH 6, p. 293.

Dallas, McHugh and Clifton were placed twelve cars back of the presidential limousine.

* Kennedy's military physician, Rear Admiral George Burkley, was generally placed in a vehicle close to the president; in Dallas, he was put in a bus twenty vehicles back from the Lincoln.

Putting all the motorcycles on the rear sides of the Lincoln would, of course, make it more difficult for a shooter at the same elevation to aim a rifle from behind and to the side, but it would open up the target from the front and side, making such a shot (for example, from the "grassy knoll") much easier. According to testimony from reporter Seth Kantor, the night before the event, the plan to have some of Will Fritz's men ride in a closed car equipped with machine guns was canceled.[37] Still another last-minute change was in the position of the photographer's truck, which was normally directly in front of the presidential limousine. For some reason, it was decided that this tradition should be broken for this motorcade, and the truck was replaced with three Chevrolet convertibles, which were placed several cars (sixth to eighth) behind the presidential limousine.[38] Up until that morning, no one in town knew exactly what the motorcade route would be because different maps had been printed in the newspapers, some showing the zigzag through Dealey Plaza, others showing the route would be straight through the plaza to a crossover past the triple underpass and on to Stemmons Freeway. Even the Dallas Police chief, Jesse Curry, testified that he was not consulted about the motorcade route; his assistant, Charles Batchelor believed that the failure of the Secret Service to keep the police advised of the exact route to be taken prevented them planning and organizing their men.

As noted earlier, the Warren Commission eventually established that Winston Lawson had previously made the cuts in the Dallas motorcade, stating that "two (2) on either side would be sufficient, about even with the rear fender of the car"[39] (i.e., four motorcycles in total, two on each side). Lawson attributed the request as having come from President Kennedy, which of course could never be proven or disproven after he was murdered.

According to Vince Palamara's research, this was categorically wrong. Kennedy had never requested such security compromises.[40] It does not take an overly creative imagination to determine who might have been the person—the one who had the unique authority, forcefulness, and chutzpah

---

37. WCH 20, p. 391.
38. WCH 6, p. 163.
39. WCH 21, p. 571.
40. Horne, p. 1403.

to have ordered these last-minute changes to the motorcycle formation—who had the temerity to make the changes while suggesting that it was JFK himself who requested them. After all the other motorcades in which he had expressed no such concerns, then suddenly here—in a city seething with hatred for him, a city that many had warned him to avoid—on that day, he decided that he would do something he had never done before and that was to order a virtual suspension of protection from both the Secret Service agents around him and the Dallas policemen on motorcycles next to his car. Such an assertion would ordinarily require a complete suspension of disbelief, yet this is precisely what the Warren Commission postulated and what we are still being asked to do by such people as Vincent Bugliosi and Gerald Posner.

Given everything we now know about what really happened in Dallas, it is not idle speculation to suggest that the Secret Service orders were put into effect by someone at the very highest level of the organization and filtered down to the street level through Floyd Boring and Winston Lawson to Emory Roberts and the others. When it appeared to that same "someone"—who was apparently having a fairly major anxiety / depressive-paranoid attack, as will be seen shortly—during the formation at Love Field that the order to reduce the number of escorts beside the limousine was not being observed, a stern reminder about it was evidently issued on the spot to the effect that the number of flanking motorcycles was not to be four on each side but only two. This is reasoned conjecture; however, it might "connect some dots" and explain the incongruities noted above as well as additional ones to be revealed shortly. In any event, regardless of who ordered the unusual formation, by the time the motorcade reached Elm Street—despite the testimony of the officers as to their general location during the motorcade—the total number of motorcycles flanking the limousine was "zero." For inexplicable reasons, during the course of the drive through the city, the motorcycle escorts were generally riding alongside the quarter panels of the Lincoln, behind its rear wheels, or between the Lincoln and the Cadillac. But by the time the limousine reached Elm Street, they were no longer riding near the Lincoln; all four of them had dropped back so far that they were directly parallel with the follow-up Cadillac. This is borne out by the Zapruder film, the Altgens photograph, and the Willis slide taken a second or two before Kennedy was shot.

Johnson's hand would be kept invisible through his having three levels of staff separating him from motorcade planning. Cliff Carter had been given much of the responsibility of getting Johnson's specific requests employed, though he claimed that "they sent Bill Moyers down to take over all charge . . . Bill Moyers was in complete charge of Mr. Kennedy's visit to

Texas."[41] The street-level advance man used by Johnson, Carter, and Moyers for the Dallas portion of the Texas trip was Jack Puterbaugh, who was described by Winston Lawson as a "civilian political advance man for the Democratic National Committee." In his summary report to the HSCA, Lawson also stated that it was Jack Puterbaugh who "recommended the Trade Mart" for the noontime luncheon. Furthermore, Lawson stated that Puterbaugh attended many of the Dallas Police and Secret Service planning meetings and was also "in charge of the protocol of the motorcade, the arranging of seating and vehicle sequence for Congressmen and other dignitaries. The motorcade was the primary focus of such protocol." Lawson also stated that Puterbaugh was in touch with "Washington" and was also possibly getting instructions from Betty Harris, who reported to Bill Moyers and was the primary local contact.[42] Needless to say, all of those names were people who reported to Lyndon B. Johnson.

One of the motorcycle policemen who was there, B. J. Martin, as noted above, stated that it was Lyndon Johnson's security contingent which made a number of changes in the motorcade at the last minute at Love Field."I guess they were Secret Service. They were sure as hell acting like they were in charge, and I know they were with Johnson, because when they got through telling us what to do, they went back to his car."[43] Jack Puterbaugh "described himself as a foot soldier that only carried out orders."[44] The origin of the "orders" Puterbaugh refers to are technically a little unclear since Cliff Carter made no mention of Puterbaugh in his testimony, and Puterbaugh likewise made no mention of Carter's involvement in the Dallas planning even though they were clearly operating as a team and both were working for Johnson. Irrespective of the technical question of the origin of Puterbaugh's orders, there is no doubt about who issued them; one need only consider who Puterbaugh worked for on this assignment and who the other man on his "team," Cliff Carter, had also reported to and had done so much to please for over fifteen years.

Carter's lack of candor in his testimony regarding Puterbaugh, and vice-versa, suggests that they were both attempting to conceal their relationship, no doubt to hide the involvement of their mutual boss. Carter's deceit carried over to other issues as well. He became caught up in a series of inconsistent

41. Transcript, Clifton C. Carter Oral History Interview I, 10/1/68, by Dorothy L. Pierce, Internet Copy, LBJ Library, p. 107(pdf).
42. Lawson memorandum to HSCA, RIF 180-10074-10396, Jan 31, 1978.
43. Sloan and Hill, "*JFK: The Last Dissenting Witness.* pp. 112–114.
44. HSCA interview with Jack Puterbaugh, RIF 180-10080-10069, April 14, 1978.

statements concerning his handling of Governor Connally's clothes. During the time that he was waiting in Parkland Hospital, nurse Ruth Standidge testified to the Warren commission that she gave the clothes to Cliff Carter and, according to Carter's interview with Manchester, he left his bag with the nurse upon departure.[45] Yet in his oral history remarks for the LBJ Library, he stated that he handed this bag of clothes to Congressman Henry Gonzalez, asking him to keep them, and his own commission statement makes no mention at all of the clothes. Since Connally's clothes were dry-cleaned before being entered into evidence, it begs the question of "who decided to destroy still another part of the 'crime scene' evidence." There were a number of other incongruities with Carter's account, all of which suggested the invisible hand of Lyndon Johnson:

• Carter stated that he "saw Rufus Youngblood in the Vice President's car . . . reach over and shove Mr. Johnson down and jumped in the back seat himself and put himself over Mr. Johnson's body."[46] This assertion was emphatically challenged by Senator Yarborough—sitting in the same backseat as Johnson—as having "never happened," as will be detailed shortly; only Johnson had stated this had happened and even Youngblood himself did not embrace it (he didn't recall it happening, but it must have *"because of President Johnson's statement to that effect")* until Johnson had apparently persuaded him to go along with it when he gave him a medal for it two weeks later.

• Carter attempted to diminish his own involvement in the motorcade planning by ascribing all the decisions to Kennedy's staff. According to him, it was the Kennedy staff who selected the Trade Mart and insisted on the motorcade route. This is contrary with Jerry Bruno's description of events in his book *Advance Man* and to practically all other accounts as referenced throughout this chapter.

• Carter denied that there were any concerns regarding President Kennedy's plans to go to Dallas, saying, "No, I didn't have any reports of anything like that. I never heard anything like that."[47] Yet, William Manchester quotes Barefoot Sanders as having said he told Cliff Carter personally that a visit by Kennedy to Dallas was "inadvisable," obviously expecting that Carter would pass on the information.[48]

• Carter said that one of the Secret Service men in the president's security car "wheeled around with his submachine gun and pointed up at one of

45. Manchester, p. 239.
46. Transcript, Clifton C. Carter Oral History Interview I, 10/1/68, by Dorothy L. Pierce, Internet Copy, LBJ Library, p. 113 (pdf).
47. Ibid., p. 106 (pdf).
48. Manchester, p. 40.

the windows of the Depository"[49] but did not fire because he could not pick out exactly the right window in time to shoot. This is contradicted by all available photographs, films, and Secret Service agent accounts.

• Carter claimed that Johnson and Katzenbach decided that Johnson should stay in Texas until Johnson could take the oath of office. This is contradicted by numerous sources as detailed elsewhere.

• Carter also stated that O'Donnell and O'Brien determined that Johnson should return to Washington using the presidential Air Force One aircraft. "The judgment seems to have been made largely on the fact that Air Force One had certain sophisticated communication equipment that Air Force Two did not have and that if a man is going to be President of the United States he's got to be in constant contact with all elements at his command. It was thought that that was not entirely possible on Air Force Two."[50] This comment seems illustrative of one that could only have come from Lyndon Johnson (completely false and baseless) and parroted by his sidekick Cliff Carter. It was contradicted by numerous sources including O'Donnell and O'Brien, as noted in the next chapter.

Another example of the wholesale cutback in Kennedy's protection can be seen on widely circulated videos of the motorcade as it commenced. Emory Roberts, aboard the "Queen Mary" following the presidential limousine, orders agent Henry Rybka, who had been running astride the limousine ready to assume his normal position on the rear bumper step, away from the vehicle as it prepared to leave Love Field (another agent on the other side of the limousine was also ordered to stay off the car, though he is not visible in the film). This video illustrates, better than any words can possibly convey, the way John F. Kennedy was abandoned in Dallas by the men who were sworn to protect him; it is essential viewing for anyone wishing to understand the reality of what happened in Dallas. *(Ref. youtube.com for video: "JFK assassination: Secret Service Standdown" showing agents being taken off their normal assignments.)*[51]

No one has studied the Secret Service protection "security stripping" issue more than researcher/author Vince Palamara; he has stated that the usual array of motorcycles was four abreast of the limousine with one placed at each fender; on many occasions there were twelve to eighteen motorcycles near the limousine. He also maintained that Gerald Behn, the head of the

49. Transcript, Clifton C. Carter Oral History Interview I, 10/1/68, by Dorothy L. Pierce, Internet Copy, LBJ Library, p. 114 (pdf).
50. Ibid., p. 124 (pdf).
51. See: http://www.youtube.com/watch?v=XY02Qkuc_f8.

White House Detail, and Floyd Boring (second in command) both assured him that JFK never vetoed or modified any Secret Service protection and that any claims to the contrary were incorrect.[52]

Another of Johnson's instructions would also be fulfilled at Love Field, when the top was removed from the limousine. According to testimony given to the HSCA, Secret Service Agent Winston Lawson stated that "on the morning of November 22, he received a call from Kellerman in Fort Worth asking about weather conditions in Dallas and whether the bubble-top on the President's car would be used or not. During that call, Lawson was told the bubble-top was to be on if it was raining, and off if it was not. The final decision in this matter was made by Bill Moyers. Moyers had been on the phone to Ms. Harris, informing her that the President did not want the bubble top. He told Harris to 'get that God-damned bubble off unless it's pouring rain.' Shortly thereafter the weather began to clear. Ms. Harris approached Sorrels about the bubble-top and together they had the special agents remove the glass top."[53]* The Discovery Channel included a rather odd description of a video they broadcast:[54]

> The limousine had a removable plastic bubble-top that was neither bulletproof nor bullet-resistant, but could be used to shield the car's occupants from inclement weather. Since the skies had cleared over Dallas on the morning of Nov. 22, Secret Service agent Winston G. Lawson ordered the top removed at the behest of President Kennedy's press assistant [sic], Bill Moyers, who knew that the president preferred to ride without it.

This text contains two points that require some elucidation or correction:

- The "bubble-top was neither bulletproof nor bullet-resistant." True enough; however, the majority of agents agreed with John E. Campion, an aide to the

---

*The use of such gratuitous profanity by an ordained Baptist minister is a little odd in the context of this situation, considering that it had been raining all morning. It begs the question of whether Moyers was the real initiator of the request, or whether he was simply passing on a demand from his boss, LBJ, known to be habitually profane and strident in practically all situations (a general exception existed whenever cameras were near, of course, in which case a broad smile replaced his scornful gaze). All things considered, it can be assumed that Moyers was merely mouthing words originally screamed by Lyndon B. Johnson, in comparable stridency.

52. Horne, p. 1403.
53. HSCA, Vol. 11, p. 526.
54. The Discovery Channel: (http://dsc.discovery.com/guides/history/unsolvedhistory/dealeyplaza/photogallery/slide_03.html).

assistant chief for security, who wrote a December 5, 1963, memorandum "Specifications of Bubble Top" that included this information: "The bubble top material of the President's limousine is $\frac{3}{4}$" thick Plexiglass."[55] It would seem that this material would, at the very least, deflect a shot.[56]

• Mr. Moyers was not JFK's assistant as indicated by the Discovery Channel; he was, of course, actually one of Lyndon Johnson's longtime assistants who had been promoted to the position of deputy director of the Peace Corps. Regardless of his title, he was in Austin on November 22 to assist in planning the next stop but was in frequent contact with Betty Harris and others in Fort Worth and Dallas.

The term "bubble top" became widely used to describe the removable top apparently because it was made mostly of plastic even though the connotation of the term was that the top resembled a bubble. In fact, the top was much more than a clear "bubble" over a big convertible; it was a very formal design with a vinyl covering, which transformed the convertible into a limousine with a very small rear window. As such, it would make it nearly impossible for a sniper to see the occupants clearly enough to aim at any of them from above. The following photographs illustrate this:

COMMISSION EXHIBIT 345

55. Palamara, Vincent M., *Survivor's Guilt*.
56. Palamara, Vincent M., *Survivor's Guilt*.

The first photograph, exhibit CE 345 of the Warren Report, shows the actual top that was carried in the car's trunk; the second shows it installed shortly after it arrived at Parkland Hospital. These photos show clearly why Lyndon Johnson's words to Bill Moyers were forcefully repeated to others: the black vinyl covering would obviously have made it impossible for anyone to have a reasonably good shot at JFK.

Still another last-minute change was the route to be taken through Dealey Plaza; instead of straight through on Elm Street and under the triple underpass or down Main Street straight through Dealey Plaza and then a sharp turn around a concrete median (or alternatively the temporary installation of planks to allow the procession to go over the four-inch curb),* the motorcade would now turn right onto Houston Street for one block before then taking a sharp (120-degree) left turn onto Elm Street, which required each vehicle to slow to a crawl, especially the stretched length presidential carriage. The Main Street to Stemmons Freeway route had been published in that morning's edition of the *Dallas Morning News,* causing confusion—between the routes published earlier and the morning paper account—and accounting for the relatively low number of people lining the streets into Dealey Plaza.

The rumors of a pending disaster were being repeated through the presidential party. Marty Underwood, an advance man who worked on the

---

* The curb was designed to impede ordinary traffic from making this same maneuver, since it created a hazard with traffic coming down Elm Street; that was not pertinent during a presidential motorcade.

planning of JFK's Texas tour stops in Houston and Austin (Lyndon Johnson took over the planning and coordination tasks only for the Dallas stop) would later state that the FBI, the CIA, the Secret Service, and the Mafia "knew (JFK) was going to be hit on 11/22/63 . . . we were getting all sorts of rumors that the President was going to be assassinated in Dallas; there were no ifs, ands or buts about it."[57] But instead of tightening security, to ensure there were no potential holes in the protection of Kennedy, nothing was done even about the known lapses. The only thing ever done about them was a campaign to deny and prevaricate about the Secret Service's errors before the Warren Commission. As noted previously, thirty years later, the Secret Service would purge many of its files related to the assassination.

The "Killing Zone"

As the presidential motorcade snaked its way through the streets of downtown Dallas then on to Houston Street, it came alongside Dealey Plaza to its left; when it reached Elm Street, it had to slow to a crawl in order to make a sharp turn, 120 degrees to the left, a maneuver which was contrary to standard Secret Service rules. The driver of the limousine, William Greer, was apparently a little surprised by this since he almost ran the car into the curb before getting it straightened back out. As the president's open-topped limousine slowly started its way down Elm Street below four buildings of more than six stories high—none of which had been secured in advance by the Secret Service—two men sat next to the sidewalk on a grassy knoll halfway down the street toward the underpass; one of them held an umbrella, which he began alternately raising and lowering as Kennedy's car approached.[58] As the limousine passed, the time on the Hertz Rent-a-Car clock atop the Texas School Book Depository read 12:30 p.m; and at that moment, an unknown series of shots rang out over Dealey Plaza.

Shock and confusion caused people who were not standing next to the presidential limousine to have many different recollections of where the shots originated. Of 178 witnesses at the scene, 61 would later say they believed that at least some of the gunfire had originated in front of the motorcade. The confusion over this point was held mostly by the witnesses farthest away, people standing closer to the corner of Houston and Elm streets. Those who were closest to the limousine were all convinced that at least some shots were fired from the "grassy knoll."[59] It is now clear that the reason for all the confusion was the variance in decibel level of each shot, depending upon each witnesses' position in the plaza and the location of each rifleman; each

---

57. Palamara, p. 35.
58. Marrs, pp. 29–33.
59. Russell, *The Man* . . . , p. 568.

had a different opinion because of the wide disparity among them as to which gunshots each of them heard and whether echoes were also heard in their position. People at the corner of Houston and Elm only heard those shots emanating from the buildings overhead; those on the grassy knoll mostly heard only the shots originating there. The man closest to the target of the shots, Secret Service Agent Roy Kellerman, stated to the Warren Commission on March 9, 1964, "A *flurry of shells* came into the car."[60] Within minutes, the whole world would know that John F. Kennedy, the thirty-fifth president of the United States, was killed on Elm Street in downtown Dallas, Texas.

Moments after the initial report—which missed the president and hit the curb well beyond the limousine, ricocheting upward and hitting James Teague as he stood below the underpass*— two more shots were fired from opposite directions, which many thought sounded like firecrackers,** and John F. Kennedy began slumping in the car and grasping his hands toward his throat. The first of these was fired from the roof of the County Records Building behind him, striking him in his back, about 5½ inches below his collar (which Gerald Ford would eventually move, through semantic gamesmanship, up to his neck in order to support Arlen Specter's desperate attempt to explain how all of this happened with only two bullets). According to SS agent Kellerman and Nellie Connally, Kennedy exclaimed, "I'm hit" at that point, just before the next shot hit him in his throat. Douglas Weldon, JD presented a compelling case that the next one (being the third shot, altogether) to hit JFK was actually fired from an above ground sewer access structure near the south end of the triple underpass, which went through the windshield (making the sound of a firecracker) of Kennedy's car and hit him in the throat.[61] He had just clutched his hands toward his throat as a result of this shot when James Altgens snapped his camera's shutter, capturing the moment in the most widely seen, highest-quality photograph taken of the assassination.

Based upon David Mantik's and Noel Twyman's work, it now appears that there were at least eight, possibly even nine or ten shots. Kennedy was hit four times—though none was "magic"—once in the back from behind (the second shot), once in the throat from in front (third shot), and two closely spaced shots to the head after the limo had been brought to a halt (fifth and sixth shots), one from behind and one from in front while another (seventh shot) from behind missed and hit the chrome strip above the

---

* This point was affirmed by a motorcycle policeman, James A. Chaney, quoted in the *Houston Chronicle* on November 24, who said the first shot "missed entirely."
** Researcher Jim Lewis test-fired high-velocity bullets through the windshields of junked cars and discovered that they make the sound of a firecracker as they pass through-(Fetzer, *Hoax . . .* , p. 436).
60. WC Report, Vol. II, p. 74.
61. Weldon, *The Kennedy Limousine (Part II of Murder in Dealey Plaza)*, pp. 151–153.

windshield, and another from the knoll was recovered from the grass (eighth shot). Connally was hit in the back (the fourth shot of the sequence) from the side as he turned to his left to see what was going on with JFK and subsequently by as many as two other shots, which (interspersed between them) hit only him. With respect to the shots that hit Kennedy, Dr. Mantik has established that the final shot to his head was a frangible bullet fired from the north end of the Triple Underpass (from another above ground sewer access structure at the end of the grassy knoll), which entered his right temple and created shock waves that blew through his skull and caused an exit wound at the rear of his damaged skull as seen in frame 374 of the Zapruder film (shown below). This caused his brains and blood to be blown out toward motorcycle policeman Bobby Hargis with such force that he thought momentarily he himself had actually been hit. The diagrams below help to illustrate this fatal wound and how all four shots hit JFK; they were originally published by James H. Fetzer in "Dealey Plaza Revisited: What Happened to JFK?" the last chapter (30) of the book, *JOHN F. KENNEDY: HISTORY, MEMORY, LEGACY*.[62]

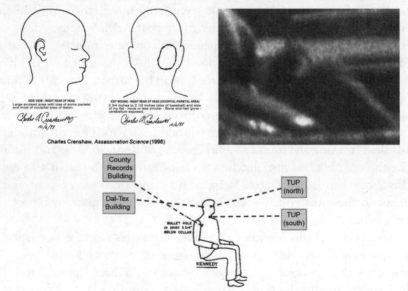

SIDE VIEW - RIGHT REAR OF HEAD
Large avulsed area with loss of some parietal and most of occipital area of lesion.

EXIT WOUND - RIGHT REAR OF HEAD (OCCIPITAL-PARIETAL AREA)
2 3/4 inches to 2 1/2 inches (size of baseball) and size of my fist - more or less circular - Bone and hair gone - cerebellum exposed.

Charles Crenshaw, *Assassination Science* (1998)

As the last shots in this "flurry" hit their mark, the vice president, crouched close to the floor of the Lincoln convertible two cars behind the president's, suddenly became the thirty-sixth president; as he must have known, this was automatically triggered on the basis of the oath he had already sworn on that cold January day 1,037 days earlier. There was never any essential need for him to even take another oath, least of all in an airplane sitting on the tarmac of Dallas' Love Field as he awaited JFK's body, which he had ordered

62. See: http://www.und.edu/instruct/jfkconference/

to be removed from the hospital and delivered to him on Air Force One. The new president had been a nervous wreck ever since arriving in Dallas, and throughout the motorcade he had hunched down in the car such that his profile was even lower than his diminutive wife's for much of the trip; his behavior would become even more strange in the hours to come and would continue to become ever more controversial, even decades later.

But just moments later, as the "smoke cleared" in Dealey Plaza, an irrefutable natural physical phenomenon occurred, which provided conclusive proof of gunfire coming from someplace other than the TSBD building. Numerous witnesses near the grassy knoll, as well as many in the motorcade itself—including Senator Yarborough, Congressman Ray Roberts, and Mrs. Cabell, wife of the mayor—smelled gunpowder as they proceeded west on Elm Street through Dealey Plaza and past the "grassy knoll."[63] The weather front moving into the area from the northwest brought gusty winds, ranging from the southwest to the northwest and north;[64] the only way anyone could have smelled gunpowder on Elm Street was from a grassy knoll or a "triple underpass" shot. In fact, moments after the shooting started, police officer M. L. Baker nearly lost control of his motorcycle from "a strong gust of wind from the north."[65] Only a wind blowing from the *east* could have possibly brought the smell of gunpowder into that area from the so-called "sniper's nest," and even that would have been unlikely because of the distance it would have had to travel. For such a pungent yet ephemeral odor to have wafted all the way down from the sixth floor of the TSBD building toward the southwest, when the wind—especially at sixty plus feet in the air—was blowing other directions, was simply impossible. Even considered apart from every other "anomaly" cited within this text, we have yet another powerful proof, if any more is needed, that the assassination was indeed a conspiracy.

The Witnesses Speak

The witnesses closest to Kennedy when the fatal bullet struck him were Jean Hill and Mary Moorman, both of whom said from the start that the shots had come from the grassy knoll. Ms. Hill said consistently that she heard from four to six shots fired from this area and that after the last shot, she saw a man run from the concrete façade toward the triple underpass.[66] Other witnesses in that area said similar things, as we will see in due course. Five journalists also confirmed that they witnessed indications that shots had come from the grassy knoll or the area around the triple underpass: Tom Wicker

---

63. Manchester, p. 156; Marrs, p. 16.
64. Bishop, 108, Marrs, 7, 16, 59, Fetzer, Murder . . . p. 33; Holland, p. 36.
65. Fetzer, *Murder* . . . p. 37.
66. WC Report, Vol. II. p. 42.

of the *New York Times*, Ronnie Dugger of the *Texas Observer*, James Vachule and Jerry Flemmons of the *Fort Worth Star Telegram*, and Mary Woodward of the *Dallas Morning News* (with a group of three others who also agreed with her) all said that shots came from near their location, behind them as they watched the motorcade in the same area.[67] Ms. Woodward was standing on the sidewalk along Elm Street within fifty feet of the Triple Overpass and stated, "Suddenly there was a horrible, ear-shattering noise coming from behind us, and a little to the right."

Ms. Woodward further stated that "instead of speeding up the car, the car came to a halt . . . I don't believe anyone was hit with the first bullet."[68] Mark Lane testified to the commission about the eyewitness' statements he had gathered, a number of which indicated that some of the first shots had come from the triple overpass, which would confirm Douglas Weldon's findings, above, that the shot to Kennedy's throat came from that direction. One of these witnesses, a reporter for the Fort Worth *Star Telegram*, stated that "Kennedy was gunned down by an assassin, apparently standing on the overpass above the freeway."[69] Ms. Woodward was another witness he quoted as saying that "the shots came from the direction of the overpass, and not at all from the Book Depository Building, which was to their left" (i.e., the direct opposite direction).[70] The wife of mayor Earle Cabell, who was riding in a car four vehicles behind the president's car, was one of many others who swore that the entire motorcade stopped as a result of the Kennedy limousine stopping. "I was aware that the motorcade stopped dead still. There was no question about that." [Later:] "As I told you, the motorcade was stopped." [Later:] "Every car in the motorcade had come to a standstill." [Later:] "we were dead still for a matter of some seconds."[71]

As demonstrated by David W. Mantik, MD, PhD, the ten witnesses closest to Kennedy as he was being shot all stated unequivocally that the limousine either completely or nearly stopped just as Kennedy was being shot in the head.[72] The anomaly this presents is that the momentary stopping of the car—what so many eyewitnesses swore to—was not reflected in the film supposedly shot by Abraham Zapruder. The fact that so many witnesses were absolutely certain of this renders the film of the assassination—generally used as the official timing record—suspect. The dilemma thus created leads inexorably to the conclusion that the film had to have been altered. As Dr. James H. Fetzer recently established, even Clint Hill, in the 2010 book

67. Ibid., pp. 42–43.
68. Ibid., p. 43.
69. Ibid.
70. Ibid.
71. Warren Commission Hearings: 7H, pp. 486–487.
72. Mantik, *The Zapruder Film Controversy*, (*Part II of Murder in Dealey Plaza*), pp. 341–342.

The Kennedy Detail, inadvertently corroborates that point inasmuch as his actions—which he has consistently described for over forty-seven years—are not reflected in the Zapruder film. Moreover, his testimony also contradicts the autopsy x-rays and other photographs:[73]

> The limo stop—during which JFK was hit twice in the head, once from behind and once from in front—was such an obvious indication of Secret Service complicity that it had to be taken out, which is undoubtedly the principal reason for fixing the film. But it had other ramifications. What Clint Hill has consistently described is not in the Zapruder film: he describes several actions in those seconds around the limo stop that were deleted from the extant film. In editing the timeline of the extant film, *it was necessary to delete his pushing of Mrs. Kennedy back into the seat—there just wasn't enough time left in the film once the limo stop had been deleted.* There is no possible way in which Clint could possibly have seen what he claims to have seen *before* the car accelerated away and passed the lead car when he was stuck on the back of the speeding limo as he is shown doing in the extant film. And from his initial reports right up to his latest "book signing" interview, he has insisted that that was when he saw those things, that he did reach Mrs. Kennedy and that he did push her down into the car, unlike what the film shows. Which means that the film is a fake.

All of these credible witnesses were either completely ignored by the Warren Commission or—such as in the case of Jean Hill, whose story will be examined closely in the next chapter—treated contemptuously by Arlen Specter and David Belin in order to try to discredit her testimony and then summarily ignored; the witnesses they decided to consider "important" enough to believe were among the most incredible, nontrustworthy, and unbelievable people they interviewed, as will also shortly become evident. The testimony about the first shot missing Kennedy will also become pertinent as we proceed through the narrative of this story.

Fifteen minutes before the assassination, one witness had been looking up at the windows of the Texas School Book Depository building. Arnold Rowland said that at about 12:15 p.m., as he awaited the motorcade, "he saw *two* men in sixth floor windows, one of them with a rifle across his chest."[74] He further stated that the man holding the rifle was not in the window of the "sniper's nest," at the right side of the building, but a window in the far left-hand side of the sixth floor. The man he saw at the right-hand side was dark complexioned, possibly a Negro.[75] When he informed FBI agents about

---

73. http://jamesfetzer.blogspot.com/2011/01/whos-telling-truth-clint-hill-or.html.
74. Ibid., pp. 169–183.
75. Summers, *Conspiracy*, p. 73.

the second man, "they told me it didn't have any bearing or such on the case right then. In fact they just the same as told me to forget it now . . . They didn't seem interested at all. They didn't pursue this point. They didn't take it down in the notation as such."[76]

About the same time that Rowland noticed the men on the sixth floor, another witness, Ruby Henderson also saw two men standing back from a window. She also noticed "that one of the men had dark hair, a darker complexion than the other." At the time, it occurred to her that he might have been a Mexican or even a Negro.[77] A third witness, Mrs. Carolyn Walther, noticed two men with a gun in an open window. "I saw this man in a window, and he had a gun in his hands, pointed downwards. The man evidently was in a kneeling position, because his forearms were resting on the windowsill. There was another man standing beside him, but I only saw a portion of his body, because he was standing partly up against the window, you know, only halfway in the window; and the window was dirty and I couldn't see his face, up above, because the window was pushed up. It startled me; then I thought, 'Well, they probably have guards, possibly in all the buildings,' so I didn't say anything. If Mrs. Walther had sounded the alarm, it would probably have been too late. She had barely noticed the second man when the President's motorcade swept into view."[78] Two films, by Robert Hughes and Charles Bronson, were made of these windows which indicate movements in more than just the "sniper's window." The Bronson film was reviewed by the FBI and dismissed as "irrelevant."[79]

Mary Mitchell (who had been standing on the southeast corner of Elm and Houston streets) testified to the Warren Commission on April 1, 1964: "Well, the president's car passed and, of course, I watched it as long as I could see it but, as I remember, immediately behind it was a car full of men with the top down and quite a few of them were standing, and I assumed they were Secret Service men, so after the car turned the corner and started down the hill, I couldn't see over the heads of the standing men for very long, so then I turned back to watch the other people in the caravan, whatever you call it, *and probably about the time the car in which Senator Yarborough was riding had just passed, I heard some reports.* The first one—there were three—the second and third being closer together than the first and second and probably on the first one my thought was that it was a firecracker, and I think on the second one I thought that some police officer was after somebody that wasn't doing right."[80] (emphasis added).

---

76. Ibid.
77. Ibid. (also, Marrs, p. 21).
78. Summers, *Conspiracy*, p. 74.
79. Ibid. p. 75.
80. Warren Commission testimony: 6H 176.

It is curious that Mary Mitchell referred to "the car in which Senator Yarborough was riding." The vice president and his wife Lady Bird were also in the car, and most people would have considered him the "primary" occupant given his office. But she didn't even mention Vice President Johnson, who should have been more visible, sitting closer to her as the car entered the intersection; after all, he was the primary "notable occupant" of the car. The reason for her curious observation—the only reasonable explanation about why she didn't remember seeing Johnson—was because he wasn't visible. He had already started ducking down behind the front seats, as if he knew in advance that danger was lurking there at the corner of Houston and Elm streets. Mrs. Mitchell, curiously, was also never questioned about this point by the Warren Commission's lawyers, yet they were eager to go off onto other "fishing expeditions" numerous times with other witnesses as noted elsewhere.

Many people in the area of the grassy knoll said that shots had definitely come from that area. Abraham Zapruder's initial reaction was that the shots had come from behind him, but for some reason he later changed his testimony to say he wasn't sure where the shots came from. Four Dallas policemen rushed up the knoll upon first hearing rifle fire. Joe M. Smith, a patrolman, climbed up the hill and said he "caught the smell of gunpowder there."[81] Officer Smith also stated that "he came across a man standing by a car. The man reacted quickly at the sight of Smith and an accompanying deputy. As Smith remembers it, 'The man, this character produced credentials from his hip pocket which showed him to be Secret Service. I have seen those credentials before, and they satisfied me and the deputy sheriff. So I immediately accepted that and let him go and continued our search around the cars . . . But he had dirty fingernails, it looked like, and hands that looked like an auto mechanic's hands. And afterwards it didn't ring true for the Secret Service . . . I should have checked that man closer, but at the time I didn't snap on it.'"[82] Seven Dallas union terminal railroad men witnessed the assassination and immediately observed a puff of smoke rising from the fence area. "Two of the men, S.M. Holland and James L. Simmons, ran from the overpass and into the railroad yard behind the fence. They found footprints behind the fence, and mud on the back bumper of a car which the gunman, or his spotter, could have stood on."[83]

The Scene at Parkland Hospital

At Parkland Hospital minutes after the shooting, a team of doctors began working exhaustively to try to save JFK's life. Their efforts were futile, of

81. Callahan, *Who Shot JFK?* p. 61.
82. Summers, *Conspiracy*, pp. 80–82.
83. Callahan, *Who Shot JFK?* p. 61.

course, since at least a third of his brain was blown out of his head—ironically, "torn into a thousand pieces and cast unto the winds" on Elm Street—and he could not have been alive when he arrived at Parkland. Within minutes, they came to the realization that there was no hope the president's life could be saved; he was pronounced dead one half hour after he had been shot, at 1:00 p.m., though it appears the conclusion came ten minutes before that but held pending the arrival of a priest.

One of the doctors, Robert McClelland, arrived at trauma room one with Dr. Charles Crenshaw, just behind Dr. Malcolm Perry and Dr. Charles Baxter. Interviewed at age seventy-nine in 2008, he described the president's face as "cyanotic—bluish-black, swollen, suffused with blood."[84] Dr. Perry asked Dr. McClelland to hold a retractor as Perry began to work futilely to save the president, and as Dr. McClelland did so, his face was eighteen inches above the president's head wound.

> McClelland looked into the head wound. Stray hairs at the back of the head covered parts of the hole, as did bits of bone, blood, and more blood clots. He watched as a piece of cerebellum slowly slipped from the back of the hole and dropped onto the cart. (In the room with his students, Dr. McClelland softly touches the rear-right part of his own head. "Right back here," he tells them. "About like this." He puts his hands together to signify the size of the wound, about the size of a golf ball. (This is the writer's characterization; most researchers agree with McClelland's own previously stated comparison to a "baseball"). Staring at the hole in the back of the president's head, "He looked at where the skull crumpled slightly around the edges. Knowing nothing else of the assassination at the time, he, too, assumed a bullet had come out of that opening."[85]

None of the doctors there, of course, had heard anything about the supposed shot from the book depository, so they had already concluded that the hole in the "right rear" of Kennedy's head was an exit wound, just as they had assumed the neck wound and temple wound were entrance wounds; they had not noticed the additional entrance wound in his back. Dr. McClelland was convinced, again, that the shot had come from Kennedy's front and to his right upon seeing the Zapruder film for the first time in 1975 and seeing how the president swayed "back and to the left."[86] About 1:30 p.m., the White House assistant press secretary Malcolm Kilduff, announcing Kennedy's

---

84. Mooney, p. 180.
85. Ibid.
86. Ibid.

murder, pointed to his own right temple to illustrate the direction from which he had been hit, saying, "He died of a gunshot wound in the brain . . . of a bullet right through the head."[87]

Dr. Charles Crenshaw had left the room briefly while Kennedy was given his last rites and the death certificate was being prepared. As he returned, he saw two pathology doctors explaining to the Secret Service agents that an autopsy was now necessary, according to Texas law. The discussion at that point was polite but forceful; however, the agents' responses were becoming even more emphatic that "*they had orders to take the President's body back to Washington, D.C.* just as soon as it was ready to be moved, that there would be no Texas autopsy . . . talking turned to shouting and hand waving escalated to finger pointing. Unable to prevail in their mission, Drs. Stembridge and Stewart angrily wheeled and stomped away. Not only were they outnumbered, but the men in suits had guns. *My impression was that someone, who had given explicit instructions to these men, wanted Kennedy's body out of Parkland, out of Dallas, and out of Texas in a hurry*" (emphasis added).[88] Can there be any question whatsoever about just who it was that was acting "behind the scenes?" Or who might have had the authority—at least thought he had the authority—to circumvent Texas law and order that JFK's body be forcefully removed from the hospital and brought back to his airplane so it could be returned to Washington with him?

The arguments grew worse until a phalanx of Secret Service agents encircled the bronze casket into which Kennedy had been placed and began forcibly taking it toward the hallway. The chief of forensic pathology, Dr. Earl Rose, had by now taken over the argument, telling Roy Kellerman, "When there's a homicide, we must have an autopsy."[89] Dr. Rose had correctly sensed the same level of pent-up anger—and the danger of continuing the argument—after ten minutes of screaming back and forth and decided to let go of the coffin just before the guns of the Secret Service were pulled from their holsters.[90] Anthony Summers stated that the guns were indeed drawn. "The Secret Service agents put the doctor and the judge up against the wall at gunpoint and swept out of the hospital with the President's body."[91]

Jim Bishop's and William Manchester's account of the surreal scene were similar: Dr. Rose was insistent that JFK's body remain at Parkland until a proper autopsy could be performed, in accordance with Texas law; seeing

---

87. Ibid., p. 83.
88. Crenshaw, p. 76.
89. Ibid., pp. 88–90.
90. Manchester, p. 302.
91. Summers, *Conspiracy*, p. 42.

that Kellerman was not backing down, he became apoplectic—furious that there was even a question about whether it would be done—and ordered Kellerman to step aside. Kellerman responded in kind, ordering Dr. Rose to get out of the way, that the body would be transported back to Washington immediately; they would have to waive their laws. [92]

After several more minutes of this back and forth squabbling over JFK's body, and the hospital's search for a justice of the peace, JP Theron Ward arrived on the scene, but by then tempers on both sides had flared, including the president's doctor, Admiral George Burkley.[93] Kellerman and the other Washingtonians were not impressed by the "JP" title or of Ward's physical presence. In the end, JP Ward would only say, "It's just another homicide case as far as I'm concerned."[94] By this time, everyone on both sides of the impasse had come to such anger that nothing that JP Ward might say could have resolved it; the tension continued to escalate as Kenneth O'Donnell glanced at Sergeant Robert Dugger of the Dallas Police, seeing that he was about to lose control and attack someone. Rose himself looked like he was ready to attack Kellerman who he continued screaming at as he flapped and swung his arms for added emphasis.[95]

As Rose and other policemen kept trying to stop them, finally, several agents led by Kellerman—with Larry O'Brien and Ken O'Donnell in front of the gurney and leading the way—shoved their way past the medical examiner and justice of the peace, ordering everyone to get out of the way, that they were waiting no longer, it was time to go.[96] Doctor Rose, in his quest to preserve the "chain of evidence," was evidently the only official in Dallas or Washington that day who remembered this fundamental rule of criminal investigations; JFK's body was only one of the more prominent items that would be compromised by the rush to return to Washington and "normalcy" that would justify a complete breakdown in practically all rules of ordinary police procedure. The most likely way that this near violent incident then ended so suddenly was just as Anthony Summers described it: Kellerman and the other agents finally put the doctor and judge "up against the wall at gunpoint" as they commandeered the casket and carried it out to the waiting hearse. This action could have only realistically been accomplished in compliance with orders that came from the highest possible authority of the U.S. government.

---

92. Manchester, pp. 297–298.
93. Ibid., p. 303.
94. Ibid., pp. 299–302.
95. Ibid.
96. Ibid., p. 304.

Three Credible Witnesses: Jack Ruby was at Parkland Hospital

About the same time as the frenzied fight over JFK's body was playing out, three witnesses saw Jack Ruby at Parkland: Veteran newsmen Seth Kantor and Roy Stamps, both of whom had known Ruby for years, and housewife Wilma Tice.[97] In his testimony to the Warren Commission, Seth Kantor said he knew Ruby personally, having worked with him on at least six feature stories about people of interest who came through his clubs. He stated that he had numerous meetings with Ruby during the period when he worked in Dallas at the *Herald Tribune*, from September 1960 to May 1962. Yet when commission attorney Burt Griffin questioned him, he repeatedly used the words "you think," or "you might have," seen Jack Ruby, as if to suggest that Kantor might have been confused on this point or perhaps not completely certain it was indeed Jack Ruby he saw.

However, Kantor would testify, under oath, that he was positive that he had seen *and* talked to Jack Ruby at Parkland Hospital. "As I had told the FBI . . . I spoke with Jack Ruby . . . [followed by three pages of inane questions about exactly which doorway he was near at Parkland when this conversation occurred] as I was walking, I was stopped momentarily by a tug on the back of my jacket. And I turned and saw Jack Ruby standing there. He had his hand extended. I very well remember my first thought. I thought, well, there is Jack Ruby. I had been away from Dallas 18 months and 1 day at that time, but it seemed just perfectly normal to see Jack Ruby standing there, because he was a known goer to events . . . And I took his hand and shook hands with him. He called me by name. And I said hello to him, I said, 'Hello, Jack,' I guess. And he said, 'Isn't this a terrible thing?' I said, 'Yes' but I also knew it was no time for small talk, and I was most anxious to continue on up the stairway . . . But he asked me, curiously enough, he said, "Should I close my places for the next three nights, do you think?'"[98] Kantor went on to say that "if it was a matter of just seeing him, I would have long ago been full of doubt. But I did talk to the man, and he did stop me, and I just can't have any doubt about that."[99]

But the sworn testimony of a man who knew Jack Ruby—who had known him for years—and *who had talked to Jack Ruby at length in Parkland Hospital* shortly after Kennedy's assassination could not persuade the staff and/or the august commissioners of the presidential commission charged with investigating the circumstances of the assassination that there was anything to it. Yet other incredible and discredited witnesses—Helen Markham, for

---

97. WC Hearings and Exhibits, Vol. XV., p. 82.
98. WC Hearings and Exhibits, Vol. XV, pp. 71–82.
99. Ibid., p. 82.

instance, is the best of several examples—were embraced by the commission as completely reliable (arguably the worst witness was the new president, who refused to testify under oath or even submit to a deposition under oath; they simply accepted Johnson's casually written statement).

The Hunt for JFK's Assassin Begins . . . and Abruptly Ends, the Same Day

By 12:45 p.m., a radio dispatcher at Dallas Police headquarters had already sent out a description (the source of which remains unclear) of a man wanted for questioning: "an unknown white male approximately thirty, 165 pounds, slender build armed with what is thought to be a .30-30 rifle."[100] Around 1:30 p.m., the hunt for Kennedy's assassin was somehow merged (how and why is also unclear) with that of the killer of policeman J. D. Tippit in the Texas Theater, a few miles southwest of Dealey Plaza. About the same time, a rifle was discovered inside a stack of boxes toward the northeast corner of the sixth floor. It was initially reported—not as the infamous 6.5 mm Italian Mannlicher-Carcano supposedly owned by Oswald—as a 7.65 mm German Mauser, according to Roger Craig and other policemen on the scene who found the rifle. According to Jim Bishop's account, "Deputy Eugene Boone yelled: 'Here is the gun!' . . . He was near the staircase leading down, farthest away from the window where the shells had been found . . . It was standing upright between two triple rows of cartons, squeezed tight."[101] Deputy Constable Seymour Weitzman, who was with Deputy Boone when the rifle was found, executed an affidavit the following day stating that the rifle found on the sixth floor of the depository was a 7.65 Mauser equipped with a 4/18 scope with a leather sling on it.[102] Deputy Sheriff Roger Craig was standing near Weitzman at the time the rifle was discovered; he said that Weitzman already thought it was a Mauser when he first looked at it then, after inspecting it closely, confirmed verbally that it was stamped "7.65 Mauser."[103]

But someone realized that this gun could not have produced the rifle shells which had been found at the "sniper's lair." In order to get around this dilemma, the FBI reports and the Warren Commission attempted to erase all references to a 7.65 Mauser and replace them with their finding that it was a 6.5 Mannlicher-Carcano, with paperwork that indicated Lee Harvey Oswald had obtained it through a mail-order transaction from his post office

100. WC Report, Vol. XXIII, p. 916.
101. Bishop, p. 254.
102. Lane, *Rush to Judgment*, p. 409.
103. This testimony can be seen in the film *Evidence of Revision* on Youtube, Part IV.

box. Deputy Sheriff Boone, in obeisance to his chief, Sheriff Bill Decker, quickly amended his description of the rifle he had been the first to find: from the high-quality Mauser to the cheap, army-surplus Italian rifle, which was congruent with the developing "official" story version.

Weitzman also later recanted his previously sworn statements that the gun was a Mauser, even though he never even saw the Mannlicher-Carcano held by the Warren Commission to confirm that it was the rifle he had seen on the sixth floor. A Dallas woman whose father was Seymour Weitzman's best friend—and who knew him intimately herself as "Uncle Sy"—stated that Weitzman was pressured at the threat of losing his job if he did not cooperate by recanting his sworn statement. She explained that the threats apparently had gone well beyond the mere loss of his job and ultimately provoked extreme stress, which caused him "blackouts" and nightmares about his wartime experiences related to being a prisoner of the Japanese and memories of his torture.[104] Here is how the Warren Commission dealt with all of the confusion in crafting its "conclusions":

> Weitzman did not handle the rifle and did not examine it at close range . . . thought it was a Mauser . . . [and eventually] police laboratory technicians subsequently arrived and correctly identified the weapon as a 6.5 Italian rifle.

Unbeknownst to anyone reading the official reports of the investigation, the Mannlicher-Carcano was actually found on a lower floor of the building, according to Frank Ellsworth, an ATF agent who had found the sniper's nest and was involved in the search for guns. "We started at the top of the building and worked our way down . . . The gun was not found on the same floor, but on a lower floor by a couple of city detectives. If I recollect right, there was an elevator shaft or stairwell back in the northwest corner. The gun was over near that, just south of it behind some boxes."[105]

Meanwhile, in the executive offices of H. L. Hunt a few blocks from Dealey Plaza, on the afternoon of November 22, a call for H. L. was received from someone in FBI headquarters who advised him that he and his family may face threats, due to a perception that he might have been involved in the assassination, and was advised to leave town as soon as possible. According to his 1981 biography, *Texas Rich*, he demurred but his son and the family's security chief Paul Rothermel Jr. urged him to accede to the FBI request. He

104. http://www.jfklancerforum.com/dc/dcboard.php?az=show_topic&forum=3&topic_id=57273&mesg_id=57273&page=
105. Russell, p. 568.

finally agreed to go to Washington saying, "I believe I can do better going to Washington to help Lyndon. He's gonna need some help."[106]

Oswald's Escape to Oak Cliff and the Shooting of Officer Tippit

About two minutes after the assassination (12:32 p.m.), Oswald was stopped momentarily by a policeman who had run into the TSBD building. He was casually drinking a Coke on the second floor, near the pay telephone installed for employees' use, essentially the same place he had been when last seen by a secretary in the building at 12:15 to 12:20 p.m.[107] This credible witness, who gave a report to the FBI, was ignored completely by the Warren Commission because her testimony did not fit their preestablished scenario.

At about the same time, Arnold Rowland saw two men in the sixth-floor windows, one of whom was holding a rifle. Rowland (whose testimony was backed up by his wife) remembered that as this happened, he heard over the police radio that the motorcade had reached Cedar Springs Road, which it had, at 12:15 p.m. Rowland was told that he was mistaken; his testimony was given to the Warren Commission, but they chose to ignore it. This was one of many similar instances where the Warren Commission demonstrated that it had no interest in perusing FBI reports that had been suppressed by bureau officials who decided against furnishing the commission certain nonconforming information to avoid contaminating the proceedings. Only fourteen minutes after the assassination, at 12:44 p.m., the first police radio broadcast of the assassin's description was made:

> Attention all squads . . . The suspect in the shooting at Elm and Houston is supposed to be an unknown white male approximately 30, 165 pounds, slender build, armed with what is thought to be a 30-30 rifle . . . no further description at this time. [The Warren Report never identified the source of this description and offered no explanation of how this description materialized.]

Unlike the implausible "official story" of how Oswald got from downtown Dallas to his Oak Cliff apartment in less than twenty-five minutes and then to the location where Officer Tippit was killed, and the many improbable (more accurately, impossible) circumstances of Oswald's arrest—the questionable witness testimony, the mishandling of the bullets and shells, the fact there were two types of bullets used, and the compelling indications that there

---

106. Russell, p. 586.
107. North, p. 377.

were two shooters of Tippit—the version offered by Officer Roger Craig is more realistic. In an unpublished memoir available at several internet sites, he described the impossibility of Oswald's movements after having been questioned by Officer Baker: walking four blocks east on Elm Street to board a city bus, ride it back in slow traffic for two blocks then exiting the bus to hail a cab, drive to a point five blocks away from his rooming house at 1026 North Beckley then walk back to that address to change his shirt and get his gun and somehow be back on the curb waiting for a bus in front of the rooming house thirty minutes after leaving Officer Baker at the Book Depository Building—at 1:05 p.m., according to his landlord/housekeeper, Earlene Roberts. Tippit was killed within five minutes of this, ten blocks in the opposite direction from where he waited to board the bus. Moreover, the description of the suspect, according to a witness to the shooting, was of a man who had black wavy hair and was taller and heavier than Oswald. But the part most inconsistent with Oswald being the shooter was the fact that he carried a pistol (revolver), yet the shells found on the scene were of two types, both of which were from an *automatic* handgun. Several authors have already established the impossibility of Oswald's supposed murder of Tippit; a good summary of the reasons why was described by Jim Marrs in his book, *Crossfire*.[108]

Within ninety minutes of the assassination, the cover-up was started by the apprehension of the designated "patsy," the "lone nut" who somehow became the number one suspect and the subject of a citywide manhunt. Lee Harvey Oswald, a.k.a. Alek Hidell, was arrested less than two hours after JFK's assassination as he sat in a Dallas theater with a defective revolver waiting for his contact to appear with papers, money, and instructions for fleeing Dallas.

Unfortunately for Deputy Roger Craig, everything he witnessed was at odds with what was being orchestrated in the background as the "official story." He was hounded continuously by Sheriff Decker for months afterward and his life threatened numerous times because he would not change his story to conform with Washington's version of events, until he was finally fired. His superiors made sure that he could not find comparable employment elsewhere and managed to scrape by for several years, narrowly escaping two obvious attempts on his life. His body was eventually found after being shot to death in what was ruled as a suicide. He can be found on Internet videos describing the events of November 22, 1963, arguably one of the true heroes of that day who refused to change his story because of orders from his superiors.

---

108. Marrs, pp. 340–350.

The (New) Presidential Party Escapes to Love Field

When Lyndon Johnson returned to Love Field, according to one of his police escorts, B. J. Martin,* "He acted scared, but that's just it—it was like he was acting, not like he was really in fear of his life. I remember hearing him yell to somebody as he was getting in the car. He said, 'We've all got to be very careful. This could be a worldwide conspiracy to kill off all our leaders.' The thing that struck me was he seemed to be in total charge already. Everybody else was kind of numb and reeling with shock, but Johnson was in full control, giving orders and telling people what to do." Chief Jesse Curry used an unmarked police car to drive Johnson, lying on the rear floor to avoid what he knew was a nonexistent sniper, back to Love Field. Agent Youngblood and Congressman Albert Thomas were also in the car, accompanied by several police motorcycle officers to clear intersections on the way, allowing the car to proceed through "pink lights." Asked if he wanted to go back to Air Force Two, the plane he arrived in, which was identical to Air Force One, Johnson said, 'No, take me to Air Force One. That's where I belong now.'"[109] He had already mentioned, at Parkland Hospital to Secret Service Agent Emory Roberts, who had said, "We've got to get in the air," that "maybe President Kennedy will need the airplane,"[110] as though there was only one airplane. Manchester noted that the confusion regarding Air Force One started at this point, even before he left for Love Field; from then on, the backup plane was almost forgotten, only JFK's airplane would do for the new president.[111]

The takeover of "Angel" was an essential part of the pre-and postassassination plans, and it was revealed while Johnson was still at Parkland by his comment, above, which said in effect, "Yes, I agree, we must get back to the airplane; but we will need to wait on JFK's body before we leave." At the heart of the controversy about his decision to take over Air Force One is Johnson's assertion that he had discussed the matter with Kenneth O'Donnell before he left Parkland Hospital. According to Manchester's account, Johnson said that O'Donnell had in fact urged him to use Air Force One and that Johnson accepted the suggestion, but only with the understanding that he would wait on board for JFK's casket and his widow. Manchester charged that, *"O'Donnell declares this version to be 'absolutely, totally, and unequivocally wrong.'"*[112] Furthermore, O'Donnell had maintained that,

---

* Under the pseudonym J. B. Marshall, in Jean Hill's book *JFK: Last Dissenting Witness.*
109. Sloan and Hill, *JFK: The Last Dissenting Witness.* p. 118–119.
110. Manchester, p. 233.
111. Ibid.
112. Manchester, pp. 234–235.

because Johnson mentioned the possibility of a conspiracy, he agreed that Johnson should leave Dallas quickly; he reiterated strongly that there was no conversation about Johnson using Air Force One, and if there had been such a conversation, he would have simply changed the Kennedy group over to the other airplane. O'Donnell repeated his insistence, in his own book, that he had never said that Johnson should shift to the other airplane. "He [Johnson] never suggested that he might wait at the airport for Jackie and the body of President Kennedy before he left for Washington. If he had made such a suggestion, I would have vetoed it . . . He never discussed with me whether he should use Air Force One instead of Air Force Two, a question which would have seemed highly unimportant at the time."[113]

According to motorcycle police officer B. J. Martin, Johnson was condescending and overtly rude with everyone when he returned to Love Field.[114] He demanded to be taken to Air Force One and that his luggage also be transferred to that plane in spite of the fact that his original plane would have been automatically redesignated as "Air Force One" since that is the code for whatever plane the president was flying on. And the planes were identical. "Both planes had the same equipment and facilities. The only difference between Air Force One and Air Force Two was the identification numbers on their tails."[115]* But he was determined to use the interior of Kennedy's aircraft as a setting for a photographic event: the new president taking his oath, with JFK's widow beside him.

His action in taking over the Kennedy plane and with him his coterie of highest level assistants—including Bill Moyers, Cliff Carter, his wife, and their luggage—resulted in overcrowding that plane. The space taken up by Johnson's people forced some of the Kennedy group, including five congressmen and Senator Yarborough, to change to the other aircraft. According to Manchester's account, as long as Kennedy was still alive, Yarborough had been treated kindly and as soon as he was dead, suddenly he was an outcast; he asked Ted Clifton why he was being kicked off the airplane and was told, "maximum security."[116] In the Boeing 707 code named Air Force Two, which Johnson had flown in that morning (since neither a president nor vice president was aboard, it would now be referred to simply

---

*According to William Manchester, "The one difference between Air Force One and Air Force Two was that Air Force One always carried a passenger manifest. It was a basic security precaution; no matter how short the flight, a presidential guest could not mount either ramp unless his name had been typed on that sheet. (p. 314).
113. O'Donnell, p. 32.
114. Sloan and Hill, pp. 118–119.
115. O'Donnell, p. 31.
116. Manchester, p. 315.

as the "backup plane"), the friction between the Texans and the non-Texans was as fierce as it was on the newly sworn President Lyndon B. Johnson's Air Force One.[117] The Kennedy party's hearts were still with their fallen leader, and with Mrs. Kennedy who was now considered the leader by default; all of them were anxious to leave, even bewildered that they had not left as soon as the coffin was brought on board. The attitude of the Johnson party was summed by SS agent Youngblood, who told Lem Johns, "When the boss says we go, *then* we go."[118] Johnson had a larger plan in mind, which required that he be sworn in before leaving Dallas, under the pretext that it was the attorney general's wish.

Floor Plan of Air Force One (aircraft 26000) (From Manchester, p. 682)

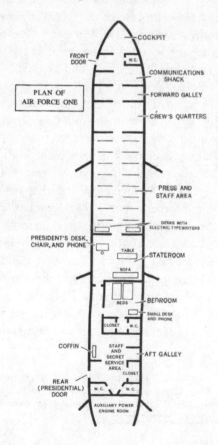

---

117. Manchester, p. 329.
118. Ibid., p. 315.

None of the crew or other staffers still aboard 26000 had expected Johnson, of course, so nothing had been done to prepare for his arrival other than Kennedy's valet, George Thomas, upon hearing the news on the television the staff had been watching, repacked JFK's change of clothes which he had previously laid out for him.[119] Since there had been no warning that Johnson was intent on taking over the airplane, when he suddenly appeared, it put the crew in a difficult and awkward position since it was embarrassing to them to be so unprepared for Johnson's arrival.[120]

As he raced from the unmarked police car, Johnson doubtlessly knew that by taking over the president's plane, he was finally and officially in control of the country as the new president. He apparently was so excited about it that he neglected to return Captain Swindal's salute as he ducked past him and raced up the boarding stairs into the cabin.[121] When Bill Moyers boarded the aircraft and first saw Johnson in the stateroom, Johnson nodded slightly but neither spoke; he reported that Johnson seemed strangely subdued and very distracted.[122]

When Godfrey McHugh arrived back at Love Field, he had heard that Johnson was on board but didn't believe it so he walked the length of the plane looking for him. He subsequently walked it again going the other direction, but still found no sign of Johnson, looking in every compartment other than the powder room adjoining the bedroom, which is exactly where Johnson had been. Given that it took McHugh three trips before finding him, it was clear that Johnson had spent considerable time in the restroom of the airplane attempting to compose himself.[123] By the time McHugh started his new search, the word had spread throughout the plane that the judge was on her way to the airport and that it had been decided by none other than Robert F. Kennedy that Johnson had to be sworn in as soon as possible; it was not something that could be put off until he returned to Washington. It was summed up by Malcolm Kilduff, to both Clint Hill and Roy Kellerman, "A judge is going to swear in Johnson. *Bobby requested it*"[124] (emphasis added to denote how the lie transformed to become the "truth").

In the meantime, General McHugh began his third search throughout the airplane for some sign of Lyndon Johnson's presence. After covering virtually the entire plane, he finally decided that he should check the powder room adjacent to the bedroom. "'I walked in the toilet, in the powder room,

---

119. Ibid., p. 263.
120. Ibid., pp. 264–265.
121. Ibid., p. 266.
122. Ibid., p. 318.
123. Ibid.
124. Ibid., pp. 311–316.

and there he was hiding, with the curtain closed.' He claimed LBJ was crying 'they're going to kill us all. It's a plot. It's a plot. It's going to kill us all. Johnson was hysterical, sitting down on the john there alone."[125] Johnson's hysteria was apparently the result of his pent-up nervousness, which had been evident in his behavior throughout the day; he had probably heard McHugh coming and might have even decided that it was time to change his demeanor to feign fear of a conspiracy, which was consistent with the script that he had planned, though there was no evidence that he was really concerned about that possibility, as will be seen shortly. In another account of this incident, Christopher Anderson stated that General McHugh found Johnson so deranged that he decided the only way to get him to snap out of his delirium was by slapping him.[126] This account of Johnson's hysteria was in sharp contrast to the many other reports, which stated that he was in complete control, steady, and resolute amidst the grieving and emotional upset of everyone else on the aircraft; all of this was not inconsistent with other accounts of Johnson's behavior, which indicated that his mood swings could rapidly go from one extreme to another as he perceived circumstances required.

But this one, an apparent nervous breakdown on board Air Force One right after the assassination deserves special attention because of the likelihood that it was a result of his finally finding enough privacy to allow himself a moment to physically release the built-up tension that he had suppressed for hours—actually, days and weeks of intense anticipation—as he planned the critical action that would save his career: the murder of JFK. Critics will point out that if McHugh had really experienced such a shocking sight—Lyndon B. Johnson in meltdown—why didn't he say anything to William Manchester in his interview with him in 1964 instead of waiting until 1978 for his oral history taken by author Gillon, which was not released until 2009? The answer may lie in the fact that Manchester, as will be detailed in chapter 9, was forced by Mrs. Kennedy to delete several pages that described the worst of Johnson's behavior in his book concerning the events on Air Force One out of fear that Johnson would make reprisals against her and Bobby.

McHugh had always disliked Johnson, and this incident did nothing to change that; the tension felt throughout Air Force One continued unabated, leading to McHugh saying loudly enough for many others to hear, that *his* president was lying in a coffin in the rear compartment.[127] It was

---

125. Gillon, pp. 127–128.
126. Ibid. (ref. Anderson, *Christopher, Jackie after Jack: Portrait of the Lady*. New York: William Morris, 1998.
127. Manchester, p. 316.

a dramatic and emotional moment, and the story was quickly repeated to most of the others on board, including Lyndon Johnson; it would eventually cost McHugh his job and even cut short his military career.[128] McHugh's description of Johnson's antics on Air Force One, as he told Robert Kennedy back in Washington, was "obscene. There wasn't any other word to use and it was the worst performance he'd ever witnessed."[129] McHugh would have certainly emphasized Johnson's nervous breakdown on board the airplane to RFK, but Bobby knew that he was in no position to use it against Johnson, especially given Johnson's friendship with Hoover; he knew that his power as attorney general was over, that he would be cut off from below by Hoover, and above by Johnson. Katzenbach would have to fill in for him from then on as the "de facto AG."

The communications gear on the aircraft recorded telephone calls but operated only when the plane was airborne. Although the technicians were able to set up the equipment to make calls, none were recorded between 1:26 p.m. when Johnson arrived and 2:47 p.m. when the airplane became airborne.[130] Of the conversations which were recorded after the plane was in the air, according to author David Lifton, many are missing completely and others have been edited. "Attempts to locate the whereabouts of the original tape recordings—attempts made by several researchers, including myself—have so far proved fruitless."[131] Johnson made numerous calls and constantly had his secretary working on making more. Most were made to Washington, to talk to (among others who could not be identified because, as noted above, these records have disappeared) Jenkins, Bundy, and Robert Kennedy. One of his Washington calls was to Abe Fortas, to ask about the Senate Rules Committee hearings on his and Baker's conduct, specifically regarding the testimony of Don Reynolds,[132] which will be reviewed in detail in chapter 9. Other calls were made to Dallas, Austin, and Houston. He also spoke to his personal tax lawyer, J. W. "Waddy" Bullion, asking for advice on what to do with his stock portfolio, considering the market's certain plunge following the assassination.[133] Pat Holloway, an attorney who worked for Bullion, stated that he took that call and listened as Johnson began telling Bullion about his number one concern at that point—at 1:00 p.m. on November 22, 1963, just as Kennedy was being pronounced dead—and it had nothing to do with John F. Kennedy. As Holloway reported it, Johnson said, "'Oh I gotta get rid of

---

128. Ibid.
129. Schlesinger, p. 675.
130. Ibid., p. 268.
131. Lifton, p. 683.
132. Ira David Wood III, *Murder in Dealey Plaza*, p. 93.
133. Ibid., p. 94.

my goddamn Halliburton stock.' Lyndon Johnson was talking about the consequences of his political problems with his Halliburton stock at a time when the president had been officially declared dead. And that pissed me off . . . It really made me furious."[134]

He also called Irving L. Goldberg, another Dallas attorney, and tried to call Federal Judge Sarah Hughes. His secretary was trying to get through to her, but she had not returned from the Trade Mart; they had only gotten as far as her law clerk, John Spinuzzi. Johnson grabbed the phone from his secretary and told Spinuzzi, "This is Lyndon Johnson. Find her," and hung up the receiver.[135] Federal Judge Sarah Hughes had called in to her office shortly after Johnson had left the message with her law clerk, Mr. Spinuzzi, then returned the call and said she could be at Love Field within ten minutes. Secret Service Agent Youngblood continued acting as Johnson's senior aide, taking care of a number of tasks, such as assigning agent Lem Johns the responsibility of identifying Johnson's staff members for the crew and, more importantly, ordering the aircraft's captain, Colonel James Swindal, to delay the departure until the arrival of the Kennedys.[136]

It is a reasonable and logical assumption, based upon Mr. Manchester's original research on this point, that it was also Johnson who ordered the Secret Service to forcibly remove Kennedy's body from Parkland Hospital before a thorough and professional autopsy was completed by doctors who were familiar with the proper methods of doing them. In fact, it is more than a reasonable conclusion: who else could have realistically done so? The Warren Report implicitly acknowledged that he had done so, according to the record of the hearings: "The president also requested that he be kept advised of the location of Mrs. Kennedy and the body of the late president and to inform him when the president's body would arrive."[137] Moreover, SS Agent Kellerman's performance at Parkland Hospital, where he stated he had "orders" to remove Kennedy's body, could only have come from one man: Lyndon B. Johnson (even though Jacqueline, for her own reasons, may have favored that as well, she certainly had no authority to issue anyone "orders"). Johnson's initial, and practiced, reaction to a number of people—Malcolm Kilduff, Bobby Kennedy, the policemen who escorted him back to Love Field—was to state his concern that the assassination might be part of some sort of Communist conspiracy. The first of these came at 1:15 p.m. in Dallas, when Assistant Press Secretary Kilduff asked Johnson to make a statement on

---

134. Baker, Russ, p. 132
135. Manchester, p. 272.
136. Ibid., p. 265.
137. WCH, Volume XVIII, p. 813.

what had happened. His response was "No. Wait. We don't know whether it's a Communist conspiracy or not. Are they prepared to get me out of here?"[138] Skeptics might be forgiven for thinking that many of Johnson's reactions in the aftermath—the hours, days, and weeks after the assassination—seemed to be rote and well practiced, anything but spontaneous.

When he later called Robert Kennedy, he expressed brief condolences but quickly turned to other matters, including his stated concern that the assassination might be part of a "worldwide plot."[139] Despite his words of concern to others, Larry Hancock observed that Johnson made numerous telephone calls and continued holding the aircraft exposed on the ground in Dallas for over an hour and a half. "Johnson was sensitive enough to his behavior over the oath that he would later make three different statements (including two of them in his Warren Commission affidavit) putting the responsibility for the delay on Robert Kennedy and Kenny O'Donnell. But Johnson's statements in both cases were adamantly denied by those individuals."[140] In his call to Robert Kennedy, Johnson offered his condolences and commented, again, that the murder "might be part of a worldwide plot." In his later statement to the Warren Commission, he said that the attorney general agreed with this assessment, although in fact, Robert Kennedy was unresponsive. Johnson said that "a lot of people down here think I should be sworn in right away . . . do you have any objection to that?" Kennedy was taken aback since he couldn't understand the need for a rush and preferred that the formal oath be deferred until his brother's body was returned to Washington. He did not respond to Johnson, so Lyndon kept talking about how he should take the oath, who would swear him in.[141] Bobby said he would look into that question and call him back.

Shortly after that, RFK called Nicholas Katzenbach, telling him of his conversation with Johnson, including the fact that he wanted to be sworn in immediately, at Love Field; Katzenbach said that he was "stunned" by this. By the time Bobby called Johnson back, the new president had already talked to Walter Jenkins and was now talking to McGeorge Bundy about the oath questions. Just as his conversation with Kenneth O'Donnell was disputed by the only other party to it, Johnson's conversation with Bobby was recalled differently by each of them. Johnson told the Warren Commission that Kennedy had advised *him* that he should have the oath administered in Texas.[142] *Kennedy denied ever saying that he should be sworn in immediately*; it

---

138. Hancock, p. 401.
139. Manchester, p. 269.
140. Hancock, p. 402.
141. Manchester, p. 269.
142. Ibid., p. 271.

was his recollection that he only told Johnson that anybody can get the oath, it's in the Constitution, and that any of the judges Johnson had appointed could do it.[143] The only logical reason for his taking over Air Force One, setting off further shock waves to everyone in the Kennedy party who were already in obvious distress, was because Johnson was determined to have JFK's body and Jackie accompany him back to Washington. It had to be something Johnson had mulled over for a long period beforehand, knowing how it would be perceived, but it would be the temporary discomfort of a few people he generally despised anyway. Their shock would be far outweighed by the unique opportunity to convey to the world that he was now in charge of his country; the pictures showing the *imprimatur* of JFK's widow acknowledging the transfer of power would ensure that the dramatic moment was flashed around the world: Lyndon B. Johnson was now officially the president of the United States and the most powerful man in the world, not to mention the universe. To forego this opportunity—even though he arguably didn't need to be "sworn in" at all since he was by definition president the moment JFK died—would mean a lost opportunity to establish the defining point that he knew would communicate his "readiness" to the world. Besides, there were other reasons he wanted JFK's body back on board the airplane and not on some autopsy table at Parkland Hospital.

Lyndon Johnson Takes Command

The motorcycle patrolman who helped flank the presidential limousine, B. J. Martin,* later accompanied the new president Lyndon Johnson, said that "he seemed to be in total charge already . . . Johnson was in full control, giving orders and telling people what to do."[144] At the same time as he was using this scenario to scare everyone into following his orders without question; he had already ordered the FBI and the police (through Chief Curry, who had remained with Johnson on Air Force One throughout the period of waiting on Jacqueline and JFK's casket) to begin guiding/coercing/ threatening witnesses into the "lone assassin" story, minimizing any talk of a conspiracy. It was reported that Johnson was on the telephone barking orders to assorted people throughout that time and had also told Chief Curry to stay with him during this entire period when the police chief would have ordinarily been at the center of the emergency investigation and the dragnet

---

*Quoted by Jean Hill under the pseudonym J. B. Marshall in her book, *JFK: Last Dissenting Witness.*
143. Ibid., pp. 271–272.
144. Sloan and Hill, *Last Dissenting Witness,* p. 118.

that had suddenly been put over the entire city.[145] Yet Curry seemed more interested in being photographed with Johnson inside the plane in several photographs; Congressman Thomas observed that, in Curry's obsession to be photographed inside Air Force One, he "was standing on tiptoes and obscuring those behind him."[146]

As the primary crime scene, the stretch Lincoln convertible known to the Secret Service as X-100 would almost immediately be compromised by its own custodians—who were also, at once, the primary investigators of the crime and deeply implicated in the events leading to the assassination—unwittingly or not. Secret Service agents had already washed most of the blood and brain tissue off the presidential limousine (i.e., the crime scene) while it was still parked at the hospital ER. On Johnson's orders, Agent Greer drove the limousine back to Love Field and had it loaded into the cargo plane, flown back to Washington, and placed back into the White House garage within hours of the assassination. A few days later, the vehicle as a "crime scene" would be completely destroyed and rebuilt (more on this point in chapter 9).

None of the Kennedy group had imagined that anyone—including even the famously audacious Lyndon Johnson—would have had the impudence to take over their plane. This came as a shock, considering the trauma they had just experienced, as Mrs. Kennedy and the JFK aides returned to the airplane. The enormous stress they were under after the murder of the president and the subsequent battle with Dr. Rose to remove the body had left them all in shock only to be faced with the fact that Lyndon Johnson had expropriated their airplane. When Jacqueline Kennedy entered the airplane unaware of the changed arrangements, she turned toward the dim corridor and stepped softly into the rear compartment where the coffin had been placed; she opened the door to the bedroom and was surprised to find the new president lying on the bed, giving dictation to a secretary. Johnson got up and the two quickly left the bedroom.[147]

When General Godfrey McHugh had thought everyone was aboard and ready to fly back to Washington, he ordered Captain Swindal to start the engines; but, no sooner than engine No. 3 was started, Johnson ordered it shut down again, saying "I've got to be sworn in here. I've talked to the Attorney General."[148] Between Swindal, McHugh, Malcolm Kilduff, and Ken O'Donnell, there was mass confusion, each countermanding orders of

145. Manchester, pp. 323–325.
146. Manchester, p. 325.
147. Ibid., 309–310.
148. Ibid.

the other. O'Donnell wrote in his book with David Powers that Johnson told him, "'We can't leave here until I take the oath of office . . . I just talked on the phone with Bobby. He told me to wait here until Sarah Hughes gives me the oath. You must remember Sarah Hughes, my old friend, the Federal judge here in Dallas. She's on her way out here now.' I was flabbergasted. I could not imagine Bobby telling him to stay in Dallas until he had taken the Presidential oath. This was no time to be waiting around at the airport for a judge to swear him into office. It was my understanding—shared, I found out later, by Bobby and by Nick Katzenbach [among others]—that Johnson acquired all the powers of the Presidency when President Kennedy died. Taking the oath is just a symbolic formality and there is no need to hurry about it. Johnson could have waited until he got to Washington and spared all of us on Air Force One that day, especially Jackie, a lot of discomfort and anxiety."[149] Johnson's bags had just been dug out of the other airplane and transferred to Air Force One, his new plane, but there was still considerable confusion about who was in charge and what the orders were; in the chaos, Godfrey McHugh, whose allegiance had not wavered when his president died, was still insistent on getting Air Force One into the air while Malcolm Kilduff, under Johnson's order, explained the multiple reasons for the delay to him and to Ken O'Donnell. The reasons included the need to wait for news reporters, the need to get the Johnson luggage switched from the other airplane, and the arrival of a Texas judge to administer the oath to Johnson.[150]

Johnson had anticipated the need to show the nation that he had taken the reins of power; the most immediate display of his taking command would be accomplished through the liberal use of photographs by the presidential photographer. This was accomplished by getting Captain Cecil Stoughton into one of the first cars to leave Parkland after Johnson left at 1:26 p.m. in a car he shared with Secret Service Agent Thomas L. Johns and Johnson aides Cliff Carter and Jack Valenti. Captain Stoughton was on the scene quickly, with two cameras and plenty of film. To add to his "instant gravitas," the pictures would need to be made on Air Force One (aircraft 26000) and they would need to show that JFK's widow, Jackie, was there standing with him as he took the oath of office, lending her grace and dignity to the moment and creating a sense of authenticity and continuity despite the hellish internal turmoil she was still dealing with. It was the description of how Johnson insisted on her presence at his swearing-in ceremony on Air Force One that

---

149. O'Donnell, p. 35.
150. Manchester, p. 313.

Mrs. Kennedy successfully had reedited and softened in William Manchester's book because it was still upsetting and distasteful to her.[151]

When Mrs. Kennedy did not immediately respond to his request that she join the rest of the party in the main cabin of the aircraft, Kenneth O'Donnell tried to urge Johnson not to subject her to the pain of the publicity of her grieving. Johnson was growing increasingly angry with her. "He (Johnson) was becoming impatient, though. Looking at his wife, he asked that someone summon her. He glanced at the bedroom door, glanced again, and said decisively, 'Just a minute. I'm going to get her.' At that instant the door opened and the widowed First Lady stepped out."[152] When she stepped out of the bedroom, into the corridor, she looked toward the stateroom and saw everyone waiting; she was bewildered by that since Johnson had told her when she first talked to him that it would be an hour before the judge got there. She hurried toward them, wondering why Johnson told her it would take an hour for the judge to arrive.[153] The anger and utter outrage felt by everyone throughout the cabin provoked by his intrusion into her privacy at this painful and agonizing ordeal, on the other hand, could never, realistically, have been foreseen or even understood by the narcissistic Lyndon Johnson.

One of the pictures which Captain Cecil Stoughton took was a bit more candid than Lyndon Johnson preferred. In the famous "wink" photo, Congressman Albert Thomas trades winks with the new president, as if to acknowledge a successful mission. Of the twenty-one photographs taken by Captain Stoughton (thirteen frames of 35 mm and eight of 120 film)[154] only one of the 35 mm negatives is, mysteriously, not preserved at the LBJ Library; the missing negative is the twelfth of the series, the "wink" photo. Richard B. Trask, in his book *That Day in Dallas*, states that he believes "*someone saw in this negative what they thought might be construed by others as an inappropriate gesture given the morbid nature of the circumstances surrounding the swearing-in, and an attempt was made to get rid of the negative.*"[155] (Emphasis added. It is left to the reader to determine who the "someone" was.) Cecil Stoughton admitted that he withheld judgment on the meaning of the wink, essentially giving Johnson another pass as hundreds, thousands, and millions of others would as well with this and other anomalies and behavioral oddities since it could not be considered as "direct evidence" of his complicity and could

---

151. Van Gelder, pp. 72–73; 82–83.
152. Dallek, *Flawed Giant*, p. 50 (citing Schlesinger, Robert Kennedy, 609; LBJ, *Vantage Point*, 13–15; Miller, *Lyndon*, 386–87, 389–90; Kenneth O'Donnell OH, Manchester, *Death of a President*, 318–23).
153. Manchester, p. 323.
154. Trask, p. 51.
155. Ibid.

arguably be merely an innocent "good luck" gesture. And besides, it isn't absolutely certain that Johnson was actually winking back to Congressman Thomas even though it was just as likely that LBJ winked first. File all of this under "Questions to Ponder."

L-R: Congressman Albert Thomas, Lady Bird Johnson, President Lyndon B. Johnson, Jacqueline Kennedy, Lem Johns (back), Congressman Jack Brooks, Bill Moyers (back wearing eyeglasses)

Although the shared winks revealed in the photo may be meaningless, at the very least, the fact is that someone—in a high enough position to make such decisions—realized that it might have revealed sinister implications and decided to discard that particular negative. At the time, the only way to duplicate a good quality photograph was by reprocessing the negative and recreating the photograph, so the obvious intent of destroying it would have been to keep any copy of it from publication. Fortunately, printed copies remained and have since been duplicated, foiling at least one obvious attempt to manipulate evidence. Captain Stoughton stayed on for eighteen months as a White House photographer, but shortly after he accompanied Mrs. Kennedy and family and friends on a trip to England to record a ceremony honoring the fallen president in May 1965, the new president effectively fired him by having him ordered transferred out of the White House, thus ending his military assignment.[156] It was reported that during the first few weeks after he became president, the White House photographer took over eleven thousand photographs of Lyndon B. Johnson.[157] The reason for the upsurge has never been officially announced; however, it has never really been a mystery either.

The friction between the Kennedy people and Johnson and his staff grew during the flight back to Washington as the two groups gravitated away from each other. As author Jim Bishop described the scene:[158]

> The Johnsons pretended that the situation did not exist. The Kennedys— which is to say Mrs. Kennedy, O'Donnell, O'Brien, Powers, McHugh— sulked in the rear compartment as though Johnson had boorishly appropriated the President's stateroom, evicting them all. They were desirous of making the President look bad. Mrs. Kennedy, having surprised the President in her bedroom, sat in the tiny breakfast nook near the casket, trembling with the vibration of the tail section. For two hours and twelve minutes, the two camps remained apart. They employed messengers to walk the corridor with whispered wishes. The alchemy of the hours had transmuted the grief of the Kennedy group to rancor; the assassination was a deep personal loss, but it was also a fall from power. The Ins were Out; the majestic were servile; the policy makers were beholden to a new man for a plane ride; a lucky shot had killed the President, but it had also paralyzed the Cabinet and the White House guard. Men who are appointed to high offices must please the man who appoints them. When he goes, they go; or they wait for the man they held in contempt to say, "I need you more than he did." . . . Conversations began and stopped abruptly. The people turned to whiskey . . . The short fat glasses of scotch and rye and bourbon jiggled their ice as Air Force One swept northeast. The empty glasses were replenished. As the busy stewards swept by, the word became: "Do it again, please." . . . *There were two separate and distinct camps aboard because Mrs. Kennedy wished it so.* (Emphasis added.)

---

156. Ibid., p. 55.
157. Zirbel, p. 134.
158. Bishop, pp. 324–326.

O'Donnell later said,

> I think Johnson sensed that he might be criticized for taking over Air Force One instead of going back to Washington earlier on his own plane, as we assumed he would do. This must have been why he later made a big point of insisting in his testimony before the Warren Commission, and in interviews with reporters, that I had specifically told him to take Air Force One when we talked before he left Parkland Hospital. *He was trying to shift the blame for his being on Air Force One to me, just as he insisted that he waited in Dallas to take the oath on the plane because Bobby Kennedy had told him to do so, which was not true at all.* I distinctly remember that when Johnson and I talked at the hospital there was no mention of which of the two planes he should use. Nor was there any mention that he was considering waiting for Jackie and the President's casket to be on the same plane with him before he left Dallas. Later a lawyer for the Warren Commission pointed out to me that Johnson's testimony that I had told him to board Air Force One disagreed with my own testimony before the commission about our conversation at the hospital. *He asked me, to my amazement, if I would change my testimony so that it would agree with the President's. "Was I under oath?" I asked him, as, of course, I was. "Certainly I wouldn't change anything I said under oath."*[159] (emphasis added)

The Newly Minted President Johnson Watching over Everyone on Air Force One

Not everyone sat transfixed to their own territory within the plane. The new president sauntered about both the main cabin and the private quarters housing the presidential suite, which he was certainly legally entitled to use now that he was the official president, regardless of what he considered the thin skins of "those Harvards and Bostons" in the previous president's party. The fact that his presence on board this aircraft had created awkwardness, friction, and frustration amongst everyone else on board didn't concern him as he went about shaving, combing his hair, and changing his shirt again in preparation for arrival at Andrews Air Force Base.[160] Some things—arguably many things—about him had never changed since his childhood and his days at San Marcos.

---

159. O'Donnell, pp. 37–38.
160. Manchester, p. 386.

For most of the flight, Johnson took over the president's office and lounge where he sat with his assistants, Cliff Carter and Bill Moyers. According to Kenneth O'Donnell, "Johnson came back once to visit with us, and told Larry and me that he wanted us to stay on with him at the White House. 'I need you more than President Kennedy needed you,' he said. We heard later that he said the same thing in exactly the same words to everybody else on the White House staff during the next few days."[161] It was a pattern which suggested that a script had been laid down well before the events of that day unfolded.

As Air Force One flew on, tapes of the conversations—which were being transmitted on four different radio frequencies—were being recorded. Researcher Doug Horne estimated that only two hours out of seven to nine hours of unedited audiotapes (i.e., about 25 percent) have been released based upon the statement of the radio operator on board Air Force One, who said: "I . . . had three phone patches going simultaneously most of the time."[162] On one of the exchanges, an unidentified voice twice says, " [unintelligible . . . or erased?]—is on 6970 . . ." Aircraft 86970 was the ex-vice presidential aircraft (Air Force Two), which left Love Field shortly after Air Force One, also flying back to Andrews AFB. Being much lighter, with only seventeen passengers and much less luggage, it reportedly overtook Air Force One and landed first. According to FBI agents James W. Sibert and Francis X. O'Neill, who had been ordered by FBI headquarters to meet the presidential jet and "to stay with the body and to obtain bullets reportedly in the President's body," Air Force One arrived forty minutes late. They stated that they were originally told the estimated time of arrival (ETA) was 17:25 (5:25 p.m.). The ETA was then revised to be 18:05 (6:05 p.m.).[163] According to Theodore H. White, "The plane slowed down so as not to overshoot the preparations of reception at Andrews Base."[164] This may come closest to the truth if "preparations of reception" can be stretched to include the task of getting aircraft 86970 unloaded in advance of the arrival of Air Force One.

Such a significant delay is congruent with the thesis that the backup aircraft, 86970, carrying the body of JFK back to Washington in a smaller, plain gray shipping casket, passed Air Force One en route, landing fifteen to twenty minutes earlier and that this casket was then flown by helicopter to Walter Reed Hospital. After the preliminary surgery described by David Lifton, it was taken via a black Cadillac hearse to the naval hospital at

161. O'Donnell, p. 38.
162. Horne, Inter-Office Memo dated October 17, 1995.
163. Lifton, p. 221.
164. White, p. 34.

Bethesda five miles away, arriving there at 6:40 p.m. (This scenario will be examined further below; however, the remaining facets of the thesis being presented do not turn on the matter of which airplane JFK's body was on; the number and kinds of anomalies related to Johnson's behavior seem, however, to be congruent with his body being switched to a lighter casket, and that it was moved to the "backup" aircraft in order to allow more time for some preliminary work on the body before the autopsy began).

As Air Force One rolled up the tarmac into its unloading position, Captain Swindal saw that Robert Kennedy was waiting in a tense half-crouch, ready to spring aboard into the front entrance as all the attention and cameras were focused on the back hatch—the president's entrance and exit. As soon as the ramp rolled into place in the front, Kennedy was inside the plane, sprinting through the staff cabin and into the stateroom. He didn't notice anyone else, including the new president, as he raced back to the private quarters in the back to find Jackie. The chaotic situation that then ensued in the process of unloading the expensive bronze casket caused the new president extreme anxiety because he resented all the attention being given to the dead Kennedy and the complete lack of attention and deference which should have now been paid to him since he was the newly sworn president.[165]

The widely and well-respected author William Manchester—wittingly or not—left many other subtle clues about the atmosphere on board the aircraft from Dallas and brought clarity and insight into the inner thoughts and worries on Johnson's mind at that time. At a time of extreme anxiety—the murder of Jacqueline's husband and father of her children and the brother of Bobby—an outrageously heinous act that caused trauma for tens of millions throughout the nation, Lyndon B. Johnson had his feelings hurt because the Kennedys, in their selfish, unthoughtful actions, did not pay him proper presidential deference. He was beside himself with anger.

According to Arthur Schlesinger's account, "'He [Bobby] ran,' Johnson later complained, 'so that he would not have to pause and recognize the new President.' Perhaps some such thought contributed to Robert Kennedy's haste. But a man more secure than Johnson would have sympathized with the terrible urgency carrying him to his murdered brother's wife."[166] Johnson lacked that inner security. "I took the oath,' he later told Kearns, 'I became the President. But for millions of Americans I was still illegitimate, a naked man with no presidential covering, a pretender to the throne, an illegal usurper.'"[167]

---

165. Manchester, pp. 387–388.
166. Schlesinger, *Robert Kennedy*, p. 675.
167. Kearns, *Lyndon Johnson*, 170.

As Larry Hancock showed, when Johnson returned to Washington, he was not actually concerned about the supposed Communist plot, which he kept pointing out to others. "Despite these expressed concerns, there is little to indicate that Johnson was acting as if this were a major concern of his. *There is not a single record of Johnson's attempting to contact the National Command Center, the White House Situation Room, the Joint Chiefs, the Secretary of Defense. Nothing shows him asking about the location of the officer with the missile launch codes. Despite his initial remark, Johnson did not make a single call or contact that would indicate he was worried about a Communist conspiracy or national security . . . During the flight back there is also not a single record that indicates that Johnson contacted or attempted to contact anyone within the national security or command structure. There is no indication that he pursued any concerns or actions in response to a conspiracy of any sort, much less a Communist conspiracy suggesting an imminent atomic first strike against the United States"*[168] (emphasis added).

Curiously, the first person to greet Johnson and shake his hand on his return to Andrews Air Force Base was James Rowley, the head of the Secret Service, who beat Johnson's other closest aides and members of the cabinet, most of whom had gathered there.[169] According to Larry Hancock, "Johnson did not speak to the Secretary of Defense until approximately 6:20 p.m. EST at the airport in Washington. He had not summoned McNamara; rather McNamara had gone of his own accord. Johnson's first remark to McNamara was, 'Any important matters pending?'"[170] *Any important matters pending?* If McNamara had answered in jest something equally inane, such as "No, just the same old, same old," would Johnson have even heard him? Could he have possibly been less concerned about the actual "state of national emergency," which he had portrayed in his public statements?

Author Noel Twyman interviewed retired Navy Admiral Taswell Shepard, one of John Kennedy's top military aides at the time of the assassination and one of the first persons to brief Johnson when he returned from Dallas on November 22, 1963. Admiral Shepard stated that "there was no sense of an eminent nuclear war" when Johnson returned to Washington that night.[171] Everyone who talked to Johnson upon his return from Dallas said that he was not concerned about the risk of a nuclear war, yet that is precisely the argument he would use over the course of several days to coerce reluctant men to accept appointments to the Warren Commission, as will be seen in

---

168. Hancock, p. 402.
169. Weldon, *Murder in Dealey Plaza*, p. 147.
170. Hancock, p. 402.
171. Twyman, p. 809.

the following chapters. Another purpose was served by this canard, which effectively trumped all the talk about a domestic conspiracy with the far more dangerous specter of an international crisis that might risk nuclear war. Anything to draw attention away from what really happened that day would buy him more time to bury the real evidence and fabricate replacements. While Johnson mouthed lame concern over a possible "worldwide conspiracy," he was clearly not thinking consciously about it when he made his escape from Parkland and returned to the airport. According to Johnson's handpicked author Jim Bishop, "The new President had overlooked The Bagman and Major General Chester V. Clifton, who understood the coded types of retaliation. If, at this time, the Soviet Union had launched a missile attack, referred to in the Department of Defense as a 'Thirty-Minute War,' it would have required a half hour for The Bagman and General Clifton to get to Johnson's side."[172]

The astonishing and bizarre contradiction between Johnson's actions following the assassination juxtaposed to what he was telling others about the ominous circumstances of worldwide peril speaks volumes about his own inner awareness of the absence of such a conspiracy. He knew intimately what had transpired, and it had nothing to do with the bogeyman favored by his friends, "the international communist conspiracy."

Oswald Fingered—U.S. Officials Overhear Air Force One Communications over the Pacific

Meanwhile, back in Dallas, the arrest of Lee Harvey Oswald set off alarms from Dallas to New Orleans and Miami and beyond U.S. shores: from Mexico City to Havana, from Tokyo to Moscow and Minsk. But one of the oddest of these alarms occurred on an Air Force Boeing 707, originally destined for Japan with cabinet members and State Department officials before being rerouted back to Washington behind both Air Force One and Two. As it was described in Theodore H. White's 1964 book, *The Making of the President-1964*, an announcement was made on board—even as all three jets were still in flight toward Andrews Air Force Base—that the sole assassin, Lee Harvey Oswald, had been arrested and that it had already been concluded that there had been no conspiracy. "On the flight the party learned that there was no conspiracy, learned of the identity of Oswald and his arrest."[173] This information was corroborated by one of the State Department officials on board the airplane, Robert Manning, in an oral history recording at the JFK

---

172. Bishop, p. 271.
173. White, Theodore H. p. 20.

Library, who said, after learning of the president's death, "The news then came in that someone named Oswald who had been in the Soviet Union had done this." That announcement came hours before Oswald had actually been charged with JFK's murder; within an hour and ten minutes of the shots in Dealey Plaza, he was being questioned as a suspect, but he wasn't formally charged with JFK's murder until 1:30 a.m. Saturday.[174] Doug Horne has analyzed this incident thoroughly and not only concluded that all traces of this information have been cleansed from what remains of the taped radio communications between the White House Situation Room and the three Air Force jets but that the information was inadvertently given to author White by an aide to Johnson.* Regardless of how he got that information, it is clearly an artifact that is connected to what transpired on Air Force One as Johnson made a decision to select the "lone nut" scenario in lieu of the "Communist conspiracy" option that had been developed by the conspirators as an option. The military and CIA rogues who had set up several fake Oswald trails to overlap with the real ones left numerous traces of an international conspiracy which had been developed to justify an attack on Cuba under the pretext of retribution for the murder of President Kennedy. These were simply traces of the original "plan B," which would have been invoked if a "conspiracy" had become undeniable, and was the preferred option by most of the military, CIA, and exile participants. But Johnson was too afraid of a major war in the Western Hemisphere; he preferred one on the other side of the world.

When Johnson returned to "the Elms" on 52nd Street, according to a *Time* magazine report in the issue dated November 29, 1963, "The first thing he saw there was a framed color photo of his beloved friend Sam Rayburn. The President saluted, then whispered: 'Well, Mr. Speaker, I wish you were here tonight.'" He probably wanted to have a toast with his departed mentor, thinking about how he had convinced "Mr. Sam" to support him three years earlier in his aggressive bid for the vice presidential nomination; he must have felt connected with Rayburn at that moment, knowing how the Speaker would have been proud of how Johnson had indeed secured his entrance into the Oval Office. Johnson phoned Hoover that evening at 7.25 p.m., according to William

---

*This situation was originally described in a 1996 book, *History Will Not Absolve Us*, by E. Martin Schotz, who noted Vincent Salandria's 1966 work, in which he posited the notion that Oswald had already been tagged as the sole assassin when this announcement was (apparently, inadvertently) transmitted to the aircraft over the Pacific. As for the tape which author White had been told contained this information, he wrote (page 20) that "It is a recording of all the conversations in the air, monitored by the [Army] Signal Corps Midwestern center "Liberty," between Air Force One in Dallas, the Cabinet plane over the Pacific, and the Joint Chiefs' Communication Center in Washington." This tape, if it still exists in its entirety, may hold the answers to many other long-lost secrets of that fateful day.

174. Fetzer (Ira David Wood III essay), p. 117

Manchester, and again from 9:10 to 9:25 p.m. that evening[175] though there is no record of either call in Johnson's official diary and no tape recording of either of these conversations has ever been made public. There were no doubt many other calls between the two during the next few weeks that would never be recorded in any diaries or audio tapes.

Johnson brought a few of his key aides—Busby, Carter, Moyers, and Valenti—with him to his house, and they talked until the early hours of the next morning about what Johnson should do the next day. According to Cliff Carter, the idea was that Johnson should address "the psychological factor that someone had picked up the torch, the country was not without its leader . . . the nation was in firm and resolute hands, this on the one hand, *and not to be overdoing on the other* . . . make everyone realize that he was going to move in and take over and yet *not to appear that he was rushing in just power-mad like a scavenger that just scoops everything out of the way*"[176] (emphasis added). Johnson clearly had the presence of mind to realize that he had to control the very element that had driven him to achieve his lifelong dream lest someone connect his imperial bearing with some other inexplicable actions during the Dallas motorcade.

Saturday Morning in the White House

Johnson's telephone call to Hoover at 10:01 a.m. Saturday, November 23, was recorded and later transcribed before someone decided that the tape was too dangerous and had to be destroyed (it is clear now that the tapes he did make during this period were staged to make it appear that he and Hoover were merely reacting to events). This particular tape was more revealing than even the person who destroyed it realized:

> J. EDGAR HOOVER: *"I just wanted to let you know of a development, which I think is very important in connection with this case—this man in Dallas (Lee Harvey Oswald). We, of course, charged him with the murder of the President. The evidence that they have at the present time is not very, very strong. We have just discovered the place where the gun was purchased and the shipment of the gun from Chicago to Dallas, to a post office box in Dallas, to a man—no, to a woman by the name of 'A. Hidell.' . . . We had it flown up last night, and our laboratory here is making an examination of it."*

175. North, pp. 412–413.
176. Transcript, Clifton C. Carter Oral Histoy, Interview I, 10/1/68, by Dorothy L. Pierce, Electronic Copy, LBJ Library.

LYNDON B. JOHNSON: *Yes, I told the Secret Service to see that that got taken care of.*

JEH: *That's right. We have the gun and we have the bullet. There was only one full bullet that was found. That was on the stretcher that the President was on. It apparently had fallen out when they massaged his heart, and we have that one. We have what we call slivers, which are not very valuable in the identification. As soon as we finish the testing of the gun for fingerprints . . . we will then be able to test the one bullet we have with the gun. But the important thing is that this gun was bought in Chicago on a money order. Cost twenty-one dollars, and it seems almost impossible to think that for twenty-one dollars you could kill the President of the United States* (Note that no comments were made about the other bullet retrieved from the body, according to witnesses, below.)

LBJ: *Now, who is A. Hidell?*

JEH: *A. Hidell is an alias that this man has used on other occasions, and according to the information we have from the house in which he was living—with his mother—he kept a rifle like this wrapped up in a blanket, which he kept in the house. On the morning that this incident occurred down there—yesterday—the man who drove him to the building where they work, the building from where the shots came, said that he had a package wrapped up in paper . . . But the important thing at the time is that the location of the purchase of the gun by a money order apparently to the Klein Gun Company in Chicago—we were able to establish that last night.*

LBJ: *Have you established any more about the visit to the Soviet embassy in Mexico in September?*

JEH: *No, that's one angle that's very confusing, for this reason—we have up here the tape and the photograph of the man who was at the Soviet embassy, using Oswald's name. That picture and the tape do not correspond to this man's voice, or to his appearance. In other words, it appears that there is a second person who was at the Soviet embassy down there. We do have a copy of a letter which was written by Oswald to the Soviet embassy here in Washington, inquiring as well as complaining about the harassment of his wife and the questioning of his wife by the FBI. Now, of course, that letter information—we process all mail that goes to the Soviet embassy. It's a very secret operation. No mail is delivered to the embassy without being examined and opened by us, so that we know what they receive . . . The case, as it stands now, isn't strong enough to be able to get a conviction . . . Now if we can identify this man who was at the . . . Soviet embassy in Mexico City . . . This man Oswald has still denied everything. He doesn't know anything about anything, but the gun thing, of course, is a definite trend.*

This discussion completely undermines the possibility of a lone gunman. Hoover's statements reflect his knowledge of a conspiracy to kill JFK and that he is already aware that someone was impersonating Oswald in Mexico City. It appears that Johnson, in other *unrecorded* calls to Hoover, had already begun his efforts to recast the investigation toward Oswald as a "lone nut" rather than as being one man in a conspiracy involving Fidel Castro. An hour and twenty minutes after the beginning of his conversation with Johnson, in which he lamented the weakness of the case against Oswald, he issued a teletype from FBIHQ to all agents that the case was wrapped up, that they were to discontinue investigating "who else may possibly have been involved." Exactly a day after the 11:20 a.m. FBI teletype, on Sunday immediately after Oswald is killed by Ruby at 11:21 a.m., J. Edgar Hoover would say to LBJ's aide, Walter Jenkins, "The thing I am most concerned about, and so is Mr. Katzenbach, is having something issued so we can convince the public that Oswald is the real assassin."[177] In one day, Hoover had come full circle and was now 100 percent confident in a case for which, just the day before, he had expressed serious doubt. This turnabout certainly wasn't due to the evidence pouring in which had pointed toward a conspiracy. Oswald had been declared the assassin, not by the investigators on the streets of Dallas, but by the new president of the United States, the only possible authority who could have realistically made such an order.

While Hoover had admitted to Johnson that the case against Oswald "is not very, very strong," he suddenly if implicitly reversed those doubts and began making strong arguments to the public that they had gotten their man; simultaneously, he began a series of actions to close down the investigation and issue a "report." In the same conversation he said a bullet from the gun was found on the president's stretcher, which would be revised later to that of Connally. Almost simultaneously with the closure of the FBI investigation was an immediate effort by the CIA to implicate Oswald in pro-Castro activities and mysterious plots during a recent trip by Oswald to Mexico City. Of course, much of this discussion undermines the mantra that Johnson and Hoover expressed in public as well as through their immediate orders to the Dallas Police to halt their investigation and to the district attorney to charge Oswald alone and stop any further talk about a possible conspiracy. To have reassured the public that there was no known international or domestic conspiracy is one thing, but to state it categorically then shift the

---

177. Scheim, p. 209; (ref. U.S. Senate Intelligence Report, *JFK Assassination*, p. 33).

evidence toward that conclusion while ignoring Oswald's Mexico visit and the implications it carried—and worse, to cut off the investigation of Oswald's New Orleans activities and his associates there and those implications—was inexcusable. Unless, of course, they already knew these were all dead ends preplanted for the purpose of "plan B" because the conspiracy was of their own making. The cover-up was now under their total control except that they still had to "act out their parts" in a way that would help to portray themselves as innocent bystanders.

Hoover's statements that the gun was fired from the fifth floor of the Texas Book Depository belie the inconsistencies that had already surfaced in the investigation. He will repeat this "mistake" in his conversation with Johnson a few days later. While he said that the gun was found on the sixth floor, he said the shells were found on the fifth floor. All of this changed after November 29 when his 'final report' was submitted; from then on, the story was changed to eliminate these discrepancies.

Saturday Morning in Dallas

It did not take long for the orders to filter through the government bureaucracy: unwritten but forcefully communicated words to the effect that "there was only one shooter, Lee Harvey Oswald; no conspiracy existed. Proceed aggressively as necessary to conform the evidence and prepare the public." As noted above, that decision was made even as the three Boeing 707s were still in flight toward Washington DC on Friday afternoon, well before Oswald had even been formally charged with the president's murder. Only an order such as this could explain an incident that occurred sometime between Friday afternoon and Saturday morning. One of the first newspaper reporters in the country to realize that something strange was going on in the aftermath of the assassination was Connie Watson-Kritzberg, a reporter for the *Dallas Times Herald*. Following her interviews with Dr. Kemp Clark and Dr. Malcolm Perry, she had written an article stating that "the front neck hole was described as an entrance wound. The wound at the back of the head, while the principal one, was either an exit or [t]angential entrance wound."

When the article appeared in print in the Saturday edition, she noticed that someone had added another sentence to the above paragraph, which said, "A doctor admitted that it was possible there was only one wound." She then asked an editor if he knew who had changed her story; he immediately knew what she was talking about and replied simply, "The FBI." Her immediate reaction—to accept the premise that it was not something too unusual, the probable result of an innocent "fact checking" between the editor and his information sources based upon a coincidental event—was shaped by the crisis atmosphere then prevalent in the newsroom and the city generally; a lot of questions would be deferred in her mind as the original scenes were replayed over and again. Connie Kritzberg was only one of hundreds of Dallas residents who experienced that same phenomenon. She told this author that she eventually concluded that this directive was subtly forced upon the newspaper, and the crudely written sentence inserted into her story, in order to begin the process of convincing the world that both shots came from one shooter, supposedly behind the president's limousine.

Unfortunately, this was merely the first instance in the case of JFK's assassination where an agency of the federal government used underhanded tactics to begin reframing the assassination into a story dictated by someone who was still in flight, as he returned to Washington DC. There would be many more instances of this to come over the ensuing days, weeks, months, years, and decades. But the fact that this one was done immediately, mere hours after the murder, makes it critically important proof of how quickly the cover-up phase was started in order to immediately put the blame on a "lone nut" despite the abundance of evidence clearly showing that multiple shooters were involved. Before the weekend was over, there were many other troubling signs of strange events happening on many fronts: Dr. Hume burning his autopsy notes in the fireplace of his recreation room, the paper bag allegedly used by Oswald to carry the oily rifle was found with no sign of oil on it, the initial FBI inspection on the rifle in which no fingerprints were found, the first reports of three police officers who found the rifle swearing that it was a German Mauser, the call from J. Edgar Hoover to Dallas SAIC Gordon Shanklin ordering that Oswald's file be sanitized followed by Shanklin ordering agent James Hosty to "get rid" of Oswald's threatening note to him and then Hosty's actions in tearing it up and flushing it down the toilet. But these were only a few of many "tip of the iceberg" events, nothing like the more astonishing—and even more revealing—things that happened then but would not be revealed until years later.

Questions Regarding Jack Ruby's Background

Jacob Rubenstein (a.k.a. Jack Ruby) was not just a castaway Mob guy from Chicago. He was directly connected to some of the highest level mafioso in the country, including the head of the Chicago Mob, Sam Giancana, who he'd known from his Italian ghetto neighborhood in that city.[178] All during 1963, Jack Ruby was trying to work out problems with the IRS and

---

178. Pegues, p. 38.

Texas revenue authorities. His nightclub business had been audited, and it was determined that "he owed the federal government excise taxes going back six years and totaling almost $40,000; and . . . owed 'an additional $20,000 in other federal taxes."[179] It may be merely a coincidence that he had been audited at this particular time, but in any event, his precarious financial condition put him into a vulnerable position vis-à-vis his friends in the Mafia. During May, he was in regular contact with Carlos Marcello's and Meyer Lansky/Ed Levinson's functionary Lewis McWillie, operating out of the Thunderbird Hotel in Las Vegas.[180] This is the same group connected to both Johnny Rosselli in Los Angeles, Sam Giancana in Chicago, and directly back to Bobby Baker in Washington, through Ed Levinson, Benjamin B. Siegelbaum, Clifford Jones, Fred Black, Mickey Weiner, and Irving Davidson. Baker is the lynchpin between all of the others, working generally through his closest associates, Davidson, Black, Jones, and Weiner[181] on one end and Lyndon B. Johnson on the other.

Just as the IRS and Texas authorities had been increasing their squeeze on him for several months, by mid-November, Ruby suddenly came into a large sum of money; only three hours before the assassination, Ruby visited his bank and talked to an official who later stated that Ruby made a deposit of $7,000 in large bills, which he had stuffed into his pockets.[182] It was reported that police detectives found two large wads of bills when they searched Ruby's apartment on November 24; he was carrying more than $3,000 in cash when he shot Oswald.[183] Three days before that, he had talked to a realtor about a new location for his club and told a friend that he was planning on moving from Oak Cliff to the much more expensive Turtle Creek section of Dallas, which would double his apartment rent. He was also looking into taking a Caribbean vacation.[184]

A reasonable deduction on the basis of all the known facts relating to Jack Ruby and his associations can be postulated as follows: The known connections between him and Mafia figures as noted throughout this book, and Ruby's subsequent attempted confession implicating Lyndon Johnson in the conspiracy, suggest a combination of Johnson's use of political influence with the IRS to "turn up the heat" on him to force him to settle his tax liabilities, and the Mob's cooperation in making him "an offer he couldn't

---

179. North, p. 355 (Ref. Blakey, G. Robert, and Richard N. Billings, *The Plot to Kill the President*, New York: New york times Book company, 1981. p. 307).
180. Ibid., p. 192.
181. Ibid.
182. Ibid.
183. Scheim, p. 149.
184. HSCA, Vol. IX, pp. 1090; 1093 and WC Vol. XXV, p. 254.

refuse." Ruby had spent a lifetime on the fringes of the Mob, and after the botched handling of Oswald, he knew that his life was no longer worth a plugged nickel, and he had no choice but to take out Oswald since he hadn't been killed during his arrest. In contrast to all of these clear connections that reveal multiple motivations, there is nothing in his background that would support the notion that a man of his ilk might be overcome with emotion for JFK's family and therefore take the actions that he did to publicly murder the assassin and be arrested for it immediately in the police station.

Shortly after Oswald died from his injuries, the Dallas authorities released information to the local television stations that confirmed their investigation was centered on the "connection between Jack Ruby and Lee Oswald." A copy of such a newscast, available at Youtube.com, reveals an early admission that police were aware of a connection:

News Anchor:
Also in the studio here is WFAA news director Bob Walker. Bob, what's new?

News Director Bob Walker:
Just learned from City Hall, from a very authoritative source, that police are working on the assumption that there, indeed, is a connection between Jack Ruby and Lee Oswald and that in some manner of speaking Oswald's murder was to shut him up. Also, they have said that they will not release in the immediate future at all, any of the information the FBI has gathered which lead them to believe so strongly that Oswald had assassinated the president. But the police and investigation now is working on the assumption that there is a definite connection between Lee Oswald and Jack Ruby and the attempt . . . and the successful attempt on Oswald's life was an attempt to 'shut him up,' this word from a reliable source at city hall.[185]

All references to any Ruby-Oswald connection would disappear as quickly as they originally surfaced after Oswald's death. Johnson's instructions to Henry Wade would have been to forcefully remind him what Cliff Carter, in his repeated calls to Wade over the previous two days, had told him, "Stop the investigation and cease all references to any possible conspiracy." There is no record of this particular call, of course—since Johnson's taping system was controlled not by his voice but by his finger—but the fact is that the "reliable source from city hall" was immediately shut down and no further mention of this aspect of the investigation was reported again.

---

185. See youtube.com: Oswald is eliminated—The Aftermath (http://www.youtube.com/watch?v=qrwZCpdvvHA&NR=1).

The WFAA television report, and others like it, reminded Johnson that to ensure his acceptance by the American public as the unquestioned leader of the nation, an official government report vindicating him was needed as quickly as possible. To put the public at ease, it would also be essential to convince the nation that the assassin—a man without any apparent motive—acted alone, and that the assassin's own killer, Ruby, also acted independently. Johnson coached and collaborated with his old friend J. Edgar Hoover who directed all facets of the early investigation. His first report was completed within one week, and within a few more weeks, the FBI's complete version would begin to be reviewed by the Warren Commission. This select group of high-level officials of Washington—mostly friends of LBJ and Hoover—was charged with giving the official government imprimatur to this hastily developed version, with Lee Harvey Oswald cast as the "lone nut." The final *coup de grace* was furnished by Jack Ruby. Johnson would soon decide that the investigation would be tightly controlled by a select number of trusted confidants within Washington rather than the Texas officials as originally planned.

November 22, 1963, only marked the first half of the entire conspiracy; the murder of JFK then kicked off the second half, which was marked by concealment and fabrication of evidence on a massive scale, culminating in a completely dishonest official report cunningly designed to point the finger of guilt away from the perpetrator(s). But the murder at halftime was only one of a very long string of official deceits—each of which was committed to keep the secrets, the CIA's "family jewels"—that would last for decades.

Phase 2 of the Conspiracy Emerges: The Warren Commission

Within days of Kennedy's death, President Johnson, FBI Director J. Edgar Hoover, and acting Attorney General Nicholas Katzenbach had agreed that a presidential commission should be established to lend credence to the FBI's report and its foregone conclusion that Oswald was the assassin, and the only assassin. Johnson had resisted such an idea initially in deference to the Dallas Police Department and the Texas state officials, for whom he was indebted because of their cooperation with every one of his requests as he planned the motorcade, and he knew that he could count on their continued cooperation.

Johnson's original plan was displaced by a new one after Oswald was murdered and new demands for congressional action put Johnson under pressure to federalize the investigation and prosecution of the crime, despite the absence of technical legal authority to do so. The idea of a presidential commission composed of a "blue-ribbon" panel to investigate Kennedy's death was first introduced to Johnson by his old columnist friend Joseph Alsop. It was soon augmented by Eugene Rostow and Dean Acheson; the entire group of three has been referred to by many researchers as the "Eastern Establishment" which operated in the background, guiding Johnson's actions. He may have had some assistance along the way, but the momentum he himself had created was the ultimate guiding force.

He knew from the start that Hoover would be the real kingpin of the cover-up because he could exercise complete control over the direction of the investigation regardless of who conducted the groundwork. Any doubt about that point would have to be reconciled with the fact that the FBI immediately took over the investigation, just as Johnson proceeded to shut down the Dallas investigation. Johnson eventually decided that it would be best to keep it under his and Hoover's direct control in Washington; as we will see, Hoover's files came in handy to control some of the distinguished men who served as commissioners.

All of Lyndon Johnson's expertise in the manipulation of successful men and women—learned early in his boyhood starting with his own father and mother, honed during his college years in San Marcos, and perfected during his early years in Washington—would finally pay off in his creation of the Warren Commission. By ingratiating himself further with these senior and august establishment men, he knew that his influence would be further strengthened now that he was the president. Influence to him meant creating new sources of subtle obligations, indebtedness, and dependencies, in some cases even potential blackmail opportunities. His Johnson treatment was by now his greatest skill; finally perfected and customized for each individual, he knew that by playing off each member's particular vulnerabilities he would create a primary psychological connection, ideally a sycophantic dependency, with them. Using either "the carrot or the stick" as necessary to influence the outcome of their deliberations, he could assure a successful result in this vital priority. The big carrot he held out for each of them was another star for their own individual legacies.

His appointment of mostly career politicians, not investigators, to the commission ensured that they would handle the job as the management of a political problem rather than a crime requiring rigorous independent investigation and resolution. Thus the final document would not be comprised of objective findings based on provable factual data so much as subjective interpretations of ambiguous data, pragmatically created and artfully worded to reflect consensus answers. All of the commission's deliberations would be subject to the effective use of his own powers of persuasion even though they might need filtering through his main connections into the boardroom: Hoover primarily, through Ford, Dulles, and McCloy. (The

"Magic Bullet Theory"—despite the continued laughable insistence of Arlen Specter to call it "fact"—would eventually become exhibit A for the "consensus answers" assertion.)

Johnson would eventually claim that he had asked Bobby for the names of two men whom he wanted to serve on the commission. According to the man that RFK himself said was a chronic liar (as documented a number of times previously), Bobby asked Johnson to appoint Allen Dulles and John McCloy. After Bobby was assassinated, ensuring that there would be no rebuttal to his assertion, Johnson began circulating a story that he had only previously divulged to his crony attorney, Abe Fortas. Johnson would then say to the publisher of his memoirs, "I could never understand why Bobby tried to put some CIA people on the Warren Commission."[186] It will never be known whether this disingenuous lie was part of his original plot, the midcourse adjustments to it, or whether the first time he supposedly uttered it—when he allegedly told it to Fortas in 1966—was also the first time he had created it.

Johnson knew that as the newly installed president of the United States—given all of his thirty-plus years of experience in gaining that office and another twenty dreaming of it, together with the help of his friend, neighbor, partner, and mentor J. Edgar Hoover—the ultimate power to control the outcome of the investigation and report would be theirs and theirs alone. He knew that the information to be fed to the commission would be tightly controlled through Hoover and that they would develop a direct channel inside the commission through at least one member, probably several of them. Much of the investigation, and the presentation of its findings to the public including the frequent "leaks," would be done by sophisticated and erudite men whose credibility was unassailable at the time. He knew that these men would ultimately fall into line because their careers depended upon it; everyone on "the team" would be convinced that convicting Oswald on the president's schedule was first and foremost the essential objective. (The commission's record itself, including the individual witnesses ignored and the evidence lost, destroyed, or fabricated would become exhibit A in that assertion). Arlen Specter was typical of the arrogant, aggressive and ambitious young staff who would work single-mindedly toward this purpose.

Finally, he knew also that the members of the commission were very busy men who had pressing schedules of their own and therefore the time they actually spent in commission meetings would be minimal. This meant that the staff members would therefore be under heavy pressure for results on

---

186. Russo, p. 362 (Ref. Weidenfeld, Lord George. *Remembering My Good Friends: An Autobiography*, New York: HarperCollins, 1994. p. 350)

a very short timetable and that they would need to obtain consensus through the normal committee protocol. These constraints would also mean that only select key issues would actually be reviewed in detail at the commission meetings and the overall plot direction would be developed within the purview of staff deliberations.

Johnson relied on his presidential clout to sell each member on being named to the commission by using the argument that the case against Oswald had already been made so "airtight" that it would not drag on interminably. Ultimately, any resistance that was made melted away when Johnson warned that "forty million* American lives hung in the balance," and they therefore had a solemn duty to God and country to accept this assignment. His appointment of Senator Richard Russell is a case study of the "Johnson treatment." Russell had been in the Senate since 1933 and would have succeeded into a leadership capacity by 1950 if he had had a more ambitious streak. Instead, he deferred his support to Johnson who had only been elected to the Senate two years before that. His decision enabled Johnson to become the most powerful man in the Senate in record time. Russell was an old bachelor and the epitome of the personality type that Johnson had long ago targeted for his most special ingratiating treatment. As he had done with Sam Rayburn before him, Johnson had sought Russell out many years before and buried him under such an avalanche of shameless patronizing that he had already effectively neutralized any natural defenses Russell might have had against such an attack. It is sufficient to observe that Russell had spent many weekends—especially Sundays—relaxing with LBJ and Lady Bird, exactly the same way as Sam Rayburn had previously been hosted. He was such a regular visitor that Johnson's daughters affectionately referred to Russell as "Uncle Dick" (joining "Uncle Sam and "Uncle Edgar"). The recording of Johnson's discussion with his old friend Senator Russell, who had objected primarily because of his dislike of the liberalism of Chief Justice Earl Warren, revealed the efficacy of the "Johnson treatment"; he simply would not take no for an answer.**

Senator Russell, despite his friendship with Johnson, was troubled early in the proceedings by the direction taken by the commission; on December 5, 1963, he wrote by hand a memo that was later found in his desk and placed in his Memorial Library at the University of Georgia:[187]

---

*He later changed this to "thirty-nine million," evidently figuring that it seemed a more precise number, obviously scientifically and meticulously determined.
** See Youtube.com: "LYNDON JOHNSON / RICHARD RUSSELL PHONE CALL (NOVEMBER 29, 1963)" at http://www.youtube.com/watch?v=3V6anKUmu9Q.

Warren asked about C.I.A. 'Did they have anything.' When I told of Mexico & Nicaraguan *NOT mentioning sums****—He mentioned 5G [$5,000] as McCone had told me. He [Warren] knew all I did & more about CIA. Something strange is happening—W. [Warren] & [Deputy Attorney General Nicholas] Katzenbach know all about F.B.I. and they are apparently through psychiatrists & others planning to show Oswald only one who even considered—this to me is untenable position—I must insist on outside counsel—'Remember Warren's blanket indictment of South.'"

As author Dick Russell shows in *On the Trail of the JFK Assassins*, Senator Russell so distrusted the FBI investigation that he decided to simultaneously conduct his own private inquiry, which came to the conclusion that Oswald did not do it.[188] Representative Boggs would later say that J. Edgar Hoover "lied his eyes out to the Commission—on Oswald, on Ruby, on their friends, the bullets, the gun, you name it."[189]

Ironically, this old friend of and mentor to Lyndon Johnson must have realized, within a few days of the assassination, that the new president was up to something very troubling—and that it was an "untenable position"— which required that he do his own investigation through his assistant, Colonel Philip Corso; Russell instructed Corso to keep no paper records of his investigation, and all briefings were to be oral. This secret information led him to believe there was a conspiracy, and he—with fellow commissioners Boggs and Cooper—demanded a private executive session of the commission to air their concerns. No transcript of this meeting was ever produced; however, the rumors at the time were that the meeting was a "no-holds barred shouting match."[190] Even with the promise that his written dissension would be published with the full report, Senator Russell had to be "arm-twisted" by Johnson into signing the report; he was later shocked to find that his dissent was not published, neither with the report nor any of the thousands of pages of (sometimes arcane) other records and hearings. In fact, the "Russell dissent" disappeared for several decades until someone found it among his papers at the University of Georgia.[191] His dissent makes it very

---

***This is a reference to a reported incident involving a Nicaraguan named Gilberto Alvarado, who said he saw Oswald at the Cuban Embassy in Mexico City talking to Consul Azcue, accompanied by a tall black man, who said "I want to kill the man." Oswald replied, "You're not man enough. I can do it." Then Alvarado said he saw the black man give Oswald $5,000 in American currency of large denominations as 'advance payment.'" (See Russell, p. 499).
188. Ibid., pp. 126–127.
189. *Texas Observer,* 11/98.
190. Russo, p. 372.
191. Ibid. p. 373.

clear that he did not believe the "single bullet theory" (which implicitly means that he thought more than three shots had to have been fired and that leads inexorably to the conclusion that a conspiracy existed).

Hoover used his assistant, Cartha DeLoach, to liaise secretly with (future president) Gerald Ford, who provided details of the commission's secret deliberations. According to another FBI assistant director, William Sullivan, Ford was "our man" on the Warren Commission.[192] The reason for Ford's willingness to cooperate with the FBI, according to LBJ's former aide Bobby Baker and reported by Anthony Summers, was because "in the year preceding the assassination, he [Baker] and Ford both had access to a 'hospitality suite' at Washington's Sheraton-Carlton Hotel rented by a mutual friend, the lobbyist Fred Black. 'Like me,' Baker said, 'Gerry Ford had a key to the suite. And sometimes Black would tell me not to use the room, because Ford was meeting someone there.'"[193] When Black was being investigated, and later prosecuted for income tax evasion, for two months in 1963, bugs were installed in the suite to pick up incriminating evidence against him. The theory advanced by Baker was that these bugs picked up compromising information on Ford, which was passed on to Edgar and from him to Johnson; Lyndon and Edgar thus had the goods on Gerry Ford, and they used it to bring pressure on him into cooperating with them to undermine the Warren Commission,[194] even going to the extreme of verbally changing the location of the entry point of the bullet into JFK's back, making it higher on the shoulder so that it would line up better with the so-called "exit" wound in his throat. This was, arguably, the most egregious case of wordsmanship in the history of the art.[195]

It was J. Edgar Hoover's original statement that became the "mission statement" for the Warren Commission: "The thing I am concerned about, and so is Katzenbach, is having something issued so we can convince the public that Oswald is the real assassin."[196] Johnson pressed the commission to complete their report as quickly as possible "so as to quiet public suspicions of a conspiracy." The commission operated in an atmosphere of concern from high government officials, including Johnson, the Justice Department, the FBI, and the CIA, that its report point to Oswald as the sole assassin and refute suggestions that any official in the United States or in any other country had planned Kennedy's death. When it delivered its findings in

---

192. Sullivan, p. 53.
193. Summers, *Official and Confidential*, p. 318.
194. Ibid.
195. Mantik, (from Fetzer's, *Murder in Dealey Plaza*), pp. 252–255.
196. HSCA, vol 3, pp 471–473.

September 1964, the commission said just that Oswald and Ruby each acted alone, "'without advice or assistance,' and that no conspiracy determined the actions of either man."[197]

To ensure that the commission would provide only a perfunctory review rather than an exhaustive analysis, Johnson's continued pressure on them to complete the report was explained as a necessity due to the presidential elections in November; Johnson had originally pressured Earl Warren to conclude the investigation in two months, by February 1964,[198] then the deadline became April, allowing for the report to be written, edited, and published in time to present it to Johnson by June 1964.[199] By May, the deadline was extended by Rankin to June 1 "so that the final report could be issued by June 30. By June 1, however, only two attorneys had completed a draft and the deadline had to be moved back."[200] On June 17, the commission announced that its hearings were completed; on June 30, it was announced that the final report would not be issued until after the Republican National Convention, which was set to begin July 13 and end July 18, 1964.[201] This tactic—of setting unrealistic deadlines and constantly moving them backward—was intended by Johnson to keep the commission, and more importantly, the staff lawyers and investigators, under extreme pressure to finish the report; this pressure would also necessarily keep them on track with the original objective of finding that Oswald acted alone by making it impossible to follow any other more plausible leads. Because of the delays in getting started and the lengthy writing process, the actual investigation lasted five months.[202] To the same end, Johnson also knew that the commission members would delegate most of the investigatory legwork and the hard tasks of drafting, collating, editing, and rewriting of the report to the staff. Their own function would be limited to interviewing witnesses in closed session and discussion of the disposition of unresolved issues and agreement to a preordained set of conclusions—including many which are inconsistent and/or incompatible to other conclusions made by the same commission—that point to Lee Harvey Oswald as the sole assassin.[203]

Lyndon Johnson and J. Edgar Hoover wasted no time in establishing the first tenet of the commission; it would be strictly subservient and beholden to

197. Dallek, *Flawed Giant*, p. 51 (ref. See two memos, Jenkins to LBJ, November 24, 1963, and shorthand note says: n.d., Special Assassination File; Miller, *Lyndon*, 423–24; Schlesinger, *Robert Kennedy*, 614–15).
198. North, p. 397.
199. McKnight, p. 101.
200. Marrs, p. 486.
201. Ibid.
202. DiEugenio, p. 115, ref. O'Toole, p. 106.
203. Ibid.

them. To firmly establish this, no direct liaison to the FBI, Secret Service, or CIA was designated, as was the case with the Justice Department for which a full-time employee had been established. Therefore when they needed FBI input, they had to go directly to J. Edgar Hoover; for example, the question of whether Oswald had been a paid FBI informant complete with monthly stipend and employee number, as had been reported; the commission referred that issue to Hoover, who simply denied it, "and that was that."[204] Undoubtedly, through Lyndon Johnson's personal instructions to Chairman Earl Warren, at the commission's first meeting on December 5, 1963, Warren laid the ground rules for the conduct of committee meetings. Most basic was the tenet that the commission would only evaluate available evidence, not gather that evidence. A corollary tenet was that it would rely upon the reports of "the FBI and Secret Service and others that I may not know about the present time." Finally, he insured the commission would be malleable and completely subservient to the new president and his FBI director by stating that "I believe that the development of the evidence in this way should not call for a staff of investigators."[205] The plan for containment and control of the ensuing investigation was complete.

By the time of that first meeting, Johnson had completely emasculated Chief Justice Earl Warren. The tenets he established above would include a few more: "He went on to say that the hearings should not be held in public. He thought that their report would carry more influence done secretly than if it were done in the open. He even suggested that the Commission hear no witnesses or even have the subpoena power, saying that this would 'retard rather than help our investigation.' At this first meeting, Warren was clearly carrying water for President Johnson when he added that one of the primary functions of the Commission was to thwart congressional committees from conducting their own hearings, which was Johnson's original goal."[206] By the time the commission received the FBI report, it was decided that it was so poor that they agreed at the second meeting that it could not be relied upon; only then was it decided that they needed subpoena power after all.

Making the commission entirely dependent upon the FBI's investigators further tightened the connection and compromised their ability to obtain untainted information. This was especially troubling when one considers that J. Edgar Hoover, personally, was the gatekeeper who monitored everything being furnished to the commission. As one researcher noted, "This was a

---

204. DiEugenio, p. 116, ref. O'Toole, p. 106; Epstein, *Inquest,* pp. 33–40.
205. DiEugenio, "A Comprehensive Review of Reclaiming History", Part 8 (http://www.ctka.net/2008/bugliosi_8_review.html)
206. Ibid.

grievous error, for once the FBI had submitted the very first reports, there was no way the stubborn, vain, unchallengeable Hoover would back down from their initial conclusion."[207] Because the FBI and Secret Service were both under fire for their security breaches in Dallas, both agencies were interested in minimizing damage and quickly finishing the commission's inquiry; likewise, the individual agents working under the collective guilt of having lost the president were interested in protecting themselves and their brother agents against the unpredictable wrath of their boss, J. Edgar Hoover. The multiple redundant conflicts of interest represented throughout this bureaucratic organizational structure are mind-boggling, although it provides at least a partial answer to the question "why was the Warren Commission so completely malleable to LBJ and Hoover?"

Any complications that would not advance the goal of a quick and controlled finish, such as a messy investigation into either a foreign or domestic conspiracy or the involvement of anyone other than the lone nut Oswald, would only prolong the investigation and risk a wholesale housecleaning starting with the top of the FBI and the Secret Service and a complete top-to-bottom reorganization of the CIA, perhaps even to the extent once threatened by JFK himself when he warned, "I will tear it into a thousand pieces and scatter it with the winds."[208] Throughout its life, Lyndon Johnson would pressure it to reach an early conclusion.

Under J. Edgar Hoover's guidance, the men Johnson appointed include two notable subgroups, the the Eastern Troika and the Southern Gentlemen. The Troika—John McCloy, Allen Dulles and Gerald Ford—was the dominant group, comprised of men who had a personal stake in the outcome and were arguably affirmatively involved in the plot (though in Ford's case, "unwittingly"). The Southern Gentlemen group–John Sherman Cooper (KY), Hale Boggs (LA), and Richard Russell (GA)—was marginalized by the Troika and fooled into believing that their objections would be recorded as such when the full report was published; as it turned out, that was only a device used by the majority to swindle them into signing the report since the dissenting opinions were never published.

The first order of business was in the selection of the general counsel who would report to Earl Warren. Rather than allow Chairman Warren to designate his own choice, Warren Olney III, as soon as Hoover and Katzenbach got wind of it, they mounted an offensive campaign through commissioners Gerald Ford and John McCloy. Hoover simply despised him because he was too much of a liberal; Katzenbach felt that he was too much of a maverick and

---

207. DiEugenio, p. 96.
208. Douglass, pp. 14–15.

could not be controlled. After a brief discussion, Warren agreed to withdraw his name from further consideration. McCloy just happened to have a short list of alternative choices on hand, one of which was J. Lee Rankin who was nominated, seconded, and voted unanimously as the commission's general counsel.[209] From then on, with assurance that everyone down the line in both agencies and the commission members were finally "on board" with the real agenda and mission, and that there were no "mavericks" around to spoil the process, the Johnson-Hoover objective to contain and direct the course of the investigation was complete.

The arrogance of most of the staff of the Warren Commission, even those taking fairly routine testimony and statements, is reflected in this statement from Senator Yarborough, given to Jim Marrs, author of *Crossfire: The Plot that Killed Kennedy*:[210]

> A couple of fellows [from the Warren Commission] came to see me. They walked in like they were a couple of deputy sheriffs and I was a bank robber. I didn't like their attitude. As a senator I felt insulted. They went off and wrote up something and brought it back for me to sign. But I refused. I threw it in a drawer and let it lay there for weeks. And they had on there the last sentence which stated: "This is all I know about the assassination." They wanted me to sign this thing, then say this is all I know. Of course, I would never have signed it. Finally, after some weeks, they began to bug me. "You're holding this up, you're holding this up" they said, demanding that I sign the report. So I typed one up myself and put basically what I told you about how the cars all stopped. I put in there, "I don't want to hurt anyone's feelings but for the protection of future presidents, they should be trained to take off when a shot is fired." I sent that over. That's dated July 10, 1964, after the assassination. To my surprise, when the volumes were finally printed and came out, I was surprised at how many people down at the White House didn't file their affidavits until after the date, after mine the 10th of July, waiting to see what I was going to say before they filed theirs. I began to lose confidence then in their investigation and that's further eroded with time.

Modified Testimony

Testimony by many eyewitnesses, whether innocent bystanders who happened to have chosen this relatively sparsely populated area to watch the motorcade

---

209. McKnight, p. 45.
210. Marrs, p. 482.

or by some of the local or federal officials accompanying President Kennedy would change quickly to "fit the pattern" that was quickly established by the plotters. Perhaps the plotters knew enough about psychology to anticipate that, immediately after the assassination of the president, most of the eyewitnesses would become affected by "post traumatic stress disorder." Depending upon their psychological makeup, it would render many of them unconfident of their own recollection of the events they experienced firsthand. The degree to which an individual might react is arguably less related to their intelligence or education than their general emotional state at the time. According to the Mayo Clinic, "Post-traumatic stress disorder (PTSD) is a type of anxiety disorder that's triggered by a traumatic event. You can develop posttraumatic stress disorder when you experience or witness an event that causes intense fear, helplessness or horror. Many people who are involved in traumatic events have a brief period of difficulty adjusting and coping. But with time and healthy coping methods, such traumatic reactions usually get better. In some cases, though, the symptoms can get worse or last for months or even years. Sometimes they may completely disrupt your life. In these cases, you may have posttraumatic stress disorder."[211] Among the typical reactions to PTSD are the following:

- Loss of self-esteem
- Feelings of worthlessness, hopelessness, and/or guilt
- Difficulty concentrating, remembering, or making decisions
- Withdrawal from friends and activities once pursued
- Persistent thoughts of death

The aggregate (or overtime, cumulative) effect of these symptoms would certainly make some people less confident in their own recollections of what they witnessed. It would uniquely explain the following nearly immediate revisions to original statements made by a number of witnesses, in most cases to reject the initial reactions in favor of a scenario that had been preestablished and immediately swung into play. This might explain why many of the eyewitnesses traveling with JFK, those who were the most emotionally attached to him, were among those who quickly adopted the "official story" in place of their own memory.

House Speaker Tip O'Neill revealed in his autobiography five years after the assassination:[212]

---

211. See Mayo Clinic website: http://www.mayoclinic.com/health/post-traumatic-stress-disorder/DS00246.
212. O'Neil, *Man of the House*, p. 178.

I was surprised to hear [Presidential aide Kenneth] O'Donnell say that he was sure he had heard two shots that came from behind the fence. "That's not what you told the Warren Commission," I said. "You're right," he replied. "I told the FBI what I had heard, but they said it couldn't have happened that way and that I must have been imagining things. So I testified the way they wanted me to. I just didn't want to stir up any more pain and trouble for the family." Dave Powers [another Kennedy aide] was with us at dinner that night, and his recollection of the shots was the same as O'Donnell's.

James Altgens, photographer of the Associated Press, wrote in an AP dispatch immediately after the assassination, "At first I thought the shots came from the opposite side of the street [i.e., the knoll]. I ran over there to see if I could get some pictures." His story quickly changed, and he eventually told the Warren Commission that he thought the shots came from behind the presidential limousine (i.e., the direction of the Depository). "I did not know until later where the shots came from."[213]

The testimony of Mr. Altgens inadvertently reveals the tactics of the commission lawyers in obfuscating and redirecting testimony when they realized that it was heading in the wrong direction:

Mr. ALTGENS: There was utter confusion at the time I crossed the street. The Secret Service men, uniformed policemen with drawn guns that went racing up this little incline and I thought . . .

Mr. LIEBELER: [quickly changing the subjects of "Secret Service men"] When you speak of the 'little incline' that means the area—the little incline on the grassy area here by this concrete structure across Elm Street toward the School Book Depository Building, is that part of Dealey Plaza too over in here, this concrete structure, or is Dealey Plaza only the name ascribed to this area here between Elm Street and Commerce Street?

The colloquy over the technical definition of what constituted Dealey Plaza served only to move the dialogue away from the mention of Secret Service men on the grassy knoll. This technique would be repeated over and over again in the direction other testimony would take whenever the discussion turned too closely to concepts not congruent with the official direction to be pursued:

Richard Dodd and James Simmons, railroad workers who witnessed the assassination from their position on the triple overpass, both complained that the information they provided to FBI agents was changed by the agents in their report to the Warren Commission:[214]

---

213. Warren Commission Hearings: 7H, pp. 517–519.
214. Warren Commission Hearings: 22H, pp. 833–835.

- Dodd told Mark Lane in a filmed interview that he told federal agents that "the shots, the smoke came from behind the hedge on the north side of the plaza" (i.e., the "Grassy Knoll"). The FBI agents incorrectly reported that Dodd "did not know where the shots came from," (CE 1420).

- The FBI agents reported that "Simmons advised that it was his opinion the shots came from the direction of the Texas School Book Depository Building." (CE 1416). Simmons has contradicted the FBI report, saying, "It sounded like it came from the left and in front of us towards the wooden fence. And there was a puff of smoke that came underneath the trees on the embankment . . . It was right directly in front of the wooden fence . . . as soon as we heard the shots, we ran around to [behind] the picket fence . . . There was no one there but there were footprints in the mud around the fence and footprints on the two-by-four railing on the fence."[215]

Another witness, J. C. Price, also reported that his statements to the FBI were completely reversed before being submitted by the FBI to the Warren Commission (19 H 492). These three witnesses were only a few of the many whose words were turned around into statements that supported a lie. There were a number of similar reports by other railroad workers on the overpass (including Nolan H. Potter, Clemon E. Johnson, Walter L. Winborn, and Thomas J. Murphy), all of whom stated that shots were fired from behind the fence on the grassy knoll. These witnesses were never called to give testimony; instead of their truths, the FBI converted their statements into lies, which were then combined into a single grand lie, and that became the foundation upon which the Warren Commission figuratively built its house. It would begin crumbling almost immediately.

The willingness of the Warren Commission to accept indirect, incorrect statements based upon unsworn hearsay from FBI reports rather than direct, sworn testimony of witnesses is clear and convincing evidence of how the commission used deliberate distortion to achieve its mission; the product of this subterfuge was that this official "Presidential Commission" not only allowed false information to be entered into the public record, it aggressively promoted it as the primary instigator. That the FBI excised all reports of gunshots from the knoll proves conclusively the unstated mission of the "president's commission" to avoid a truthful accounting of events in favor of the preordained verdict of Oswald, alone, as the assassin. Even two police officials would later make statements contradicting what they stated originally:

215. Marrs, *Crossfire*, pp. 57–58.

- Jesse Curry, the Dallas chief of police, broadcast over his car radio, "Get a man on top of that triple underpass and see what happened up there," immediately after the shots were fired. Yet by the very next day, he told reporters from the *New York Times* that although he was driving the lead car of the motorcade, he "could tell from the sound of the three shots that they had come from the book company's building near downtown Dallas."[216]

- Bill Decker, the Dallas sheriff, was riding with Curry in the lead car, and according to the police transcript, Decker called over Curry's radio, "Have my office move all available men out of my office into the railroad yard to try to determine what happened in there and hold everything secure until Homicide and other investigators should get there." When Decker testified to the Warren Commission, he did not reveal, nor was he ever asked, where he thought the shots came from.[217]

The immediate and widespread effort to reform eyewitness' testimony, documented over and over again by the early researchers cited previously, was only the first of the inconsistencies and anomalies to emerge after the publication of the Warren Report. The enormous scale of distortion that soon became obvious to most people with a minimally critical mind was the catalyst which created the most doubt in the public mind about the findings of the commission.

Commission Staff's Efforts to Publish Voluminous Report

Its decision to publish a 912-page book just before the 1964 presidential election, followed afterward by twenty-six more volumes and fifty thousand more pages of documents, was designed to show the public that the investigation was thorough and complete; in truth, this was done to obfuscate the fact that they had explored only one very narrow lead, effectively excluding all others. In order to "paper the files," the staff was, evidently, instructed to include thousands of pages of extraneous material having nothing to do with the pertinent issues. This effort apparently led to someone gathering miscellaneous debris collected during the course of the "investigation." Some examples of this are legendary:

- Three pages devoted to David Belin's efforts to elicit from Mrs. Barbara Rowland that she got As and Bs in high school and that her husband had

---

216. *The New York Times*, November 24, 1963.
217. WCR, 23 H 913.

fudged his high school grades to her when they were courting since she later saw one of his report cards and noted that it had some Cs on it; also included was a review in minute detail of his entire work history.[218]

- Jack Ruby's mother's dental records from 1938, including a comment from the dentist that "patient states she has teeth but not wearing them." Evidently, at least someone on the staff had a rather perverse sense of humor to have gratuitously included such a document obviously intended to disparage Jack Ruby's mother, Fannie Rubenstein. But this was not the only instance of the commission's staff attacking the integrity of completely innocent American citizens.

- Finally, among many other such irrelevant files, there is yet another enigmatic item buried in the thousands of pages, which relates to a nail file purportedly owned by Lee Oswald's mother.

It may be that the real reason these items were included was that someone was trying to leave a clue that the entire report was thrown together in such haste that everything in it is suspect. Or they were merely following orders from on high to publish every single item in the commission's files—even the round ones beneath every desk. Yet there were many relevant facts which the commission decided to ignore in its report, some already noted; another was the fact that two of its attorneys (Coleman and Slawson) went to Mexico City and listened to the CIA tapes of the Oswald imposter. However, no mention of this detail was anywhere to be found in the final report or any of the twenty-six volumes of hearings and witness depositions.[219]

The lack of a conclusive verdict and the virtual impossibility of ever attaining one is obviously an indisputable fact of life for anyone attempting to evaluate this case. But the question of when, if ever, we will have actually reached the finality of the "case closed" situation must ultimately be measured against the proven facts that much of the evidence at the time, and subsequently thereafter, was destroyed, altered, or fabricated. This alone should serve as the "proof" of the fallacy of the "lone assassin" myth and with it the entire conclusion of the Warren Commission Report. In retrospect, the one singular and spectacular success of the Warren Commission Report is arguably that it succeeded in buying enough time to ensure that enough evidence would disappear or be "fixed," the key players would die off either naturally or otherwise, and the cloud of confusion left in its wake would make a real and convincing verdict forever impossible.

---

218. WCR, Vol. 6, pp. 177–179.
219. Newman, *Oswald and the CIA*, pp. 634–635.

Presenting the Warren Report to the President
(and the Skeptical Nation)

The presentation of the Warren Report to President Johnson was celebrated by newspapers and news magazines throughout the United States and the world as the end of a long and arduous task conducted by a large staff of lawyers and their assistants who completed their charge in record time and whose work, once and for all time, resolved the "crime of the century." None of this was really "new" news since Hoover had seen to it that the FBI reports had already been leaked to the press months before followed by periodic leaks of other materials to keep the nation's thirst for more knowledge about it quenched and to prepare it for a preordained verdict. Unfortunately, time and a steady outpouring of inconsistencies, anomalies, and obvious lies would prove those assertions not only incorrect but outrageously baseless. The release of the original report was timed to coincide with a cover page article in *Life* magazine on October 2, 1964. The introductory piece was written (at least his name was listed as the author) by Gerald Ford, one of the members of the commission; the lead paragraphs said,[220]

> The most important witness to appear before the Warren Commission in the 10 months we sat was a neat, Bible-reading steam fitter from Dallas. His name was H. L. Brennan and he had seen Lee Harvey Oswald thrust a rifle from a sixth-floor window of the Texas School Book Depository and shoot the President of the United States.
>
> In the shock and turmoil that followed, Brennan had headed for a policeman and given him a description of the man he had seen in the window. The police sent out a 'wanted' bulletin based on that description. About half an hour later, as police interrogated the assembled employees

---

220. *Life* magazine, October 2, 1964, p. 42.

of the Depository, the manager, noting that Lee Harvey Oswald was missing, had checked the personnel files for Oswald's address and description. The police then issued their second wanted bulletin based on the new information. After this second bulletin was issued, Officer J. D. Tippit stopped Oswald on the street and Oswald shot him dead.

The two descriptions differed in some details—although Brennan later identified Oswald in a police lineup—and it was this discrepancy which set off the first of the countless rumors concerning the President's assassination: namely, the story that two men were involved.

Thus, both here and abroad began the cascade of innuendo, supposition, imagination, twisted fact, misunderstanding, faulty analysis and downright fantasy that surrounded the tragic death of John Fitzgerald Kennedy.

The last paragraph may ironically be the most truthful of them all, if the context is reversed, but Ford actually intended to apply those words to the critics of the Warren Report, who were merely trying to understand the truth of what happened in Dallas. Much of the confusion which Ford—not known to be a particularly articulate man—referred to was caused by this sort of double-talk. It quickly developed that, though Brennan did view the lineup, he never positively identified Oswald or anyone else for that matter despite having proclaimed that he could do so. He even told the FBI that he "'*could not positively identify Oswald as the person he saw fire the rifle*' and this was after Brennan had seen Oswald's picture on television."[221]

Brennan had described the man he saw "from the belt up" as a "slender white male in his early thirties wearing 'light colored clothing.'" He further said, "I heard what I thought was a backfire. It ran in my mind that it might be someone throwing firecrackers out of the window of the red brick building [the Depository] and I looked up at the building. I then saw this man I have described in the window and he was taking aim with a high-powered rifle. I could see all of the barrel of the gun. I do not know if it had a scope on it or not. I was looking at the man in this window at the time of the last explosion. Then this man let the gun down to his side and stepped out of sight. He did not seem to be in any hurry . . . I believe I could identify this man if I ever saw him again."[222]

Author Marrs then noted that "much later, it was determined that Brennan had poor eyesight and, in fact, a close examination of the Zapruder

---

221. McKnight, p. 398 (Ref. *Warren Commission Report*, Vol. 3, pp. 143–147 *Hearings before Commission*, For Brennan's statement to the FBI that he could not positively identify Oswald, see Gemberling Report, November 30, 1963, FBIHQ Oswald File, 105-82555-505, Section 21, 11, 13).
222. Marrs, pp. 25–26.

film shows that Brennan was not looking up at the time of the shooting."
Furthermore, Brennan's job foreman, Sandy Speaker, told Marrs:[223]

> They took [Brennan] off for about three weeks. I don't know if they
> were Secret Service or FBI, but they were federal people. He came back
> a nervous wreck and within a year his hair had turned snow white. He
> wouldn't talk about [the assassination] after that. He was scared to death.
> They made him say what they wanted him to say.

Jim Marrs also reported that Brennan's supervisor Sandy Speaker, a combat
marine veteran, said that he heard "at least five shots and they came from
different locations."[224] Mr. Speaker had not talked about the matter since
1964, until he spoke to Marrs about twenty-five years later; he told Marrs
that he had gotten a call early in that year from another coworker, A. J.
Millican, who was almost in tears and who told him never to talk about
the assassination. Millican said he had just received an anonymous call
threatening not only his life but the lives of his wife and her sister. He
said the caller told him to also warn Speaker to keep his mouth shut. Mr.
Speaker then told Marrs, "That call really shook me up because Millican
was a former boxing champ of the Pacific fleet. He was a scrapper, a fighter.
But he was obviously scared to death. And I still don't understand how
they got my name because I was never interviewed by the FBI, the Secret
Service, the police or anyone. They must be pretty powerful to have found
out about me."[225] Of the group of workers that accompanied Mr. Speaker
to watch the motorcade during their lunch break, only Brennan claimed
to have seen the man he described (but couldn't identify) alone in the
Depository window. That would account for why he was the only one of
the group to have been interviewed by the FBI and why they did not want
to hear anyone else since they claimed to have either seen more men or
heard more shots than the official story being promulgated by the FBI and
sanctioned by the Warren Commission.

After noting the tremendous help the commission received from the
various federal agencies such as the FBI and Secret Service (the CIA wasn't
mentioned), Ford said in the article, "The full details of Oswald's nearly
three years in the U.S.S.R. will remain covered in mystery until and unless
the Soviet government opens its files completely. It has not done so yet."
Almost fifty years later, it is astonishing to read his account, which so clearly
sidesteps the facts now known about Oswald's training by the CIA and ONI

223. Ibid., p. 26.
224. Ibid., p. 29.
225. Ibid., p. 319.

preparatory to his trip to the Soviet Union yet blames the Soviets for the lack of knowledge of his life and times in that country. It is an interesting read in the context of everything that has since become known about Oswald (and Ford), and one thing does become clear after reading this material now: Congressman Ford was simply following a script that had been laid out well before the shooting started.

The Rebuttals Begin

The official report of the Warren Commission was immediately subjected to strong criticisms and ridicule by those few who actually read it; their incredulity led many others to discredit the veracity of its conclusions. Although it took fifteen years, Congress eventually conceded that there were most likely at least two gunmen involved in the assassination, possibly more. But it took another twenty years, and the production of an acclaimed movie on the subject, for Congress to decide to make public a mountain of evidence and information which had been heretofore officially sealed for up to seventy-five years by Lyndon Johnson's edict. By this point, however, there had been so much misinformation—and official disinformation—published that massive public confusion had displaced any meaningful "official version" of the real truth of this defining moment of U.S. history. It appears that this is exactly what Lyndon Johnson, the genius at manipulating people and planning very complex scenarios, had planned all along.

The book *Whitewash*, originally self-published in 1965 by Harold Weisberg, set the baseline as the first rebuttal of the Warren Report, showing that it utterly failed in its purported mission as the final word on solving the JFK assassination. Forty years later, a student of Weisberg's, Gerald McKnight, brought his mentor's arguments up to date with the publication of *Breach of Trust—how the Warren Commission Failed the Nation and Why*. Numerous others have added even more dimension to the record of the failures, omissions and fabrications of the Warren Report, which show conclusively its lack of credibility. One such author, Henry Hurt, in *Reasonable Doubt: An Investigation into the Assassination of John F. Kennedy* (1985), concurred that the Warren Report was a whitewash.

Professor McKnight established that the Warren Report was tantamount to a grandiose exercise in public relations—with a worldwide audience—developed to "prove" that Oswald alone assassinated President Kennedy; this was clearly the only objective from the start, even before the Warren Commission was established and functioning. He noted that the commission's own records—together with thousands of other items it ignored, or had been kept from seeing, or had been fabricated—show that there were two conspiracies: the one that it left still unsolved about the persons and events actually involved in the assassination itself as well as the secondary one into which its very own existence had become an inseparable part—the cover-up.[226] Moreover, the research done by McKnight established that the Warren Commission embraced the FBI's lone-gunman theory from the outset. The FBI repeatedly suppressed or actively ignored any and all evidence not congruent with that presumption. Its implied mantra throughout the perfunctory investigation was to ignore crucial leads, discount contradictory evidence, and select witnesses primarily on the basis of their willingness to cooperate in testifying consistently with the politically correct, preapproved findings; a related objective was to harass and ridicule those witnesses who did not conform to their agenda.[227] The inevitable conclusions of this body would be established early on and remain constant until the finish, which were then summarized as follows:

- "The Commission has found no evidence that either Lee Harvey Oswald or Jack Ruby was part of any conspiracy, domestic or foreign, to assassinate President Kennedy."
- "In its entire investigation the Commission has found no evidence of conspiracy, subversion, or disloyalty to the U.S. Government by any Federal, State or local official."

Despite its stated additional conclusion, "the Commission has investigated each rumor and allegation linking Oswald to a conspiracy which has come to its attention, regardless of source," the fact that it purposely culled its witness list of anyone who claimed that they heard more than three shots, or that they heard shots from the grassy knoll, renders this a specious claim. Though most people assumed that Oswald was involved in some way, possibly as one of the assassins, his lack of a real motive (his enigmatic past notwithstanding), his choice of weapon, and the surfeit of questions surrounding every facet of the investigation all contributed to the public skepticism that grew almost immediately after the commission published its report.

Beyond the detailed instances of incompetence or malfeasance of the FBI's handling of the investigation, there was even more troubling evidence of subtle conflicts of interest between the FBI and the Secret Service vis-à-vis the commission members and its staff that are addressed by Professor McKnight. Throughout his book are references to the fact that the commission itself and J. Lee Rankin, its general counsel, were beholden to the FBI and

---

226. McKnight, p. 354.
227. Ibid., p. 89, for example.

J. Edgar Hoover, which caused them to have to be exceedingly deferential to him, lest he become upset and withhold his and/or the FBI's assistance to the commission.[228] Rankin was acutely aware that the commission's timetable and its mandate (ostensibly to find out the truth of the assassination, but in reality to return a "guilty" verdict for the dead Oswald, with plenty of paper to back it up), required that they have the FBI's full cooperation. To do so, his first priority was to avoid alienating the cantankerous Hoover. "From March to September 1964, there were many occasions when a deferential Rankin tried to smooth the director's ruffled feathers. His placatory efforts never mattered in any fundamental way because the director and his agency perceived the commission as an adversary and a threat that had to be contained. When Rankin gushed about the superior quality of FBI testimony before the commission, Hoover dismissed the compliments. 'They were looking for FBI "gaps," he huffed, 'and having found none yet they try to get "syrupy.""'[229]

Among the many errors and incongruities of the Warren Report noted by Professor McKnight and numerous others the following few are noted in summary fashion in the interest of brevity and because they are thoroughly analyzed in numerous other books:

- **The "magic bullet" theory**. This is the single most controversial, widely criticized, and thoroughly discredited "conclusion" of the report. None more clearly divides the Warren Commission supporters ("Lone Nut Theorists") from the researchers who believe the "Single Bullet Theory" was borne more of a need to fill a vacuum than it was a rational and objective attempt to reconstruct the crime. This conclusion postulates that one shot hit Kennedy near the top of his back (which required a clever parsing of words, with help from Gerald Ford, to move the bullet wound on JFK's back to a point high enough to be called his shoulder[230]), which then came out the front of his neck, went through Connally's back, came out of his chest, smashed his right wrist, and caused a puncture wound in his left thigh. After doing all of this bone-breaking damage, the nearly pristine bullet was supposedly found on a gurney in the hospital, which was not even used to carry either Kennedy or Connally. The many issues regarding the origin and subsequent handling of this bullet renders the conclusions made about it utterly impossible.[231]

---

228. Ibid.
229. Ibid., p. 106.
230. Mantik, (from Fetzer's *Murder in Dealey Plaza*), pp. 252–255.
231. McKnight (Chapters 8 and 9 are dedicated in their entirety to the "Single-Bullet Fabrication").

- **More bullet controversy**. Parkland Personnel Director O. P. Wright stated in 1967 that the bullet he saw on the day of the assassination did *not* look like the bullet that later became CE-399. This statement directly conflicted with the FBI memo of July 7, 1964, which said that Wright had told an FBI agent that the bullet looked like the one he had inspected on November 22, 1963. By this time, of course, the matter had been officially put to bed.[232]

- **Kennedy's moving back wound**. Dr. Humes, who testified that he stuck his finger in Kennedy's back wound and found that the path only went one to two inches into his flesh, would lead one to conclude that the actual bullet to Kennedy's back was a "short" charge not powerful enough to go farther. It certainly didn't turn upward and exit his throat, or anywhere else, and proceed to then make five more entries and exits in Connally. The shot was in his *back*, not the back of his neck, despite the best efforts of Arlen Specter and Gerald Ford to move the wound through their attempts to obfuscate the facts. Specter continually referred to this back wound as being "on the lower part of the neck."* Arlen Specter can be found on a number of internet videos (such as one titled: "FBI Agent, Specter on JFK Back Wound") continuing, decades later, to say that the wound was on JFK's "neck", which is a complete deception. As he also demonstrated on the same referenced video, his own political skills were sharply honed, including such creative, paradoxical idioms, as, "Sometimes, truth is stranger than fiction," probably meant to blur the lines between the two opposites. There are many ways to interpret that particular sentence, but they all depend upon the meaning and context of the word "truth", as well as whom the speaker is.

   In his partial defense, Specter's point of view was not derived from an analysis of any actual photographs of the bullet in Kennedy's neck, but only of an artist's (H.A. Rydberg) rendering which (quite inaccurately) showed the wound in the lower neck, so far from the actual entry point that it clearly demonstrates that the artist didn't see the photograph either, and was drawing it based upon Gerald Ford's clever parsing of words. It is possible the artist used Dr. Humes' ambiguous description of the wounds—which were stated four months after the autopsy and also without the benefit of ever reviewing the autopsy photographs. The reason the Commission decided that the actual photographs would be withheld from the view of anyone, including the very witnesses and investigators who were charged with finding the truth, was as a favor to the Kennedy family; it is clear that such a directive could have only come from Earl Warren, or, more likely, the man to whom

---

*See, for example, WCR vol. 2, p. 352.
232. Hurt, p. 79, North, p. 378.

he reported. Specter's final words on the subject were included in an April 30, 1964 memo to Lee Rankin: "Some day, someone may compare the films with the artist drawings and find a significant error." [233]

- **Oswald's Marksmanship**: Two of the three shots attributed to Oswald were perfectly fired, supposedly by an average shooter even in his Marine Corps days who was armed with an extremely poor-quality, antique Italian Army surplus rifle equipped with a defective scope. No one, including the best "master marksmen" in the nation, has ever been able to duplicate the alleged shot-making skills of this man who was never considered, by those who knew him in the Marine Corps, ever interested enough in target practice to even become an expert rifleman.

The many other substantive issues raised by McKnight and others relating to the Warren Report are clear evidence of an extensive effort by the FBI to substitute evidence and create, in behalf of those who were orchestrating the massive cover-up, a set of evidence that conformed to the preestablished objective of finding Oswald guilty of the crime. In reality, the documents produced by the Warren Commission were intended to achieve the objective of satisfying the man who conceived and executed the crime in the first place: Lyndon B. Johnson. The tentacles of Johnson's and Hoover's power over other men led the commissioners themselves—and the entire staff, mostly unwittingly—to spin a web of obstruction and obfuscation, which was manifested in the production of a document that was touted as being a "296,000-word report [which] is itself only a summary of two dozen 500-page volumes"[234]

In the early part of the Warren Commission's proceedings, in February 1964, Earl Warren responded to a reporter's question about when all the testimony would be made public, saying, "Yes, there will come a time. But it might not be in your lifetime."[235] This rather candid response revealed more than Earl Warren probably intended. But now, going on three generations later, it is time that all the testimony and physical evidence—properly labeled as real or fabricated—be made public.

---

233. Also see: http://mcadams.posc.mu.edu/shootft.htm.
234. Life magazine, October 2, 1964, p. 44.
235. Lifton, p. 225.

Chapter 8

A MORE PLAUSIBLE
SCENARIO

*If I told you what I really know, it would be very dangerous to this country.
Our whole political system could be disrupted.*

—J. EDGAR HOOVER

November 22, 1963: An Hour in Johnson's Life

One-half hour before John F. Kennedy was assassinated, Lyndon Johnson
was the beleaguered vice president in a world of trouble with two Senate
investigations proceeding against him and Bobby Baker; the attorney general
was intent on removing him from office as he fed incriminating information
about Johnson, both to Senate investigators as well as *Life* magazine. One-
half hour after JFK was assassinated, all of that changed as the nation gave
him unconditional support as its new president; he was now in a position to
stop all the investigations and begin putting his long-planned strategies in
place to become elected in his own right less than a year later.

Only by becoming president on November 22 could Johnson have
survived without finally paying his penalty. Had there been any further delay
(tentative alternate plans had already been planned and discarded in Chicago
and Miami in the previous weeks), Johnson would have been exposed in the
continuing Bobby Baker investigation and would have likely been impeached
and prosecuted after that.[1] On that very day, he knew that the man Bobby
Baker had a run-in with, the insurance salesman Don Reynolds, was
scheduled to testify in closed session of the Senate Rules Committee, giving
documented evidence of just a few of the illegal financial dealings, bribery
and extortion; he also knew that this testimony would not remain secret
for long if it were not stopped immediately. He was doubly upset because
he knew that if he were still running the Senate, these investigations would
have never been launched; now, they were in full swing, headed toward
what appeared to be certain censure by the Senate and probable indictment

---

1. (Ref. for example, Chapter 5, the story recently told by James Wagenvoord, an assistant
editor of *Life* magazine in November 1963).

by the Justice Department. If things got out of control at this point, the investigations might have automatically led into further scandals involving other associates, including congressmen who might be implicated in the far-reaching financial scandals and then back up through his friends'—Bobby Baker's and Fred Black's sex clubs—directly to the president, even possibly bringing down the entire administration. He knew, of course, that there would be no sanctuary in that scenario for himself, given that Kennedy's downfall would also inevitably bring himself down along with everyone else. To say that JFK's assassination and LBJ's ascension changed the course of American history is a major understatement on many disparate levels.

Love Field, Dallas, Texas: The Morning of November 22, 1963

The Johnson-Connally feud with Senator Yarborough had already boiled over several times since Kennedy's arrival, and Lyndon Johnson was in one of his famous funks. The most likely explanation for his strange behavior all during the motorcade was that he was very nervous about all the plans he had worked on the last several weeks—the most complex project he had ever commanded—yet grateful for the help he was receiving from key associates in Washington. When he arrived at Love Field, he would have noted the early signs of a successful execution, seeing that the bubble top had been removed as he had ordered Bill Moyers to ensure and that Puterbaugh was completing the last-minute changes in the motorcycle formation and moving the vehicle sequence of the motorcade to keep photographers well back instead of their usual place near Kennedy's limousine. As the motorcade began moving from the tarmac, he knew his orders were materializing now as he watched Emory Roberts order Henry Rybka to stand down instead of preparing to mount the rear bumper of the president's limousine.

His most trusted men had made their presence known; all of them were with him in Texas. Besides Puterbaugh, there was Cliff Carter who, a few months before, had accepted his order to return to Texas to help prepare for the Texas trip. Both had been very effective in standing in for—and protecting—Johnson in making sure the motorcade was "set up" in all respects according to Johnson's wishes. Carter's devotion to Johnson would be given the ultimate test today, and for the next several days, as he dutifully handled one task after another as requested by his leader. Carter had been Johnson's closest assistant—closer even than Walter Jenkins—for the entire period of his vice presidency, serving another role as his advance man on every trip Johnson had made during that entire period. Carter and Puterbaugh had worked together well in the weeks leading up to this day, ensuring the motorcade route that brought it down Main Street before turning up Houston Street to the 120-degree turn onto Elm Street, instead of the other alternatives (simply going down Elm Street in lieu of Main Street or following Main Street straight through Dealey Plaza and onto Stemmons via a temporary ramp over a small curb).[2] Mac Wallace would also be in Dallas that morning but remain as invisible as he could be made to be. His sloppiness in executing his missions was something that would have to be minimized, and for thirty-five years afterward, it seemed that it was. As will be seen shortly, however, Mac Wallace had left a fingerprint on one of the boxes that would remain classified as "unknown" until a fingerprint expert named Nathan Darby determined, over thirty years later, that it matched Mac Wallace's fingerprint.

Lyndon Johnson would also be glad to see that the Dallas Police Department had ordered most of their men to duty at Love Field, leaving only light protection the rest of the way; even the policemen posted at the major intersections would disappear at the point where the motorcade turned north on Houston, at the edge of Dealey Plaza, "the weakest link in downtown Dallas."[3] As William Manchester later noted, there were only a few scattered patrolmen around Dealey Plaza, though there had been 365 policemen at Love Field and 60 stationed at the Trade Mart.[4] As he had directed, the Dallas Police Department and the county Sheriff's Department were told to end motorcade protection at Houston Street because from there on, the Secret Service was to take over, though no actual Secret Service agents were posted anywhere around there other than those in the motorcade. It was only a short distance from the triple underpass to the ramp leading to the freeway; however, it left the motorcade completely unprotected for that critical distance designated as the "killing zone." Johnson knew also that there would be men posted there with Secret Service credentials who would ensure that no well-meaning bystanders would get in the way and spoil the planned getaway of the men behind the picket fence. They were also instructed to note everyone taking pictures of the motorcade and immediately begin confiscating them after the operation was completed.

After leaving the airport, according to Senator Yarborough as chronicled by William Manchester, Johnson did not enjoy being in the motorcade as he rode through Dallas, staring glumly at the people who had come out to greet the presidential party.[5] Shortly after the motorcade started, Johnson abruptly

---

2. Twyman, pp. 844–845 (interview with Johnson's mistress Madeleine Brown).
3. Manchester, p. 149.
4. Ibid.
5. Manchester, p. 134.

leaned forward toward the front seats and ordered the driver to "turn the radio on." Hurchel Jacks obeyed the vice president, turning the volume up so that Johnson could hear a local station broadcasting the progress of the motorcade through the city.[6] Listening to the local radio station was a pretext for Johnson to lean forward during parts of the entire ride—making his actions when his car approached Elm Street, by then, not seem all that unusual to his fellow passengers—while virtually ignoring the crowd lining the streets. Riding forward on the seat and hunching down like this would put him into the ideal position to quickly fall behind the front seat as the car approached Elm Street. By this point, he would switch his attention to a hand-held wireless "walkie-talkie," shared with Secret Service Agent Youngblood, according to Senator Yarborough. This would give him further excuse to duck down below the rear seatbacks feigning hearing difficulties. This kind of conniving, as part of his overall long-term planning, was precisely what Lyndon Johnson excelled in throughout his life; the objective of his behavior in the motorcade, as we shall see shortly, was to take himself out of the line of fire when the shooting began.

By noon in Dealey Plaza, three cars somehow had gained entrance into the parking area adjacent to the railroad yard, which had supposedly been closed by the police at 10:00 a.m. Lee Bowers, a railroad switchman, was sitting in a tower overlooking the parking lot at that time. He had a good view of the area between his tower and Elm Street. In sworn testimony, he stated there was a lot of activity going on in the area of the picket fence, with strange cars coming in and out and strangers loitering around inside the fenced area. He saw two men as they arrived in the parking lot to take up positions along the fence area. He added, "These men were the only two strangers in the area. The others were workers whom I knew." He saw that one of the men had a handheld "walkie-talkie," which he was talking into sporadically.[7] Though their movements looked very suspicious to him, he decided that they were probably involved in the presidential security detail.

The logistics of the "crime of the century" had been worked out by men who held some of the highest offices of the government and involved about a dozen; they also had access to an assortment of the best equipment available to carry out their mission. But most did not know any more than that which they needed to know to perform their own part. Only three at the top, another three or four in the middle, and as many again at the bottom, including the actual shooters, were aware of the real agenda. The others were part of the loosely accountable, compartmentalized world of covert operations

6. Ibid., p. 136.
7. Twyman, p. 19, 759.

and had no knowledge of the ultimate objective of their assignments. Many were veterans of "Operation Mongoose" and were now actively involved in *ZR/RIFLE* or "Operation 40," but this operation was only supposed to be a failed assassination attempt, for vague purposes to them. The only unifying object of their diversionary mission was the promise of being the catalyst for a new and energized retaliatory attack on Cuba to finally achieve the permanent removal of Fidel Castro.

According to an interview conducted by Dick Russell, Gerry Patrick Hemming told him that the Cubans were brought into the picture in the middle of November 1963:[8]

> The week before the assassination, Felipe Vidal Santiago told my group that some people had approached him to go to a big meeting in Dallas that week," Hemming said. "We warned him and some other people not to go, that something funny was up. I'd heard of other meetings, where the conversation got steered around toward hitting JFK instead of Fidel. I'm talking about . . . some people in Dallas. It's hard to say exactly who this select group of Cuban exiles was really working for . . . For a while, they were reporting to Bill Harvey's ex-FBI CIA guys. *Some were reporting back to Hoover*, or the new DIA [Defense Intelligence Agency]. There was a third force—pretty much outside CIA channels, outside our own private operation down in the Keys—that was doing all kinds of shit, and had been all through '63.

The men coming into place in Dealey Plaza that morning were working on a covert operation that had been cloned from the earlier efforts to assassinate Castro and invade Cuba. The operation was modified in the final days once the final nod was given by the commander of the operation. One of the lower-level contract agents involved in the conspiracy was Lee Harvey Oswald, selected months ago to become, in his own words after the realization had dawned on him, the "patsy" of the operation. He had been deluded into thinking that this was the culmination of his lifelong childhood dream: becoming a spy like the exciting character on the television series *I Led Three Lives*.* Oswald was not one of the actual assassins, however; he personally liked John F. Kennedy. Many researchers agree that the Altgens photo (to be reviewed shortly) shows Oswald standing at the entrance to

---

*Based upon a book by Herbert Arthur Philbrick titled *I Led Three Lives: Citizen, 'Communist', Counterspy*, which was made into a movie and television series called *I Led Three Lives*, starring Richard Carlson and Ed Hinton, loosely based on Philbrick's experiences.
8. Ibid., pp. 623–624.

the building and that of course would mean he fired no shots at all. A more likely scenario for the errant shot would be that it was not fired from the TSBD building at all, but rather from a lower floor of the Dal-Tex building; this would explain why it was not so much a "wild shot" but rather one which narrowly missed hitting its mark, instead it hit the edge of the gutter directly in front of the limousine. As Dr. James H. Fetzer has established, Oswald's weapon could not have fired the shots that killed JFK; he was not even on the sixth floor at the time, and Oswald passed his paraffin test showing he had not fired a carbine.[9] Furthermore, it is improbable that Oswald had even been on the sixth floor of the TSBD after noon that day for several reasons, including the testimony of Officer Marion Baker and Oswald's boss, Roy Truly, both of whom stated that Oswald was very calm and not out of breath, which anyone would have been after running down four flights of stairs, something he would have had to have done if he had been a shooter, in order to meet them on the second floor only ninety seconds after the final shots were fired. Another was that Carolyn Arnold saw Oswald on the first floor at 12:15 p.m. and about the same time Arnold Rowland saw a man standing at a window with a rifle, but this was the corner of the other side of the building (the southwest corner) on the sixth floor. Josiah Thompson established this in 1967; he also postulated that John Connally was hit from a different shot than the president. Thompson's work helped to prove there were multiple shooters and simultaneously demolish the "single bullet theory" as well.

Sometime after the shots were fired, it must have occurred to Oswald that he was being played as a "patsy," and if he didn't get out of there immediately, he would probably be shot dead upon capture. A "suspect description" of unknown origin, which loosely matched Oswald, was broadcast as an "All Points Bulletin" about then; Ruby might have been the source. It appears that Ruby had told him to meet him at the Texas Theater as soon as possible that afternoon but he had to go back to his apartment first to retrieve his pistol, for his own self-protection. Oswald headed back to his apartment to get it as well as change his shirt. The plan after that, he had been told, would then be to reconnoiter at Redbird Airport with pilots who would then fly him to Mexico with papers and visa for entry into Cuba to begin preparing for the coming U.S. invasion. Oswald thought that, finally, he would achieve his ultimate lifetime goal: becoming a full-time, well-paid spy just like his hero from *I Led Three Lives*. Ruby had expected that the police would track him to the theater and kill him when he drew his pistol; unfortunately for Ruby, it didn't work out that way.

---

9. Fetzer, Murder, pp. 361–370.

Oswald had quietly prepared for his part in the mission, starting back in New Orleans accompanying his handlers, primarily David Ferrie, Guy Banister, and Clay Shaw, on several "test" training missions. George de Mohrenschildt, like his counterpart Clay Shaw, a sophisticated and urbane man having a long history of CIA connections, had also helped to pave the way for a number of actions, including moving Oswald from Fort Worth to Dallas and securing him a job through others not aware of the pending assassination. Both Shaw and de Mohrenschildt had taken their orders directly from the man controlling the details of the operation from his CIA position in Mexico, under the code name of Maurice Bishop, David Atlee Phillips. Phillips, as did his peer David Morales, in charge of the operational and logistical end of the plan, took his orders from Bill Harvey who reported only to two men at the highest levels of the CIA, James Jesus Angleton and Cord Meyer. According to information furnished by E. Howard Hunt during negotiations related to a possible film expose—which was finally scuttled because of his excessive monetary demands—Harvey and the others were being guided primarily by Cord Meyer, operating out of his London CIA offices.[10] In turn, David Ferrie and Guy Banister, the point men in New Orleans, were guided by Harvey to groom Oswald for his coming role in Dallas.[11] Moreover, it is clear from the evidence cited that Oswald knew of his initial role in a simulated assassination with the intent of forcing Kennedy to invade Cuba.[12] He knew that it was only for his own good that he did not know details on the overall mission; his objective was simply to perform his task well, and he would be whisked off to his next mission, assured of safe passage to Cuba and that his young family would be taken care of in his absence, probably better than he could have done himself, he reckoned.

The highest levels of the operation had set the "stage" in many ways, beginning with the virtually complete elimination of the normal protection given to the president. In addition to the absence of more than a few patrolmen, no effort had been made, as was the norm, to see to it that all the windows in the buildings around Dealey Plaza were closed and that normal security checks of personnel within those buildings had been made. The motorcade route—which could have alternately gone straight down Main Street to a temporary crossover onto the Stemmons Expressway and the Trade Mart—would require the limousine to go into a 120-degree turn at the Elm Street intersection, which ensured that the vehicle would slow to a crawl. Shortly

---

10. JFK Lancer symposium, Nov. 2007, David Giammarco presentation.
11. Twyman, pp. 706, 727–729.
12. Ibid.

after that, the driver would be instructed over the radio to slow down, even stop, at a place in the road next to a man with an open umbrella now marked with a big white X.

Meanwhile, as the limousine lurched to a brief halt, the snipers, including a Corsican sharpshooter and a Mafia hit man—expert shooters using expensive, highly accurate automatic rifles with equally precise telescopic sights—let loose a volley of at least five more shots, the first one at almost the same time as the missed shot, hitting Kennedy in the throat, the next hitting him in the back. As Kennedy reacted to that by leaning to his left, another similarly placed shot missed him and hit Connally in the back. The last volley consisted of one from the back, hitting Kennedy in the back of the head and causing his body to jerk forward; within a fraction of a second, the last shot was fired from behind the fence on the grassy knoll. This was the instantly fatal shot, which hit him in the right front side of his head, violently pushing it backward while exploding his skull and causing most of his brain tissue from the right side of his skull to splash backward, hitting the motorcycle policemen riding to the left rear corner of the limousine.*

Lee Bowers, watching from the railroad yard tower, told Mark Lane, "At the time of the shooting . . . there was a flash of light or, as far as I am concerned, something I could not identify, but there was something which occurred which caught my eye in this immediate area on the embankment. Now, what this was, I could not state at that time and at this time I could not identify it, other than there was some unusual occurrence—a flash of light or smoke or something which caused me to feel like something out of the ordinary had occurred there."[13] There was no question in the mind of Lee Bowers that a shot, possibly more than one, was fired from the area of the wooden stockade fence. It is interesting that Bowers also told of the men's use of a walkie-talkie.

Inside the Vice Presidential Car: Noon to 12:29 p.m.

As the motorcade proceeded down Main Street to the turn on Houston Street, the nervous anticipation must have been overwhelming for Johnson and had

---

* This sequence offers a more viable explanation of (i) the entry wound in Kennedy's throat, rather than being an "exit" wound as claimed by the Warren Commission; (ii) a more plausible reason for the delay between Kennedy's and Connally's reactions in lieu of the "single bullet theory"; (iii) an explanation of why Kennedy's head briefly jerked towards the front, followed immediately by a forceful backward movement; (iv) and the real reason for the first shot— hitting the curb and ricocheting upwards to graze James Tague's face, which should have been the easiest to aim—having been missed so wildly, was because it did not emanate from the "snipers nest" but from another location entirely.

13. Lane, *Rush* . . . p. 32.

rendered him sullen and morose. From the many descriptions of Johnson's actions and behavior that day, it is clear that he was extremely stressed and apparently in the "depressive" phase of his manic-depressive illness noted earlier and to be examined further in the final chapter. William Manchester, writing one to two years after the event—perhaps not realizing the real depth of, or the reasons for, Johnson's dour mood (how much he did realize will not be known until the year 2067, as noted elsewhere)—described him as having sat in the backseat of the convertible throughout the ride through Dallas as he sought solace by pretending to listen to the car's radio; before the shots, his prestige had all but disappeared amidst the daily news of investigations closing in on him.[14] Apparently, Mr. Manchester had not become fully aware of the real reason for Johnson's worries; yet there were glimpses, between the lines, of his considerable discomfort with the new president.

Despite the fact that the Johnson car lagged behind the Queen Mary by one and a half car lengths (to make the vice president's appearance a 'separate event' from the president's),[15] Johnson hunched himself down at various times throughout the motorcade as it made its way through Dallas, at times leaning forward pretending to listen to the radio. According to Manchester's account, Johnson had remained hunched down in the car throughout the ride down Harwood Street, to Main Street, and Dealey Plaza as he continued listening to the Dallas radio station.[16] Meanwhile, Senator Yarborough, who was waiving jubilantly and repeatedly calling to onlookers, "Howdy, thar" throughout the trip, said that Johnson was clearly not enjoying this bit of politicking; he said that Johnson appeared "saturnine."[17]

Clearly, Senator Yarborough—as most politicians of clear conscience would in this situation—was enjoying the event, in contrast to the morose and dour Johnson who obviously had other things on his mind. When the motorcade turned right from Main Street onto Houston Street, after the first few cars had passed, people in the crowds noticed that Johnson's profile in the convertible was unusually low, even lower than his diminutive wife Lady Bird's, who sat next to him.

As the president's limousine began proceeding down Elm Street after slowing to practically a complete stop as it made the turn, in the second car behind, Lyndon Johnson, Lady Bird, and Senator Yarborough were just entering the intersection as the first shot rang out. Johnson, who had already

---

14. Manchester, p. 228.
15. Ibid., p. 134.
16. Manchester, pp. 145, 134.
17. Ibid., pp. 151–152.

been slouching down in his seat as he pretended to listen to the radio on the car's dashboard, had by now disappeared from view.[18] As noted in the previous chapter, Johnson was already practically invisible to onlookers and was below the front seat back of the car even before the shooting started. Mary Mitchell stated that she heard the first shot just as Senator Yarborough's car entered the intersection, obviously because she had not seen Johnson in the car.

As will be detailed shortly, Officer B. J. Martin stated that other police officers riding motorcycles close by the Johnson convertible in the motorcade said that he had slouched down in the seat and continued shrinking along Houston Street as he sat lower and lower in the seat. "According to the guys who were escorting his car in the motorcade, our new president is either one jumpy son of a bitch or he knows something he's not telling about the Kennedy thing . . . he started ducking down in the car a good thirty or forty seconds before the first shots were fired."[19] Johnson's profile had disappeared completely by the time the car turned onto Elm Street.

The Hidden Key to Unraveling the Crime of the Century

The famous Altgens photograph (below) captured the moment Johnson's car completed its turn onto Elm Street, just before anyone other than Kennedy had time to react to the first shot. The millions of eyes which looked at it either didn't notice something very peculiar about it or disregarded an anomaly that was written off as a blur in an otherwise very clear photograph: Lyndon Johnson was not in it. He had already disappeared completely out of sight. As he knew he had to be all along the motorcade route, he would have to remove himself from the line of fire sometime before the turn onto Elm Street. He did so under the pretext of listening to the radio or a walkie-talkie even *before* the first shot rang out. Johnson, in a prepared statement to the Warren Commission, invented an unsupported explanation for the incident:

> I was startled by a sharp report or explosion, but I had no time to speculate as to its origin because Agent Youngblood turned in a flash, immediately after the first explosion, hitting me on the shoulder, and shouted to all of us in the back seat to get down. I was pushed down by Agent Youngblood. Almost in the same moment in which he hit or pushed me, he vaulted over the back seat and sat on me. I was bent over under the weight of Agent Youngblood's body, toward Mrs. Johnson and Senator Yarborough . . .

18. Manchester, p. 145, Sloan and Hill, *JFK: The Last Dissenting Witness* p. 112.
19. Sloan and Hill, *JFK: The Last Dissenting Witness* p. 112.

Youngblood himself apparently could not remember what he did in the most important action he ever undertook. The Warren Report stated that he "was not positive that he was in the rear seat before the second shot, *but thought it probable because of President Johnson's statement to that effect.*"[20] (Emphasis added.) It is not possible that Youngblood had already shoved Johnson down at that point, based upon his own statement in his report to Chief Rowley dated November 29, 1963, when he stated that after the first report (sound of a shot):[21]

> I noticed that the movements in the Presidential car were very abnormal and, at practically the same time, the movements in the Presidential follow-up car were abnormal. I turned in my seat and with my left arm grasped and shoved the Vice President, at his right shoulder, down and toward Mrs. Johnson and Senator Yarborough. At the same time, I shouted "get down!" I believe I said this more than once and directed it to the Vice President and the other occupants of the rear seat. They all responded very rapidly.

Two facts plainly visible in the photo belie Johnson's claim to have already been shoved down by Youngblood: First, Youngblood's comment that he *"noticed . . . the movements in the . . . follow-up car were abnormal"* (in the Altgens photo, no such discernible reactions can be noted) and second, Youngblood's statement that, at the same time he shoved Johnson down, he yelled to both Lady Bird and Senator Yarborough to "get down" and that they "all responded very rapidly." Yet neither of the other rear seat passengers had reacted whatsoever at the instant this photograph was taken. At the very least, if Youngblood had already done all of this at that moment, one might expect a look of surprise or shock or fright or bewilderment in their faces, but they both have stoic, even blasé, expressions. They look like they might have become a little tired of all the forced smiling, perhaps a little glad that the end of the parade was in sight; but their expressions clearly reflect the fact that neither of them had heard, or at least reacted, to anything, including the shouts of Rufus Youngblood. Obviously, the reality of gunfire had not yet been recognized.

The only possible reason for Johnson's prevarication (together with the apparent fact that he had persuaded Youngblood to, albeit hesitatingly and probably reluctantly, partially agree with his deception but with a caveat that said essentially, "since the President says so, it must be true") was to provide "cover" for the fact that he was not in the photo. Unfortunately, Youngblood

---

20. Warren Commission Report, p. 52.
21. See: http://www.jfk-online.com/youngblood.html.

was not properly schooled in the finer nuances of the art of deception and hedged on that point since his testimony, unlike Johnson's, was under oath. To add to the confusion from Johnson's "testimony," Senator Yarborough insisted that Youngblood never even left the front seat; he maintained that the agent merely turned around and talked to Johnson in an undertone and that there was no room for him to have come into the backseat in any case. "It just didn't happen . . . It was a small car (relative to the Presidential Lincoln). Johnson was a big man, tall. His knees were up against his chin as it was. There was no room for that to happen."[22] Dave Powers had glanced back to the car and confirmed Yarborough's account. The driver of Johnson's car, Hurchel Jacks, said that after the shot, Youngblood "asked me what that was and at the same time he advised the Vice President and Mrs. Johnson to get down."[23] In other words, according to Jacks, Youngblood's first reaction, after asking Jacks his opinion of the noise, was to merely shout "Get down!" It appears, by the testimony of Youngblood, Jacks, and Mrs. Johnson, he didn't reach into the back until at least after the remaining shots, if he even did it then; according to Yarborough, sitting in the backseat next to Lady Bird, Youngblood never came into the backseat at all. All of this is simply another example of the confusion surrounding Johnson's hyperbole that he stated, in a prepared statement in lieu of a sworn deposition or testimony, "He vaulted over the backseat and sat on me. I was bent over under the weight of Agent Youngblood's body.".[24]

Anyone who has ever sat in the backseat of a standard (nonstretch) Lincoln, as plush and nice as it may be, can attest to the fact that it is still only slightly bigger than a standard-sized Ford. To think that Agent Youngblood could have pushed Lyndon Johnson, as big as he was, to the floor, with two others sharing that space, and sat on him and neither of them still be noticed in the Altgens photograph is simply "hogwash," to use a Texas colloquialism. But the reality of the situation was lost on Lyndon Johnson, not because of the shock and mayhem everyone else experienced, but because he knew well in advance what to expect—and nervously anticipated it all morning—and had prepared for it; the most compelling explanation of why Johnson was so nervous all morning but so confident after the killing of JFK was because he knew it would happen, where it would happen, and when it would happen.

---

22. Marrs, pp. 249–250 (Also See *The Senator who Suspected a JFK Conspiracy:* http://www.geocities.com/senatoryarborough/.
23. WCH, Vol. XVIII, p. 801.
24. Manchester, p. 166.

All of these pesky discrepancies would be written off by him much as he once told Doris Kearns when she caught him in a lie. "Oh these journalists, they're such sticklers for details!"[25] As his own press secretary George Reedy, later reflecting on Johnson's lack of credibility, explained, the truth for Lyndon Johnson was whatever he deemed it to be and in this case he apparently felt that he needed to embellish the facts with a little added drama. There was evidently a sliver of reality left in his consciousness since he was aware of the perjury implications of lying under oath, ergo his decision to reveal his "recollections" as casually as possible (he simply sent the Warren Commission a memo to explain all of this). For many people, it was unclear why he thought that seemingly innocuous difference in how Agent Youngblood reacted—whether he had simply turned around, yelled "Get down," and then covered himself with his arms and shoulders, versus his jumping over the seat back and sitting on him—was important enough to risk perjuring himself under oath if the commission had insisted on it (as absurd as such a scenario would appear).

But lie about it he did, according to everyone else offering testimony in direct conflict with the new president. This particular anomaly has now become much more clear: Lyndon Johnson had apparently inspected the Altgens photograph and seen its incriminating implication; lest he be called upon to explain it to others, he knew he had to come up with a justification for his absence from the photo. His refusal to give sworn testimony to the Warren Commission about his reactions to the shots in Dealey Plaza was clearly based on his fear of having to commit perjury; he knew that if anyone ever looked closely enough at the Altgens photograph, the only reasonable justification for his absence in the photo was because he was crouching behind the seat, and the only possible explanation for that was that he was shoved there by agent Youngblood. Senator Yarborough said that Youngblood held a small walkie-talkie over the back of the car's seat and that he and Johnson both put their ears to the device. He added, 'They had it turned down real low. I couldn't hear what they were listening to.'"[26] Additionally, Ira David Wood III further confirmed Yarborough's account:[27]

> In the motorcade's Vice Presidential limousine, Lyndon Johnson is later described as having his ear up against a small walkie-talkie held

25. Kearns, p. 30.
26. Manchester, p. 166.
27. Fetzer, Wood, *Murder in Dealey Plaza Part I: 22 November, 1963: A Chronology*, p. 32.

over the back seat, "listening to the device which was 'turned down real low,'"[28] "Lyndon Johnson's Secret Service detail is already '*on the alert*' . . . the agents seem poised for immediate action. "Local Dallas newspaper reporters have been joking all morning about when and where "*the shooting will start.*'"

That exact moment was captured by James "Ike" Altgens, a photographer for the Associated Press. This is a very clear, professional-quality photograph showing the first four cars of the motorcade. When cropped down to show only the Johnson-Yarborough car, all the occupants are clearly visible except for two: Secret Service Agent Jack Youngblood, whose position behind the motorcycle precludes his image; however, it does show clearly that he had *not* yet positioned himself over the seat to cover Johnson. There is no image whatsoever of Lyndon B. Johnson in this famous photograph, who should be quite visible, seated to the left of the clearly visible Lady Bird and Senator Yarborough, both of whom were seated to his [LBJ's] left in the rear seat and arguably should have been less visible than him given his size and position in the car, while they were seated behind the driver. The spot where LBJ is supposed to be shows only the midbody portions of people standing on the sidewalk beyond the car (a bit of distortion between the images through the windshield vs. those above it is caused by the curvature of the windshield).

If he were only concerned with listening to the car's radio, as reported by Manchester—or subsequently, the Secret Service walkie-talkie, as reported by others—he would not have needed to fall completely behind the seat and onto the floor of the car to do so. Yet his complete absence in this photograph—*well before any other person in any of the four cars in Altgen's photograph had reacted*, except only for President Kennedy grasping his throat—is compelling evidence that, until now, has not been presented for public scrutiny. The millions of viewings of this photo were focused on JFK's first reaction to being shot, not on Johnson's absence, which obviously occurred even before the first shot. Given the situation in the motorcade, there was no rational explanation for Johnson's actions throughout the motorcade—especially having a need for listening to an AM radio broadcast of the motorcade, and then listening to a walkie-talkie—that required him to practically lie on the floor of the car just before reaching Elm Street. That is, no reason other than the one which should be obvious: he was afraid the shooters might fire off a volley at him instead of shooting only Kennedy, as they had been ordered to do, by him.

---

28. Also see Zirbel, p. 254.

This photo, with the noted reports from witnesses, should be *prima facie* proof of Lyndon Johnson's foreknowledge of the assassination. If one accepts the premise that a conspiracy existed, then anyone who knew of it in advance, yet did nothing to stop it, was at least complicit in it—in his case, arguably its main perpetrator. Only Lyndon Johnson was in a position, at 12:30 p.m. on November 22, to ensure that the crime would be covered up, and all those involved in it would escape prosecution. By "connecting the dots" between this photo, available since November 22, 1963, and statements from eyewitnesses about the conduct of Lyndon B. Johnson on that fateful day, a piece of the mosaic emerges that shows convincingly Johnson's self-incriminating actions at the precise moment of John F. Kennedy's assassination. This photograph could have once been admissible in court as "best evidence" of the most credible and reliable kind; it is now only interesting hearsay, and the case is no longer litigable. But it is still compelling and irrefutable "circumstantial" evidence of Johnson's complicity.

Dealey Plaza, 12:30–12:31 p.m. November 22, 1963:
The Altgens photo, taken seconds after the first shot:

Altgens photo of Lincoln turning onto Elm Street,
1–3 seconds after the first shot was fired.

**Cropped and blown-up part of Altgens photo of LBJ's car:
Where is LBJ?**

*The Altgens photograph—revealing Lyndon Johnson's not-so-mysterious
prescience about the imminent assassination of JFK—is clearly the long hidden
but always present "Rosetta Stone"; the key to finally solving the crime of the
twentieth century.*

*There can only be one reasonable explanation: it is the smoking gun—the key
to finally solving the crime of the twentieth century. But it is the juxtaposition
of this close-up version of the Altgens photograph with the statement of Police
Officer B. J. Martin:*

> *According to the guys who were escorting his car . . . he started ducking
> down in the car a good 30 or 40 seconds before the first shots were
> fired . . .*

*. . . that is the long hidden but always present "Rosetta Stone," proof that Lyndon
Johnson knew before his car entered the intersection of Elm Street that his time
had finally come, within moments he would be the president of the United States.*

The Altgens photo blown-up further showing no sign of LBJ—only the crowd in back of the car.

This photograph was coincidentally taken by Mr. Altgens one to three seconds after JFK had been shot since he had already, reflexively, grasped his hands toward the front of his neck. According to Fletcher Prouty, "By cross-referencing this remarkable photograph with the Zapruder film chronology, it is possible to determine that this picture was taken 3.6 seconds after the first shot was fired and 3.2 seconds before the last shot."[29] The exact moment is debatable since most researchers agree with the Warren Commission (about the only point of agreement between the two sides) that the "first shot" did not even hit JFK, it being the one which hit the curb well beyond the limousine, causing a fragment to hit James Tague in the neck.

The weight of the evidence, as previously noted, indicates that two shots followed quickly immediately after the shot that hit Tague: one from the top of the County Records Building, which hit JFK in the back, and an instant later, another from in front of the limousine, from the south end of the triple underpass, which went through the windshield of the car and hit Kennedy in the throat. In fact, on good quality copies of the photograph, the windshield crater and peripheral cracks are visible, meaning that the shot had to come before Zapruder 313, or well before the "head shots." Kennedy can also be seen holding his right hand close to his mouth as his left hand is reaching toward his throat as though he is trying to dislodge a bullet from his throat. This would also explain why the bullet did not penetrate deeply

---

29. Prouty, p. 31.

into Kennedy's throat since the windshield would have taken away most of its momentum. Practically no witnesses were looking back in that direction as the motorcade made its way down Elm Street, though some did state that they heard what they believed was a shot from that direction. According to Douglas Weldon, several witnesses reported seeing a shot from that area, or smelling the distinctive odor of gunpowder in that area.[30] In testimony to the Warren Commission, Mark Lane quoted a witness who stated that "On the other side of the overpass a motorcycle policeman was roughriding across some grass to the trestle for the railroad tracks, across the overpass. He brought his cycle to a halt and leapt from it and was running up the base of the trestle when I lost sight of him."[31] Naturally, that bit of testimony was not rigorously pursued, so there will never be resolution of where this mysterious shot came from. Persuasive evidence of a shot from the south knoll has been presented,[32] but the facts that all eyes were pointed the other direction and all the ears in the area were hearing echos of shots as the sound waves bounced back from the high-rise buildings on the hill above have caused the existence and identity of this shooter to have become another loose end that may never be resolved.

According to Richard Trask, "Beginning at about Z189, the President's hand acts in a manner inconsistent with his previous waving motion. Willis's 10 year-old daughter . . . had been running down Elm Street, and at about Z190, she suddenly stops and looks towards the direction of her parents . . . and [years later] stated, 'I stopped when I heard the shot.'"[33] The math would indicate that the "first shot" came at this point, Z189, 6.8 seconds before the last, at frame 313, though it missed its target wildly. It is also known that Kennedy had not yet been hit one second later, at frame 202, because that moment was captured in the Phil Willis slide 5. Comparing the position of his arms in the Altgens photo with frames in the Zapruder film (see Twyman, photo section between pp. 144–145) it would appear Kennedy was hit in the throat about one second after Willis snapped the shutter on his camera, at about Z220. This would account for Kennedy's reaction four frames later at Z224, just as the limousine emerged from behind the Stemmons Freeway sign. Altgens snapped his camera shutter 1.7 seconds after that, at Z255,[34] and his photograph shows Kennedy's reaction. Before leaving this point, it is important to understand the obvious: The hole in the windshield occurred *before* the fatal shots to the head were fired, so it can't be argued that

---

30. Fetzer, (Weldon) *Murder* . . . p. 152.
31. WC Hearings, Vol II, pp. 42–43.
32. The Education Forum (Ref. Malcolm Wallace, Part 1).
33. Trask, Pictures... pp. 64–65.
34. Ibid. p. 312

480 •LBJ: THE MASTERMIND OF THE JFK ASSASSINATION

"fragments" from those shots caused the damage to the glass; furthermore, it clearly couldn't have been caused by the (ridiculous) "magic bullet." Ergo, even the most simplistic analysis possible, on this single point, renders the entire Warren Commission conclusions as thoroughly debunked.

The Altgens photograph clearly shows Senator Ralph Yarborough (on the right side of the photo) behind the driver and Lady Bird, both still smiling, in the rear seat; neither they nor the motorcycle policemen have yet reacted to the first shot. Yet Lyndon Johnson has already disappeared from view even though he had been seated next to Lady Bird on the left side of the picture (right side of car). If he had been asked about this anomaly, Johnson's rebuttal to this question might, predictably, have been, "Well, that would have been after Youngblood shoved me down." The prosecutor—in a fair and perfect world—could have then rejected it immediately, pointing out to him that such an action would have certainly produced great shock and surprise on the faces of the driver, Herchel Jacks, Senator Yarborough, and most importantly, his own wife, Lady Bird. Yet the look on all three of their faces remains stoic (Jacks), happy (Yarborough), or relaxed and pleasant (Lady Bird); it is undoubtedly the very last moment that such expressions would remain. By then, Lady Bird had probably grown a little tired of Lyndon's antics with the radio and walkie-talkie and had become used to his being partially hunched down throughout the motorcade, as noted earlier in William Manchester's account. Since the repeated descriptions of Johnson's strange behavior throughout the motorcade in Manchester's book obviously did not come from Lyndon—ergo, nor Lady Bird—it stands to reason that they came from Senator Yarborough who made similar statements about it to other authors.

To understand Johnson's behavior throughout the motorcade, it is necessary to factor in his well-established manic-depressive patterns and, on November 22, 1963, overcome with worries and fears of something going wrong, he was definitely in a depressive cycle, as will become clearer shortly. It is also pertinent to consider at this point Johnson's long history of cowardice when put into a position of fear of bodily harm. Once when he got into a verbal fight over a game of poker in San Marcos, the other boy lunged at him and, instead of squaring off and preparing to defend himself, he fell back on a bed and began kicking his feet in the air like a girl, threatening to kick the boy if he tried anything. Vernon Whiteside witnessed this spectacle and said, "You know, every kid in the State of Texas had fights then, but he wouldn't fight. He was an absolute physical coward."[35] It was Johnson's

---

35. Caro, *The Path*, p. 156.

innate cowardice which caused him to duck at that moment and to provide, almost five decades later, photographic evidence that he knew in advance where and when the shooting would commence.

The people on the sidewalk at the back of the car are partly visible, through the windshield, beyond the car. SS Agent Youngblood is not visible; he is behind the motorcycle policeman on the left. Although this photo would, in many cropped variations, be published in thousands of newspapers around the world within hours of the assassination of JFK, it was consistently done with various captions alluding to the last few moments of Kennedy's presidency or his happy and beaming persona. Unfortunately, the understandable interest and focus on John F. Kennedy's first reaction to being shot, clearly into his throat, from the front, helped Lyndon Johnson in his efforts to obscure his own reaction and explains fully why he would attempt to postulate—but not swear to—his complete surprise.

A similarly cropped, close-up view of the Altgens photograph focused on the vice presidential car and the following Secret Service car with the rear door open was published by Robert J. Groden in his 1993 book, *The Killing of a President,* but no mention of the missing LBJ was made.[36] Like Groden, many people either never noticed Johnson's absence or routinely decided to ignore it as not substantive evidence of anything and assumed there must be some explanation for it, either excusing Johnson's disappearance or writing it off as some photographic anomaly despite the fact that this flaw didn't affect anyone else's image. Even Fletcher Prouty overlooked the implications of this photograph when he stated, "Lyndon and his bodyguard are sitting in their seats in this photo, but are partially obscured by the edge of the car on the left."[37] He must have meant that they were obscured by the windshield of the police motorcycle; however, that also is an unsatisfactory explanation, given the wide space to Lady Bird's right (to her left as one looks at the photo) which is where Johnson should have been. He was clearly not just "obscured," *he wasn't even in the photograph!*

This photograph might explain a few other curiosities concerning Johnson's actions in the days that followed:

• On Saturday morning, he asked Hoover whether anyone had shot at him, revealing why he had been so uncomfortable during the motorcade. He had been worried that the shooters would fire off a round or two at him.

---

36. Groden, *The Killing of a President*, p. 15.
37. Prouty, Op. cit.

This high level of nervous anxiety would explain his odd behavior during the motorcade when he kept "hunching down," pretending to listen to the radio broadcast. His nervousness during the motorcade and later—on board Air Force One, when General McHugh found him in the toilet area in the middle of nervous breakdown—is quite explainable; the answer to the paradox suggests that his paranoia that day was not entirely baseless, it was connected to a real source of concern.

• Johnson personally oversaw all of the evidence being shuttled back from Dallas starting on the very evening of the assassination. He had to have seen the Altgens photograph among the first artifacts brought to his attention and probably would have looked for all images of himself before looking at anyone or anything else. On a good-quality, large-format print of this photo, magnifying glass in hand, he would have seen that he was not visible in the photo. It was that knowledge that would explain why he chose not to appear before the Warren Commission to testify and not even provide them a sworn statement. The most casual statement he could make, a simple letter to the commission, would have to suffice. Not only did he not have to swear as to his actions, this maneuver ensured that he would never face cross-examination as well.

• Two weeks later, on December 4, 1963, he presented Secret Service Agent Youngblood a medal for his purported actions in immediately throwing Johnson to the floor and sitting on top of him to protect him from gunfire, possibly saving his life. This ceremony completed his diabolical plot since it allowed him to implant the notion into millions of minds the "truth" of that story while luring the hapless Mr. Youngblood into his scheme; after all, given the pomp and circumstance of such a nationally publicized award for his fast-thinking, heroic actions, how could "Ruf" Youngblood possibly counter the president's recollection of events. This further explains Youngblood's curious statement to the Warren Commission, cited above, concerning that event. He really didn't think he was "in the rear seat before the second shot, *but thought it probable because of President Johnson's statement to that effect.*" This statement speaks volumes and provides an underlying subtle hint that Johnson had planted a factoid that was not based in truth. If it were really true, Youngblood would have had no reason to waffle on whether or not he did what he was purported to have done (of course, if he had done this, he would have also been captured in the Altgens photo doing it). Agent Youngblood was merely one of the "pissants" Johnson used throughout his life to advance his own purposes, and for every man for whom Johnson had sized up, he knew intuitively what the man's weaknesses were, and how best he could exploit them. In Youngblood's case, he saw a proud and patriotic man who valued service and sacrifice; what better way to "buy him off" than bestow the highest medal of honor of the Treasury Department? He had told James Rowley, probably one of his co-conspirators, upon his return to Washington, "I want you to do whatever you can, the best thing that can be done, for that boy."[38]

It is ironic—albeit instructive, as to how many people reacted in the process of dealing with the horror—that even the photographer Ike Altgens failed to see this otherwise inexplicable discrepancy: the complete disappearance of Lyndon Johnson at the precise moment of the first rifle shot of the ensuing volley. Altgens never mentioned even seeing the anomaly and possibly didn't even notice it. Yet apart from that, he was quoted as saying, "He had yet to see indisputable evidence to the contrary that Oswald did not kill the President."[39] While he admitted difficulty in understanding how one person could have accomplished the assassination, he felt that it was inappropriate to reach conclusions other than those that were officially sanctioned by his government. Yet he himself had taken a picture that would be more revealing of what actually happened than all the other pictures and film combined. This disconnect illustrates how he—and millions of his fellow citizens—treated the crime; they were simply too afraid to even think about an even greater danger possibly lurking in the background.

This collective preference, suddenly afflicting millions of Americans to shut out any doubts about what they were being told by the still-trusted authorities—together with the quick and easy alternative solution being foisted upon them by J. Edgar Hoover—offered them the comfort they needed in a time of extreme fear and anxiety. The secure feeling that the government could be trusted to find the answers leading to a resolution meant that justice would prevail, and the hated "lone nut" Oswald would be found guilty, even if only posthumously.

The contrary thought was simply too outrageous—too horrible and unthinkable—to allow one's mind to even ponder. Many people could simply not bear the thought that the United States had experienced not only the assassination of their president but a concerted conspiracy and *coup d'état*. In fact, some people even refused to talk about it; the weight of such thoughts was simply too heavy to consider. It was easier to put it aside with the thought that the wheels of justice of a trusted government would quickly find justice for the murderer(s) of the president. Yet when the government presented its findings, at least 75 percent of those Americans—then and now—would not believe their own government's version of events. The wholesome trust

---

38. *Time* magazine, November 29, 1963.
39. Trask, p. 75.

Americans still had in their government in 1963 seems rather anachronistic now, a quaint memory of life before November 22, 1963; it would start its gradual disintegration immediately after that date, fall further after the Warren Report was issued ten months later, and finally go into freefall as the truth began emerging, thanks to the original authors and researchers who expressed doubt from day one.

Someone was evidently very worried that the Altgens photo might reveal too much and decided it should be specially cropped before being presented to the Warren Commission. That same someone was no doubt the same person who decided to further muddy the waters by claiming that Youngblood's reaction was so fast that if anyone saw the photo of the Johnson car and noticed his absence, his alibi was already on record: it was Youngblood's lightning fast response, which caused him to be shoved to the floor, in spite of the fact that this did not square with the testimony of others, even his own wife's. The cropped photo is yet more proof of the disturbing pattern of the Warren Commission being given fabricated and selectively culled evidence. Exhibit CE 203 was the version of the Altgens photograph furnished to the commission; it included only the picture of the presidential limousine. Johnson's car was eliminated entirely.

COMMISSION EXHIBIT 203

Warren Report exhibit CE 203

The importance of the discoveries related to this photograph—that the motorcycle patrolmen's statements regarding Johnson's actions have been vindicated by photographic evidence showing that Johnson had indeed disappeared below the car's seatbacks and that the photo had been severely cropped for the Warren Commission—cannot be overstated. On the basis of this "best evidence," it should be obvious to anyone—even those convinced that Lee H. Oswald was the only shooter—that Lyndon B. Johnson was aware of the imminent assassination.

Johnson has long been suspected by many of being at the very least behind the cover-up, a case already made by other authors and summarized here, though many simply attributed it to his fear of confronting Cuba and the Soviet Union in such a way as to lead to a nuclear war. With this new perspective on old evidence, it can now be presumptively concluded that his involvement went well beyond that: Lyndon Johnson was clearly aware of the pending assassination. Now, the only question is, just how much did he know about it, and was he, in fact, the creative and conniving mind behind it? The evidence presented here—including the many other books and materials cited within, the result of millions of hours of research by all of the cited authors and many others cited by them in turn—shows conclusively what many people already knew but could not prove: JFK's assassination was carefully planned and choreographed by Lyndon B. Johnson, with the very sophisticated assistance of key members of the CIA, the FBI, and an assortment of operatives associated with the Mafia and/or of Cuban origin.

The Flurry of Telephone Calls Continues—from LBJ's Aides, then Lyndon Himself

District Attorney Wade acknowledged and discussed the calls he received; the calls to the other Texas authorities—such as Dallas Police Chief Curry, Captain Will Fritz, Sheriff Decker, and Texas State Attorney Waggoner Carr—as attested to by others who they had confided in, were just as real. The message was that the president was worried about the consequences of alleging a conspiracy on the part of the Russians; as Wade relayed it, such an allegation "would hurt foreign relations if I alleged a conspiracy—whether I could prove it or not . . . I was to charge Oswald with plain murder."[40] Wade even admitted going to city hall to see Captain Fritz to tell him the same thing even though Fritz had already gotten the word directly from Johnson, who had advised him that he had already gotten his man and that no further investigation was necessary.[41] On Johnson's direct orders, his aide Cliff Carter phoned Henry Wade, Dallas district attorney, three times Friday evening, November 22, repeatedly ordering him to stop making allusions to

---

40. Marrs, p. 356.
41. Twyman, p. 793.

"any word of a conspiracy—some plot by foreign nations—to kill President Kennedy."[42] Such a connection, it was said, "would shake our nation to its foundation." Something had happened which caused that very threat to be dropped despite the fact that Johnson himself had already expressed it as a possibility, and it was never investigated further. Although he was the first to express it as a possibility, and would continue doing so for several days as he recruited members of the Warren Commission, he and J. Edgar Hoover both ordered the investigators to drop it. Johnson would not speak of it again for several years before making several statements in which he admitted never believing the Warren Commission's "lone nut" conclusion.

Given everything else we know about Lyndon Johnson's actions on and after November 22, 1963, one can almost hear him explain to Captain Fritz how it is necessary to wrap up the case with Oswald as the only suspect, putting an end to the nightmare then and there to calm the fears of the American citizens and to avoid a nuclear confrontation with Cuba and Russia that might kill forty million Americans within an hour (i.e., the very same argument that he was taped a few days later using with Senator Russell and which he had by then already used on Chief Justice Warren). In 1963, few police officers in America would reject his nation's president, making such a small request when he was being so profoundly challenged.* He might have even suggested to the two lawmen that the country might even be better off if some outraged citizen decided to take care of Oswald himself so the country would not have to be subjected to a long drawn-out trial at which the suspect gets off on some technicality. By playing on their emotions, he might have even set the stage for Ruby to perform his role. If anyone was capable of manipulating other men to achieve his own objectives, as we have amply seen in the previous chapters, and will do so again in the rest of this book, there was no other man alive in 1963 who was nearly as skilled at this as Lyndon B. Johnson.

After two days of suggestions and friendly cajoling—reminders that "you have your man"—*the Dallas Police were finally ordered to stop their investigation completely and to turn over all evidence to the FBI*, which was being put in charge of the entire investigation.[43] Hoover used his power as head of the FBI to secretly punish many of the personnel in Dallas and New

---

* The distinction was made regarding the year 1963, because at that time, police chiefs, like their fellow citizens, had much greater respect for the institution of the presidency, regardless of its current incumbent, than is generally true today; therefore, the context of why a police chief would knowingly accept a dubious request from a politician should be considered.

42. Ibid.

43. Sloan and Hill, *JFK: The Last Dissenting Witness*. pp. 120–121.

Orleans, though the real reason for it was for Hoover's own cover to hide the facts of how the FBI records were cleansed of any damning evidence of involvement with setting up Oswald.[44] It had become clear to many of the Dallas policemen, including B. J. Martin, that "Lyndon Johnson forced Captain Fritz to back down when he initially would not yield. His exact words were, 'You can't keep running a homicide investigation when the president of the United States calls you on the phone and tells you point-blank to stop.'" Martin knew this was the truth because "that's the only way 'old Cap' would've ever quit before he finished a job. The worst part is, he's the only man alive who could've gotten to the bottom of this damned thing. Now nobody'll ever know the truth."[45]

Penn Jones also reported that Captain Will Fritz told his friends "when the President of the United States called me and *ordered* the investigation stopped, what could I do?"[46] Just before the scheduled transfer of Oswald from the police station to the county jail, Jesse Curry, the Dallas chief of police who was to oversee the transfer, had a telephone call from Mayor Earle Cabell who kept him on the phone until Oswald had been shot by Jack Ruby.[47] Mayor Cabell was the brother of General Charles Cabell of the CIA, who had been fired by JFK after the Bay of Pigs.

Eyewitnesses Revisited

Turning the tables on the Warren Commission's tactic of suborning perjury from eyewitnesses, by forcing many of them to revise their testimony in order to be congruent with a preordained, fabricated story, here we will allow them to speak the truth as they best remember it before they were intimidated, threatened, or ignored by the FBI, Secret Service, or Dallas Police. By virtue of accepting their compelling stories, including their reports of this intimidation, their testimony essentially replaces the tainted testimony of others and thus allows the resulting distortions to be eliminated and the record corrected. Doing so also results in the automatic elimination of many of the "anomalies" already identified.

A common thread that many of the key eyewitnesses in Dealey Plaza would later reveal was the immediate presence of men who claimed to be with the Secret Service. If, in fact, they had been with the Secret Service, and they had used their usual procedures along a motorcade route at an obviously

44. North, pp. 395–397.
45. Sloan and Hill, *JFK: The Last Dissenting Witness.* pp. 120–121.
46. Jones, vol. III, p. 101.
47. Groden, p. 245.

dangerous site like Dealey Plaza, they would have ordered all the windows in the TSBD, the County Records, and the Dal-Tex buildings to be closed and sealed and would have had a man in the plaza to ensure that they stayed closed.[48]

But according to numerous researchers, including James W. Douglass, the "only 'Secret Service Agents' present in Dealey Plaza when the shots were fired were imposters and killers, bearing false credentials to facilitate their escape and coerce witnesses into handing over vital evidence that would vanish. The vacuum created by orders from Washington was immediately filled. When the president's security was systematically withdrawn from Dealey Plaza, his assassins moved swiftly into place."[49] A few weeks after the assassination, it became clear that the existing Secret Service credentials— the engraved identification books—had been compromised: all agents were instructed to turn in their current identification books, and they were replaced with all new sets.[50] The HSCA report documented several instances of fake Secret Service agents at Dealey Plaza, as reported by author Twyman:[51]

> The committee did obtain evidence that military intelligence personnel may have identified themselves as Secret Service agents or that they might have been misidentified as such. Robert E. Jones, a retired Army lieutenant colonel who in 1963 was commanding officer of the military intelligence region that encompassed Texas, told the committee that from 8 to 12 military intelligence personnel in plainclothes were assigned to Dallas to provide supplemental security for the President's visit. He indicated that these agents had identification credentials and, if questioned, would most likely have stated that they were on detail to the Secret Service. The Committee sought to identify these agents so that they could be questioned. The Department of Defense, however, reported that a search of its files showed 'no records...indicating any Department of Defense Protective Services in Dallas.' The committee was unable to resolve the contradiction.

Roger Craig

As Sheriff Decker had ordered, Deputy Roger Craig had been standing alongside other deputies in front of the courthouse at 505 Main Street.

---

48. Douglass, pp. 272–273 (Ref. Ratcliffe, David T., *Understanding Special Operations*, p. 206).
49. Ibid., p. 273, Twyman, pp. 762–769.
50. Bolden, pp. 54–55.
51. Twyman, p. 763.

After the president's limousine had passed and made the turn from Main to Houston and then slowed almost to a stop to make the 120-degree turn onto Elm Street, he heard the first shot. He quickly ran across Houston toward the plaza and heard two more shots. For ten minutes, he scanned the area for evidence until at 12:40 p.m., he heard a shrill whistle from the opposite side of Elm Street. In his testimony to the Warren Commission, he described what he saw next:[52]

> About this time I heard a shrill whistle and I turned around and saw a white male running down the hill from the direction of the Texas School Book Depository Building and I saw what I think was a light colored Rambler station wagon with luggage rack on top pull over to the curb and this subject who had come running down the hill get into this car. The man driving this station wagon was a dark complected white male. I tried to get across Elm street to stop the car and talk with subjects, but the traffic was so heavy I could not make it. I reported this incident at once to a Secret Service officer, whose name I do not know, then I left this area and went at once to the building and assisted in the search of the building. Later that afternoon, I heard that the city had a suspect in custody and I called and reported the information about the suspect running down the hill and getting into a car to Captain Fritz and indentified the subject they had in custody as being the same person I saw running down this hill and get into the station wagon and leave the scene.

In his unpublished memoir *To Kill a President* (available on the Internet at a number of sites), he also wrote that he immediately noticed this because of the incongruity of seeing two men in an obvious hurry attempting to flee the scene, in contrast to the fact that everyone else was running toward it. He also stated that he regretted not getting the idenity of the "Secret Service" man to whom he reported the incident who seemed interested only in the part about the Rambler wagon. Since the Secret Service denied having any agents in Dealey Plaza at that point, it seems clear that this man had been stationed there in advance by the conspirators for no purpose other than reassuring eyewitnesses that everything was under control by the appropriate authorities when in fact it was being administered by the conspirators.

Craig saw the man who had run down the hill and gotten into the car a few hours later in the office of Captain Will Fritz. It was the recently

---

52. WCH Vol. 19, p. 524.

arrested Lee Harvey Oswald. When Fritz told Oswald that Officer Craig had seen him enter a *car* on Elm Street after the assassination, Oswald replied, "That *station wagon* belongs to Mrs. Paine . . . Don't try to tie her into this. She had nothing to do with it."[53] It was that comment that indicates it was the real Oswald, not his look-alike, who Craig had seen minutes after the assassination. Oswald then said, "Everybody will know who I am now,"[54] as if his "cover" in the intelligence community had been blown, a real bummer in his mind (yet portrayed by Warren Commission investigators as exactly opposite the real feeling he had experienced; instead it was made to seem as though he were bragging about his newfound notoriety).

Between Deputy Craig's sighting of Oswald the first time on Elm Street and the second time in Fritz's office, he had become involved in the search of the Texas School Book Depository and was with Seymour Weitzman when a rifle was found on the sixth floor of the Texas Book Depository by Deputy Sheriff Eugene Boone. As previously noted, the other officers were later forced to recant their sworn statements that the rifle was a Mauser; Craig's refusal to do so would eventually cost him his job, his family, and his life. Although Roger Craig was interviewed by Assistant Counsel David W. Belin for the Warren Commission, he "was disturbed by Belin's habit of turning off the tape recorder at key points in the questioning . . . *Craig said his testimony had been changed in fourteen places, even apart from critical omissions.* Several of the changes seemed designed especially to keep Craig's descriptions of the station wagon and its driver from serving as bases for their identification."[55]

Julia Ann Mercer

About 11:00 a.m., Julia Ann Mercer was stalled in traffic on Elm Street, just beyond the triple underpass, a few hundred yards from where the white *X* in the street marks the spot where JFK was shot in the head. She noticed a green pickup truck parked such that its right side was on top of the curb to her right. As she watched, a man walked to the back of the truck, reached into the bed, and pulled out a rifle case wrapped in paper. She didn't immediately recognize the driver; they had eye contact as she inched past the truck. Three days later, when she saw his picture on television and in newspapers, it was Jack Ruby, the man who killed Oswald, whom she recognized as the same

---

53. Horne, 1114.
54. Ibid.
55. Douglass, p. 451 (note 309).

man she had seen Friday morning in the truck.

Carolyn Walther

A few minutes before the arrival of the president's motorcade, Carolyn Walther, standing across Elm Street from the TSBD building at the corner with Houston Street, looked up at the upper floors of the building, and focused on a light-brown-haired man in a white shirt who was leaning out of one of the southeast corner windows. What caught her attention was that he was also holding a rifle, pointed down toward the street as he looked down Houston Street from where the motorcade was about to emerge.[56]

Moreover, the scene became ever more mysterious when she noticed another man lingering in the background. She couldn't see his head behind the closed and dirty glass of the double-sashes, which were in the upper position. Only through the open window could she see him, wearing a brown suit coat, standing behind the man with the rifle.[57]

James Richard Worrell Jr.

Standing directly across the street from Carolyn Walther, directly in front of the TSBD, James Worrell Jr. was looking down Houston Street the entire time that the procession was making its way toward the intersection. He had no reason to look back and upward to the building until he heard the first shot. Just as the vice presidential auto was coming into the Elm Street intersection, he heard the shot and turned immediately to look up and saw the barrel of a rifle protruding from the window, firing toward the president's car. He was too close to the building to be able to see inside; he looked back toward the car and saw the president slumping down in the seat. He was shocked, and his immediate reaction was to run up the street, but he stated that he heard *at least four shots*. He looked back and saw a man in a sport coat running out the back of the TSBD, his coat opening and flapping in the breeze. He did not follow him because he was so terrified that he felt he had to get out of the area.[58]

56. Ibid. p. 275.
57. Ibid.
58. Ibid.

S. M. Holland

At his Warren Commission deposition, S. M. Holland testified that he viewed the motorcade from the railroad bridge overlooking Elm Street and that during the assassination, he heard four reports, three of which sounded like they came from "the upper part of the street," toward the Texas School Book Depository, but one of which (either the third or the fourth) came "from under those trees" on the grassy knoll. When he looked toward the knoll area, he said, "A puff of smoke came out about six or eight feet above the ground right out from under those trees . . . like someone had thrown a firecracker, or something out, and that is just about the way it sounded. It wasn't as loud as the previous reports or shots." It was "just like somebody had thrown a firecracker and left a little puff of smoke there; it was just laying there," he told investigator Josiah Thompson two years later. "It was a white smoke; it wasn't a black smoke or like a black powder. It was like a puff of a cigarette, but it was about nine feet off the ground."[59] Seconds later, the odor of burnt gunpowder permeated the air around the grassy knoll, as reported by numerous witnesses as we will shortly see. Holland then ran "around the end of this overpass, behind the fence to see if I could see anyone up there behind the fence . . . Of course, this was this sea of cars in there and . . . I ran on up to the corner of this fence behind the building. By the time I got there, there were 12 or 15 policemen and plainclothesmen, and we looked for empty shells around there for quite a while."

There was another thing that Holland saw which he found very suspicious even though he couldn't find anyone on the Warren Commission who felt there was anything at all odd about it. He testified that behind the fence, at what he estimated to be the same location as the place where he had seen the puff of smoke rise into the air, "there was a station wagon backed up toward the fence, about the third car down, and a spot, I'd say 3 foot by 2 foot, looked to me like somebody had been standing there for a long period . . . and also mud upon the bumper of that station wagon. . . . [It looked] like someone had been standing there for a long time . . . It was muddy, and if you could have counted them, I imagine it would have been a hundred tracks just in that one location. . . . [There was] Mud on the bumper in two spots. . . . as if someone had cleaned their foot, or stood up on the bumper to see over the fence. . . . Because, you couldn't very well see over it standing down in the mud, or standing on the ground."[60]

Holland also told author Thompson that the first, second, and fourth shots had a similar sound to them while "the third shot was not so loud; it

---

59. Warren Commission *Hearings,* Vol. VI, pp. 245–46.
60. Ibid.

was like it came from a .38 pistol, compared with a high-powered rifle." The third and fourth shots, he said, were nearly simultaneous. Holland believed that the third shot was fired from behind the stockade fence on the knoll, from the point where the puff of smoke originated. He took Thompson to the location where he saw the smoke, behind the stockade fence.[61] Holland's supervisor Richard C. Dodd confirmed much of what he said and added that "there were tracks and cigarette butts laying where someone had been standing on the bumper looking over the fence."[62]

Richard Randolph Carr

High overhead, in the sixth floor of the new courthouse building under construction at the time, Richard Randolph Carr saw a man on the top floor looking out of the second window from the southeast corner of the TSBD, whom he later described as a "heavyset individual" who was wearing a hat, a tan sport coat, and horn-rimmed glasses. Moments later, he heard what he thought was a car backfire, or a firecracker, followed by two other similar sounds in quick succession. He thought the sounds were coming from the triple overpass or grassy knoll areas and looked that direction to see people falling to the ground. He quickly ran down the stairs and out onto Houston Street where he saw the man he had just seen in the window now running toward him but repeatedly looking backward, over his shoulder. He continued watching the man run as he turned on Commerce Street and walked down to Record Street, getting into a Rambler station wagon parked on that street. He saw that the driver was a young dark-skinned man, possibly either a "Negro" or Latino, and the car proceeded north on Record Street to Elm Street where it went one and half blocks before it was spotted next by Deputy Roger Craig and four other witnesses as it stopped to pick up the other passenger.[63]

Four Other Witnesses to the Rambler Scene

Helen Forrest was on Elm Street near the grassy knoll and said that she "saw a man suddenly run from the rear of the Depository building, down the incline, and then enter a Rambler station wagon." She was also certain that it

---

61. Thompson, p. 122.
62. Ibid.
63. Douglass, p. 275.
64. Ibid. p. 276 (Ref. Michael L. Kurtz, *Crime of the Century: The Kennedy Assassination from a Historian's Perspective,* Knoxville: University of Tennessee Press, 1993; p. 132).
65. Ibid. (Kurtz, p. 189).

was Oswald, saying, "If it wasn't Oswald it was his identical twin."[64]

James Pennington was near Helen Forrest and corroborated her account.[65]

Marvin C. Robinson had to jam his brakes on his Cadillac to avoid hitting the Rambler when it suddenly stopped in front of him.[66]

Roy Cooper, an employee of Robinson, was driving in back of his boss and witnessed the near accident and saw the man who looked like Oswald jump into the backseat before the Rambler roared off toward Oak Cliff where J. D. Tippit would soon be killed.[67]

Mary Moorman

Mary Moorman was with her friend Jean Hill near the curb opposite the grassy knoll when the motorcade began its way down Elm Street. Mary had taken four or five Polaroid pictures as the limousine came closer and closer to them, handing each one to Jean to process as she prepared and shot the next photo. By the time they finished, all of the prints except one had been given to Jean. Because of what happened before their eyes, Mary had kept the last one; she later processed it herself after Jean ran to the other side of the street and up the knoll looking for a shooter. The last photograph was taken directly toward the grassy knoll just as the final shot was made, capturing the shooter, dressed as a police officer, another man standing behind him to the right, and a third man in front of the stockade fence, Army Corporal Gordon Arnold, identifiable by his army cap. This photograph was arguably one of the two most important photos taken of the assassination. However, the Warren Commission successfully avoided publishing it or interviewing Ms. Moorman.

Jean Hill

The witness closest to the presidential limousine, Jean Hill, was standing on the curb opposite the grassy knoll, having sweet-talked a young police officer into letting her and her friend Mary Moorman cross the street so that she could be assured of getting some good photos of the president as well as her boyfriend, who was riding a motorcycle alongside the limousine. She had left her bright red raincoat on well after the sun had come out just so that he would not miss seeing her. Jean had taken them to process the prints, stripping the

---

66. Ibid. (Kurtz, p. 189).
67. Ibid.
68. Sloan and Hill, *JFK: The Last Dissenting Witness,* pp. 20–23.

paper coverings, and then brushing them with a finishing chemical. She then put them into a pocket of her raincoat thinking, incorrectly, that she would have plenty of time to look at them later.[68]

As the final shots were fired, Jean's eyes fixed on a sight that would stay with her the rest of her life. "A muzzle flash, a puff of smoke, and the shadowy figure of a man holding a rifle, barely visible above the wooden fence at the top of the knoll, still in the very act of murdering the president of the United States . . . [then] Jean detected an abrupt flurry of movement to her right, and her eyes darted in that direction, fixing themselves on a point at ground level near the school book depository. Somebody was running. A lone man in a brown coat was running as hard as he could go, past the frozen, motionless figures of the stricken onlookers, straight toward the position of the shadowy gunman holding the rifle."[69] That man looked exactly like the man she would see two days later on live television as he emerged from the shadows with a revolver already held straight out toward Lee Harvey Oswald, a suspect being held in another policeman's murder as well as for JFK's assassination, a man named Jack Ruby. "Despite her friend's shouts to her to hit the ground, she reacted instinctively to find out where the shots were coming from, to see just who was behind the fence shooting at the president, so she ran across the street, up the small hill and around the end of the fence, only to see a uniformed policeman putting a rifle away in some kind of a carrying case. But why, no other policeman had a rifle, why did he have one? And why should he be back here behind the fence?"[70] She was then shocked, numb, conflicted, and confused by the sight; after all, this was a policeman, there to protect us, and of course policemen could carry guns.

The next thing she knew, a burly man came up to her, clamped her shoulder tightly, and announced, "Secret Service," as he briefly flashed a badge of some kind at her before sticking it back in his pocket. When she tried to break free, another plainclothesman gripped her other shoulder and jammed his hand into her coat pocket, grabbing the Polaroid prints she and Mary had just taken. Jean objected strongly, saying, "Those are my pictures! Who do you think you are?" The man shoved the pictures into his pocket, saying, "We know who we are, the question is, who are you? That's what we're going to find out, so just start walking and keep smiling—just like we are all good friends. Otherwise, you're in big trouble." The men then led her across the plaza into the Criminal Courts Building where she was grilled for hours about what she "thought" she saw and was told over and over that she was mistaken, that "you

68. Ibid.
69. Ibid., p. 24.
71. Sloan and Hill, *JFK: The Last Dissenting Witness*. pp. 25–29.

496 •LBJ: THE MASTERMIND OF THE JFK ASSASSINATION

couldn't have seen any such thing." The interrogator growled at one point, "If you know what's good for you, you'll keep quiet about it. It would be very foolish of you to ever repeat what you're saying outside of this room."[71]

Jean Hill was also videotaped in a number of interviews regarding her experiences and emphasized a number of points that were in direct conflict with the "official story," including the fact that within fifteen minutes of JFK's assassination, the alleged Secret Service agent told her that there were only three shots and that she was obviously confused when she maintained that she heard at least four shots, possibly as many as six.[72] She was already being warned that she had to change her story to conform to the "three shots" or she might be harmed; "something 'very bad' may happen to you if you do not change your story."[73] She also stated that she definitely saw the brake lights on Kennedy's limousine and that the car had almost stopped completely at the point of the fatal head shot. According to the same film, a total of twenty-eight witnesses agreed that the limo stopped at least momentarily, although this is not reflected in the Zapruder film, which indicates the film was tampered with to avoid this truth from emerging.[74] In 1965, J. Edgar Hoover admitted that critical frames in the film were not printed in correct sequence and explained this reversing of the Zapruder frames as a "printing error."[75] The handling of the Zapruder film will be examined more closely in the next chapter.

Jean Hill would finally sneak out of the building when her interrogators took a break, after having been there over eight hours. Later, she would discover that other witnesses experienced similar treatment, including Gail and Bill Newman and Charles Brehm. She had written lengthy notes about her experience and given them to her boyfriend, B. J. Martin, the Dallas patrolman who had flanked JFK's limousine during the motorcade. Shortly afterward, someone broke into his locker and stole the notes she had given to him to read.[76] Her life from that point on would never be the same. She was grilled for hours about what "she thought she saw" and repeatedly told that she could not have possibly seen a gunshot from behind the fence and that if she "knew what was good for her," she would stop repeating such false testimony. She finally snuck away when they had taken a break but was harassed for months by the FBI into changing her testimony, which she never did.[77]

---

72. See Youtube.com: Jean Hill: JFK Assassination Eyewitness (http://video.google.com/videoplay?docid=6966129980059644433).
73. Ibid. (19 min. 50 sec. to 20 min. 30 sec.).
74. Ibid. (at 50 minutes).
75. Marrs, p. 67.
76. Sloan and Hill, *JFK: The Last Dissenting Witness*, p. 66–67.
77. Sloan and Hill, *JFK: The Last Dissenting Witness*, General Theme.

As she waited to give her testimony, she endured months of threatening telephone calls. Someone deliberately tried to run her son off the road as he rode his motorbike, and in another incident, persons unknown tampered with the tie-rods on her automobile, causing her to crash the almost new car off an expressway and into a tree. Investigators told her that she and her eleven-year-old daughter survived only because the wet, muddy ground caused the car to decelerate quickly before it crashed into the tree.[78]

Because of the intense intimidation and constant surveillance that Jean Hill had received from the FBI and the Secret Service in the following weeks, she tried to avoid testifying to the Warren Commission but finally relented to an interview in Dallas by Arlen Specter. This proved to be an enormously traumatic event because Specter aggressively tried to get her to revise her testimony to be compatible with the official version of events that had already been scripted. The insulting and condescending treatment she received from Arlen Specter for not cooperating with him in rewriting her story left her perplexed, confused, and disgusted that no one wanted to hear her story of the truth of what happened. She maintains in her interview that Specter's behavior was contemptible, that she was coerced and bullied and her testimony cut up, splintered, and fragmented, with much of it taken "off the record" and not introduced. She stated that he became angry with her because she would not change her testimony to conform to his storyline and finally told her, "Look, we can make you look as crazy as Marguerite Oswald and everybody knows how crazy she is. We could have you put in a mental institution if you don't cooperate with us."[79] Like Jean Hill, numerous other witnesses reported similarly aggressive and condescending treatment by Specter, Belin, and other investigators, as well as the fact that their testimony was changed so much that it could not even be recognized as their words. Substantive, factual changes were made which completely changed their testimony without their permission.[80]

Officer B. J. Martin

In her book *JFK: The Last Dissenting Witness*, Jean Hill gave her boyfriend, escort motorcycle Officer B. J. Martin, the pseudonym of "J. B. Marshall," which was intended to protect his real identity and his reputation since he was a married man at the time. Martin was the Dallas motorcycle patrolman who had ridden beside JFK's limousine; after several months of enduring

---

78. Sloan and Hill, *JFK: The Last Dissenting Witness,* p. 150.
79. Marrs, pp. 483–484.
80. Ibid.

the intense postassassination inquiries during which all involved policemen were pressed to conform to the official line, he told of fellow police officers who were near Johnson's car who had reported some very strange behavior on his part throughout the parade. Because of veiled threats that had been made beginning immediately afterward—and continually for many more years—Martin's statements had been suppressed for thirty years before being published and have still not been made widely known in the fifteen years since then:

> "According to the guys who were escorting his car in the motorcade, our new president is either one jumpy son of a bitch or he knows something he's not telling about the Kennedy thing", J.B. had drawled. . . They say he started ducking down in the car a good 30 or 40 seconds before the first shots were fired. . . . One of them told McGuire he saw Johnson duck down even before the car turned onto Houston Street, and he sure as hell wasn't laughing when he said it [At Love Field, before the motorcade left]. . . while Kennedy was busy shaking hands with all the well wishers at the airport, Johnson's Secret Service people came over to the motorcycle cops and gave us a bunch of instructions. The damnedest thing was, they told us the parade route through Dealey Plaza was being changed. . . It was originally supposed to go straight down Main Street, but they said for us to disregard that. Instead, we were told to make the little jog on Houston and cut over to Elm. . . but that's not all. They also ordered us into the damnedest escort formation I've ever seen. Ordinarily, you bracket the car with four motorcycles, one on each fender. But this time, they told the four of us assigned to the president's car there'd be no forward escorts. We were to stay well to the back and not let ourselves get ahead of the car's rear wheels under any circumstances. I'd never heard of a formation like that, much less ridden in one, but they said they wanted to let the crowds have an unrestricted view of the president. Well, I guess somebody got an 'unrestricted view' of him, all right."
>
> "Are you sure it was Johnson's Secret Service that told you all this?" Jean asked. Surely, there had to be some mistake here, she thought.
>
> "I guess they were Secret Service. . . . They were sure as hell acting like they were in charge, and I know they were with Johnson, because when they got through telling us what to do, they went back to his car. Oh, and that's another thing. They changed up the order of the cars in the motorcade before we started out. Originally, the car carrying Johnson was supposed to be right behind Kennedy's

car, but they decided to put a carload of Secret Service in between the two main VIP cars. That didn't make a helluva lot of sense to me either, but it might at least explain why Johnson was so ready to duck . . . maybe he forgot about putting that Secret Service car between him and Kennedy. . . If he knew there was going to be shooting, maybe he was thinking he was a lot closer to the intended victim than he really was."[81]

In April of 1964, Jean Hill asked Martin a question that had been lingering in her mind for sometime, "'I want you to refresh my memory about something you told me a while back . . . You said you escorted Johnson back to Love Field from the hospital that day . . . I was just wondering how he acted.' 'Well, . . . he acted scared, but that's just it—it was like he was acting, not like he was really in fear of his life. I remember hearing him yell to somebody as he was getting in the car. He said, 'We've all got to be very careful. This could be a worldwide conspiracy to kill off all our leaders.' The thing that struck me was he seemed to be in total charge already. Everybody else was kind of numb and reeling with shock, but Johnson was in full control, giving orders and telling people what to do.'" Martin also commented that "our new president's up to his neck in this mess . . . he either caused it to happen or knowingly allowed it to happen . . . he did everything possible to make the Dallas police back off the case and leave it to his hand-picked 'investigators.'"[82]

Dallas Police Captain Will Fritz

Author Jim Bishop described Captain Will Fritz, head of the Homicide Division of the Dallas Police Department, as "a big bifocaled man with hyperthyroid eyes who wore a cowboy hat. He was shrewd as captain of Homicide, but he had the potential pensioner's attitude of obeying the boss without question."[83]

But Captain Fritz was changed by JFK's assassination—more correctly, its stunted investigation—in a way that clearly tortured him for the rest of his life. Until then, he had been a much-respected homicide detective who "lived by the book" and knew how best to get information from his prisoners. Captain Fritz had been a proud man of very high integrity who would have never cut short an investigation for politically based reasons. His reputation was that of an effective interrogator and a careful, thorough investigator whose percentage of successful arrests for murder over a ten-year period was 98

81. Sloan and Hill, *JFK: The Last Dissenting Witness,* pp. 112–14.
82. Ibid.
83. Bishop, p. 94.

percent. Fritz gained nationwide attention when he headed the investigation of the assassination and was the first person to question suspected assassin Lee Harvey Oswald just hours after Kennedy was shot on November 22, 1963. It was immediately after this interrogation that he received the first telephone call from Cliff Carter on Air Force One, suggesting that they "had their man" and noting all the reasons to shut down the investigation. Hours later, though he still did not elicit a confession from Oswald, Fritz said he had all the proof he needed to convict, and before midnight, he formally charged Oswald with the president's murder.

The new president's aide Cliff Carter, as requested by his boss, made a number of calls Friday afternoon from Air Force One and the White House later in the evening. Johnson realized that it was essential to get control over the police investigation at an early stage while curtailing public announcements by the local officials who might say things not helpful to their mission. He called Dallas District Attorney Henry Wade, Police Chief Curry, Captain Fritz, and State Attorney General Waggoner Carr to request that they avoid making any official statements or discussions relating to conspiracy. If anyone questioned his authority to make such requests, he used President Johnson as the authority for the request; he also brought pressure on Curry to retract statements made by FBI agent Hosty regarding Oswald's known Communist affiliations, and Curry did so.[84]

In the calls that Fritz received from Cliff Carter in the White House between Friday evening and Saturday afternoon after the assassination, he was repeatedly advised to cease the investigation. He was told, "You have your man." As noted above, "finally, he received a person to person call from the new president *who specifically ordered him to cease further investigation.* [Officer Frank B.] Harrell not only confirmed Fritz's remarks to researchers, but also relates that *Fritz was ordered to stop the interrogation of Oswald*"[85] (emphasis added). For years after the assassination, Fritz rarely spoke of the case and turned down repeated offers for books and articles. A former Dallas newsman who became a correspondent for CBS News, Bob Sirkin, wrote an article a few years ago about conversations he had with Captain Fritz in regard to these points:

August 22, 2003
HELLO, CAPTAIN FRITZ HERE
By Bob Sirkin

---

84. Hancock, p. 289.
85. Hancock, p. 404 (ref. Twyman, *Bloody Treason: On Solving History's Greatest Murder Mystery*, pp. 793–795.

In September of 1977, I was preparing to leave WFAA-TV in Dallas for a new position as a Correspondent for ABC News, based in Atlanta. I had a final task to complete before leaving town. I needed to arrange a meeting with a legendary, retired Dallas Police Captain; the first man to interrogate Lee Harvey Oswald following his arrest on November 22, 1963, for assassinating the President of The United States.

I met Captain Will Fritz for breakfast, at a small, shabby downtown Dallas cafe. Fritz was old, frail and in failing health. But his mind was razor sharp. Fritz lived nearby, at a residential hotel, not far from Dallas Police Headquarters; the place he worked for the better part of his life. We took a booth toward the rear of the cafe.

Over plates of bacon, eggs and toast, I asked Fritz the burning question: "Captain, would you consider sitting down with me, for an on-camera interview about that phone call you took from the White House on November 22, 1963? With that, Fritz dropped his fork on his plate, raised his head and stared at me long, hard and coldly. "Not now. Maybe I'll write something, someday," Fritz curtly replied. Disappointed, I finished my breakfast, politely said good-bye to Fritz and left for my new position in Atlanta.

A few years later, Will Fritz passed away. Here's what Fritz, reportedly, took to his grave: After completing a marathon interrogation of Lee Harvey Oswald, Fritz was told that there was a call holding for him from the White House. On the line, the newly installed President of The United States, Lyndon Johnson. President Johnson reportedly told Fritz . . . *"You've got your man, now we'll take it from here."*

A short while later, the FBI seized full control of the most famous murder investigation in U.S. history. The FBI was also about to seize control of the main suspect, Lee Harvey Oswald, before he was fatally shot by Jack Ruby in the basement of police headquarters.

Mary Ferrell of Dallas, perhaps the world's most renowned JFK Assassination researcher and archivist had petitioned the Warren Commission and House Select Committee on Assassinations to release Will Fritz's testimony. *In parts of it, Fritz alludes to the LBJ phone call. But details remain sealed . . .*

Following his death, some members of Fritz's family told me how despondent he was over the FBI snatching the Oswald investigation from him. Unknown, is whether Fritz, given the opportunity, could have gleaned from Oswald details of the alleged cover-up . . . and could have determined whether Oswald acted alone.

It is abundantly clear that Fritz's testimony is considered too dangerous to be revealed; as with the Win Scott and the George Joannides documents and others which remain under seal—assuming they haven't already been destroyed, as many other documents have already been—they are coincidentally those which contain real truths that would lead directly to the exposure of the real story.

Gordon Arnold

There were other witnesses who were treated similarly to Jean Hill, Gordon Arnold among them; he was turned away by men who quickly flashed a badge, mouthed the words "Secret Service," and ordered him away from the area despite the fact that there were no actual Secret Service agents assigned to that area. Mr. Arnold, who was on leave from the army, had been looking for a good spot to take a film of the motorcade, first choosing the railroad overpass at the end of Dealey Plaza. Arnold was stopped by a well-dressed man who showed him a Secret Service badge. A Dallas police officer and a county deputy sheriff reportedly encountered a second such "agent" on the grassy knoll immediately after the shooting. Arnold then found a good spot a few feet in front of the stockade fence. As the motorcade approached and he began filming, he felt a shot whiz past his left ear. He threw himself to the ground in an automatic reflex, probably as a result of his army training. Arnold's film was also confiscated immediately afterward by a uniformed police officer.[86] Senator Ralph Yarborough, sitting in the same car as Lyndon Johnson (who is by then lying flat behind the front seat-backs, according to the police escorts beside his car),[87] saw Mr. Arnold "hit the dirt" and thought his reaction was that of an experienced "combat veteran."

The Killing of Officer J. D. Tippit: Crumbling the Old (Faux) "Rosetta Stone"

Warren Commission Attorney David Belin called the Tippit shooting the "Rosetta Stone" to the JFK assassination. "After all, Oswald killed that policeman. Why would he do that if he hadn't killed the President?"[88] In fact, that was the only thing that connected Oswald to JFK's murder, yet it has become clear to anyone examining the evidence that there is nothing that connects him to Tippit's murder, and in fact, the evidence actually clears him completely. The evidence suggests that there were in fact two shooters

---

86. Fetzer, *Murder in Dealey Plaza, Part I: 22 November, 1963: A Chronology,* Wood III, Ira David, p. 41.
87. Sloan and Hill, *JFK: The Last Dissenting Witness,* pp. 112–14.
88. Marrs, p. 340.

because there were two different bullet types/brands extracted from his body. It remains unclear whether the murder of Tippit had anything at all to do with Kennedy's assassination. A more likely scenario was that it was simply retribution by the husband of the woman Tippit was known to have been sleeping with. The Warren Commission was only interested in selecting enough pieces of "evidence" to link the shooting to Oswald despite the fact that the vast preponderance of evidence did not support such a link. Their conclusion was based on selecting the least credible witnesses of the shooting and ignoring the ballistic evidence:

- The chief witness for the Warren Commission was Helen Markham whose credibility was questioned even by the commission lawyers. She claimed to have talked to the dying Tippit for twenty minutes, yet medical authorities said he was killed instantly. She said she saw Tippit's killer talk with the policeman through his patrol car's right-hand window before shooting him, although pictures taken at the scene show that window was shut. She was hysterical at the time and subsequently could not identify Oswald in a lineup. Later, in her testimony before the Warren Commission, Markham stated six times she did not recognize anyone in the police lineup that evening before Commission Attorney Joseph Ball prompted her with a hint of how to answer. "Was there a Number two man in there?" Markham responded, "Number two is the one I picked . . . When I saw this man I wasn't sure, but I had cold chills just run all over me . . ."[89] She was hysterical on November 22 and again as a witness months later, although in a quite different context.
- Joseph Ball, the commission's own senior counsel, referred to Markham's testimony as "full of mistakes" and characterized her as "utterly unreliable."[90]
- Other witnesses at the scene—William Scoggins, Ted Calloway, and Emory Austin—stated that they never saw Mrs. Markham in the minutes immediately following the shooting.[91]
- A number of other witnesses were excluded by the commission in deference and favor to a witness who was criticized by its own staff as being unreliable; some of these included Mr. and Mrs. Donald Higgins who lived across the street, Acquilla Clemons and Frank Wright, other neighbors, and T. F. Bowley who used Tippit's police radio to inform the dispatcher of the shooting. Ms. Clemons saw two men standing near the police car, one of the men with a pistol, waving away the other. The other man, running away toward Jefferson Street, was described as "kind of short,

89. Ibid.
90. Summers, Anthony, *Not in Your Lifetime*, Warner Books, 1998, p. 68.
91. Ibid.

kind of heavy." The second man was described as tall and thin, wearing a white shirt and khaki slacks. Neither description was close to being that of Lee H. Oswald. Frank Wright stated that he had come out of the house midway through the episode, just in time to see a man circling around the police cruiser and get into an old, gray car on the other side of it, then driving off rapidly.[92]

The problem with the other witnesses, all much more credible than Ms. Markham, was that they told of seeing two shooters, clearly not what the FBI wanted to hear. In fact, J. Edgar Hoover explicitly ordered the special agent in charge of the Dallas bureau office not to permit his agents to question Acquilla Clemons or Mr. and Mrs. Wright, a fact later revealed when the FBI memo from Hoover to Gordon Shanklin was noted in Michael Kurtz's book, *Crime of the Century*.[93]

The other, even more compelling, exculpatory evidence that contradicted Oswald's involvement in the Tippit shooting related to the inconsistencies with ballistics evidence. While the initial report radioed in by Patrolman H. W. Summers indicated the suspect (who was said to have "black wavy hair, wearing an Eisenhower jacket of light color, dark trousers, and a white shirt, none of which matched Oswald), had a different kind of handgun. Moments later Sergeant G. Hill reported that "the shell at the scene indicates that the suspect is armed with an automatic .38 caliber, rather than a pistol." It is sufficient to state that there is a major difference in an "automatic," rather than a "pistol," which was a term used to mean a "revolver."[94] Additionally, the Dallas coroner had removed four bullets from Tippit's body and found that three were copper coated, manufactured by the Winchester Western company. The fourth was a lead bullet without a copper jacket, made by the Remington-Peters company. This evidence alone indicated that there were *two* different gunmen involved.[95]

The Dallas homicide unit sent only *one* bullet to the FBI lab, which initially found that the bullet did *not* match Oswald's revolver. The commission eventually questioned why all four bullets were not processed and, months later, they were dug out of the files of the Dallas homicide division; the next evaluation was inconclusive as to whether they matched Oswald's gun. Another discrepancy related to the cartridges was that Officer J. M Poe had scratched his initials into the two that he had obtained from

92. Garrison, p. 228.
93. Ibid., p. 229.
94. Ibid., p. 230.
95. Ibid., pp. 230–231.

witness Domingo Benavides, yet there were no such markings on any of the four, including additional markings which Sergeant W. E. Barnes had added to the two shells.[96]

The severe mishandling of the ballistic evidence and the carefully selected "witness" testimony proved conclusively the blatant manipulation of evidence by the Dallas homicide unit in the Tippit case: attempting to conceal three bullets, the disappearance of at least two, and likely all four, of the automatic cartridges found at the scene and the failure to aggressively pursue the testimony of the most credible witnesses who saw two assailants are all clear indications that the Dallas Police attempted to tie Oswald to the murder of Tippit and thus provide a linkage to the assassination of President Kennedy.

Telltale Signs of the Complicity of Key Military Officers

Author Twyman interviewed Col. L. Fletcher Prouty, who had been stationed at the Pentagon through the early 1960s. Prouty told him that "the Pentagon was in shock and dismay when JFK was elected. He said that this happened from the very beginning, immediately after the election (not just after the Bay of Pigs or the Cuban missile crisis). He said that many, or most, military people in the Pentagon had contempt for Kennedy, but there were also people like himself who admired him."[97] Prouty also emphasized the disgust of many top-level military officers with specific actions taken by Kennedy and McNamara, directly referencing the TFX contract, saying that General Curtis LeMay was enraged when they took over and soon cancelled the decision to award the $6.5 billion contract to Boeing and awarded it to General Dynamics, though Johnson was actually to blame for the switch.

Colonel Prouty told Noel Twyman that Colonel Howard Burris, Johnson's military aide, was one of the most important of the Pentagon men during that time, which would have given him a high level entrée into highly secret places along the Potomac other than the Pentagon.[98] Prouty explained to Twyman that when the White House trumped the military chiefs by taking over the awarding of the TFX contract, it created a chasm between the career officers and McNamara, and further, to Kennedy, that "was a major item for consideration as to the motive in the assassination."[99] He went further, to suggest that there was someone else that Twyman had not mentioned, someone who might be a "hot item." When Twyman then mentioned the

96. Ibid., pp. 233–234.
97. Twyman, p. 538.
98. Ibid., p. 539.
99. Ibid.

"back channel" connection to the CIA's Vietnam assessments—information that neither McNamara nor JFK even had access to—and read him a "TOP SECRET—EYES ONLY" July 20, 1961, memorandum written by Colonel Howard L. Burris, LBJ's military aide, Prouty exclaimed, "*There is the hot item*"(emphasis added). Burris at that time was one of the most important of the Pentagon men.[100] Prouty said that he and Burris had been friends and neighbors for a while, but that the last he knew of Burris was that he retired in 1964 and later became a wealthy oil man with operations in Saudi Arabia, Iran, and other countries throughout the world. The circumstances of his retirement shortly after the assassination, followed by his stunningly quick success as a lobbyist and international businessman in the oil industry, make Colonel Burris one of the most enigmatic, yet least researched and little understood figures closest to Lyndon B. Johnson as of November 1963.

One of Colonel Burris's early assignments, in May 1961, was to accompany Johnson on the trip to Vietnam. To prepare for that trip, he was rehearsed on how to control LBJ and told what he could say or could not say to the vice president. What he found suggests that he thought Johnson had a rather provincial and shallow understanding of the culture, economy, history, and concerns of Southeast Asia in general and Vietnam in particular. As reported in a previous chapter, Colonel Burris said that "*I don't think he had a really deep perception and comprehension of what the whole scene was about.*"[101] This trip—despite Johnson's miserable performance, as previously described—would mark the start of what would become Johnson's secret back-channel to the CIA, which provided him unfiltered intelligence information unavailable to either McNamara or Kennedy. Author Gus Russo confirmed this when he stated that Burris had personally told him that "Johnson had back-channel sources at the CIA that kept him apprised of such matters."[102]

Still another connection to the CIA was the discovery, by Russo, that the unlisted phone number of Howard Burris was found in George DeMohrenschildt's address book.[103] An explanation for this was discovered by researcher/author Larry Hancock, among records which indicated that Burris was reporting to the directorate of plans by 1963 while working on the TFX program (undoubtedly at the behest of Johnson). He was still a liaison to the vice president and had become embroiled in a prolonged feud with Johnson's aide Walter Jenkins regarding actions Burris felt were essential to prepare the vice president to assume the presidency; one of his concerns was

100. Ibid. p. 539.
101. Newman, *JFK and Vietnam.* p. 91.
102. Russo, p. 74.
103. *Who is Jim DiEugenio?* by Gus Russo. John F. Kennedy Assassination News, Commentary, & Opinion. http://jfkfiles.blogspot.com/2008/09/who-is-jim-dieugenio.html

establishing his own position in the chain of command, including acquiring an office close to Johnson in the EOB rather than within the Pentagon. It was Jenkins who suggested to Burris that he meet with de Mohrenschildt, according to those same records[104] though the purpose of that specific meeting is still unclear.

Colonel Burris went to Texas on November 21, 1963, as Johnson had directed him, though his statement about the reason for this is yet another puzzle, considering that Johnson and Kennedy never discussed issues of substantive foreign policy, especially on political trips unrelated to such subjects. He said, "I was to be there at that [Friday night] meeting. Johnson had asked me to prepare a briefcase full of 'Eyes Only' documents for the meeting."[105] According to author Russo, this material was to be used by Johnson in his planned confrontation with JFK on foreign policy issues, a subject which he had steadfastly ignored for most of the past three years. Furthermore, it has been well established that the big "welcome" party planned at the LBJ Ranch, with dozens of people in attendance, would have precluded any such meeting. The fact that there were so many questions raised by all of this suggests that it was merely another diversion, but it didn't end there. Burris told author Russo of catching a flight back to Washington the next day on a two-seat fighter jet in which he had to seize the unfamiliar controls and take over flying and landing the jet after the pilot lost consciousness (his previous flying experience was as the commander of [four engine] bomber units in England and France twenty years earlier).[106] That story was told thirty-five years after the event, evidently for the first time; the fact that he submitted an expense report at the time for a return trip on a commercial airline from San Antonio, via Chicago, to Washington suggests that he was either playing games with Russo or simply lying about the entire episode for some reason, which will doubtlessly never be known now that he is deceased. One explanation for why Johnson wanted Burris at his ranch with top secret reports concerning Cuba and the Soviet Union might have been related to the possible need for a Cuban invasion in case the "lone nut" option could not be used.

Colonel Howard L. Burris seems to have done very well for himself when he retired shortly after the assassination. Even before his retirement, within a month of the assassination, he took a long-term leave and travelled

---

104. U.S. Senate Committee on rules and Administration. *Construction of the District of Columbia Stadium and Matters Related Thereto.* Washington, DC: U.S. Government Printing Office, 1965, pt. 12, p. 1101.
105. Russo, p. 285.
106. Ibid. p. 562 (e/n 36).

to Germany and Austria. His thirty-year career is interesting in many respects, not the least being his rapid promotions—from second lieutenant to colonel—in the first three years, but no further promotions for the next twenty-seven years; it is an understatement to say that this was "unusual," unless possibly this was only a "cover" that helped to insinuate him into multiple international circles. He began working as a consultant/lobbyist for Martin Marietta and McDonnell-Douglas shortly afterward and continued to keep in close contact with the new president Johnson and his aides—one in particular, Cliff Carter—for the rest of Johnson's term. There were no indications of great wealth in Burris's past, yet somehow, working apparently part-time as a lobbyist, he managed to acquire such affluence that he was able to build a palatial estate on 149 acres overlooking the Potomac River, which he called Heritage Gardens, estimated to have cost $15 million in 1968. During this interim period, Burris had become very close to Richard Helms, and both of them became very close friends with the shah of Iran. In fact, his son, Howard Lay Burris Jr., was married for a while to Princess Shahrazad Pahlbod, the niece of the late shah of Iran—which reflects the closeness of his father's relationship with the CIA director who had been a longtime friend of the late Shah.[107]

There were a number of other very visible peripheral ties relating to the involvement of key, high-level military officers in JFK's assassination in Dallas, including the following: [108]

- General Charles P. Cabell, the brother of Dallas Mayor Earle Cabell, after being fired by Kennedy as deputy director of the CIA, he called Kennedy a traitor. This was not simply excusable hyperbole from an armchair philosopher, coming from a general in the U.S. Army, it is incendiary and unprofessional conduct and should be taken as seriously as the literal context of the remark. But then, he was not alone in that, General LeMay, [and Generals Power and Willoughby all] had a habit of doing the same thing.

- An army intelligence officer accompanied Dallas Police Lieutenant Jack Revill on a ride to the Dallas Police Station and was evidently his source for an incorrect address for Lee Harvey Oswald, "605 Elsbeth." Oswald had lived at "602 Elsbeth" the previous year, but the only file which had contained the incorrect address was later determined to have been in the filing cabinet of the 112th MI group, located in Dallas.

---

107. U.S. Senate Committee on rules and Administration. *Construction of the District of Columbia Stadium and Matters Related Thereto*. Washington, DC: U.S. Government Printing Office, 1965, pt. 12, p. 1101.
108. Marrs, pp. 309–311.

- Immediately after JFK's body was taken by Secret Service agents out of Parkland Hospital, the military assumed custody of it and remained in control of it through the transport by air and ambulance/hearse to military hospital(s) for autopsy, funeral, and burial. A team of high-level military officers were on hand to monitor the entire procedure and in fact, controlled the military doctors performing it, as we will examine below, ordering them to refrain from normal procedures used in the most routine homicide investigations.[109] Any tampering with Kennedy's body, regardless of when and where it might have been, could have only been accomplished with the acquiescence of these high-level military brass—under their direct orders to do so, in fact, as will become apparent below. Additionally, to be seen shortly, a very complex "shell game" involving the ornate casket in which JFK's body had left Parkland Hospital would play out between the time it left there and when it arrived back at Bethesda in that same coffin. The logistical moves related to this—confirmed by numerous enlisted men who had been sworn to secrecy and who abided by this for many years—could only have been accomplished by very high-level military officers.

CIA Presence in Dealey Plaza

Colonel Prouty also advised author Twyman that Edward Lansdale had been sent to Dallas where his picture was taken in Dealey Plaza (walking beside and in the *opposite* direction of the "tramps" and two "policemen" carrying shotguns, not rifles—which they were doing very casually and unprofessionally—in one widely viewed photograph). Prouty sent this and other photos to Gen. Victor Krulak, who also knew Lansdale very well; he confirmed Prouty's assertion. "That is indeed a picture of Ed Lansdale. The haircut, the stoop, the twisted left hand, the large class ring. It's Lansdale. What in the world was he doing there?"[110] The purpose of such a trip, assuming that he had no role in the assassination, was not clear at the time; but that was over thirty-five years ago, and the fog has lifted sufficiently now to allow the implications to become apparent: Edward Lansdale's role appears to have been that of a "field commander."

His high-level intelligence and military connections were described in chapter 3, and Lansdale's long history of creating complex manipulative schemes affecting many thousands of indigenous people in far-off lands earned him the nickname, "the Ugly American." Edward Lansdale was probably

109. Law, p. 144.
110. Letter from Victor Krulak to Fletcher Prouty dated March 15, 1985 (http://www.ratical. com/ratville/JFK/USO/appD.html)

the single most experienced man in America in planning the most cunning and deadly covert military operations of the era, from the Philippines, to Vietnam, and finally, Cuba.[111] When JFK refused to appoint him to be the ambassador to Vietnam in 1961, a position which he coveted and practically assumed he would be given, he was furious. Eventually, he was put in charge of Operation Mongoose, a position at the center of a cauldron filled to the brim with CIA operatives and anti-Castro Cubans, all of whom hated JFK. In that capacity, he would direct—or participate in—the activities of such men as William K. (Bill) Harvey, George Joannides, David Atlee Phillips, and David Sanchez Morales, among others.

But Edward Lansdale was not the only CIA man in Dealey Plaza that day.* Other photos show a half dozen or more CIA officials, including Lucien Conein, Grayston Lynch, Ted Shackley, Tracy Barnes, and William "Rip" Robertson (in the Altgens 4 photo) and E. Howard Hunt were also present (in the Rickerby photo; his son, Saint John Hunt told this author that he agrees that the man in a three-quarter-length trench coat crossing Elm Street shortly after the assassination with many others "does resemble his overall appearance," although he hasn't conclusively determined that it was him). All of this begs the question: What were so many spooks doing in Dealey Plaza that day? Even Joseph Milteer, the right-wing reactionary caught on tape discussing the planned assassination in Miami the week before (previously noted), was photographed in Dealey Plaza. Chauncey Marvin Holt, who appears to have been the third tramp and who prepared fifteen sets of forged Secret Service IDs for use in and around the plaza, told James Fetzer that he had seen "more mercenaries and assassins in Dealey Plaza [before JFK was taken out] than you would at a Soldiers of Fortune convention". The most likely explanation, as Chauncey told Fetzer, was to create a load of "red herrings" if an investigation were to pursue those who were there.[112] The CIA officials, by contrast, were probably there to pay their last respects to a man whose death they had helped to plan. The killing of a president, after all, was a historic event, which they wanted to witness. These inferences regarding the motives of so many men, though somewhat speculative, are also reasonable presumptions in light of the many indications of CIA collaboration presented throughout this synopsis.

---

* See Fetzer, James H., "Dealey Plaza Revisited: What Happened to JFK" p. 368 (or Google "Familiar Faces in Dealey Plaza", for several websites which detail the presence of numerous CIA operatives; one such is at http://bottleofbits.info/econ/faces/familiar_faces.htm)

111. For a lengthier background of Lansdale, see: http://www.historynet.com/ed-lansdales-black-warfare-in-1950s-vietnam.htm

112. Author's Jan. 2011 correspondence with James H. Fetzer.

Confusion at Bethesda Naval Hospital

When Air Force One arrived at Andrews Air Force Base in Washington, the coffin was quickly unloaded and placed in a gray Pontiac navy ambulance to convey it, with Jacqueline and Bobby Kennedy, to the Bethesda Naval Hospital. A helicopter departed the area shortly thereafter even though it was never officially acknowledged as having any role in the operation—although the use of helicopters to convey the coffin to Walter Reed Hospital had been discussed by military officers in Washington with others on board Air Force One as it flew back from Dallas. In a memo dated October 17, 1995, former AARB investigator Doug Horne (now researcher/author, as previously noted) wrote Jeremy Gunn, the general counsel for the AARB, summarizing his findings from a review of the recordings; excerpts of that memo follow:[113]

- Onboard Air Force One on the return flight to Washington, Secret Service Agent Kellerman, and later General Ted Clifton (Military Aide to the President) make it clear that their desire is for an ambulance and limousine to take President Kennedy's body to Walter Reed General Hospital for autopsy "under guard . . . ," as specified by General Clifton. Gerald Behn, Head of the White House Secret Service Detail, counters that a helicopter has been arranged to take the president's body to the National Naval Medical Center at Bethesda for autopsy, and that all other personnel will be choppered to the South Grounds of the White House.

- Ultimately, the president's physician, Admiral George Burkley (on Air Force One), sides with Gerald Behn (at the White House) in support of a Bethesda autopsy and persuades the Surgeon General of the Army, General Heaton (in Washington) to cancel arrangements for a Walter Reed autopsy.

- Once it becomes clear that Bethesda is to be the site, two things happen: first, both Admiral Burkley and General Clifton insist that the president's body be transported to Bethesda by ambulance, even though Gerald Behn at the White House informs General Clifton that President Kennedy's Naval Aide, Captain Shepard, has assured him that it will be no problem for the helicopter to carry the heavy casket; second, even though Admiral Burkley and General Clifton insist on ambulance transport of JFK's body to Bethesda, Gerald Behn at the White House subsequently orders Roy Kellerman: "You accompany the body aboard the helicopter."

- Finally, General Clifton insists and then repeats, in great detail, orders for a forklift and platform at the left rear of the aircraft for the casket, a

113. Memorandum from Doug Horne to Jeremy Gunn dated October 17, 1995 describing the audio tapes, captioned "Air Force One Audiotapes from November 22, 1963." http://www. history-matters.com/archive/jfk/arrb/staff_memos/pdf/DH_AirForceOne.pdf

personnel ramp at the left front of the aircraft for President Johnson and other passengers' debarkation, and another personnel ramp at the right front of the airplane (the dark, unlit side of the aircraft where there is a galley door) for the departure of Jacqueline Kennedy.* These concerns are mirrored at flight's end in a conversation from Colonel Swindal (Air Force One pilot) to Colonel Cross (USAF also) on the ground.

• Background chatter can be heard at one point, discussing a "limousine and ambulance at Andrews," and later in the same background conversation, something about a "black Cadillac" . . . [in another call] "SAM Command Post" calls Air Force One and a "Colonel Arnbuck (phonetic) from OPS" expresses a concern from the Chief of Staff (General LeMay?) as to whether President Johnson and Mr. Kennedy's body is onboard the aircraft. This question is followed immediately on the tape by the confusing tug-of-war over who will control autopsy arrangements, etc.

On more than one occasion during the flight, personnel in Washington specifically ask whether Mrs. Kennedy is on board. "A.F. Command Post" first asks this question, immediately before the "Chief of Staff's Office" inquires about the whereabouts of President Johnson and Mr. Kennedy's body. Subsequently, "Air Force Command Post" asks who the top people on board are. "Winner" (a Mr. Hatcher at "Crown") later asks if Mrs. Kennedy is on board. During the flight, Admiral Burkley assumes that Mrs. Kennedy will accompany the body; General Clifton very carefully arranges separate debarkation arrangements from the aircraft for Mrs. Kennedy and Gerald Behn (head of White House Secret Service Detail) attempts on two occasions to separate all passengers on Air Force One from JFK's body after arrival (desiring to send the body alone to Bethesda on a helicopter and all other personnel to the South Grounds of the White House). The significance of this repeated concern about Mrs. Kennedy's whereabouts and her plans upon landing is a source of controversy among some researchers.

Immediately after Behn orders Kellerman to "accompany the body aboard the helicopter," the following exchange takes place: Kellerman: "I was unable to get ahold of Payne and Bob Burke [names are phonetic approximations]." After a break, the words, "Payne and Burke at the ranch,"

---

* Editorial notes: (1) The fact that Jacqueline Kennedy never used the ramp at the right front of the aircraft has caused at least one researcher to question the real motivation for its placement; (2) An Air Force document titled: "Historical Highlights of Andrews Air Force Base, 1942–1989" states that "the body of the slain President was removed to Walter Reed General Hospital," which further fuels the controversy over the movements of the president's body after Air Force One landed at Andrews.

are heard; it is unclear whether the speaker is Kellerman or Behn. Finally, an unidentified speaker says, "Payne and Burke were not notified." The meaning or possible significance of this exchange, if any, is not known.

One last noticeable exchange worth reporting is from "Wing" (Brigadier General Godfrey McHugh, USAF, Kennedy's Air Force Aide) to "Slugger" (Capt. Cecil Stoughton, USAF, White House photographer who photographed both the swearing-in of LBJ onboard Air Force One in Dallas, *and* the onloading of JFK's casket at Love Field): Wing asks that Crown relay to Slugger that he must meet the aircraft as soon as possible after arrival Andrews, and that if he cannot do this, he is to see Wing as soon as possible after arrival, or contact him in any way feasible. The urgency and importance of this matter to Wing is very clear from his tone of voice. Later, Crown informs Wing that Slugger remained on the ground in Dallas. One of the many conversations not on the LBJ transcript which *is* on the edited tape reads as follows:

> Andrews(?): Air Force One, this is very important.

> Slugger: This is Capt. Stoughton in Dallas.

> Air Force One: Warrior advises he is unable to speak with you at the present time and asks would you please call the White House in about 30 minutes. (Note: It is unclear what this is all about, and additionally unclear why Warrior is the party unable to speak with Slugger, when it was Wing who asked to speak with him in the first place.)

A particularly intriguing question arises from the "unidentified voice," which twice made statements about someone being on "6970," the designation of the previous "Air Force Two." Given that there were only seventeen passengers on board that aircraft, none of whom were military officers (although a few Secret Service agents were aboard), it might have been "Lancer" (JFK) whose name was erased. Still another mysterious comment caught on tape, from Roy Kellerman to Gerald Behn, was "I'm sure the Volunteer boys will go over his car and so forth."[114] This is clearly a reference to the need for Lyndon's "boys" to examine the limousine and make whatever fixes it might need to support the official storyline, and if that proved difficult, then to have the car rebuilt to hide whatever unwanted information it might hold.

---

114. Horne, p. 1101.

Transporting JFK's Corpse: A More Likely Explanation

One possible—admittedly bizarre, yet given Johnson's capacity for audacious and outrageous conduct, realistic—interpretation from this *edited* transcript, based upon the other known facts and anomalies presented, suggests the following scenario:

- Kennedy's body was taken from the ornate bronze coffin and put into a light shipping casket then moved to the "backup" aircraft formerly designated by LBJ as "Air Force Two," (aircraft 86790) during a fourteen-minute period when the casket was unattended, as Mrs. Kennedy was forced to attend Lyndon's swearing-in ceremony. At this point, both airplanes were parked next to each other and the passengers had already been seated and were waiting to take off. When Judge Hughes arrived, Johnson was intent on emptying the aft compartment of the plane, saying, "We'll get as many people in here as possible." He dispatched men to round up witnesses. Valenti, Youngblood, Roberts, and Lem Johns were sent into the staff area to extend a general invitation, and then he himself went in. Gesticulating broadly, he announced, "If anybody wants to join in the swearing-in ceremony, I would be happy and proud to have you."[115] It appears that Johnson's mood swings were by then bouncing from one extreme to another: dour and morose in the motorcade to hysterical shortly after boarding the airplane and now, barely an hour later, celebratory and magnanimous as he encouraged everyone on board to witness him swearing to uphold the constitution.

  Many of the Kennedy group were in no mood to watch Johnson being sworn in, but his efforts to empty the aft compartment, where the coffin was, and fill the stateroom—already insufferably hot and stuffy—with more people have to be considered more than a little odd.

- Johnson's real intent was to keep the Kennedy people from the aft compartment, where the coffin had been secured, and move them into the forward, staff compartment while he "swore" that he would uphold the constitution. While Johnson was being sworn in, the entire party was either with him in the stateroom or in the forward compartments, leaving the rear of the plane behind the closed corridor door empty; the exception, of course, would be for anyone Johnson dispatched to have Kennedy's body switched to another, smaller and lighter, shipping casket, which would then be moved to the backup aircraft.

- The backup aircraft followed Air Force One in the takeoff queue but overtook it in flight and reportedly landed well ahead of it at Andrews (the

---

115. Manchester, p. 320.

"leapfrogging" had been a common practice so that the vice president would arrive first in order to greet the president). This was confirmed by the FBI agents who interviewed the head of the Secret Service White House Detail, Gerald Behn, who stated that "Air Force Two passed Air Force One in flight."[116] The official Secret Service reports indicate that Air Force Two arrived at Andrews after Air Force One; however, the two contradictory statements cannot be reconciled. Given that Behn's statement indicated that Air Force Two passed Air Force One in flight, it implicitly means that Air Force Two landed first. This was probably an indiscreet comment to make to the FBI agents, Sibert and O'Neill, but has to be considered more factual than the "official" Secret Service records, many of which have been widely discredited, as will be seen throughout the remaining chapters. In view of the massive fabrication of other evidence already cited, it is not far-fetched to suggest that the arrival time of "86790" was incorrectly recorded.

• Once Air Force Two (a.k.a. "backup aircraft" or "86790") landed at Andrews, the body was immediately removed and taken by helicopter to Walter Reed Army Hospital, which could have been reached within five to eight minutes, allowing for at least forty-five minutes for preautopsy "surgery"—as (inadvertently) verified in the FBI report—before being sent on to Bethesda in a black Cadillac hearse and delivered to the rear door at 6:35 p.m., consistent with the testimony of three witnesses.

The assertion that JFK's body had been moved to the "backup" aircraft is supported by David Lifton's original finding that the typed report submitted by FBI agents Sibert and O'Neill, who were dispatched to the autopsy to retrieve any bullets found inside his body, had been "*typographically altered* to replace 'Air Force 6790' with 'Air Force One'*"[117] (emphasis added). Despite this finding, Lifton did not believe ultimately that the body was moved to Air Force Two because of the Secret Service's logs, which showed that it landed almost one-half hour after Air Force One. My own opinion is that, given all of the other distortions and fabricated evidence, which are only summarized herein, it is not unreasonable to suggest that these records were also changed. The changes made in the FBI report, as such an example, are shown below:

---

* In the days before computers, to avoid retyping an entire report (or, to "revise" one done by someone else) it was customary to use a quick drying white substance called "White-Out" to "correct" the copy.

116. Lifton, p. 679.
117. Lifton, p. 638.

At approximately 3 p.m. on November 22, 1963, following the
President's announced assassination, it was ascertained that
Air Force One, the President's jet, was returning from Love
Field, Dallas, Texas, flying the body back to Andrews Air Force
Base, Camp Springs, Maryland. 3As FRANCIS X. O'NEILL, JR.
and JAMES W. SIBERT proceeded to Andrews Air Force Base to
handle any matters which would fall within the jurisdiction

Lifton wrote, "Thus, it was my theory that the Sibert and O'Neill report, as originally typed, read that the body was aboard 'Air Force 6790, the President's jet . . .' It should be noted that 6790 was Lyndon Johnson's jet, and he was now 'the president.' This typographical alteration suggested there had been a change in Sibert and O'Neill's understanding as to which plane carried the body from Dallas to Washington and arrived at Bethesda before they did. Exactly what Sibert and O'Neill asked Gerald Behn at the White House on November 27, 1963, must remain a matter of speculation. But they did record the response—a response which suggests they may have been told that the body was aboard *Air Force Two*, and that *Air Force Two* passed *Air Force One* in flight."[118]

The fact that the FBI agents took the trouble sometime later to go back and make this "correction" to their typed report indicates not only that it was a very important point but suggests that the reason it was even mentioned in the first place was because they had inquired about how the body arrived in Bethesda before they did. This is a very reasonable deduction given that— had the point not been raised as an "issue" in the first place—it would have been routinely typed "Air Force One" originally, and there would have been no reason to have to make such an obvious and glaring "correction."

The tapes of conversations between people on Air Force One and on the ground (White House) reveal a lot of confusion about where JFK's body was to be taken; almost all references to the location of the pending autopsy refer to Walter Reed (Army) Hospital and there is considerable talk about transporting JFK's casket, and other people, by "chopper" to Walter Reed. Despite the fact that Jacqueline had requested, early on, that it be done at Bethesda, the recorded conversations continued to refer to Walter Reed as the destination for the casket. Even as late as 5:58 p.m., as Air Force One taxied onto the tarmac, Lyndon Johnson's secretary, Marie Fehmer, continued making chronological notes for the new president; the final entry on these notes was "5:58 Arr. Andrews—Body w/Mrs. K. to Walter Reed."[119] Ms.

---

118. Ibid., p. 642.
119. Lifton, p. 690.

Fehmer (now Mrs. Andrew Chiarodo) told David Lifton that "I'm sure someone told me, but . . . I have no way of remember[ing] who."[120]

David Lifton's book, published in 1980, still stands as the original definitive work on this aspect of the manipulation of JFK's body; Noel Twyman's 1997 book, William Matson Law's 2005 book, and Douglas Horne's 2009 five-volume work all added to that base. The above probable scenario is simply a condensed version of their meticulously researched analysis. One exception is that of my disagreement with David Lifton's decision to accept the "official Secret Service records," which indicated that Air Force Two arrived after Air Force One, despite the statement of Gerald Behn who implicitly said the opposite when he said *Air Force Two* passed *Air Force One*. That distinction either opens up or rules out the possibility of the body having been moved to Air Force Two (a.k.a. "backup aircraft" or "86790") as noted above. By moving JFK's body to a lighter shipping casket, it could also be disguised to make it appear as a plain crate, just another piece of cargo that had to be moved from Air Force One in order to make room for the Johnson party's luggage. In this thesis, the body was moved while both airplanes sat side by side on the tarmac in Dallas—amidst mass confusion as baggage was moved from one plane to the other, back and forth—all while Johnson gathered together practically everyone on Air Force One to watch him take the oath of office to uphold the Constitution of the United Sates of America.

In fact, the heart of this thesis is that Johnson had all of this meticulously planned for months; as we have demonstrated throughout this book, he was a genius at planning very manipulative, complex, and extensive scenarios to dupe others and had done it time after time. It is clear that the "miscommunications" between himself, Kenneth O'Donnell, and Robert F. Kennedy were all part of his plans to create a very chaotic situation at Dallas Love Field in order to set the stage for remaking JFK's wounds to support the "lone gunman" scenario. His master plan had also called for a number of otherwise inexplicable actions, among them:

- The huge number of telephone calls that he and his assistant Cliff Carter initiated aboard *Air Force One*, mostly to Washington officials; the priority for them at this point would have been to ensure that JFK's body was modified as necessary to show that he was only shot from behind;
- The numerous phone calls which Cliff Carter made to Dallas County Sheriff Decker, Captain Fritz and District Attorney Henry Wade, telling them to quit talking about "conspiracy" and to start closing down their investigation;

120. Ibid.

- Invoking "top secret" security measures for everyone involved in transporting and/or modifying the body and conducting the autopsy; everyone involved was sworn to secrecy and made to understand that they would suffer severe penalties if they failed to conform to these orders.

Further, this thesis is based upon the following purposes to Johnson's actions:

- All of his actions at Love Field were part of his grand scheme; nothing he did was spontaneous and without some underlying purpose. By taking over Air Force One and holding it on the tarmac while he waited for JFK's body to arrive with his widow, he could force the Secret Service agents to quickly secure the body, wresting it away from the hapless Dr. Rose and eliminate any chance that a rigorous, well-executed autopsy would be performed. He had clearly planned this weeks before, knowing that a "special" autopsy would be necessary, one that would obliterate any evidence that Kennedy was shot from anywhere but from behind; the doctors to be used in this would have been preselected by their superiors beforehand, probably on the basis of utilizing only those who would be absolutely obedient and vulnerable to their unconditional control.
- While the attention of everyone on board was distracted to his swearing-in "ceremony," JFK's body was removed from the big heavy casket and moved into a small shipping casket resembling an ordinary crate, which would then be moved with other baggage to *Air Force Two,* Johnson's old airplane, which he would never have to suffer the embarrassment of riding in again. This explains why he insisted on having the baggage moved from one plane to another as reported by Manchester (clearly not something that he should have been concerned with at all given all the other events of the day and the fact that both planes would be flying back to Washington at practically the same time anyway).[121] It was critical to the need to make any "fixes" necessary to fit the "lone nut disaffected communist" theory, which was his preference all along, against the "Communist conspiracy conducted by Cuban sympathizers" option favored by some in the military and intelligence communities to provoke an invasion of Cuba.
- The remaining pieces would then follow: get the body to Andrews first, "chopper" it to Walter Reed to make whatever "final adjustments" might be necessary, redeliver it by a waiting hearse to Bethesda for "preautopsy" reviews and x-rays, create even more chaotic conditions at Bethesda so the body could be put back into the "false-decoy" ambulance, which would then reconnect with the original "decoy ambulance" carrying the ornate

---

121. Manchester, p. 239.

Dallas casket (after Bobby and Mrs. Kennedy got out of it at the front of the hospital). Only after such a "shell game" played out—in a zany "hide and seek" chase around the Bethesda Navy Hospital grounds that ended only minutes before 8:00 p.m.—would the original ambulance, with JFK's body finally back in the original bronze casket, drive up to the rear loading dock of the hospital. Almost simultaneously, the truck conveying the "casket team" finally made its way back, just in time to carry the coffin into the hospital.

If all of that sounds a little outrageous, rest assured that it conforms to the stories of many witnesses, as we will see shortly; it is also not nearly as outrageously unbelievable as numerous aspects of the "official version" foisted on a credulous nation in 1964, the most outlandish of which was the absurd "Magic Bullet Theory" invented by Arlen Specter, which was then entered, arguably fraudulently, into official evidence as commission exhibit 399. All of this despite the questionable provenance of the bullet and its being in practically pristine condition, as only a bullet shot into thin air, a barrel of water or a very sizeable box of loose cotton might emerge. Jack Ruby probably knew where it came from, but no one thought to ask him.

The pilots and other military officers who participated in the transfer in Dallas would of course, have been sworn—and warned—to keep their silence, on the basis of "national security" reasons due to highly sensitive matters that were naturally well over their "need to know." So the statements they made to Lifton and others to obfuscate or "not remember" what happened are understandable. If the doctors at Bethesda could be influenced to hide the truth, which has been proven beyond a doubt as we shall see, then it is not far-fetched to suggest that the same phenomenon existed all along the way, from the time the casket left Parkland Hospital, and is at the heart of the dichotomy between Parkland doctors and Bethesda doctors. This would also apply to the arrival time logged in for *Air Force Two*. Rather than 18:30 (6:30 p.m. EST) the logged number might have been fudged because a normal flight time of two hours and fifteen minutes from Dallas to Andrews was more likely, which would mean that it arrived *before Air Force One*, given that the latter aircraft was slowed in flight to allow the "backup" aircraft to do its customary "leapfrog" and arrive ahead of the master ship, a common procedure as explained elsewhere. Yet, regardless of which aircraft JFK's body arrived on, its movement after arrival in Washington was, nonetheless, not exactly as depicted in the news reports of the time.

At the Morgue: A Colossal Hearse "Shell Game" Plays Out

The maneuvering to return JFK's body to the casket in which it left Parkland Hospital in Dallas—after it had been removed during Johnson's swearing-in on the tarmac of Love Field—took on an (almost) comical aspect at Bethesda Naval Hospital when three different ambulance/hearses appeared on the scene. The first one was a black Cadillac hearse at approximately 6:35–6:40 p.m. from which a "plain gray shipping casket" was removed and immediately taken into the morgue. Inside was the president's body in a military-style zippered body bag. This casket was received by First-Class Petty Officer Dennis David, who stated that it was accompanied by six or seven civilians who he assumed were Secret Service agents. A navy hospital corpsman, Paul O'Connor, and x-ray technician Jerrol Custer both confirmed that the body was nude except for a sheet wrapped around only the head; that there was a huge hole (4" × 7") in the back and top of the head; and the brain was almost completely gone except for residual tissue.[122]

In the meantime, the gray Pontiac navy ambulance carrying the ornate bronze coffin from Dallas arrived approximately fifteen to twenty minutes later, at 6:55 p.m., dropping Jacqueline and Bobby Kennedy off at the front door before delivering the bronze casket to the rear of the building. In a bizarre scene, as Jacqueline entered the building at 7:05 p.m. through the front lobby, Jerrol Custer passed her "carrying exposed x-ray film of JFK's body that had already been taken. This despite the fact that JFK's body was supposedly outside in a bronze casket in the navy ambulance. We now have a corroboration of Dennis David's story *"mutually corroborative evidence from three extremely credible witnesses . . ."*[123] (emphasis added).

To add even more drama to the clearly broken "chain of custody" of JFK's body, a carefully planned "mix-up" occurred on the hospital grounds when the truck with the seven men serving as the casket team could not keep up with the gray Pontiac navy ambulance after Robert and Jackie Kennedy got out of it at the front of the hospital; another identical Pontiac decoy hearse was entering the area at the rear at the same time, and the men in the pickup became confused regarding which was which. For one hour, from 7:00 p.m., when Mrs. Kennedy exited the hearse, until nearly 8:00 p.m., when the casket team carried the bronze casket into the morgue, as reported by Lt. Sam Bird's report,* there was an inexplicable break in its custody.[124]

---

* Bird was in charge of the unit, which was from Company E, First Battalion, 3rd Infantry, Fort Meyer, Virginia.
122. Lifton, pp. 601–607; Twyman, pp. 171–172.
123. Twyman, p. 173.
124. Lifton, pp. 389–422.

It appears that the "shell game" being played out with multiple gray Pontiac ambulances was planned by someone who had studied the art of illusion as practiced by magicians, something that in fact the CIA had done in the previous decade as part of the *MK/ULTRA* operation.

One of the men assigned to the "casket team" recalled that the reason they became lost and confused was because the ambulance/hearse left the front of the hospital and sped away; they tried to catch up with it, spending "ten to fifteen minutes" at speeds up to 50 mph on the hospital grounds and another fifteen minutes trying to get back to the building from where they started. When they returned to the rear entrance they were advised that the casket had still not arrived so they returned to the front entrance (twice, apparently); it returned for the second time to the rear entrance shortly before 8:00 p.m., finally finding the ambulance with the bronze casket.[125] The driver of the ambulance was not from the casket team, nor was he any other enlisted man; *he was an admiral, Calvin B. Galloway, the man in charge of the entire medical center, the immediate superior of Commander Humes who would perform the "autopsy"*[126] (emphasis added).

The scene around Bethesda Naval Hospital, described by many of the witnesses to it, is, admittedly, bizarre. However, through attempting to understand and explain these anomalies while giving the witnesses due credibility, it becomes apparent that the entire scenario was explainable. It was considered essential that the body be made to conform to a preconceived plot; to facilitate that end, it had to be subjected to certain adjustments to hide the evidence of any gunshots from the front (e.g., the resizing of the hole, so that it extended toward the top and front of the skull) to make it congruent with the ideal plot of two shots from behind. After that was done, the "shell game" was played out by secretly moving the body out of the hospital room after the "adjustments" were complete, into another "decoy" standard-issue navy ambulance, which met the original Pontiac ambulance in some other part of the hospital grounds; after the body was transferred back to the original coffin and ambulance, Admiral Galloway personally returned it just before 8:00 p.m. to the rear entrance. The result of this "sleight of hand" scenario explains generally how the subterfuge created long ago in Lyndon Johnson's mind was executed. It also reconciles most of the "irreconcilable differences" extant, which relate to noted anomalies between the credible witness statements and the incredible story represented in the Warren Commission Report.

---

125. Ibid., p. 626.
126. Ibid., p. 416.

Doug Horne, in his five-volume, eighteen-hundred-page work, *Inside the Assassination Records Review Board: The U.S. Government's Final Attempt to Reconcile the Conflicting Medical Evidence in the Assassination of JFK*, has conclusively established the presence of unequivocal evidence of a U.S. government cover-up of the medical evidence in the Kennedy assassination; his research (based upon previous works cited) proves that the Zapruder film was in fact altered within a few days of the assassination in a manner consistent with that to be described in chapter 9. In an interview with author Dick Russell, for his 2008 book *On the Trail of the JFK Assassins*, Horne stated that [127]

> I am now convinced—and this insight didn't really come to me until 2006, when I did much of the writing on the manuscript I'm putting together about all this—that Humes and Boswell, who were there at the morgue with the president's body well before the autopsy started and prior to Dr. Finck's arrival, were involved in a covert deception operation from the very beginning. I believe they were told, for national security reasons, to destroy or suppress any evidence that the president was shot from the front and to record only evidence that he was shot from the rear—even if they had to manufacture some of it.
>
> I don't think Finck was initially a part of the deception; the great irony is that even though he was a board-certified forensic pathologist, I believe he was a victim of the Humes-Boswell covert operation. At some point, after the fact, I believe Finck suspected this, but felt he was in so deep by this time, and realized he was so compromised, that he decided not to blow the whistle officially; instead he left a few clues in the record over the years for "CYA" purposes . . . The main point I am trying to make here is that Humes and Boswell had possession of the president's body much earlier in the evening than the official record indicates, and undertook activities to alter the evidentiary record that they did not reveal to Finck.

Jerrol Custer told William Matson Law in 1998 that "*the Officer of the Day said to me he was coming in from Walter Reed.* I took the films and the cassettes to the morgue, and I set everything up. We sat there and waited and waited; they said, 'He should be arriving at any moment.' They brought him in, in the [shipping] casket, put the casket down and opened it. So we proceeded to remove the body from the casket and place it on the autopsy table . . . the head was completely covered by a plastic bag and there was a sheet around it.

---

127. Russell, *On the Trail* . . ., p. 281.

The sheet, of course, was bloodied and nothing was ever mentioned about that"[128] (emphasis added). Custer said he "double loaded" the x-ray machine with two films, so that "if one film is a little bit too dark, one film is just right . . . I ran [i.e., processed] one film and put the other film in the light-proof box [and later] ran the films in the light-proof box, those were all good too. I put them in one of the mailing folders [and kept them there] for a 'Couple of months.'"[129] When author Law asked him what happened to those extra films, Custer said "I destroyed them . . . Because of the gag order that I had signed. I didn't destroy them right away. After I'd thought on it and pondered on it a little bit, and thought, 'Well, if these films happened to surface along the line somewhere, they're going to trace them back to me. And guess whose body is going to wind up in jail.' I never thought that later on down the road that they could have been worth millions. Or they could have solved the whole problem."[130]

It should be noted here that *all* navy personnel were immediately ordered, verbally, and subsequently very formally, in writing, not to speak of anything they saw that night to anyone else, under threat of court martial. According to David Lifton, "A group of men, in civilian clothes . . . were keeping very careful track of who was entering and leaving the room. This group, between six and ten in number, was stationed in the anteroom to the morgue, where the chillboxes were."[131]

Researcher/author Doug Horne told Dick Russell about how he and his colleagues tracked down an ex-marine sergeant who was in charge of the security detail at the morgue. He and his team were not the honor guard, with the white gloves and dress uniforms described by William Manchester, but they formed a physical security detail from the Marine Barracks in Washington DC, dressed in Marine Corps working uniforms, and carrying weapons:[132]

> The sergeant's name was Roger Boyajian, pronounced "Boy-gen." He had retained an original onion-skin carbon copy of the after-action report that he wrote on November 26, 1963, the day after JFK's funeral, and had shared its contents with Ms. Cunningham. A document like this one that is contemporaneous is priceless, because it's not distorted by fading memories, by time—or by anyone's subsequent theories about the assassination. So I interviewed Boyajian

---

128. Law, p. 111.
129. Ibid., pp. 122–123.
130. Ibid.
131. Lifton, pp. 607–08, 631.
132. Russell, *On the Trail . . .*, p. 282.

on the phone, and he then mailed me a photocopy of that document, and authenticated it with a letter written above his signature.

He'd gotten to Bethesda really early, before the president's body arrived. One of the entries in his report reads: "1835—President's Casket Arrives." That means 6:35 PM, and indicates that he took notes; every military man in those days had what's called a "wheel book," a little green U.S. government memoranda notebook that fits into your back pocket. The thing is, that's a mind-blowing entry, because it is a well-documented fact that the light-gray Navy ambulance, with the president's bronze casket from Dallas inside, didn't arrive at Bethesda until approximately five minutes before seven, and it sat outside in front of the main building, for about 12 minutes or so before being driven around to the back of the morgue. HSCA interviews of FBI agents James Sibert and Francis O'Neill revealed that these two men, assisted *only* by two Secret Service agents, helped carry in this heavy bronze casket (using a dolly), *without* the assistance of the joint service casket team (which was not present when this happened); and a 1964 FBI report provides a time marker for this event of about 7:17 p.m. Yet here was Sergeant Boyajian, four days after the assassination, placing the arrival time of the president's body almost forty-five minutes *earlier*. (emphasis in original)

There were so many witnesses who were on the scene at Bethesda who have independently come forward and agreed on the fact that Kennedy's body had come in between 6:35 and 6:40 p.m. that they cannot be ignored. Now Roger Boyajian joins Dennis David, Paul O'Connor, Floyd Riebe, Jerrol Custer, and Captain John Stover; even Dr. Boswell "confirmed to Dennis David that he and his sailors had indeed carried the president's body into the morgue early that evening."[133]

The scenario described here is merely a synthesis based upon the original research performed by authors Lifton, Twyman, Law, and Horne, fitted to conform with known anomalies of the situation and the previously inexplicable actions of Lyndon Johnson. The premise of this thesis is that JFK's body arrived in a shipping casket on board the backup aircraft perhaps fifteen minutes before Air Force One's arrival and was transported by helicopter first to Walter Reed Hospital, then on to Bethesda Navy Hospital in the black Cadillac hearse after an initial review of the wounds on the body and the initial modifications, which is not to say that additional modifications were not made when it arrived at Bethesda (as noted by David Lifton, a helicopter

---

133. Ibid., p. 283.

was taking off very near Air Force One just as it arrived at Andrews Air Force Base).[134] Dennis David told author David Lifton that "he was told the black hearse he saw coming from the rear gate had come down Fourteenth Street. A check of a map of Washington showed that a few miles away was Walter Reed Army Medical Center."[135] This suggests that the helicopter was used to move the body to Walter Reed; after possibly some of the "adjustments" were made there, it was transported to Bethesda in the black Cadillac hearse, arriving there at approximately 6:35–6:40 p.m.

Author David Lifton—whose original research over thirty years ago was ridiculed by many at the time, but which has now been largely vindicated—interviewed Floyd Albert Reibe, a photographer's assistant who had taken many photographs of Kennedy's corpse. Before he would say anything at all, he reminded Lifton that everything about it had been declared "top secret" and refused to speak about it until Lifton convinced him that the order had been rescinded, reading to him the pertinent part of the House Select Committee document. The statement he had signed on November 27, 1963, included the warning:[136]

> "I have read and fully understand them and am aware of the disciplinary action possible in the event that I disobey these orders . . ." He further said that "Captain Stover called down and told Mr. Stringer that he and myself [were] to come on up, and I think just about everybody who was at the autopsy that night was up there—all navy personnel, and he explained to us the Secrecy Act, *and [word] came down from the White House, [they] wanted this kept top secret and nobody must talk about it* . . ." (emphasis added)
>
> LIFTON: He actually used the words *'the White House'.*?
>
> Reibe: Yes.

The reason that Reibe and the others were given for the "top secret" orders was "security." He had no reason to suspect anything sinister was going on, even as his photos were destroyed, as he assumed that it was because they raised some kind of "security" concern, just as the casket team was told the "decoy ambulance" served a "security function."[137]

The photos included some of JFK lying on his stomach, showing the back wound, and six pictures of internal portions of the body; none of them

---

134. Lifton., p. 683.
135. Ibid., p. 681.
136. Ibid., pp. 638–639.
137. Ibid., p. 639.

is in the collection stored in the National Archives. The reason was that Secret Service agents seized the film and exposed it to light, destroying all images he had taken.[138]

Reibe told David Lifton that JFK's body had arrived in a plain shipping casket with turnbuckles and thumbscrews, designed so that "the whole lid came off."[139] He further said that it was his recollection that the body was contained in a body bag . . . "a dark bag that opened with zippers" and that the word around the hospital—though he did not see it himself—was that it had come in by helicopter.[140] The helicopter transport would ensure that the body arrived well before the navy ambulance carrying Bobby Kennedy and Jacqueline Kennedy.

JFK's Autopsy

By the time the autopsy began on JFK's body, many other links to high-level military officers would suddenly materialize. Twenty-eight (28) civilians and/or high-level military brass were in attendance and in total control of the 'autopsy' was General Curtis LeMay, with the president's doctor Admiral Burkley directing the medical aspects of the autopsy: Paul O'Connor, a laboratory technologist who assisted in the autopsy of President Kennedy said, *"I remember Curtis LeMay sitting there [in the gallery at the JFK autopsy] with a big cigar in his hand."*.[141]

None of the medical officers had ever experienced such a large number of observers who had mysteriously inserted themselves into the autopsy procedure in a relatively small autopsy room. This prompted Navy Commander Humes to ask at the outset, "Who's in charge here?" An answer came from the back, "I am." The fact that the highest-ranking military man there—the Air Force representative of the Joint Chiefs of Staff—was General Curtis LeMay, would suggest that it was he who responded to Commander Humes' question.[142] However, according to William M. Law's interview with O'Connor, it seems that Admiral Burkley, the president's personal physician, "came in and was very agitated giving orders to everybody, including higher-ranking officers."[143]

David Lifton interviewed James Curtis Jenkins, a laboratory technician at the autopsy table "touching elbows" with Dr. Finck, who said he saw a

---

138. Ibid., pp. 636–637.
139. Ibid.
140. Ibid., 637–638.
141. Law, William, *In the Eye of History*, p. 35.
142. Russell, p. 571.
143. Law, p. 35.

"huge hole" in Kennedy's head, "'at least one-third of the skull was gone when Kennedy was brought in' a hole which extended toward the rear, and with fragments that seemed to be hanging on, and which seemed to have been exploded toward the rear, Jenkins formed the opinion that President Kennedy had been shot in the head from the front . . . But then, the next day, said Jenkins, 'I found out that supposedly he was shot from the back. I just, you know, I just couldn't believe it, and have never been able to believe it.'"[144] Jenkins went on to describe the scene between the doctors and the civilians, asserting that the men in civilian clothes seemed to have a "preconcluded" idea of what the evidence had to support and were growing angry with the physicians who were hestitating to agree with their findings. His opinion was that doctors would say that the purported shot was "not possible" and then be chastised for being insubordinate; the men in suits were becoming very irritated that the doctors were initially resistant to the portrayal of the assassination which their findings was supposed to describe.[145] Apparently, their persistence eventually paid off, given the numerous traces of inexplicable contradictions between the reports they rendered versus the statements cited by other witnesses. Lieutenant Colonel Pierre Finck was the army doctor who assisted Dr. Humes and another navy doctor, Commander J. Thornton Boswell, in the autopsy. Colonel Finck was subpoenaed a few years later by Jim Garrison about that experience. A portion of his testimony is included below to illustrate the surreal—bizarre is more descriptive—nature of the president's autopsy scene:[146]

> COLONEL FINCK: Well, I heard Dr. Humes stating that—he said, 'Who is in charge here?' And I heard an Army General, I don't remember his name, stating, 'I am.' You must understand that in those circumstances, there were law enforcement officials, military people with various ranks, and you have to co-ordinate the operation according to directions.
>
> QUESTION: But you were one of the three qualified pathologists standing at that autopsy table, were you not, Doctor?
>
> COLONEL FINCK: Yes, I was.
>
> QUESTION: Was this Army General a qualified pathologist?

---

144. Lifton, p. 610.
145. Ibid., pp. 611–612.
146. Douglass, pp. 312–313 (Ref. "Testimony of Dr. Pierre Finck," February 24, 1969, in the trial of Clay Shaw; Appendix A in James DiEugenio, Destiny Betrayed: JFK, Cuba, and the Garrison Case. New York: Sheridan Square Press, p. 291).

COLONEL FINCK: No.

QUESTION: Was he a doctor?

COLONEL FINCK: No, not to my knowledge.

QUESTION: Can you give me his name, Colonel?

COLONEL FINCK: No, I can't. I don't remember.

QUESTION: How many other military personnel were present at the autopsy in the autopsy room?

COLONEL FINCK: That autopsy room was quite crowded. It is a small autopsy room, and when you are called in circumstances like that to look at the wound of the President of the United States who is dead, you don't look around too much to ask people for their names and take notes on who they are and how many there are. I did not do so. The room was crowded with military and civilian personnel and federal agents. Secret Service agents, FBI agents, for part of the autopsy, but I cannot give you a precise breakdown as regards the attendance of the people in that autopsy room at Bethesda Naval Hospital.

QUESTION: Colonel, did you feel that you had to take orders from this Army General that was there directing the autopsy?

COLONEL FINCK: No, because there were others, there were Admirals.

QUESTION: There were Admirals?

COLONEL FINCK: Oh yes, there were Admirals, and when you are a Lieutenant Colonel in the Army you just follow orders, and at the end of the autopsy we were specifically told—as I recall it, it was by Admiral Kenney, the Surgeon General of the Navy—this is subject to verification—we were specifically told not to discuss the case.

The testimony became a little more adversarial for the next several minutes as Dr. Finck tried to be responsive but not revelatory in his statements, and his interrogator repeatedly needed to ask the judge to intervene with direction to Dr. Finck as they got closer and closer to the point:

QUESTION: I will ask one more time: Why did you not dissect the track of the bullet wound that you have described today and you saw at the time of the autopsy at the time you examined the body? Why? I ask you to answer that question.

COLONEL FINCK: As I recall I was told not to, but I don't remember by whom.

QUESTION: You were told not to, but you don't remember by whom?

COLONEL FINCK: Right.

QUESTION: Could it have been one of the admirals or one of the generals in the room?

COLONEL FINCK: I don't recall.

QUESTION: Do you have any particular reason why you cannot recall at this time?

COLONEL FINCK: Because we were told to examine the head and the chest cavity and that doesn't include the removal of the organs of the neck.

QUESTION: You are one of the three autopsy specialists and pathologists at the time, and you saw what you described as an entrance wound in the neck area of the president of the United States who had just been assassinated, and you were only interested in the other wound but not interested in the track through his neck. Is that what you are telling me?

COLONEL FINCK: I was interested in the track, and *I had observed the conditions of bruising between the point of entry in the back of the neck and the point of the exit at the front of the neck, which is entirely compatible with the bullet path.* [Emphasis added to Finck's unsupported statement, in contradiction to the known evidence.]

QUESTION: But you were told not to go into the area of the neck, is that your testimony?

COLONEL FINCK: From what I recall, yes, but I don't remember by whom.

Navy medical corpsman Paul O'Connor, who helped the doctors with the autopsy, stated, "I was upset by the way the autopsy was conducted and by the fact that we weren't able to do certain critical things like probe the throat wound that we thought was a bullet wound. We found out it was a bullet wound years later."[147]

Corpsman O'Connor, in an interview several years later, described how the military brass, crowded into the small room, would not permit the doctors to probe the throat wound, which everyone in Dallas had said was an entrance wound. "It got very tense. Admiral [Calvin] Galloway [the

---

147. Law, p. 45.

chief of the hospital command] started getting very agitated again, because there was a wound in his neck . . . and I remember the doctors were going to check that out when Admiral Galloway told them, 'Leave it alone. Don't touch it. It's just a tracheotomy.' He stopped anybody from going further. Drs. Hume and Boswell, Dr. Finck, were told to leave it alone, let's go to other things . . . O'Connor further stated that Admiral George Burkley, the president's physician, also blocked the doctors from probing the neck wound and a back wound, claiming to be acting in behalf of the family, none of whom were present at the autopsy."[148]

Doug Horne concluded that it was Doctors Humes and Boswell who conducted the earlier surgery to modify the head wound, enlarging it to make it appear that the fatal shot came from the rear and exploded the entire right side of the head; they had also removed evidence in JFK's right temple of a shot fired from the front—the grassy knoll—in accordance with apparent orders from their superiors. Moreover, he also concluded that a number of small bullet fragments were removed at the same time and that a large bullet fragment was removed from JFK's back.[149] Horne also determined that, after the autopsy ended at about 11:00 p.m. new and misleading photographs were taken which showed the back of JFK's head as seeming to be intact, something that was not seen by any of the witnesses, either in Dallas or Bethesda. It was only then that the body was passed to the Gawler's Funeral Home personnel to begin preparing it for the services being planned to commence that morning. It was through the use of "special effects" that such photographs could be made for the obvious purpose of purporting to show that there was no "exit wound" in the back of the head, in direct contradiction of the statements of numerous eyewitnesses.[150]

Doug Horne's exhaustive research not only supports much of the material in this book but goes many steps further. His new work also establishes many other conclusions regarding the facts of the cover-up and references many other sources. One such reference involves his detailed explanation and analysis of the conclusions of independent researcher David Mantik, who is both an MD (radiation oncologist) as well as a PhD in physics; Horne has already stated that Dr. Mantik "has conclusively proven, with his exhaustive optical density measurements of the x-ray materials in the archives, that the three head x-rays in the autopsy collection are not originals but are forged composite copy films that are simply modifications of the authentic skull x-rays. My [Horne's] own hypothesis and reinterpretation of the medical

---

148. Douglass, pp. 312–313 (also, refer to p. 465, note 576).
149. Russell, *On the Trail . . .*, pp. 285–286.
150. Ibid., p. 285- 286; Horne, pp. 998–1000

evidence necessitates that the original head x-rays were exposed only after Humes and Boswell had completed their clandestine postmortem surgery on the skull to remove bullet fragments from the brain and enlarge the head wound."[151] Dr. Mantik's expert analysis of the two lateral skull x-rays proved conclusively that "a very dense optical patch [was] superimposed on the copy films over the occipital-parietal area behind the ear to mask the blow-out or exit wound seen in Dallas in the back of the head." In layman's terms, Dr. Mantik's work has documented the fact that the x-rays are forgeries— altered films created from the original skull x-rays, designed to intentionally distort the depiction of how President Kennedy was killed.[152] In addition to author Horne's new work, Noel Twyman previously included a very detailed layman's interpretation of Dr. Mantik's findings in chapter 14 of his book.[153]

The tangled mess that remains of John F. Kennedy's autopsy records can only be understood in the context of how the above descriptions of the hurried and extemporaneous orders were issued to make his wounds fit a predetermined script caused so much confusion in the military officers, doctors, and pathologists who received those orders. The fact that the autopsy conclusions seem to have evolved over a period of time was apparently caused by a succession of changes in orders leading to multiple versions of autopsy reports; the result was incrementally differing conclusions about the nature of the president's wounds. The intentional fabrications of the x-rays were another facet of the widely based conspiracy to cover up the real cause of Kennedy's murder. In the next chapter, it will be shown that other photographs, as well as the famed Z film, were similarly altered, beginning within hours of the assassination. The conclusions reached will prove overwhelmingly that the hand of Lyndon B. Johnson, aided continually by J. Edgar Hoover, was behind all of the evidence tampering.

The Final Changes to the Plan

The operation went according to plan but for the botched killing of Oswald; it came too late to silence his real voice, which meant that all the phony tapes that had been fabricated to convince the world that his orders came from Castro could no longer be used to justify the invasion. That was probably just the backup, "plan B" anyway; Johnson's preferred plan appears to have been the "lone nut" story, which would avoid the invasion but would require a lot of last-minute "fixes" to make the evidence and witnesses conform to the

---

151. Ibid., pp. 291–292.
152. Ibid.
153. Tyman, pp. 223–241.

tale. It would also require that all of the other planted documents that had been ready for release would need to be destroyed, since they had suddenly become too hot to handle. There were a number of them: Agent Hosty's note, which Hoover and Shanklin ordered destroyed, the FBI cable warning of an assassination attempt that was found in New Orleans, the Mexico City photos, tapes, and transcripts—all had to be destroyed or discredited. The decision to ditch the plan to blame the assassination on Cuba and Russia was made by Johnson and Hoover when it became apparent that the voice on the tape was clearly not that of Lee Harvey Oswald. This tape, fourteen minutes in length, was made at 10:01 a.m. Saturday morning, November 23, 1963, and their conversation was noted in the previous chapter; it was apparently a victim of the hurried plan to destroy all of the evidence containing original recordings and photographs and other evidence of Oswald's visits to Mexico.

The planted evidence trails were used in another way, however. Johnson used them to convince other leaders of the danger of a nuclear war with Cuba and the Soviet Union, which might "kill 39 million Americans." His goal became one of enlisting the support of other national leaders—specifically those he named to the Warren Commission—to cooperate in burying the affair for the good of the country. By sealing the vaults containing the evidence until the year 2039, he would prevent the truth from emerging for at least seventy-five years, and even beyond that, since the trails would be so cold by then that the real truth would be lost forever. By then, thanks to the help he would enlist of unwitting "historians," his enduring legacy as a great president worshipped by millions would be assured.

Though some of the high-level plotters feared that a crime involving so many men could not be contained, the two men at the highest level of planning knew that the secondary conspiracy, to "cover up" the first, would need to be even more precisely executed in order to protect everyone connected to the first phase, "the execution," to ensure ultimate success. Their confidence grew out of the knowledge that they would have ultimate control of the subsequent investigation. They would make maximum use of the federal government's well-developed protocols for maintaining secrecy and the CIA's ability to manage evidence, and people, outside the rules. Eventually, they would screen all physical evidence to ensure that it was congruent with the predetermined verdicts to be reached; that which was not would be destroyed or modified or ignored as necessary. After the screening process, all key evidence would then be stored away for seventy-five years (based, ironically, on the immediate need to maintain "national security'), to allow the Agency plenty of time to perform whatever editing and altering that was required to prepare it for the more credulous of the future historians. By the end of that fateful day, as the stories coming from Dallas switched from "many signs of a conspiracy" to a single "lone nut," the massive cover-up phase of the conspiracy had begun. By Saturday morning, Lyndon Johnson had chosen the course and would permit neither further speculation about a "conspiracy," nor any efforts by investigators, to follow leads in that direction. His basic instincts told him to stay as far away from that as possible, since that might expose the truth.

It is now, finally, time to throw out all of the pseudo evidence created under the watchful eyes of Lyndon Johnson and J. Edgar Hoover and replace it with the credible testimony of the witnesses so long denied their truthful stories: the bystanders in Dealey Plaza, the emergency room doctors at Parkland Hospital, the attendants in Bethesda who told of the horrible scene of decoy ambulances playing a massive "shell game" to move JFK's body around the back lot to get it back to the original casket, the many others who have come forth to describe their peripheral involvement in processing secret photographs, modified films, and documents or their own stories which, combined together, form a complete and believable account of what really happened. The truth has emerged from the common threads woven together throughout this book to reveal a tapestry that more accurately portrays the events of nearly fifty years ago: it was nothing less than a clever takeover of the U.S. government by a man who marshaled the resources of the very government he commanded to execute a secret *coup d'état* that would remain covered up for at least two generations.

PART V

Postassassination Intrigue

Chapter 9

THE COVER-UP CONTINUES

In a loud, hysterical voice he said, *"John, that son of a bitch is going to ruin me.*

If that cocksucker talks, I'm gonna land in jail. . . . I practically raised that motherfucker, and now he's gonna make me the first President of the United States to spend the last days of his life behind bars." He was hysterical . . . *"We're all gonna rot in jail. Tell Nat to tell Bobby that I will give him a million dollars if he takes this rap . . . Bobby must not talk. I'll see to it that he gets a million-dollar settlement."*

—LYNDON JOHNSON TO SPEAKER OF THE HOUSE JOHN McCORMACK
PLEADING WITH HIM TO INTERVENE WITH BOBBY BAKER—FEBRUARY 4, 1964, IN
McCORMACK'S OFFICE

Lyndon Johnson Destroys the Evidence

By 8:00 a.m. Saturday morning, Evelyn Lincoln was in the West Wing packing up her things. The head of the Secret Service White House Detail, Jerry Behn—who was not the most well-liked Secret Service man on the roster—had come into the office. Mrs. Lincoln greeted him, with a not-so-well-disguised, condescending, and bitter, "Jerry, there's something new" remark, which he did not acknowledge.[1] Around eight thirty, the new president, Lyndon B. Johnson, unexpectedly appeared; he asked her to come into the Oval Office and then used his standard "I need you more than you need me" statement, only this time he followed it with a request to have his own staff begin moving into the offices within the hour, saying that he had an appointment at 9:30 a.m.[2] Robert Kennedy arrived shortly after this encounter and, seeing Johnson coming toward the Oval Office, "spread his arms at the doorway and shrieked to the new President that he could not

---

1. Manchester, p. 453.
2. Ibid.

536

enter. 'Don't come in here! . . . You should not be here! You don't deserve to be here."[3] Bobby later confirmed that a confrontation took place and that he was merely trying to keep Johnson away while his brother's belongings were being packed and removed from the office, which is what he clearly explained to Johnson.[4] Bobby had to explain to Johnson that it would take a little time to crate up the considerable personal property that JFK had left behind before turning over the office to him. He asked Johnson, "Can you wait?" Johnson allowed that he could wait a little while then stated that he personally did not want to occupy the White House already, but that "his advisers were insisting upon it." [5] (This assertion, though an obvious lie, ironically reveals more of the real truth of what was going on at that moment, considering everything said before about Johnson's "whoppers.") Almost as soon as JFK's portrait was removed from behind Evelyn's desk, a huge gold-framed portrait of Lyndon Johnson was swiftly hung.[6]

After leaving the West Wing, Johnson went to McGeorge Bundy's office around 9:00 a.m., and according to both Manchester's book and Johnson's diary, he met with DCI McCone for a short briefing. It was so short that it was almost nonexistent, according to McCone's aide Russell Jack Smith, who had accompanied McCone to the White House and found the new president in the basement secretarial area outside Bundy's office. Larry Hancock quotes Mr. Smith: "Johnson stood among the typing and ringing telephones to talk briefly with McCone and Smith and 'had no interest whatever in being briefed.' After some inconsequential chatting, he turned back into Bundy's office. This narrative only underscores Johnson's apparent lack of any real concern about any national security implications of the assassination."[7]

Within twelve hours of the assassination, Johnson and his aide Cliff Carter had succeeded in having all pertinent evidence at the crime scene seized and sent to Washington. Starting with the illegal transfer of Kennedy's body—essential to the plan so it could be modified to fit the "official scenario"—the other evidence moved to Washington included Kennedy's clothing, the bloodstained limousine, the murder weapon and the "magic bullet," and all other ballistics evidence. Since the hole in the front windshield of the limousine did not conform

---

3. Russo, p. 383 (Ref. David, Lester and Irene David. *Bobby Kennedy, The Making of a Folk Hero.* New York: Dodd, Mead & Co., 1986, p. 215).

4. Ibid.

5. Manchester. pp. 454–455.

6. Manchester, pp. 454–455.

7. Hancock, pp. 290–291 (ref. Smith, *The Unknown CIA; My Three Decades with the Agency*, Potomac Books, 1989, p. 163.

to the official version of events being propagated, it was replaced initially with a piece of glass which—unlike the windshield that had been seen by a number of witnesses who saw a hole completely through the glass[8]—only showed cracks emanating from a small nick. Three days later, the limousine was secretly shipped to Detroit to be cleaned and repaired, and a few weeks later it was sent to Cincinnati to be completely rebuilt. In his article "A Study of the Presidential Limousine," Doug Weldon cites Gary Shaw, who stated in his book *Cover-Up* that "within 48 hours of the shots in Dealey Plaza the Kennedy death car was shipped to the Ford Motor Company in Detroit and completely destroyed as far as evidence was concerned."[9] Only two men in the country had the authority to make these decisions to destroy the crime scene: One was James J. Rowley, head of the Secret Service; clearly, though, a prudent man, one with a modicum of concern for his career, would not have been willing to make such a decision to tamper with evidence involving the "crime of the century." The only other man was his new boss, who was also the new president, President Lyndon B. Johnson. The man given the responsibility for doing the glass replacement work on November 25, 1963 George Whitacre Sr., finally, near the end of his life, gave in to requests to reveal the secret he had held for thirty years; he can be seen on video with Doug Weldon, a JFK researcher.[10]

Several weeks after the car was repaired, it was decided that merely fixing the damage was not enough; the car was taken to Cincinnati where it was completely renovated and bulletproofed; it was as though budgetary constraints prevented the purchase of a replacement, making it necessary to rebuild JFK's car according to new specifications because only it would do as the presidential limousine. The car was completely rebuilt, including "a souped-up motor, two and a half tons of new steel plating, three-inch glass, and bulletproof tires, but Johnson rarely used it."[11] In fact, a new limousine was built and delivered a few years later to Johnson. JFK's limousine continued to be used through the presidencies of Nixon, Ford, and finally the Jimmy Carter administration. This completely rebuilt incarnation of the limousine is now on display at the Ford Motor Company's headquarters museum in Detroit.

Hoover Throttles the FBI Investigators

Four minutes after the assassination, J. Edgar Hoover received word that Kennedy was "perhaps fatally wounded," and he shortly called Robert Kennedy

---

8. See "Bullet Holes in the limousine and extra bullets in Dealey Plaza (http://www.youtube.com/watch?v=UtFoPCKVp-8&feature=player_embedded).
9. See Kennedy Assassination Chronicles: www.maryferrell.org/mffweb/archive.
10. See youtube.com: Limo to Detroit, Parts 1 and 2.
11. Ibid., p. 631.

on their direct line—that had not been used in months—and advised him that the president had been shot. Twenty minutes later, Hoover phoned again to deliver the final blow. "The president's dead," he said and promptly hung up. Kennedy would remember, his voice was oddly flat—"not quite as excited as if he were reporting the fact that he had found a Communist on the faculty of Howard University."[12] Later that day, according to ex-FBI agent William W. Turner, "when Robert [Kennedy] arrived at his office, he picked up the hot line phone. Hoover was in his office with several aides when it rang . . . and rang . . . and rang. When it stopped ringing, the Director snapped to an aide, 'Now get that phone [which RFK had installed so he could talk to him instantly] back on Miss Gandy's desk.'"[13] The day after JFK's assassination, the FBI stopped sending any reports or other information to the Organized Crime Section of the Justice Department.[14]

Except for his call to RFK and James Rowley, head of the Secret Service, Hoover called only one other man that afternoon: Billy Byars, Texas oil millionaire and member of the "Del Charro Set" who joined Hoover once a year for a gambling and party holiday in La Jolla, California. Byars's gambling partners included Clint Murchison Sr., H. L. Hunt, and Sid Richardson, all of whom had been frequent guests at Benny Binion's "Legendary Top of the Hill Terrace" in the 1950s.[15] Richardson, Murchison, and Hoover were only an arm's length away from Jack Ruby, through their mutual friend Joe Campisi, who eventually replaced Joseph Civello as the Mafia leader of Dallas; both Campisi and Civello were Carlos Marcello's deputies in Dallas and the heads of Dallas's relatively small Mafia family. As noted by author John H. Davis, this was "a reality that J. Edgar Hoover tried to keep from the attention of the Warren Commission and which the commission itself suppressed by not mentioning it in its report or published exhibits."[16] The way Hoover kept his association with Mob leaders and the oil millionaires secret was by having a special detail of FBI agents accompany him to ensure that mobsters would not come up to him in public at the racetrack.[17] He evidently found that to be easier than simply avoiding them in the first place. Hoover would later say to Byars's son, "If I told you what I really know [about the assassination], it would be very dangerous to the country. Our whole political system could be disrupted."[18] It is one of the least

---

12. Summers, *Official and Confidential*, p. 314.
13. Turner, p. 95.
14. Scheim, p. 249.
15. Scott, p. 206; Marrs, p. 394.
16. Davis, John H. p. 403.
17. Scott, pp. 207–208.
18. Summers, *Official and Confidential*, p. 330.

noticed points—and most remarkable ironies—of this story that this was probably the only issue on which J. Edgar Hoover and Robert F. Kennedy ever agreed. According to author David Talbot, Bobby once said "If the American people knew the truth about Dallas, there'd be blood in the streets."[19]

Shutting Down the Mexico-Cuba Option

In his landmark book *Plausible Denial*, author Mark Lane succinctly described the brilliance of Harvey's plan, which provided for a quick way of connecting Oswald to the assassination—and the dual purpose potential to be the catalyst for a Cuba invasion in the event a "conspiracy" could not be denied—but which could be efficiently jettisoned as a "lead" by the FBI when it had served its usefulness:

> *In September 1963, the CIA, having planned to assassinate President Kennedy,* established a false trail, a charade that would inexorably lead to Lee Harvey Oswald after the murder in Dallas. The plan was brilliantly conceived. Not only would it implicate an innocent man in the crime and thus spare the CIA from responsibility, but it would focus attention upon Oswald, a man with connections to the FBI. The FBI connection would freeze J. Edgar Hoover into inaction because of fear that his bureau might be terminally embarrassed.[20]

On December 12, Hoover pressured the Mexico City LEGAT to shut down its continuing investigation and on December 18 directed the New Orleans field office to shut down the investigation of David Ferrie and his connections to Oswald, Banister, Shaw, and Carlos Marcello. All of this explains why the Warren Commission's report about Oswald's activities in New Orleans was superficial and abruptly ended before his connections to Ferrie, Shaw, and Banister were traced. Specific other actions would quickly follow, including the removal of all documents relating to Oswald's journeys to Mexico[21] from his file and the shutdown of any further investigations into his Mexican activities. As reported by Thomas Mann, a career diplomat in the State Department, "The message I received from Hoover, very soon after the assassination, was, 'We don't want to hear any more about this case. And tell the Mexican government not to do any more investigating; we just

---

19. Talbot, p. 268.
20. Lane , *Plausible. . .*,p. 54.
21. Russell, p. 491.

want to hush it up.'"[22] Ambassador Mann had apparently been coached by his superiors to deny the existence of any evidence pointing to a conspiracy because of the fear of war with Cuba and the Soviet Union. Lawrence Keenan, the FBI agent Hoover sent to Mexico City to discredit the Gilberto Alvarado, claim that he had seen Oswald accepting money from someone at the Cuban Embassy, said that "The most vivid memory I have is that of Ambassador [Thomas] Mann telling me 'The missiles are going to fly.'"[23]

Keenan was sent to Mexico City two days after the assassination, armed with practically no knowledge of the CIA activities leading up to that point, and given no support by the CIA's men—Win Scott and David Phillips— once he arrived; the interagency rivalry created an "impenetrable wall between the CIA and the FBI. There was not enough trust to coordinate the investigation,' Keenan points out. 'There was absolutely no conversation between myself and [Win] Scott. It just wasn't done."[24] In 1993, Keenan told his interviewer on the PBS Frontline radio:[25]

> The information at the time was definitely that it was no conspiracy. The crime was already solved. There was definitely a feeling that there was not going to be any investigation pursuing this. Within a few days . . . [it was confirmed that] this was a single assassin and there was no thought of any further investigation. The idea was to wrap this thing up as soon as possible . . . Any idea that Oswald had a confederate or was part of a group or a conspiracy definitely placed a man's career in jeopardy.

The cover-up plan, as designed by its chief architect, was working flawlessly after that first day, when the many signs of the faux conspiracy (plan B) had already surfaced; now the shift away from that and back to plan A had been effectively implanted, as evidenced by the words of Lawrence Keenan, so that every man involved in any way in the cover-up phase of the conspiracy knew what the object of their work product was to be: everyone knew implicitly, if not explicitly, that there was to be no investigation into any conspiracy—not only one of foreign origin, but domestic as well—and ignoring that directive would only mean the end of their career.

When the commission met on December 5, Hoover sent them a not-so-subtle message about who was really in charge of them by refusing to even send a representative; when he sent them a copy of the FBI's "final report" on December 9, 1963, he included a demand that all members publicly agree

---

22. Ibid., p. 453.
23. Russo, p. 357.
24. Ibid. pp. 357–358.
25. Ibid. p. 358.

with his conclusions. The commission was stymied by Hoover's intransigence and came to the realization that, without its own investigative staff, they were dependent upon the FBI files. On December 16, they issued a request for specific files; on the same day Hoover met privately with Johnson "for an off the record luncheon in an obvious effort to deflect the Commission's demand," successfully delaying a response for almost one month.[26]

As detailed by author Mark North, "On January 27 the chief counsel and other members apparently view the Zapruder, Hughes and Nix films. On January 22 and 27 they meet in secret session, openly discussing the reality of the situation. Hoover is essentially charged with obstruction of justice. The seriousness of the situation appears to overwhelm some members of the group."[27] After two more months of such wrangling, the commission's staff attempted to entrap Hoover into admitting there were connections between Oswald and the Mafia; Hoover's response was to release derogatory information on Rankin's staff assistant, Norman Redlich, to the press as Hoover marshaled his supporters to demand "full-security investigations" by the Bureau of all staff members. The commission was stunned by the ferocity of Hoover's counterattack and instructed Rankin to abandon his plan to confront Hoover at the hearing. When he finally does appear before the commission, on May 14, members Ford and Dulles managed to keep a muzzle on Rankin, preventing him from pursuing his line of questioning about the FBI's obstructed investigation into Oswald's Mafia and Mexico City connections.[28] Lyndon Johnson, who had originally called for the completion of the Warren Commission's review by February, then pressed Earl Warren to conclude the proceedings by April.[29] After repeated delays and rescheduling, as described elsewhere, eventually they would conclude the investigations by late June, allowing the last few months for the staff to write and publish the voluminous report.

The FBI's Incriminating Actions

Among the other incriminating actions already noted, author Noel Twyman, in meticulous detail, chronicled the numerous incriminating actions taken by the FBI (read: Hoover) to throw off any remaining signs of an honest and open investigation:[30]

26. North, p. 398.
27. Ibid., pp. 398–399.
28. Ibid., pp. 399–400.
29. Ibid., p. 401.
30. Twyman, pp. 773–774.

- The FBI cooperated with the Dallas Police in falsely pinning the murder of Police Officer J. D. Tippit solely on Oswald when ballistic and testimonial evidence showed overwhelmingly that at least two people and two guns were involved; also, the timing of Oswald's movements would have been yet another impossible feat for him.
- Hoover knew very soon after the assassination that separate shots had hit Kennedy and Connally; therefore it had to have been a conspiracy.
- The FBI cooperated with the CIA to suppress evidence of an Oswald impersonator in Mexico City; the tapes between Johnson and Hoover reveal that Hoover knew there was an Oswald imposter.
- No mention was made of H. L. Hunt in any of the FBI reports to the Warren Commission even despite his obvious linkage to many incriminating actions which he had made against Kennedy; the only action taken by the FBI was to urge him to leave Dallas and to assist him in relocating to Washington where he asked to go so that he could "help Lyndon."
- One of the events which implicated H. L. Hunt was the gunrunning operation going on in Dallas, which involved militant Cuban exiles, the Minutemen, John Thomas Masen, and Jack Ruby; John Elrod's arrest on November 22, 1963, would have led directly to H. L. Hunt and General Edwin Walker, both friends of J. Edgar Hoover.
- The FBI concealed information in its possession shortly after the assassination concerning the French OAS terrorist Jean Soutre, who was in Dallas on November 22, and was expelled shortly thereafter; only an inquiry by French intelligence agencies inadvertently exposed this event over fifteen years afterward. FBI documents also show that both Michel Mertz and Michel Roux were also in Dallas the day of the assassination; Soutre had connections to E. Howard Hunt, General Walker, and General Willoughby.
- Finally, as detailed below, the FBI and Secret Service had taken possession of the Zapruder film and the Nix film by the time they were altered; evidence already published, as described below, shows that Lyndon Johnson and Hoover knew about—even directed—Z film alterations during the long weekend of national mourning of JFK's murder in Dealey Plaza.

The Fabrication of Photographic Evidence: "The Z Film"

Researchers Jack White and Jim Marrs, who interviewed French freelance journalist William Reymond, prepared a compelling video titled, "The Great Zapruder Film Hoax," which proves conclusively that the Zapruder film was, in fact, altered. This 57.5-minute film, and other similar films, can be seen at Google Videos by doing a search with that title. For the last fifteen minutes of the video (starting at 42.38), Jim Marrs interviews Mr. Reymond regarding his knowledge of the original, unedited, version of the Zapruder film. This is compelling new evidence of the tampering of the film, which we shall further explore below, as to exactly how this occurred. Another facet not mentioned in the film, but noted by Twyman as additional evidence of the film tampering, was the impossibly quick turn with which limousine driver William Greer turned his head at two points in the shooting sequence. Twyman's detailed study of this aspect proved that these head turns were supposedly done twice as fast as the professional tennis players he hired could complete similar head turns.

Mr. Reymond's statements regarding the original Zapruder film, which he believes was actually purchased by H. L. Hunt two hours after the assassination, was used to create the copy later sold to *Life* magazine and hidden for decades. The story that Mr. Zapruder told others, about him having sold the original to *Life*, was either a subterfuge by him or in fact what he believed had happened, unaware that the original and three "first-generation copies" of it had actually been made after being hastily edited from the original. There are various interpretations of how the Zapruder film was altered and the intention of the plotters in making the alterations, but the consensus of many researchers is that frames were deleted from the film in order to portray the gunshots as coming only from the rear and to hide evidence that Kennedy was shot from the front; additionally, it was intended to cover up the fact that the limousine practically stopped just as the final shots were being fired.

According to Richard B. Trask, "Through Agent Sorrels' efforts, by the evening of November 22 the Secret Service now had two first-generation copies of Zapruder's film. At 9:55 p.m. Agent Max D. Phillips hastily hand-lettered a brief memo to Secret Service Chief James Rowley enclosing one of the two copies of the film to Washington. Phillips noted, 'According to Mr. Zapruder, the position of the assassin was behind Mr. Zapruder.' . . . Late that night or early Saturday morning the Secret Service, through Inspector Thomas Kelly, loaned the Dallas FBI the second first-generation copy of the film. Unable to have copies made locally, some time after 5 p.m. on Saturday, Shanklin in Dallas was instructed by Washington to send the film immediately to FBI headquarters on a commercial flight. That same night Shanklin forwarded the film requesting that the FBI lab make three copies—one for Washington and two for the Dallas FBI office informing them that, 'It is felt one copy should be sufficient,' and that 'You are cautioned that the film is for official use only.' Although a *Life* magazine representative later stated that on Saturday, November 23, he had obtained both Zapruder's original and first-generation copy, he only bought print rights to the film and it is likely that Zapruder retained one copy, especially in light of the fact that Zapruder later testified that Sorrels came to his office quite a few times to show the film to different people. From Saturday afternoon, November 23, until about November 26, Sorrels did not have a copy of the film, the two having been sent to Washington, and he most likely needed to view Zapruder's copy. It also seems probable that others, including CBS's Dan Rather, saw the film in Zapruder's office on November 25 as the reporter broadcast a description of its contents that day as if he had just viewed it that same morning."[31] As Dick Russell described it, "Dan Rather, at the time a local news reporter in Dallas, had been the first journalist to see the twenty-second-long 'home movie' taken by dressmaker Abraham Zapruder. Rather proceeded to tell a national TV audience that "the second shot the third shot total but the second shot hit President Kennedy and there was no doubt there, his head . . . went forward with considerable violence . . ."[32]

In fact, the footage eventually released showed precisely the opposite. In his book *The Camera Never Blinks*, Rather later defended his 'mistake,' saying it had happened because his viewing of the film was so hurried.[33] In considering how such a mistake might be made, one option is the most obvious—that Dan Rather purposely misrepresented what he had seen—but another less obvious, yet arguably more likely answer to this paradox, is that the film itself was edited after Rather had seen it. If the frames involving the actual shot from the front were excised—which would have also been some of the same frames that would be deleted to hide the fact that the limousine had momentarily stopped—and those frames were then replaced by doctored frames intended to prove a shot from the rear; it is axiomatic that another (unintended) result would be a change in how Kennedy was first thrust forward and in the next instant, thrown violently backward and to his left. The rush of getting all of this done in a limited time frame, to satisfy the demands of the conspirators, would have added to the sloppiness of the altered product.

Another long-held secret bearing on Rather's report from Dallas—which was done Sunday evening, only two days after the assassination—was revealed a few years later, when it was disclosed that many of the major news organizations, including his employer, *CBS*, (along with *Life* and *Time* and the *New York Times*) had been participating in the CIA's Operation Mockingbird, described in chapter 3, to facilitate "the company's"

---

31. Trask, *Pictures* . . ., pp. 80–81.
32. Ibid., p. 87.
33. Russell, *On the Trail* . . ., p. 34.

propaganda to the masses. Carl Bernstein, of Watergate fame, wrote in a *Rolling Stone* article about those media organization's ties to the CIA.[34] Regardless of which option one might consider as the key to solve the matter of why Rather's statement was diametrically opposite of what the extant Zapruder film showed, the implications of the CIA's involvement could not be more sinister.

A Possible Explanation of Dan Rather's Misstatement: How the Z Film was Altered

In 1967, Josiah Thompson published his first book *Six Seconds in Dallas* in which he called the Zapruder film "the nearest thing to 'absolute truth' about the sequence of events in Dealey Plaza." Over the years, doubts began to arise after the film became widely available in the late 1970s. Only prints of selected frames were available before the film was first shown on television twelve years after the assassination, in 1975. As more and more of the film's anomalies came under scrutiny, the arguments for and against the "alteration" thesis grew.

There is abundant evidence, if one can train his or her mind to accept it, that the Zapruder film was altered to portray JFK's murder as having been caused by three shots from behind while eliminating in the process three (3) to five (5) other shots.[35] Altogether, there were four objectives: (1) to attempt to make it show that all shots came from the rear (which was plainly a failure), (2) that only two (originally three until that proved even more impossible) shots hit Kennedy and Connally and (3) to eliminate evidence that Greer had stopped, or nearly stopped, the limousine just as JFK was being executed and (4) delete the earliest frames, which showed Greer's difficulty in completing the 120-degree turn from Houston to Elm Street; a maneuver which conflicted with a Secret Service dictum against using a route which required such a turn.

Many people who have long accepted the premise of a conspiracy in the assassination have still not been persuaded that the film was altered. The dissension over the issue evolved during the 1990s into what can now be characterized as a raging battle between the two groups during the decade beginning in the year 2000. Some of the highlights from the continuing feud include:

- The 2000 book *Murder in Dealey Plaza,* edited by Dr. James Fetzer, in which the essays by Doug Horne, Jack White, and David Mantik argued persuasively for the alteration thesis.

---

34. Ibid., p. 37.
35. Twyman, Noel, *Bloody Treason* (e-version), Appendix F.

- The case was further strengthened by the original authors and joined by additional pro- and antialterationist authors—among others, David Healy; John Costella, PhD; David Lifton; Noel Twyman; Rich DellaRosa; Josiah Thompson, PhD; and Gary Mack—in Dr. Fetzer's 2003 sequel, *The Great Zapruder Film Hoax: Deceit and Deception in the Death of JFK.*
- David R. Wrone's 2003 response, *The Zapruder Film: Reframing JFK's Assassination,* attempted to disprove the theories advanced in the earlier books.
- Harrison E. Livingstone, in his 2004 book *The Hoax of the Century: Decoding the Forgery of the Zapruder Film,* recast the arguments for alteration.
- Josiah Thompson's three-part response to the earlier works was posted on the Mary Ferrell Foundation Web site in 2007: "Bedrock Evidence in the Kennedy Assassination."
- Doug Horne's massive 2009 five-volume book devoted over 180 pages to a grand finale, conclusive end—"Case Closed" last word—on the subject.

The problem I have in addressing this issue is that to thoroughly do so would require many more pages than could be fitted into this book. Besides, it is unnecessary. Doug Horne has proven his case; one needs to only acquire his volume IV to understand why. Noel Twyman is in substantial agreement with Horne's position, but has gone further, in naming both Lyndon Johnson and J. Edgar Hoover as having been involved in the plot and in the cover-up, though he failed to determine that Lyndon Johnson was the mastermind of the conspiracy.[36] This book merely adds that last element in a case that has already been proven beyond a reasonable doubt.

The summary analysis, below, of how the Zapruder film was acquired and altered before being copied was originally developed by senior Assassination Records Review Board (ARRB) analyst Douglas P. Horne following an interview he, with three other ARRB staff, had conducted with the former manager of the CIA's National Photo Interpretation Center (NPIC), Homer McMahon. As noted earlier, Horne's complete five-volume study *Inside the Assassination Records Review Board: The U.S. Government's Final Attempt to Reconcile the Conflicting Medical Evidence in the Assassination of JFK,* published shortly before the manuscript for this book was completed, includes, in meticulous detail, a strong argument in support of the thesis. Noel Twyman's research, cited below, shows the general steps taken to revise the Zapruder film and other photographic records of the assassination to fit the mosaic Johnson created. The long-suppressed truth of how the Zapruder film was confiscated by the FBI and modified with help from the Secret

---

36. Ibid. (see also Appendix G)

Service in such a way as to reflect a contrived story about three shots being fired from the TSBD building has now emerged.

The NPIC was created by the CIA to analyze and interpret photos taken by the U-2 spy plane, and the scope was later expanded to include photos taken from satellites. The center was started by Arthur C. Lundahl who had started his career in 1953. By 1963, it had been relocated from its original location to Building 213, a seven-story concrete building in the Washington Navy Yard at First and M Streets SE. The interpreter's use of tools became more and more sophisticated, and they built a library of images that enabled them to compare a specific place with what it looked like at some point in the past.[37] According to author Ronald Kessler, NPIC used computers to analyze the images and (quoting from William E. Burrows in his book *Deep Black*), the computers "were 'routinely being used to correct for distortions made by the satellite's imaging sensors and by atmospheric effects, sharpen out-of-focus images, build multicolored single images out of several pictures taken in different spectral bands to make certain patterns more obvious, change the amount of contrast between the objects under scrutiny and their backgrounds, extract particular features while diminishing or eliminating their backgrounds altogether, enhance shadows, suppress glint from reflections of the sun and a great deal more."[38]

In summary, the story developed by Horne and Twyman involved a Secret Service agent named Bill Smith delivering to Homer McMahon, the head of the NPIC, a day or two after the assassination but before Kennedy's funeral, an 8 mm amateur movie of the assassination. The film was the same type—a double 8 Kodachrome II, unsplit, which meant the overall width was 16 mm. Smith requested that 5" × 7" blow-up prints be made of selected frames. This and other subsequent meetings were first described by Doug Horne in reports about interviews with McMahon and his assistant Ben Hunter in the 2000 book *Murder in Dealey Plaza*.[39] There were a total of four meetings and two telephone call reports during the summer of 1997, all conducted by ARRB staff including Doug Horne.

McMahon maintained that he produced the requested prints, "perhaps as many as 40, but not more than about 40." McMahon described the work as "an all night job" and said they were instructed by Bill Smith that this was top secret, and not to tell anyone, even their supervisor, about what they did. Bill Smith told McMahon to select frames that would show only three shots from behind, which was what they wanted to see; he explained himself,

---

37. Kessler, The CIA . . . pp. 69–70.
38. Ibid. p. 70 (Ref. Burrows, *Deep Black: Space Espionage and National Security*, Random House, 1986, p. 219).
39. *Murder in Dealey Plaza*, edited by James H. Fetzer, PhD, pp. 311–324.

"*You can't fight City hall*" (emphasis in original). In a separate interview of McMahon's assistant Ben Hunter by Horne and ARRB staff, after watching the film a number of times he stated his opinion that *President Kennedy was shot 6 to 8 times from three different locations*, but that this was ultimately ignored (emphasis added).

In his latest work, Doug Horne described a new revelation that he personally discovered in 2009:[40] On Saturday evening, November 23, 1963, a day before "Bill Smith" brought the Zapruder film to Homer McMahon for the requested prints, Dino Brugioni—who had been chief of the NPIC Information Branch and was author of *Eyeball to Eyeball*, an account of the Cuban missile crisis referenced elsewhere in this book—had received the film from two Secret Service agents and used it to create briefing boards. It was found that the briefing boards now in the Archives are not the ones created on that first night, but the ones done on the second night. Horne concluded that there were specific reasons for the two events, one of which was that the Secret Service wanted to ensure that the technicians who saw and worked on the exhibits during the first event, on Saturday night, would not participate in the second event on Sunday night; they wanted a completely different cast of characters to conduct the work in the second event. His conclusion was that Dino Brugioni and his crew were working from the true camera original version on Saturday night and Homer McMahon and his crew were working from an altered Zapruder film created Sunday in an optical printer at the "Hawkeye Plant" at Kodak headquarters in Rochester, New York. The reason this had been done at this top secret, CIA funded facility was because "blowing up a small 8 mm film frame to 40 times its original size for the making of internegatives would have required *the highest quality product available*, otherwise the resulting [altered film] would have been degraded."[41] These witnesses to both events confirm with authority how the Zapruder film was altered over the weekend following the assassination, even before JFK's cold body was interred in Arlington on that gray, cold, and windy Monday, November 25, 1963.

As noted by Noel Twyman, "McMahon said that [the prints were] mounted by others on briefing boards at NPIC and delivered first to John McCone at CIA and then to Lyndon Johnson at the White House."[42] Gus Russo in his book *Live by the Sword* confirmed much of McMahon's testimony, and went one step further, in his interview of NPIC photo analyst Dino Brugioni[43] on January 27, 1998:

40. Horne, *Inside the ARRB* . . . . Vol. IV, pp. 1230–1239.
41. Ibid.
42. Twyman, Appendix F (Mobipocket ebook) p. 2654 [1/2010].
43. Twyman, Appendix F [January 2010] (Ref. Russo, *Live by the Sword*, pp. 330–340).

The night after the murder, the Secret Service brought over to the CIA a copy of an 8mm home movie taken of the murder, the "Zapruder film." Now, in another part of the CIA's headquarters, the National Photographic Interpretation Center, the Agency's top photo analyst, Dino Brugioni, watched in horror as the top of the president's head exploded in a shower of crimson. Brugioni recently recalled: *There were six or seven of us at the meeting. We were asked to time it, which was difficult because the camera was spring-loaded. We also developed still frames, which we enlarged and mounted on a large board which [Director] McCone took over to President Johnson. Later, we had the U-2 photograph Oswald and Marina's residences in Minsk. We gave the photos to Richard Helms.*[44]

When it's all added up, the essence of the testimony and statements shows that the new president was up to his ears in directing the entire cover-up operation to delude the public. By then, with the help of his friends J. Edgar Hoover and H. L. Hunt, the fabrication of the photographic records of the entire assassination and JFK's bungled autopsy would have been well under his control. Johnson and Hoover didn't have to commiserate too long about what to do with the piles of photographic artifacts which had been collected from the witnesses, many of whom were forced to hand over the films and photographs, never to see them again; in other cases, when the photos were returned to the owners, they noted that alterations were made to the evidence while in FBI custody.[45] Though all three of them were extremely delusional, and Johnson was probably suffering from manic periods of paranoia, they knew that all traces of their criminal acts had to be hidden, throughout the photographic evidence before them. Because of the involvement of the renegade CIA officials and high-level military officers, they knew their own identities would be protected through the existing security protocols of secret classifications, the requirement that everyone involved be sworn to secrecy, and of course, the invocation of all the precepts of covert operations.

The Zapruder film was the most important artifact presented to this trio, and it was essential that it be edited such that it would corroborate the official story. The process followed to effect the changes would have involved changes dictated by Johnson to a military officer, who would have taken detailed notes referenced to each film and frame; the film would then be dispatched to one of the facilities having the required K-II equipment.[46] Though the identities of

---

44. Russo, pp. 339–340.
45. Ibid., p. 338.
46. Twyman, Appendix G (e-book version).

everyone involved in the photographic fabrications have not been established, it has been clearly established by Horne and Twyman that it was done. In Twyman's case, an imminently qualified expert, Dr. Roderick Ryan, a highly credentialed expert filmmaker in Hollywood, was recruited to conduct independent analysis of the film; he determined that the blood spray had been "painted" on the film.[47] Following this lead, Doug Horne consulted with other film experts in his latest work. He described the results of their review: "The considered opinions of our two film restoration professionals, who together have spent over five decades restoring and working with films of the late 1940s, 1950s, and 1960s (when visual effects were done optically—not digitally), in that one moment superseded the statements of all those in the JFK research community who have insisted for two decades now that the Zapruder film could not have been altered, because the technology did not exist to do so. Our two restoration experts know special effects in modern motion picture films far better than Josiah Thompson, or David Wrone, or Gary Mack, or Robert Groden, or me, for that matter; and their subjective opinion [better—professional judgment] trumps Rollie Zavada's as well—a man who has absolutely no experience whatsoever in the postproduction of visual effects in motion picture films. And while Rollie Zavada, a lifetime Kodak employee receiving retirement pay from his former employer, would certainly have an apparent conflict of interest in blowing the whistle on Zapruder film forgery if his former employer was involved in its alteration, our three Hollywood film professionals had no vested interest, one way or the other, in the outcome of their examination of the 6K scans on August 25, 2009."[48]

Anyone interested in pursuing this issue further should obtain volume IV of Doug Horne's book referenced above. His compelling account of how he went from believing the Zapruder film was authentic to becoming convinced that it had been altered, and could no longer be relied upon as a reliable record of the assassination, is persuasive additional proof of the existence of a widespread, immediate cover-up put together by the highest level, top secret U.S. military and intelligence organizations. While I agree with most of his conclusions, I've noted elsewhere specific points of his conclusions for which I disagree.

Conclusions Based on the Z Film

The most likely explanation for the obvious incompatibility of Dan Rather's description of the Zapruder film—which was made, according to an analysis by

---

47. Twyman, pp. 154–160.
48. Horne, *Inside the ARRB*, Vol. IV, p. 1361.

Richard Trask, on Saturday, November 23, and gave the first radio interview on that date and then repeated the description again in a radiocast on Monday, November 25[49]—is that the film he saw was the original, unaltered Zapruder film. Both of the dates noted were before the film alterations could have been completed. It was during this period that Johnson, Hoover, and Hunt were sorting through all the photographic evidence and issuing instructions and orders to make the required modifications.

Given everything else Johnson and Hoover did during those seventy-two hours, it is not a stretch to suggest that they were not merely looking at modified photos and deleted frames from film footage; they were clearly involved from the start in deciding which photos and frames would be deleted or altered and which would be made available to the press. These sessions would have doubtlessly included not only the Zapruder and Nix films but the autopsy photos and the films and photographs confiscated by the fake Secret Service agents in Dealey Plaza, who spread out immediately to find everyone with a camera. A number of witnesses independently and immediately reported this had happened to them, such film and photos never having being returned to them (including Gordon Arnold, Jean Hill, Mary Moorman, and Beverly Oliver, among others). Just as many actual photographic records disappeared, newly fabricated films and photographs were created to bolster Johnson's "official storyline."

The statements indicating Lyndon Johnson was personally involved in reviewing the photographs, movie films, and other evidence is completely consistent with other reports of him micromanaging the evidence in the days immediately following the assassination. Senator Ralph Yarborough had been shocked to find out how closely he was reviewing artifacts and evidence; he found that Johnson had set up a process to review all vital assassination information even before it ever went to Attorney General Robert Kennedy or the Warren Commission.[50] It is the insightful observations by people such as Senator Yarborough that lend additional credence to the conclusions formed in this book about Johnson's absolute control over all aspects of the cover-up operation; he was the final arbiter in the decisions of what evidence would be used and what would be discarded, what would be tagged for rebuilding or fabricating and what would be "inadvertently" lost or destroyed.

This evidence shows that Johnson and Hoover—and probably H. L. Hunt as well, since he had quickly departed Dallas for Washington DC after having been called there by J. Edgar Hoover—participated in directing the Z film alterations throughout the weekend following Kennedy's murder.

---

49. Trask, p. 86.
50. Marrs, p. 482.

Johnson no doubt knew in advance—undoubtedly having even preplanned the general steps—the need for having body alterations made to support the favored "lone nut" theory if that option was selected, which it was, as described below. By the time the photos began coming in, Johnson must have also wished he could have also gotten to the Altgens photo a little earlier, to have his picture pasted into the spot where he should have been. It is obvious that the reason for his dissembling, contrived "testimony" to the Warren Commission was due to his absence in that photograph, as evidenced by his claim concerning agent Youngblood's fictitious act of immediately slamming him to the floor. Based upon these stunning revelations, it should now be clear to all that there were three people—two following the script laid by the other—who were jointly orchestrating this particular vignette. But it was all according to the grand play—a masterpiece of design and execution—which had been developed over a period of nearly four years by the most brilliant, and evil, political force the country had ever seen: *Lyndon B. ("Bull") Johnson, determined at all costs to fulfill his lifelong dream, in the only realistic way possible for him to become president of the United States.*

Fast Forward Four Years: The Jim Garrison Investigation

Between the tangled story about Dan Rather's report from Dallas concerning the Zapruder film, the fact that the film was kept under wraps by *Life* for the next twelve years and the later developments about Operation Mockingbird, a further enigma occurred four years after the assassination. Having concluded in November 1966 that the single-bullet theory did not hold up, both *Time* and *Life* paradoxically decided to stop further reporting on anomalies of the Kennedy assassination two months later. This was exactly the same time that the Garrison trial was getting underway in New Orleans. It is abundantly clear now that a lot of high-level officials in the CIA, the FBI, the Justice Department, and the White House were very worried about what might be revealed in that trial and nothing was spared in getting it shut down before it got out of control.[51] Whatever his excesses or mistakes, the plain fact was that D. A. Garrison was getting much too close to people and evidence that had not been sufficiently buried.

On February 16, 1967, Hoover had been shown an article from the New Orleans *States-Item* about the reinvestigation being launched by Garrison into the Kennedy assassination, and that one of his chief suspects was David Ferrie, who had known Lee Harvey Oswald for at least eight years and was then working for Carlos Marcello. Author John H. Davis

---

51. Horne, *Inside the ARRB*, Vol. IV, p. 1361.

described what happened next. "FBI cable traffic during the last two weeks of February reveals that news of the Garrison investigation convulsed Hoover. Immediately he began marshalling his allies in the government and the media in a discreet, behind-the-scenes effort to discredit Garrison and undermine his investigation."[52] His "allies in the government" would have certainly included President Johnson and James Angleton, and clearly many others on down the hierarchy. Immediately after that, Garrison arranged to put Ferrie up at the Fontainbleau Hotel but for some inexplicable reason, he left the hotel on February 21 and returned to his apartment.[53] In the early hours of the next morning, Ferrie was found dead, the coroner later ruling it of "natural causes" despite the existence of two typed suicide notes found in the apartment, neither of which had been signed. Garrison had good reason to question that verdict, though the autopsy pointed to a burst blood vessel in the brain. One of the medications he had found in Ferrie's apartment was Proloid®, which he recognized as being used to raise metabolism, not something that a man also taking drugs for hypertension should be taking. It was well known among those who knew him that Ferrie had very high blood pressure, "over 200" according to Layton Martens.[54] Garrison discussed this with a forensic pathologist at Louisiana State University and found that such a person taking a large dose of this medicine would indeed die of a brain aneurism, just as Ferrie had.[55] Ferrie's worst fears seem to have materialized: Someone apparently forced him to ingest this medication and then watched and waited while he died. Whoever did so could have made it look more like a genuine suicide through a suicide note that spelled out that intent, and then forced Ferrie to sign it, but perhaps all of that seemed unnecessary. Perhaps the strange "suicide notes" were merely intended to add a little more confusion to the scene and provide a secondary explanation in case the "natural causes" one didn't work. The coroner, despite many things that pointed to murder, ruled that "there is no indication whatsoever of suicide or murder." According to Harold Weisberg, the contents of Ferrie's home included various guns and military equipment and a hundred-pound bomb; but another item found, three blank U.S. passports, is something that would ordinarily have been practically impossible for a small-time, part-time crook to possess.[56] On Wednesday, March 1, 1967, the postassassination questions came to a boil with the arrest of Clay Shaw in New Orleans for his alleged role in the Kennedy assassination. This followed a lengthy investigation by

---

52. Davis, Mafia Kingfish . . . p. 324
53. Garrison, pp. 163–164.
54. Russo, p. 402.
55. Garrison. pp. 164–165.
56. Hurt, p. 265; Weisberg, *Oswald in New Orleans*, p. 163.

District Attorney Jim Garrison who was attempting to show not that David Ferrie and Clay Shaw and others were guilty of the murder of JFK, but that a conspiracy to murder the president was hatched there in New Orleans and that their paths and connections to that conspiracy could be shown.

President Johnson was very interested in what was going on in New Orleans, gathering information through someone within the investigation who was connected to John Connally, as well as a New Orleans reporter covering the story, Rosemary James, who was married to Jack Valenti's cousin.[57] Before Ferrie's death, Johnson had gotten his new acting U.S. attorney general, Ramsey Clark, to look into the Garrison case. In one of the oddest of the many strange actions of David Ferrie, when he was served the subpoena to testify to Garrison, Ferrie went to the local FBI office to report this development. Clark later informed Johnson that "Ferrie wanted to know what the Bureau could do to help him with this nut [Garrison],"[58] essentially revealing a connection to the FBI that had thus far been hidden. But this was not the kind of news Johnson wanted to hear; it seemed that the President was a bit disappointed with Clark—the son of his old friend Tom Clark—who was picked to replace Bobby Kennedy. In fact, Johnson would tell writer Leo Janos later that he was disappointed by Clark's apparent ineptness:

> "I asked Ramsey Clark to quietly look into the whole thing. Only two weeks later, he reported back that he couldn't find anything new." Disgust tinged Johnson's voice as the conversation came to an end. "I thought I had appointed Tom Clark's son—I was wrong."[59]

Evidently, Johnson—frustrated by Ramsey Clark's inability to close down Garrison's investigation any other way—decided to unleash multiple attacks on the DA's character and methods, unfortunately including a circuit through the voice of Ramsey Clark, pressing him so hard to do so that his mouth started the attack before his brain had evaluated the logic behind his charges: Clark immediately launched an attack on Garrison, claiming that Shaw had already been exonerated by the FBI, implicitly meaning that they had actually investigated his ties to the others—including Oswald—involved in the preassassination planning. One newsman asked Clark directly if Shaw was "checked out and found clear?" "Yes, that's right," replied the attorney general. Clark also said the Justice Department knew what Garrison's case involved and did not consider it valid. The attorney general obviously did not realize the implications of his statement; Jim Garrison wasted

---

57. Russo, p. 404.
58. Ibid. p. 402.
59. Ibid. p. 400 (Ref. Leo Janos, *Atlantic Monthly*, July 1973).

no time in explaining it to him: "The statement that Shaw, whose name appears nowhere in the twenty-six volumes of the Warren Commission, had been investigated by the federal government was intriguing. If Shaw had no connection to the assassination, I wondered, why had he been investigated?"[60] This was ludicrously inconsistent with the entire story they had heretofore fabricated, of course, so Clark had to back off within a day of this pronouncement, conceding that his statement was "erroneous." That episode did more than merely belie the direct lie; it came close to revealing the larger lies; it barely missed inadvertently exposing the truth of JFK's assassination.

Shortly afterward, on another level evidently created by Johnson through the CIA, an orchestrated attack on Garrison was mounted by the major news media—led by NBC, CBS, *Newsweek,* and *Time* magazines—accusing him of attempting to intimidate witnesses, engaging in criminal conspiracy and inciting felonies such as perjury, criminal defamation, and public bribery. As they did this, they were simultaneously, for inexplicable reasons, deciding that they would no longer allow their reporters to pursue questions about the Warren Commission findings; from that point on, they adopted the "official line." Subsequently, *Playboy* magazine published an interview with Garrison to evaluate these charges:[61]

> PLAYBOY: All right. The May 15 issue of *Newsweek* charged that two of your investigators offered David Ferrie's former roommate, Alvin Beauboeuf, $3,000 and an airline job if he would help substantiate your charges against Clay Shaw. How do you answer this accusation?
>
> GARRISON: Mr. Beauboeuf was one of the two men who accompanied David Ferrie on a mysterious trip from New Orleans to Texas on the day of the assassination, so naturally we were interested in him from the very start of our investigation. At first he showed every willingness to cooperate with our office; but *after Ferrie's death, somebody gave him a free trip to Washington. From that moment on, a change came over Beauboeuf; he refused to cooperate with us any further and he made the charges against my investigators to which you refer.* (emphasis added) Fortunately, Beauboeuf had signed an affidavit on April 12,—well after the alleged bribe offer was supposed to have been made—affirming that "no representative of the New Orleans Parish district attorney's office has ever asked me

to do anything but to tell the truth. Any inference or statement by anyone to the contrary has no basis in fact." As soon as his attorney began broadcasting his charges, we asked the New Orleans police department to thoroughly investigate the matter. And on June 12th, the police department—which is not, believe me, in the pocket of the district attorney's office—released a report concluding that exhaustive investigation by the police intelligence branch had cleared my staff of any attempt to bribe or threaten Beauboeuf into giving untrue testimony. There was no mention of this report, predictably enough, in *Newsweek*.

Reactions in Washington DC to the 1967 Garrison Trial

As Jim Garrison prosecuted the Clay Shaw trial in New Orleans, Helms was also said to have routinely started his daily 9:00 a.m. meetings at CIA headquarters with questions like "How is the Shaw trial going? Are we giving them all the help they need? Is everything going all right down there?"[62] This information was revealed by a former CIA agency staff employee, Victor Marchetti, who said that comments like "We'll pick this up later in my office," or "talk to me about it after the meeting" were used to tightly control who was privy to certain information. When he tried to find out more about what was going on, he was told that "Shaw, a long time ago, had been a contact of the Agency. He was in the export-import business . . . he knew people coming and going from certain areas; followed by, 'well, of course, the Agency doesn't want this to come out now because Garrison will distort it, the public will misconstrue it.'"[63] If there is any doubt about how scared the CIA brass was about the possibility of Garrison getting too close to the truth, and had to be stopped, that account should put the matter to rest. From the start, the Agency had done everything it could to ignore requests for information from the Warren Commission, and when it did finally comply, provided phony documents and/or photographs.*

By the same token, President Lyndon B. Johnson, and his acting attorney general, Ramsey Clark, were also following developments in the trial very closely. On February 20, 1967, Clark and Johnson discussed again the investigation that Garrison had launched. Louisiana Congressman Hale Boggs, a former member of the Warren Commission, had commented to

---

* There are numerous sources which validate the CIA's fabrication of evidence. One example: Garrison, pp. 72–75.
62. Garrison, p. 273.
63. Ibid., pp. 273–274.

several people that he believed that the assassination might be linked directly back to Lyndon Johnson. Clark seems a little shocked by Johnson's uncharacteristic equanimity, as described by Max Holland:[64]

> Still, Clark is already discomfited by one "nutty" aspect of the story, namely the rumor that Garrison is allegedly linking Johnson with the conspiracy. As fantastic as this rumor sounds, its source is credible. It comes via Representative Hale Boggs, whose district encompasses much of New Orleans, putting him in a position to know whereof he speaks. Boggs, of course, was also on the Warren Commission, which puts him in a bit of a dilemma. Whereas he might be inclined to speak out against Garrison (whom he apparently dislikes) and denounce the DA's probe, it is risky to attack a prosecutor who shares the same jurisdiction. To Clark, any allegation about Johnson's involvement is an early indicator that Garrison might be deranged.

It perhaps comes as a surprise to Clark that Johnson treats the whole matter with considerable equanimity, not even swearing or muttering to himself when Clark brings up Bogg's story. The president's reaction is in marked contrast to his response last October when the insinuation first surfaced. As it turns out, the news from New Orleans is far from the wildest story making the rounds. Johnson asks Clark if he has heard about an even more fantastic rumor in Washington, one that was conveyed personally to the president by syndicated columnist Drew Pearson, considered something of a renegade by his Washington peers. The story, which Johnson heard a month earlier, is that after the 1961 Bay of Pigs debacle, the CIA sent men into Cuba to assassinate Fidel Castro, who then retaliated. And as if the implications of that weren't staggering enough, Pearson also says that Robert Kennedy concocted the plots against Castro, as they occurred in the days when he was "riding herd" on the Agency for his brother.

> CLARK: I had heard that Hale Boggs was sayin' that he—Garrison—was sayin' that . . . or privately around town [was saying] that it [the assassination] could be traced back [to you] . . . or that you could be found in it some place, which . . . I can't believe he's been sayin' that. The bureau says they haven't heard any such thing, and they['ve] got lots of eyes and ears. 'Course, that was a [credible] fella like Hale Boggs. But Hale gets pretty emotional about people that he really

---

64. Holland, The Kennedy Assassination Tapes pp. 389–394 (Hear it on the Internet at: http://www.impiousdigest.com/index00.htm).

doesn't like, and people who have fought him and been against him, and I would be more inclined to attribute it to that. Either that, or this guy Garrison [is] just completely off his rocker.

JOHNSON: Who did Hale tell this to?

CLARK: *[somewhat in disbelief]* Apparently Marvin [Watson].

JOHNSON: *[aside to Watson]* [Did] Hale tell you that—Hale Boggs—that this fella [Garrison], this district attorney down there, said that this is traced to me or somethin'?

WATSON: Privately he [Garrison] was usin' your name as having known about it [the assassination]. I said [to Boggs], Will you give this information to Barefoot Sanders? Ramsey was out of town, this was Saturday night. He [Boggs] said, I sure will. So I asked the operator to get Barefoot and Ramsey together, and they did.

After that exchange, the course of the conversation turned to the even more "fantastic rumor" about the assassination attempts on Castro.

Johnson's reaction to this news speaks volumes. The fact that these comments were coming from one of the members of the Warren Commission, a highly respected congressman, is particularly insightful. His death by plane crash in a desolate part of Alaska a few years later, and one year after his lambasting of Hoover on the floor of the House of Representatives, followed by the mysterious disappearance of many of his records related to his work on the Warren Commission from Tulane University, only adds to the mystery of what Hale Boggs really knew. The Los Angeles *Star*, on November 22, 1973, reported that before his death, Boggs claimed he had "startling revelations" on Watergate and the assassination of JFK.

CBS News correspondent George Herman asked Clark about the death of David Ferrie in a March 12, 1967, interview on *Face the Nation*. When asked why documents concerning Ferrie had been classified by the FBI and the Justice Department, Clark lied, "No, those documents are under the general jurisdiction of the General Services Administration." In 1968, Clark—no doubt acting at the behest of President Lyndon B. Johnson, appointed a panel of four medical experts to examine various autopsy evidence on JFK's death, and it dutifully concluded that Kennedy was struck by two bullets fired from above and behind, one of which traversed the base of the neck on the right side (right where Gerald Ford had moved the wound); the second one having entered the skull from behind and destroyed its upper right side (which would be consistent with how the skull had been modified at one of the two military hospitals in Bethesda, Maryland). On his last day as attorney general, January 25, 1969, he ordered the Justice Department to withhold from Garrison the x-rays and photographs from the autopsy of John F. Kennedy, undoubtedly making permanent a procedure that had already been in effect for the last two years.

In Defense of Dr. Crenshaw's Assertions

For thirty years, Dr. Charles Crenshaw kept his memories of the tragic weekend of JFK's assassination to himself. During those three decades after he and the other Parkland Hospital doctors tried to save the president's life, then his assassin's, they continued a *de facto* "conspiracy of silence."[65] He and the other Parkland doctors would not necessarily agree on every fact involved in these events—and none of them had even realized that Kennedy had been shot in the upper back, since his body was laid on his back the entire time in Trauma Room One—but they were nearly unanimous in their agreement about two wounds the president did suffer:

- The nonfatal wound in his throat, no larger than the "tip" of Dr. Crenshaw's little finger, was an entry wound;
- The shot that entered his right front side above the hairline had come from his front, and had produced a large "fist-sized" hole in the rear of his head; the right rear of his brain was gone, according to Dr. Crenshaw.

While twenty-one out of twenty-two witnesses at Parkland Hospital agreed in their earliest statements about these conclusions, including Drs. Malcolm Perry and Kemp Clark, the "men in suits," in this case the Secret Service, forced Dr. Perry and then Dr. Clark to change their testimony. According to author James W. Douglass, "As Dallas Secret Service Agent Elmer Moore would admit to a friend years later, he 'had been ordered to tell Dr. Perry to change his testimony.' Moore said that in threatening Perry, *he acted 'on orders from Washington and Mr. Kelly of the Secret Service Headquarters.'* . . . Moore [admitted that he] 'badgered Dr. Perry' into 'making a flat statement that there was no entry wound in the neck' . . . [and said] 'I regret what I had to do with Dr. Perry' . . . [but] he had been given 'marching orders from Washington . . . I did everything I was told,

---

65. Crenshaw, p. 109.

we all did everything we were told, or we'd get our heads cut off.'"[66] In April 1992, almost twenty-nine years after the assassination, Dr. Crenshaw finally broke his own silence:[67]

> I believe there was a common denominator in our silence—a fearful perception that to come forward with what we believed to be the medical truth would be asking for trouble. Although we never admitted it to one another, we realized that the inertia of the established story was so powerful, so thoroughly presented, so adamantly accepted, that it would bury anyone who stood in its path . . . I was as afraid of the men in suits as I was of the men who had assassinated the President . . . I reasoned that anyone who would go so far as to eliminate the President of the United States would surely not hesitate to kill a doctor.

After Crenshaw's book rose to number one on the *New York Times'* bestseller list, he was attacked mercilessly by people who were not interested in the truth being revealed. Ultimately, it was the *Journal of the American Medical Association* (*JAMA*) that leaped into the fray to attempt to discredit one of their members. They first tried to deny that Dr. Crenshaw was even in Trauma Room One with President Kennedy; that scurrilous charge was quickly addressed by records submitted by Dr. Crenshaw, including Warren Commission testimony establishing that five different doctors and nurses specifically mentioned seeing him working with them to revive the president. There is no question that he was there and in 1994, a court agreed, awarding Dr. Crenshaw and his coauthor, Gary Shaw, a sum of money and ordering *JAMA* to publish a rebuttal article. There is more to the story of JAMA's egregious attempt to reinforce a discredited theory by attempting to deny the truth, but due to space limitations, and the fact that the point has now been adequately covered, the matter will be suspended; enough has been said for the reader to ponder who was behind the motivation for the slanderous treatment of Dr. Charles Crenshaw.

But the real reason for the attempt to discredit Dr. Crenshaw had nothing to do with his involvement with other doctors working on John F. Kennedy; it was really about what he said regarding a telephone call received during the time he assisted Dr. Shires in trying to save Lee Harvey Oswald's life. Dr. Crenshaw stated that Lyndon Johnson personally called the hospital about an hour after Oswald had been admitted, asking him to secure

---

66. Douglass, pp. 309–310 (Ref. Douglass's interview with James Gochenaur and HSCA tape-recorded interview with Gochenaur May 10, 1977).
67. Douglass, p. 310 (Ref. Crenshaw, *JFK: Conspiracy of Silence*, pp. 153–154).

Oswald's "deathbed confession." Practically everyone in the country knew about Oswald's shooting almost immediately after he was shot at 11:21 a.m. (12:21 p.m. in Washington), whether or not they personally saw it on live television in real time on Sunday morning. Johnson had heard about it on his way back from one of his rare appearances in a church, when Secretary of State Rusk informed him. The call which Johnson made to Dr. Crenshaw was made at the full height of his excited reaction to the news that the assassin had been shot, and he thought that getting Oswald's "confession" would help to put a lid on any further investigation.

It should by now be clear that Lyndon Johnson would not hesitate to make such a call, any more than all the other calls he made that weekend. To those critics of Dr. Crenshaw's statements, who continue defending the myth of a guiltless Johnson, the claim that he did not have sufficient time to do so because he was in his limousine on his way to the Capitol is simply a disingenuous attempt to further obfuscate the truth. There was plenty of time for such a call after he arrived at the Capitol. What the critics leave out from Manchester's account is that, when Bobby and Jacqueline met briefly with Johnson in the Blue Room, Johnson was already highly agitated about Oswald's being wounded, informing Bobby for the first time and saying, *"You've got to do something, we've got to do something. We've got to get involved. It's giving the United State a bad name around the world"*[68] (emphasis added). It is entirely in keeping with Johnson's obsessive-compulsive/manic behavior for him to remain in this hyperactive, frenzied state of mind throughout the forty-minute trip to Capitol Hill, no doubt irritating everyone else in the limousine. According to Manchester, the limousine reached Capitol Hill at 1:47 p.m., after which the "Band plays 'Hail to the Chief' at 1:52."[69] Between that time and 2:07 p.m., when Oswald was pronounced dead, was a fifteen-minute interlude during which Kennedy's coffin was being carried into the Capitol rotunda. At 2:00 p.m. Washington time, 1:00 p.m. in Dallas, Oswald had been in the emergency room for one hour and fifteen minutes, which is consistent with Dr. Crenshaw's statement that the call came at least an hour after the operation had begun; he would die shortly after Crenshaw returned to the operating room, at 1:07 p.m. Dallas time.

Entering the Capitol was a routine homecoming for Johnson; he practically owned the place, at least in the part of his enigmatic mind where he kept his most private thoughts. He had access to many offices there, including, of course, the "Taj Mahal," also known to reporters as the "Nookie

68. Manchester, p. 518.
69. Manchester, pp. 518–519.

Room," which he coerced from the new majority leader, Senator Mansfield, who Johnson thought was unworthy of such splendor. A quick whisper to his wife to excuse himself for a few minutes for whatever reason (e.g., a restroom stop) would have freed him to go there to use the telephone to make this short call; after Dr. Crenshaw took it, the call was over within half a minute.[70] Johnson wanted Dr. Crenshaw to take a message to the operating surgeon, Dr. Shires. "I want a death-bed confession from the accused assassin. There's a man in the operating room who will take the statement. I will expect full cooperation in this matter," he said firmly.[71] Such a call, made from a telephone in his office at the Capitol Building, would not have been placed through the White House switchboard; therefore no record of it would have existed. Not that the existence of records of Johnson's telephone calls should matter regardless; he seems to have figured out ways to make calls that never appear in the official logs. For example, one such call, according to William Manchester, was made by him to J. Edgar Hoover at 7:25 p.m. on Friday evening.[72] He also conferred with Hoover from 9:10 to 9:25 p.m. that evening.[73] However, there is no record of either call in Johnson's official diary, nor has a tape of either conversation been made public. There is no question but that Johnson and Hoover talked frequently by telephone throughout the first several days and weeks after the assassination and that only a few of their conversations were actually taped. Readers are urged to view the video interview of Dr. Crenshaw on YouTube.com to consider his veracity, as compared to that of LBJ and his apologists. (See "LBJ's Phone Call to Parkland Hospital.")

Closing the Files—the Bobby Baker Scandals

Even before he returned to Washington, Johnson talked to Abe Fortas about Don Reynolds's Senate testimony, and as soon as Johnson returned to Washington, he contacted B. Everett Jordan to find out more about what Reynolds had said regarding his testimony incriminating him (LBJ). He found that his worst fears had come true. Reynolds's testimony, under oath, included his revelation of the $100,000 bribe for fixing the TFX contract, clearly the most worrisome of all the charges for Johnson. The same evening, Johnson also spoke to Abe Fortas about Senator Williams, vowing to punish him with an IRS audit (which he did, to no avail; aside

---

70. Crenshaw, pp. 132–133.
71. Ibid.
72. Manchester, p. 405.
73. North, pp. 412–413.

from the inconvenience and time required to answer the questions raised, it was eventually found that the IRS owed him $87).[74] Johnson's own most valued lawyer—the brilliant legal strategist Abe Fortas, who had practically single-handedly manipulated the legal process to enforce Johnson's stolen 1948 Senate election (see chapter 1)—resigned immediately as Baker's lawyer to help Johnson in his latest imbroglio, replaced by the renowned Mafia defense attorney, Edward Bennett Williams.[75] When Johnson tried to press the Democratic leadership of the Senate to halt the investigations, they tried to get Johnson to pull other strings and use whatever "secrets" he might obtain against the Senate Republican leadership to put a halt to the continuing investigation. Baker was amused to observe that before long, Senator Hugh Scott (R-PA) began to soft-pedal criticism of him, to the point of even starting to praise the new president. "'I have so much desire not to damage the Republic. I think Lyndon Johnson is a fine, can-do president, a man of action. I believe he is sincerely advancing a program he believes is in the best interest of this country.' There was good reason for Senator Scott's conversion, as I learned through the White House grapevine: LBJ had threatened to close down the Philadelphia Navy Yard unless Senator Scott closed his critical mouth."[76]

As noted by Peter Dale Scott, "Thanks to what one senator called 'string-pulling by Johnson and Abe Fortas,' only a highly bowdlerized version of the Reynolds testimony reached the public and the press, who declined to pursue the matter." One of the strings pulled by Johnson and Hoover was simply having the FBI stop cooperating with the Justice Department: "As soon as Johnson became President, Hoover and the FBI stopped sending the Justice Department reports on the Bobby Baker case."[77]

Johnson was even more effective in closing down the parallel Senate investigation of the TFX contract, by Robert Kennedy's former Senate boss Senator McClellan. The McClellan subcommittee had closed its TFX meeting on November 20, 1963, with the chairman's undertaking 'to resume hearings next week'; *Business Week* predicted that Fred Korth would be the next witness. But the hearings promised for 'next week' were not resumed until 1969, after Johnson left office; and Korth never had to testify."[78] The nationally syndicated columnists Drew Pearson and Jack Anderson, obviously

---

74. Lasky, *It Didn't Start . . .*, pp. 135–137.
75. North, p. 402.
76. Baker, *Wheeling*. p. 402.
77. Scott, p. 222 (ref. Gentry, *Hoover*, 559n; William W. Turner, *Hoover's FBI*, Los Angeles: Sherbourne Press, 1970, p. 185; New York: Thunder's Mouth Press, 1993, p. 174.
78. Scott, pp. 221–222.

among the most well-connected pundits in Washington, predicted that result within a day of JFK's assassination:

> WASHINGTON—It will be interesting to see whether Sen. John McClellan, D-ARK., really tries to find out how much Bobby Baker knows about the TFX controversy. The stern Senate Investigation chairman has promised to look into published reports that Baker threatened to expose some TFX skulduggery if his own get-rich-quick activities are scrutinized too closely. McClellan's investigators will have quite a trail to follow. But if they follow it carefully it will take them through the Quorum Club , which Bobby founded, and lead them in the direction of of Vice President Lyndon Johnson.

In the weeks after Kennedy was killed, rumors began to circulate that Johnson had organized the assassination since he had the best motive for wanting Kennedy dead. If he had *not* been the instigator, the thinking went, it would have been in his best interest to insist on a full and open investigation of the assassination independent of his direction or involvement. This would have been the best way to have cleared his name convincingly then and there, effectively ensuring that it would not haunt the country for decades (centuries, probably) afterward. If he had, in fact, been completely innocent, he should have easily seen that this course was essential. The fact that he forced the close of multiple investigations against himself, that he involved himself with major decisions to limit, destroy, and obfuscate evidence—minutes, days, weeks, and months afterward—clearly ties Johnson to multiple cover-ups of the assassination of JFK.

Senators John Williams and Hugh Scott (both of whom had unblemished public reputations, despite Johnson's and Hoover's search for private skeletons in their respective closets) were also pressured to end the Senate inquiry. Other witnesses were allowed to appear before the Senate Rules Committee but most refused to testify. The committee later stated that Don Reynolds was unwilling to continue testifying, which Senator Curtis said was a lie; he had left the country, afraid for his life. By New Year's Day, 1964, barely six weeks after the assassination, Johnson was still trying to control or stop the Congressional hearings investigating different facets of the still emerging scandal. Starting in January, his anger at Senator Williams grew daily, exponentially, and prompted him to use every tool in his massive toolbox, including news leaks to Drew Pearson, wiretaps, and break-ins by the FBI and IRS tax audits on Williams, threatening to get enough on him "to send the bastard to jail." The "bastard," Senator Williams, was a plain and soft-spoken former chicken feed dealer, operating without a staff of investigators, funds, or the power of subpoena, who simply tried to purge Washington of a particularly unsavory clique of political wheelers and dealers.[79]

Johnson vowed to flood Delaware with enough money to defeat "the son of a bitch" Williams when he came up for reelection the following year (which he tried to do, even making a campaign appearance there for his opponent and pleading with voters saying, "Give me men I can work with!")." For a state having only three electoral votes, a major effort was made to unseat the Republican incumbent, which was to prove, again, unsuccessful, as Williams won reelection by seven thousand votes.[80] Victor Lasky was among the few authors who investigated Johnson's brazenly illegal actions further; most others continued to maintain a "hands-off" approach to the new president either because of fear, or undue deference to the new president during his honeymoon period, or because they were saving their hypocritical venom for his successor after the comparatively lesser episode of presidential illegalities called "Watergate":[81]

> Even before the story broke into the headlines, Williams knew that his curiosity about the case had triggered someone pretty high up in Washington to "get" him. Strangers posing as Washington investigators were poking around his home town, asking questions about such things as the kind of farm subsidies the senator was collecting. Williams knew immediately that an effort was being made to prove he was benefiting from legislation he helped pass. But Williams remained unafraid and more determined than ever to pursue his inquiries into corruption in high places . . . Then one night in February 1964 he met with an official in the Johnson administration who had something frightening to say. "I couldn't risk going to your office," he told Williams, 'but I can't stomach what they're doing to you. Senator, your mail is being intercepted. *Every letter you write to any federal official asking about the Baker case is immediately routed to a special handler. He sends the Senate Rules Committee copies of any information sent to you. Sometimes he even checks with the Committee before deciding whether your inquiry is to be answered at all. You'd better be careful about what you put in writing* [emphasis added]. . . . Also in the works was a campaign of character assassination. Williams was called a "crackpot" by Democratic members of the Rules Committee. Drew Pearson wanted to know why Williams had not been outraged by Eisenhower's acceptance of expensive gifts . . .

---

79. Lasky, *It Didn't Start* . . ., p. 131 (citing John Barron, *The Case of Bobby Baker and the Courageous Senator,* The Reader's Digest, September 1965).
80. Lasky, *It Didn't Start* . . ., pp. 135–137.
81. Ibid., pp. 132–135.

The Washington Post helped the LBJ cause by publishing a false, unchecked story alleging that the senator had been using hidden microphones in his office to record interviews.

Don B. Reynolds continued his testimony before the Rules Committee on January 9, 1964; the hearings proceeded during the rest of January with Reynolds testifying, under oath, about other shocking stories involving Johnson. "He spoke of the time Baker opened a satchel full of paper money which he said was a $100,000 payoff to Johnson for pushing through a $7 billion TFX plane contract. So much pressure had been exerted to get the contract for Texas based General Dynamics that Republicans called the TFX the 'LBJ.' Another Reynolds story described how Johnson, making an official trip to the Far East as Vice President, drew $100,000 in counterpart funds while in Hong Kong. This is money earned by the U.S. government in foreign countries and can only be spent there. According to Reynolds, Johnson had spent all that money 'in a period of twelve to fourteen hours buying gifts for people who were loaded.'"[82]

Lyndon Johnson excelled in behind-the-scenes political blackmail and, thanks to his friend J. Edgar Hoover's extensive files, which yielded dirt on practically everyone in Washington, the compound effect was devastating for anyone who got in his way. Now he launched an all-out attack on Don Reynolds, the "damned fool insurance salesman"; he obtained Reynolds' military file from the Pentagon in a particularly egregious, illegal action, then leaked information to the columnists Drew Pearson and Jack Anderson. As orchestrated by Johnson, on February 5, 1964, the *Washington Post* reported that Reynolds had lied about his academic record at West Point and revealed that he had been a supporter of Joseph McCarthy (as had the Kennedys; McCarthy had even learned his attack methods from Johnson, as noted in chapter 1). The files also claimed that Reynolds had accused business rivals of being secret members of the American Communist Party and had made anti-Semitic remarks while in Berlin in 1953. At the same time as these stories were printed, the *Washington Star* printed an editorial stating that the administration (i.e., Johnson) had tried to peddle the same derogatory information about Reynolds to them, calling it "a rather clumsy and half-hearted effort to smear Mr. Reynolds and otherwise deflect the impact of his disclosures away from the President."[83]

This release of Reynolds' personal information was not only illegal, but it also created a sympathetic backlash in favor of Reynolds. It also

82. Lasky, *It Didn't Start . . .*, p. 131.
83. Mollenhoff, p. 313–314.

provided support to Senators Scott, Williams, Curtis, Karl Mundt, and other Republicans for their arguments to vigorously pursue the Baker case despite the obvious White House meddling.[84] A few weeks later, the *New York Times* also reported that Lyndon Johnson had used information from secret government documents to smear Don B. Reynolds and had been applying pressure on newspaper editors to suppress information regarding Reynolds' Senate testimony. Senator Williams pointed out that Reynolds had left the Air Force with an honorable discharge, and he had an "excellent record" in the State Department with "thirteen or fourteen promotions . . . No one raised the question about discrediting this witness until after he gave some damaging testimony."[85] At a National Press Club luncheon, GOP Chairman William Miller suggested a broad investigation of the considerable advertising revenues the LBJ Company reportedly had received from large defense industries. "'How many times did North American Aviation advertise over the LBJ station?' Representative Miller wanted to know."[86] As the hearings wore on, the damaging evidence against Johnson became more muffled and Reynolds became more circumspect due to Johnson's smear campaign against him. As Reynolds told Senator Williams, *"My God! There's a difference between testifying against a President of the United States and a Vice President. If I had known he was President, I might not have gone through with it.".*[87]

In a Senate speech on February 3, Senator Hugh Scott (R-PA) said he had received "veiled threats" for pushing the Bobby Baker probe. The Pennsylvanian declared that he would push for a full investigation and calling of "all witnesses, no matter how many veiled threats may be conveyed to members of the Rules Committee." He spoke on the Senate floor of the "shocking" leak of confidential information about Reynolds. Since some of the information came from the Air Force files, he wrote to Secretary McNamara, "I am doubly concerned that leaks of internal memoranda can apparently be used to destroy witnesses whose testimony becomes embarrassing. The situation is particularly serious when it's realized that this information was denied to proper officials of the United States Senate . . . In a House speech, Representative Gross charged that the Johnson administration had engaged in an 'outrageous' attempt to 'intimidate' Reynolds and other witnesses who might give testimony that embarrassed the White House . . . The Army-Navy-Air Force Journal declared that the leaking of the Reynolds file seriously 'undermined' the confidential status of military files . . . A

---

84. Mollenhoff, p. 312–316.
85. Ibid.
86. Ibid., p. 312.
87. Curtis, pp. 243.

Washington Evening Star editorial spoke of the 'smear' and disclosed that persons connected with the White House had tried to peddle derogatory information and allegations about Reynolds to the Star."[88]

In the middle of everything else that Johnson was doing "behind the scenes" to derail the Senate investigations, the wife of the government accountant who had been assigned to investigate Bobby Baker's finances, mysteriously turned up dead, found by her children in her bathroom. Her autopsy was inconclusive, yet no criminal investigation was conducted.[89] Of course, this could have been merely one more coincidence, unrelated to Johnson's manic actions to put the brakes on the continuing investigation, but the apparent lack of interest in even looking into the matter suggests otherwise. The Democratic members of the Senate Rules Committee, outnumbering the Republicans by a 6–3 majority, were pressured by Lyndon Johnson to end the hearings aimed directly at himself and his connection to Bobby Baker. The three Republicans desperately tried to subpoena Walter Jenkins to testify under oath and be cross-examined regarding the charges made by Don Reynolds about the "gifting" of the stereo. In fact, they had submitted a list of more than fifteen witnesses, including Jenkins; their requests were voted down by the six Democrats, who were trying to kill the investigation completely to avoid further embarrassment to Johnson and their own Congressional leadership. Johnson continued applying pressure on everyone on the Hill he could talk to; one of his recorded telephone calls was to Senator Hubert Humphrey:[90]

> JOHNSON: This is just between me and you and God, now; don't tell a human.

> HUMPHREY: No.

> JOHNSON: But Dick Russell just called me and said that the leadership was treating Everett Jordan outrageous, and that he was ready to throw in the towel and that . . . [Everett] Dirksen ought to be told that if he wants to go into campaign contributions, why, we can look into a lot of campaign contributions. *We can authorize the FBI to go into all the Republican ones that have ever been made.*

---

88. Ibid., pp. 312–313.
89. Hancock, p. 309.
90. Text and audio of tape on the Web site which accompanies the book by Robert D. Johnson, *All the Way with LBJ: The 1964 Presidential Election* (Cambridge University Press): "http://allthewaywithlbj.com/lbj-and-the-bobby-baker-scandal/".

HUMPHREY: Mm-hmm.

JOHNSON: And we'll do it with the administration if he wants to do that—that we've got nothing to hide, that Bobby Baker hasn't got any campaign contributions. Then he said, "Will you call Mike [Mansfield] and Hubert?" I said, "I can't tell you who I'll call, because I don't want to call anybody that I can't talk to. But I'll call somebody. And I don't want 'em to say the White House is directing this thing."

HUMPHREY: Mm-hmm.

JOHNSON: He said, "Well, they want to call a bunch of new witnesses, and [Carl] Curtis is going to offer an amendment that any senator could call a witness"—which would be outrageous—instead of a majority, and they want to do that so they can call Walter Jenkins, and call a bunch of other people.

HUMPHREY: Mm-hmm.

JOHNSON: *Of course, I wouldn't let Walter Jenkins go; I'd just defy 'em.* But they oughtn't to be put on that spot, and make that a campaign issue for the rest of the year. It's deader than hell now; if they'd leave it dead. Every poll they took—they took one, I noticed, in Salem, New Jersey yesterday, and 1 percent have ever heard of it. The rest of 'em don't pay any attention. (emphasis added).

Johnson was obviously mortified that the committee might try to subpoena his aide Walter Jenkins to get his testimony under oath, under threat of perjury, regarding his role and knowledge about this aspect of the Baker scandal. As seen in the previous chapter, Johnson had a tremendous fear about having to testify under oath about anything he did, as though that kind of testimony would be turned against him as a way to convict him in the absence of anything else sufficiently incriminating to indict him; clearly, he had the same attitude toward allowing Jenkins to do the same thing, testifying essentially as his surrogate. According to Rick Perlstein,[91]

> In late January [of 1964] when Republicans tried to get Walter Jenkins, Johnson's most intimate aide, to testify before a Senate subcommittee investigation, Johnson put in the fix. Two psychiatrists

---

91. Perlstein, p. 309.

appeared to testify that an appearance would—literally—kill him. [Republican] Carl Curtis moved to call Jenkins to the stand anyway. He lost 6 to 3 in a party-line vote. That was a good thing for Johnson: 'I've got considerably more detail on Reynolds' love life,' Jenkins told the President about the man who linked him to Bobby Baker. 'Well, get it all typed up for me,' Johnson replied—not the kind of shady behavior Jenkins wanted to be asked about under oath. Curtis lost again when he moved to make the record of the session public. The investigation closed without a single Administration witness being called.

Johnson Throws a Congressional Hissy Fit

By February, Johnson was getting more and more nervous about the course of the congressional investigations. Naturally, in most cases, the conversations regarding the bribery, blackmail, political influence peddling, and other illegal activities that transpired on Capitol Hill were closely guarded secrets only known to those complicit in the activities (except those recorded by Hoover's men of course). Unfortunately for Lyndon Johnson, as a result of his inability to be discreet when under pressure, there was one major exception in his case, which was told by a firsthand witness to it, Robert N. Winter-Berger, in his book *The Washington Pay-off.* This impromptu conversation—a result of Baker's insistence on the additional payment of $5,600 by Ralph Hill for the rights to the renewal of his contract noted above—occurred on February 4, 1964, in a surprise appearance by the new president Lyndon Johnson in Speaker of the House John McCormack's office in the Capitol. Speaker McCormack, for the record, was a longtime friend and collaborator with both Lyndon B. Johnson and J. Edgar Hoover, and an enemy of John F. Kennedy, who "view[ed] each other with personal disdain."[92] Mr. Winter-Berger had an appointment with Speaker McCormack at 4:00 p.m. on Tuesday, February 4, to discuss his public relations concerns regarding his effort to win the nomination for the vice presidency in the coming elections.[93]

Ordinarily, Winter-Berger attended meetings with Speaker of the House John McCormack only in the company of Nathan Voloshen, a friend and business associate-lobbyist who later pled guilty to influence peddling and conspiracy. He had been a longtime associate of John McCormack,

92. North, p. 109.
93. Winter-Berger, pp. 64–69.

who, when he was Speaker of the House, rented a portion of his offices to Voloshen for $2,500 per month and allowed him unlimited use of those facilities and his staff in exchange for this and other favors, including a weekly supply of Havana cigars and creams and lotions from Saks Fifth Avenue for his wife which the secretaries called "Voloshen's Lotions." On that day, however, Voloshen had a conflicting appointment which required him to be in New York, but he urged Winter-Berger to go ahead with the meeting with McCormack without him.

The meeting began on schedule, in McCormack's massive office across the corridor from the House chamber. After only five minutes, the private door to the inner office opened and Lyndon B. Johnson strode in, with a look of "such anguish" as he had never seen before. Winter-Berger sat stunned by what was happening before his eyes, not knowing whether to stay seated or excuse himself and exit quickly; neither gave him any hint about that choice, so he stayed seated:

> *Johnson disregarded me, but I can never forget the sight of him, crossing the room in great strides. In a loud, hysterical voice he said: "John, that son of a bitch is going to ruin me. If that cocksucker talks, I'm gonna land in jail.". . . Things couldn't be worse, and you know it. We've talked about this shit often enough. Why wasn't it killed, John?" When Johnson looked up at McCormack, I could see he was crying. He buried his face again. . . "I practically raised that motherfucker, and now he's gonna make me the first President of the United States to spend the last days of his life behind bars." He was hysterical. . . . "How much money does the greedy bastard have to make?" Johnson said. "For a lousy five thousand bucks, he ruins his life, he ruins my life, and Christ knows who else's. Five thousand bucks, and the son of a bitch has millions.". . . "He should have given him the goddamn machines," Johnson said. "He should have known better. Now we're all up shit creek. We're all gonna rot in jail." "We'll think of something," McCormack said. He rubbed Johnson's shoulder. "Please. Calm down. Control yourself."*
>
> *In a burst, Johnson said: "It's me they're after. It's me they want. Who the fuck is that shit heel? But they'll get him up there in front of an open committee and all the crap will come pouring out and it'll be my neck. Jesus Christ, John, my life is at stake!. . . . He's got to take this rap himself. He's the one that made the goddamn stupid mistake. Get to him. Find out how much more he wants, for crissake. I've got to be kept out of this. . . Oh, I tell you, John, it takes just one prick to ruin a man in this town. Just one*

person has to rock the boat and a man's life goes down the drain.
And I'm getting fucked by two bastards—Bobby and that Williams
son of a bitch. And all he wants is headlines." "It'll pass, Lyndon,"
McCormack said. "This will pass."

Johnson got angry. "Not if we just sit around on our asses and think
we can watch it pass. You've got to get to Bobby, John. Tell him I expect
him to take the rap for this on his own. Tell him I'll make it worth his
while. Remind him that I always have." "All right, Lyndon."

All during this session, McCormack tried to position himself to block the
view between Johnson and Winter-Berger, who had continued to be tempted
to make his escape, and there were several occasions when he probably could
have done it discreetly. Johnson broke down, crying hysterically, a few times,
making so much noise himself that he would not have noticed it if Winter-
Berger left; but he sat transfixed, unable to move. He sat in amazement of
the scene that was unfolding before him. After one of Johnson's tantrums, he
suddenly became quieter and, apparently for the first time, he became aware
of Winter-Berger's existence, asking McCormack softly,

"Is he all right?" McCormack said. "Yes. He's a close friend of Nat's."
Johnson looked up at McCormack, his expression changing to a look of
discovery. "Nat can do this," he said. "Nat can get to Bobby. They're
friends. Have Nat get to Bobby." McCormack seemed relieved. "Yes,
Lyndon. I'd prefer that. I don't think this is a good time for me to get
in touch with Bobby." "Yes," said Johnson. "Get Nat. Let's talk to him.
Is he around?"

McCormack told Johnson that Nat was in New York, but agreed to get him to
be an intermediary to work with Bobby Baker. Winter-Berger agreed to meet
with Nat the next morning; Johnson asked him to take him a message,

Johnson said, "Tell Nat that I want him to get in touch with Bobby
Baker as soon as possible—tomorrow, if he can. Tell Nat to tell Bobby
that I will give him a million dollars if he takes this rap. Bobby must
not talk. I'll see to it that he gets a million-dollar settlement. Then
have Nat get back to John here, or to Eddie Adams later tomorrow, so
I can know what Bobby says."

Winter-Berger continued writing all of this out, saying repeatedly, "Yes, sir."

Then McCormack said, "Tell Nat to tell Bobby Baker not to try to get in
touch with me, I don't want to have any meeting with Baker." Johnson
said: "Tell Nat this is urgent, and I want him to get on it right
away."

With this, Johnson was now relieved enough to calm down. He and McCormack then left for the White House in McCormack's chauffer-driven car; Winter-Bergen left as well, on his way to New York to carry the bribery offer from the president of the United States—albeit with two intermediaries between him and the recipient—to his old friend and associate, Bobby Baker. Lyndon Johnson, in another instance of hysteria prompted by his realization that he was in danger of being indicted along with Baker, admitted his long-term criminal involvement. It is yet another "dot" on the matrix that can be connected to the hundreds of others which point to him as a criminal mastermind. In this case, the price of his own protection which he offered to pay was a nice round number: one million U.S. dollars.

It is not difficult to imagine Johnson having similar tirades at other equally distressing times when he felt himself in legal jeopardy. From the time that the Bobby Baker affair first began appearing in the news four months prior to this conversation, there were no doubt many similar occurrences of the same reaction; Johnson even admitted as much when he shouted, *"We've talked about this shit often enough. Why wasn't it killed, John?"*

On another front about this time, Johnson arranged for Secretary of State Dean Rusk to write to a judge who was adjudicating a trial involving Baker's—and his partners'—involvement with a Dominican Republic scam, to request that the judge suppress audio taped evidence implicating Baker *in the interest of national security*.[94] Several months before this, before the assassination, Johnson and Baker had made a trip to the Dominican Republic, which was related to a business deal involving Johnson's leverage within the Department of Agriculture and gaining approval for a slaughterhouse owned by Clint Murchison (which had a history of failed inspections due to unsanitary conditions) to sell its product on the Haitian market; getting the USDA's inspection approved was part of the deal that netted Baker a "finder's fee" of a half cent per pound of beef sold.[95]

One week after Johnson's meltdown in Speaker McCormack's office, an internal FBI memorandum written to FBI Assistant Director Alan Belmont on February 13, 1964 partially explains how Lyndon Johnson was finally able to shut down the Justice Department's investigation into Bobby Baker and, with it, the Senate investigations as well. The memo was captioned "ROBERT G. BAKER / CONFLICT OF INTEREST / FRAUD AGAINST THE GOVERNMENT" and stated, "There is attached

94. Hancock, p. 315 (ref. Baker, *Wheeling* . . . p. 211)
95. Ibid. p. 316.

hereto information received from the Washington Field Office which indicates that (redacted) advised the Washington Field Office that President Lyndon B. Johnson had confiscated the Robert G. Baker file from the U.S. Department of Justice while Attorney General Robert Kennedy was on his recent peace mission trip. (Redacted) stated this information came to him from Senator John Williams of Delaware. (Redacted) stated as a result of this action, the Senate Rules Committee investigating the Baker matter was at a complete standstill because it was not receiving any further information from the Justice Department."

On March 16, Senator Hugh Scott made a speech on the Senate floor charging that the six Democrats on the Rules Committee were lining up for a political vote to kill the investigations. "It is not an investigative decision. It is a political decision. This investigation is embarrassing to members of the Democratic Party. The majority members of the Rules Committee are not watching facts; they are watching the calendar. The November elections are approaching, and they are determined to put this skeleton back into the closet." He accused his Democratic colleagues of having "attached to themselves blinders for their eyes, plugs for their ears, and handcuffs for their wrists. So equipped, they have stumbled into, through and around one of the most sordid scandals in Washington . . . The investigators have been directed to skip evidence on party girls; they have been directed to skip evidence on political contributions; they have been directed to skip evidence on abortions* . . . The request to call Mr. Reynolds [in an open hearing] was refused, and the request to call an important witness, the head of a telephone answering service who would establish that Mr. Jenkins had made certain calls to Mr. Reynolds, was refused."[96]

Shutting Down the Senate Investigations

As the (by now, crippled) Senate investigations wore on through the remainder of 1964, the Republicans managed to keep the scandals alive while the Democrats continued to portray Bobby Baker as an embarrassing loose cannon, amazingly disconnected from anyone else in the party, including the president. As both sides geared up for the 1964 election, the news of the scandal almost dried up entirely, though the GOP tried to move it back to the front pages through vague charges that "something is wrong" with respect

---

* This was, evidently, a reference to a service offered the party girls before *Roe v. Wade* made the procedure legal.
96. Mollenhoff, p. 315.

to the state of Washington morality. On September 11, *Time* reported, in an article titled "Investigations: That Lingering Aroma" that the issue had not quite gone away:[97]

> With a sort of *'heh-heh-now-let's-see-what-you-Republicans-can-do-about-it'* air, the Democratic majority on the Senate Rules Committee last May declared its investigation into the shenanigans of former Senate Democratic Secretary Bobby Baker at an end. The majority report found no real wrong doing on the part of Baker or, perish the thought, his longtime sponsor, Lyndon Johnson.
>
> But the aroma from the Baker case has refused to fade away, mostly because of the efforts of Delaware's G.O.P. Senator John J. Williams, who has fashioned a highly successful Senate career from his lone-wolf investigative abilities. Among Williams' gum shoe disclosures . . . [was] all sorts of chicanery in the farm soil-bank program, which was altered after Williams' disclosures.

Time's September report detailed how a $35,000 payoff made by contractor Matt McCloskey to Bobby Baker was set up to allow him to claim it as a business expense, deductible from the profit he banked from the construction of the D.C. Stadium. On December 11, 1964, *Time* updated the affair in an article titled "Investigations: Parties & Payments":[98]

> Anyone who has followed the Bobby Baker case even vaguely knows of charges of a political payoff to help finance the 1960 presidential campaign and of reports that Baker used shapely party girls to help smooth the way for his shady deals. Last week, the fact that there was indeed a lot of loose change floating around—$35,000, to be exact—was confirmed beyond a doubt, to whatever purpose it may have been used. And the Senate Rules Committee, reopening its hearings into the Baker affair, also began pinning down some of that party-girl talk. . . . Star witness was Insurance Man Don Reynolds, 48, an old business buddy of Baker's. . ."I," said Reynolds, "was the bagman in this thing from beginning to end. The bagman is the man pushed around for having been the medium . . . I was low man on the totem pole." Of the $35,000, Reynolds said, he kept $10,000 for himself, and "Bobby told me that $15,000 was to go for the presidential campaign and the other $10,000 was to go for political purposes as he and

---

97. *Time* magazine, September 11, 1964. See: http://www.time.com/time/magazine/article/0,9171,830631,00.html#ixzz0XmKQLfNs.
98. *Time* magazine, December 11, 1964. See: http://www.time.com/time/magazine/article/0,9171,897373,00.html#ixzz0XmGG9TRO.

Mr. McCloskey saw fit—mostly Bobby." Reynolds said that Baker further told him to "stick the money in a bank you don't ordinarily use, so those people snooping around will have a hell of a time locating it." [Reynolds] produced some impressive documents to support his story: 1) an invoice in the amount of $109,000 sent to McCloskey by Reynolds, 2) a check for $109,000 sent to Reynolds by the McCloskey company, and 3) a bill for only $64,000, the performance-bond premium minus Reynolds' regular $10,000 commission, sent to Reynolds by the insurance company for which he was agent.

That left it all pretty much a case of Reynolds' word against McCloskey's. And as far as Bobby Baker was concerned, that was how it would stay. Appearing under subpoena before the committee last week, Baker invoked not only the Fifth Amendment, but the First, Fourth, and Sixth refusing to answer more than 40 Rules Committee questions.

The following March, *Time* reported on how the Senate closed down the hearings of the Rules Committee under the pretext of an "FBI Report" that was a thinly disguised whitewash, which seemed to be written by someone in the White House:[99]

> In fact, the report was not written by the FBI at all, but rather by a team of Justice Department functionaries who boiled down hundreds of pages of raw FBI interviews. *Unlike Reynolds, none of the persons interviewed by the FBI were under oath. The only part of Reynolds' testimony that has at any time been tested by a sworn statement from an adversary witness turned out to be true: that was Reynolds' claim that he had purchased advertising time on a Johnson-owned Austin TV station in return for selling insurance on Johnson's life.* The claim was recently corroborated in substance by former White House Aide Walter Jenkins.

Through the skillful parsing of words, this report—falsely labeled an FBI report—seemingly vindicated the real culprits, Baker and Jenkins, while portraying Don Reynolds as a liar, even though he had receipts and documents backing up every one of his charges. According to a follow-up article in *Time* four months later, the Senate finally yielded to Johnson's pressure, which was probably applied in much the same way as he used in his tirade with Speaker McCormack in February.[100]

---

99. *Time* magazine, March 12, 1965. See http://www.time.com/time/magazine/article/0,9171,839285,00.html.
100. *Time* magazine July 9, 1965. See http://www.time.com/time/magazine/article/0,9171,833902,00.html.

The "Watchdog" Loses His Fangs

Senator Williams appeared on the television program, *Face the Nation,* stating he regretted that the Rules Committee had ended the hearings "without pursuing some of the many leads . . . left dangling." He called Reynolds "an excellent witness," and lamented that "there was . . . what appeared to be a determined effort to discredit him . . . based on some leads from high sources . . ." Moreover, he suspected that "it may be an effort to intimidate any future witness that may want to testify before the Committee."[101] He defended Reynolds from the Johnson "leaks" of the FBI's findings of dirty laundry in his closet (noted above) and pointed out that he had "an excellent record" in the State Department "with 13 or 14 promotions" and had served commendably in the Air Force, leaving as a Major and an honorable discharge.[102] Senator Williams, a simple man from the rural part of south Delaware, who went to Washington with a commitment to fight political corruption, passed his information to the three Republicans on the ten-member Rules Committee. Being outnumbered, though, their push for a full investigation into Johnson and Baker was stopped by the Democrat majority.[103]

The role of Bobby Baker in assisting Johnson to build his empire has never been quantified, basically because of the refusal of Senate Democrats to permit any further probing of that sordid affair. But President Kennedy had incorrectly assumed that Johnson had not been "on the take since he was elected" as vice president. Before that, however, as he told Ben Bradlee, "I'm not so sure." He conceded that he knew Johnson, only a heartbeat away from the Presidency, had been improperly "tooling around the country in Grumman corporate jets. Exactly one month later, John Kennedy's heart stopped beating, and the nation had a new President."[104]

The investigations unleashed by Johnson on Senator Williams were centered on making him seem like a cad, rather than the soft-spoken former chicken-feed dealer who tenaciously, gallantly—but credulously—tried to expose high-level corruption in Washington. More salacious rumors began to circulate from a mysterious source that Senator Williams was connected somehow to Carole Tyler, one of the party girls from the Quorum; when Ms. Tyler took the stage to defend herself, she revealed that she had important information about Senator Williams' sex life. She turned up at a Nashville press conference, reading a prepared statement:[105]

---

101. Mollenhoff, p. 316.
102. Ibid.
103. Hersh, Seymour, *The Dark Side of Camelot,* pp. 406–407.
104. Lasky, *It Didn't Start . . .,* p. 125.
105. Ibid., pp. 139–140.

"I wonder what you would think if you knew that the principal instigator of the Senate investigation was seen by me on July 6 at 6:30 A.M. with a lady—not his wife—just after they finished breakfast. And just think, this is the gentleman who has been criticizing the Senate Rules Committee for not going into the so-called sex angle of the Baker case.* I leave it to his conscience, if any, as to why he was with this lady—not his wife—at such a time near a summer resort."

Asked to name the senator, Miss Tyler responded, "I think you know who I mean." Actually, Miss Tyler had been telling the truth. She did, in fact, see the senator with a lady not his wife. The lady happened to be his granddaughter, whom he was accompanying to her home following a weekend at the beach. But Williams refused to dignify the attack by commenting on it at the time.

Behind the scenes of this soap opera, it became apparent that Johnson's fixation with "getting" Senator Williams was, by this time, becoming a maniacal obsession, which his aides realized was running the risk of destroying his own credibility. Despite Johnson's efforts to stop the Senate investigation, the pressure brought by Senator Williams made it difficult for the Democratic majority to close the matter; they finally managed to take it out of play by referring it to the Criminal Division of the Justice Department. When the division failed to get Hoover's cooperation to "wire" an informant who was about to confer with Baker—he actually reported this request to Johnson, who immediately stopped it—the Justice Department lawyers then routinely asked for help from the Bureau of Narcotics, which complied immediately.

In the meantime, Baker thought he had escaped by having taken the Fifth Amendment and presumed he was "off the hook." He was wrong about that and in 1967 was finally indicted on seven counts of tax evasion, one count of theft, and one count of conspiracy to defraud the government. This upset Johnson, who then ordered his aide Marvin Watson to get a complete rundown on former assistant attorney general Herbert J. Miller, who had ordered the use of wiretaps and bugs to investigate Baker. At the FBI, DeLoach wrote an internal memo outlining the request and stating that it should be done "as discreetly as possible," and any reports should address "whether any of these individuals were close to Bobby Kennedy."[106] Baker was found guilty but managed to stall his prison term for several years while

---

* Though the Baker case was replete with sex angles, the fact was that Senator Williams never called on the Rules Committee to investigate them.
106. Ibid., pp. 140–141.

he appealed the conviction. The man who Johnson referred to as his "son" began serving his sentence in January 1971, at Lewisburg Penitentiary, until his parole after seventeen months in 1972.[107]

Baker himself wrote a sad ending to the story: "One Sunday evening I was consulting with Abe Fortas at his home when Lady Bird Johnson called . . . I hardly heard her. I was thinking: *LBJ's right there by her side, but he won't talk to me because he wants to be able to say he hasn't.* I knew that Johnson was petrified that he would be dragged down . . . LBJ was already nervous because of the previous Estes scandal and the resignation of a Texas friend, Fred Korth, who'd quit as secretary of the Navy following conflict-of-interest accusations. So I'd not expected to hear much from him. In fact, from the moment I resigned in October of 1963 until I visited him at his ranch to see a dying man, almost nine years later, we spoke not a word and communicated only through intermediaries."[108] After Baker's release from prison, in September 1972, Walter Jenkins, who had also been reunited with his mentor, telephoned and arranged for him to visit Johnson at his home in Texas.

During this visit, Johnson told Baker that he wanted to come to his aid, "But Bobby Kennedy would have crucified me . . . If there was any way in the world I could have turned off the investigation when I became president, I'd have gladly done it. But I knew it would be politically disastrous, and perhaps even legally disastrous." The next morning, Johnson raised the question that bugged him the most: "LBJ gave me a sideways look and said, 'Bobby, what's gonna be in that book I hear you're writing? Is it gonna be one of those kiss-and-tell books?' Baker replied that he was "still in the outline and research stage, that the book hadn't yet been fully formed in my mind."[109] Baker undoubtedly reassured Johnson that he was safe. He acknowledged that, if he had revealed the information he knew about in its entirety, there would have been extensive recriminations to many of his old political friends. He added that he could not "chirp like a canary" and further stated that "I would not have liked myself very much had I turned informer." Neither did he say anything about the influence of the million dollars Johnson agreed to pay him, which was negotiated by Nat Voloshen.

Fast Forward: March 1978

Fifteen years later, in a revealing interview with Michael Gillette for an Oral History documentary for the LBJ Library, about the Bobby Baker

---

107. Ibid.
108. Baker, Bobby, p. 182.
109. Ibid., p. 272.

investigations, Senator Carl Curtis spoke candidly about Lyndon Johnson's invisible "footprints" behind the closure of the Senate investigation into Baker's criminal activities:[110]

> "Everything would appear as though Lyndon didn't know the investigation was going on. He had the ability to direct things and not be anywhere near the scene. No, he didn't get caught interfering with that investigation at all."

That characteristic of Johnson was at the heart of all of his maneuvers and manipulations throughout his career. It was there in the stolen 1948 election; it was true of his dealings with Billie Sol Estes; it was obvious in the Bobby Baker scandals even before Senator Curtis spelled it out for Mr. Gillette. And it was axiomatic in Johnson's long-term plot to become president at the expense of John F. Kennedy's life.

In his autobiography *Forty Years against the Tide*, Senator Curtis described the attempted investigation into the activities of Lyndon Johnson through his associates Bobby Baker, Walter Jenkins, and Fred Black. Curtis was a member of the Senate Rules Committee chaired by Senator Williams, which was in the process of secretly interviewing Don Reynolds as JFK was being assassinated. He spent two years trying, unsuccessfully, to get the case investigated. Moreover, Curtis confirmed the information from Burkett Van Kirk, the Republican counsel to the committee, which was that most of the incriminating information came from Robert F. Kennedy, who was planning to get Johnson dropped as vice president. He also revealed that much of the information on Baker came from a "bug" placed on instructions by RFK in Fred Black's Washington hotel suite.[111] (Perhaps Senator Curtis was unaware that Hoover was already taping that room.)

According to Curtis, Johnson pressured the seven Democrats to vote against hearing the testimony of important witnesses, including two women who had been secretaries to Bobby Baker: Margaret Broome and Carole Tyler. The word went forth that Broome could not be relied on to keep quiet, so the six Democrats on the committee voted against allowing her to appear. It was understood, however, that Carole Tyler, who had become Baker's mistress, was a "safe" witness, despite the allegations by Reynolds that she was deeply involved in handling funds which were earmarked for

---

110. Oral history interview with Carl Curtis for the Johnson Library, October 3, 1978. Interviewer: Michael Gillette.
111. Curtis, Carl T., *Forty Years against the Tide*, p. 248.

bribery, and had traveled extensively on Serve-U Corporation business. Tyler did testify but refused to answer questions on the ground that she might incriminate herself (Tyler later died in the strange crash of a small airplane on the beach in front of Baker's Carousel Motel in Ocean City, Maryland). Senator Curtis described Baker, Jenkins, and Black as "contact men." He added, "Contact-men existed primarily to obtain for their clients and themselves some share of the vast pool of riches in the possession of swollen centralized political bureaucracies. The more impressive a contact-man's political connections, the better he and his clients would fare."[112]

When Baker was finally brought to trial for his misdeeds, one of the scams brought before the jurors—which illustrates the practically unlimited potential scope of his under-the-table dealings, clearly the conceptual baby of Lyndon Johnson, who provided him the tools and coached him in the amorality which ensured its success—resulted from his pressing California savings and loan association to contribute $100,000 to senatorial campaigns. He kept $80,000 for himself, in order to help fund his own finances, which were depleted by his investment in the Carousel Motel.[113] Baker then suggested to Senator Robert Kerr, who had stepped up to fill the "influence peddler" void after Johnson became vice president, that some of the savings and loan executives would be willing to put up $200,000 if their taxes were not increased. According to Drew Pearson, "On Nov. 9, 1962 Bobby Baker brought in the first installment—$100,000 in greenbacks—and laid it on Sen. Kerr's desk . . . Kerr counted out the money and stacked it in three piles on his desk. He put $50,000 in one pile to go to the Oklahoma campaign. He put $10,000 in another pile to go for contingent expenses. And he put $40,000 in another pile, which he gave to Bobby Baker. He told Baker at the time that he should begin looking out for himself and that this was a gift."[114] It isn't clear which of his sponsors—the senator whose political influence was being purchased, Johnson followed by Kerr—was the more generous with their "finder's fee," but this transaction was probably typical of how these funds were shared. The meaning of the term "contingent expenses" can probably be inferred to be a provisional amount for legal fees in the "worst case" scenario.

Having as their main political connection the new president of the United States reflects the height of the pinnacle of their careers reached by these power brokers, pimps, and lobbyists.

---

112. Ibid.
113. *Bobby Baker Trial Begins*, Associated Press, January 10, 1967.
114. Pearson, Drew. *Issues in Baker Trial*, January 7, 1967.

Jack Ruby's Statements of Johnson's Involvement . . . and His Quick Death by "Cancer"

In March 1965, Jack Ruby conducted a televised news conference in which he stated the following:

> "Everything pertaining to what's happening has never come to the surface. The world will never know the true facts of what occurred, my motives. The people who had so much to gain, and had such an ulterior motive for putting me in the position I'm in, will never let the true facts come above board to the world." When asked by a reporter, "Are these people in very high positions Jack?" he responded "Yes."[115]

Jack Ruby intimated that Lyndon B. Johnson was responsible for the assassination when he added that, had Adlai Stevenson been the vice president, it would have never happened. "When I mentioned about Adlai Stevenson, if he was vice president there would never have been an assassination of our beloved President Kennedy." Asked if he would explain it again, Ruby continued, "Well, the answer is the man in office now (Lyndon Johnson).[116] While waiting for his appeal for his first trial to be adjudicated, Ruby wrote a sixteen-page letter, which he gave to a fellow prisoner to smuggle out of jail. This letter wound up in the hands of researcher Penn Jones. The following excerpts indicate that Ruby repeatedly leveled the charge that Lyndon Johnson was behind the assassination:[117]

> First, you must realize that the people here want everyone to think I am crazy, so if what I know is actually [*sic*], and then no one will believe me, because of my supposed insanity. Now, I know that my time is running out . . . they plan on doing away with [me] . . . As soon as you get out you must read Texan looks at Lyndon [*sic: A Texan Looks at Lyndon: A Study in Illegitimate Power*, by J. Evetts Haley] and it might open your eyes to a lot of things. This man [Johnson] is a Nazi in the worst order. For over a year now they have been doing away with my people . . . don't believe the Warren report, that was only put out to make me look innocent in that it would throw the Americans and all the European country's [*sic*] off guard . . . There are so many things that have been played with success that

---

115. Jack Ruby's Press Conference: (http://www.youtube.com/watch?v=we2eucWXqjg).
116. Ref. Jack Ruby—Part 2 @ 5:35 (http://www.youtube.com/watch?v=FDDxYOqyqlc&feature=related).
117. Marrs, *Crossfire*, pp. 430–431 (ref: Penn Jones, *The Continuing Inquiry*, November 22, 1978 and December 22, 1978).

it would take all nite to write them out . . . I am going to die a horrible death anyway, so what would I have to gain by writing all this. So you must believe me . . . Johnson is going to try to have an all-out war with Russia and when that happens, Johnson and his cohorts will be on the side-lines where they won't get hurt, while the Americans may get wiped out. The only way this can be avoided is that if Russia would be informed as to [who] the real enemies are, and in that way they won't be tricked into starting a war with the U.S. One more thing, isn't it strange that Oswald who hasn't worked a lick most of his life, should be fortunate enough to get a job at the Book Bldg. two wks before the president himself didn't know as to when he was to visit Dallas, nowhere would a jerk like Oswald get the information that the president was coming to Dallas. Only one person could have had that information, and that man was Johnson who knew weeks in advance as to what was going to happen because he is the one who was going to arrange the trip for [the] president, this had been planned long before [the] president himself knew about [it], so you figure that one out. The only one who gained by the shooting of the president was Johnson, and he was in a car in the rear and safe when the shooting took place. What would the Russians, Castro or anyone else have to gain by eliminating the president? If Johnson was so heartbroken over Kennedy, why didn't he do something for Robert Kennedy? All he did was snub him.

According to Jim Marrs,[118] Deputy Sheriff Al Madox said, "We had a phony doctor come in to [the Dallas County Jail] from Chicago, just as phony and queer as a three-dollar bill. And he worked his way in through—I don't know, whoever supplied the county at that time with doctors . . . you could tell he was Ruby's doctor. He spent half his time up there talking with Ruby." Ruby told me, "Well, they injected me for a cold. It was cancer cells." DPD Officer Tom Tilson said that "it was the opinion of a number of other police officers that Ruby had received injections of cancer." Bruce McCarthy, who operated an electron microscope at Southwest Medical School near Parkland Hospital, was asked to analyze Ruby's cancer cells and explained there are two types of cancer cells: cilia (which affect the respiratory system) and microvilli (affecting the digestive system). McCarthy identified Ruby's cells as microvilli, indicating they originated in the digestive system. He was shocked when it was announced that Ruby died from lung cancer.

---

118. Ibid., pp. 432–433.

On October 5, 1966, the Texas Court of Appeals reversed Ruby's conviction and granted him a new trial. Ruby realized that this could mean he could get a five-year sentence; he could be out on the streets as soon as the trial was over, having already served three years of his time in jail. On December 7, they decided the trial would be held in Wichita Falls.[119] This realization would have caused many people back in Washington to become very nervous. Only two days later, on December 9, Ruby was taken to Parkland Hospital. He had suddenly come down with a persistent cough and nausea. The doctors initially decided it must be pneumonia. The very next day, however, cancer was diagnosed. After some testing, it was decided that Ruby's lung cancer was no longer curable.

Though many believe Ruby died of cancer, he didn't. On January 2, 1967, a blood clot formed, forcing the doctors to put Ruby on an oxygen mask. The next day, at 9:00 a.m., Ruby had a spasm; ninety minutes later, he was declared dead. Dr. Earl Rose, the man who had done the autopsy of Tippit and Oswald and should have done the autopsy on the president—but for the orders of Lyndon Johnson to hijack JFK's corpse—discovered that the heaviest concentration of cancer cells was in the right lung, with traces of white cancerous tumors throughout the body. According to the doctors who treated Ruby, his cancer had originated in the pancreas, but Rose saw a normal pancreas. Rose listed the immediate cause of death to be pulmonary embolism (i.e., a massive blood clot) that had formed in the leg, had gone through the heart, and had ended in his lung. Ruby's body was flown to Chicago, where he was born, and buried in the Westlawn Cemetery, next to his parents.

Before his death, Ruby had made at least three suicide attempts. He tried to hang himself, he split his skull by running into a wall, and at one time unscrewed the light bulb and threw water over his feet, trying to electrocute himself, only discovering the lightbulb was too high to reach while standing. One of the doctors assigned to Ruby was Dr. Louis Joy Ion West, a psychiatrist who had worked with the CIA's MK/ULTRA program, which involved the use of LSD and other experimental psychological procedures. Dr. West was brought in mysteriously, by persons unknown, as he had no previous connection to Ruby or Dallas. If Ruby was in some way administered LSD, this would explain Ruby's pitiful attempts to go jumping up and down, trying to reach the lightbulb and thus kill himself or to split his skull.[120]

In a second letter Ruby wrote and had smuggled out of jail, he stated,[121] "They found some very clever means and ways to trick me and which will

---

119. Ibid., p. 432.
120. Coppens, This Is Not America p. 222.
121. Marrs, p. 431 (ref: Copy in files of researcher J. Gary Shaw).

be used later as evidence to show the American people that I was part of the conspiracy in the assassination of president . . . *They alone planned the killing, by they I mean Johnson and others . . . In all the history of the United States never has a president been elected that has the background of Johnson. Believe me, compared to him I am a Saint.*" (Emphasis added.)

The Kennedys Stifle Manchester to Appease Lyndon Johnson

In March 1964, Jacqueline Kennedy and Robert Kennedy entered into an agreement with author William Manchester to write "an extensive account describing the events of and surrounding the death of President Kennedy on November 22, 1963."[122] The reporters covering this announcement had no idea of the disaster that was about to ensue. That result was almost guaranteed by the looseness and ambiguity of the letter of understanding written by Robert Kennedy, the top legal official of the United States having a staff of thousands of attorneys, and signed by the author he had chosen for the project. Later correspondence between the two continued the confusion, including a telegram sent by RFK, which stated that "members of the Kennedy family will place no obstacle in the way of publication of his work."[123]

The entire controversy stemmed from Manchester's account of Lyndon Johnson's behavior after the assassination, including his taking over Air Force One, then forcing Mrs. Kennedy to participate in his swearing in ceremony. The Kennedys did not want the unvarnished truth revealed because it would only exacerbate the poor relationship between them and Johnson, and run the risk of harming Robert Kennedy's image and political career. As the controversy became public, Bobby's prescience on that point proved to be correct, but not in the way he feared; instead, he came to be seen as a ruthless, vindictive, mean-spirited man who would countenance "book burning" where it suited his needs. Johnson, ironically, was seen as the hapless victim of the Kennedy's stridency, despite the fact that it was his own boorish behavior and his rude, insensitive, and arrogant actions that caused the rift in the first place.

Though William Manchester made a number of mistakes in the epic account he rushed to have published, his account is veritable and almost intact, in spite of tremendous pressure on him to delete much of his treatment of Johnson. Ultimately, he agreed to some changes "in passages deemed distasteful by Mrs. Kennedy" to soften the criticisms of Johnson. But the

---

122. Van Gelder, p. 19 (quoting from a press release dated March 26, 1964 from the "Office of the Attorney General").
123. Ibid., p. 37.

early changes proved to be inadequate to appease them, even though they had personally not reviewed the manuscript. It was clear that Manchester had correctly described Johnson's actions; however, the changes requested were based on political points, which RFK's strategists (including Richard Goodwin, Edwin Guthman, John Seigenthaler, Pierre Salinger, Arthur Schlesinger Jr., and Theodore Sorensen) had asked for, before excerpts were published in *Look* magazine. Lawrence Van Gelder described the tension between the Kennedys, Johnson, and Manchester in his book, *Why the Kennedys Lost the Book Battle*:

> In the first installment, the Kennedy strategists sought changes affecting 288 words; in the second, 270; in the third, 2,737; and in the fourth, 3,177. It was clear that the deletions sought were proportional to Lyndon Johnson's mounting prominence in the narrative. Johnson had not been interviewed by Manchester. Two appointments were made, then cancelled. Johnson did, however, see written questions from Manchester. He did not answer all of them. His testimony before the Warren Commission had not stressed any friction aboard Air Force One . . . Kennedy told Manchester, the author said later, that Sorensen had advised him to file suit because the manuscript endangered his political future . . . . But efforts to induce Manchester to change his manuscript did not cease . . . . the author said there came what he later called "the largest wave, of 111—the suggestion that 111 passages be deleted. These were clearly political. They were not made by the Senator, who had not read the manuscript, but by one of his representatives . . . ." "Of course," the author said later, "we were still cutting. But with these people when you cut something, nobody ever says, 'Thank you.' They look at the rest and try to think: 'What else can we cut now.'"[124]

In the end, Jacqueline Kennedy got the most important deletions she had asked for, including a significant softening of Johnson's demand that she appear and be photographed for his swearing-in ceremony. Altogether, Manchester agreed to delete a total of seven pages from the book at Mrs. Kennedy's request.[125] It should be noted that Manchester had already eliminated two hundred pages, "which I felt was personal or which would injure the prestige of people now in public office."[126] When he originally wrote Mrs. Kennedy after completing the book, he admitted that, "I tried

124. Ibid., pp. 61–63.
125. Van Gelder, pp. 82–83.
126. Ibid., p. 31.

desperately to suppress my bias against *a certain eminent statesman who always reminded me of someone in a grade-D movie on the Late Show,* the prejudice showed through . . ."[127] (Emphasis added.) Author Van Gelder allowed that "there was little doubt about the identity of the unnamed person."[128] Ironically, it was Lyndon Johnson who had created the animosity which caused the controversies Manchester recorded, yet it was also he who benefited from the public reaction against this account, apparently because it was considered unnecessarily harsh and unfair to the new president. Once again, Johnson escaped the elusive atonement which he richly deserved because of the public's disbelief that his behavior could have been as bad as Manchester had apparently presented it. Johnson had Moyers, Reedy, and others pull all the strings they could to turn the situation around within the press corps; he knew that, as president, he would automatically be imbued with the deference that automatically attaches to the presidency, which was the biggest prize of all: an unlimited supply of "benefit of the doubt," which for him was the currency he had used throughout his lifetime.

Harper and Row published the reedited *Death of a President,* and it became a best seller. *Look* set new records for magazine sales in its serialization of the book. William Manchester banked $650,000 in 1967 and obtained new book contracts for future revenue. Robert Kennedy got nothing except a drop in his favorable polling numbers, which had been on the ascendancy for the two previous years. "It was Robert Kennedy who bore the brunt of public outrage and whose future was drastically altered by the dispute."[129] While getting no concessions from Manchester, RFK also "lost prestige among the liberals, who considered him a book burner and were chagrined at the revelation, that same month, of Kennedy's role as a wire-tapper [of Martin Luther King]. The newly wooed Southerners, particularly in Texas, resented Manchester's portrayal of Dallas as a spawning ground for violent psychotics. Party leaders around the country . . . now viewed Kennedy as a bungler or worse. 'I never thought much of Lyndon,' explained one leading Texas Democrat. 'But now I understand what he's gone through. The Kennedys have so displayed that they've put their ambitions ahead of patriotism, I'm obsessed with the necessity to support Lyndon.'"[130] Such a sentiment—to say that one "now understands what Lyndon has gone through"—is sad indeed.

Ultimately, Manchester agreed to withhold the censored pages for 100 years, until the year 2067. According to author Van Gelder, the material

---

127. Ibid., p. 68.
128. Ibid.
129. Ibid., p. 91.
130. Ibid., pp. 123–124.

in these pages indicates that it "dealt almost entirely with Johnson: his part in the events of Novmber 22, 1963; his relationships with members of the Kennedy family; his image as a crude and boorish Texas cowboy, wiping his muddy boots in the halls of Camelot."[131] Some of the specific points included, among other things:[132]

> "members of the Kennedy party—in effect holding Johnson responsible for the assassination—refused to sit with him on the return flight from Dallas; that he had been brusquely blocked off from the coffin when the plane landed at Andrews AFB; that his general conduct toward Mrs. Kennedy on the plane was heavy-handed; that he had insisted she appear for his oath-taking and prior to the settlement of the lawsuit, it was leaked that Schlesinger—within hours after the assassination—had inquired about dumping Johnson as a candidate in 1964."

Whatever might have prompted Schlesinger's actions to try to dump Johnson will apparently never be known, at least until 2067, if even then. Manchester's agreement with the Kennedys was to keep the deleted pages under seal for one hundred (100) years; perhaps my grandson, born in 2007, will still be around to discover what was so damaging to the 1967 relationship between Lyndon Johnson, Bobby, and Jacqueline Kennedy that required these deleted pages to be withheld from the public for that long. It is likely that those deleted passages contain great insights into Johnson's role based upon his immediate actions after the assassination.

The Wallace Fingerprint: Identified Thirty-five Years Later . . .

The primary role of Johnson's hit man, Mac Wallace, was to ensure that the "right" shells were in place and all others on that floor were picked up. Wallace's fingerprint was identified three decades later as being a "match" to one left on a box in the sniper's nest. Researcher/author Walt Brown called a press conference in Dallas in May 1998 to announce that a previously unidentified fingerprint at the "sniper's nest" had been linked to Malcolm Wallace by an expert fingerprinting analyst. Using the 1951 fingerprints from Malcolm Wallace's arrest for the murder of Doug Kinser, a certified fingerprint examiner, A. Nathan Darby, positively matched Wallace's print with a copy of a fingerprint labeled "Unknown," which had been lifted the day of the assassination from a carton by the southeast sixth floor window

---

131. Van Gelder, 92.
132. Van Gelder, 72–73.

of the Texas School Book Depository. This carton was labeled "box A," and also contained several fingerprints identified as those of Lee Harvey Oswald. Mr. Darby, a member of the International Association of Identifiers, signed a sworn, notarized affidavit stating that he was able to affirm a 14-point match between the "Unknown" fingerprint and the "blind" print card submitted to him. The generally accepted standard requires only a 12-point match for legal identification. Since cardboard does not retain fingerprints for very long, it is clear that Malcolm E. Wallace had left his fingerprint on "box A" on the sixth floor of the Texas School Book Depository early on November 22, 1963.[133]

Critics of this identification have said that there was too much missing from the partial fingerprint being studied to attach 100 percent certainty to the results despite Darby's unequivocal certitude. For this reason, the evidence has never been conclusively settled one way or the other during the intervening twelve years; one reason for that may be because neither the FBI nor the Texas DPS will release the fingerprints for further testing in the absence of a specific pending case to attach it to. Evidently, solving the murder of a former president is not sufficient justification for the release of this public record.

Lyndon Johnson's Gamesmanship

In 1967, Marvin Watson, a Johnson aide, confided to an FBI official that his boss now felt that there was conspiracy in the assassination of President Kennedy. The FBI official wrote: "[Johnson] was now convinced there was a plot in connection with the assassination. Watson stated the president felt that CIA had something to do with this plot."[134] In the fall of 1968, shortly before he would leave the White House for good, Johnson volunteered a piece of information to the ABC newsman Howard K. Smith: "I'll tell you something [about John Kennedy's murder] that will rock you," he said. "Kennedy was trying to get to Castro, but Castro got to him first." "I was rocked, all right," Smith later recalled; he begged for details. But Johnson refused to provide any, saying only, "It will all come out one day."[135]

Six months after Johnson's death, *The Atlantic* published an article by one of his former speechwriters, then a *Time* bureau chief, Leo Janos, *The Death of the President*. The interview, taken toward the end of Johnson's life, was done with the understanding that the end was coming soon. Johnson made a comment that would expand on his statement made five years earlier

---

133. Also see McClellan, Exhibits A,B,C,D,E,F,G,H and I.
134. Marrs, p. 209.
135. Schlesinger, p. 701–702 f/n. (Ref. Howard K. Smith, ABC News Broadcast, 6/24/76).

to Howard K. Smith. Johnson told Janos that in his opinion, President Kennedy's assassination had been the result of a conspiracy organized within Cuba in retaliation for the various U.S. plots against Castro. "I never believed that Oswald acted alone, although I can accept that he pulled the trigger," he said to Janos.[136] Additionally, he said that once taking office, he had discovered that the CIA "had been operating a damned Murder Inc. in the Caribbean."[137]

Between these three rather provocative canards, Johnson had planted three distinct potential geneses of the plot: the CIA acting alone, Castro, and the Mafia in cahoots with the CIA. They were the primary three theories being discussed at the time, including at Jim Garrison's trial of Clay Shaw. As with practically everything else Johnson had ever said, there was a "self-serving" aspect to these comments; in this case, he was simply trying to divert attention from himself and toward other, mutually exclusive, alternatives. In the first statement to Janos, he said, "I *never* believed that Oswald acted alone . . ." (Emphasis added.) That means that he lied to the American public multiple times (not surprisingly or out of character, of course) presumably to keep from alarming the country. If he never believed his own Warren Commission, then he was with the majority opinion on that issue, but that begs the question: Who then might have been behind it? If he meant in the latter part of the statement exactly what he said, that he stumbled upon this information about assassination attempts on Castro after he became president, the implication is that all of this was a complete surprise to him. That is highly unlikely, considering the number of confidants and back channels he had throughout the Pentagon, the CIA, FBI, and other intelligence agencies. He would have surely been aware of these incidents, at least right after they had been deployed, if not before. It has been reported that within the administration after the Bay of Pigs, it was common knowledge that President Kennedy made his brother the driving force behind the effort to overthrow Castro.[138] Johnson was certainly part of that administration; even though he was kept at bay by many insiders, he still had many other contacts who would have made him aware of activities by his nemesis, Robert F. Kennedy. While it is possible he did not know of Robert Kennedy's most secret plans in 1963, to think that he was unaware of the previous efforts against Castro before his taped conversation with Ramsey Clark on March 2, 1967, and another with John Connally on March 13, 1967, would require a complete suspension of disbelief.

---

136. Holland, Max, The Assassination Tapes. The Atlantic Magazine, June 2004.
137. Ibid.
138. Ibid.

Giving him the "benefit of the doubt" on that point, and assuming he really believed that Castro was behind the assassination, suggests that he purposely ignored even the possibility of a retaliatory attack by a Communist country ninety miles from the U.S. shore. Against such a "real threat" next door, the subsequent bullying and bellicose threats which would soon lead to an all-out war with a nonthreatening third world country nine thousand miles away—under the full force of American military power over the ensuing decade, at an enormous loss of life and limb to our soldiers, sailors, and airmen—makes even less sense. As troubling as all of that is, it is even more disturbing when one considers the juxtaposition of these two separately unfolding policies as they occurred in real time, beginning in November 1963 and continuing throughout the end of his term in 1968. Castro, for his part, made a number of entreaties to Johnson through William Attwood and Lisa Howard, who were the still-active "back channel" conduits through which Kennedy had tried to negotiate privately with Castro; Johnson ignored these attempts and continued ignoring Castro. His UN Ambassador, Adlai Stevenson, also tried to get Johnson to make an effort to resume communications, to no avail. Castro then enlisted the help of his Cuban Minister of Industry, Ernesto "Che" Guevara, who met with Eugene McCarthy at Lisa Howard's New York apartment in December 1964 to try to establish a relationship: Johnson ignored that as well.[139]

Lyndon Johnson showed little interest in dealing with, or removing, Fidel Castro. He told Dean Rusk, Maxwell Taylor, and John McCone a week after the assassination, on December 2, 1963, that South Vietnam is "our most critical military area right now."[140] Furthermore, according to David Kaiser, Johnson "never seriously considered the alternatives of neutralization and withdrawal (from Vietnam). Johnson, in short, accepted the premises of the policies that had been developed under Eisenhower—premises whose consequences Kennedy had consistently refused to accept for three years."[141] The real reason for Johnson making his stand in Vietnam, rather than Cuba, may have been as simple as his not wanting to give Robert Kennedy the satisfaction of taking action toward an invasion of Cuba. As absurd as that might sound, it is entirely consistent with all the other actions Johnson ever took, nearly always based on the narrow trajectory of what was best for himself, personally, as demonstrated repeatedly throughout this text.

His last statements regarding the assassination were simply intended as yet another smoke screen or puzzle for those who write history books to

---

139. Douglass, pp. 90–92.
140. Kaiser, David. pp. 288–290.
141. Ibid.

interpret. He made this statement knowing that most people held the view that there had been a conspiracy even though there were many different ones from which to choose. This was simply another attempt by him to muddy the water by selecting the one he thought was most salable in the hope that posterity would come to settle on that one, thus deflecting the real one—the factual one which he feared that someone would figure out and might someday become established as the one most commonly held. In other words, he was simply planning to game the system for eternity, just as he had so expertly done for his entire forty-plus-year career. He probably went to his grave thinking that his superior intellect and manipulative skills— including his treasured "Johnson treatment"—would continue protecting his reputation well after his death. Just as George Reedy would eventually explain for posterity, Johnson would tell a story that he had come to believe was the truth; if he really believed it, and if everyone else believed it too, then wouldn't it become official history, what all those nitpicking journalists and historians would pass on as representing the truth?

EPILOGUE

[When we pull out] of Vietnam in 1965: I'll become one of the most unpopular presidents in history. I'll be damned everywhere as a communist appeaser. But I don't care. If I tried to pull out completely now from Vietnam, we would have a Joe McCarthy red scare on our hands, but I can do it after I'm reelected. So we had better make damned sure that I am reelected.

—JOHN F. KENNEDY

Just get me elected, and then you can have your war.

—LYNDON B. JOHNSON
(TO THE JOINT CHIEFS OF STAFF AT A 1963 CHRISTMAS PARTY)

Summary

In the first several chapters of this book, we saw the innate defects of Lyndon Johnson's character and how they were to become his most defining traits. His learned behavior—the manipulative skills, the ability to lay elaborate plans to accomplish his goals, the ingenuity of categorizing everyone by their weaknesses for future exploitation—coupled with his natural abilities and manic-driven quest to achieve his goals provided him the platform from which his entire career was launched.

By 1958, at the age of fifty, Lyndon B. Johnson had accomplished a nearly unbelievable rise to the pinnacle of political power in the United States, yet he had come to believe that the chasm between where he was—the majority leader of the U.S. Senate—and where he aspired to be was practically an impossible hurdle. His mentors in Congress, Representative Rayburn and Senator Russell, had convinced him that his Southern ties would prevent him from winning the presidency. By this time, his constant battles with the highs and lows brought on by his bipolar disorder—which grew unchecked by medical attention for the entire course of his political career—left him with a great fear of rejection, afraid to run for the office he had always been obsessed with achieving.

In 1960, he so feared losing the nomination for the presidency that he didn't announce his candidacy, and did no campaigning, until five days before the Democratic convention. Even then, he seemed to know that the campaign was over before it started; his only hope of beating John Kennedy was exposing his health problems. However, that did not work inasmuch as he could not produce the "proof" that it required; that would risk revealing his source for the information. Other than the most negative attacks on JFK and his father, Johnson's presidential "campaign" was virtually nonexistent.

In contrast to his presidential "noncampaign," his campaign for the vice presidential nomination was stunning in its ferocity. The array of armaments he deployed in Los Angeles—for a position no one had ever before striven for—was formidable, unmistakably well planned, and precisely executed. He used every tactic imaginable, from the persuasive powers of Phil Graham and Sam Rayburn to the blackmail material from the files of J. Edgar Hoover to the use of threats and intimidation by Johnson himself. He vowed to kill any legislative initiatives Kennedy might ever send to the Hill. The overpowering blitz was so effective that it became an offer Kennedy "could not refuse." Lyndon Johnson desperately wanted the vice presidential nomination— arguably a "step down" from his position as majority leader—because he knew it would be the only means by which he would ever reach the White House. In 1960, he was fifty-two years old; if Kennedy had lived and been reelected in 1964, by the end of his term in 1968, Johnson would have been sixty years old, almost the end of his expected life given his family history. That wouldn't do; he knew he had to create another plan to ensure his ascendancy before then.

During his almost three-year term as the vice president, Johnson would do everything he could to sabotage Kennedy behind his back. In foreign affairs, it included disagreements on Cuba and the Soviet Union and, most significantly, Vietnam. In the domestic arena, the primary issue was how he attempted to slow the progress of civil rights legislation and keep it as ineffective as possible, only months before he would reverse course and force congress to pass the most sweeping reforms in history.

His real objectives during the period 1961–63 were focused on taking high-level risks to continue his side businesses of selling the value of his political influence through associates, underworld figures, and lobbyists. He even compromised other administration officials to assist him to perpetuate these scandals, in one instance persuading Orville Freeman, the secretary of agriculture, to relax regulatory rules in order for his friend and benefactor Billie Sol Estes to carry out massive financial fraud. The traces of Johnson's hand in the criminal activity of a number of men, culminating in that of Estes and Bobby Baker—including the murders of several men uniquely vulnerable to the will of only one man, Lyndon B. Johnson—lead to the inescapable conclusion that he was capable of the most heinous crimes imaginable. In

Dallas that day, he had key men positioned such that they would be available at the right times and the right places to ensure the plan was well executed. Only two of them—Cliff Carter and Malcolm Wallace—would know what was really going on; the others on hand, Connally, Moyers, Jack Puterbaugh, and a few lesser aides, would not. They were only following what might have been, for anyone else, strange and inexplicable orders, such as Moyer's assignment to request the removal of the bubble top that otherwise would have protected John F. Kennedy.

Johnson's behind-the-scenes manipulation of his men to prepare for the complete suspension of ordinary protection of the president—and his secretive charter of men to be selected by Angleton and his associates, purposely done with limited knowledge of operational details on his own part—would create the scene of the crime and presence of the assailants on the last day possible for salvaging his career. His plans for "phase 2" were designed to sew up the investigation and use the Texas judicial system to pronounce the designated "lone nut" the guilty party. At any later time, his nemesis, Bobby Kennedy, would have closed in on him and served an indictment rather than merely feeding information to congressional committees and *Life* magazine. His last day for achieving his lifetime obsession was, ironically, also the last day for him to thwart his grandmother's prognostication. Rather than end his lifetime in prison, as she had predicted, he would end it in the White House, in accordance with what he had always believed was his rightful destiny.

He had always favored the "lone nut" option since it would avoid the risk of World War III, an event which would certainly have carried with it the possibility of nuclear war, and of course the Soviets could be expected to aim their first missiles at 1600 Pennsylvania Avenue. However, there were many men at the highest levels of the military and intelligence organizations who preferred a head-on confrontation with these enemies, promising to annihilate them with a "first strike." To keep that option on the shelf, multiple trails to the assassin would be planted in Dallas, New Orleans, and Mexico City to justify an immediate invasion of Cuba; this would serve the purpose of plan B (required in the event that a "conspiracy" was undeniable) but would need to be covered over in the event that plan A prevailed.

Other trails—the supposed mail-order purchase of guns which were allegedly shipped to Oswald's post office box in Dallas (even though he had given no authorization for mail to "A. Hidell" at that location) and the newly created allegation that Oswald was the "shooter" of the retired right-wing General Walker—were so immediately established as to create the impression that they were just a little too convenient for reality. Since Oswald had not been immediately killed—and his voice, which had now been recorded, was clearly different than the "Oswald" voice recorded by the CIA—it quickly became apparent that the Castro-inspired conspiracy option had to be scuttled. As the new president settled in for the flight back to Washington, an impromptu decision was made which officially deemed Oswald the assassin; phase 2, the cover-up, was redirected to prove that the assassin was a poor misguided communist "lone nut," and Castro had nothing to do with it.

Cliff Carter had already begun calling the Dallas authorities to tell them as much, starting with the instruction that "you have your man" and no further investigation was necessary. Allen Dulles, probably knowing the real source of the assassination, stood ready to lead the charge that it was indeed merely a "lone nut" who killed the president when he prepared his notes for the first meeting of the presidential commission. In the meantime, it was time to "heal the country" and put the matter aside while the official government commission did its work. The citizens were assured that the government was in good hands, and the leaks from the commission performed their function of mollifying an entire population. The presidential commission dutifully returned its verdict: the dastardly deed was merely the work of a misguided fool and he had been killed by another misguided but patriotic citizen, and now, all the rest were safe from both of them. With that, the case was, almost, closed. The fact that it was not is testimony to the relentless work of hundreds of researchers and authors previously cited who have successfully dismantled the lie piece by piece.

The objectives set forth at the beginning of this book have been completed; Lyndon B. Johnson uniquely met every one of the criteria for evaluating who might have been behind the assassination of John F. Kennedy:

- Who had the most to gain?
- Who had the least to lose?
- Who had the means to do it?
- Who had the apparatus in place to subsequently cover it up? and
- Who had the kind of narcissistic/sociopathic personality capable of rationalizing the action as acceptable and necessary, together with the resolve and determination to see it through?

The massive body of information about the Kennedy assassination—including the hundreds or thousands of books, the materials collected by researchers for more than four decades, the partially released secret government files—have produced a more complete understanding of the forces, which culminated in Kennedy's murder. Some of the evidence has been there all along, including the Altgens photograph taken two to three seconds after Kennedy was hit in the throat in one of the first shots. Most of the rest of it, as attested to by the books listed in the bibliography, have spanned the forty-five-year period

1964–2009, and it has emerged very slowly despite the best efforts of many people to obfuscate facts and cloud the memories of those who witnessed the actual event.

How does one begin to explain the persona of Lyndon Johnson? To start a description by saying he was the thirty-sixth president of the United States automatically evokes the respect normally accorded to a person who achieved that high and majestic office. That the path he took to achieve it was different than any other man before (or after) him is worthy of more than an asterisk. His ascendancy came on the back of John F. Kennedy, just as his engineered (albeit flawed) "legacy" was bought with IOUs from JFK's bank of favors. His legacy should reflect his real persona: an egomaniacal, duplicitous politician dedicated only to his pursuit of the presidency; worse, it was only to satisfy his own vanity rather than for any altruistic, public-spirited, or patriotic reasons, though he sought to convince his "subjects" otherwise. His character should be at least partially defined by the ever-higher stolen elections all along the way—from his college days on through his clearly fraudulent election to the Senate in 1948—all of the steps in his ascendancy were tainted by fraud. His reputation as a magnanimous and gregarious respected world leader was as bogus as the voter fraud, illicit fund raising, and influence-peddling activities that "won" him his high offices. Historians credit him with his "people skills," but if one looks beneath the semipolished veneer—beyond the Texas colloquialisms, past the bluntness and sarcasm, the gross and demeaning behavior to others, and the ruthless disregard for legal and moral boundaries—the man should be known for what he was: a world-class criminal whose own grandmother had him pegged since he was a child when she predicted that he would one day end up in the penitentiary.

Resolving the Unsolved Murders

The series of murders for which Lyndon B. Johnson has been implicated were mostly committed in the 1960s, but the first two were in the early 1950s. A brief review of them is necessary in order to understand the context of how the future president of the United States apparently became involved in such extreme and despicable conduct. It should be observed that the early murders were sufficiently detached from Johnson so as to keep him at a safe distance by his attorney crony Ed Clark. While that would remain part of the modus operandi for the later murders, enough traces of his own hand and his direct motives would later appear to make the connections ever stronger until the final murder, that of John F. Kennedy. As one examines the details of each of the murders, the question inevitably arises, "Who would have had the motive to be behind this murder?" The answer, insofar as anyone else who might have had a motive, will of course vary by the individual victim. But when the focus is adjusted to a macro level—the entire group of the murdered people previously named—there is really only one person who would have conceivably benefited by *all of them*. The invisible hand of Lyndon B. Johnson can be seen behind each murder described: from Doug Kinser in 1951 to his own sister Josefa in 1961 (both intended to keep Josefa out of the news, which might expose himself to ridicule, a career-ending scandal, or the penitentiary). The remaining murders (except for the last one, of course) were of men connected to the Billie Sol Estes scandals, which were inexorably linked to Johnson because they had threatened to implicate him directly in fraud against the government as well as a number of businessmen. This, of course, would mean a prison term for him; but worse, in his view, was the loss of any possibility of him becoming president, which in his mind was his lifetime destiny.

The fact that he was never charged or convicted of them should be considered a mere technicality, just as others who have committed murder but were never convicted of them; due to other failures of the justice system, Johnson "got off." The random effectiveness of the American system of justice—which in the case of Johnson allowed him to continue enjoying his freedom to engage in ever higher, more deadly lawlessness and evade justice—should not mitigate the validity of arguments demonstrating that he was, nevertheless, guilty of numerous crimes. The evidence against Johnson is admittedly of a "hearsay" and circumstantial nature, thanks to his success at the time in having it suppressed. Nevertheless, many people have been convicted of murder on far less such evidence, in some cases, even in the absence of the body and/or the murder weapon. In the murders of the people who uniformly got into Johnson's way—and only Johnson, in the context of the entire group—the bodies were found, but the evidence was manipulated in such a way as to protect him from prosecution.

In the last one, John F. Kennedy's assassination, Lyndon Johnson would clearly have a bigger, more obvious motive than anyone else. In fact, his motive—coupled with those of the various accomplices noted within—would dwarf those of the hapless Lee Harvey Oswald. The motive of the president's accused killer, despite the enormous creativity of the Warren Commission and its staff to try to invent one, was never established. He had none; in fact, he had left several indications, as noted elsewhere, that he actually liked Kennedy. While it is impossible now to convict Johnson of the earlier murders, that should not be considered as an impediment to consider all of them— they all remain open, "unsolved cold cases"—as specific intrinsic evidence of a pattern. If the use of murder as a tool to accomplish his objectives during desperate times worked effectively once then twice and again and again, it follows that the use of the same tool could be rationalized by an obsessive and sociopathic mind to gain the object of his lifetime goal.

During his time as president, of course, Johnson had never consulted a psychiatrist, but he did in the final months of his life because the burden of carrying his crimes evidently became too much for him. According to his one-time attorney whose insights into Johnson's persona were described in his book, *Blood, Money & Power*, Barr McClellan stated that a trust arrangement was negotiated for the psychiatrist who treated Johnson to define what was to be considered privileged, but that after his death, and Lady Bird's death, he would be in a position to reveal his findings, though that has never been done. According to McClellan's insights into what Johnson told his attorney Don Thomas, it was understood that Johnson told Thomas about all the previous murders, as well as the assassination of Kennedy. He cited the investigations launched by Bobby into his criminal past and how they were closing in on him, closing out all of his options, as well as the Congressional hearings that were doing the same.[1]

The matter of Lyndon Johnson's mental health will be considered further below as it lies at the center of his successful political rise over nearly four decades to the same extent as his dramatic fall, which began immediately after being elected in the greatest landslide victory of all time. The events which the reader has become familiar with since the first pages of this book require one to reconsider Johnson's widely held public persona and the high esteem in which he is still held in many quarters. An honest evaluation of Johnson's actual imprint on American history requires one to consider this other evidence, which is not presently widely known about his past. Most historians and biographers prefer to avoid any allegation against him unless it can be proven through court documents, which show that a properly adjudicated legal case established the allegation as absolute fact, or have multiple credible sources for every assertion made against him; to dismiss the assertions of Madeleine Brown and Billie Sol Estes among others because they are considered disreputable—despite the fact that their statements are consistent and believable given the independently verifiable supporting material and witnesses—is to ignore substantive, provable information bearing on Johnson's involvement. If anyone should be considered disreputable, it should be Johnson himself based upon his proven record of the most outrageous lies and deceits, a summary of which appears throughout this book. Everything he accomplished—not the least of which, his "presidential commission"—should be examined with a jaundiced eye approach wherein everything he considered as "fact" is assumed to be suspect.

---

1. McClellan, 274–283.

Given Johnson's single-minded obsession with becoming president of the United States and the intensity of his resolve to achieve it—seemingly catapulted to higher and higher levels each time he repeated it, to himself or, occasionally, others—he is clearly the single individual most responsible for setting the assassination forces in motion. He would not have been able to achieve his objective without the willingness of others, many of whom, admittedly, may have already begun plotting on their own. But the others, whether they were high or low in the pecking order, acting from their base as a renegade CIA, FBI, or Secret Service member, disaffected Cuban exile or Mafia leader, were not in a position to ensure that they would get away with the crime. Only one person had the wherewithal to accomplish that. The totality of the evidence points toward Lyndon Johnson as the primary instigator, the uniquely positioned single person behind all the forces which led to John F. Kennedy's assassination. The twin "keystones" of this mass of evidence detailed in earlier chapters become clear only when they are juxtaposed together; then they become the compelling "smoking gun" which moves the circumstantial evidence from being merely "persuasive" to "convincing" and beyond a reasonable doubt:

- The statements of motorcycle patrolman B. J. Martin, who stated that according to the guys who were escorting his car in the motorcade . . . *[Johnson] started ducking down in the car a good 30 or 40 seconds before the first shots were fired . . . One of them told McGuire he saw Johnson duck down even before the car turned onto Houston Street, and he sure as hell wasn't laughing when he said it.*

- The Altgens photograph taken a few seconds after Kennedy was shot shows clearly that practically no one else had reacted except for Kennedy himself as he instinctively tried to grab his own neck. *A closer examination, however, shows that one person had already reacted by disappearing below the seat backs even before the first shot, thus providing clear photographic evidence of the veracity of Patrolman Martin's statement.*

It is said that the "best evidence"—in terms of the prosecution of a legal case— is that which is most certain, and the example generally used is photographic evidence that has not been tampered with. The Altgens photograph, arguably the single most famous still photograph of the assassination, has been there all along and would have been impossible to have been altered. Johnson himself probably noticed its implications and would have therefore liked to get it altered if he could to put himself back in it. Since that was obviously not possible—having it cropped to eliminate him and the car he was in—a censored version was entered as evidence for the Warren Commission.

The police testimony, although now considered hearsay, would have been admissible at the time if given under oath soon after the crime. But that was, of course, not done because there was no real investigation and the perpetrator of the crime had become the de facto chief justice of the land, having displaced the official chief justice of the Supreme Court to temporarily head the kangaroo court established to cover up the "crime of the century."

There is only one realistic explanation which fits all of the real facts of JFK's assassination, including Lyndon Johnson's absence from the Altgens photograph: he knew that Dealey Plaza was to be the killing zone. As soon as the motorcade turned on to Elm Street, he knew that bullets would be flying from three different directions. It also explains the heated argument he had with Kennedy at the hotel the morning of the assassination as he tried to replace Connally with Yarborough in the president's car; he tried to avoid putting his friend Connally in the line of fire but had no problem with having the hated Yarborough sitting in front of Kennedy. He knew the shots would all be aimed toward JFK; however, he was also aware that he had his own enemies, and he couldn't count on not being in the line of fire himself, even for an accidental missed shot. So he did what he had to do: he ducked, either through earlier well-thought-out planning or as a last-minute instinctive self-preservation act, even before the first shot was fired, which explains why he was so nervous throughout the motorcade.

Johnson's unseen hand, in the form of many of his aides and accomplices, was actively controlling the Dallas motorcade route (Puterbaugh), the change in motorcycle police protection (Rowley, Boring, Roberts, and Puterbaugh), the removal of the bubble top (Moyers), as well as halting the Dallas investigation (Carter) within hours and the FBI investigation (Hoover) within days. Ensuring that the final verdict of guilt would be assigned to the now-dead "lone nut" would also come from men completely under his control; that objective—originally intended for a Texas venue, changed in midcourse to the more venerated but equally controllable federal level—was the pièce de résistance of his entire plan. The evidence of all of these facts, along with all the other circumstantial evidence presented here, proves beyond a shadow of a doubt that Lyndon B. Johnson, at the very least, had foreknowledge of John F. Kennedy's assassination. More than any other person, he had the means, motive, and opportunity to have been the singular key conspirator-instigator and the mastermind of the operation. The factual evidence presented here renders the long-debated official conclusions suspect because so much of it is simply part of the lie created by Johnson. Accepting this premise means that many of the cover-up actions once considered as too unbelievable must now be considered as the most plausible accounts. Such factually supported assertions can be summarized as follows:

- A widely based conspiracy existed to assassinate Kennedy, including the involvement of a number of Secret Service personnel—as well as a number of "fake" Secret Service agents—to eliminate normal protection of the president in the Dallas motorcade.

- The Zapruder film, and other films and photographs, were altered for the purpose of showing that Kennedy was shot only twice from behind, through deletion of frames showing his brains being blown out the back of his head—which was the same footage that showed how the limousine stopped momentarily as the fatal shots hit Kennedy's head—false debris was "painted in" to attempt to portray the brain matter being ejected upward instead.

- Johnson ordered his personal aide Carter to pressure Dallas Assistant DA Alexander and DA Wade to not charge Oswald with "conspiracy." It was at this point that he clearly had reached a decision to drop the "Castro did it" option, for which much evidence had been created, and go with the "lone nut" option.

- The body of JFK was taken at gunpoint—as only a "presidential" directive could have assured—away from Parkland Hospital before a real autopsy could be performed then later removed from the heavy bronze funeral casket and subjected to alterations to also show that shots came only from the rear.

- Autopsy records, photographs, and x-ray film have been destroyed and replaced with fabrications on Johnson's orders. As Larry Hancock pointed out, "In a [1967] conversation with attorney General Ramsey Clark, Johnson expressed his displeasure with Dr. James Humes' referring to a photograph that did not officially exist."*

- Also as shown by Larry Hancock, Johnson "personally issued orders to place Bethesda personnel under a gag order in regard to the autopsy; Captain John Stover, commanding Officer of the National Naval Medical School, reportedly received this instruction from Admiral Buckley on orders from the White House."[2]

- As previously documented, much of the "evidence" used by the Warren Commission was fraudulent, just as many of the witnesses it used threatened to provide incorrect testimony to support its predetermined verdict. Only a well-defined comprehensive plan established well in advance of the operation could possibly have ensured this result.

---

* Hancock also pointed out that Dr. Humes lost his credibility more than once: (1) he admitted destroying both his notes and his first version of the autopsy report; his assistant, Dr. Boswell also lost his notes the night of the autopsy; (2) his less-than-forthcoming interviews with the ARRB; (3) his loss of the lawsuit filed by Dr. Crenshaw; and (4) his "in your face" display of the gold presidential cuff links during his testimony, which were given to him personally by President Johnson during the interviews. (Hancock, 308, 561)

2. Hancock, 307.

- In the aftermath of the assassination, the "invisible hand" quickly produced a "verdict" for the hapless "patsy" followed by a curtailed and corrupted "investigation," which was given over to a commission which completely accepted the tainted FBI reports, added their own distorted analysis, and fabricated evidence based largely on the most incredible witnesses—creating fanciful if outrageously absurd "theories" in the process—and dutifully added the *imprimatur* of the U.S. government to its report back to the instigator of the entire crime; only Lyndon B. Johnson was in a position to control every aspect of the pre- and postassassination conspiracies.

Eleven years after the assassination, *New York Times* reporter Seymour Hersh interviewed James Angleton, who made a rather enigmatic and cryptic remark which seemed to be an acknowledgement of sorts of CIA involvement in the assassination. David Talbot describes Hersh's comments about that incident:[3]

> "A mansion has many rooms . . . I'm not privy to who struck John. What did the cryptic remark mean? I would be absolutely misleading you if I thought I had any fucking idea," says Hersh today. "But my instinct about it is he basically was laying off [blame] on somebody else inside the CIA, and the whole purpose of the conversation was to convince me to go after somebody else and not him. And also that he was a completely crazy fucking old fart."

The preponderance of the evidence at this point in time indicates that James Angleton was deeply involved in the preassassination conspiracy in many ways as previously described but clearly with respect to moving Lee Harvey Oswald into position. The postassassination cover-up appears to have been handled primarily by Allen Dulles and Richard Helms. Perhaps this division of responsibilities was all worked out in advance, within the "many rooms" of the big mansion in Langley. There were many people put into long-term positions, which enabled them to control the Johnson "legacy" for decades, including a number who were employed in Langley, Virginia. One of them was Johnson's long-term secretary, Marie Fehmer, who acknowledged being a high-ranking CIA officer in 1989 to Jane Pauley on the *Today* show, having moved directly from the White House to her new position at the end of Johnson's term. Interestingly, her mother Olga Fehmer had been a friend of Mrs. George (Jeanne) de Mohrenschildt and Abraham Zapruder, all of whom worked together at Nardis of Dallas in the 1950s.[4]

In his reconciliation of his own book with that of Doug Horne's, Noel

---

3. Talbot, 274
4. See: http://www.ciajfk.com/news4.html

Twyman wrote, "Doug Horne concludes that 'the National Security State killed President Kennedy . . .' I can't argue much with him on that, but it could not have happened without bringing Lyndon Johnson and J. Edgar Hoover into the plot before the fact, if they were not themselves the master planners, along with H. L. Hunt, General Charles Willoughby, CIA's Bill Harvey, James Angleton, and the French Connection—but this isn't the National Security State—at least as I think of the term—[is it] a question of semantics, perhaps? Maybe it's what the National Security State could sink to if given the necessary evil people in the right positions, and in the right circumstances."[5] The closeness of Twyman's and Horne's conclusions are now narrowed down to "a question of semantics," and the combination of their views is essentially congruent with the conclusions of this book; it may be that the assassination was indeed the product of a "national security state," but if so, the head of that entity in 1963 was arguably Lyndon B. Johnson, carrying out a plan he first conceived at least in 1960, if not before. It is this key point that becomes the key to the "chicken or egg" question. Lyndon Johnson's planning began well before John F. Kennedy was even nominated to become president, and much before JFK's actions in the Bay of Pigs, the Cuba missile crisis, the Laos and Vietnam issues, his "peace speech" and the nuclear test ban treaty had thoroughly upset the many men who came to question his ability to run the federal government apparatus of the United States.

Reassessing Lyndon Johnson's Reign

Lyndon B. Johnson's "accidental presidency" should be considered according to the charges contained in this book and regarded for what it was: a *coup d'état*; a deeply insidious subversion of the democratic process, the result of a criminal enterprise with other men who, deluded to think that their actions were patriotic, conspired to murder the thirty-fifth president of the United States, John F. Kennedy. The resulting impact on the United States was both immediate and long-term. Within a few years, it produced a tragically misbegotten war with a contrived enemy sold on the basis of pseudo patriotism to establish U.S. dominance throughout the world. Pundits still use the term "Vietnam quagmire" as the default benchmark for unfortunate comparisons to military conflicts in which a legitimate United States national interest actually exists. The U.S. "image" around the world, including the self-image by its own citizens, was greatly and permanently diminished by the illegitimate presidency of Lyndon B. Johnson, and this lingering bruise is

---

5. Twyman, Appendix G (Mobipocket ebook version), 3660

ample proof of the long-term effects of Johnson's deceit.

Lyndon B. Johnson was initially protected by the natural inclination of American citizens at the time to assume only the best about the new president; after all, he had advanced to the number two position over many years and had been presumed to have been "vetted" by his Texas constituents who kept elevating him to higher and higher positions (although it was accomplished through stolen elections and elaborate lawyering, this was not known outside of Texas). Then, according to his carefully drawn plan, the American people would follow his guidance following the traumatic event that thrust Johnson out of a downward spiral leading to prison and into the presidency of the United States; during the following year he would be assured of their support, just as he began reassuring them with his masterful performance as a new president thrown into office by the horrible act of "the lone nut." In the meantime, the ruling class on Capitol Hill decided collectively to bury any suspicions they may have held as individuals about the moral turpitude of the new president for fear of pursuing any further investigations against him. If the evidence against him in the Bobby Baker or other scandals were to rise to an impeachable offense coming on the heels of the assassination, a constitutional crisis might have ensued, especially if all of his crimes had been revealed. And if he were to be found involved in the murder of JFK, the crisis might have been far worse than that; a collective decision was reached, probably silently and discreetly, that it might be best to "let sleeping dogs lie."

Lyndon Johnson had relied on what he felt was the inherent sophistry of his subjects—"pissants" he called them—to accept a story that he knew would be the one most comfortable to them: the sole assassin was a misguided communist, a screwball. He knew that the real story of his coup d'état would be so unbelievable and incomprehensible to most of them that the alternative would be an easy sell; it was the one which least terrified the entire nation.

As he prepared for the 1964 election, competing with a man he portrayed as a "warmonger," he had continued assuring the nation that he was capable of running the country maybe even better than his predecessor had. Suddenly, in July, 1964, the long-dormant and stalled civil rights legislation had finally gotten passed, and he was (at least he was portrayed to be) skillfully handling the terrible Vietnam "problem" as he valiantly tried to keep American youths from being called to war again while he carefully protected the national security interests of the United States. Only a man having mastered the art of duplicity could be portrayed as trying to keep the country out of the very war that he was simultaneously working to create, just as he began championing the long-suppressed civil rights legislation, which he had stymied for decades. By the time of the landslide 1964 election, when

"All the way with LBJ" became the ubiquitous battle cry heard throughout the country (comparatively few remember "In your heart you know he's right," advanced by his opponent), he was safely ensconced as the confident and magnanimous leader and president that he always knew, in his own mind, he would be; now he only needed to expand the "legend" from his own mind to those of everyone else.

It wasn't until he became president that he began to rally Congress to pass the very civil rights legislation he had personally stymied for three years, which was also a concept he had fought for twenty-three years before that. He knew that he needed to have landmark legislative accomplishments during his first year as president to support his own run for the presidential election of 1964. There can be only one reason that Johnson continued, throughout his vice presidency, to block Kennedy's attempts—no matter how tepid they might have been—toward the adoption of more aggressive civil rights reform: he wanted to save it as his own "place in history." That was all he cared about, the only thing that kept him motivated to become president throughout his lifetime and, once there, it was not sufficient to be merely "one of many presidents"; he had to be considered the best one ever so that his place in history would be guaranteed. But to have a legacy at all necessarily meant that he had to become president in the first place, and in those nearly three years he spent holding an office he detested, his resolve to carry through with his planned takeover was steeled by polishing a meticulously crafted plan he had created to accomplish just that.

Rather than being the primary catalyst of the new legislation, he was, ironically, thrust into a position as the beneficiary of the public's remorse for JFK's assassination and the collective guilt for the long-simmering civil rights battles that symbolized the last smoldering vestiges of the nation's sorry history of slavery. At last, the nation in mourning could look at itself in the mirror of history and do what it needed to do to redress old wounds and make peace with itself. That Lyndon "Bull" Johnson could foresee all of this is debatable, but his ability to manipulate people—a single person or dozens, thousands, or millions at a time—has been proven; he benefited from the growing sense of outrage felt especially by younger people at the unfairness of the water hoses aimed at students simply attempting to register for college or black people denied service at lunch counters. The time for civil rights legislation had come, and the man responsible for it, more than any other, Martin Luther King Jr., would soon become the martyr for his cause. Lyndon B. Johnson had cleverly but merely been put into the position of taking much more credit for the passage of this legislation than should have been bestowed, given the extreme methods he used to accomplish his objectives. The *New York Times* went so far as to give the lion's share of credit for its passage—not to Lyndon Johnson—to Everett Dirksen, the Republican senator and minority leader.

The greater the number of threats, rumors, and innuendo from the "Bostons" in the White House, fed more and more ferociously by his own paranoia and sensitivity to criticism, the more he realized that he was out of options; he had to proceed with the plan in order to reach his destiny (and, of course, to stay out of prison). Another aspect he obviously factored in was that, in addition to securing his "legacy," it would simultaneously divert attention away from any doubts harbored by people about his own complicity in the crime of the century, as the "mastermind" who put it all together. This was undoubtedly one of the first entries on his list of "Great Society" legislation begun well before November 22, 1963.

The Final Demise of Lyndon Johnson

In October 1972, Johnson invited his "son" Bobby Baker to visit him on his ranch. Baker later wrote, "I was so unprepared for LBJ's appearance when we entered his bedroom, I'm afraid my face registered shock. Lyndon Johnson was very fat, most pale, and white-haired; he'd aged far more than his infrequent newspaper photos had led me to expect. There was an oxygen mask by his bed, which he frequently used to aid his breathing; he was removing it from his face as we walked into the room . . . [he thought] 'Jesus, the poor man looks terrible. This isn't the Lyndon Johnson I knew,'"[6] Within a quarter of an hour, Johnson was dressed in his new "twenty buck" double-knit britches and a Western-style outfit, driving Baker and his wife around the ranch, playing the part of a country squire, "tooting his automobile horn as he drove among grazing cows, pointing out his irrigation system, driving up a paved road to gesture toward his restored birthplace a mile or two from the LBJ ranch house. He constantly smoked and gulped Cutty Sark; throughout our visit he kept a portable bar handy."[7]

Barr McClellan described Johnson's need for deep psychotherapy to find relief from his guilty conscience and how the psychiatrist had "gotten rid of the demons" he had long ago buried in the back of his mind. According to this rendition of the very real story also reported elsewhere, the closest he came to admitting an involvement in Kennedy's assassination was to lay the blame mostly back on his chief attorney Ed Clark: "'That dear old Ed-ward is a son of a bitch,' he lisped, again mimicking Clark. 'Just think. At one time, he was

---

6. Baker, 262
7. Ibid. 263

ready to ride "ol' Sparky" for me.' Johnson was referring to the electric chair at the state prison. 'Hell of a man,' he continued. 'Willing to give all for me. You just gotta admire that . . . Yessir. That man's got balls!'"[8] According to McClellan, the attorney Don Thomas was given a number of million-dollar funds to be paid over time for certain witnesses who knew things that might compromise the closely guarded secrets. One was put up for a mistress and others set up for local officials including a judge. Controls were put into place to maintain secrecy and prevent anyone from being able to trace it in the future, and of course to ensure that all transactions were subject to the attorney-client privilege. The funds would continue flowing as long as the recipients kept their mouths shut and themselves out of the newspapers. The people managing all of this would also monitor their charges so that if anyone started talking "out of school," then the money would stop and nothing could be done to prevent that.[9] Indeed, this might explain why, according to Madeline Brown's account in her book *Texas in the Morning*, her own monthly stipend stopped after several years without explanation and without recourse; she had by then begun talking to others about her days and nights with Lyndon.

According to McClellan's account, which he obtained directly from his former attorney colleague Don Thomas, Johnson also blamed the Pentagon for bad advice on Vietnam; never mind that others, as noted previously, had given both him and Kennedy clear warnings about the futility of getting involved in a land war in Asia or the fact that he would intimidate his own advisors from disagreeing with his preconceived opinions. One example of his condescending, belittling treatment of his military advisors was provided by Lt. General Charles Cooper (USMC, Ret.) who attended a meeting between President Lyndon Johnson and the Joint Chiefs of Staff early in 1965 and described Johnson's reaction to the advice he had just received:[10]

> "He screamed obscenities, he cursed them personally, he ridiculed them for coming to his office with their "military advice." Noting that it was he who was carrying the weight of the free world on his shoulders, he called them filthy names-shitheads, dumb shits, pompous assholes-and used "the F-word" as an adjective more freely than a Marine in boot camp would use it. He then accused them of trying to pass the buck for World War III to him. It was unnerving, degrading."

The fact that he consistently refused to follow the military's advice on what was

---

8. McClellan, 277.
9. Ibid., 278–279.
10. Cooper, 4

actually necessary to win his war was also something he couldn't acknowledge according to this account of his dying days.[11] Johnson purportedly admitted to Thomas that he told the psychiatrist "'about the killings' . . . At first, Clark had done most of the dirty work on his own, keeping Thomas 'out of the loop.' When he had to act it was through trusted relatives or compromised public officials to protect Johnson from any involvement in the necessary crimes. In the 1948 election, Clark had to enlist Thomas. No one else could add the needed votes. Then, in the early fifties, Clark had drawn Thomas deeper into the web, making him the chief contact with John Cofer, the firm's attorney for criminal matters . . . In his heart, he knew the most terrible of all crimes had likely been told. The assassination of a president simply could not be 'contained.' If the doctor knew, that was it. The word would be out. Thomas was sure the doctor knew because, being the outstanding psychiatrist he was, the patient was the only concern. He had to find out what troubled Johnson. The killing of John Kennedy was, he was sure, the primary cause of Johnson's paranoia. That was followed by Vietnam and its paranoia with even more depression. Together, they led to the collapse of his presidency . . . 'You know full well what was happening back then. They were closing in . . . Investigations everywhere. Hearings all over the damned hill."[12] This "factional" account described by McClellan, written as his honest interpretation of what he believes his fellow lawyer experienced with Johnson, is admittedly not conclusive as to what transpired, but it is the closest, most persuasive account of Johnson's dying days that we have and will probably ever have.

The general thrust of McClellan's description of Johnson was affirmed by D. Jablow Hershman in her book *Power Beyond Reason: The Mental Collapse of Lyndon Johnson*, who wrote that "the United States was being led by a man who already was or rapidly was becoming psychotic. LBJ's grandiosity, megalomania and paranoia reached dimensions that could no longer pass for normalcy. Signs of grandiosity and paranoia were present before LBJ became President, but assuming responsibility for the war in Vietnam appears to have been more stress than he could bear as 1966 wore on."[13] Furthermore, Hershman concluded, "LBJ's manic furies and incapacitating depressions, his pathological ego, megalomania and paranoia were products of his manic depression. Unfortunate though they were for him and the people with whom he came in contact, their effects became tragic when he took over the conduct of the Vietnam War . . . The effect on LBJ was catastrophic. His

---

11. McClellan, 280–281.
12. Ibid., 281–282.
13. Hershman, 212.

illness worsened past the point of psychotic collapse. The consequences were fatal, if not for him, certainly for those who died in Vietnam in his needless war—LBJ's war—for he would not accept guidance from the advisors who might have imparted some degree of sanity to his decisions."[14] The chilling description presented by author Hershman of Lyndon B. Johnson's real persona makes a compelling case for the need of a better vetting process for candidates for the presidency and vice presidency.

Some of the visitors to his ranch after he retired independently described him with the following adjectives: "The most moody person I've ever known," "odd," "crazy," and "psychopathic." Author Hershman said that when Lady Bird was away, he vacillated between paranoia, depression, and rage as the torment of his long-repressed loneliness overwhelmed him.[15]

According to author Dorothy Davis, "Many depressives frequently plan their deaths on the anniversary of a significant event."[16] It is interesting that Johnson died on the most significant anniversary of his life, at the ending of what would have been his second term, two days after Richard M. Nixon was sworn into office for the second time. But since he had to vacate the White House four years before his second term would have ended, he returned to his ranch where he pretended to find solace and comfort, but in reality, he was forced to encounter the loneliness and isolation and raging despair that would render him a four-year battle with a fate worse than death: his loss of presidential power, which he had worked all of his life to achieve. Doris Goodwin reportedly confirmed that Johnson tried to will his own death in his last few years at the LBJ Ranch,[17] apparently so that he would die on the anniversary of his being sworn in as president after winning the 1964 election. It appears that he knew somehow that his death would be worth one last major "benefit of the doubt" because of the automatic deference that past presidents are due; it would finally give him the peace that had been so elusive, knowing that he would never have to respond to any inquiries about the crime and therefore would also ensure that he would never be tried and convicted of the murder of JFK. That knowledge was probably the only solace he could find, and it made him seek eternal peace for his troubled soul.

Johnson's disease was as responsible for his political success in the early years as it was responsible for his self-destruction as president. It accounted for his single-minded obsessiveness in wanting more and more power, money, and glory and his turn to the criminal activities necessary to attain those goals. It contributed to his crude, vulgar, and obnoxious behavior to others

14. Ibid., 291.
15. Ibid. 241–243
16. Davis, Dorothy, 170.
17. Twyman, 830.

and his condescending, belittling, and arrogant treatment of his subordinates. The worst, of course, was that it fueled his compulsion to become president at all costs, including the murder of John F. Kennedy because he was the only person standing in the way. Almost as bad, however, was that his disease was the catalyst that caused Lyndon Johnson, who was determined not to become "the president who lost Asia to communism" or lose any war, to put himself into a position to do both.

Though his grandmother didn't use the precise clinical terms to describe Lyndon, her prescience about his eventual probability of serving time in prison revealed what she observed about his essential character traits. His grandmother's observations would have related to behaviors he had already manifested by the age of five: manic energy, poor concentration, mischievousness, arrogance, and defiance. Even then, he had developed a reputation for arguing and haranguing his playmates to the extent that they just wanted to get away from him.[18] His sister Rebekah recalled that he bossed everyone else around—even his mother—as though he were the head of the family.[19] When teachers tried to discipline him, "he spit at them and walked out."[20] A lady who tutored him in his early schooling called him "a real hellion."[21] After an entire lifetime spent "on the edge" of making excuses and lying about matters both large and small and constantly striving to achieve his childhood dream, the anxieties this produced, combined with his other psychological issues (whether they were merely those of a typical person diagnosed with bipolar disease, paranoia, or sociopathic personality disorder or some combination of all three), caused his condition to worsen after he left the Oval Office and returned to the LBJ Ranch. Between the anxieties playing out in his mind and the loneliness of life on the ranch—not the ordinary loneliness many people occasionally feel but the kind that is exacerbated by the sociopath's extreme fear of being alone—he had consigned himself to a life of misery in his last four years.

The narrative in this and previous chapters, which relates to Johnson's psychological state, is not intended to be considered as a definitive psychological or psychiatric analysis of his condition; except for citations to other authors, it is presented as the author's "speculative or conjectural" commentary and must be considered as such. The comments are, however, based upon reasoned interpretations of Johnson's actual behavior at specific

---

18. Ibid., 27.
19. Kearns, 87.
20. Dallek, Lone Star . . . , 43.
21. Ibid.

events as cited. An excerpt from the *Encarta Dictionary* on "personality disorder" reads as follows:

> People with antisocial personality disorder act in a way that disregards the feelings and rights of other people. Antisocial personalities often break the law, and they may use or exploit other people for their own gain. They may lie repeatedly, act impulsively, and get into physical fights. They may mistreat their spouses, neglect or abuse their children, and exploit their employees. They may even kill other people. People with this disorder are also sometimes called sociopaths or psychopaths . . . Antisocial personalities usually fail to understand that their behavior is dysfunctional because their ability to feel guilty, remorseful, and anxious is impaired. Guilt, remorse, shame, and anxiety are unpleasant feelings, but they are also necessary for social functioning and even physical survival. For example, people who lack the ability to feel anxious will often fail to anticipate actual dangers and risks. They may take chances that other people would not take. Antisocial personality disorder affects about 3 percent of males and 1 percent of females. This is the most heavily researched personality disorder, in part because it costs society the most. People with this disorder are at high risk for premature and violent death, injury, imprisonment, loss of employment, bankruptcy, alcoholism, drug dependence, and failed personal relationships.

One does not need a PhD in psychology or an MD in psychiatry to understand the meaning of these layman's words. A person having taken only a high school or undergraduate level course in psychology can readily understand by now that Lyndon B. Johnson met every one of the criteria noted above. Many people still persist in their belief that, though Johnson was fiercely ambitious and admittedly a chronic liar, he was not depraved enough to murder his predecessor; clearly, by now, it is time to reassess that point based upon everything else previously written. Lyndon B. Johnson was paranoid and a sociopath who suffered from manic depression.[22] According to Gerald Tolchin, PhD and professor of psychology, "Johnson may well have been the most psychologically unstable person ever to assume the presidency. He was a tragic figure pursued by demons, real and imagined . . . It appears likely that Lyndon Johnson suffered from bipolar (manic-depressive) disorder throughout his life, a condition that grew worse as he grew older, peaking just as he reached the zenith of his

---

22. Hershman, 16.

influence and power."[23]

The historical record shows that a number of men, between 1964 and 1968, realized that Johnson's mental health was in serious trouble. In May, 1964, Robert F. Kennedy expressed concern for the country's future because of Johnson's state of mind, asking Arthur Schlesinger, "How can we possibly survive five more years of Lyndon Johnson? Five more years of a crazy man?"[24] One year later, in July, 1965, Richard Goodwin stated, "Early that same month, I was sitting in Bill Moyers's office . . . when Bill walked in, his face pale, visibly shaken. 'I just came from a conversation with the president,' he said. 'He told me he was going to fire everybody who didn't agree with him, that Hubert [Humphrey] could not be trusted and we weren't to tell him anything; then he began to explain that the communist way of thinking had infected everyone around him, that his enemies were deceiving the people and, if they succeeded, there was no way he could stop World War Three'. . . 'Suppose he really does go crazy,' I said. And then, answering my own question: 'I tell you what would happen if we went public with our doubts. They could assemble a panel of psychiatrists to examine the President, and he would tell them how sad it made him that two boys he loved so much could have thought such a thing, and then explain his behavior so calmly and reasonably that when he was finished, we would be the ones committed. Indeed, what could be done—what could anyone do—about a man who was always able to impose an immensely powerful and persuasive simulacrum of control to mask his growing irrationalities?'"[25]

Evidently, all of these men were aware—unbeknownst to anyone else in the rest of the country, yet suspected by many—that, in fact, the country was being run by a man incapable of controlling even himself in a rational manner, to say nothing of the nation's affairs, which he was then trying to radically change for all time. Years later, decades after his death, the case would be made that in fact, Johnson suffered not only from what is now referred to as "bipolar" disease but more generally, a combination of paranoia and sociopathic disorders.

Facets of his apparent underlying afflictions—e.g., sociopathic personality disorder—are rarely treatable, much less curable. It is something which apparently remained undiagnosed throughout all but the last two years of his sixty-four-year life, mostly because he did not wish to be treated for it (why would someone of his obvious stature and brilliance need to see a psychiatrist?) and no self-respecting doctor could make such a diagnosis without even interviewing the patient as long as he was still alive; it was not until he was

23. Ibid., 6.
24. Schlesinger, *RFK.* . . p. 836
25. Goodwin, Richard, pp. 402–403

dead that the analysis began. So the patient afflicted an entire country with the remorse that he would not—could not—come to terms with himself.

Lyndon B. Johnson could be made a case study for future psychological textbooks—in the sections dealing with extreme narcissism, egomania, paranoia, bipolar and sociopathic disorders—and the compound effect of multiple disorders—and how a person, left untreated for decades, could take over the government not only in a third world country but in a superpower nation. This is not merely some esoteric exercise; a good case has been made for the premise that many of the world's tyrants were afflicted by mental disorders similar to Lyndon Johnson's, including specifically, Napoleon Bonaparte, Adolf Hitler, and Joseph Stalin.[26] Perhaps the nation, and we as individuals, would be better equipped to cope with people like Lyndon Johnson in the future if this were done posthumously in his case.

The Jury Is Charged

It is now well past the time for the fraudulent "evidence" to be thrown out and a reevaluation of the thirty-sixth president be undertaken. The enormous destruction Lyndon Johnson caused after his coup, by inserting the American military machine into a faraway land to fight its nonthreatening indigenous people—where more than two million Americans were sent to fight in their civil war, of whom over 58,000 never returned and over 350,000 more were seriously injured; where two Vietnamese civilians for every enemy soldier died, a total of 3.8 million Vietnamese or 14 percent of their entire population[27]—was a direct result of his ascension into the presidency of the United States. Should not this be sufficient to embarrass the nation and cause the removal of his name from the monuments, lakes, expressways, parks, buildings, and the space center, which have been named after him? It is also clear that at the very least, the case presented here should cause the government to at least force the release of the remaining FBI and CIA files, which have still not been made public nearly two decades after they were ordered to be. An accounting of all the official misdeeds, including the fabricated photos and films, the destruction of files, and the harassment of witnesses should quickly follow. A thorough cleansing of the national conscience is in order after all of these years to enable Americans to reconcile the personal tragedy suffered by John F. Kennedy, and the national tragedy suffered by the country at large, at the hands of Lyndon B. Johnson.

The damage caused by Lyndon Johnson and his intrinsic dishonesty with

---

26. Hershman and Julian Lieb, MD, *A Brotherhood of Tyrants: Manic Depression and Absolute Power*. Amherst, NY: Prometheus Books, 1994.
27. Hershman, 11.

the American people is incalculable. His role in creating the level of cynicism and mistrust of government that exists today has been well hidden for over forty years; it was through his pernicious behavior and ability to mesmerize his peers with velvet gloves while commanding his subordinates with an iron fist that he was able to wrest control of the government of the United States. He did it through outright cajolary, cruelty, bombastic speeches, blatant disregard of the laws he was charged with upholding, and ultimately, murder. Until the real story of the thirty-sixth president is exposed and the complete truth of his crimes against the United States and the world are acknowledged, there will always be questions lurking about the trustworthiness of the government itself.

This concludes the posthumous indictment of the thirty-sixth president of the United States of America, Lyndon B. Johnson. The "defense case" has already been presented multiple times over nearly fifty years by many credulous authors combined with the virtual absence of critical reporting by the news media, which had collectively worked so many years to protect his secrets and burnish his reputation as a great politician. It is not whimsy to posit—indeed, it has already been proven beyond a doubt—that for reasons that can only be imagined, the major news media of the time came to Johnson's defense in 1967 to assist the Johnson administration and the CIA to attack Jim Garrison and simultaneously began adopting the "official line" on JFK's assassination while ridiculing those who kept bringing forth evidence which cast doubt on that line. And it is not unreasonable to suggest that a widely based media cover-up was launched at that time that still exists today; so successful has it been that merely questioning such outrageously absurd "official truths" as the "Magic Bullet Theory" renders one a "conspiracy theorist" who is unable to accept the "conventional wisdom" that the government has decreed to be the factual record. It is enough to make one suspect that Lyndon Johnson had foreseen this eventuality too and had planned its outcome over fifty years ago.

Thankfully, there were also a courageous few who were more intellectually honest, who delved into the darker side of his character and helped by providing much of the documentation which has been presented here: each of these incidents represents a dot on a very large historical matrix. The dots have finally been connected; the puzzle has been completed. A more complete story of Lyndon Johnson has been written, at least enough of it to provide a little balance to the lopsided "biographies" already written about the man, which artfully avoid revealing anything about his real character.

The verdict of the jury—the American people—awaits.

BIBLIOGRAPHY

*What is to be feared is not so much the immorality of the great as the
fact that immorality may lead to greatness.*`
—ALEXIS DE TOCQUEVILLE, *DEMOCRACY IN AMERICA*

Baker, Bobby with Larry L. King. *Wheeling and Dealing, Confessions of a
Capitol Hill Operator.* New York: W. W. Norton & Company, Inc.,
1978.

Baker, Judyth Vary, *Me & Lee.* Oregon: TrineDay, 2010.

Baker, Russ, *Family of Secrets; The Bush Dynasty, America's Invisible
Government and the Hidden History of the Last Fifty Years.* New York:
Bloomsbury Press, 2009.

Beschloss, Michael R. *Reaching for Glory.* New York: Simon & Schuster,
2001.

Beschloss, Michael R. *Taking Charge: The Johnson White House Tapes.* New
York, Simon & Shuster, 1997.

Bishop, Jim. *The Day Kennedy Was Shot.* New York: Greenwich House, 1968,
1983.

Bolden, Abraham. *The Echo from Dealey Plaza.* New York: Harmony Books,
2008.

Bradlee, Ben. *A Good Life: Newspapering and Other Adventures.* New York:
Simon & Schuster, 1995.

Brown, Madeleine. *Texas in the Morning: The Love Story of Madeleine Brown
and President Lyndon Baines Johnson.* Baltimore: The Conservatory
Press, 1997.

Brugioni, Dino A. *Eyeball to Eyeball—The Inside Story of the Cuban Missile
Crisis.* New York: Random House, 1991.

Bryant, Traphes. *Dog Days at the White House: The Outrageous Memoirs of the
Presidential Kennel Keeper.* New York: Macmillan Publishing, 1975.

Bugliosi, Vincent. *Reclaiming History: The Assassination of John F. Kennedy.*
New York: W. W. Norton & Company, 2007.

Bullion, John L. *In the Boat with LBJ.* Plano, TX: Republic of Texas Press,
2001.

Burleigh, Nina. *A Very Private Woman: The Life and Unsolved Murder of
Presidential Mistress Mary Meyer.* New York: Bantam Books, 1998.

Callahan, Bob. *Who Shot JFK?* New York: Fireside Books, 1993.

Caro, Robert A. *The Years of Lyndon Johnson—The Path to Power*. New York: Alfred A. Knopf, 1982.

Caro, Robert A. *The Years of Lyndon Johnson—Means of Ascent*. New York: Alfred A. Knopf, 1990.

Caro, Robert A. *The Years of Lyndon Johnson—The Master of the Senate*. New York: Alfred A. Knopf, 2002.

Clifford, Clark. *Counsel to the President: A Memoir*. New York: Random House, 1991.

Collier, Peter, and David Horowitz. *The Kennedys* New York: Summit Books, 1984.

Cooper, Charles G., with Richard E. Goodspeed, *A Marine's Story of Combat in Peace and War*. Victoria, Canada: Trafford Publishing, 2002.

Crenshaw, Charles A., and Gary J Shaw. *Trauma Room One: The JFK Medical Cover-up Exposed*. New York: Paraview Press. 2001.

Curtis, Carl T., and Regis Courtemanche. *Forty Years Against the Tide: Congress and the Welfare State*. Chicago: Regnery Gateway, 1986.

Dallek, Robert. *Lone Star Rising: Lyndon Johnson and His Times 1908–1960*. New York: Oxford University Press, 1991.

Dallek, Robert. *Lyndon B. Johnson: Portrait of a President*. New York: Oxford University Press, 2004.

Dallek, Robert, *Flawed Giant: Lyndon Johnson and His Times 1961–1973*. New York: Oxford University Press, 1998.

Davis, Deborah, *Katherine the Great*. New York: Harcourt, Brace and Jovanovich, Inc. (1979).

Davis, John H. *Mafia Kingfish: Carlos Marcello and the assassination of John F. Kennedy*. New York: McGraw Hill, 1989.

Davis, John. *The Kennedys: Dynasty and Disaster 1848–1983*, New York, McGraw-Hill, 1984.

Day, James M. *Captain Clint Peoples, Texas Ranger*. Waco, TX: Texian Press. 1980.

DeGregorio, William A. *The Complete Book of U.S. Presidents*, Wings Books, 1991.

DiEugenio, James. *Destiny Betrayed—JFK, Cuba, and the Garrison Case*. New York: Sheridan Square Press. 1992.

DiEugenio, James, and Lisa Pease, (Ed.). *The Assassinations*. Los Angeles: Feral House. 2003.

Douglass, James W. *JFK and the Unspeakable: Why He Died and Why it Matters*. Maryknoll, NY: Orbis Books. 2008.

Dugger, Ronnie. *The Politician—The Life and Times of Lyndon Johnson: The Drive for Power, from the Frontier to Master of the Senate*. New York: W. W. Norton & Company 1982.

Fensterwald, Bernard Jr., with Michael Ewing. *Coincidence or Conspiracy?* New York: Simon & Schuster, 1965.

Fetzer, James H. *The Great Zapruder Film Hoax: Deceit and Deception in the Death of JFK.* Chicago: Catfeet Press, 2003.

Fetzer, James H., PhD.(Ed.) *Murder in Dealey Plaza.* Chicago: Catfeet Press, 2000.

Fonzi, Gaeton. *Greater Philadelphia Magazine.* August 1, 1966.

Fonzi, Gaeton *The Last Investigation.* New York: Thunder's Mouth Press, 1993.

Garrison, Jim. *On the Trail of the Assassins.* New York: Warner Books, Inc. 1968.

Giancana, Sam, and Chuck Giancana. *Doublecross.* New York, NY: Warner Books,1992.

Gillon, Steven M. *The Kennedy Assassination—24 Hours After: Lyndon B. Johnson's Pivotal First Day as President.* New York: Basic Books, 2009.

Goodwin, Richard N. *Rembering America: A Voice From the Sixties.* Boston: Little, Brown and Company, 1988.

Groden, Robert J. *The Killing of a President—The Complete Photographic Record of the JFK Assassination, the Conspiracy, and the Cover-up.* New York: Viking Studio Books, Viking Penguin, 1993.

Groden, Robert, and Harrison Livingstone. *High Treason.* Baltimore: The Conservatory Press, 1989.

Guthman, Edwin O. and Jeffery Shulman. *Robert Kennedy in His Own Words.* New York: Bantam, 1988.

Hack, Richard. *Puppetmaster—The Secret Life of J. Edgar Hoover.* New Millennium Press: Beverly Hills, CA, 2004.

Halberstam, David. *The Best and the Brightest.* New York: Random House, 1972.

Haley, James Evetts. *A Texan Looks at Lyndon—A Study in Illegitimate Power.* Canyon, Texas: Palo Duro Press, 1964.

Hancock, Larry. *Someone Would Have Talked.* Southlake, TX: JFK Lancer Productions & Publications, Inc. 2006.

Hersh, Burton. *Bobby and J. Edgar: The Historic Face-Off Between the Kennedys and J. Edgar Hoover That Transformed America.* Carroll & Graf, 2007.

Hersh, Seymour M. *The Dark Side of Camelot.* Boston: Little, Brown and Company, 1997.

Hershman, D. Jablow. *Power Beyond Reason: The Mental Collapse of Lyndon Johnson.* Fort Lee, NJ: Barricade Books, 2002.

Hershman, D. Jablow and Julian Lieb, MD, *A Brotherhood of Tyrants: Manic Depression and Absolute Power.* Amherst, NY: Prometheus Books, 1994.

Holland, Max. *The Kennedy Assassination Tapes.* New York: Alfred A. Knopf, 2004.

Horne, Douglas P. *Inside the Assassination Records Review Board: The U.S. Government's Final Attempt to Reconcile the Conflicting Medical Evidence in the Assassination of JFK.* Amazon, 2009.

Hunt, E. Howard with Greg Aunapu. *American Spy: My Secret History In The CIA, Watergate & Beyond.* Hoboken, NJ: John Wiley & Sons Inc., 2007.

Hunt, Saint John. *Bond of Secrecy,* Published electronically: http://www.saintjohnhunt.com/index.html.

Hurt, Henry. *Reasonable Doubt: An Investigation into the Assassination of John F. Kennedy.* New York: Holt, Rinehart and Winston, 1985.

Israel, Lee. *Kilgallen.* New York: Delacorte Press, 1979.

Johnston, James P. and Roe, Jon. *Flight from Dallas: New Evidence of CIA Involvement in the Murder of President John F. Kennedy.* Bloomington, IN: First Books, 2003.

Jones Jr., Penn. *Forgive My Grief,* vols. I-IV. Self published, Waxahachie, TX. (I. 1966; II. 1967; III. 1974; IV. 1976).

Kaiser, David. *American Tragedy—Kennedy, Johnson, and the Origins of the Vietnam War.* Cambridge, MA: The Belknap Press of Harvard University Press, 2000.

Kantor, Seth. *The Ruby Cover-up,* New York: Zebra Books, 1978.

Karnow, Stanley. *Vietnam: A History.* New York: Viking Press, 1983.

Kearns Goodwin, Doris, *LYNDON JOHNSON and the AMERICAN DREAM, New York: St. Martin's Press, 1991.*

Kessler, Ronald. *In the President's Secret Service: Behind the Scenes With Agents in the Line of Fire and the Presidents They Protect.* New York: Crown Publishing Group, 2009.

Kessler, Ronald. *Inside the CIA,* New York: Pocket Books, 1992.

Kessler, Ronald. *Inside the White House.,* New York: Pocket Books, 1995.

Kessler, Ronald. *The Sins of the Father: Joseph P. Kennedy and the Dynasty He Founded.* NY: Grand Central Publishing, 1997.

Lane, Mark. *Plausible Denial.* New York: Thunder's Mouth Press, 1991.

Lane, Mark. *Rush to Judgment: A Critique of the Warren Commission's Inquiry into the Murders of President John F. Kennedy, Officer J. D. Tippit and Lee Harvey Oswald.* New York: Holt Rinehart & Winston, 1966.

Lasky, Victor. *It Didn't Start with Watergate.* New York: The Dial Press, 1977.

Lasky, Victor. *JFK—The Man and the Myth.* New York: The MacMillan Company, 1963.

Law, William Matson, with Allan Eaglesham. *In the Eye of History: Disclosures in the JFK Assassination Medical Evidence.* Southlake, TX: JFK Lancer Productions & Publications, Inc., 2005.

Lifton, David. *Best Evidence—Disguise and Deception in the Assassination of John F. Kennedy.* New York: Macmillan Publishing Co., Inc., 1980.

Lincoln, Evelyn. *Kennedy and Johnson.* New York: Holt, Rinehart and Winston, 1968.

Livingstone, Harrison Edward. *Killing the Truth: Deceit and Deception in the JFK case* New York: Carroll & Graf Publishers, 1993.

Livingstone, Harrison Edward. *Killing Kennedy—And the Hoax of the Century.* New York: Carroll & Graf Publishers, 1995.

Mahoney, Richard D. *Sons & Brothers—The Days of Jack and Bobby Kennedy.* New York: Arcade Publishing Co., 1999.

Manchester, William. *The Death Of A President.* New York: Harper & Row, 1967.

Margolis, Jon. *The Last Innocent Year: America in 1964 [The Beginning of the "Sixties].* New York: William Morrow and Company, Inc., 1999.

Martin, David C. *Wilderness of Mirrors.* Guilford, CT: The Lyons Press, 2003.

Martin, Ralph G. *Henry and Clare: An Intimate Portrait of the Luces.* E Rutherford, NJ: Putnam, 1991.

Marrs, Jim. *Crossfire: The Plot That Killed Kennedy.* New York: Carroll & Graf Publishers, Inc. 1989.

May, Ernest R., and Philip D. Zelikow. *The Kennedy Tapes: Inside the White House During the Cuban Missile Crisis.* Cambridge, MA: The Belknap Press of Harvard University Press, 1997.

McClellan, Barr. *Blood, Money & Power—How LBJ Killed JFK.* New York: Hannover House, 2003.

McGhee, Millie. *What's Done in the Dark.* Rancho Cucamonga, CA, 2005.

McKnight, Gerald D. *Breach of Trust—How the Warren Commission Failed the Nation and Why.* Lawrence, KS: University Press of Kansas, 2005.

McMaster, H. R. *Dereliction of Duty: Lyndon Johnson, Robert McNamara, the Joint Chiefs of Staff, and the Lies That Led to Vietnam.* New York: HarperCollins Publishers, 1997.

Meagher, Sylvia. *Accessories After the Fact.* New York: Warner Books, 1992.

Melanson, Philip H. *Lee Harvey Oswald and U.S. Intelligence.* New York: Praeger Publishers, 1990.

Mellen, Joan. *A Farewell to Justice.* Dulles, VA: Potomac Books, Inc., 2005.

Mollenhoff, Clark R. *Despoilers of Democracy.* Garden City, NY: Doubleday & Company, Inc., 1965.

Montague, Ludwell Lee. *General Walter Bedell Smith as Director of Central Intelligence, October 1950–February 1953.* University Park, PA: Penn State Press, 1992.

Mooney, Michael J. *The Day Kennedy Died.* Dallas, TX: D Magazine, November 2008.

Morley, Jefferson. *Our Man in Mexico: Winston Scott and the Hidden History of the CIA.* Lawrence, KA: University of Kansas Press, 2008.

Morrow, Robert D. *First Hand Knowledge—How I Participated in the CIA-Mafia Murder of President Kennedy.* New York: S.P.I. Books, 1992.

Newman, John M. *JFK and Vietnam: Deception, Intrigue and the Struggle for Power.* New York: Warner Books, Inc., 1992.

Newman, John M. *Oswald and the CIA.* New York: Carroll & Graf, 1995; Updated in 2008 to include Epilogue "The Plot to Murder President Kennedy: A New Interpretation" beginning on page 613: *Oswald and the CIA: The Documented Truth About the Unknown Relationship Between the U.S. Government and the Alleged Killer of JFK* (Paperback). New York: Skyhorse Publishing, 2008.

North, Mark. *Act of Treason: The Role of J. Edgar Hoover in the Assassination of President Kennedy* New York: Carroll & Graf Publishers, Inc., 1991.

O'Donnell, Kenneth P., and David F. Powers, with Joe McCarthy. *Johnny, We Hardly Knew Ye: Memories of John Fitzgerald Kennedy.* Boston: Little, Brown, 1970, 1972.

O'Neill, Thomas P. *Man of the House: The Life & Political Memoirs of Speaker Tip O'Neill.* New York: Random House, 1987.

O'Toole, George. *The Assassination Tapes* New York: Penthouse Press, 1975.

Palamara, Vincent M. *Survivor's Guilt: The Secret Service and the Failure to Protect the President,* Vol. 4 No. 1.(http://www.assassinationresearch.com/v4n1.html).

Palamara, Vincent M. *The Third Alternative—Survivor's Guilt: The Secret Service and the JFK Murder* (self-published, 1993).

Parmet, Herbert. *Jack: The Struggles of John F. Kennedy.* New York: Dial Press, 1980.

Pearson, Drew. *Drew Pearson's Diaries, 1949–1959.* New York: Holt, Rinehart and Winston, 1974.

Pegues, Stephen, *Texas Mafia* (Unpublished manuscript, limited circulation 1997).

Perlstein, Rick. *Before the storm: Barry Goldwater and the Unmaking of the American Consensus.* New York: Hill and Wang, 2001.

Popkin, Richard H. *The Second Oswald.* New York: Avon Books, 1966.

Posner, Gerald. *Case Closed.* New York: Random House, 1993.

Prouty, L. Fletcher. *JFK: The CIA, Vietnam, and the Plot to Assassinate John F. Kennedy.* New York: Skyhorse Publishing, 2009.

Prouty, L. Fletcher. *The Guns of Dallas.* Gallery Magazine, October, 1975.

Reedy, George. *Lyndon B. Johnson: A Memoir.* New York: Andrews and McMeel, Inc., 1982.

Reeves, Richard. *President Kennedy: Profile of Power.* New York: Simon & Schuster, 1993.

Roemer Jr., William F. *Roemer: Man Against the Mob.* New York: Ballantine, 1989.

Russell, Dick. *On the Trail of the JFK Assassins—A Revealing Look at America's Most Infamous Unsolved Crime.* New York: Skyhorse Publishing, 2008.

Russell, Dick. *The Man Who Knew Too Much.* New York: Carroll & Graf Publishers, 1992.

Russo, Gus. *Live by the Sword: The Secret War Against Castro and the Death of JFK.* Baltimore, MD: Bancroft Press, 1998.

Russo, Gus, and Stephen Molton. *Brothers in Arms—The Kennedys, the Castros, and the Politics of Murder.* New York: Bloomsbury, USA, 2008.

Salinger, Pierre, *With Kennedy.* Garden City, NY: Doubleday & Company, Inc., 1966.

Sample, Glen, and Mark Collom, *The Men on the Sixth Floor.* Sample Graphics, Second Edition 1997.

Scheim, David E. *Contract on America: The Mafia Murder of President John F. Kennedy.* New York: Zebra Books/Kensington Publishing Corp., 1989 (Paperback).

Schlesinger Jr., Arthur M. *A Thousand Days.* Boston: Houghton Mifflin, 1965.

Schlesinger Jr., Arthur M. *Robert Kennedy and His Times.* New York: Ballentine Books, 1978.

Scott, Peter Dale. *Deep Politics and the Death of JFK.* Los Angeles: University of California Press, 1993.

Sherrill, Robert. *The Accidental President.* New York: Pyramid Publication, Inc., 1968.

Shesol, Jeff. *Mutual Contempt: Lyndon Johnson, Robert Kennedy, and the Feud That Defined a Decade.* New York: W. W. Norton & Company, 1997.

Sloan, Bill, with Jean Hill. *JFK—The Last Dissenting Witness.* Gretna, LA: Pelican Publishing Company, Inc., 1992.

Smith, Malcolm. *John F. Kennedy's 13 Great Mistakes in the White House.* Smithtown, NY: Suffolk house, 1980.

Stich, Rodney. *Defrauding America* 4th Edition, Alamo, CA: Silverpeak 2008.

Sullivan, William C. with Bill Brown. *The Bureau: My Thirty Years in Hoover's FBI*. New York: W. W. Norton & Company, 1979.

Summers, Anthony. *The Kennedy Conspiracy*. London: Warner Books, 1998. (Previously titled as *Not in Your Lifetime*. New York: Warner Books, 1998 and *Conspiracy*, New York: McGraw-Hill Book Company, 1980).

Summers, Anthony. *Official and Confidential—The Secret Life of J. Edgar Hoover*. New York: G. P. Putnam's Sons, 1993.

Swearingen, M. Wesley. *To Kill A President*. Self Published, 2008.

Talbot, David. *Brothers*. New York: Free Press, 2007.

Thompson, Josiah. *Six Seconds in Dallas*. New York: Bernard Geis Associates for Random House, 1967.

Trask, Richard B. *Picture of the Pain*. Davners, MA: Yeoman Press, 1994.

Trask, Richard B. *That Day in Dallas: Three Photographers Capture on Film the Day President Kennedy Died*. Danvers, MA: Yeoman Press, 1998.

Trento, Joseph J. *The Secret History of the CIA*. Roseville, CA: Prima Publishing, 2001.

Turner, William W. *Hoover's FBI*. New York: Thunder's Mouth Press, 1993.

Twyman, Noel. *Bloody Treason—The Assassination of John F. Kennedy*. Rancho Santa Fe, CA: Laurel Publishing, 1997.

Valenti, Jack. *This Time, This Place: My Life in War, the White House, and Hollywood*. New York: Harmony Books, 2007.

Van Gelder, Lawrence. *Why the Kennedys Lost the Book Battle*. New York: Award Books, 1967.

Waldron, Lamar and Hartmann, Thom. *Ultimate Sacrifice*. New York: Carroll & Graf Publishers, 2005.

Watson, W. Marvin, with Markman, Sherwin. *Chief of Staff: Lyndon Johnson and His Presidency*. New York: Thomas Dunne Books—St. Martin's Press, 2004.

White, Theodore H. *The Making of the President—1964*. New York: Atheneum Publishers, 1965.

Winter-Berger, Robert N. *The Washington Pay-off*. Secaucus, NJ: Lyle Stuart, Inc., 1972.

Wolfe, Donald H. *The Last Days of Marilyn Monroe*. New York: William Morrow and Company, Inc., 1998.

Zirbel, Craig I. *The Texas Connection*. Scottsdale, AZ: The Texas Connection Co., Publishers, 1991.

Periodicals

Austin American-Statesman: February 27, 1952; June 19, 2000.

Dallas Times Herald, March 31, 1986; May 20, 1989.

Esquire magazine, December, 1966.

Human Events, August 25, 1960.

LIFE magazine, October 11, 1963; November 22, 1963; August 21, 1964; October 2, 1964; June 18, 1965; August 7, 1970.

New York World Journal Tribune, Weisberg, Harold. "Oswald in New Orleans" February 28, 1967.

The New York Times, May 29, 1962, June 20, 1962, , November 24, 1963.

The New Republic, Murray Kempton: "May We Have Some Facts, Please?" June 13, 1964.

Playboy Magazine, vol. 14 no. 10 "Interview with Jim Garrison," October 1967.

The Texas Observer, August 2, 2003.

TIME magazine, May 25, 1962; July 20, 1962; November 29, 1963; December 13, 1963; March 12, 1965; October 29, 1965; December 22, 1975; August 15, 1977.

US. News and World Report, August 5, 1963 "Is U.S. Giving up in the Arms Race?"

Vanity Fair, October 2009.

The Washington Post, July 19, 1961; November 27, 1963; December 1, 1963; February 5, 1964.

The *Washington Evening Star*, June 9, 1964.

Internet Websites

[The] Arlington National Cemetery Website

[The] Billie Sol Estes Website

[The] B-26 Marauder Historical Society

[The] CIA Website

[The] Citizens for Truth about the Kennedy Assassination (CTKA) Website

[The] Education Forum

[The] Fair Play Magazine Website

[The] History Matters Website (Bradford, Rex).

JFK/Deep Politics Quarterly Website

[The] JFK Lancer Forum

[The] JFK Library Website

[The] LBJ Library Website

[The] Mary Ferrell Website

[The] Mayo Clinic Website

[The] PBS Website

[The] Sixth Floor Website

[The] Spartacus Educational Web site

[The] Lew Rockwell Website

[The] USS Liberty Veterans Association Website (http://www.gtr5.com/evidence/warcrimes.pdf)

Youtube Videos (Referenced in Footnotes)

Other Sources

JFK Library, Boston, MA

LBJ Library, Austin, TX

U.S. Government Printing Office, Washington, DC

House Select Committee on Assassinations (HSCA)

Warren Commission Report (WCR)

Warren Commission Hearings (WCH)

INDEX